Dissident Marxism and
Utopian Eco-socialism in the
German Democratic Republic

Historical Materialism Book Series

The Historical Materialism Book Series is a major publishing initiative of the radical left. The capitalist crisis of the twenty-first century has been met by a resurgence of interest in critical Marxist theory. At the same time, the publishing institutions committed to Marxism have contracted markedly since the high point of the 1970s. The Historical Materialism Book Series is dedicated to addressing this situation by making available important works of Marxist theory. The aim of the series is to publish important theoretical contributions as the basis for vigorous intellectual debate and exchange on the left.

The peer-reviewed series publishes original monographs, translated texts, and reprints of classics across the bounds of academic disciplinary agendas and across the divisions of the left. The series is particularly concerned to encourage the internationalization of Marxist debate and aims to translate significant studies from beyond the English-speaking world.

For a full list of titles in the Historical Materialism Book Series available in paperback from Haymarket Books, visit: www.haymarketbooks.org/series_collections/1-historical-materialism.

Dissident Marxism and Utopian Eco-socialism in the German Democratic Republic

The Intellectual Legacies of Rudolf Bahro, Wolfgang Harich, and Robert Havemann

Alexander Amberger

Translated by
Carla Welch

Haymarket Books
Chicago, IL

First published in 2024 by Brill Academic Publishers, The Netherlands
© 2024 Koninklijke Brill NV, Leiden, The Netherlands

Published in paperback in 2025 by
Haymarket Books
P.O. Box 180165
Chicago, IL 60618
773-583-7884
www.haymarketbooks.org

ISBN: 979-8-88890-349-0

Distributed to the trade in the US through Consortium Book Sales and Distribution (www.cbsd.com) and internationally through Ingram Publisher Services International (www.ingramcontent.com).

This book was published with the generous support of Lannan Foundation, Wallace Action Fund, and the Marguerite Casey Foundation.

Special discounts are available for bulk purchases by organizations and institutions. Please call 773-583-7884 or email info@haymarketbooks.org for more information.

Cover art and design by David Mabb. Cover art is an adaption developed from *Luibov Popova Untitled Textile Design on William Morris Wallpaper for Historical Materialism*, edition of 100, screen print on wallpaper (2010).

Printed in the United States.

Library of Congress Cataloging-in-Publication data is available.

Contents

Foreword VII
Acknowledgements X
Abbreviations XI

1 **Introduction** 1
   1 Research Question and State of the Art 1
   2 The Concept of Political Utopia 9
   3 Political Utopia Since the 1960s 19
   4 Time, Place, and Actors 24
   5 Political Utopia and the GDR 30
   6 Meadows and the GDR 36
      6.1 *The Economic Situation in the GDR* 36
      6.2 *The Club of Rome and Post-materialist Discourse* 45
      6.3 *The Apocalypse as a Problem of Imperialism* 54

2 *Communism without Growth?*: **Wolfgang Harich and the Eco-dictatorship** 68
   1 Harich and His Era 68
   2 The Primacy of Nature: Harich's Return to Archistic Utopia 87
      2.1 *The Archistic Utopian Tradition* 88
      2.2 *Harich's Utopian Construct* 98
      2.3 *Situating* Communism without Growth? *in Utopian History* 109
   3 How *Communism without Growth?* Was Received 138
      3.1 *Reactions from SED Circles* 138
      3.2 *Reactions to the Book in the West* 151

3 **Rudolf Bahro's *The Alternative in Eastern Europe*** 162
   1 Bahro's Life: Exploring the Realms of the Possible 162
   2 The Origins of *The Alternative* 181
      2.1 *Frustration* 181
      2.2 *Mentors and Companions* 182
      2.3 *His Dissertation* 188
      2.4 *Bahro and Dutschke* 190
   3 *The Alternative* 193
      3.1 *Criticism and Analysis* 193
      3.2 *Utopia in* The Alternative 209

        4   Bahro and Utopianism   236
            4.1   *Up to 1980*   236
            4.2   *Post-1980*   245
            4.3   *A Post-materialist Philosophy of Praxis*   247
        5   *The Alternative* as an Alternative?   254
            5.1   *Impact in the* GDR   254
            5.2   *Reception of Bahro's Work in the West*   264

4 *Tomorrow*: Robert Havemann in Pursuit of the Third Way   283
        1   The Life of Robert Havemann   283
        2   The Origins of *Tomorrow*   298
        3   Havemann's Classical Utopia   304
            3.1   *Critique of Industrial Society and World Systems*   304
            3.2   *The Third Way via Utopia*   308
        4   Havemann's Utopian Ideas and Their Place in Utopian History   324
            4.1   *Tomorrow in the Context of Havemann's Political Works*   324
            4.2   *Situating the Book in Utopian History*   343
        5   The Reception of *Tomorrow* in the East and the West   366
            5.1   *The East*   366
            5.2   *The West*   372

5 Conclusions   379

    Bibliography   399
    Index of Names   421

Foreword

Even today, the inextricable link between the history of opposition in the German Democratic Republic (GDR) and the names Robert Havemann, Wolfgang Harich, and Rudolf Bahro is irrefutable. These individuals were more than just dissidents in a highly ideologised state who, using Marxist arguments, developed an immanent critique of the dogmatic rigidification of the German version of a Soviet-type system of domination. Indeed, one of the main reasons they were so well known was also due to the fact that they became victims of merciless persecution at the hands of the GDR government. Havemann was isolated from the outside world, placed under house arrest and Stasi surveillance, Harich was incarcerated for eight years and Bahro for one. These acts of repression attracted the attention of the Western media, particularly in West Germany during the Cold War, and brought these men international fame. Yet, this renown centred on the dissidents' immanent criticism of the outdated GDR structures and largely overlooked the dimension of their arguments that was at least as important as the critique itself – the utopian alternative to the structures being criticised, as portrayed in Havemann's novel *Tomorrow*, in Harich's interview *Communism without Growth?* and in Bahro's social science essay *The Alternative in Eastern Europe*.

Alexander Amberger can be credited with remedying this lack of comparative analysis by evaluating substantial print and non-print sources, including archive materials and Stasi documentation. In terms of methodology, as a paradigm for the analysis of his material, he chose to draw on Thomas More's classical utopia. According to this concept, political utopias are imaginary projections of either an ideal or a frightening society. They can be interpreted as better or worse alternatives to the undesirable developments, identified and criticised in the author's society of origin. This is a plausible approach insofar as the lines of argumentation pursued by all three dissidents followed this pattern. They not only criticised the GDR's structural shortcomings but also showed how a society might look in which the root causes of the aberrations identified have been eliminated. It does not go without saying, however, that this concept of utopia will be used in the current study. In fact, the concept of the classical utopia is not entirely compatible with the theories of Marx and Engels or, drawing on the philosophy of praxis, their claim to validity in accordance with the 11th of Marx's *Theses on Feuerbach*.

That said, Amberger is right to point out that there is a difference between Marx and Marxism. The founding fathers of historical materialism may have focused primarily on a critique of the capitalist political economy and marginalised the depictions of the classless society they strived to achieve. Yet, Marxism frequently flouted this *Bilderverbot* or ban on images. Typical examples of this are Bebel's *Woman and Socialism* and Alexander Bogdanov's utopian novels *Red Star* and *Engineer Menni*. If the concept of classical utopia can claim to be capable of adaptive flexibility, then, as Amberger points out, we can also say the same of Marxism. With regard to the claim to validity rooted in the philosophy of praxis, the three authors at the centre of this study invoke the concept of 'concrete utopia', first used by Ernst Bloch, with its emphasis on the utopian motivation to act.

In the context of the classical utopia, Amberger finds this assimilation perfectly acceptable, since even the claim to validity of More's *Utopia* in the form of a regulative principle should not be misinterpreted as idealistic and noncommittal. Even if he believed it would be impossible and indeed undesirable to translate this utopia into a social reality one-to-one, he certainly did not exclude the option of implementing, albeit with some caution, top-down reforms based on utopian ideals.

The classical utopia as defined by More can nevertheless help structure the present study. The basis of the present analysis is quite clear, given that the utopian phenomenon of a fictitious alternative image of society is always inextricably linked with the utopian author's critique of discernible aberrations in his society of origin and that this quite frequently includes biographical elements. Amberger's work pursues this approach rigorously. In his 'Introduction', he not only describes in detail the reasoning behind his choice of the classical model of utopia; but he also depicts the socioeconomic and structural ecological problems in the GDR criticised by all three authors. This critique was the starting point for Havemann's, Bahro's and Harich's gradual distancing from the GDR regime, ultimately leading them to develop a fictitious alternative to the stagnation and ossification of the mechanisms of reproduction in 'actually existing socialism'.

In the concluding part of the book, the author conducts a comparison of the utopian texts written by Havemann, Harich and Bahro. He sums up by stressing the importance of the challenge-response pattern or the notion of critique-alternative for the three authors. Within the concept of classical utopia, Amberger successfully manages to situate the fictitious alternatives to the GDR's actually existing socialism between the two poles of the archistic (authority-driven) and the anarchistic (free from authority) approach. Harich's eco-dictatorship clearly possesses archistic traits. In many respects, Havemann's more libertarian construct is very much in accord with the anarchistic approach and Bahro's *Alternative in Eastern Europe* constitutes a hybrid of archistic and anarchistic elements. Amberger, however, goes on to reduce the classical utopian approach to the hegemonic post-materialist interpretation, which has prevailed since the 1970s. This proved to be an essential step given the apparent overlap between Havemann, Harich and Bahro, in other words, their shared examination of the issue of ecology, something which has been subject to public debate ever since the publication of Meadows's *The Limits to Growth*.

According to Amberger, however, this common feature should not be allowed to obscure one all-important difference. The distinguishing feature of post-materialist utopian discourse in the US context was the fact that it was highly self-reflexive. The positive utopian image of society was conceived in the knowledge that it could also fail and become the opposite of what was intended. There is no sign of this at all in Bahro, Havemann or Harich's utopian texts. Drawing on Rousseau's positive human image, Havemann and Bahro do not see positive utopia or eutopia as a fragile construct that departs from an altruistic image of a 'New Man'; more to the point, man's lust for power and his aggressiveness barely feature in their utopian works. Admittedly, some overlap between Harich's approach and Arnold Gehlen's anthropology can be seen. Harich's vision of environmental communism, however, does not anticipate the development of self-destructive tendencies, for example when no mechanisms are in place to curb power.

There is also another difference. Given the fact that they focus more heavily on the issue of growth than post-materialist utopian authors such as Ursula K. Le Guin, Ernest Callenbach and Marge Piercy, it might be more accurate to describe Havemann, Bahro and Harich's utopian antitheses as 'post-growth utopias'. As such, once liberated from their GDR mantle, they could still claim to be of relevance today. Amberger summarises a key finding of his analysis:

> Their utopias are both anachronistic and could not be more relevant today. They are anachronistic because the historical context in which they emerge has very little to do with the present. Yet they are relevant because of their relationship with critique of growth and the development of post-growth models.

At this juncture, we could add that Alexander Amberger has produced a study that enriches utopia research, bringing present and future ecological disasters and imagined alternatives into focus. But more than this, his work is also instrumental in giving us a better understanding of how oppositional thinking in the GDR emerged and of the restrictive conditions under which this thinking had to be verbalised.

Richard Saage
Berlin, April 2014

Acknowledgements

Rudolf Bahro, Wolfgang Harich, and Robert Havemann are three of the most well-known critics of the politics of the SED. In the historical analyses of the lives and works of these men carried out to date, however, the eco-socialist utopias developed by these authors have played no more than a peripheral part. In light of this, the main aim of my book was to bring these texts out of the shadows and discuss their importance in utopian discourse as well as their relevance today. The publication of this work would not have been possible without the financial support of the Rosa-Luxemburg-Stiftung, for which I am exceedingly grateful.

These three critics of the GDR are no longer with us. However, many of those who had dealings with them and can provide first-hand reports of their experiences are still alive today. My thanks also go to those whose expertise and knowledge were so instrumental to this book.

A debt of gratitude is also owed to the Stasi Records Archive and the archive of the Robert Havemann Society for preparing and supplying me with invaluable archive material. Grit Gernhardt, Dr Andreas Heyer, and Dr Peter Welker helped me tremendously by editing my work. To them, and to the examiners of this manuscript at Martin Luther University Halle-Wittenberg, Professor Richard Saage and Professor Matthias Kaufmann, I also owe thanks.

Last but not least, I am endlessly grateful to my family, who patiently stood by my side with words of encouragement throughout the seven years it took to give life to this book.

Abbreviations

ADMV	German Motorsports Association
APO	Extra-Parliamentary Opposition
ARD	(West) German public broadcaster
BStU	Federal Commissioner for the Records of the State Security Service of the former German Democratic Republic (Stasi Records Agency)
CDU	Christian Democratic Union of Germany
Comecon	Council for Mutual Economic Assistance
CPSU	Communist Party of the Soviet Union
ČSSR	Czechoslovak Socialist Republic
DKP	German Communist Party
ESG	Protestant Student Community
FDJ	Free German Youth
FDP	Free Democratic Party
FRG	Federal Republic of Germany
GDR	German Democratic Republic
GNU	Society for Nature and the Environment (GDR)
HDS	University Initiative Democratic Socialism
HU	Humboldt University
IPW	Institute for International Politics and Economics
Jusos	Young Socialists in the SPD
KGB	Committee for State Security of the Soviet Union
KPD	Communist Party of Germany
KPD/AO	Communist Party of Germany (*Aufbauorganisation*)
KPD/ML	Communist Party of Germany (Marxists-Leninists)
KWI	Kaiser Wilhelm Institute
MfS	Ministry for State Security (Stasi)
MIT	Massachusetts Institute of Technology
ML	Marxism-Leninism
ND	*Neues Deutschland*
NDR	Norddeutscher Rundfunk (radio and television broadcaster)
NÖSPL	New System for Economic Management and Planning
OV	*Operativer Vorgang*, a Stasi file on suspected enemies of the state
PDS	Party of Democratic Socialism
RAF	Red Army Faction
RIAS	Radio in the American Sector
SBZ	Soviet Occupation Zone
SED	Socialist Unity Party

SPD	Social Democratic Party of Germany
SPÖ	Social Democratic Party of Austria
UN/UNO	United Nations
USSR	Union of Soviet Socialist Republics
VAO	*Vorlauf Operativ*, a preliminary Stasi file prior to the opening of an OV
VdN	Persecutee of the Nazi regime
ZDF	Zweites Deutsches Fernsehen (German public broadcaster)

CHAPTER 1

Introduction

1   Research Question and State of the Art

Over 30 years ago now, the system of 'actually existing socialism' that had prevailed in East Germany collapsed. Since then, the role of opposition figures and their impact on the end of the German Democratic Republic (GDR) has been the subject of much debate. Given the short time interval between these developments, the debate is politically and emotionally loaded, and much of the research conducted on this subject tends to be conspicuously one-sided. Some former dissidents tend to overrate the opposition, even going so far as to glorify it, while those who were against it at the time continue, to this day, to downplay its role, while condemning it at the same time.[1] Neither approach makes a particularly helpful contribution to an objective reappraisal of history. In fact, beyond these politically tinted interpretations, a closer look at the history of the opposition shows that it might be more fitting to place certain elements of it in an international context. But what exactly do we mean when we refer to the 'opposition' and 'dissidents' here? Ultimately there are 'still ... no definitions of resistance and opposition in the GDR that come close to being widely accepted'.[2]

The political scientist Walter Euchner provides a general definition of opposition as being 'forces that antagonize the ruling power within a given polity'.[3] This definition encapsulates different forms of opposition, which can be distinguished by their degree of legality. The pluralist systems found in Western democracies have a legal form of parliamentary opposition rooted in the constitution. In this context, there are also different types of extra-parliamentary opposition, some of which fall outside the scope of the existing legal framework and are thus persecuted in accordance with the law. In authoritarian actually existing socialist countries, there was no credible constitutional opposition.[4] There may have been several parties and mass organisations with representation in the GDR parliament (the *Volkskammer*); critics of the system, however, were denied access to the system. The only space for oppositional activity

---

1   See Richter 2012.
2   Kowalczuk 1999, p. 67.
3   Euchner 1993, p. 7.
4   See Neubert 1999, p. 35.

was therefore extra-parliamentary, the domain beyond the legal political field. Moreover, there was not just *one* single opposition in the GDR; instead there was a plethora of barely connected heterogenous opponents and critics of the system spanning a broad political and ideological spectrum.[5] Only a small part of this spectrum comprised individuals who could be referred to as Marxist oppositionists. The actions and arguments of these individuals were not aimed against socialism and the GDR per se; neither were they in favour of relinquishing the socioeconomic achievements of the system. Their focus was rather on changing the prevailing conditions. In other words, they were not inherently opposed to the system. And yet they were still denied legal access to power. They were against the ruling individuals and structures, criticising their omnipotence and certain aspects of their policies. Excluding critical forces from power and instead choosing to persecute them therefore proved to be a grave mistake on the part of the ruling powers. The result was that the entire system remained monolithic and lacked the momentum and progressive stimuli that constructive criticism would have provided.[6] In its place, illusions of the proletariat as a historical subject, despotism and the suppression of the real misery caused by the system defined the behaviour of a large part of the political and economic elite.

The Marxist opposition were not in fact enemies of the system, although they did call for change for the better and restructuring. What they certainly did not want was for the GDR to emulate the capitalist social system that prevailed in the West. This left them stuck between a rock and a hard place; persecuted by the government and yet, at the same time, criticised by the anti-communist opposition for their Marxist ideas. Bearing this in mind, the commonly used term 'dissident' and the associated stigma does not really apply to the critics of the system at the centre of this study. That said and even though they never saw themselves in this light, the book does still occasionally use the term dissident since it was one that was ascribed to them, predominantly from the outside, by

---

[5] 'In all its historical diversity, opposition and resistance in the SBZ/GDR took many forms, from objection to individual protest, from conscious, pointed rebellion to social democratic, Christian democratic and liberal resistance, organised into definitive groups …, from communist dissidence to internal party opposition, from political strikes to spontaneous mass action and unrest, from the creation of openly active groups and civic initiatives to resistance members holding conspiratorial meetings and initiating proactive measures.' Gutzeit 1997, p. 11. See also Geisel 2000, p. 28f.

[6] 'In fact, totalitarian systems seem less able to weather political and economic crisis than liberal systems with a pluralist structure that institutionalise government control, as well as an alternative government and alternative policy positions as an integral function of the system' (Euchner 1993, p. 17).

the Western media or other political actors, for example. In the context of this book, the term is used not to describe someone who is fundamentally opposed to the system but rather a critic of realpolitik, one who was not diametrically opposed to this form of politics but was simply unable to identify with it.

In the context of actually existing socialism, Marxist dissidents called for changes in and to the status quo but were themselves not in a position to demand or implement these changes by legal means. With the political elite being so seclusive, dissidents were forced to seek access to power via the alternative public sphere, if all else failed even by entering into a Faustian pact with anti-communist actors in the Federal Republic (FRG). Ilko-Sascha Kowalczuk also noted that another distinctive characteristic of the dissidents in the GDR was the fact that 'they expressed their resistance openly, consciously accepting the disadvantages and the persecution this entailed, to some extent creating an organised movement'.[7]

Rudolf Bahro, Wolfgang Harich and Robert Havemann have commented publicly on their own self-perception as opposition figures or dissidents, at the same time distancing themselves from media reports describing them as such. In this sense, the Marxist opposition is vastly different from non-communist dissidence.

For the purposes of my study of these three unconventional thinkers, however, their ascribing themselves to the role of opposition figures is of minor importance only. Here, it is their political utopian works, discussed in chronological order, that take centre stage. They can by all means be situated within the international historical context in which utopian thinking emerged. The works in question are:

1) Harich's *Communism without Growth? Babeuf and the 'Club of Rome'*,[8] published in 1975.
2) Bahro's *The Alternative in Eastern Europe*,[9] published in German in 1977 and in English translation in 1978.
3) Havemann's *Tomorrow. Industrial Society at the Crossroads*,[10] published in 1980.

Despite their many differences, what these texts have in common is that they were all written during the second half of the 1970s against the backdrop of international ecological and post-growth discourse. This discourse evolved in the context of the social and political movements that came to be popularly

---

7 Kowalczuk 1999, p. 58.
8 Harich 1975.
9 Bahro 1978.
10 Havemann 1980b.

associated with the year 1968 and the onset of the global economic crisis in the early 1970s.[11] The book entitled *The Limits to Growth. A Report for the Club of Rome's Project on the Predicament of Mankind*, authored by a team of researchers led by MIT's Dennis Meadows[12] and published in the USA in 1972, generated lively debate about growth worldwide,[13] and the GDR was no exception.

At the same time, the discourses on the environment and feminism also revived the political utopia. The addition of new elements, including environmental issues, enriched the genre. Martin d'Idler observes that the ecological utopia subgenre originated in the most advanced industrial countries of the Western world.[14] This makes the unique case of ecological utopias in the GDR all the more fascinating. The fact that they were not written in a capitalist environment but rather came about in an authoritarian socialist country contradicts the conservative critics of utopias who claim that they are *a priori* totalitarian.[15] If this were the case, it would have resulted in a paradoxical situation[16] where the opposition to an (allegedly) totalitarian state (the GDR) had been attacking that very state using totalitarian means. Although it is possible to fight fire with fire, the fact that this was not the case here – the political utopias written by the GDR dissidents were (with the exception of some elements of Harich's draft) in fact anything but totalitarian – flies in the face of the conservative criticism, demonstrating that they completely misunderstood the nature of modern utopias.[17]

An authoritarian system such as the GDR's, based on the claim to omnipotence of a single party and particularly its elite, did not actually forbid people from *thinking* differently. On the contrary, it even encouraged criticism and, in relation to this, the development of alternatives. Although dissenting opinions were ignored or persecuted, they were not forbidden, as is clearly illustrated in the old song *Die Gedanken sind frei* (Thoughts are free), which had such a

---

11   See Idler 1999, p. 135 f.
12   Short for Massachusetts Institute of Technology. For other acronyms, see List of Acronyms.
13   See Idler 1999, p. 33.
14   See Idler 1999, p. 14.
15   Referred to explicitly in Popper 1997, p. 515 ff. For more on this, see also Saage 2000, p. 45 and Saage 2010, p. 31.
16   The paradox of this situation was defined by Günter Gaus in 1985: 'Wherever utopias still exist, they have degenerated into clichés. You only need to look at socialist states. In truth, they do not correspond to the utopia that people once saw as being synonymous with the term socialism. And here in the West, we even go as far as to condemn utopia, while at the same time continuing to measure actually existing socialism against the utopia we refuse to believe' (Heym 1990, p. 211).
17   See, for example, Fest 1991, p. 94 ff.

formative influence on the identity of the opposition. Left-wing opposition, the conceptualisation of alternatives, and utopianism permeated the history of the GDR.[18] Anton Ackermann in the 1940s, Harich and the other 'conspirators' of 1956, the ostracised Ernst Bloch, the crackdown on artists and creative professionals in 1965, the dissidents of the 1970s, all the way up to the alternative thinkers of the 1980s, such as Lothar Kühne and Rolf Henrich, played a pivotal role.

This list could be continued *ad infinitum*. For the purposes of the present study, however, the scope will be limited to 1970s post-materialist utopias with a focus on ecology and critique of growth.[19] This does not imply that utopian thought in the GDR was also confined to these areas but rather that Bahro's, Harich's and Havemann's works occupy their own unique position, which is why it makes sense to analyse each individually as well as compare them with one another. By the same token, to allow for scientific analysis and comparability, precise criteria are required and Bloch's concepts, Kühne's architectural criticism or Henrich's anthroposophical socialist approach, in particular, would go beyond the bounds of these criteria. Moreover, these approaches were developed under different conditions and so do not fall within the same comparative framework that encompasses the three selected works. After all, this

---

18 Werner Mittenzwei subdivided the GDR opposition into two currents, the anti-communist and the Marxist. He considered the latter to be the more important of the two, 'because it produced policy programmes, comprehensive concepts and theories. Its most important representatives were Wolfgang Harich, Robert Havemann and Rudolf Bahro. Yet, it was not just their actions that won them a place in history, but also their theoretical views. However much their views changed over time, their Marxist perspective consistently dominated. That said, there were still breaks in their theories. They were not able to reach the masses with their opinions, but people gathered around them and, in small circles, they managed to disseminate their ideas in society, despite the oppression' (Mittenzwei 2003, p. 309f.).

19 The term ecology is defined in the broadest sense as the relationship between different life forms in their environment. This relationship is determined by interdependencies, and in their entirety, these make up an ecosystem, in which the population of living beings regulates itself by means of resource distribution. When it matures, the ecosystem achieves a state of ecological equilibrium. Several 'specific ecosystems' (e.g. a forest, a pond etc.) together make up the global ecosystem. See Weigmann 2003. Industrialisation and the development of modern man transformed both the individual specific ecosystems and the global ecosystem, with the latter being at risk of losing its relative state of equilibrium. Ecological discourse addresses how this development impacts the relationship between humans and the environment (the term 'eco' comes from the Greek 'Oikos' = house(hold)). In his book *The Age of Ecology*, Joachim Radkau argues that it is not possible to precisely define the terms 'environment' and 'nature' in the sense of a Weberian ideal-type. See Radkau 2014, p. 118.

book is not intended as a history of GDR utopianism but rather an analysis of three specific utopias within their historical and geographical contexts.

In examining this subject matter, different issues come to light. The first question that arises is why the three dissidents who claimed to be Marxists resorted to political utopia, a genre that had in fact been discredited by Marxist-Leninist doctrine.[20] Marx and Engels considered social utopianists to be dreamers – with the right intentions fundamentally but with no scientific basis for the ideas they postulated.[21] As the proletariat and class antagonism

---

20 Alongside specific passages from the Communist Manifesto, it was predominantly Friedrich Engels's *Socialism: Utopian and Scientific* which sought to draw a distinction between Marxism and utopia. This short book was an independently published extract from *Anti-Dühring*, which first appeared in French, the German version not being published until 1882. At the time, *Anti-Dühring* was banned under the repressive Anti-Socialist Laws. However, it was easy enough to disseminate the excerpt from the book and this 'played ... a significant role in the dissemination of scientific socialism among revolutionary workers', as a 1987 philosophy textbook from the GDR put it. It also stated that *Anti-Dühring* was published in the midst of 'conflict between Marxism and the various pseudo-socialist theories, a theoretical battle that Marxism ultimately won'. It was said that Engels had thus drawn a line between Marxism and 'bourgeois social reformism and petty-bourgeois socialism' and in so doing deduced that the 'utopian theories of socialism ... could not grasp socialism as a historical necessity that is the result of the social relation of capital'. The social utopianists in contrast were said to have presented idealistic concepts as the absolute truth, which they would automatically achieve through their 'own strength' – without acknowledging the historical role of the proletariat. See Academy of the Social Sciences of the Central Committee of the SED (ed.) 1988, p. 152.

21 Marx and Engels considered the works of the social utopianists to be anticipatory wishful dreams, which were not underpinned by any kind of analysis of capitalism, and the means of achieving those dreams to be flawed. 'Marx and Engels were not the only ones to remain silent, although a few allusions were made ..., about what the fully developed socialism of the future would be like. It is equally important to note that their critique of utopia was perceived by many later Marxists as a form of the ban on images, condemning the notion that socialism can be conceived both with the senses and as something tangible on the basis that this was "unscientific". The fact that this extreme rejection was instrumental in the dogmatisation of Marxism, depriving it of those very qualities that would prevent it from being reduced to economism and determinism, can hardly be disputed. Marx's and Engels's critique of utopian thought, exercised in the name of "scientific socialism" had a lasting effect on the theory formation of the European left. However, it would also be true to say that this critique was not influential enough to put an end to utopian discourse altogether' (Saage 2000, p. 398). Oskar Negt critically argues: 'The fact that Engels banished utopian socialism from the community of human motives for action for the purpose of satisfying a self-imposed ideal of scientific certainty in the context of justifying the intellectual mode of production, is one of the most historically significant fallacies of the twentieth century. The development of socialism from utopia to science is an arch deception, an error that reaches ominously from the faith in science of the nineteenth century to the need for a world view of the twentieth' (Negt 1998, p. 60f.).

developed further, utopia became anachronistic, making those who continued to adhere to the concept no more than reactionary sectarians.[22]

At the time, Marx's and Engels's focus was also on the claim to exclusive representation in leading the workers' movement and the distinction between purportedly scientific and unscientific socialism. Although Marxist discourse subsequently did have certain utopian elements,[23] the hegemonic doctrine, particularly of the Eastern European systems shaped by Stalinism, continued to discredit utopia as unscientific.[24]

But it is not only a comparison between Bahro's, Harich's, and Havemann's utopias and Marxism that provides us with new insights. Comparing them with works from Western post-materialist utopian discourse is equally enlightening. Another important area of study is the impact the texts have had in the East and the West, specifically in light of the authors' biographical contexts. This line of inquiry is particularly revealing when it comes to establishing the authors' motivation for writing their utopian works as well as some specific ideals based on the authors' individual character traits.

Political utopias must always be understood and analysed in the context in which they were written. This is why it is so important to examine the conditions of actually existing socialism and explore the possibilities and forms of the genre in this context. To date, there has been no extensive comparison of the utopias authored by Bahro, Harich and Havemann, nor one which explicitly considers their position in (discourse) history. Although numerous scholarly works about the three opposition figures have emerged from research on the history of the GDR, they rarely focus on the authors' political utopias.

Andreas Heyer, for instance, has published various essays on Harich's and Havemann's texts.[25] And the articles by Richard Saage on utopian research, which also cover Bahro, Harich and Havemann, deserve a mention here, too.[26] In addition, there are several more recent studies, which do not, however, follow the analytical research approach of the classical utopia. One such publication is Gert Röhrborn's *Dissidenten als geistige Schrittmacher* (Dissidents

---

22 See Marx and Engels 1975a, p. 514 ff.
23 See Heyer 2006b, p. 18 ff.
24 'To this day, the type of orthodox Marxism established in actually existing political systems, which sees itself as a science that has the capacity to draw valid conclusions over the course of history, has a tense relationship with utopia, which in any society invariably goes beyond the status quo' (Biesterfeld 2006, p. 144).
25 See Heyer 2006a; 2009; 2010a; 2010b.
26 See Saage 2008; 2010.

as intellectual pioneers) (2008), which addresses the impact of the three utopias on the GDR opposition. Even as early as 1996, Bucknell University's Peter Morris-Keitel published a work about Havemann's vision of eco-socialism. Another noteworthy contribution here is by Sandra Thieme who, in 2000, published a comparative study of the utopian visions introduced by Ernest Callenbach in his book *Ecotopia* and those outlined by Havemann in *Tomorrow*. The study formed the basis of her dissertation, defended at the University of Münster in 2004 and entitled *Perspektiven ökologisch-nachhaltiger Entwicklung. Zur Aktualität utopischen Denkens*[27] (Prospects of environmentally sustainable development. The pertinence of utopian thinking).

To place the GDR utopias in their historical context, I will draw on the main texts by GDR opposition figures as well as individual studies on philosophy, history, ecology, sociology of power and analysis of the GDR system. I will also refer to literature on the aforementioned research focuses published in the GDR.

Each of the book's chapters contains numerous bibliographical references to the life and works of the three opposition figures. Guntolf Herzberg and Kurt Seifert authored an extensive biography on Rudolf Bahro, which also meets scientific standards.

Similar biographies for Harich and Havemann have yet to be written. Although several biographical books have been published on each of these opposition figures, these were written either by the individuals themselves or by friends and family and so are to a greater or lesser extent subjective or, for various reasons, too sketchy to meet the requirements of a comprehensive scholarly biography.[28] For this reason, I will be drawing on a number of shorter texts in combination with these biographies.[29]

---

27   Laitko 2010c, p. 2. See also Morris-Keitel 2004 and Thieme 2000; 2004. In her dissertation, Thieme studied four utopian texts: *Tomorrow, Ecotopia, bolo'bolo* (Widmer 1983) (P.M.) and *The Solar Economy* (H. Scheer). Thieme's concept of utopia was thus very broad. In terms of conceptual definitions, she limited herself to the terms ecological and (very broadly understood) utopian. Thieme devoted an entire chapter to *Tomorrow*, in which critique of the GDR was only given marginal consideration. Her research interest was geared much more towards Havemann's critique of capitalism and the links with the present. See Thieme 2004, p. 121.

28   Some more recent biographical texts are as follows: on Havemann: Hurwitz 2012; Florath and Theuer 2007a; Havemann, F. 2007; Havemann, K. and Widmann 2003. On Harich: Harich, A. 2007, Harich 1999 and 1993; Prokop 1997.

29   'All in all, Havemann's theories were relatively well researched, particularly compared to those developed by other opposition figures in the GDR. Other works, more comprehensive publications in particular, on the context in which Havemann's thinking is to be interpreted are essentially non-existent' (Heyer 2010b, p. 32).

INTRODUCTION

For all three opposition figures, the study takes the most important, freely accessible primary literature into account, which goes well beyond the three individual utopias mentioned above. This literature can be found in many libraries but can also be easily obtained second-hand. My analysis of the three utopias also incorporates specific texts and documents from the Stasi Records Archive and the archives of the Robert Havemann Society, records which are seldom used, if at all. The latter include a broad range of reviews on the three books. Furthermore, several edited volumes of materials from conferences and colloquia held in recent decades on the three opposition figures provide insights into specific aspects. Finally, interviews with eyewitnesses also helped me to answer several of my questions.

2   The Concept of Political Utopia

People have been writing and reading utopias for centuries. Utopian authors engage in a critical reflection of the prevailing circumstances and, drawing on this, develop an alternative model of society in which the flaws and potential that the present offers are fleshed out and incorporated into an ideal vision for the future or a fictional island. As a result, the history of the genre also reflects phases of human history. The genre is thus synonymous with a society that is normatively (more) just, given that 'for more than two thousand years the exploitation of man by man has been abolished in utopias. Social utopias contrasted the world of light with night, broadly pictured their land of light, with the sparkle of justice in which the man who is oppressed feels uplifted, and the man who goes without feels content'.[30] Drawing on Niklas Luhmann's systems theory, Arno Waschkuhn defines political utopias as dialectical negations with a corrective function that are anchored in society and serve to strengthen 'society's immune system'.[31] He also contends that '[u]topias are mind-broadening speculations over possibilities'.[32]

Utopias criticise the present in a more or less covert manner. This is exactly why it has been and continues to be possible for authors living and writing in authoritarian systems and dictatorships to be critical of the status quo. By disguising the text as fiction or (supposed) satire, the authors are able to criticise

---

30   Bloch 1986, p. 475f. This characterisation does not take dystopias into consideration, however.
31   Waschkuhn 2003, p. 232. For a critique of Waschkuhn's not uncontroversial book *Politische Utopien* (Political utopias), see Heyer 2010a, p. 51 ff.
32   Waschkuhn 2003, p. 3.

the ills that readers of utopias are all too familiar with. On the one hand, this covert approach protects the authors as they are not being blatantly critical (to bring any kind of credible charge against would inevitably mean opening up to debate the criticism made in such writings).

On the other hand, this approach also attracts a large readership of individuals who can identify with the criticism. At the same time this alternative world instils hope that alternatives to the existing model of society do exist and that these are worth fighting for. Each utopia is a product of the times in which it is written.[33] These texts reflect the epoch's social, economic and cultural flaws,[34] and the post-materialist utopias penned by the GDR dissidents were no exception.

For the purposes of an analysis and comparison of the texts, a working definition of the concept of utopia is needed. In the study of utopianism, there is no one-size-fits-all definition; on the contrary, there are almost as many dif-

---

33   The modern form of this genre emerged during the Renaissance when the utopian legacy of the ancient world was resurrected by Thomas More's *Utopia* (published in 1516). Other important utopias of this period included Tommaso Campanella's *The City of the Sun* and Francis Bacon's *New Atlantis*. The earlier texts were dominated by the desire for order linked with a critique of what were to some extent rather chaotic circumstances at the time. The (largely French) utopias of the Age of Enlightenment built on the early works mentioned above. They responded to social ills of absolutism and countered these with alternative, normatively better visions of society. The most important utopian authors of the time included Louis Armand Lahontan (e.g. *Dialogues with a Savage*) and Louis-Sébastien Mercier (*The Year 2440*). Historically, the Age of Enlightenment was followed by the Age of Industrialisation, which brought major social upheaval in its wake, something that proved to be fertile ground for the emergence of political utopias. The utopian works penned at the beginning of this era by authors such as Charles Fourier, Henri de Saint-Simon and Auguste Blanqui followed the social utopia classics like Étienne Cabet's *Journey to Ikaria*, Edward Bellamy's *Looking Backward: 2000–1887* or William Morris's *News from Nowhere*. The actual dictatorships of the twentieth century, which frequently legitimised their political power by claiming to be implementing political utopia, plunged the genre into a major crisis. The most well-known dystopias or black utopias by Yevgeny Zamyatin (*We*), Aldous Huxley (*Brave New World*) and George Orwell (*1984*) showed that the utopian genre could also be self-critical, even destructive, if this is what social realities demanded. After the end of World War II, political utopia seemed to fall victim of its own tragic attempts to become reality. It was not until the late 1960s that the appearance of post-materialist utopias rescued the genre from this 'exile'. These are but a few examples taken from the history of political utopia. A chronological list of the classic works can be found in Idler 2007, p. 287 f. A comprehensive insight into the history of political utopias since the modern age from a political sciences perspective is provided by Richard Saage in his four-volume series *Utopische Profile* (Utopian profiles) over a sizeable 1,600 pages plus.

34   See Saage 2003, p. 6.

ferent descriptions of the concept as there are researchers.³⁵ Political science research, on the other hand, continues to rely on the description of utopia established by Thomas More in his book *Utopia*. His work not only lent the entire genre its name), (from the Greek 'ou' meaning 'not' and 'topos' meaning 'place'), but many of its characteristic elements could also be identified in later utopias. For the purposes of this book, these elements will be used as analytical categories. That is not to say that Bahro's, Harich's and Havemann's texts will be shoehorned into the template of a book that is almost five centuries old. Rather, the intention is to situate the texts in an equally enduring tradition and to identify them as part of the evolution of utopian thought, thus illustrating the genre's capacity to 'learn' and adapt. This means that in Bahro, Harich and Havemann's texts, negative experiences of earlier utopias are integrated, negated and sublated, thus proving that the political utopia genre, too, is continuously undergoing a process of learning and adaptation.³⁶

But what exactly is utopian thought and what are political utopias? Utopian thought constitutes a way of thinking that does not *automatically have to correspond with* a comprehensive concept for society.³⁷ Ernst Bloch, who used a very broad concept of utopia, identified this utopian way of thinking virtually every time anyone's thoughts went beyond current realities. Opting for this definition, however, would make it virtually impossible to analyse or compare Bahro's, Harich's and Havemann's texts from a political sciences perspective, though they do include elements of Bloch's concept of utopia. In the chapters that follow, these elements are therefore not treated as methods but rather as objects of investigation.³⁸

---

35   In his three-volume *Der Stand der aktuellen deutschen Utopieforschung* (The state of the art in contemporary German utopian research), published between 2008 and 2010, Andreas Heyer provides an overview of the sheer breadth of these approaches from the German-speaking world alone.

36   'Many utopias explicitly adopt elements from other outlines, such as the concept of collective ownership as a way of resolving the social question; on the other hand, they also attempt to change and improve earlier utopias, at times even going so far as to propose complete counter-visions. And thus a closely interwoven utopian discourse emerges' (Idler 2007).

37   In utopian studies, the distinction between utopia and utopian methodology was carved out by Raymond Ruyer and Hans-Jürgen Krysmanski in the mid-twentieth century. See Heyer 2008a, p. 100.

38   Harich wrote in the 1980s for instance that he admired Bloch for his 'political and social engagement' but did not accept him as a philosopher. See Harich 2004, p. 106. Further, Harich described Bloch as a fashionable philosopher who had never been a Marxist. See Harich 2004, p. 296. And described him as taking an approach of 'uncritical idealism'. He

Richard Saage, a political scientist specialising in the study of utopianism, identifies three authoritative concepts of utopia that are relevant for the twentieth century. Firstly, the very broad concept of 'concrete' utopia which goes back to the works of Gustav Landauer[39] and is used by philosophers such as Bloch and Karl Mannheim. This concept also includes chiliasm and eschatology and cannot be explored using a single cohesive research model. Secondly, there is the 'utopian paradigm based on the theory of totalitarianism' adhered to by Karl Popper, who discredited utopias as being related to totalitarianism, thus completely ignoring the twentieth century post-materialist utopias that were critical of totalitarianism. Thirdly and lastly, there is what is referred to as the 'classical utopian concept'.[40] This was a term coined by Richard Saage as an analytical tool for the purposes of political science research on utopia. Saage names the concept 'classical' because it is rooted both nominally and substantively in the classic of the genre: More's *Utopia*. Drawing on Norbert Elias and Max Weber, Saage therefore defines the 'classical utopian concept' as an ideal-type that can be used 'as a heuristic tool'.[41] He identifies two key advantages to using this concept: It enables us to measure utopias against this ideal-type, in other words to 'clearly define and differentiate them', and it also allows us to 'identify ... hybrid forms' and interpret them.[42] According to this conception:

> Political utopias are fictional inner-worldly societies ..., which are compressed either into an ideal or a frightening image. Their aim is to provide an accurate critique of existing institutions and socio-political relations, which they contrast with a well thought out and rationally plausible alternative. ... They ... are always oriented towards the future.[43]

Consequently, classifying backward-looking genres as political utopias would be just as inaccurate as placing mythical or historically romanticising concepts in this category.[44] The methodological basis of the analysis of Bahro's, Harich's

---

claimed Bloch was 'the philosophical exponent of expressionism and the various other related aspects of "left-wing" pseudo-avantgardism in art and literature', something which was also reflected in his concept of utopia. See Harich 2004, p. 116 f.
39 See Bloch 1976, p. 17 and p. 146. See also Heyer 2006b, p. 104 ff.
40 See Saage 2003, p. 512 f.
41 Saage 2005, p. 292.
42 See Saage 2005, p. 293.
43 Saage 2000, p. 46 f.
44 In the GDR, Bahro, Harich and Havemann identified as Marxists, rejecting regressive concepts such as these. In this respect, Saage's concept of utopia lends itself well to their utopias.

and Havemann's utopias that follows draws on Saage's concept of utopia, one that is tried and tested in utopian research in the political sciences.⁴⁵ That said, our specific context – political utopia as an instrument used by *Marxist* critics of the system within a state that derives its legitimacy from *Marxist philosophy* – requires this methodological approach to be expanded to include Marxism. Richard Saage in fact explicitly excludes Marxism from his ideal-type classical utopia because Marx and Engels, as the founding fathers of Marxism, 'leave the question of differentiated structure of the body politic in fully developed socialism open: despite the fact that reference to this is actually at the very heart of the political utopia'.⁴⁶

Saage rejects the claim that Marx and Engels were themselves utopianists.⁴⁷ Although I would agree with this assessment,⁴⁸ we have to assume that not only utopian discourse has the capacity to learn and adapt but that Marxism has a similar ability when it comes to utopia. Marx and Engels were not utopianists – they disassociated themselves from utopia too clearly for us to draw this conclusion and, although their writing does include utopian elements, these components are peripheral in the overall context of their work.⁴⁹ That said,

---

45 On this, see Idler 2007, p. 16 f.; Saage 2005.
46 Saage 2000, p. 48.
47 See Saage 2000, p. 24 f.
48 Marx and Engels refused to predict the communism of the future using imagery, which they believed would convey a (false) expectation to communist supporters. They did not regard such a visual depiction of the future to be important for the transition to communism because, according to the laws of development in their historical philosophy, communism, being the next level of development after capitalism, was an absolute certainty. Leszek Kolakowski expressed it in the following way: 'God speaks through the *Phenomenology* [*of Spirit*; magnum opus of Georg Wilhelm Friedrich Hegel], history speaks from the *Communist Manifesto*; the subject and the object of great science converge' (Kolakowski 1974, p. 16 f.).
49 Iring Fetscher, a scholar of Marxism, wrote: 'In Karl Marx's *Foundations of the Critique of Political Economy* (1857/58) he allows himself – in contrast to his more cautious wording in *Capital* (1867) – in some places to describe in more detail the way of life of the people in a post-capitalist society: labour will have lost its burdensome character and will have become a pleasing activity. Thanks to many years living under the conditions of capitalism, "industriousness" will have become a general characteristic of all human beings. The "time available" to nurture scientific and artistic skills will lead to the emergence of what could almost be described as an "übermensch"' (Fetscher 2004, p. 168). 'In some places, however, Marx arrives at utopian formulations. For instance, when he describes how fully rounded individuals will be repositories of "the accumulated knowledge of man". This vision of the future is not centred on the property question. Nor does it focus on "macrosocietal planning". In fact, it is based on fully developed social individuals' (Fetscher 2004, p. 172). Rolf Schwendter also noted: 'In the writings of Marx himself, we find, albeit spread across his complete works, at least 50 comments which could be described as actual uto-

Marx and Engels *should not be seen as synonymous with Marxism*. Marxism is, in fact, the further development of their ideas in theory and practice, and we have seen numerous different trends evolving over the last 150 years. As with the history of utopia, Marxism also comprises archistic and anarchistic models of society. Similarly, in Marxist discourse, the treatment of utopias can also be identified: the spectrum of approaches included an orthodox adherence to the ban on images, the desire to utopianise according to Bloch, and utopian visions of society in line with More's classical utopian model, which are, however, decidedly Marxist. Works that deserve a mention here are, for instance, August Bebel's *Woman and Socialism*, Alexander Bogdanov's *Red Star* and *Engineer Menni*, and, last but not least the utopian outlines developed by the Marxists Bahro, Harich and Havemann.

Socialist Unity Party (SED) ideology or Marxism-Leninism still essentially adhered to the ban on images despite the fact that imagery depicting utopian ideas could nevertheless be found in literary and scholarly publications in the GDR. This rarely corresponded with the classical concept of utopia, however. Any outlines published comprised images that were intentionally distant, as though viewed through a telescope, and were contextualised using the SED's realpolitik. A clear example of this was the utopian predictions regarding the possibilities of chemistry and space travel in the 1960s.[50]

---

pian; lacking in context, not particularly original, but unquestionably far removed from a ban on images' (Schwendter 1994, p. 11). On this, also see Kolakowski 1974, p. 11f.

50 After these dreams had faded, utopia continued to be viewed as something that fell between the 'ban on images' and the concept of 'concrete utopia'. A good illustration of this is the introduction to the anthology of classical utopias written by Joachim Walther in 1987. Here he wrote: 'It was Engels who subjected utopias to a thorough analysis and evaluation in his *The Development of Socialism from Utopia to Science*, which was clearly a programmatic text, even going by its title. His critique encompassed all utopias that were not based on a division of society into classes, the inevitability of the class struggle and the social revolution, including those conceived by Owen, Saint-Simon and Fourier because they were not staunch advocates of the interests of the proletariat and, instead of seeking to liberate the working class as a first step, their ambition was to free the whole of humanity. These immature theories corresponded with the immature class position. The objective contradictions, which had not been clearly acknowledged, must be removed from people's heads. With thoughtful rationality rather than revolutionary practice. Ever since, what utopia lacks has been expressed in clear terms' (Walther 1987, p. 12). Once Marx and Engels had published their insights into utopias, this genre no longer held much weight. Apart from the utopias penned by Bellamy and Morris, the works were unoriginal (Walther gave the example of Herbert George Wells). Then there were the black utopias, although with their 'fatalistic doom and gloom and lack of outlook' these were not at all useful. That said, Walther deemed distant utopian goals combined with practical policies in the here and now to be both useful and necessary. See Walther 1987.

When Richard Saage writes, therefore, that Marx and Engels, as the founding fathers of Marxism, 'leave the question of differentiated structure of the body politic in fully developed socialism open: despite the fact that reference to this is actually at the very heart of the political utopia',[51] this applies solely to Marx and Engels and not to the Marxists Bahro, Harich and Havemann. The reason being that, unlike Marx and Engels and unlike the proponents of the concept of the 'concrete utopia', Bahro, Harich and Havemann deliberately posed 'the question of differentiated structure of the body politic in fully developed socialism'. Thus, they took up the classical utopian line and at the same time opened Marxism up for utopia again, which, despite being repeatedly dismissed, has always remained an important latent element.

Their texts clearly signal that the proclaimed renunciation of purportedly unscientific utopia deprived Marxism of an important progressive element. Admittedly, the historical schematism of Marx's theory of social formation, whose heyday coincided with the peak of Stalinism in the 1930s, does indeed comprise religious-chiliastic utopian elements. However, at the same time, it makes a farce of utopia because it neglects to include any criticism, one of the key elements of the genre. Bloch had already highlighted this shortcoming, but his utopianisation of Marxism and his appropriation of utopia for Marxism was reminiscent of Goethe's ballad *The Sorcerer's Apprentice*, in which the eponymous character is no longer able to control its exploits. Bloch's borderless concept of utopia is not a suitable research tool. That said, his influence on GDR philosophy remains an important subject of study.[52] Unlike Bloch, Bahro,

---

51 Saage 2000, p. 48.
52 Bloch, whose book *The Principle of Hope* was also published in the GDR in the 1950s, fell from grace after 1956. The 1957 publication of the book *Ernst Blochs Revision des Marxismus. Kritische Auseinandersetzung marxistischer Wissenschaftler mit der Blochschen Philosophie* (Ernst Bloch's revision of Marxism. A critical study by Marxist scientists of Bloch's philosophy) bears witness to this. However – or perhaps precisely because of this – Bloch's utopian philosophy had a considerable influence on the critical left-wing thinkers in the GDR. Even after Bloch migrated to West Germany, *The Principle of Hope* continued to be read and discussed among critics of the SED, causing his concept of utopia to remain influential for critical thinkers in the GDR. Thus, Bloch also shaped Bahro's, Havemann's, and Harich's utopian thought, though the latter noticeably distanced himself from Bloch's philosophy in his final years. Harich, for instance, wrote: 'Bloch attempted ... to merge his religious teleologism, which suited his Messianic eschatology, with an expressionist style of thinking and writing and elements of Marxist thought. A brilliant mix: exceedingly interesting, often incredibly inspiring, but philosophically extremely questionable, much of it even frivolous, charlatanism and stylistically, of virtually unsurpassable affectation. Bloch was able in jest to portray himself as a cathedral where Marxism was "no more than" the Holiest of Holies. And at times he degraded Marxism, driven by some kind of

Harich and Havemann managed to avoid the putative mistake of developing an excessively unbounded concept of utopia. The utopias they outlined were more or less closed, and, at the same time, were quite clearly Marxist. In the history of utopia, this positions them with other well-known Marxists who already ignored the ban on images at a much earlier stage.[53]

But let us return now to the characteristics of the classical utopia. As well as drawing a distinction between archistic (authority-driven) and anarchistic utopias,[54] Saage employs different structural levels for analytical purposes. What must now be explored is the form of critique Bahro, Harich and Havemann each practiced in the context of the time and historical location of their writing. To what extent was this critique of the present reflected and extrapolated by the three authors in their utopian outlines? Related to this, we must also ask ourselves what ideal of the common good formed the normative basis for their respective visions of the future and how, where applicable, they integrated this ideal into the graphic representation of their utopias. Besides the normative level, material aspects also played a pivotal role for utopian visions. Particularly because we are talking about Marxist utopias here, another question to be addressed is how socioeconomic relations, which – in Marxist terminology – represented the material basis for the normative superstructure, were designed. In this context, this inevitably includes the issue of ownership of the means of production, but also of private property per se. What role does the economy play in the different dimensions of Bahro, Harich and Havemann's utopias? And, building on this: What political and institutional notions and premises ensue from this economic conjecture?[55]

The role that each utopia assigns to work is another aspect of the material realm. In this context, the following questions arise: What is the importance of work? Does the word have positive or negative connotations? Who works? What purpose does work have? Is work something that is done individually or collectively? Is there a compulsion to work? How is motivation generated? What types of relaxation are envisaged?

---

exasperation with what he referred to as the "narrow gauge," to no more than a side nave in the Bloch cathedral' (Harich 2004, p. 120). On this, see also Amberger 2013.
53   On this, see also Heyer 2006b, p. 25 ff.
54   Saage's concept of utopia draws on anti-egoistic utopias, which means that in his view, there can be no 'positive egoistic utopias'. Even anarchistic concepts, however individualistic they may be, were based on the principle of social solidarity, something that archistic concepts were built on anyway (albeit controlled hierarchically from 'above'). And this is the point of overlap between these two different forms. See Saage 2003, p. 7.
55   See Saage 2000, p. 49; Saage 2003, p. 62; Idler 2007, p. 15.

In terms of needs, it is important to establish: Does luxury exist? If it does, then for whom? What value is attributed to consumption? What is said about the consumption or waste of resources? Does asceticism or the obligation of asceticism exist? What role do clothes and fashion play? What is the relationship between egotism and an awareness of necessity?

And finally, on the role of technology: What is the significance of technology for social development? Is there generally a faith in technology or does scepticism prevail? What role do chemistry and nuclear power play? What is the attitude towards medicine and death? Does technology serve humankind? Is the concept of nature instrumental? Beside these concerns I also examine the importance ascribed to aspects such as sexuality, gender equality, family, art and religion.[56] The concept of classical utopia also includes the politically integrative side of utopias: 'Characteristic of this type of utopia is the fact that it is fundamentally based on gender relations, spanning sexual morals, forms of "family", the status of women, and even the creation of a "new" type of human being, a "new" man. The political community, in the narrowest sense, generally provides information about the institutions of consensus-building as well as about citizens' political participation and decision-making. Statements on whether utopia will have political elites and how these are recruited are not infrequent either. Lastly, every political utopia contains commentary, some more detailed than others, on education, justice, religion, art, and foreign affairs, in particular the topic of war and peace. Of paramount importance is recognition that political utopias are defined by the claims to validity they make. Essentially this is a matter of how the author envisages the transition from the utopian ideal to reality'.[57] After all, according to Waschkuhn, many authors perceived their utopias as actual blueprints intended to be implemented.[58] However, it should be noted that utopias that come to fruition can no longer be referred to as utopias in the literal sense, as the word 'utopia' means 'non-place' or nowhere.[59]

Saage describes three criteria that political utopias must fulfil to be regarded as such by the 'classics'. Firstly, they must have the classical utopian structure; secondly, they must offer a vision of an alternative society that reflects the zeitgeist of the epoch, and in so doing, achieve a certain degree of prominence. And thirdly, the utopia must be representative of the utopian thinking of the era, regardless of whether this emerges at the time the utopia is written or later on.

---

56   See Saage 2003, p. 64 ff.
57   Saage 2000, p. 50.
58   See Waschkuhn 2003, p. 3.
59   See Saage 2000, p. 46.

Besides this classical ideal-type, Saage also considers other outlines that contain elements of classical utopianism, that fail to fall into the category of political utopia. These can take on various forms, from literature, to discourse to (totalitarian) reality.[60]

Taking these criteria as the basis for analysing the three texts I have chosen gives us the following starting point: Although only the lengthy utopian chapter of Havemann's *Tomorrow* takes the form of a literary narrative, Harich's and Bahro's books undoubtedly also fulfil the criteria belonging to classical utopia because of their discursive examination of the status quo and their depiction of socioeconomic alternatives.[61] They meet these criteria by presenting utopian counter-visions reflecting the thinking of the epoch and by reaching a degree of prominence that enables them to be representative of the era.

> According to the self-portrayal of the utopian construct, it is not restricted to the medium of the novel. ... [It] has ... also always been articulated in social philosophical essays or dialogues.[62]

This openness towards other genres is Saage's defence against accusations that he limits the concept of political utopia to the classical *Staatsroman* or the political novel. Regardless, Saage underlines the historical dynamics of classical utopia, its adaptability to the relevant historical circumstances and its openness to elements, which, in this field of research tend to be ascribed to the broader concept of the 'concrete utopia'.[63] Expanding the concept of the classical utopia to include elements of the motivating function of the 'concrete utopia' – and thus combining it with a cautious openness towards the

---

60   The Soviet Union, for example, certainly had elements which would fall under the concept of classical utopia, although, as a whole, it could not be classified as an achieved utopia. See Saage 2003, p. 10 ff.
61   'The approach to ecological utopias, in particular, shows that utopian thinking is in no way limited to the novel' (Heyer 2008b, p. 87).
62   Saage 2003, p. 381.
63   The representatives of the classical approach bemoaned that reducing utopia to its intention would inevitably result in an inflated conception, which, due to the arbitrariness of its content would make it unusable as a research paradigm. The opposing side responded that the classical approach used an excessively narrow definition of the phenomenon and shoehorned it into the concept of the classical political novel. This methodological dualism does not necessarily need to be resolved. After all, it does have the advantage that scholars in utopia studies can make a reasoned choice, depending on the specific subject of their research. However, we must remember that ... the classical concept of utopia undoubtedly absorbed elements of concrete utopia over the course of its evolution, for instance in the shape of chiliasms, popular visions of paradise etc. They gave the classical

demand Marxist practical philosophy places on utopia – allows for a more precise analysis, also of the outlines Bahro and Havemann developed, which erred towards the concrete utopia both in style and intention. This utopian concept will, therefore, form the basis of the rest of this book.

3   Political Utopia Since the 1960s

In utopian discourse, the relationship between humans and nature played an important role even before the post-materialist era.[64] Although in the sixteenth and seventeenth-century renaissance utopias, an instrumental understanding of nature still predominated, some of the utopianists who followed Rousseau went on to counterpose the 'natural' to early capitalist reality, positing that people should forgo luxury.[65]

> Consequently, the critique of utopias at that time vehemently attacked the exploitation of the workers and condemned the stark contrast between the extremes of luxury and hardship. The responsibility for this was believed to lie in the capitalist economy, characterised by competition and private ownership of the means of production as it was. Moreover, other much criticised aspects included the waste of resources resulting from crises of abundance and the uncoordinated (anarchistic) mode of production employed as well as the inferior quality of the mass-produced goods resulting from the overwhelming focus on exchange value rather than use value.[66]

That said, as Martin d'Idler observes, the majority of the utopianists in the age of industrialisation, with the exception of William Morris, were not opposed to human dominance over nature. Even in the dystopias of the early and mid-twentieth century, nature was completely controlled by humans and subjugated to their needs.[67]

---

      utopia the very emotional dimension that had always been inherent in it, in other words, in times of need and desperation, the ability to convey something akin to hope on a subjective level' (Saage 2010, p. 30f.). On this, see also the debate on the pros and cons of the concept of classical utopia in the journal *Erwägen, Wissen, Ethik*, no. 16, Stuttgart 2005, pp. 291–355.

64   On this, see Heyer 2008b, p. 86f.
65   See Idler 1999, p. 58ff.
66   Idler 1999, p. 62.
67   See Idler 1999, p. 65ff. Although it is important to add here that, in addition to the future

While the authors of social utopias in the early twentieth century still rhapsodised about the potential to completely control nature thanks to technical advances, thus abandoning the ideas of asceticism of earlier representatives of the genre,[68] by the middle of the century, the positive utopias found themselves in crisis, triggering a step change in the discourse. The dystopias described earlier now served as a response to fascism, Stalinism, war, etc. After World War II, it seemed as though this genre had come to an end. In the 1960s, however, the discourse underwent yet another sea change that would continue to this day.[69] The positive utopias experienced a renaissance, albeit with certain dystopian elements. This involved a dialectical sublation of the classical utopia, which was augmented by including dystopian elements alongside ecological and feminist influences.[70]

There were two key factors behind the rise of these post-materialist utopias. The first was the ideational normative impact of those involved in the protests of 1968, who forged and represented the values, and their ideas were authoritative for the discourse of the time. The quantifiable damage to the environment inflicted by humans and their technology, on the other hand, had a tangible empirical impact. This value shift and the socioeconomic problems that emerged paved the way for the rise and success of ecological utopias.[71]

Andreas Heyer observes:

> It is a tribute to the genre of utopia that it managed to successfully integrate into its paradigm postmodern needs and expectations, on the on hand, and ideas and opportunities, on the other. Since the late-1960s we have therefore seen more and more ecological and feminist utopias being published, many of which in fact addressed both dimensions at the same time. This resulted in an important change in utopian discourse itself, with modern utopias generally factoring in the notion of their own failure ever since. In other words, utopias no longer constitute static, strictly archistic closed societies but rather dynamic and evolving entities, albeit with a certain amount of inherent fragility as a result.[72]

---

societies they constructed, Yevgeny Zamyatin, Aldous Huxley and George Orwell's dystopias also depicted natural external worlds, which the ruling powers perceived as anachronistic and normatively reprehensible, and which served as a temporary refuge for the respective protagonists.

68 See Saage 2000, p. 307 ff.
69 See Idler 1999, p. 11.
70 See Saage 2003, p. 326.
71 See Idler 1999, p. 84.
72 Heyer 2006b, p. 117 f.

INTRODUCTION

Thus, more recent utopias broke with the characteristic of a holistic, rigid system that previously typified them, now incorporating the conflict lines as well as the social heterogeneity.[73]

As Waschkuhn points out, in reference to the newer utopias:

> Despite all the differences between their utopian counterworlds, one thing they have in common is the dissociation of utopia from a belief in progress rooted in the philosophy of history, as well as the radical decentralisation of political, social and economic institutions and the reconciliation of technology and nature, which corresponds in particular to a strict ethic renouncing consumption and, anticipating something that would come much later, also the formula of sustainable development.[74]

Ever since, these 'post-materialist'[75] utopias have shaped the discourse. They take up the tradition of positive utopias once again and propose alternatives, albeit against a different backdrop. Thus, they detach themselves from the rationalism and reasoned thought of the classical social utopias and replace these elements with, for instance, nature mysticism.[76] The aspiration is to achieve a balance between humankind and nature.

> In sum, we can conclude that the ... positive utopias after World War II jettisoned the primacy of unlimited economic growth, in which the tradition of the nineteenth century in particular had originated, along with their global market orientation. To some extent, they returned to models of a 'decelerated economy'. Moreover, new life was breathed into the notion of economic autarchy, an ideal that nonetheless seemed out of reach. At the same time, the pursuit of the satisfaction of needs suppressed profit-oriented economic incentive. The goal is to aspire to a 'Third Way', one that lies in between capitalism and state socialism, although this would be approached in entirely different ways.[77]

---

73 See Waschkuhn 2003, p. 223.
74 Waschkuhn 2003, p. 13.
75 On this term, see Saage 2000, p. 358.
76 Here, Martin D'Idler was not wrong to distinguish between nature mysticism and nature rationality of the type described by Callenbach. The latter is, according to Idler – in contrast to nature mysticism – not regressive but rather founded on harmonious coexistence between human beings and the natural environment on the basis of human reason. See Idler 1999, p. 118.
77 Saage 2000, p. 364.

Technology plays a different role now. Aware that technological progress is accompanied by a negative dialectic, manifest in the alienation and destruction of humankind and the environment, we now strive to use technology more cautiously.[78]

In post-materialist utopias, provided that it neither becomes an obligation nor alienates people, physical work has positive connotations. Out of a sense of social responsibility and because it contributes to a personal feeling of wellbeing, intellectuals now perform physical work as well. Work serves as relaxation, is fun, and is an autonomous activity carried out without state or rather collective coercion.[79] For the sake of conserving resources, people abstained from consumption and accepted a reduction in the material standard of living. Renouncing consumption is seen in a positive light from an ethical perspective.

> The needs that are to be met are thus post-materialist in the literal sense of the word, in that they balk at the uninhibited consumption of goods which prevails in the industrialised countries of the West.[80]

As a substitute for consumption, these societies engage in drugs, sex and love, art and music, for instance. The 'primacy of ecology' prevails.[81] Methods of family planning such as free contraception change the structure of society. Monogamy and small families are considered anachronistic and are supplanted by new concepts such as raising children in groups. Gender equality is also achieved.[82]

This pursuit of participation and individualisation stands in opposition to the technological state, which tries or tried to incorporate individuals into sociotechnical superstructures. It is here that we can observe the antagonism between emancipation and étatism. Competitiveness, consumption and egoism are criticised, a value shift towards more quality of life begins. Elites are called into question and participatory alternatives conceived.[83]

In post-materialist utopias, there is no longer a process of history directed towards a final state, as described by Georg Wilhelm Friedrich Hegel.[84]

---

78 See Saage 2000, p. 366f. Modern ecological utopias are opposed to 'Luddism' and call for a rational approach to technical progress. See Idler 1999, p. 39.
79 '... all post-materialist utopias break with the Puritan work ethic ...' (Saage 2003, p. 337).
80 Saage 2000, p. 373.
81 Saage 2000, p. 374.
82 See Saage 2000, p. 375.
83 See Saage 2003, p. 448f.
84 'Utopias no longer find themselves in an ahistorical space, i.e. they are consciously derived

'Accordingly, Western-style industrialisation, celebrated well into the twentieth century by the older utopianists as the materialisation of world-historical progress, is no longer understood as the foundation but rather as the downfall of utopian society'.[85] Nevertheless, it is important to note that the break with the Hegelian philosophy of history in the Marxist-leaning utopias penned by Bahro, Harich and Havemann was nowhere near as explicit as this and the moments of self-reflection also much less distinct. That said, they did exceed the limited paradigm of Marxism-Leninism, and this makes them all the more pertinent for contemporary discourses. They combined the two historical phases of development of 'scientific socialism' with archistic or anarchistic utopia and embedded each of their utopian scenarios within these two phases, though Harich completely revised the Marxist philosophy of history on the basis of ecological principles.

In sum, although the configuration of the different elements varies, the newer utopias all feature certain key aspects: the decentralisation of politics and the economy; the fact that science and technology no longer exclusively serve economic prosperity; the positive role of work as an individual, emancipatory act; the renunciation of (superfluous) consumption and luxury; the revaluation of sexuality and the arts; a greater focus on the emancipation of women; and finally, the calling into question of the philosophy of history in the sense of faith in progress. The dissonance between individuality and collective reason is, however, not resolved, the possibility of coercion remains, and the danger of disenfranchisement continues to exist.[86]

According to Waschkuhn, even the more recent utopias –

> cannot necessarily be interpreted as individualistic visions, because superego categories such as nature and the (female) sex are interwoven with the new normative homogeneity of the common good (at times even enriched by the holistic myth of nature), and thus they no longer allow for a diversity of the criteria of distribution – as always based on a more solid and more considered view about what form the good life might take. Individual consciousness is controlled by social consciousness, albeit with the inclusion of elements of reflexive scepticism.[87]

---

from European history, they appear as an extension of the positive or negative trends of the present. As a result, the history of utopia itself also remains open' (Heyer 2006b, p. 142).
85   Saage 2000, p. 383.
86   See Saage 2000, p. 405 f.
87   Waschkuhn 2003, p. 231.

Moreover, in terms of the purpose of utopia, there was a break with the classical utopian tradition:

> [u]topias no longer claimed to provide the best social structure of all, instead seeking to make a contribution to social discourse about the shape of the future. The ecological utopias published since the 1970s, however, left no doubt that the society of the future had to be geared towards the needs of humankind, not only socially but also environmentally.[88]

In his study on modern ecological utopias, Martin d'Idler remarks that it is problematic for scholars to clearly interpret the impact of post-materialist utopias today, first of all because not enough time has passed and, secondly, because the most actively involved individuals tend to belong to an opaque subculture (anarchists, environmental activists) and so appear heavily shielded. Idler goes on to say that the effects and causal relationships are, in this case, also difficult to prove empirically.[89] Though this assertion is largely correct, it has to be modified somewhat for the GDR because, when it comes to the opposition's impact during the 1989/90 period, certain effects can in fact be identified.

4   Time, Place, and Actors

The GDR and actually existing socialism in the sphere of influence of the Soviet Union constituted quite a unique scenario with regard to political utopia and the possibilities for its development. The intellectual narrow-mindedness of the dogmatic scientific community provided fertile ground for (sub)cultural niches, in which the potential for political utopia was harnessed and brought to fruition. Consequently, utopia was a clear thread running through the history of the GDR opposition, starting with Ernst Bloch, who brought his utopian writings to the GDR from his exile in the United States and was forced to leave the country again for the self-same works, extending to the key actors of the 1989 revolutionary period who developed ideas and concepts of a Third Way as an alternative to capitalism and actually existing socialism.

---

88   Idler 1999, p. 11.
89   See Idler 1999, p. 124.

The specific circumstances of 1989/90 were one reason why the potential for utopia failed to come to fruition. However, the reasons for this also lie in a much earlier era, that of the Soviet Occupation Zone (SBZ) at the end of the 1940s, a period that, to a certain extent, the dissidents also criticised in their utopias. In any event, during the almost 44 years of the SED's existence, there were constant deviations and deviants from the course, both within and outside the party.

Temporally speaking, in the broadest sense, my analysis of Bahro's, Harich's, and Havemann's utopias covers the years from 1945 to 1990 and, more specifically, the second half of the 1970s. Ultimately, the utopias did not occur extemporaneously but were closely linked with the political, social, economic, environmental, as well as historical, philosophical and cultural developments in the GDR. Moreover, this objective situatedness should be supplemented with a subjective one in the form of biographical details about the dissidents themselves.

Another reason for my decision to focus the analysis on the second half of the 1970s is that an international ecological discourse emerged at this time. Up until this point, there had been no ecological utopias in the GDR.[90] Moreover, the 1970s represented the heyday of Marxist dissidence. In the 1980s, in contrast, it was the opposition that emerged around and on the physical premises of the church that was most influential.[91] In addition, the 1980s environmental movement had less of a theoretical orientation but was much more practical in its approach. The era of intellectual dissidents hiding behind their desks was

---

90 Even Ernst Bloch, the 'founding father of utopia in the GDR', cannot, despite the passages from his book that strive for a harmonious relationship between humans and nature, be called a pioneer or even an author of ecological utopias. On the contrary, his understanding of nature was primarily instrumental, and the question of the environment played a peripheral role in his work. See Idler 1999, p. 68f. Regarding Bloch's worship of technology and his positive position on civilian use of nuclear power, Joachim Radkau writes: 'The "peaceful atom", which seemed to fit in with the "swords into ploughshares" slogan, did help to drive out fears of the atom bomb; the common emphasis on peace, typical of the early postwar decades, may be found both in the in the "Göttingen Manifesto" of 1957 (composed by West German nuclear physicists) and in the French "atomic pope" Fréderic Joliot-Curie. The most fanatical expressions figure in *Das Prinzip Hoffnung* ..., the magnum opus of the prophet-philosopher Ernst Bloch, who sees nuclear energy ... as right up there alongside solar energy' (Radkau 2014, p. 68f.). On the one hand, the GDR's Marxist intellectuals welcomed the civilian use of nuclear power, but publicly opposed military use, particularly by the US, on the other. Besides Bloch, Havemann and Harich are particularly worth mentioning in this context.

91 See Geisel 2000, p. 51f.

a thing of the past. Now the pragmatists shaped the opposition. Hence, the three selected texts originate in a period which furnishes them with a discursive frame, while providing justification for the decision to limit the study to this period of time.

In the same way that any analysis of post-materialist utopias in the Western hemisphere generally tends to take Ursula K. Le Guin's novel *The Dispossessed: An Ambiguous Utopia*, Ernest Callenbach's *Ecotopia* and Marge Piercy's *Woman on the Edge of Time* as examples, three important works by Bahro, Harich and Havemann must be referred to in any examination of the unique context of the GDR.

There were undoubtedly many other utopian authors in the GDR.[92] In addition to the political utopias penned by Ernst Bloch, who has already been mentioned above, Rolf Henrich, Christa Wolf, Stefan Heym, Lothar Kühne, Helmut Seidel, Michael Brie and many others,[93] there is also a broad spectrum of lighter works of fiction written by authors such as Gerhard Branstner or Gert Prokop. Although these novels were described by their publishers as utopias, they ought to be classified primarily as futuristic and science fiction literature. These works unmistakably contain political utopian elements or, in the case of Prokop's *Wer stiehlt schon Unterschenkel* (Who steals legs?) (1977) and *Der Samenbankraub* (The sperm bank robbery) (1983), what are clearly elements of ecological dystopia. What they lack, however, is a critique of actually existing socialism and the development of an alternative system. For this reason, these books fall outside the scope of the present study. Given that it did provide a critique of contemporary capitalism, we should not reject *a priori* the idea of situating GDR fantasy literature in the history of the utopian genre. That said, this critique often entailed little more than contrasts between capitalism and models of (real) socialism.

Havemann, Harich, and Bahro, for their part, were all from the higher echelons of the SED and, although they ultimately distanced themselves from the party doctrine and came into conflict with the party leadership, they nonetheless never completely turned away from the idea of socialism and remnants of loyalty or sympathy for the ruling party remained. As dissidents who themselves identified as Marxists living in a state which drew its legitimacy from Marxist doctrine, the conflicting priorities they faced were instrumental in making their political utopias unique. Their aim was not to abolish the GDR

---

92 See Heyer 2009, p. 5f.
93 The brochure entitled *Linke Utopien – die Zukunft denken* (Left utopias – imagining the future) by Kinner and Wurl 2006 provides a good overview here.

but rather, consistent with historical dialectics, to sublate society into a state in which the achievements of socialism are maintained and advance to a higher level.

These critics of the system aimed to synthesise the successes of the bourgeois revolutions and the advantages of actually existing socialism against a backdrop of 'Limits to Growth'. To achieve this, the three authors developed different concepts: While Harich's utopia was a global eco-dictatorship based on archism and asceticism, Havemann and Bahro geared their utopias towards anarcho-communist counter ideologies to the GDR system, albeit very distinct in their individual forms.

Moreover, the peculiarity of left-wing critics in the socialist state was of particular importance to the authorities. How the texts were received by the government bodies bears witness to this. On the one hand, the left-wing opposition were unwelcome rivals competing for the favour of the socialist-minded members of the population and yet, at the same time, they legitimised the existence of the organs of repression and gave the powers that be an enemy figure that was used to justify national surveillance.[94] The three dissidents came from within the ranks of the SED, the very party that then shunned them. From that moment on, at the very latest, they had nothing else to lose and felt free to posit their ideas publicly, partly also because the authorities' treatment of the opposition was less harsh following the shift in foreign policy at the start of the 1970s. Clearly, the GDR did not suddenly become a pluralist constitutional state once it had signed the Helsinki Declaration in 1975, and, in fact, a permanent atmosphere of tension continued to prevail between the authorities and the dissenters, although the former gradually began to lose power partly as a result of foreign policy and economic factors.

Consequently, the party began to rely on strategies of prevention and exclusion, which frequently only resulted in bad publicity for the SED leadership. It was due to German singer-songwriter Wolf Biermann's expatriation that he first became known to the broader public, for example.[95] Although the powers

---

94 'Utopia is the most dangerous challenge to power and yet, at the same time, is also its lifeblood. ... Every church depends on its heretics. The preachers of heresy, the rebels and dissidents are the life source of every dogmatically structured faith community, whether religious or secular. They almost always act in the name of the original purity, the true and unadulterated doctrine. They invoke the writings of the founders of religion, comparing them with reality, and call for a return *ad fontes* (to the sources). They are the thorn in the side of the rich and flaccid temple priests. It is over their bodies that the powerful warm their cold bones. Nobody needs the heretic more than the inquisition' (Hertle and Wolle 2004, p. 128).

95 See Havemann, K. and Widmann 2003, p. 16 f.

that be made many such strategic errors, it still seemed impossible for the system to break the mould and free itself from its rigid structure, resulting in it frequently being wrong footed:

> Havemann's call in 1976 for independent opposition parties or 'a newspaper independent of government organisations and able to publicly criticise all political and economic processes' to be permitted had no chance given the position of the SED leadership. However, it did make it clear what direction the reforms would have had to take to make the GDR government more stable and the leadership more secure.[96]

Based on their seemingly papal claim to sole representation and infallibility,[97] the system and the political leadership appeared to be completely resistant to criticism. The existence and demands of the opposition were not subject to self-criticism, but rather simply attributed to the hostile influence of the West.[98] This was as true of the Prague Spring as it was of the East German uprising of 1953.[99] In hindsight, even some of the leading Stasi cadres have said that the treatment of Marxist dissidents was not the right course of action. Take retired colonel Reinhard Grimmer, for example, who says:

> If the actions of these individuals were aimed at achieving change and reform in the GDR by means of constructive criticism, then dialogue, open and honest confrontation and mutual understanding should have been decisive. Forcing them into a 'hostile corner', as was frequently the case, only ever had counterproductive consequences.[100]

---

96 Weber 1991, p. 140.
97 Here, reference is being made to the conflict between the SED and Ernst Bloch over his demand for a new philosophy drawing on Marx's 11th Thesis on Feuerbach. See Amberger 2013, p. 568ff., Zwerenz, I. and Zwerenz, G. 2004, p. 165.
98 See Grimmer 2003, p. 256.
99 See Grimmer 2003, p. 178ff.
100 Grimmer 2003, p. 250. And the retired Lieutenant Colonel of the Stasi, Wolfgang Schmidt writes: 'The measures introduced by the Stasi in the form of years of intensive surveillance impacted many renowned cultural professionals, particularly writers such as Christa Wolf, Stefan Heym, Stephan Hermlin, Franz Fühmann, Günther de Bruyn and Volker Braun. The intention was mainly to prevent a possible renunciation of the GDR or the exploitation of such individuals for Western propaganda purposes as well as to support the efforts of the SED and responsible state functionaries in promoting constructive cooperation based on trust. The measures escalated following the expatriation of Wolf Biermann in November 1976. The protests sparked by this move not only highlighted that the GDR should have put up with Biermann, but also quite rightly that the method of expatriation was ques-

The legal situation in the GDR was far from tolerant of regime opposition, however, and a series of elastic legislative clauses[101] provided for considerable scope when it came to criminal prosecution. That said, the more prominent the opposition figure and the longer the GDR had been existence, the less harsh the criminal prosecution.[102] Opposition figures were not the only ones to have sanctions imposed on them, however. Members of the SED themselves were not immune and for the duration of its existence, the Socialist Unity Party doled out 800,000 party sanctions that sought to 'keep party members in line'.[103] The oppressive nature of this political climate is something that has to be borne in mind when studying dissidents' attempts at literary and philosophical escape.

The political leadership's goal to create a socialist society went hand in hand with a strong emphasis on educating young people in keeping with the state doctrine. To this effect, the official state youth organisation, the Free German Youth (FDJ), was an omnipresent force and young people who deviated from the norm quickly ended up in conflict with the government authorities. The 'hippies' who were disparagingly referred to as 'layabouts' even in the more conservative FRG had even less freedom in the GDR. Their culture was perceived as undesirable and contrasted sharply with the stuffy middle-class ideal of the members of the FDJ.[104] Accordingly, the ideas of the hippy culture which had such a formative influence on ecological utopia conflicted with state ideology. And the same applied to post-materialist utopia. In fact, environmental protection issues in the GDR were given very little attention because the process of economic catch-up in the context of systemic rivalry with the West left no space

---

tionable. The subsequent exclusion of critical writers from the GDR association of writers (*Deutscher Schriftstellerverband*) including Stefan Heym, instigated by the SED leadership, proved to be short sighted and counterproductive. It was patently a grave political mistake' (Schmidt 2003, p. 632 f.).

101 'In December 1957, the *Volkskammer* amended the German Criminal Code, creating new legal ways of persecuting political opponents. Up until then, political offences could only be prosecuted under Article 6 of the Constitution. Now the new law defined state treason, espionage and collecting information as crimes. Moreover, links with "other states and their representatives or groups conducting a struggle against the workers' and farmers' power", in other words, connections with practically any non-communist organisation, was punishable with up to three years in prison. With sections of the law on "anti-state propaganda" and "incitement of popular hatred" and "state defamation", even telling political jokes was potentially a criminal act. The new law also made "inducing others to leave the GDR" punishable. For serious cases of state treason, espionage and diversion, the death penalty was even reintroduced' (Weber 1991, p. 83 f.).
102 See Schmidt 2003, p. 652.
103 Zwerenz and Zwerenz 2004, p. 195.
104 See Hertle and Wolle 2004, p. 136.

to reflect on the environment. The dangers of continued exponential growth as illustrated by the Club of Rome in the early 1970s, was met with ignorance or resistance in the GDR. Very few intellectuals tackled the issue, and along with Bahro, only Harich and Havemann took the notion of limiting or halting growth seriously as a viable alternative. Although their responses were quite different, they all had 'indisputably utopian qualities'.[105]

In sum, at the time, the GDR was an extremely ill-suited location for ecological utopias – and yet, they still appeared.

5 Political Utopia and the GDR

Was the GDR a political utopia? Despite one or two areas of overlap, the answer to this question is a definitive no, for two reasons: firstly, the GDR was not utopian in terms of its self-defined ideological aspirations and secondly, actually existing socialism does not adequately meet the criteria of a classical political utopia.

Invoking the 'classics of Marxism', the GDR defined itself as anti-utopian. Across the philosophical publications that appeared in the GDR, the general consensus was that social utopia, although a necessity in the past, had become anachronistic since the achievement of socialism. In the *Philosophisches Wörterbuch* (Dictionary of philosophy) published in 1985, for instance, the entry for the term 'utopia' reads: 'Since scientific socialism signifies the end of utopia and this has thus lost its original dimension in socialism, not only is the term utopia no longer applicable but the utopian novels of the nineteenth and twentieth century are also essentially anachronistic'.[106] Drawing on Marx's and Engels's critique of utopia, this thus implied that, henceforth, anyone who continued to adhere to utopianism was deemed to be reactionary.[107]

---

105   Saage 2008, p. 153.
106   Buhr and Klaus (eds.) 1985, p. 1254.
107   Thus, Gottfried Handel considered Ernst Bloch a '... bourgeois philosopher who saw himself as a Marxist'. Handel 1983, p. 107. And was critical of Bloch's utopianism: 'Bloch's idealistic utopian view of socialism also proved its lack of a solid foundation both in theory and political practice, particularly in times where imperialism was exacerbating the class struggle. Bloch sympathised with counter-revolutionary endeavours in Hungary and Poland in 1955 [*sic!*] and advocated for revisionist activities in the ČSSR, which were outlawed in 1968. Bloch's political involvement in these situations can be traced back to his intellectual affinity with concepts that the revisionists propagated as "human socialism" and the right-leaning social democrats as "democratic socialism" and which conflict with actually existing socialism' (Handel 1983 p. 109f.).

INTRODUCTION

This rejection of utopia was not an SED invention but derived from the anti-utopian ambitions of Soviet ideology, whose 'classics' – Lenin, Marx and Engels – argued polemically against the utopianists, accusing them of being unscientific in their analysis of historical processes. They also contested the accusation that Marxism itself was utopian.[108]

While certain utopian elements could still be identified in Lenin's thinking and also in the ideas of some of the earlier Bolsheviks, such as Alexander Bogdanov,[109] by the end of the 1920s at the very latest, when Stalin came to power, a rift became evident: 'In the first half of the 1930s, the utopianism-inspired ideas of the left-wing post-revolutionary phase were eliminated, not only in ideology but in all areas of life and culture, and were replaced by what was referred to at the time as "Leninist" ideology'.[110]

The Stalinist and later post-Stalinist system that prevailed in the Soviet Union witnessed a gradual process of the 'erosion of utopia',[111] as Hans Günther described it. Though utopian elements and images occasionally cropped up, these served primarily ideological purposes and generally disappeared again after some time.[112]

Stalin's break with Marxism, which resulted from his belief in the possibility of a form of socialism confined to national borders, led to the loss of utopia, which was no longer desired as an alternative to reality. Calls to redeem the utopian ideal were countered with terror tactics. By prohibiting ideas and opinions, reality was portrayed as having no alternative.[113]

As an ideology, actually existing socialism was not dynamic. Here, there is a clear similarity with the older utopias, which also described a rigid historical end state. That said, the argument can be made that at least these utopias tended to depict a harmonious society oriented towards the common good, something that cannot really be said of the GDR, and that in modern utopias the homogeneity dogma was replaced by more dynamic concepts.

---

108 'Marx and Engels substituted a utopian fiction of the future society as seen from the perspective of the suppressed, with the premise of the fundamental predictability of the socialist alternative, which had different theoretical prerequisites to utopia. While the latter comprises anticipatory wishful dreams, the former is based on forecasts, on the extrapolation – admittedly corroborated by history in Marxist discourse – of facts and trends in existing society' (Saage 2000, p. 24f.).
109 See Saage 2003 p. 52 ff.
110 Günther 1985, p. 379.
111 Günther 1985, p. 378.
112 See Günther 1985, p. 388.
113 See Negt 1998, p. 57 f.

But what of the argument that the founding generation of the GDR held utopian ideals that they perceived as having real prospects of success? Many of those returning from exile harboured real hopes of creating an independent German state furnished with characteristics from the tradition of utopian socialism. The most prominent of these returnees with clear connections to utopianism was undoubtedly Ernst Bloch. But many other intellectuals – for the most part those who had been exiled in the West – returned to the SBZ full of expectation, among them Anna Seghers, Bertolt Brecht, Stefan Heym, Walter Janka and Paul Merker.

Initially a relatively independent fresh start did indeed appear feasible. A climate of freedom evolved, which was hardly surprising after 12 years of fascism.[114] But even in those days, appearances could be deceptive. Wolfgang Leonhard reported that, in early May 1945 (before the capitulation of the Nazi regime), in reference to the creation of the Berlin district administration under the Soviet commandant, Walter Ulbricht had said to his comrades-in-arms, including Leonhard himself: 'It's quite clear – it's got to look democratic, but we must have everything in our control'.[115] Although this quote only referred to the specific situation regarding recruitment immediately after the war,[116] it still showed that the Soviet occupying powers were making their demands known internally, even at this early stage.

From then on, the SBZ/GDR was a Soviet satellite state and was dominated politically, economically and culturally by the hegemonic power. Ulbricht later felt the impact of this, when, in the 1960s, the Moscow government blocked his course towards more national autonomy, enabling Honecker to come to power.[117]

After World War II, the Stalinist system was transferred to the new countries of the Eastern Bloc, factoring in country-specific conditions, with, for instance, several parties being permitted in the SBZ/GDR. At the start, for example, the SED was

> ... not established on the basis of the Soviet model; the principles of Marxism for example were adhered to, whereas Leninism was not. Of course, in day-to-day practical politics the SED was still the extended arm of the

---

114 On this, see Schivelbusch 1997.
115 Leonhard 1958, p. 303. On this, see also the *Tulpanov Report* published in 2012.
116 And not on the 'destruction of bourgeois democracy', as Ehrhart Neubert 1999, p. 34 claimed. According to this interpretation, the Nazi regime was a bourgeois democracy, destroyed by the Red Army.
117 See Weber 1991, p. 106, Frank 2001, p. 387 ff.

Soviet occupying powers. With the help of the Soviet Union, the SED was able to fill key positions in the administration, police force, economy and mass media.[118]

Moscow's influence was unmistakable. And since, as shown above, Stalinism had broken with utopia, we cannot refer to the GDR as a utopia either. Indeed, the GDR was not a utopia in the classical sense because a utopia is defined as a situation where 'the better alternative to the given status quo represents a *fictional concept*: it is this difference and only this difference that establishes its claim to be a regulatory principle of political practice, a source of knowledge that can provide guidance and give direction for people's actions'.[119] Given that a utopian outline is something imagined, an ideational counter-project to what exists, it must 'inevitably lose its ideality when it enters reality'.[120]

Ernst Bloch likewise rejected the possibility of utopia and its realisation occurring simultaneously. The purpose of utopia is to serve as the seed of revolutionary processes. Subsequently, these processes would go on to become thickly encrusted with ideology.[121] He described utopias as roadmaps for the future that are anchored in the present. This concept was diametrically opposed to that of ideology.

> In the simplest sense, the difference between utopia and ideology is that ideologies do not have a utopian component, that ideologies are groups of ideas reflecting and justifying the existing society. Utopias, in contrast, are or at least should be and generally are, ideas and perceptions held by groups that undermine and break up existing society or at least pave the way for its destruction with the dream of a better world, a better society.[122]

This also rebuts the thesis posited in the conservative critique of utopia, according to which the systems that evolved in the aftermath of the October Revolution were utopian or rather utopias that had come to fruition. There could be

---

118 Weber 1991, p. 24. On this, see also Christina Trittel's dissertation *Die Landtagsfraktionen in Sachsen Anhalt von 1946 bis 1950*, Wiesbaden 2006.
119 Saage 2008, p. 151.
120 Heyer 2006b, p. 9.
121 See Bloch 1980, p. 68f.
122 Bloch 1980, p. 70. That said, this quote also illustrates the difficulties in narrowing down Bloch's concept of 'concrete utopia'.

no truth in this because utopia's function as a normative corrective measure to the status quo, a function that is firmly anchored in the concept of the classical utopia, is not fulfilled.[123] According to this concept, utopias cannot be achieved in reality. The realisation of a utopia would be synonymous with its end, thus prompting the creation of new utopias, which, in turn, function as a normative corrective measure for the existing utopia. Even if the GDR had been a real utopia, by 7 October 1949 at the latest, the term 'utopia' could no longer have been used to describe it.

This does not, however, mean by implication that the GDR system had no elements of the utopian tradition, or no utopian content at all. Although the conclusion Matthias Krauß reached in his comparison of the GDR with More's *Utopia* may be somewhat questionable in terms of the methodology he used: 'If utopia is the best of all worlds, then the GDR must have been better than the best of all worlds'.[124] A sober comparison of the GDR system with the classical utopian tradition does, however, reveal parallels with the archistic type of utopia.

The first of these parallels can be found with the political economic system. In the GDR, this was a highly centralised system headed by a functionary elite which asserted a vanguard claim to control the economy and society. Planned economies can also be found in many classical utopias of the archistic tradition, including those by Thomas More, Étienne-Gabriel Morelly, and Gracchus Babeuf. Centralism is correlated with anti-individualism, which is also part of the classical utopian tradition. The stifling effects of this centralised system on innovation are said to have played a crucial role in the ultimate demise of the GDR.[125] The elite's claim, especially prevalent during the early years of the GDR, that it should shape society in its entirety, and the belief that nature and people could be controlled and planned with technology led to the creation of a huge surveillance apparatus and to the plundering of nature without any possibility of effective opposition by environmentalists. The lack of supervisory authorities resulted in a blinkered, self-righteous elite, which ultimately led to the ossification of the entire system.[126]

The architecture of actually existing socialism exhibited certain parallels with the buildings depicted over the history of utopia, both being rooted in anti-individualism. Symptomatic of this are the new high-rise blocks of flats

---

123 See Heyer 2006b, p. 71f.
124 Krauß 2008, p. 21.
125 See Saage 2002a.
126 See Saage 2003, p. 540.

which often formed entire (satellite) towns (such as Berlin-Marzahn, Halle-Neustadt or Leipzig-Grünau). This type of architecture had already been criticised in one of the first dystopian novels, Yevgeny Zamyatin's *We*, which was published as a reaction to the post-revolutionary situation in Russia. However, more frequently, the dystopia seemed to be the genre of choice when it came to examining the police and surveillance apparatus. These organs of repression were (at least in part) devised and implemented for all those who refused to adapt to the desired social structure.

Adherence to the philosophy of history, the ruling elite's belief in the completeness of history, also directly contradicted Marxism. Describing the historical dynamics, Bloch writes:

> Since Marx, the abstract character of utopias has been overcome; world improvement occurs as work in and with the dialectical coherence of the objective world, with the material dialectics of a comprehended, consciously manufactured history.[127]

Although the GDR was not cut off from progress, over its more than 40-year history, the lofty goals and ambitions it set gradually diminished. The stagnation was most evident after the removal of Ulbricht. While Ulbricht had still maintained certain socio-political visions, once he was ousted, a seemingly bourgeois consumerism came to the fore. From an economic policy perspective, the consequences were catastrophic. In terms of civil and human rights, in contrast, the Honecker era saw a relaxation of restrictions that also impacted the concept of man.[128]

The image of the 'New Man' is one of the most important characteristics of political utopia. In the Soviet Union, the Stalin era brought an anthropological rift, with the Russian-Asian peasantry opposing the Bolsheviks' desire for progress at all costs. For Stalin, the concept of the 'New Man' was pivotal and he saw a 'comprehensive polytechnic education'[129] as an important part of its formation. As early as 1928, Stalin extolled the virtues of the engineer, putting him on a pedestal as the 'New Man', essential for building communism, part of the bigger whole and anti-individualistic in his actions.

This anti-individualism played a very important role, even being incorporated into the 1977 Soviet Constitution. The individual was required to adapt to

---

127   Bloch 1986, p. 583.
128   See Weber 1991, p. 131 ff.
129   Saage 2003 p. 536 f.

the 'interests of all workers' and their individual (basic) rights were to be subordinated to this collective right. For the opposition this meant that anyone not acting in compliance with this principle would have their basic constitutional rights revoked.[130] Even with Ulbricht at the helm, the GDR still strived for an ideal of humanity, the achievement of which was largely dependent on shaping young people.[131] Here, the notorious highpoint was the 11th Plenum of the Central Committee of the SED in December 1965 with its policy of cultural crackdown or 'clear-cutting' (*Kahlschlag*). This pressure on young people to conform dwindled after Ulbricht was removed from power but never completely disappeared.

Thus, the GDR did have certain utopian elements, although there was little evidence of the progressive characteristics of utopia emphasised by philosophers such as Ernst Bloch. Over the years, the GDR became increasingly inflexible, moving into a holistic end state, just as earlier utopianists had imagined. This lack of flexibility and momentum in a world which was perpetually moving forward was ultimately the GDR's downfall.

6   Meadows and the GDR

6.1   *The Economic Situation in the GDR*

It is impossible to explain the economic development of the SBZ/GDR without first situating it in the global historical context. From 1945 to 1990, external factors permanently shaped the history of East Germany, ultimately also playing a pivotal role in its demise. Were it not for the GDR's dependence on the Soviet Union, a relationship declared to be friendly, on the one hand, and on the West as a much maligned and yet necessary trade partner, on the other, the GDR would not even have been conceivable.

---

130   See Saage 2003, p. 535 ff.
131   Werner Mittenzwei describes Ulbricht's cultural and human ideal as the means for the achievement of these goals: 'Ulbricht's cultural policy comprised an eclectic mix of elements he adopted from Soviet arts and cultural policy and what he personally thought was good and fitting for the educated nation he was striving to create. He remained unimpressed by the workers' culture of the 1920s. Modern art concepts were alien to him. Nor could he envisage that every generation of artists had to hold their predecessors to account, to kill off their "artistic fathers". Or as the young Peter Hacks put it: "Whatever you inherit from your forefathers you must reject in order that you might take ownership of it." For Ulbricht this was barbarism. He advocated the concept of continuity, which sought to prevent every form of provocative artistic productivity. Like a disciplinarian task mas-

The foundation was laid early on, when the gap between the economy and standards of living in this part of the former German Empire (whose economy and infrastructure were already weak) and West Germany started to widen due to the high reparation payments to and lack of reconstruction assistance from the Soviet occupying powers to the East.[132] Industrial development and the associated emergence of a working class had, for decades, already been far more advanced in West Germany than in the predominantly agrarian Prussia. Although many of West Germany's industrial plants were also destroyed during World War II, its industrial infrastructure and skilled workers never totally disappeared. Since, compared to the SBZ, West Germany barely had to pay any reparations to the occupying powers, and because – in stark contrast – the Marshall Plan provided huge financial reconstruction assistance, enabling the country to replace the destroyed industrial facilities with machinery featuring first-rate, state-of-the-art technology, the FRG was able to embark on a period of economic growth, now widely referred to as the 'economic miracle'. What this does not mean, however, is that the GDR economy was destined to fail from the word go, just that it found itself in a catch-22 situation. On the one hand, there was the 'economic miracle' in West Germany, which was one reason behind the mass emigration of hordes of GDR citizens. And, on the other hand, the stringent economic policy guidelines issued by Moscow made it virtually impossible for the GDR to put different methods or alternative socialist models to the test. Torn between the population's material wishes and Soviet directives, in the 1950s and '60s, the SED leadership under Ulbricht attempted to steer a course in the direction of successful economic policy. Initially, the focus was on the reconstruction of the industrial facilities that had been destroyed by the war or dismantled and the machinery used to pay reparations to the USSR. And, to a certain extent, the efforts were successful, although they could not match the successes of the FRG. Once the reparation payments had all been settled in 1954, the GDR economy experienced marked growth. Vehicle production, for instance, thrived.[133] Towards the end of the decade, the SED leadership had become so confident that it even went as far as to assert that

---

ter he attempted to hammer the best of art and literature into the working class in order for it to constitute an educated nation' (Mittenzwei 2003, p. 260). In 1956, Harich criticised this Stalinist method of moulding human beings. After the 20th Party Congress, he wrote, full of hope: 'There is therefore no doubt that the misunderstandings and false dogmas ... belong just as much in the past as Stalin's bombastic architectural facades and the miserable clichés of the aesthetic of his engineers of the human soul' (Harich 1956, p. 656f.).

132   See Roesler 2002, p. 20.
133   See Prokop 2006, p. 77.

the GDR would have caught up with West Germany in terms of per capita consumption by 1961.[134] The GDR also benefited from help from the Soviet Union, which, because of the GDR's special status during the Cold War, now granted the country privileged support. But this all changed when, with the construction of the Berlin Wall in 1961, the grounds for this privilege ceased to exist and the Soviet Union itself was hit by economic crisis. At the same time, Leonid Brezhnev replaced GDR patron Nikita Khrushchev as General Secretary of the Communist Party.[135] Given this clear-cut status quo, on the other hand, it then became easier to focus unimpeded on the development of the economy.

At this time, the Communist Party of the Soviet Union (CPSU) resolved to build communism within the next 20 years,[136] whereby the focus was on creating a broad range of goods that would help the USSR outstrip Western industrial countries. The GDR's walled-in population was now to benefit from an economic boom with the all the associated improvements in material quality of life. With this in mind, in June 1963 the 'New Economic System of Planning and Management' was announced. This included creating material incentives for the development of small private businesses to increase economic growth, innovation capacity and labour productivity.[137] Rather than focusing on quantity, the economic policy pursued in the 1960s was aimed at increasing efficiency. There was great faith in the possibilities of science and progress. Almost messianic hope was placed in the potential of the chemical industry.[138] Given the shortage of raw materials such as steel or coal in the GDR, the intention was to produce a wide range of goods with the help of chemicals. The state and party leadership considered this to be the path to success and assumed at that point, not entirely erroneously, they were in the process of creating a competitive, indeed more attractive economic model as an alternative to capitalism.

> In 1968, Walter Ulbricht coined the dialectically astute phrase 'to overtake without catching up'. What he meant by this was that the GDR would be able to catch up with capitalism from a technological perspective, without having to endure the negative socio-political developments that accompanied progress. Ulbricht's maxim was often ridiculed and fre-

---

134 'The Federal Republic repeatedly served as a yardstick for the GDR, the mirror image, the *tertium comparationis*, the dialectic counterpart, like light to dark. The GDR drew its historical legitimation from the existence of the other German state. It defined itself through the FRG, both politically and ideologically' (Hertle and Wolle 2004, p. 259).
135 See Roesler 2002, p. 24.
136 See Hertle and Wolle 2004, p. 110.
137 See Weber 1991, p. 119 ff.
138 See Hertle and Wolle 2004, p. 117. See also Kaminsky 1999, p. 26.

quently misconstrued. This was essentially the last attempt to articulate the utopia of the global triumph of socialism in concrete terms, to portray it as an everyday routine. In his later years, Ulbricht recognised that the decision between socialism and capitalism would be made in the realm of labour productivity and pinned his hopes on the supposed superiority of his system resulting from national government planning in scientific innovation.[139]

Towards the end of the decade, however, the rise of actually existing socialism came to a halt. In 1970, the GDR faced supply shortfalls resulting from the neglect of the consumer goods industry. Subsequently, the country was forced to import consumer goods at high prices, a decision that, in turn, increased the GDR's external debt.[140]

Similar phenomena were observed in other Eastern Bloc countries which had experimented with reform in the 1960s. After the violent suppression of strikes and protest actions by Polish workers responding to attempts at economic restructuring in December 1970, it was decided in 1970/71 that a U-turn was needed in the economic and social policy of all Eastern Bloc countries with the exception of Romania.[141]

The 1970/71 workers' uprisings in Poland also gave the SED leadership something of a scare, galvanising it to change tack on economic policy with a view to nipping any further social unrest in the bud.[142] Although there was certainly nothing to complain about when it came to economic growth (five percent in 1970),[143] the economic policy priorities did not enable the government to meet demand for consumer goods. At the 8th Party Conference of the SED in June 1971, the first to be held under Ulbricht's successor Erich Honecker, Honecker established new premises in economic policy, calling for the 'unity of economic and social policy' and referring to the GDR as a 'developed socialist society', thus making the goal to achieve communism a distant prospect.[144] Investment

---

139   Hertle and Wolle 2004, p. 116.
140   See Hertle and Wolle 2004, p. 158 f.
141   Steiner 2007, p. 165.
142   See Klenke 2007, p. 6.
143   See Steiner 2007, p. 274.
144   'The loss of the communist utopia, the shifting of its time horizon to an uncertain point in the future, brought the complexity and contradictions of society into sharp focus. According to its own Marxist-Leninist theory, if the party leadership were to give up the goal of equality and freedom in exchange for a future that would soon be attainable, it would no

in the technology sector was scaled back in favour of improving the quality of life of the workers. The resources that were freed up were used to improve the population's living conditions in an attempt to boost their work motivation. In other words, the resources were invested in 'human capital' rather than in economic infrastructure. The hope was that the increased motivation would boost labour productivity, allowing the investment to be recovered in the medium term.[145]

Hence, the new government under Honecker sought primarily to improve the supply situation and upgrade social security.[146] This would be achieved through a centralised economy with production geared towards quantity over quality ('more-is-better ideology') in huge industrial complexes known as *Kombinate*.

The departure from the subtly market economy-oriented approaches pursued in the Ulbricht era culminated in 1972 in the nationalisation of the remaining 11,000 small and microenterprises, most of which filled artisanal niches.[147] The negative impact of this measure on the capacity to supply the population with consumer goods was palpable:

> Now it was the job of the economic planners to take care of the '1,000 little things' that made up everyday necessities, things which, so far, flexible small and medium-sized enterprises had managed to produce on their own and which now gradually disappeared from the shelves.[148]

Attempts were made to bridge these gaps by 'requiring the companies and industrial complexes that were part of heavy and primary industries to pro-

---

longer be in a position to claim legitimacy. The SED resorted – like the other communist parties – to the concept of a "developed socialist society". Although this was the necessary precursor to communism, it was quite clear that, in political practice, this goal was not being pursued' (Meuschel 1991, p. 39).

145 See Steiner 2007, p. 168.
146 The socio-political measures included, for instance, an increase in the (minimum) wage and pensions, more holiday, financial support for parents and more childcare facilities. 'What was striking was that the substance and standards of socio-political measures continued to be geared towards the needs of working-class families in the interwar years, the period during which most of the members of SED leadership had been politically socialised. The majority of the population measured their own life circumstances against the standards that had been achieved in the West. This discrepancy inevitably became a new source of disgruntlement' (Steiner 2007, p. 197).
147 See Hertle and Wolle 2004, p. 167 ff.
148 Hertle and Wolle 2004, p. 170.

duce consumer goods'.[149] As a result, the state increased its share in industrial goods production from 82 to almost 100 percent in the course of a year.[150]

It was not the policy of centralisation that was the main contributory factor in the decline of the GDR economy, however. In fact, international factors had a crucial impact which was impossible to cushion because domestic political and ideological directives thwarted flexible and appropriate political and economic action. The GDR found itself in a debt trap. Imports from the West (primarily consumer goods and industrial equipment) increased external debt. However, the anticipated boost in motivation as a result of an improvement in the workers' general standards of living failed to materialise.[151] Additionally, the resultant massive deterioration in the terms of trade had a major impact on the GDR economy with its heavy dependence on foreign currency and exports.[152] The price of imported goods increased, while export goods failed to bring in the desired foreign exchange revenues. This, in turn, saw external debt continue its upward trend.[153] Since the SED wanted to avoid social unrest among the population at all costs, cuts in spending on social security or consumer goods imports were not an option. Moreover, the promise to freeze consumer prices prevented the government from adjusting commodity prices to the global market and, as a result, government subsidies were needed to make up the difference.[154]

But this wasn't the only context where the SED's promises proved expensive. The housing construction programme adopted in 1973 swallowed up significant financial resources and led to discontentment among those groups of the population that were unable to benefit from the programme:

> State subsidies for housing increased from 2.1 billion East German marks in 1971 to 16 billion in 1988. In the same period, the pooling of resources for new residential construction accelerated the decay of the existing older buildings.[155]

---

149 Hertle and Wolle 2004, p. 173.
150 See Weber 1991, p. 141.
151 'This policy was expected to improve employee performance. However, because the socio-political regulations were not explicitly linked to corresponding incentives, it did not produce the desired results. The fact that employees' individual performance failed to bring about a better standard of living, nor the social security that was seemingly promised, had a negative impact on performance motivation over the long term' (Steiner 2007, p. 188).
152 See Nawrocki 1975.
153 'Between 1975 and 1982 alone, the GDR's hard currency debt increased from 8.9 billion DM to 26.1 billion DM' (Roesler 2002, p. 27).
154 See Steiner 2007, p. 165, p. 187.
155 Hertle and Wolle 2004, p. 185.

The brunt of the housing construction programme was borne by the owners and tenants in the older apartments who had to cope with the worsening conditions. As much as 40 percent of existing older buildings were still privately owned. Added to this was the fact that the capital city were given priority, resulting in losses in the districts, which had to reassign construction capacities.[156]

The aim of Ulbricht's economic policy had been to improve efficiency. Under Honecker, this approach became a thing of the past and instead there was a return to quantitative growth on the assumption that, against the backdrop of the Cold War, whoever produced the most would ultimately be the victor. A textbook from the Higher Party School of the CPSU, a translation of which was published in the GDR in 1974, describes the approach:

> The quantitative characteristic of economic competition find their concentrated expression in the pace of economic growth. Inextricably linked to the rapid development of social reproduction is the consolidation of the economic and political power of the socialist economic system as well as its capacity to decisively influence the course of world history.[157]

The hope was that the economic crisis in the West was a sign of the imminent decline of capitalism and, at the same time, it was assumed that the GDR's own marked growth would soon enable it to overtake actually existing capitalism. Here the 'more-is-better' ideology was of the essence:

> The most important benchmarks in economic competition between the socialist and capitalist system is the size of production capacity and the quantity of products that each of the systems is able to produce.[158]

The fact that a quantitative growth approach such as this constituted an all-out risk to the economy and was also incredibly harmful to the environment is something that society certainly felt the effects of. But it was no longer possible to abandon the chosen path. In the course of the struggle over which system was the more successful, the East attempted to defeat the West at any cost, in the process completely abandoning the path of effective economic management and concentrating increasingly on the expansion of the consumer sector.

---

156 See Hertle and Wolle 2004, p. 185.
157 Party Academy of the Central Committee of the Communist Party of the Soviet Union (ed.) 1974, p. 377.
158 Party Academy of the Central Committee of the Communist Party of the Soviet Union (ed.) 1974, p. 385.

At the 9th Party Congress in 1976, the SED presented a new statute and a new party programme. Honecker's previous call for 'unity of economic and social policy' was once again heralded the right path to take.

> The party leadership thus made the tacit assumption that the specific life aspirations of the workers in the GDR were not fundamentally different from those of their counterparts in Western industrial, capitalist societies, leading them effectively to conceive a socialist consumer society of sorts. This decision was dictated by circumstances and, in this respect, with a view to retaining power, it was the right one at the time. That said, it also contained a significant element of defensive retreat from the supremacy of Western consumer ideals.[159]

Consumer promises, however, were increasingly being made at the expense of state debt. The state simply could not afford the wage and pension increases, the expansion of the service sector and the manifold socio-political concessions to the citizens. Although this risk was acknowledged by some of the state functionaries concerned with economic affairs at the time, the SED leadership under Honecker, could not and did not want to withdraw the concessions.[160]

Initially, this seemed to be the right policy:

> For a long time, the centrally planned economy was so successful that an international study conducted as late as the end of the 1970s came to the conclusion that, with its economic development, the GDR had 'outdone fully fledged market economies'. But the GDR's growth had a fatal flaw. As in other Eastern Bloc countries, compared to Western capitalist societies, the GDR needed substantially more resources to produce the same volume. Throughout its existence, the GDR's marginal capital coefficient, a term used to describe the effectiveness of investment, was almost always above that of the Federal Republic. The extensive growth was an expression of the system's dominant tendency towards waste. Companies' projected figures were based on production volumes, but their calculations underestimated the resources that would be required. This led to the emergence of the 'more-is-better ideology': The bigger the outlay needed to manufacture a product, the higher its designated value.[161]

---

159   Wolle 1999, p. 48.
160   See Wolle 1999, p. 50.
161   Klenke 2007, p. 6.

Another factor that had a negative impact on the GDR's economic development was the system of annual plans, which proved to be obstructive, hampering long-term planning and innovation.[162]

Towards the end of the 1970s, the full extent of the GDR's failed economic policy became evident. The country had missed its opportunity to enter the microelectronics market. There was a lack of innovation and investment. The West rapidly moved into the lead in the research and development field and it was no longer financially feasible for the GDR to catch up.

'Computerisation dramatically changed the global economic environment to the disadvantage of the Comecon countries.'[163] The GDR invested a small fortune in a microelectronics programme, but to no avail. It proved impossible to manufacture products that could compete on the global market. 'Instead of being a driver of growth, microelectronics became an overly expensive white elephant ...'.[164]

Besides the investment in the IT sector, huge sums were also spent on importing raw materials. Thanks to price lags resulting from the Comecon trade agreements, the GDR felt the effects of the 1973 oil price crisis later than the West – but when it did hit, the country certainly knew about it. Although it was still possible to export petroleum products at a profit, this left only scarce resources for domestic use. The GDR was almost entirely dependent on its own lignite to meet the country's energy requirements.[165]

Added to this were the enormous costs resulting from the new round of the arms race in the late 1970s. The increased defence spending but also the rising cost of the social system and consumer goods were such a huge burden on the state budget that investment in research and development was

---

162   For a summary of the steps involved in the planning process, i.e. how plans between companies, combines and political decision-makers were drawn up, see Judt 1998, p. 125 f. See Steiner 2007, p. 175.
163   Klenke 2007, p. 7.
164   Hertle and Wolle 2004, p. 228.
165   See Hertle and Wolle 2004, p. 197. 'Indeed, the early GDR did have an unparalleled competitive edge – the largest uranium deposits in the world. Unfortunately, the GDR was forced to export its uranium to Russia at no profit. ... In its place, the GDR imported Soviet oil – until, in 1981, Moscow cut its crude oil exports [to the GDR – author's addition] by two million tonnes. This news is said to have almost brought Erich Honecker to tears. The only options he was left with were brown coal and begging. Honecker's entreaties to the Russian envoy Konstantin Russakov are documented: "I plead with you to ask Comrade Brezhnev straight whether 2 million tonnes of crude oil is worth the price of instability in the GDR and the destruction of our people's trust in the Party and state leadership"' (Finger 2011, p. 27).

nigh on impossible.¹⁶⁶ And so, a decade after Honecker came to power, global market prices for additional imports and lending rates ultimately left the GDR dependent on Western lenders. Moreover, the high subsidies used to ensure price stability tore gaping holes in the budget, although it would have been virtually impossible for the government to adjust prices to the increased costs without provoking discontent among the population. Consequently, prices were not increased any further until 1989, causing 'government subsidies ... for food, consumer goods and transport tickets ... to rise to more than 50 billion Deutschmarks'.¹⁶⁷ And, at the same time, the 1980s also saw the GDR economy go into decline.

The constraints that burdened the system precluded every possible solution to the crisis. In order for the GDR to obtain the foreign currency it urgently needed to pay back its debts, it even exported to the West at prices that were below the production value.¹⁶⁸ This huge financial burden meant there were insufficient funds for investment and the country saw its economic infrastructure deteriorate.¹⁶⁹

6.2   *The Club of Rome and Post-materialist Discourse*

However, even in the capitalist West, the 'economic miracle' was not destined to last forever. The late 1960s saw a fundamental change in the structure of industrial nations. The West experienced its first severe crisis since the end of World War II. The technology-obsessed industrial society showed the first signs of crumbling and the transition to the service economy commenced. In his 1973 book *The Coming of Post-Industrial Society*, Daniel Bell attempted to capture this transition. According to Bell, in just a few short decades, the type of society he referred to as 'post-industrial' would shape the social fabric in a great many different countries, irrespective of the dominant ideology or religion.¹⁷⁰ He forecast the emergence of the knowledge and service society and the gradual decline in the importance of the manufacturing sector. He believed that the increase in 'brain work' would go hand in hand with a change in social structure. In the same way that industrial society brought 'semi-skilled workers', this new society would be accompanied by the emergence of a 'knowledge class'.¹⁷¹

---

166   See Steiner 2007, p. 180.
167   Hertle and Wolle 2004, p. 209.
168   'The share of trade with the Western world in GDR foreign trade as a whole increased between 1980 and 1989 from 27% to 51%' (Roesler 2002, p. 27).
169   See Hertle and Wolle 2004, p. 210 f.
170   See Bell 1976.
171   See Bell 1976, p. 15 ff. Bell's theory was rejected by the SED since it was based on cross-system development rather than the class struggle.

The value shift that this brought in its wake was closely correlated with the prevailing problems of the (capitalist) world order, some of which continue to exist even today. This post-materialist[172] transformation put topics on the political agenda that up until then had been either of peripheral importance or not even part of the debate, issues such as pacifism, the environment or women's emancipation.

The crisis of the bourgeois capitalist world of ideas came hand in hand with an economic crisis in the West. All this brought a renaissance of utopian and dystopian scenarios in its wake. This shift was not exclusive to left-wing political niches but even occupied major global corporations, a fact exemplified by the Club of Rome and its commissioning of the much-discussed Meadows Report.[173]

Founded in 1968, the Club of Rome consists of 100 current and former heads of state, scientists, business leaders and dignitaries from a wide range of different countries. The official objective of this non-democratically elected group is to advise on 'the most critical problems facing humanity; analysing the interrelationships of these problems'.[174] To examine this, in the early 1960s, the Club of Rome commissioned a team of researchers led by American scientist Dennis Meadows from the MIT to produce a report about the condition and future of humanity. The report was funded by the automobile manufacturer Volkswagen. Moreover, the co-founder of the Club of Rome, Aurelio Peccei, was a Member of the Board for the Italian car manufacturer Fiat. This, along with the close relationship the Club of Rome had with industry, engendered scepticism about the study from parties on the left of the political spectrum in the West and particularly from the GDR. A more in-depth discussion on this will be presented in the next section.

First though, since Wolfgang Harich drew heavily on the contents of the 1972 Meadows Study in *Communism without Growth?* and Bahro and Havemann both also referred to it, more detail on the report itself would be pertinent at this stage.

---

172 'This term circulated mainly though the work of the American political scientist Ronald Inglehard: *The Silent Revolution: Changing Values and Political Styles among Western Publics*, Princeton 1977' (Radkau 2014, p. 451). In the form of a chronology table, Radkau (ibid.) provides a useful overview of the most important events, works and debates at the beginning of the 'eco-age' around 1970.

173 Although Joachim Radkau saw the book's success as being largely due to the fact that it captured the zeitgeist that had been evolving over many years: '[T]he environmental boom began considerably earlier and provided the background for the huge success of *Limits to Growth*. Two decades before, most of the world's inhabitants would have thought it a banal truth that there were limits to growth' (Radkau 2014, p. 101).

174 Meadows 1972, p. 7.

The Meadows Report analysed five trends with a global impact: 'accelerating industrialization, rapid population growth, widespread malnutrition, depletion of non-renewable resources, and a deteriorating environment. These trends are all interconnected in many way'.[175]

Meadows and his colleagues forecast that, if these trends were not stopped, in a century they would inevitably result in the collapse of the human world order. In light of this, change was urgently needed, and the sooner the better. All five trends would be subject to exponential growth. In other words, their growth would accelerate increasingly rapidly (the intervals between doubling would grow shorter each time) and would, in contrast to simple linear growth, literally explode.[176] According to the report, this would have fatal consequences.

The aim of the MIT study was to extrapolate existing trends. The scientists involved were perfectly aware of the complexity of the problem and thus emphasised that it would be impossible to provide precise forecasts.[177] With the help of computers, they carefully calculated different combinations of developments,[178] yielding a dystopian collapse scenario that would arise if limits to growth were surpassed:

> In this run the collapse occurs because of non-renewable resource depletion. The industrial capital stock grows to a level that requires enormous input of resources. In the very process of that growth it depletes a large fraction of the resource reserves available. As resources prices rise and mines are depleted, more and more capital must be used to obtain resources, leaving less to be invested for future growth. Finally, investment cannot keep up with depreciation, and the industrial base collapses, taking with it the service and agricultural systems, which have become dependent on industrial outputs (such as fertilisers, pesticides, hospital laboratories, computers, and especially energy for mechanization). For a short time, the situation is especially serious because population, with the delays inherent in the age structure and the process of social adjustment, keeps rising. Population finally decreases when the death rate is driven upward by lack of food and health services. The exact timing of these events is not meaningful, given the great aggregation and many uncertainties in the model. It is significant, however, that growth is stopped

---

175 Meadows 1972, p. 21.
176 See Meadows 1972, p. 25 ff.
177 See Meadows 1972, p. 94 f.
178 See Meadows 1972.

> well before the year 2100. ... We can thus say with some confidence that, under the assumption of no major change in the present system, population and industrial growth will certainly stop within the next century, at the latest.[179]

According to the researchers, technological advances alone would not have been enough to prevent the fatal consequences of exponential growth.[180] Their position was entirely in keeping with the post-materialist zeitgeist at the time. They were not making a plea for 'Luddism' and certainly conceded that technology held substantial potential to solve problems. What they did condemn, however, was blind faith in technology and naivety when it came to potential side effects of new technologies. According to the MIT experts behind the report, the exponential growth would be stopped by 'negative feedback loops' at some point anyway. Consequently, they believed a wiser decision would be to take timely steps to regulate growth.

According to the report, stability could only be achieved by limiting all five factors, in other words by stopping growth incrementally. However, these steps had to be taken as soon as possible and should seek to achieve a state of global equilibrium:[181]

> Thus, the most basic definition of the state of global equilibrium is that population and capital are essentially stable, with the forces that tended to increase them or decrease them in a carefully controlled balance. There is much room for variation within that definition. We have only specified that the stocks of capital and population remain constant, but they might theoretically be constant at high level or low level – or one might be high and the other low. ... The longer a society prefers to maintain the state of equilibrium, the lower the rates and levels must be.[182]

The equilibrium described does not have to be synonymous with stagnation. It is much more of a 'dynamic equilibrium',[183] with freedom and not extern-

---

179 Meadows 1972, p. 126.
180 See Meadows 1972.
181 See Meadows 1972.
182 Meadows 1972, p. 172.
183 'By choosing a fairly long-time horizon for its existence, and a long average lifetime as a desirable goal, we have now arrived at a minimum set of requirements for the state of global equilibrium. They are: 1. The capital plant and the population are constant in size. ... 2. All input and output rates – births, deaths, investment, and depreciation are kept to a minimum. 3. The levels of capital and population and the ratio of the two are set in

ally imposed constraints at its core. The following excerpt in particular bears witness to the post-materialist content of the Meadows Study:

> Population and capital are the only quantities that need to be constant in the equilibrium state. Any human activity that does not require a large flow of irreplaceable resources or produce severe environmental degradation might continue to grow indefinitely. In particular, those pursuits that any people would list as the most desirable and satisfying activities of man – education, art, music, religion, basic scientific research, athletics, and social interactions – could flourish.
>
> All of the activities listed above depend very strongly on two factors. Firstly, they depend upon the availability of some surplus production after the basic human needs of food and shelter have been met. Secondly, they require leisure time.[184]

These factors thus determined the amount of population and capital in the state of equilibrium. By controlling technological advance and maintaining the same production volume, it was also possible to further increase the amount of leisure time people had. But this would be driven by entirely different motives if everything were to occur against the backdrop of impending ecological collapse.

The Meadows Commission identified a particular need for technological improvement in the area of recycling technologies, research into regenerative energy sources, the medical field and in the development of sustainable products. But this technological advance first had to be freed from the growth mechanism and the growth imperative.[185] The MIT researchers considered it highly unlikely that the society they had depicted would actually see the light of day. But, since their aim was to spark a debate and illustrate alternatives, they nevertheless decided to create an outline for an alternative model of society. They conceded that a social order of this type would also limit human freedoms (by controlling births and conserving raw materials, for example). On the other hand, though, it would also result in new freedoms such as protection

---

        accordance with the values of the society .... An equilibrium defined in this way does not mean stagnation. ... The three points above define a dynamic equilibrium, which need not and probably would not "freeze" the world into the population-capital configuration that happens to exist at the present time. The object in accepting the three statements above is to create freedom for society, not to impose a straitjacket' (Meadows 1972, pp. 173–4).

184   Meadows 1972, p. 175.
185   See Meadows 1972.

from environmental pollution, hunger and overpopulation, and would provide access to new creative and emancipatory opportunities.[186] '[L]ong-term goals must be defined and short-term goals made consistent with them'.[187] And here we cannot fail to be reminded of Ernst Bloch's call for a utopia.[188]

Many parts of the report fall into the category of early 1970s post-materialist discourse[189] and it thus had nowhere near the strong industry focus that many left-wing critics claimed. In fact, it could be argued that the conservative connotations were based on a selective interpretation of the book, one which is very clearly illustrated by the afterword in one of the German-language editions, written by Heinz Riesenhuber, a Christian Democratic Union (CDU) politician in the Kohl government. According to Riesenhuber's interpretation, population growth was the biggest problem, with capitalist growth, in contrast, no more than a peripheral issue. Accordingly, he tended not to place the blame on the Western power elites but rather took the third world governments to task, which he called on to take steps to control population growth.[190] This position is somewhat reminiscent of Thomas Malthus's theory,[191] according to which overpopulation was to blame for the distress of the lower classes.[192]

After the Meadows Study, which was the first report to the Club of Rome, sparked an international furore, a second report followed in 1974. This report was authored by Mihailo Mesarović and Eduard Pestel and entitled *Mankind at the Turning Point*. These two authors incorporated far more than the original five factors in their computer calculations as, unlike the MIT researchers, their views were based more heavily on the assumption of a heterogeneous world, on the simultaneity of the nonsimultaneous. They shared the belief that if the world were to carry on as it was, it would inevitably end in catastrophe. The alternative they proposed, however, was 'organic growth' that factored in the different stages of development in the different regions of the world. As a basis for their analysis, they created a 'multi-level model'.[193]

---

186   See Meadows 1972.
187   Meadows 1972, p. 182.
188   See Bloch 1980, p. 71f.
189   See Saage 2003, p. 473.
190   See Riesenhuber undated, p. 202ff.
191   'That the increase of population is necessarily limited by the means of subsistence. That population will invariably increase when the means of subsistence increase. (To be absolutely sure, we can add: except for when some form of hindrance irresistibly impinges – an extremely rare occurrence!) [...] And that the superior power of the population it repressed, and the actual population kept equal to the means of subsistence, by misery and vice' (Malthus 1809, p. 27).
192   For a critique of Malthus, see Jackson 2009, p. 6f.
193   See Mesarović and Pestel 1975.

They considered growth to be a complex process, which is why simple solutions such as an immediate halt to growth were not suitable. Mesarović's and Pestel's 'organic growth' model stood in opposition to the concept of exponential growth. In light of the world's heterogeneity, they believed a total halt to growth would be misguided. Regional differences and development paths thus also had to be taken into account. They asserted that a 'General Plan' for the vital change from indiscriminate to organic growth had to be developed as a matter of urgency.[194] They were critical of the fact that mankind had become so accustomed to using technology to exploit and subordinate nature and that it was now dependent on these accomplishments. However, nature was retaliating. If the fragile global ecosystem were to topple, then mankind, too, would be at risk. A new way of thinking was therefore required and a more balanced relationship with nature had to be found.[195]

According to Mesarović and Pestel, apart from this change in values and norms, a restructuring of international relations was equally crucial. If no action is taken, the chasm between the North and the South will only continue to grow. The longer we take to respond to the problem, the more costly it will become. Development aid is thus urgently needed. But this should be invested in the creation of small-scale workplaces and decentralised employment instead of being used to finance high-cost large-scale projects, which only succeed in exacerbating the problems of urbanisation in developing countries. However, it is debatable whether policymakers would be able and willing to change their mindset here.[196] Only if Western industrial societies reduce their growth to a globally sustainable level – something that would inevitably involve people in these countries restricting their lifestyles for the sake of development aid – can the world's problems be solved.

However, Mesarović and Pestel were not calling for a global distributive state. Their proposal was more about creating a new world economic system where capital and labour is used effectively, adapted to regional differences, and within the limits of the available resources. In such a system, there would be no place for nationalism and sustainability would be essential.[197]

> We are not the Developed World; we are actually the overdeveloped world. Economic growth in a world where regions are underdeveloped is fundamentally contrary to mankind's social, moral, organizational, and

---

194 See Mesarović and Pestel 1975.
195 See Mesarović and Pestel 1975.
196 See Mesarović and Pestel 1975.
197 See Mesarović and Pestel 1975.

scientific growth. At this moment in history, we are facing an enormously difficult decision. For the first time in man's life on earth, he is being asked to refrain from doing what he can do; he is being asked to restrain his economic and technological advancement, or at least to direct it differently from before; he is being asked by all the future generations of the earth to share his good fortune with the unfortunate – not in a spirit of charity, but in a spirit of necessity. He is being asked to concentrate now on the organic growth of the total world system.[198]

Individuals in the 'civilised' world were alienated by this, however. For the developing world to follow the same path towards 'civilisation' as the West would be a grave error. Mesarović and Pestel asserted that these countries needed new and alternative paths, adapted to their own regional structure. The world should not become one homogenous unit; instead, regional particularities must be used to the advantage of each respective region, with all the regions cooperating in the process. They proposed using technological means in the form of a 'planning instrument' to prevent or curb future crises. Moreover, there should be no governing elite but instead broad control and cooperation among the people within a global framework.[199]

It can thus be seen that the Second Report to the Club of Rome also contained idealist links with post-materialist discourse. This included calls for a change in values which politicians were not really in a position to achieve. And yet, these very politicians were Mesarović's and Pestel's main target audience.[200]

Besides the two Club of Rome reports, Harich and other authors of eco-utopias also drew on the *Doomsday Book* written by British journalist Gordon Rattray Taylor. This book was published in English in 1970, with the German translation appearing in West German bookshops a year later under the title *Das Selbstmordprogramm*.[201] In other words, even before the Meadows Commission had released its report, Taylor had presented a disastrous vision of the future depicting a world completely destroyed by mankind. His book was entirely in keeping with the zeitgeist: 'In the sixties, American discourse on

---

198 Mesarović and Pestel 1975, pp. 141–42.
199 See Mesarović and Pestel 1975, p. 139 ff.
200 More than 40 years later it is now primarily the civil societies, social movements and NGOs of today, interconnected by technological advancements, that strive for non-étatist cooperation on a global level, with the aim of solving impending global problems. At the time the book was written, these movements were still in their infancy. They are rooted in the protests of 1968 with their post-materialist discourses.
201 On the *Doomsday* discourse in West Germany, see Hermand 1991, p. 134 ff.

INTRODUCTION

environmental problems was increasingly characterised by horror scenarios ..., which culminated in around 1970 in an almost eruptive breakthrough in ecological thought'.²⁰² Without recourse to computer calculations, Taylor also forecast a collapse of the ecosystem should mankind fail to change its behaviour. He warned against the consequences of population explosion, blind faith in technology, and wasteful use of resources. He attacked urbanisation, instead calling for decentralised settlements. This represented a clear overlap with post-materialist utopias, as did the references he made to nature mysticism in his depictions of experiences of nature as 'quasi-religious experiences'.²⁰³ Taylor, too, advocated global action, if necessary, by drastic means. Taylor's ideas certainly bore some archistic features; in some cases, we might even describe them as eco-Stalinist.²⁰⁴

The works referred to here symbolise a value shift, which manifested itself in the post-materialist discourses. The Meadows Commission's criticism of existing representative democratic government systems was also in line with this shift. At the heart of this critique were doubts as to whether representative democratic governments were even capable of resolving the existential problems of humanity.

Opinions on this were divided. Unlike Harich, who demanded increased centralism, more coercion and étatism, the Club of Rome authors called for accelerated decentralisation, which was entirely consistent with the post-materialist model. These ideas tied in closely with Bahro's and Havemann's eco-utopias. They saw a global, pluralist network of various different stakeholder levels as being of central importance, safeguarded and controlled through the grassroots involvement of the citizenry.²⁰⁵ Harich and Taylor, in contrast, did not believe that mankind had the ability to effect such transformation. They argued that, for the purposes of saving humanity, authoritarian means had to be employed to suppress and ultimately completely quash consumer appetites and materialist thinking.

The texts described here are just a small selection of the discourses prevalent at the time that centred on the destruction and protection of the environment.²⁰⁶ This issue can also be found at the heart of post-materialist ideas,

---

202   Uekötter 2010, p. 290.
203   See Taylor 1972, pp. 250–51.
204   Wolfgang Harich was also one of the environmentalists accused of being an eco-Stalinist. However, he responded with self-deprecation. See Prokop 1996, p. 61. On the contradiction between Stalinism and environmental protection and the associated critique of the concept of eco-Stalinism, see Amberger 2011b, p. 13 f.
205   See Saage 2002a.
206   See Hermand 1991, p. 134 ff.

since, without a functioning ecosystem to underpin them, social relations simply become impossible. Despite technological progress, mankind still remains dependent on nature. Should the environmental crisis get worse, then, in all probability, social problems too would increase.[207] Taylor's book and the reports to the Club of Rome sparked a wide-ranging debate about the limits to growth and the accompanying problems of environmental pollution. Post-materialist discourse originated in the movement of '68 and saw to it that, a good ten years later, green parties were founded and entered parliament in a great many Western democracies. This bears witness to just how much post-materialist thinking grew in importance in a mere ten years.[208] But how did the actually existing socialist part of Germany respond to these dismal future scenarios disseminated by Western scientists and journalists?

6.3 The Apocalypse as a Problem of Imperialism

In light of the SED's economic policy course and the problems the GDR economy was evidently facing in the 1970s, the reports to the Club of Rome represented something of a challenge. The findings directly contradicted the GDR's economy policy objectives. That said, it was not as if environmental problems had always been taboo in the GDR. Quite the contrary, in fact: In the early 1970s there were open and frank discussions on the subject.[209] In May 1970, the *Volkskammer* adopted a *Landeskulturgesetz* or law on national culture which, despite the name, was an environmental law and represented the GDR's commitment to environmental protection. A year later the Ministry for Environmental Protection and Water Management was created. Over the course of the 1970s, various other laws or implementing ordinances on the protection of water and clean air were passed, as were a number of regulations on the utilisation and safe disposal of waste products. The government also made sure that sanctions were in place for non-compliance on the part of businesses.

In terms of air pollution, 1976 saw the first emissions limits set, with both short-term and long-term limits being made more stringent in 1979. Companies that exceeded these statutory limits had to pay a penalty (*Staub- und Abgasgeld*) calculated on the basis of the difference between the maximum permissible and actual emissions as well as the duration of the company's failure to stay below the maximum permissible levels. With active involvement of the *Kammer der Technik* (Chamber of Technology), the GDR government developed methods for the protection of soil, water, and clean air. However, once the

---

207 See Idler 1999, p. 13.
208 See Idler 1999, p. 21.
209 See Neubert 2000, p. 213.

INTRODUCTION

research had been concluded and the laws and regulations fleshed out, the next step was to translate all this into active environmental protection. It was at this point that it became clear that 'mobilising reserves' and 'imposing fines' was not going to be enough. Effective pollution control required investment sums running into billions. But it was impossible to squeeze any more out of the already trimmed down spending for the reproduction and expansion of industrial installations. At best, the money would have to be taken from the budget for the 'Main Task',[210] e.g. from the residential construction programme. However, no-one in the Politburo was willing to advocate such a move. Environmental protection as part of the 'Main Task' was de facto dead in the water. Instead, environmental problems were increasingly 'resolved' by attempting to conceal their gravity. Any issue related to the environment became 'classified information'.[211] Testimony to this shift in approach is the fact that the 'environmental reports', which until 1974 had been publicly available, were then entrusted solely to the *Ministerrat* (Council of Ministers) and, from 1982 went exclusively to Erich Mielke, Günter Mittag, and Willi Stoph under the strictest of secrecy.[212]

This shows that the problem was subject to a gradual cover-up, a process driven by the growing contradictions[213] between lip service and the imper-

---

[210] Translator's note: The 'Main Task' or *Hauptaufgabe* was the economic policy announced at the 8th SED Congress in June 1971. Its aim was increased production of consumer goods and increased material well-being to provide a higher standard of living for the population.

[211] Roesler 2003, p. 19ff. On this, Joachim Radkau writes: 'It created an environment ministry as early as November 1971, sixteen years before the Bundesrepublik and at least on paper its environmental laws were certainly impressive. Left-wing eco-activists in the West were convinced that the private-profit motive was the ultimate reason for the damage to the environment; this was music to the ears of the GDR leadership, and for a long time its assurances that East Germany's ecological problems were a "legacy of imperialism" – or that the horrors of the "chemical triangle" went back to Walter Rathenau rather than Walter Ulbricht – sounded more or less credible. In the early 1970s, which are generally regarded as the best period of the GDR, the Honecker leadership appears to have seen environmental protection as a special opportunity for the planned economy to prove its worth. But that all came to an end in 1974, after the first oil crisis; the officially celebrated "weeks of socialist land culture" were written out of the annual timetable, and in 1976 it was decided to abolish the environment council within the Academy of Sciences. We should not forget that, had it not been for the broad movement in society (and the Federal Environmental Agency inspired by it), the eco-age would have ended in West Germany too with the top-level meeting at Schloss Gymnich called by Chancellor Helmut Schmidt on 3 June 1975' (Radkau 2014, p. 367). See also Barthel 2001.

[212] See Roesler 2003, p. 20.

[213] See Neubert 2000, p. 212f.

atives of realpolitik. Political realities meant that it was impossible to implement these environmental regulations without simultaneously jettisoning the growth objectives altogether. An article written in *Die Zeit* in 1983 described the dilemma:

> The statutory environmental regulations are good, but compliance is lacking. Companies would rather pay high penalties than implement costly environmental protection measures. What is required is economic growth and improvements in standards of living and this should be seen as the primary goal of the oft-cited 'policy of the Main Task'. Environmental propaganda is limited to small-scale civic initiatives, with citizens tending to green spaces, and waste collection with scrap metal, paper, and glass being separated for recycling.[214]

That said, it is worth pointing out that the GDR introduced a comprehensive recycling scheme (SERO), where people were paid for bringing materials to SERO shops, long before the FRG – albeit motivated more by a latent shortage of raw materials than environmental awareness. However, '[t]he SERO system was at least indirectly geared toward environmental consciousness and served to protect the environment'.[215]

Nevertheless, reality looked gloomy – quite literally. The massive air pollution could largely be blamed on the wasteful use of resources in the energy sector. Since fuel costs for consumers were not based on market prices, they were often far too low. Plus, the lack of any real cost disadvantages for consumers that did not take any energy conservation or insulation measures, they barely exerted any pressure on political decision-makers to put efficiency improvement measures in place. Much of the blame for air pollution could be placed squarely on the crude lignite used for fuel and the severe industrial soot and sulphur dioxide emissions. Owing to the lack of filtration systems and sewage treatment plants, water pollution was also an issue and wastewater was often discharged into rivers and streams untreated. On top of this, the mining industry tore holes in the countryside with its huge opencast pits, rarely adequately recultivating the land, if at all, not to mention the radioactive mining waste dumped on slag heaps. And then there were all the illegal rubbish dumps pumping toxic substances directly into the groundwater, further exacerbating the desperate state of the environment.[216]

---

214   Menge 1983.
215   Barthel 2001, p. 16.
216   See Wolle 1999, p. 211f. Supply bottlenecks in the energy sector resulted in the develop-

When it came to practical policymaking, the SED was thus all talk and no action, unable to follow up on the pledges in its political programme with any kind of tangible measures. The party legitimised its leadership ideologically by claiming that it was destined to rule, to serve as the vanguard of the working class. Here, it invoked the works of Marx, Engels and especially Lenin. However, it was precisely this comparison between Marx's and Engels's writings and the prevailing reality that the opposition was able to use to push the SED into a corner and challenge its legitimacy. Similarly, when it came to the destruction of the environment, the opposition was also able to draw on the Marxist 'classics'. Contrary to the frequently heard claims that Marxism placed a blind faith in technology and progress and perceived nature as no more than an object to be surrendered to humankind for exploitation, there are in fact passages in Marx's and Engels's works that very clearly bear witness to their respect for nature. It was not until the Bolsheviks came to power that these warnings were no longer heeded,[217] a development that went on to shape every country governed by this type of political system.

Marx and Engels had the foresight to recognise that industrialisation would result in the destruction of nature. They saw the antagonism between long-term conservation of the environment and short-term interests of profit.[218]

---

ment of nuclear energy: 'So long as the GDR had high-quality brown coal as well as cheap oil from the Soviet Union, it had no pressing need for nuclear energy; a word from Ulbricht in the early 1960s was enough to cancel the development of its own reactor types, much to the annoyance of East German technologists. But after 1980 at the latest, the days of brown coal and cheap oil were over. With the GDR completely reliant on Soviet reactors, the party leadership approved the "state nuclear energy plan" (1983), but it remained unclear how the country, already threatened with bankruptcy, was to fund this programme, the most ambitious in its history. For the time being, it was dependent on brown coal deposits, which had been mined to such an extent that they were ironically called "potting compost". Expensive filtering systems were by now unthinkable' (Radkau 2014, p. 367). So nuclear energy was more of a last resort than technical reverie: 'Erich Honecker told Western interlocutors at the time that, if the GDR had had black coal reserves, it would have given up nuclear energy. This was not the position of the minister responsible for economic policy Günter Mittag, but insiders let it be known that Honecker was not one of those for whom nuclear energy embodied progress in the "scientific-technological revolution". Not by accident did he come to power in 1971 as a critic of the techno mania of the late Ulbricht era' (Radkau 2014, p. 366).

217 See Saage 2008, p. 152.
218 See Marx 1976, p. 638f. 'The accusation sometimes heard today that the classics of Marxism could never have imagined the problems of human ecology, otherwise they would have been far less certain about the future and less confident in progress, misses the point in two respects. Firstly, Marx and Engels were always aware of the problem, from their younger years until the end of their lives, and they also described it in their writings.

However, they did not develop strategies to combat this capitalist exploitation because they believed that revolution imminent.[219] They implicitly assumed that under socialism, or rather communism, the problem of environmental devastation would cease to exist.[220] Marx believed that the destruction of nature was a side effect of industrialisation:

> Large-scale industry and industrially pursued large-scale agriculture have the same effect. If they are originally distinguished by the fact that the former lays waste and ruins labour-power and thus the natural power of man, whereas the latter does the same to the natural power of the soil, they link up in the later course of development, since the industrial system applied to agriculture also enervates the workers there, while industry and trade for their part provide agriculture with the means of exhausting the soil.[221]

In his *Dialectics of Nature*, Friedrich Engels also emphasised that the exploitation of the earth's resources would inevitably have negative consequences for mankind: 'Let us not, however, flatter ourselves overmuch on account of our victories over nature. Each victory, it is true, in the first place brings about the results we expected, but in the second and third places has very different, unforeseen effects which only too often cancel the first.'[222]

And thus, every bit of progress brings dangers and negative effects. The social scientists and economists in the GDR who scrutinised the Club of Rome's critique of growth drew on Marx's and Engels's ideas. But they took their line of argument further, also criticising capitalist exploitation, although they let the GDR off the hook since it did not adhere to the capitalist laws of profitability. They argued that the blame for the apocalypse should be placed squarely on

---

Secondly, their certainty about the future and their confidence in progress did not apply to a human society limited to exploitative regimes, in general, and capitalism, in particular, whose interest in maximizing profit they very explicitly described as the root cause of their ecological 'problematique' (as the Club of Rome liked to call it)', Hollitscher 1980, p. 28 f.

219 See Fetscher 2004, p. 184 ff.
220 '*Anticipation* of the future – real *anticipation* – occurs in the production of wealth only in relation to the worker and the land. The future can indeed be anticipated and ruined in both cases by premature over-exertion and exhaustion, and by the disturbance of the balance between expenditure and income. In capitalist production this happens to both the worker and the land' Marx 1989b, p. 442.
221 Marx 1981, p. 950.
222 Engels 1987b, p. 460 f.

imperialism's shoulders. These scientists adhered to the SED ideology, according to which socialism had already been achieved in the GDR. In their eyes, the Meadows Report was no more than an attack by Western capital, itself thrown into crisis, targeting the class enemy from the East that was rapidly gaining ground.

The topic of the Club of Rome per se was thus not entirely hushed up in the GDR. There were certainly reactions from SED circles but these statements were rarely made by the leading politicians themselves, instead coming from scientists working for the SED Central Committee and publishing their findings through GDR publishers. These articles were approved for publication by the Central Committee and as such can be interpreted as an indirect official response from the political elites to the Club of Rome's findings.

At this juncture, it would be pertinent to describe some of these writings in more detail, especially given the in-depth treatment of them by Harich in particular. One of the initial reactions that fell into this category was *Das Gleichgewicht der Null. Zu den Theorien des Nullwachstums* (State of equilibrium. Theories of zero growth) by Jürgen Kuczynski. This paper was published in 1973 and was the 31st book in a series of publications entitled *Zur Kritik der bürgerlichen Ideologie* (A critique of bourgeois ideology) by the Akademie publishing house. In his book, Kuczynski, who was one of the most renowned social scientists and economists in the GDR and frequently came to blows with the dogmatic adherents of the ideology of the SED, made a vehement attack on Meadows's zero-growth proposal. In his view, it only served to cover up the crisis of capitalism and ignored the fact that, in large parts of the world, people were living in hunger and misery. In truth, Kuczynski claimed, this was just a jealous, aggressive response from Western capital to the fact that socialist states had now achieved greater economic growth.

Kuczynski viewed bourgeois society as a homogenous whole, thus neglecting to consider the differences between industry and environmentalists. The latter he disparagingly regarded as traitors and accomplices of capital. According to Kuczynski, capitalist growth was not as dynamic and healthy as economic growth in socialist states. He went on to argue that the socialist economy had already reached an equilibrium long ago, while, not through want of trying, capitalism had yet to achieve the same.[223] In fact, he claimed that the price explosion since the early 1970s had even exacerbated this nonequilibrium. Capitalism's growth phase was over, he said, 'stagflation' – the simultan-

---

223 See Kuczynski 1973, p. 15 ff.

eous increase in inflation and stagnation of production – had kicked in and economic growth was on a downward trend. The emerging theories of zero growth only served to disguise this defeat.[224]

Kuczynski then attempted to also expose post-materialist transformation as a capitalist strategy, condemning the fact that, while many advocates of these theories were critical of capitalism, they ruled out socialism an alternative, instead leaning towards the Third Way of zero growth.[225]

Finally, Kuczynski voiced targeted criticism, claiming that although the productivity of US agriculture had rapidly increased, the area under cultivation, conversely, had been permanently reduced so that ultimately, the per capita output remained constant thus keeping prices stable. In other words, it would have been possible to harvest a lot more to combat world hunger but, for the sake of price stability, the government neglected to do this. This created an artificial zero growth by subsidising non-work, which, according to Kuczynski, was evidence of the 'parasitical' nature of capitalism.[226] Moreover, growth did not necessarily equate to expansion. Here there was a difference between quality and quantity. And capitalism is a very good illustration of this because capitalist growth is purely quantitative and irrational, which implies a lot of unnecessary duplication of effort and a high degree of waste.[227]

Kuczynski also talked about population growth but stopped short of calling for a halt to growth, instead demanding aid for developing countries to tackle this problem. He argued against mandatory regulations, advocating instead for the population to be provided with incentives.[228]

Kuczynski then went on to discuss the Meadows Report specifically. He welcomed the idea of limiting population growth in developing countries but contended that we should be prepared to suspend this measure at a later date. His view on resource scarcity, however, was that it was unproven. He claimed that Meadows was simply creating unnecessary panic since, in reality, new sources were constantly being discovered, natural resources were still in plentiful supply under the seafloor, continuous technological developments were opening up new opportunities for raw material extraction, and, thanks to recycling technologies, raw materials would no longer be in such short supply in the future. In truth, Kuczynski argued, this panic was being used to conceal the root cause of the resource scarcity, in other words the fact that uncontrolled capitalist

---

224 See Kuczynski 1973, p. 21.
225 See Kuczynski 1973, p. 22.
226 See Kuczynski 1973, p. 26 f.
227 See Kuczynski 1973, p. 33.
228 See Kuczynski 1973, p. 39.

exploitation was destroying countless resources. Kuczynski was also an advocate of using nuclear energy for power generation in the future.[229]

The fact that he failed – or was unwilling – to understand both the post-materialist value shift and Meadow's intentions can be seen in his polemic in the following: 'Humanity appears to be confronted with a choice: improving the material standard of living and reducing the chance of a healthy life in old age – or a return to the way of life of prehistoric man with clean, unpolluted air'.[230]

Ultimately, neither Meadows nor the majority of Western critics of capitalism wanted to return to an archaic way of life. According to Kuczynski, in the West, environmental protection was no more than ideology.[231] 'The problem of the environment in capitalist states is not, as is claimed by the authors of the study, caused by advances in science and technology and the growth of the population, but rather the capitalist mode of production, its subjugation to the profit principle'.[232]

Kuczynski thus lets the actually existing socialist states off the hook and blames the capitalist West for all the problems, while he sees the socialist states, with their planned economies, as aspiring to achieve an equilibrium between production and the environment for the good of society. For now, however, this requires concessions: 'Faced with an adversary that is increasing its economic potential with virtually no environmental protection measures in place, it follows that it is far, far easier to catch up and overtake capitalism while, at least to a certain extent, neglecting the environment, than it would be to attempt to catch up and overtake while ensuring an adequate level of environmental protection'.[233]

Here he was clearly referring to the imperatives of bloc confrontation. Kuczynski did not believe that capitalist accumulation and zero growth were compatible. For him, this would automatically mean the end of capitalism.[234] Only under the mantle of socialism would the side effects of technical progress be anticipated and given due consideration.[235] Under socialism, the only thing that counted was the 'growth of the common good', and at the time this was tied to scientific and technological growth. This situation might be different 'in a few hundred years', when the material level has increased to such an

---

229 See Kuczynski 1973, p. 45 ff.
230 Kuczynski 1973, p. 51.
231 See Kuczynski 1973, p. 51 f.
232 Kuczynski 1973, p. 52.
233 Kuczynski 1973, p. 56.
234 See Kuczynski 1973, p. 59.
235 See Kuczynski 1973, p. 63.

extent that 'the increase in material production' can be reduced. One thing that has to be borne in mind, however, is that an increase in non-material needs requires a certain level of material growth, producing more books to read or instruments to play, for instance. 'In principle and in general, it holds that socialist society is a growth society, which, as a matter of course, clearly grows in equilibrium, and whose growth for the increasing good of the population is unlimited'.[236]

Kuczynski argued that socialist society was still in the process of being built, and that growth was a natural part of this, whether in housing construction, appliance manufacture, the service sector, or in industry and agriculture. Due to the system rivalry with capitalism, the GDR could not afford the exorbitantly high costs of environmental protection. Later, in developed socialist society, the costs of environmental sustainability would be internalised in the production process. Regarding Meadows, Kuczynski came to the conclusion: 'This means that all the problems the authors raised as "fundamental world problems" are, in socialist countries, in fact not problems at all, or will be solved in due course. In a socialist world, where socialism prevails everywhere, these problems will be resolved quickly'.[237]

In *Communism without Growth?*, Harich was highly critical of Kuczynski's text, accusing him of being short-sighted and naive. Similarly, Harich also attacked *Qualität des Lebens* (Quality of life), a pamphlet written by Hermann Grosse and Manfred Puschmann in 1974, two economists in the employ of the Central Institute for Socialist Economic Management within the Central Committee of the SED. They, too, stressed that capitalism was in crisis and that actually existing socialism therefore needed to offer a high quality of life that would also be an attractive alternative for workers from the West.[238] They described the Club of Rome's aim in similar terms to Kuczynski:

> Obviously, the defenders of the *Limits to Growth* have been startled by the crisis-ridden and, in large parts of capitalist society, even catastrophic development. They feel besieged the successes of socialist states and frightened by the increasing actions of the working class, young people and progressive elements of the intelligentsia, demanding codetermination in society, social security and humane living conditions. They are looking for an escape route and are propagating limits to growth.[239]

---

236 Kuczynski 1973, p. 69.
237 Kuczynski 1973, p. 71.
238 See Grosse and Puschmann 1974, p. 6f.
239 Grosse and Puschmann 1974, p. 58.

INTRODUCTION 63

To achieve this, a crisis was artificially created and instrumentalised:

> The environmental hysteria stirred up by imperialist ideologues including their so-called 'environmental crisis' are thus just as much a social problem as the increasingly pervasive social insecurity, alienation of young people and inflation in capitalist societies. Capitalism treated and continues to treat nature in an aggressively consumptive manner and in the self-serving interests of profit; its behaviour toward the natural environment is rapacious.[240]

Thus, the ecological problem is a social problem and as such also rooted in the conditions that prevail in capitalist society. The situation in the GDR was quite different, however:

> In the socialist countries themselves a whole set of environmental protection measures had already been introduced. Within Comecon, the international community of socialist states all worked on developing and implementing programs to study and protect the environment against adverse effects. This also reflected the genuine humanism of the socialist way of life and the tireless concern for the common good.[241]

The consequences of the disastrous environmental policy that was implemented in reality were suppressed even more rigorously than in Kuczynski's text – if we recall, the last time an 'environmental report' was published was the year the Grosse and Puschmann publication appeared. By way of contrast, the Grosse and Puschmann pamphlet sang the praises of the planned economy's environmental policy and the GDR's environmental laws and regulations.[242] The authors claimed that the GDR had achieved socialism, and, consequently, there was no more overexploitation of the environment. They more or less completely omitted to include any kind of self-critical view on their own environmental destruction. Had they admitted that overexploitation of the environment also continued in the GDR, this would have risked pushing ideology to its limits. This would have raised the question of whether either Marx was wrong or the GDR was in fact not an example of complete socialism. And this might also have explained why in actually existing socialist states the Meadows

---

240 Grosse and Puschmann 1974, p. 125.
241 Grosse and Puschmann 1974, p. 124.
242 See Grosse and Puschmann 1974, pp. 58 and 127f.

Report was either generally ignored entirely or attacked.²⁴³ This was made particularly clear in a speech given by the SED's *Chefideologe* or chief ideologue, Kurt Hager on 3 December 1975 at Humboldt University of Berlin to commemorate the 50th anniversary of the publication of Engels's *Dialectics of Nature*. Hager saw:

> ... the rule of man over nature ... in capitalism not as the result of society working in accordance with a sensible overarching plan, but rather as spontaneous and isolated actions of individual capitalists, companies, corporations, monopolies etc. for the purpose of achieving maximum profit. Since profit is the driving force of capitalist production, this inevitably takes the form of uncontrolled overexploitation of productive forces and reckless plundering of nature.²⁴⁴

To substantiate his argument, Hager referred to 'the underutilisation of production capacities' in the West. At the same time, he claimed that unemployment had permanently increased. In addition, there was the issue of uninhibited expropriation of natural resources, especially in the energy sector. Nonetheless, according to Hager: 'Bourgeois scientists recognise the symptoms of this development. They see it as the so-called ecological crisis of humanity'.²⁴⁵ He implied that they perceived the problems as having anthropological rather than materialist roots and, quoting from the report by Mesarović and Pestel, he indicated that there was not much time left to salvage the situation.

> Yet, what is portrayed as an ecological crisis of mankind is in fact above all the inability of capitalist society to overcome antagonism between humans and the natural environment resulting from private ownership of the means of production and natural resources, along with the pursuit of profit .... At the same time, the prevailing propaganda announcing an 'ecological crisis of humanity' served the ideological purpose of making the general crisis of capitalism ... seem like a crisis of humanity and declaring the much-needed revolutionary renewal of society through the transition to socialism superfluous. The reactionary ideological purpose of the theory of the ecological crisis consists of substituting the socialist revolution with environmental protection.²⁴⁶

---

243   See Saage 2008, p. 151.
244   Hager 1975, p. 44 f.
245   Hager 1975, p. 46.
246   Hager 1975, p. 47.

In contrast, according to Hager, socialism offered the chance to resolve the antagonism between nature and the human mode of production. Through organisation and planning, socialism would enable mankind to take their way of life and their existence to a higher level.

> Through the emergence and development of socialism in the Soviet Union and in the socialist world system, this prediction by Engels has, in practice, already come true. The transition to socialism provides mankind with the chance to genuinely address and ultimately solve the problems related to the relationship between nature and society caused by capitalism. We do not in any way deny the existence of grave environmental problems.[247]

Hager saw socialism or rather communism as the only system capable of overcoming ecological problems. And he regarded the actually existing socialist states to be well on their way to achieving this. He believed that, with efficiency improvements under socialism, these problems could be tackled. Hager went on to describe his visions of a future form of communism where nature and society are in equilibrium. This would be:

> ... neither a wasteful nor an ascetic society. Its growth and thus the chance of it satisfying the needs of its citizens will depend on the steady increase of all growth factors, including the potential of scientific research, the level of education, and the involvement of all members of society in the resolution of social problems. This will allow for rational treatment of existing raw materials and energy sources as well as the exploitation of as yet undiscovered resources.[248]

Hager and the SED ideologues predicted that the communism of the future would include the dialectical sublation of the contradiction between the human mode of production and the natural environment. Indeed, even during the transitional phase, referred to in formation theory terms as 'socialism' or 'the dictatorship of the proletariat', the sublation of this contradiction was already being pursued. At least that is the theory. In reality, however, the chosen economic course led to an all-or-nothing scenario. This strategy was based on credit-financed investments and the expectation of subsequent refinancing accompanied by productivity increases. To abandon the growth path

---

247 Hager 1975, p. 48.
248 Hager 1975, p. 50.

would have been impossible under global political conditions that prevailed at the time without risking state insolvency. To follow the necessary growth path made the overexploitation of natural resources in the GDR unavoidable.

With its materialist objectives, the economic policy of the seventies, which was consumer goods based out of necessity, was diametrically opposed to any critique of growth and even more so to post-materialist or postgrowth discourses.[249] In the conflict between the economy and ecology, the decision had fallen on the side of economic priorities. However, the SED had underestimated the extent to which their critics had appropriated the question of survival. They could label the actual conflicts between the economy and the environment and draw on the general sense of misery.[250] Thus, contrary to the insidious cover-up of the real state of the environment, a movement was emerging in the GDR that was attempting to expose this sensitive issue. And Harich's *Communism without Growth?*, though not a seminal work for the movement, appeared at its very inception.[251] What is striking, however, is that, along with the later environmental groups that appeared during the 1980s, this book took on a special standing among the critics and opponents of the SED. Stefan Wolle is quite right in saying: 'Since the SED combined both economic and political power, it was able to classify any reference to environmental sins as "subversive" and criminalise and muzzle independent environmental groups'.[252]

Nonetheless:

> ... the environmental movement in the GDR differed from the human rights or peace groups in a number of important aspects. For instance, in the history of ideas, there was nothing that connected the environmental movement specifically to the GDR. The roots of the movement were essentially the same as those of the environmental movement in the West, much as the faith in progress, technology, and growth of the socialist mode of production, and the resulting attitude towards the natural environment was not fundamentally different from that of capitalism. Environmental activism in the GDR was therefore, just as it was in the West, substantially shaped by general criticism of civilisation that cuts across systems as well as 'post-materialist' re-evaluations, under which system-specific aspects of environmental destruction were largely subsumed.[253]

---

249 See Saage 2003, p. 454. See also Idler 1999, p. 44.
250 See Neubert 2000, p. 212 f.
251 See Röhrborn 2008, p. 55.
252 Wolle 1999, p. 210.
253 Jordan and Kloth 1995, p. 145 f.

The topic galvanised more than just those who were critical of or opposed the system. And it was not limited to the alternative church opposition either. Rather, concerns about the destruction of the natural environment also extended to mainstream society, with many GDR citizens unwilling to simply accept what was happening. However, since the SED did not necessarily regard environmentally aware citizens as oppositional, they were not *a priori* targets of political persecution. Instead, the SED, attempted to channel the movement into apolitical institutions. To this end, the *Gesellschaft für Natur und Umwelt* (Society for Nature and the Environment, GNU) was founded in 1980 as part of the *Kulturbund* (Cultural Association). Just five years after it was set up, the GNU already had more than 50,000 members, organised into 1,500 working groups. There was also a Minister for the Environment as well as government environmental policy councils, committees and inspections. That said, all these institutions were subordinate to the primacy of the crisis-ridden economy and the pressure of state debt, such that they had no more than a marginal impact at the local and municipal level, for instance in urban beautification projects.[254]

In conclusion, the ecological problem was not categorically suppressed in the GDR but rather the difficulties in dealing with the issue became a constant matter of concern for the SED, something it attempted to get to grips with through a tactical combination of concealment and institutionalisation.

---

254   See Jordan and Kloth 1995, p. 147 ff.; Radkau 2014, p. 369.

CHAPTER 2

Communism without Growth?: Wolfgang Harich and the Eco-dictatorship

1   Harich and His Era

To this day, Wolfgang Harich is regarded as one of the GDR's most controversial thinkers. On the one hand, he never fully came to terms with the reality of the German Democratic Republic. And yet, he could not bring himself to leave, despite the fact that he suffered more injustice at the hands of the Socialist Unity Party (SED) than many other critics of the system.

Harich was born in Königsberg on 9 December 1923. His grandfather on his mother's side (Wyneken) was editor-in-chief for the *Königsberger Allgemeine Zeitung* daily. Harich's father, Walther, a literary scholar and author of several books,[1] moved with his family to Neuruppin because he did not see eye to eye with his conservative father-in-law.[2] In her memoirs, Harich's widow Anne wrote of her husband that in the mid-1980s when she met him, he treated her children in an 'authoritarian manner'[3] and that his behaviour towards his new stepchildren was at times harsh. This demeanour stemmed from his own childhood: 'His strict authoritarian upbringing taught him to be obedient'.[4] The authoritarian spirit instilled in him was something he was unable to free himself from till the day he died. It was also reflected in his writing, particularly in *Communism without Growth?*. Even in his final years, Harich adhered to strict self-imposed rules. His widow described how, when she first met him, he was a real pedant, following a strictly regimented daily routine, reluctant to change any of his habits.[5]

Returning now to Harich's younger years, after Neuruppin, his family moved to Berlin, where the young Wolfgang, at the time a mere secondary schoolboy, began to attend philosophy lectures given by Eduard Spranger and Nicolai

---

1 For an account of the works of Harich's father, see Wirth 2007, p. 56 ff.
2 See Harich, A. 2007, p. 38 f.
3 See Harich, A. 2007, p. 15.
4 Harich, A. 2007, p. 16.
5 See Harich, A. 2007, p. 19 f.

Hartmann.[6] It was at this time, around 1942, that Harich encountered communist ideas for the first time when he received a copy of Lenin's work *Materialism and Empirio-criticism*. Harich himself stated that this was a book that made a huge impression on him.[7] In 1942, Harich was drafted into the armed forces, only to desert two years later to join the efforts of a Berlin resistance group.

Five days before the official end of World War II, Wolfgang Leonhard paid Harich a visit in Berlin-Wilmersdorf. At the behest of Walter Ulbricht, Leonhard was to find candidates for Berlin's postwar district administrations. Harich was at top of the list for Wilmersdorf. He politely declined, offering instead to take on responsibilities in the cultural field.[8] His offer was accepted, paving the way for his career in the Soviet Occupation Zone (SBZ)/GDR.[9] In February 1946, Harich joined the Communist Party of Germany (KPD) and soon after became a member of the SED. At this time he was a prolific journalist, writing for a number of publications including the *Tägliche Rundschau*, the *Kurier* and the *Weltbühne*.[10] After graduating with a degree in philosophy and literature, he took up a teaching position at Humboldt University of Berlin (HU), then going on to complete his doctorate on the philosopher Johann Gottfried Herder in 1951. A year later, Harich accepted a professorship in philosophy at HU, at the same time working as an editor for the Aufbau-Verlag publishing house.[11] Harich was instrumental in the establishment of the *Deutsche Zeitschrift für Philosophie* (German journal of philosophy), which he co-published and occasionally acted as editor-in-chief for.

Even at this early stage, Harich had a somewhat tense relationship with the philosophical direction the SED was moving in, coming into direct conflict with the party in 1952 over lectures on Georg Wilhelm Friedrich Hegel he was holding at Humboldt University, during which he (unwittingly) criticised Stalin's critique of Hegel. This resulted in a reprimand from the party.[12]

This was not the end of the conflict, however. In fact, a dispute over the reception of Hegel, among other things, led Harich to resign from his professorship in 1954, although he did still continue with his well-attended lectures.

---

6   Hartmann's philosophy was to accompany Harich his whole life. It is no coincidence that Harich's last major work was a Hartmann monograph.
7   See Harich, A. 2007, p. 60.
8   See Leonhard 1996, p. 223 f., Prokop 1996, p. 33.
9   Although his first ventures into the cultural policy field were unsuccessful, with one example of this being his acquisition of the newly founded *Weltbühne* magazine. See Schivelbusch 1997, p. 264 ff.
10 See Götze 1996.
11 For an account of the early years of this publishing house, see Mittenzwei 2003, p. 35 ff.
12 See Harich, A. 2007, p. 120, Sieber 2008, p. 54 ff., Heyer 2011, p. 51 ff.

Harich also opposed the SED's cultural policy and the formalist doctrine related thereto. This meant that he was all the more delighted about the 20th Congress of the Communist Party of the Soviet Union (14–26 February 1956) and the subsequent de-Stalinisation debates. The notion that this could make the situation worse[13] was not something he considered at the time.

Wolfgang Harich was a widely educated and critically minded intellectual. Like Bloch, Harich was concerned with practical philosophy, in other words the link between Marxist thought and practical action. He demonstrated great drive and ambition, although he did appear to be somewhat naïve when it came to realpolitik.[14] His biographer Siegfried Prokop writes:

> There is no way his conflicting personality structure did not play a role here – he was relentlessly self-confident, exuding an aura of ease, and yet at the same time he was also obedient and accepting of his position under certain authorities. Harich could also be quite boyishly inept, expecting strict instructions and trying not to make mistakes. Self-flagellation and self-criticism, sometimes even with elements of Bolshevik discipline, could not be ruled out.[15]

Yet Harich did not shy away from confrontation with dominant individuals and ideologies. The clearest illustration of this combination of critical thinking and failure in real life can be seen in the events of 1956, when the 20th Congress of the Communist Party of the Soviet Union brought about changes in the political and cultural landscape throughout the Soviet Union's sphere of influence,[16] including the GDR, where it led to a political 'thaw'.[17] This was reflected

---

13 See Herzberg 2000, p. 174.
14 Werner Mittenzwei characterised him as follows: 'Gifted in a multitude of ways, whether as an editor or polemic publicist and boldly generalising philosopher, he could have been the greatest philosopher since Bloch, had his academic career been allowed to continue uninterrupted. However, his talent was characterised by two different traits which, when brought to bear with the same drive, had destructive consequences. He put forward his generalisations with polemically provocative vigour. His theoretical considerations, as thorough as they were, were naively implemented in practice. He was not afraid to take risks' (Mittenzwei 2003, p. 121). In her memoirs, Anne Harich was critical of this image that Mittenzwei portrayed of her husband: Harich, A. 2007, p. 304f.
15 Prokop 1997, p. 113f.
16 Wolfgang Leonhard commended Khrushchev's course of action at the party congress, in particular his secret speech: 'We had hope, and this hope was not entirely unfounded, as Khrushchev achieved a great deal. I regard the speech he gave on 25 February 1956 not as a half-hearted announcement, but as one of the most significant speeches in the history of communism' (Leonhard 2006, p. 4).
17 In this context, the term was coined by Ilja Ehrenburg. See Kuczynski 1993, p. 16.

in intellectuals gradually beginning to criticise various structural features of the Stalinist system that they perceived as negative.[18] This 'thaw' initially culminated in what was referred to as the 'freedom conference' in March 1956, with Ernst Bloch making the closing remarks, thus ending the tradition of Kurt Hager being the last to take the podium. The intelligentsia pinned their hopes on overcoming the dogmatism and schematism of Marxism.[19]

Soon afterwards, Harich penned a text for Volume 4/1956 of the *Deutsche Zeitschrift für Philosophie* under the title 'Vademekum für Dogmatiker' (Vademecum for dogmatics), the political fallout of which saw the journal attempt to mitigate criticism by giving it the alternative header of 'Kleines Vademekum für Schematiker' (A short vademecum for schematics), which would, however, never be published in the GDR. The article was not rediscovered until 2005 when it was uncovered in a Stasi Record Agency archive. The book article comprised 16 theses, in which Harich criticised the dogmatism of the prevailing philosophy at the time and made a case for a philosophy of praxis, which displayed similarities with the concepts framed by Bloch, Lukács,[20] Havemann and Kolakowski. 'Harich imagined Marxist philosophy as a living science'.[21]

This text was a cornerstone in two respects: firstly, it paved the way for the debates on political theory within what was referred to as the *Plattform für den besondern deutschen Weg zum Sozialismus* (The platform for the distinctive German path to socialism) which brought together the results of discussions among the 'Harich group', which led to the arrests made in late 1956. Secondly, by spring of the same year, the text had already drawn Harich to the attention

---

18 Extensively analysed and presented by Herzberg 2006.
19 The speeches given by Harich and Bloch can be found in the ledger of minutes of the party congress. They show that, in his speech, Harich was critical of Bloch for not taking the opportunity to address the political upheaval in the Eastern Bloc in his opening speech. See Deutsche Akademie der Wissenschaften zu Berlin (ed.) 1956. Also see Rauh 2006, p. 752.
20 Anne Harich believed that, over the course of his life, her husband felt the greatest philosophical affinity to Georg Lukács. See Harich, A. 2007, p. 135. In a discussion with her in the mid-1980s he said: 'I was imprisoned on 29.11.1956. Everything they asked of me at the time, I revealed before the court. Only on one issue did I refuse to acquiesce: I refused to turn my back on Lukács academically, I remained loyal to him, as my teacher, as my ally in Marxist philosophy. And they never forgave me for this. They did not want me to admit my affinity with Lukács publicly. That was 30 years ago and I am still being punished for it' (Harich, A. 2007, p. 147). But it was not only within his family that he professed his support for Lukács. In fact, he also publicly acknowledged his support in the 1980s, for instance in his article 'More respect for Lukács!' (published in 1988 in the West German magazine *Kultur und Gesellschaft*). Florath took an opposing stance, accusing Harich of being disloyal to Lukács. See Florath 1994, p. 61.
21 Prokop 2005.

of those who would later become his prosecutors and judges.[22] That said, his 16 theses contained 'absolutely no genuine historical, let alone political references to GDR socialism and/or to the SED as the sole ruling party'.[23] This is why the text actually ended up not being used in the case against him, instead disappearing into the Stasi's 'poison cabinet'. Similarly irrelevant for the trial (probably because Walter Ulbricht did not have access to it)[24] was the *Memorandum* that Harich had written for the Soviet ambassador Pushkin. In this text, entitled *Studien zur weltgeschichtlichen Situation* (Studies on the global historical situation), Harich criticised Ulbricht and demanded his removal as well as a break with antidemocratic and Tsarist-style Stalinism.[25] In contrast with these two texts, Harich's *Plattform* played a decisive role in the show trials of 1957.

To this day, exactly what happened within the 'Harich group' remains unclear. As late as the 1990s, Wolfgang Harich and Walter Janka even continued their dispute over who had control of the narrative as rivals in court. In his 2006 book *1956 – DDR am Scheideweg* (1956 – The GDR at a crossroads), historian Siegfried Prokop attempted to reconstruct a detailed chronology of events, which can be summarised as follows:

Over the course of 1956, the intelligentsia grew increasingly critical of the party leadership. In late June, the leadership, represented by Hager, took a more combative step by inviting the editors-in-chief of the intellectual press to participate in a debate. Among them was Wolfgang Harich, who consequently

---

22   In 1957, following Harich's imprisonment, Kurt Hager stated that the struggle against dogmatism that took place after the 20th Party Congress was positive and productive. 'However, in summer last year, at a number of institutes and universities, there were already unprincipled discussions and attempts to abandon the fundamental principles of Marxism-Leninism that were upheld by history'. According to Hager, revisionism was being propagated under the guise of the 'struggle against dogmatism'. 'It is no coincidence that Agent Harich's counter-revolutionary career started when he abandoned the Marxist world view. As early as 1954, at a meeting of Marxist philosophers, Harich was the target of fierce criticism owing to an attempt he had made in the literary journal *Sinn und Form* to link the ideas of the fascist anthropologist Arnold Gehlen with those of Marxism. In July 1956, Harich formulated 16 theses "on the question of the further development of Marxism", in which he called for dialectical materialism to be re-established, and appropriated the imperialist slogan of Stalinism, declaring that Marxism was by no means universally valid, but rather "was at a stage of development which essentially corresponded to the needs of the class-conscious proletariat in the capitalist era". Harich thus renounced Leninism, instead adopting the thesis of the imperialist ideologues that Marxism was only right for the nineteenth century' (Hager 1956, p. 534).
23   Rauh 2006, p. 753.
24   See Prokop 1996, p. 19.
25   See Harich, A. 2007, p. 61 ff.

discussed his reform ideas with a group of colleagues from the Aufbau-Verlag publishing house. It was from this discussion group that the *Kreis der Gleichgesinnten* (circle of the like-minded), also known as the 'Harich group', evolved. The group included intellectuals such as Gustav Just, Heinz Zöger and the head of the Aufbau-Verlag, Walter Janka. Harich was, without a doubt, the intellectual heart of this group, however. On 22 October, Harich mentioned Janka's name in the presence of some Soviet acquaintances and referred to Paul Merker as a 'German Gomułka'.[26] Those who were part of the discussion saw clear signs of an imminent revolution in the GDR.

Three days later, Harich met with the Soviet ambassador Georgy Pushkin to discuss the aforementioned *Memorandum*. Janka and the other critics at the Aufbau-Verlag, who were counting on the support of the ambassador, had high hopes for this meeting. But things turned out very differently. While Harich was critical of SED policy direction under Ulbricht as well as of the public reporting on events in Poland, Pushkin defended the party line and Ulbricht's *Deutschlandpolitik* or intra-German policy. Nonetheless, the critics continued to pin their hopes on progressive forces in Moscow.[27] It was after this that Harich made his gravest mistake: On 1 November he made contact with the Social Democratic Party (SPD) in West Germany, as he saw the GDR as being on the brink of witnessing events similar to those that were unfolding in Hungary. He believed that only the SPD had the requisite authority to keep the population of the GDR in check. He made contact with the SPD's regional association in West Berlin (rather than the party's intelligence unit the *Ostbüro*, which overtly worked against the GDR).[28] His contact there Josef Braun (aka 'Freddy', who was in fact a GDR agent) directed him to Comrade Weber (in reality Peter Wandel, Head of the *Ostbüro* of the SPD). According to Prokop, this is ultimately how the fateful contact was made with the *Ostbüro* against Harich's will and without his knowledge.[29]

On 7 November, Harich was summoned to Walter Ulbricht's office, who warned him that he would not tolerate a 'Petőfi club' in the GDR.[30] However, the group of intellectuals continued to work on ideas and measures in opposition to Ulbricht.[31] On 15 November, some of the group met with the Minister

---

26 Władysław Gomułka (1905–1982) was a ray of hope at the top of the Polish Communist Party, having strongly advocated for de-Stalinisation and reform in 1956.
27 See Prokop 2006, p. 143ff. On the Harich of 1956, also see Herzberg 2006, pp. 489–510.
28 For more on this see Zwerenz, I. and Zwerenz, G. 2004, p. 28.
29 See Prokop 2006, p. 157f.
30 See Klein, Otto and Grieder 1996, p. 259.
31 'Ulbricht the politician regarded Harich as one might a deeply religious person from

for Culture Johannes R. Becher where they were openly critical. The next day, further criticism was voiced at a meeting of editors, also attended by Johannes R. Becher.[32]

A week later, on 21 November, another meeting took place at Walter Janka's house in Kleinmachnow that proved to have a decisive impact on the subsequent show trial. Paul Merker arrived first, followed by Just and his wife, Zöger and Harich. The topics of discussion included: criticism of Ulbricht and Stalinism, of the socialist planned economy and social inequality, of the party-state apparatus as the implementer of Stalinism and the need for it to be dismantled, 'targeted criticism' of different members of the Politburo, German reunification in cooperation with the SPD,[33] and lastly Harich clarified his own ideas, prompting Janka and Just to urge him to put them in writing. The next day, Becher also asked Harich to put his ideas down on paper in order that they might be discussed with the SED experts. On 25 November, Harich visited Bernhard Steinberger, where he was also introduced to Richard Wolf. Harich had a copy of his *Plattform* with him, which elaborated on his ideas in written form.

> On the one hand, the paper called for a radical democratisation of the SED, the removal of the top functionaries' privileges, the establishment of religious and intellectual freedom, permission for small and medium-sized commercial entities to operate, the introduction of workers' councils in socialist enterprises, trade unions and mass organisations that are independent from the party, free elections and general legal certainty. On the other hand, however, Harich was against socialist ownership structures being abolished. Moreover, Harich envisaged elections based on unified lists of candidates from the democratic bloc, which, in turn, he saw as securing the rule of what would then be a reformed SED. Specifically, this meant that, from the very start 'strict adherence to the principles of democratic centralism' would be necessary. ... [German – author's addition] unity must be achieved as quickly as possible, and in the West, the SPD should push through anti-capitalist and anti-fascist policy.[34]

---

another century, a seducer, a dissenter, a deviant, a frivolous intellectual thrill seeker' (Mittenzwei 2003, p. 140).

32 See Prokop 2006, p. 175 ff.

33 The hopes Harich placed in the SPD were also fuelled by the party's *Deutschlandpolitik* (intra-German policy). See Klein, Otto and Grieder 1996, p. 260.

34 Neubert 2000, p. 107. Harich's *Plattform* is still providing food for thought to this day. Bernd Florath, for instance, views *Plattform* as deeply undemocratic: 'Harich's *Plattform* would

Together, Harich, Steinberger and Wolf analysed the situation in the GDR and the possible actions they could take. Harich, however, kept quiet about his meetings with the SPD, which he already regretted having. It was decided that Steinberger would draft a 'minimum programme' intended for nonconformist members of the Central Committee. Harich, on the other hand, was keen to continue working on the 'maximum programme', which was not something meant for public consumption. In the firm belief that anti-Stalinists had now come to power in Poland, they were seeking to exert influence in the GDR through the media in Poland, not least because the West German route would have had a discrediting effect on their campaign.

As regards Harich's *Plattform*, the Stasi presumably discovered a copy during a search of Harich's premises, which was then presented to Ulbricht on 26 November. Harich and Steinberger were the only ones who had a copy of the document, with Wolf and Manfred Hertwig only having read excerpts. With a view to establishing new contacts, Harich planned to travel first to Hamburg and then on to Poland. On 26 November, he flew to Hamburg where he met with the publishers Rudolf Augstein, John Jahr and Hans Huffzky, amongst others. Harich had pinned his hopes on change in the GDR which would see the SPD come to victory in the West German parliamentary elections in 1957. This would provide the basis for the reunification of the socialist Federal Republic of Germany and the de-Stalinised GDR, creating a democratic socialist Germany. At least that was Harich's pipe dream.

Back in the GDR, disaster was already looming for the critics of the system. On 27 November, Ulbricht insisted that, in the next issue of the weekly *Sonntag*, Zöger print articles that were self-critical, a move that sparked a dispute among the members of the editorial team. Ernst Bloch accused Johannes

---

never have meant an end to Stalinism. At best, it offered a detailed rational, centralist model as an alternative to real Stalinism with its repeated irrational twists and turns' (Florath 1994, p. 67). Werner Mittenzwei put forward a contradictory position: 'Although this blueprint involved a revolution from above, Harich worked on the basis of a socialist understanding of democracy that had a whole new quality' (Mittenzwei 2003, p. 137). And, to validate the text, he noted: 'Notwithstanding all the weaknesses and limitations, the political naivety of the timing, Harich's *Plattform* is still the most comprehensive programme of any opposition movement since 1989. In his time and in light of the difficulties he faced, even the reformer Gorbachev had no tangible solutions, no better developed programme' (Mittenzwei 2003, p. 139). Andreas Heyer acknowledges that Harich was calling for more democracy, dialogue, freedom of expression, the separation of politics and the economy etc. He had turned against Marxist-Leninist historical determinism and the party's claim to omnipotence and infallibility. However, since these were the two central pillars of its claim to legitimacy, Harich was treading on dangerous ground. See Heyer 2007b, p. 536 ff.

R. Becher of having left Georg Lukács high and dry when he had banned Walter Janka from paying him a visit.³⁵ But it was no use, the fate of the critics of the system was sealed and now the powers that be hit back. The politically ailing Walter Ulbricht in particular sought to intimidate and silence his various opponents within the party.³⁶ At this point, Harich and Janka's behaviour meant that they were the ideal pawns to be sacrificed in a show trial.³⁷ On 29 November 1956, Harich and his girlfriend were arrested. The 3 December issue of *Sonntag* printed Zöger's self-critique, sparking a fierce debate at the publishing house. Three days later, Janka was also arrested. On 11 December, the Politburo rejected Kurt Vieweg's draft agricultural reform as 'damaging to the party'.³⁸ In January 1957, the party leadership of the Institute for Philosophy at the University of Leipzig launched a revisionist campaign against Bloch. On 8 March, Gustav Just was arrested while he was testifying at Harich's trial and the very next day Harich, Steinberger and Hertwig were all sentenced. All three were stripped of all of their academic titles. Finally, on 26 July 1957, sentences were passed against Janka, Just, Zöger and Wolf.³⁹ Shortly before this, in the first issue of the *Deutsche Zeitschrift für Philosophie* since Harich was removed from his post as editor-in-chief, Walter Ulbricht published an article in which he presented the subversive effect of the 'like-minded' in the worst possible light and thanked the security agencies in the GDR for their vigilance.⁴⁰

The legal proceedings against the 'Harich group' bore similarities with the many Stalinist show trials that had been taking place since 1936, beginning with the Moscow Trials in the Soviet Union but then followed in other countries of the Eastern Bloc at the end of World War II. The most famous of these trials are associated with the names László Rajk in Hungary in 1949 and Rudolf Slánsky in Czechoslovakia in 1952. Both men received the death penalty.

After the 20th Congress of the Communist Party of the Soviet Union in 1956, many intellectuals thought they had seen the back of show trials, which made it all the more of a shock for Harich, Janka and the others when, in 1957, they found themselves at the centre of one. Although the most brutal expressions

---

35 See Prokop 2006, p. 192 ff.
36 'Officially, the SED could not go back on de-Stalinisation. However, in order to nip the unrest it had created in the bud, all dissenters were accused of "revisionism", a "Third Way" between socialism and capitalism, which purportedly split the antifascists united front' (Neubert 2000, p. 106).
37 See Frank, M. 2001, p. 260.
38 For more information on Vieweg's agricultural programme, see Herzberg 2006, p. 474 ff.
39 See Prokop 2006, p. 212 ff.
40 See Ulbricht 1956, p. 531 f.

of Stalinism were abolished after the party congress and did not emerge again until 1989, the fundamental mechanisms of the system remained in place.

Particularly worth noting here is the ban on parliamentary parties which the Bolsheviks intended to use in 1921 to force party unity during the era of the post-revolutionary struggles. Contrary to an original announcement, this ban was never repealed and from then on served as an instrument for discipline, which 'not only hampered new ideas and thoughts but even made the conditions for these a punishable offence. After securing a victory, which is something it desperately wanted, the revolution then failed'.[41] Fritjof Meyer sums up the consequences: 'And thus the history of socialist opposition within the Bolshevik Party came to an end; any political disputes that came after this, albeit cloaked in socialism by the opposition, as well as the ruling group, and indeed the whole of society, were simply a power battle within the ruling bureaucracy'.[42]

From then on, anyone who defied the party line was liable to be prosecuted. The severity of the penalty depended on the circumstances and was determined on the basis of ambiguous legal definitions. After Stalin's demise, opposers of the regime faced long prison sentences rather than the death penalty. The mechanism remained in place, however, and was also used in the proceedings against the those involved in the 1956 opposition.

The reasons for the conflict between Janka and Harich that continued until the day they died were rooted in the show trial against Janka and other defendants, in which Harich was a witness for the prosecution (Harich's trial had taken place earlier). At the close of his testimony, in which he spoke of the theses and proposals that had been discussed within the group, Harich named his comrades.[43] He later justified his actions by stating that he had not said anything that the Stasi had not already known before the arrests. But for Janka, in particular, these statements weighed heavily, and he held it against Harich until his death.[44] In his memoir he wrote: 'Without his statements, the Stasi would not have been able to bring an even half-way convincing charge against me and the other co-defendants Just, Zöger and Wolf'.[45] In Harich's moral defence, it should be added here that, while in custody awaiting trial he was threatened

---

41 Zwerenz, I. and Zwerenz, G. 2004, p. 302.
42 Meyer 1975, p. 175.
43 See Hoeft 1990, p. 54 ff.
44 See Janka 1989, p. 89 ff.
45 Janka 1992, p. 339. Falck 1999, in contrast, saw Harich as a victim of a conspiracy organised by Janka and Ulbricht.

with the death penalty.⁴⁶ Something else worth remembering is that, of those on trial, Harich was punished most severely, receiving the longest prison sentence and being stripped of his philosophical and academic reputation. For decades to come, the accusations made by the prosecution 'against the young Marxist philosopher from the GDR would remain unchanged, having been preserved and codified in the history of the party. In the party's last official self-portrayal of the GDR history of philosophy published in 1988, *Philosophie für eine schöne neue Welt* [A philosophy for a brave new world] Harich is not mentioned at all, not even in a negative or hostile light'.⁴⁷

Harich was given amnesty in 1964 and was released from prison with just two years of his ten-year sentence remaining. Walter Ulbricht refused to grant permission for him to resume his academic career. Since for Harich, a dyed-in-the-wool Communist, moving to West Germany was not an option,⁴⁸ he found himself a new field of work in the Akademie Verlag publishing house in Berlin, where he worked on the publication of an edition of the works of Ludwig Feuerbach. At the same time, Harich continued with his study of Jean Paul, which he had begun whilst in prison and later documented in several books.⁴⁹

> His book *Zur Kritik der revolutionären Ungeduld* [A critique of revolutionary impatience], published in Basel in 1971, led to him becoming involved in the West German student movement. In this book, Harich examines the student leader Daniel Cohn-Bendit, who Harich saw as a neo-anarchist par excellence. The book was inspired by Hans Magnus Enzensberger and Karl Markus Michel in spring 1969. An abridged version appeared in *Kursbuch*, Volume 19, in December 1969.⁵⁰

Alongside his preoccupation with political theory and philosophy, Harich also became involved in current affairs. He was particularly interested in global political events in the late 1960s and the related new social and political movements. In addition to his aforementioned critique of the renaissance of anarchist ideas, he soon began to reflect on environmental issues, too. Prokop: 'As the first environmental activist in the GDR, from 1971, he focused on ecological

---

46 See Janka 1992, p. 339.
47 Rauh 2006, p. 755.
48 See Harich, A. 2007, p. 306 and p. 309.
49 See Mittenzwei 2003, p. 242.
50 Mittenzwei 2003, p. 242. For a more detailed account of the history of this book's publication, see Amberger 2011c, p. 14 f., BStU, MfS, AP, 4578/71, vol. 9, p. 324 ff.

issues'.[51] In 1975 this culminated in what was probably his most important book *Communism without Growth?*. His interest in ecological problems, however, continued right up until his death, which meant that they also featured in his later works.[52]

In the GDR of the 1970s, his environmental warnings fell on deaf ears, leaving Harich resigned in the face of his own powerlessness.[53] This was one of the reasons why he made a personal appeal to Erich Honecker on 8 March 1979 requesting permission to leave the country. Just four days later, his request was granted. The SED even presented him with unexpected 'gifts': he was given a certificate of invalidity and a long-term visa (which allowed him to return to the GDR at any time), his doctoral title was reinstated, and he was granted the right to retain East German citizenship.[54]

Harich became involved in the nascent green movement in both Austria and West Germany. By doing so he refused to accept the role of GDR dissident, frequently pointing out that he was still a citizen of the GDR, as he did in an interview published in the Austrian journal *Neues Forum* in summer 1979.[55] Harich never managed to settle down in the West, however. His influence and success there was limited, which could partly be attributed to the fallout of Stefan Heym's novel *Collin*,[56] which was published just as he was starting to build up his own personal circle. He was also attacked by Wolf Biermann[57] who

---

51 Prokop 1996, p. 22. According to Alexander Reich, Harich's initial exposure to ecology was actually a decade earlier: 'Harich discovered the subject of ecology in 1948. As a student of philosophy, he combed through the new "leading science" of biology in search of evidence of Stalin's "lapidary theses" on "dialectical and historical materialism"; first basic feature: nature as a "coherent, unified whole", in which "things and phenomena are organically linked, dependent on one another and determine one another"' (Reich 2009). Harich's biographical addition to this is enlightening: 'However, what at the time seemed very remote was any notion of future science, any thought of environmental destruction, environmental pollution, any thought that this ecology could possibly have anything to do with politics. ... I would never have imagined that one day this science would bring forth warnings of ruin. ... But after reading the two Club of Rome reports at the beginning of the 1970s ..., you can imagine that, for a person who has had an interest in ecology for over 30 years ..., this new realisation and warning is like a bolt from the blue' (Harich 1980, p. 75).
52 For more on this, see Amberger 2011b, Hofbauer 1996.
53 See Harich 1979c, Amberger 2011b, p. 8f.
54 See Harich 1979b, p. 17, Harich, A. 2007, p. 182f.
55 See Harich 1979b.
56 *Collin* addressed the history of the 'Harich group'. Although the main protagonists in the book all had different names, with a little background knowledge they are easily recognisable. The novel takes Janka's perspective. The role assigned to Harich is therefore not a favourable one.
57 Even before his expatriation, Biermann took action against Harich. Peter Hack's proposal

denounced him as a 'traitor' in an article published in *Die Zeit*, accusations that Harich claimed were based on slander spread by Walter Janka.[58]

In 1981, the financial difficulties Harich was facing on top of his tattered reputation led him to return to the GDR disillusioned. But no-one was waiting for him. Even his own daughter Katharina had had distanced herself, as described by Anne Harich:

> She did not know what to say to her father. For so many years they had had no contact at all. Katharina Harich had severed all contact with her father, placing more trust in the Havemann-Biermann circle, which Walter Janka was a sporadic member of. This circle was vehemently against Harich and viewed anyone who had anything to do with him as suspicious and being on the wrong side, i.e. the side of the traitors. Any attempt to have a conversation with her father or at least help him in his hour of need might have resulted in her being rejected by her own circle of friends. I am really not sure. The contempt for Harich after his imprisonment was like a legacy that was continued through accomplices and that did not even stop at his own child.[59]

After his return to the GDR, Harich had no choice but to withdraw and live a secluded life. Siegfried Prokop wrote that the isolation saw Harich descend into a psychological pit and that the persecution complex he had suffered from since his imprisonment had only grown worse, causing him to seek treatment at this time.[60] The SED leadership granted him a disability benefit, but he was still not welcome to return to the university. He was left with no other option than to work from home. Nevertheless, he remained in contact with a number of high-level academic and cultural functionaries, with

---

to accept Harich as a member of the PEN Club in 1975 failed due to opposition from Otto Gotsche and Wolf Biermann. See Harich, A. 2007, p. 191. This is also verified by Gerhard Zwerenz 1996, p. 27.

58   See Harich, A. 2007, p. 188 f.
59   Harich, A. 2007, p. 190 f. From an article by Bernd Florath, who had been an associate of Havemann since 1971, we can surmise what was thought and said about Harich within Havemann's circle. Florath accused Harich of 'egomania' and that his ideas, even in the texts he wrote in 1957, were elite and centralistic in nature. See Havemann, K. and Widmann 2003, p. 75 ff., Florath 1994, p. 62 ff. Harich was enraged by the article and called the accusations 'ahistorical'. In Harich's view, Florath was passing judgement from today's perspective and not based on the situation at the time. Moreover, the *Plattform* had only been a first draft for the debate and not a fully developed concept. According to Harich, it was therefore wrong to criticise it. See Prokop 1997, p. 110 f.
60   See Prokop 1997, p. 156.

Gregor Schirmer, Lothar Berthold and Klaus Höpcke asking him to write a book about Nietzsche in the early eighties, for instance.[61] Klaus Höpcke, the Deputy Minister of Culture and Head of the Administration for Publishing and the Book Trade, also known as the 'Minister for Books', had a relatively good relationship with Harich at this time. He did him small favours and took time to meet and converse with him.[62] But in 1987, Harich fell out with Höpcke, too, when the Nietzsche debate resulted in tensions in the GDR.[63] Harich developed genuine feelings of hatred towards anyone in the GDR who sought to even slightly revise the perception of Nietzsche. In fact, according to Schirmer, Harich went as far as to describe such men as Klaus Höpcke, Stephan Hermlin, Manfred Buhr and Manfred Naumann as 'his worst enemies'.[64]

Despite all these setbacks and vilification, Harich wanted to become a member of the SED again, partly because he thought this would give him an opportunity to introduce his ideas and opinions about Nietzsche, Jean Paul and Lukács more effectively.[65] The ruling party did not yield to his wish, however, and Harich, finding the SED's position on Nietzsche scandalous, withdrew his application of his own accord. It was not until 1990 that the appeal against Harich's 1957 verdict was upheld and the GDR supreme court announced his rehabilitation. From 1992, Harich set up and chaired the 'Alternative Commission for German Contemporary History'. Harich was extremely unhappy about how the process of German unification was executed in reality. The one thing he had always longed for did not happen as he had imagined. His perception was that the process of unification was defined by the conservatives' primitive anti-communist desire for revenge, something that sickened him.[66] He wished to take a stance against the process and show his solidarity

---

61 See Harich, A. 2007, p. 192.
62 See Harich, A. 2007, p. 209 f. Also see Harich 1979c.
63 See Harich, A. 2007, p. 249. The SED wanted something of a thaw in their cultural policy and also to honour important non-socialist German thinkers, including Nietzsche, within the framework of the legacy and tradition debate. Harich, who saw Nietzsche as a pioneer of fascism, was vehemently opposed to him being honoured.
64 See Harich, A. 2007, p. 341.
65 See Harich, A. 2007, p. 294.
66 See Prokop 1997, p. 171 f. Günter Gaus praised Harich's work during this period: 'The GDR did not, of course, resemble the country it liked to portray itself as. But what country does? That said, in the second half of its existence, it did not continuously resemble the bleak pictures painted by the rather stupid winners of history after 1989. Among other things, the German *Wende* took away our ability to see nuances. Harich's Alternative Commission of Enquiry into the History of the German Democratic Republic was a must if the Germans were, in retrospect, to do justice to even the simplest of historical truths. But is this really what they wanted?' (Gaus 1999, p. 293).

with the shunned former GDR functionaries,⁶⁷ but without positioning himself unilaterally on their side:

> The aim of the Alternative Commission was to make the historical debate more objective. The intention was to replace the bias that defined the debate with multidimensionality and nuance. The Commission sought to conduct a critical historical analysis of contemporary German history in its entirety. This also included a critical examination of the GDR's political system with all its empty rituals and democratic deficit. This reappraisal of contemporary German history must leave no stone unturned, no subject, no essential fact overlooked. From the very start, Wolfgang Harich rejected nostalgia in any form.⁶⁸

For a brief period after the *Wende* or Peaceful Revolution, Harich was part of a small splinter group of the German Communist Party but he soon cancelled his membership once he caught wind of North Korean donors. He was not keen to become a member of the Party of Democracy Socialism (PDS) in the early 1990s because Janka was on the party's Council of Elders.⁶⁹ Only once Janka had left the party in 1994 did Harich eventually join, not least because he did not wish to come to the end of his life with no party-political affiliation. Indeed, he did not live much longer after this. With Harich's death on 15 March 1995, the world lost one of the most controversial German Marxists of the twentieth century.

Was Wolfgang Harich a dissident or an opposition figure?⁷⁰ He himself rejected both labels. In an interview with the *Kölner Stadt-Anzeiger* on 12 May 1978, he stated that he had no intention of using oppositional political activities to

---

67 As the spokesperson for the Alternative Commission of Enquiry, in 1994, Harich was critical of how the PDS treated the old SED cadres. He accused the PDS of 'humiliating' the former members of the Honecker government during the *Wende*. In his opinion, the party leadership showed a lack of solidarity towards the old SED cadres, who, despite the justified criticism directed at them from among their own ranks, still should not be passively surrendered to their political opponents as scapegoats. Harich also regarded the purging of all former Stasi employees from within the party as wrong, as this would only face anti-communist protest from opponents. Harich praised Egon Krenz for his level-headed behaviour in the autumn of 1989 when he made a unilateral decision to prevent bloodshed. In Harich's opinion, this had earned him the honour that would be paid to a national hero as he did no less than Stauffenberg and, unlike Stauffenberg, was actually successful. See Harich 1994a, p. 47 ff.
68 Prokop 1997, p. 176.
69 See Prokop 1997, p. 172 f.
70 For more on this, see Amberger 2011c.

achieve his ecological objectives in the GDR but instead would seek to fulfil those objectives by way of legal petitions or communications. When it came to international relations, Harich was a realist who, given the global political context, saw growth of the military in the GDR as inevitable – but not the growth of mass consumption, and this was something he used lawful means to oppose.[71] Writing about the period 1979 to 1981, which Harich spent living in the West, Siegfried Prokop observed: 'During this time, Harich resisted all efforts by the Western media to instrumentalise him as a dissident against the GDR and socialism. Since then, the general consensus among the conservative bourgeois ruling elite was that Harich was a "peculiar" or "eccentric dissident".'[72]

And Alfred Schmidt was of the opinion that

> Harich was probably one of the first Marxist philosophers to take issue with Marx's God of history, 'the growth of productive forces'. He was concerned about this new problem that classical Marxism was helpless in the face of. In the *Frankfurter Rundschau* of 21 June 1979 Harich explained: 'I have entirely different concerns to those opposition figures in the East who people like to call dissidents. I am increasingly and almost singularly occupied by thoughts of the terrible global crises, which, if things carry on as they are, we will have to deal with as early as the 1980s'.[73]

In an interview with the *Berliner Extradienst* on 19 April 1974, Harich complained that he felt the Western media had exploited his 'dissident' status: no one in the West had ever been interested in the works he had written before his arrest and, for political reasons, these had been 'undervalued'.

> There were never any reviews of these works, nor did I receive any offers to purchase the rights to publish. Once I had been released from prison,

---

71 See BStU, MfS, AP, 4578/71, vol. 7, p. 28 ff. Elsewhere in the files, there is information labelled HA XX and dated 22 May 1978 about the Harich interview published in the *Kölner Stadt-Anzeiger*. The interview had been approved 'by the Department for International Relations of the Ministry for Foreign Affairs' with no knowledge of its content. When the interview was published, Harich said that he stood by his statements and that these were not directed at the GDR. However, he was furious that he had been wrongly declared an oppositionist in parts of the article that he had not even approved (header, short biography). What is more, the newspaper had also included incorrect information about his age and term of imprisonment. As a result, he stated that he would no longer be giving interviews of this type in future. See BStU, MfS, AP, 4578/71, vol. 8, p. 86 ff.
72 Prokop 1996, p. 22.
73 Schmidt 1999, p. 498.

> I discovered that I had suddenly become 'overvalued' in the West, that they had discovered my genius. Fortunately, I am not a megalomaniac. I am also not one to resort to unfair means for reasons of self-promotion. Otherwise, instead of working, I would be spending all my time polishing my long since dusty crown of immortality.[74]

Harich frequently uttered such polemic remarks against those dissidents who did not distance themselves to the same degree as he did from the Western media. Comments like this reveal the arrogance that the majority of GDR oppositionists accuse Harich of to this day. It was difficult to pin him down. He professed his commitment to the SED and was opposed to capitalism. He refused to take on the role of dissident – whether for the Western media or the SED critics in the GDR. A clear illustration of this can be found in reports submitted to the Stasi by unofficial collaborators about two lectures Harich held on 26 June and 3 July 1978 for the protestant student community (*Evangelische Studentengemeinde*, ESG) in Greifswald on the issue of the environment (at the time, the Lubin nuclear power plant, the first and only one in the GDR, was in the process of being constructed). At the first of these lectures, Harich presented on *Communism without Growth?* and the Club of Rome: 'Off the record, it was reckoned that the majority of the participants considered Harich's lecture, his theses and theories, difficult to understand, comprising purely abstract theories, with barely any resemblance to real social conditions, almost utopian and absurd seeming. In particular, the theses he put forward on *Communism without Growth?* were seen as philosophical nonsense which contradicted the laws of science but, on the other hand, were also considered food for thought.'

Harich's failure to say anything negative about the realities of the GDR disappointed the majority of those present. On the second ESG evening, too, Harich advanced the theses from *Communism without Growth?* The unofficial collaborator took the view that here, too, Harich's positive views on the GDR failed to meet the expectations of the majority of the around 25 participants.[75]

Anne Harich described his motives: 'As a lone wolf, he no longer wanted to be accused of dissent and so his only option was to make nice with the party authorities if he wanted to continue to influence the destiny of the GDR, and he took great care not to be co-opted by the West as an outsider, an oppositionist. And because he never turned to the West for help, he was never a true dissident.'[76]

---

74 BStU, MfS, AP, 4578/71, vol. 7, p. 138 ff.
75 BStU, MfS, AP, 4578/71, vol. 8, p. 57 ff.
76 Harich, A. 2007, p. 148 f.

Indeed he had no interest in being an opposition figure because he did not want to land up in prison again, which is why he sometimes had a panic-stricken response to attempts to appropriate him and use him against the SED leadership. One particular episode illustrates this very clearly:

> It was April 1978, a few months after Rudolf Bahro had been imprisoned. A woman named Kirsten Rowe, who he had never met before, turned up at his apartment. She gave him a letter from Carl Amery, who was attempting to mobilise prominent residents of East Berlin in support of Bahro. At the same time, a radio broadcast was given on the subject. The Committee for the Defence of Freedom and Socialism also played a part here. There was talk of taking measures, something which Harich saw as an attempt at provocation.[77]

Harich himself reported that, after the woman from the Committee for the Defence of Freedom and Socialism had visited, he had been afraid that he was being lured into a trap and so immediately contacted Mr Lohse, who he saw as an 'instructor' of the Central Committee. This Mr Lohse was, in fact, called Lohr and was a Stasi Major.[78] Harich agreed his tactical approach with Lohr, meaning the Ministry for State Security influenced Harich's actions, albeit indirectly and conspiratorially. Werner Mittenzwei describes Harich's special position within the SED opposition movement:

> Wolfgang Harich occupies a prominent position in the history of the GDR opposition movement. He made the biggest sacrifices and presented the most comprehensive concept for the transformation of societal conditions in Germany. His personality and his theories were a reflection of the huge insurmountable contradictions of the time. Even his naivety expressed the helplessness of the people during the Cold War era. It was him that made the most courageous contribution to the unity of his fatherland.[79]

Siegfried Prokop, too, was full of praise for Harich:

> Harich is one of the most important left-wing intellectuals of this century. He never lost sight of the significance of the national question. Unlike

---

77 Prokop 1997, p. 143.
78 See Becker 1994.
79 Mittenzwei 2003, p. 310.

other representatives of the SED opposition, such as Robert Havemann and Hermann von Berg, Harich was always aware of the key political importance of the SPD in Germany. The various political camps, particularly the Stalinists and the old conservatives, bitterly opposed Harich. Politicians and the media accused him of being a Stalinist, Trotskyist or revisionist. But none of these labels and stigma were accurate. Harich in fact embodied a broad spectrum, from the anti-fascist educated middle class of his respectable parental home to the green movement to undogmatic communism.[80]

In the reappraisal of GDR history, however, these positive opinions of Harich are few and far between. The more dominant picture is of Harich as an authoritarian scatterbrain. Portraying him as an anti-democrat and a utopianist discredits Harich's entire political thought. In his monumental *Geschichte der Opposition in der DDR 1949–1989* (The history of the opposition in the GDR, 1949–1989), Ehrhart Neubert writes about Harich's ecological ideas, for instance: 'Apart from the fact that the theory was a tragic expression of the internalised oppression which Harich experienced, and that he now over-eagerly offered it as a remedy, the utopian character of this theory deprived it of any political relevance, meaning it was not appreciated by the members of the opposition'.[81]

Harich was neither a dissident nor a critic of the status quo, neither a Stalinist nor a liberal democrat. According to his widow, he was critical of the bloody suppression of the Tiananmen Square protests in Beijing in 1989 and welcomed Mikhail Gorbachev's efforts to deescalate tensions as well as his disarmament and democratisation project.[82] On the other hand, he in no way identified with Western capitalist democracy. He could be described as a non-conformist communist who, despite eight years in prison and substantial political aspersions after that, remained committed to Marxist and Leninist doctrine. He was keen to be of use to the SED, to help the party with suggestions for improvement. But from the mid-1950s, the party was no longer interested in his help. By this point at the latest, a class of functionaries had emerged the majority of whom disliked Harich's activities. Harich stood no chance against this group, in part because he did not consider himself a dissident, an enemy of the system and could therefore not expect to be shown any solidarity by fellow oppositionists.

---

80   Prokop 1996, p. 25.
81   Neubert 2000, p. 213.
82   See Harich, A. 2007, p. 379 ff.

2   The Primacy of Nature: Harich's Return to Archistic Utopia

In 1975, a book written by Wolfgang Harich appeared in West Germany, issued by the Rowohlt Verlag publishing house. It was not the first of his works to be published in the West. Alongside various journal articles, his *Jean Pauls Kritik des philosophischen Egoismus* (Jean Paul's critique of philosophical egoism) (1968), *Zur Kritik der revolutionären Ungeduld* (Toward a critique of revolutionary impatience) (1971) and *Jean Pauls Revolutionsdichtung* (Jean Paul's revolutionary poetry) (1974) had also been printed. This book, however, was something special. While Harich's 1971 analysis of anarchism was, to a great extent, consistent with the SED's stance on the West German extra-parliamentary opposition (APO),[83] and his Jean Paul books undoubtedly won recognition among literary scholars, this book, entitled *Communism without Growth? Babeuf and the 'Club of Rome'*, was a contribution to contemporary environmental discourse.

This time, Harich's arguments were not quite as consistent with the SED view as in 1971 and he was also writing for a different target audience to 1968 and 1974. And this time he managed to achieve recognition in a debate that had so far been largely dominated by contributions from the USA. His text was an independent German contribution on how the Club of Rome had been received and also brought about a 'major renaissance'[84] of archistic utopia. Harich successfully pulled off the feat of connecting the (rigid) ideology of Marxism-Leninism with the two Club of Rome reports and other literature from Western environmental discourse, cleverly using the French revolutionary and utopian socialist Gracchus Babeuf as the link between the two. A construct of this type inevitably sparked dissent.

But what did Babeuf have to do with the Club of Rome? In the first instance, very little, given that he lived from 1760 to 1797 and would never have been aware of the problems of the twentieth century. Harich's focus therefore was

---

83   In this book, Harich deals with the anarchist part of the APO and points out the differences between anarchists and communists. Harich's argumentation draws on the criticisms of anarchism formulated by Lenin in his 1917 *State and Revolution*. According to this account, the communists first wanted to build socialism and then allow the state to wither away – the anarchists, on the other hand, wanted to abolish the state immediately. The anarchists, however, did not yet have a plan. This was to be the next step after the old apparatus had been destroyed. The Marxists, in contrast, would establish a new state based on soviets to complete the revolution. Lastly, the Marxists wanted to prepare the workers for revolution through the bourgeois state, while the anarchists did not wish to use this potential. See Lenin 2014, p. 154f.

84   Heyer 2009, p. 9.

not on Babeuf's specific political ideas but on his archistic utopia, which Harich attempted to recontextualise in contemporary discourse.

2.1   *The Archistic Utopian Tradition*

Fundamentally, the history of political utopia can be divided into two strands of development: the utopias that take an étatist, archistic approach (with a strong centralist state coupled with the subordination of the individual or their sublation to the collective) and the utopias that follow the anarchistic school of thought, rejecting étatist models. 'The antagonism of archistic and anarchistic approaches is one of the factors which, in utopian tradition, guaranteed the dynamic of the entire genre'.[85] Rolf Schwendter notes that it is in times of chaos and suffering that archistic utopias play a particularly strong role in shaping discourse because this is when people are most receptive to regulatory concepts.[86]

The schism between archistic and anarchistic utopias occurred during the French Enlightenment when, for the first time, there was a break with the utopian étatism in the tradition of Plato and More. This rift has continued to this day, defining the utopian discourse within the workers movement at the beginning of the twentieth century.[87] Over the course of its development, the utopian genre lost its attraction and importance because of its association with totalitarian systems and their atrocities. It was not until post-materialist discourse that a renaissance of utopia was ushered in, although only the anarchistic form emerged as an antithesis to dystopia.[88] Nevertheless, Harich sought to revive the archistic utopian tradition.

To this end, he took recourse to Babeuf, who had proposed a radical étatist concept of equality. Many of Babeuf's ideas reappear in Harich's *Communism without Growth?* and as such will be described in more detail below.

---

[85]   Heyer 2009, footnote no. 8, p. 8.
[86]   'These visions for the future particularly resonate during structural crises. In general, these utopias of social order reveal the downside of a society bursting with competition, chaos and conflicts of interest, which block the necessary solutions to their problems' (Schwendter 1994, p. 22). According to Harich's archistic approach, uncoordinated and decentralised action by individual states to solve ecological problems can be seen as a downside.
[87]   See Heyer 2009, footnote no. 8, p. 8.
[88]   The archistic utopian tradition, of which Babeuf should also be seen as a representative, did not manage to survive the twentieth century. We must agree with Richard Saage when he writes that the collapse of actually existing socialism also sealed the fate of the archistic utopia. Although a renaissance of this type of system cannot be entirely ruled out, the hope principle is likely to be *a priori* negated in such a society. This also means, however, that the anarchistic line in utopian history should not be ignored because society will always require corrective measures. See Saage 2002a.

François-Noël Babeuf[89] was born into a poor family in France on 23 November 1760. He received no more than a basic education, married in 1782 and went on to have several children who died in early childhood. Babeuf initially worked as a land surveyor. This provided him with financial security but, through his work with taxes and land registries, he learnt a lot about the decadence of the nobility. As a consequence of the French Revolution, Babeuf lost his livelihood.[90] After the fall of the Robespierre in July 1794, the Thermidors came to power, a development that Babeuf initially welcomed. However, he soon publicly opposed the new rulers, leading him to be arrested and imprisoned. During his time in prison, he met other political prisoners with whom he planned a conspiracy. Once he was released from jail in 1795, he played a leading role in the creation of a conspiratorial circle of opposition figures. The movement grew rapidly but the government hit back and put a stop to the conspiracy with the help of informers. Babeuf was arrested and, along with 64 other defendants, appeared before the courts in 1797. He represented himself in court.

His defence plea during the trial, in which he made reference to the radical French philosophers of the Enlightenment, Morelly, Rousseau and Mably,[91] is regarded as a plea for absolute equality.[92] He denied the charge of conspir-

---

[89] Babeuf called himself Gracchus from 1793. See Bambach 1991, p. 37. A short biography can be found in Höppner and Seidel-Höppner 1975b, p. 49 ff.

[90] See Scott 1988, p. 7 f.

[91] Babeuf defended his attacks on private ownership by arguing that Rousseau and Mably had already rejected the concept without being ostracised – quite the contrary, in fact. See Babeuf 1988, p. 72 ff. Similarly, he also referred to Diderot's book *The Basic Law of Nature* without being aware that this was in fact written by Morelly (something which was not yet known at the time). See Babeuf 1988, p. 89 f. 'Rousseau himself did not necessarily see a society of small property owners as the be-all and end-all, but rather as the best of the options that were – still or already – available, as he saw the abolition of private ownership and a return to the "golden age" of the primordial classless community as an attractive but impracticable idea. In 1755, Morelly, whose life remains shrouded in mystery to this day, surmounted this obstacle in his *Code of Nature*; the book rejected the aim not only of abolishing the existing feudal privileges, but also of eradicating any kind of class differences. However, his precise utopia was written in the style of the popular science fiction novel and failed to show the path that might lead to such a utopia. ... Even the noble pessimist Mably (1709–1785) extolled in various parts of his varied works a society of equals with an economy based on common property, which only he perceived as being concordant with the laws of nature and humankind's need for happiness, and which, unlike Morelly, he believed had no chance of being achieved in real life, which is why, for practical reasons, he gave partial achievement preference. Dismissed by contemporaries as scholarly shenanigans, both ideas from the far left would go on to be food for thought during the revolution; their readers including Buonarotti and Babeuf' (Markov and Soboul 1989, p. 61).

[92] See Scott 1988, p. 15 ff.

acy, saying this would only apply in the case of a minority opposing a majority. Given that the ruling Thermidors were themselves a minority, ruling without having been given the mandate to do so by the majority of the people, opposition was both justified and democratic.[93]

Finally, Babeuf presented his objectives, which drew on the concept of contractualism. He argued that, in its natural state, the land had not been subject to private ownership and that it was not until private ownership came about that the 'owners and slaves', the 'happy and unhappy' emerged. Moreover, this inequality was further consolidated and reinforced through the law of inheritance. Lastly, he saw wage inequality as the third reason for social inequality.[94] Babeuf believed that many of society's ills had their origins in private ownership and that these ills could only be entirely eradicated if the underlying ownership structures were removed, too. 'It is clear, then, from all that has been said, that everything owned by those who have more than their individual due of society's goods, is theft and usurpation. It is therefore just to take it back from them.'[95]

Nor did Babeuf baulk at employing instruments of repression in the event that those who saw themselves as entitled to a better wage for better performance should refuse to abolish private ownership. In a letter written from prison in 1795, Babeuf describes in detail how he envisages the abolition of the market and the future distribution: 'No more merchants and businessmen unless they limit themselves to that which, in our own words, they actually are, that is to say genuine facilitators of distribution. Once all those who contribute to the production and processing of goods work for the collective warehouses and each and every one sends the product of their individual labour there in the flesh, once the facilitators of distribution are no longer deployed for their own benefits only but for the good of the big family, once every citizen is provided with the same manifold share of the entire production of the whole association as reward for that which he has contributed to its improvement or reproduction, in my view, trade will not be abolished but rather on the contrary, it will be perfected because it will offer advantages to everyone'.[96]

However, it is not just goods that are to be coordinated and allocated by the administration, but also labour.[97] This would unburden people of their worries and stabilise society, also making it possible to keep population growth in check:

---

93 See Babeuf 1988, p. 39.
94 See Babeuf 1988, p. 62f.
95 Babeuf in Fried and Sanders (eds.) 1964, p. 66.
96 Babeuf 1975a, p. 58.
97 See Babeuf 1975a, p. 58.

Everything is adjusted and proportioned according to current and anticipated needs, based on the probable growth of society, which is relatively easy to estimate. Actual demand is precisely calculated and fully met thanks to the fast shipment of goods to all regions irrespective of distance. ... Production loses its private character once all productive activities are practiced for the benefit of the big family. Each individual workshop is part of a main workshop, each product, each good is managed by the big warehouse and then assimilated into the collective fund of the Republic. ... I am able to work in peace and without burden and do no more than that which is absolutely necessary, at no detriment to the body. That which I can do will be sufficient for myself and my kin, of that I am certain: what more could I wish for? If I invent a machine ..., if I have mastered a trick which can help me do something faster and better, then ... I rush to inform the association .... The invention ... provides me and all those whose work it makes easier with leisure, and this leisure is then no longer ominous inoccupation but rather pleasant free time. ... Competition, which never spares a second thought for perfection, submerges carefully manufactured products into the masses of cheap rubbish, which wish for nothing less than to pull the wool over the public's eyes, since knockdown prices only become possible by forcing the worker to debase his craft and workmanship with botch jobs, sucking the life out of him, at the same time demoralising him with this show of unscrupulousness. ... Competition fabricates blindly, unperturbed by the risk of not finding buyers and having to destroy huge quantities of raw materials, which could have been put to good use but are now wasted resources that are devoid of value. ... But will I be concerned in the future when my profession introduces a machine that makes hundreds of poor workers superfluous? No, I will not .... For me and for everyone, a decent livelihood is guaranteed, protected from all the vicissitudes, whims of fashion, speculations and price increases. ... With ... the strict duty to contribute being one of the cornerstones of association and the right to be provided for, there can no longer be voluntary idlers in its midst. ... Nobody will have the right to live at the expense of others.[98]

What in Babeuf's works is levelled against the social injustice of his time, against the stark contrast between the privileges and the opulent behaviour of the new rulers, on the one hand, and the suffering of the masses, on the

---

98   Babeuf 1975b, p. 60 ff.

other, was taken up by Wolfgang Harich 180 years later and adapted to the ecological crisis which was, and still is, related to the North-South problem of hunger. Harich's demand for equality was directed at the decadence of the industrialised countries of the world. The parallels between the excerpt quoted from Babeuf's letter and Harich's utopia are striking. Even capitalism's wasteful consumption of natural resources was something that Babeuf had already addressed even though, at the time, the effects of this phenomenon could in no way be equated, either qualitatively or quantitatively, with those identified by the Club of Rome.

Unlike some of his followers – certain groups among the Babouvists – Babeuf himself was not opposed to technical progress. He rejected 'Luddism' and recognised the opportunities for human emancipation provided by the increase in leisure time and security achieved through mechanisation. Babeuf's rejection of luxury should also be understood against this background. For Babeuf, luxury was reprehensible solely in the context of the low development of productive forces at the time – he no longer rejected it once it could be available to everyone[99] as it was '[n]ot the development of productive forces per se that was a problem for Babeuf, but rather its social form'.[100] Later, Harich too became preoccupied with this uneven development, rejecting luxury amid concerns over the ecological threat as well as the need to align the level of development of poor countries with that of the industrialised states, a stance that positioned him closer to the Babouvists than to Babeuf.

Babeuf derived his demand for equality from natural law.[101] Here, he drew on Morelly's *Code of Nature*[102] believing absolute equality to be achievable through a centralised administration. To substantiate his argument, he gave the example of the military where this model functions very effectively. In Babeuf's view, only such a strict administration would be in a position to offer people a good life.[103]

---

99   See Höppner 1985, p. 194.
100 Bambach 1991, p. 45.
101 'Like both Morelly and Rousseau, B.'s departure point was the basic idea from the Era of the Enlightenment that private property occurred as a result of unlawful appropriation and that the origin of ownership resulted in the destruction of the natural equality between people' (Franz 1983a, p. 59).
102 See Babeuf 1975b, p. 71 ff.
103 'Only an administration of this type can bring about universal, immutable and unadulterated happiness, *collective happiness, the very purpose of society*. This administration will cause boundary stones, fences, walls and locks to disappear; disputes, trials, theft, murder and all forms of crime; courts, prisons, gallows, punishment and despair, which causes all this harm; envy, resentment, gluttony, pride, deceit, falsehood, in short all that is immoral;

Given that Babeuf's ideas stemmed largely from the history of utopia or the French Enlightenment, their historical significance can be found in the radical philosophy of praxis approach they took, rather than in his ideas, works and speeches. Babeuf was a revolutionary. His merit lies in his steely determination to implement his ideas in practice,[104] to make his utopia 'concrete'. His commitment to revolutionary change distinguished him from many of the other social utopianists, something that was also commended by Marx and Engels.[105] But their positive view of Babeuf was limited to his revolutionary methods and did not extend to his concept of communism as, in the words of Ernst Bloch, 'Marx mocks the "raw, ascetic egalitarianism" of Babeuf'.[106]

This view was also in keeping with the reception Babeuf received in the GDR. The attitude towards the French social utopianist was described in a book published in 1975, for example: 'Indeed, the Babouvist concept of a transitional dictatorship is no more than an embryonic form of what we understand as the dictatorship of the proletariat today'.[107] Babeuf's aim was to secure the common good and, by means of centralism and equality, prevent chaos, suffering and anarchy. 'It was this and the harmonisation of relations to be brought about by the eradication of social inequality that Babeuf held to be the grand prize of the communist order'.[108]

For his concepts of equality, Babeuf himself drew primarily on the ideas of Étienne-Gabriel Morelly, an early French communist thinker and social utopian novelist born in 1715. Morelly proposed two utopian models: the liberal *Basiliade* and the strictly étatist *Code of Nature*.[109] In the latter, he depicted an egalitarian society dominated by a scarcity of goods. As Babeuf would after him, Morelly founded his concept of communism in reality.[110] Both thinkers

---

   moreover (and this point is undoubtedly the crucial one) above everything else the gnawing maggot of universal worry that lives in each and every one of us about the fate that awaits us tomorrow, next month, the following year, in old age, and about that of our children and grandchildren' (Babeuf 1975b, p. 79f.).
104 See Bambach 1991, p. 37, Heyer 2007a, p. 19.
105 See Heyer 2007a, p. 5f.
106 Bloch 1986, p. 576. Marx and Engels wrote in their *Manifesto of the Communist Party* in 1847/48 that the early proletariat and its means of production would not have the necessary level of maturity: 'The revolutionary literature which accompanied these first stirrings of the proletariat is necessarily reactionary in content. It teaches a general asceticism and a crude egalitarianism' (Carver (ed.) 1996, p. 27).
107 Höppner and Seidel-Höppner 1975a, p. 93.
108 Höppner and Seidel-Höppner 1975a, p. 85.
109 For a comparison of the two texts from the perspective of utopian history, see Saage 1999.
110 See Franz 1983b, p. 674f. The mid-eighteenth century saw a caesura in the history of uto-

thus created a 'utopian Leviathan'.[111] 'Morelly provided a construct in which the individual is eliminated entirely and integrated into a new society or rather becomes completely dependent on this new society in all areas of life. In the name of reason, the state encroaches on the lives of individual members of society and uses rigid punishment to force them to behave in a way that is in line with the system'.[112]

Morelly, too, was opposed to private ownership, believing its existence to be the root of all evil.[113] He called for the centralised distribution of products, it being the only way of guaranteeing equitable provision for everyone. In his utopia, luxury had been overcome.[114] He also saw coercion as a means to an end:

> Supported by the advancements in world history inaugurated by nature, the utopian project loses its contemplative character, becoming a political action plan that seeks to achieve a 'permanent state of good' (Morelly) for humanity in the future. The implications of this aspiration did not become apparent until the twentieth century, when ideologies for the legitimisation of totalitarianism believed they could justify the suffering and sacrifice of entire generations as a 'historical necessity' in the interests of a supraindividual promise of salvation.[115]

Referring to Morelly, Arno Waschkuhn noted: Many elements of this utopia became reality in the form of principles underpinning the actually existing socialism that developed 200 years later; principles such as the socialisation

---

pia – a shift away from spatial utopia to temporal utopia. This expanded the function of utopia, as the primary focus was no longer solely on criticising the status quo but on depicting a possible ideal for the future, one that should be strived for. Linked to this was the emergence of transformation strategies. See Waschkuhn 2003, p. 12.

111 Saage 1999, p. 56. The term 'Leviathan' was defined in the eponymous book written in 1651 by Thomas Hobbes. Hobbes outlined a means to 'legitimise governance through the consent of individuals, among whom a state of equality prevails' (Speth 2003, p. 97). Here, the governance of the Leviathan is in no way limited or constrained by supervisory authorities: 'The Leviathan only has to provide protection and order and to do this, according to Hobbes, it is also allowed to suppress freedom of expression and of religion ... However, Hobbes's solution results in state absolutism, in which all democratic aspirations are suffocated. Individuals depriving themselves of the right to decide precludes any democratic self-determination' (ibid, p. 98).

112 Heyer 2006b, p. 12.

113 See Morelly 1846, p. 116. Unlike Rousseau or Robespierre, Morelly and Babeuf reject the institution of private property outright.

114 See Morelly 1846, p. 166 f.

115 Saage, 1999, p. 66.

of ownership, the universal obligation to work (or the right to work), the purported rational control of production and distribution, equality of education and educational utilitarianism.[116]

The dynamics of the antagonism between archistic and anarchistic utopias is a common thread throughout the history of the labour movement, shaping the 'classics' of Marxism, although Marx and Engels themselves refuted the accusation that they were social utopianists and fiercely criticised early utopian socialism.[117]

This analogy becomes particularly apparent when we consider the two-stage theory of the development of communism. According to this theory, to achieve communism, society must first pass through a period of transition known as the 'dictatorship of the proletariat', which must still be archistic, while the communist end state is of anarchistic nature. Karl Marx introduced this strategy in his *Critique of the Gotha Programme*.[118] He described this transitional phase as inevitable:

> The question then arises: what transformation will the state undergo in communist society? In other words, what social functions will remain in existence there that are analogous to present state functions? This question can only be answered scientifically, and one does not get a fleahop nearer to the problem by a thousandfold combination of the word people with the word state. Between capitalist and communist society lies the period of the revolutionary transformation of the one into the

---

116 Waschkuhn 2003, p. 88.
117 See Engels 1989.
118 Here, Marx outlined the two development phases of communism: 'Besides, one worker is married, another not; one has more children than another, etc., etc. Thus, given an equal amount of work done, and hence an equal share in the social consumption fund, one will in fact receive more than another, one will be richer than another, etc. To avoid all these defects, right would have to be unequal rather than equal. But these defects are inevitable in the first phase of communist society as it is when it has just emerged after prolonged birthpangs from capitalist society. Right can never be higher than the economic structure of society and its cultural development which this determines. In a higher phase of communist society, after the enslaving subordination of the individual to the division of labour, and thereby also the antithesis between mental and physical labour, has vanished; after labour has become not only a means of life but life's prime want; after the productive forces have also increased with the all-round development of the individual, and all the springs of common wealth flow more abundantly – only then can the narrow horizon of bourgeois right be crossed in its entirety and society inscribe on its banners: From each according to his abilities, to each according to his needs!' Marx 1989a, p. 87.

other. Corresponding to this is also a political transition period in which the state can be nothing but *the revolutionary dictatorship of the proletariat*.[119]

Lenin's definition of this concept was far more precise. In *The State and Revolution*, he wrote that after the revolution, the revolutionary state must be preserved until all class distinctions are completely eliminated. The aim of abolishing the state was one that the anarchists also shared, but Lenin – unlike the anarchists – saw this as an impossible achievement without the dictatorship of the proletariat, which he felt was necessary to suppress reaction.[120]

> Only in communist society, when the resistance of the capitalists has been completely crushed, when the capitalists have disappeared, when there are no classes (i.e., when there is no distinction between the members of society as regards their relation to the social means of production), *only* then 'the state ... ceases to exist' and 'it becomes possible to speak of freedom.' Only then will a truly complete democracy become possible and be realized, a democracy without any exceptions whatsoever. And only then will democracy begin to *wither away* owing to the simple fact that, freed from capitalist slavery, from the untold horrors, savagery, absurdities, and infamies of capitalist exploitation, people will gradually *become accustomed* to observing the elementary rules of social intercourse that have been known for centuries and repeated for thousands of years in all copybook maxims. They will become accustomed to observing them without force, without coercion, without subordination, *without the special apparatus* for coercion called the state.[121]

In the first stage of development, the dictatorship of the proletariat, the archistic utopian tradition dominates, while in the second stage, which is communism itself, the anarchistic line will re-emerge. Marx and Engels claimed to have turned socialism into a science that was aimed at legitimising its distinction from utopia. The fundaments of this claim were postulated in Engels's *Socialism: Utopian and Scientific* where he described the withering away of the state after the communist revolution as a result of seemingly objective dialectical laws of history.[122]

---

119   Marx 1989a, p. 95.
120   See Lenin 2014, p. 98 ff.
121   Lenin 2014, p. 127.
122   See Engels 1989, p. 324 f.

In light of all this, the contradiction between archistic and anarchistic utopia was consequently resolved during the two stages of development. If you look at both the theory behind the 'actually existing socialist practices and the dictatorship of the proletariat, this transitional phase is in fact reminiscent of Babeuf's "barracks" communism'.[123] Both Babeuf and Lenin considered the use of force as a means of achieving the rule of the proletariat, or rather of its 'vanguard'. True communism, the end state that Lenin described, has remained a utopia, while his 'dictatorship of the proletariat' became reality under the Stalinist-style Bolshevik dictatorship and collapsed after more than 70 years without ever having achieved its ultimate goal of true communism.[124]

In recent decades there have been various alternative attempts at developing theories to fathom this communist end state, some of which even included strategies for achieving it. The majority of the proposed models were based on a state of anarchy, which Marx, Engels and Lenin saw as being the final stage of development. Almost no one dared to bring the end state forward to the first stage, i.e. into the dictatorship of the proletariat. The notion of 'actually existing socialism' was simply too unacceptable and unattractive for anyone to choose it as an ideal.

Communism without Growth?, however, was Harich's attempt to do just that. To this day, his thought experiment is seen as one of the last contributions to the tradition of archistic utopia.[125]

---

123 Peter Ruben believed that actually existing socialism could be clearly attributed to Babeuf and not the Asiatic mode of production (a hypothesis supported by Bahro, for instance): 'In the twentieth century, the position of modern communism on private productive assets remained unchanged since it was established by Babeuf. The transformation of the Bolshevik faction of Russian social democracy into the Russian Communist Party (formally constituted in March 1918) is clearly a preservation of Babeuf's programme and not "Asiatschina", as Western European ideologues who were unable to identify Russia's European position believed' (Ruben 1999, p. 15).

124 A decisive factor here is the schematic theory of history posited by Stalin in his paper entitled 'Dialectical and historical materialism' in the *History of the Communist Party under the Soviet Union (Bolsheviks). Short course* in 1938. In this article, the history of humankind is divided up into five formations and with regard to socialist development, the role of the party is formalised as a subject of transformation. See Stalin 1945; see also Hedeler 2011, p. 35 ff.

125 On page 175 of the book, Harich refers to *Communism without Growth?* as a utopia. See Harich 1975, p. 175. In an interview with the *Kölner Stadt-Anzeiger* newspaper on 12 May 1978, when asked whether his concept of egalitarian communism was not a utopia, Harich replied: 'Utopia or not – the only alternative is the destruction all life on Earth in the foreseeable future' (BStU, MfS, AP, 4578/71, vol. 7, p. 28 ff.).

2.2 Harich's Utopian Construct

Communism without Growth?, which bore the sub-title *Babeuf and the 'Club of Rome'*, was not a 'self-contained' book, but in fact a collection of interviews and letters exchanged between West German Social Democrat Freimut Duve and the erstwhile loyal SED member and 1956 leader of the opposition Wolfgang Harich. In parts of the book, Harich is still very critical of the SED, but his critique comes from a completely different perspective and with a very different intent to 1956.

Duve, who later became an SPD member of parliament, wrote the introduction to the book, describing the problems of the era and introducing the readers to Harich's concepts. The first Club of Rome report, published in 1972, highlighted the problems that unlimited growth could cause for humankind and the environment. The report sparked a debate among intellectuals the world over. Taking up this debate, however, Duve came to the sobering conclusion that policymakers in both the West and the East had so far failed to address these issues seriously. On the contrary, in fact, economic growth was seen as dogma in both the FRG and the GDR, and Harich was the only one there prepared to break with this taboo. Harich believed that the transition to communism could happen in the West first, although the ideal of socialism would have to be geared towards a strictly archistic distributive state. Citing Babeuf, Duve goes on to say that this ascetic state is the only thing in a position to solve the ecological and distributional problems of the time.[126] In Duve's words: 'Harich does not say so in so many words but the consequence of his apocalyptic utopia is most certainly a total police state in control of global supply, which he evidently endorses'.[127] In saying this, Duve is criticising Harich's virtually unquestioned faith in the Club of Rome and disputing the feasibility of implementing its concepts in the short term. Duve also highlights Harich's most obvious shortcoming in respect of the question of power: 'No matter what, those in charge of managing scarcity will inevitably end up with the real power. By pinning his hopes on communism, Harich is neglecting other forms of government including the Babeuf-style ascetic communist dictatorship'.[128]

And this captures the main essence of Duve's introduction. The introduction is followed by the book's first interview entitled 'Dialektischer Materialismus und Ökologie' (Dialectic materialism and ecology), in which Harich bemoans that the Frankfurt School confines Marxism to social issues and fails to consider its potential when it comes to solving ecological problems. Harich's view was

---

126 See Harich 1975, p. 7f.
127 Harich 1975, p. 9.
128 Harich 1975, p. 10.

that this narrow interpretation must be expanded and a new type of universal scholar capable of thinking beyond existing disciplines is needed to replace the orthodox Marxists. Here, Harich drew on Robert Jungk, who had hoped for 'a new version of the "renaissance man"'.[129]

The second interview in the book, 'Marx und Malthus' (Marx and Malthus) is devoted to the growth problem. Although Malthus was fiercely criticised by Marx and Engels for representing a reactionary ideology, according to Harich, the risks of unbounded population growth invoked by Malthus needed to be addressed again from a social sciences perspective.[130] Referring to a letter written by Engels in 1881, in which he takes a positive view of the feasibility of regulating population growth under communism,[131] Harich is critical of Jürgen Kuczynski who in his work *Das Gleichgewicht der Null* (The balance of the zero) advocates restricting population growth in the Third World, yet wants to accelerate it in the GDR.[132]

In reference to the 'concrete' nature of his utopia, Harich writes:

> With the level of development in productive forces achieved so far, I deem the immediate transition to communism to be feasible, and, in light of the ecological crisis, urgently necessary. However, I no longer believe that there can ever be a total communist society living in over-abundance, like the one we Marxists have been striving for up till now. This is one aspect of our approach that has to be corrected.[133]

Harich called for the end of capitalism and an end to population growth, which he believed would only be possible in a communist state: 'Since Marxism is humanity that has become science and not a mechanical calculation, it must discard the barely sustainable maximum population size as one of its criteria. Only a population which is optimum in size from a biological, economic and cultural perspective can be the standard for Marxism'.

---

129   See Harich 1975, p. 18 ff.
130   See Harich 1975, p. 23. On the neo-Malthusian discourse at the time, see Radkau 2014, p. 108.
131   See Harich 1975, p. 26 f.
132   See Harich 1975, p. 31. Kuczynski writes: 'The majority of us Marxists believe that parents should decide how many children they want to have. This does not mean that society cannot take measures to make it easier for parents to have a larger or number of children' (Kuczynski 1973, p. 39). Here Kuczynski was thinking of incentives like providing a better living space or bonuses, rather than coercion.
133   Harich 1975, p. 32 f.

According to Harich, seen from a global perspective, this population size was 'exceeded a long time ago'.[134] It is easier to regulate needs in a socialist society than a capitalist one, as the former has no powerful interest groups to prevent the government from pursuing a regulatory path and distribution can be implemented in a socially just manner.[135] Since world peace is the primary socialist foreign policy doctrine, wars over resources will no longer be waged. If the population size in a given country is too low, people from more populous areas should be encouraged to move there. 'And one day, in order to achieve a more equal distribution of the earth's population, which would certainly be advisable for ecological reasons, a world communist government will conduct global-scale resettlement measures anyway'.[136]

Such forced resettlement measures as a means to an end were one of the main reasons behind the eco-Stalinist accusations directed at Harich after his book came out. To mitigate the problems inherent in the 'resource question', Harich advocated recycling technologies.[137] Moreover, unlike the SED leadership, he was not daunted by ideological barriers: he believed that, to fight against the destruction of the environment and the population explosion, communists must also seek non-communist allies (with the exception of 'monopoly capital') such as the Club of Rome, for instance.[138]

In Harich's utopia, the issues of sexuality, reproduction and 'the woman's question' went hand in hand, since, unlike animals, human beings have control over their own procreation, which is why Harich called for the birth rate to be regulated. 'This scale of moral values gives the right of a human female to orgasm precedence over the destiny to reproduce that she shares with animal females'.[139] For the purposes of pleasure, therefore, sexuality should certainly play an important role and should not be controlled by the state.[140] Procreation, however, should not be down exclusively to the parents' wishes. Harich

---

134   Harich 1975, p. 37.
135   'Harich combined the demand for zero growth with the idea of fair distribution of scarcity, with rationed distribution. This idea came to him in late 1973 while he was living in the FRG. The oil crisis had led to petrol rationing – the first indication of a deeper global economic crisis' (Hofbauer 1996, p. 49).
136   Harich 1975, p. 41.
137   See Harich 1975, p. 43.
138   See Harich 1975, p. 46.
139   Harich 1975, p. 47.
140   The invention of the contraceptive pill enabled the 1968 generation to link population control and sexuality: 'By then, birth control was losing the sourly misanthropic and puritanical overtones of the old Malthusianism. The protection of wild nature was no longer associated with the repression of the natural wildness within human beings: an epochal change in the relationship between man and nature' (Radkau 2014, p. 68).

set out his thoughts on this four years later in an essay entitled *Das Weib in der Apokalypse* (The woman in the apocalypse).

In the chapter headed 'Der Club of Rome im Urteil der Kommunisten' (The Club of Rome as viewed by the communists), Harich looked at how the Club of Rome study was received in the Eastern Bloc, coming to the conclusion that, among the party intelligentsia in the Soviet Union there was a clear receptiveness to the results and that theories of zero growth were also being discussed. In the GDR, on the other hand, with the exception of Kuczynski's leaflet, the issue was not discussed and the Club of Rome was discredited as a class enemy. Scholars who were loyal to the party line continued to adhere unreservedly to the growth paradigm.[141]

Harich argued for radical equality in line with Babeuf's concept: 'Communism means equal distribution, implemented consistently and radically'.[142] To support his argument, he cites the original Marxist texts: alongside the aforementioned letter from Engels, he draws directly on passages from Marx himself. Harich saw Marx as having praised the economic prosperity that accompanied the bourgeoisie, albeit with reservations: 'Capitalism, states Marx in *The German Ideology*, makes productive forces into destructive forces. And it is precisely this that we are currently experiencing'.[143] Harich then goes on to quote from Marx's *Capital*, coming to the conclusion that Marx also regarded the protection of nature as a central paradigm of socialism.[144] Taking the old Marxist texts that the SED leadership had used up till then as ideological justification for the presence of growth in actually existing socialism, Harich sought to legitimise his own demands, which were, in fact, in conflict with those of the state leadership.

Harich even went as far as to claim that today, Marx would think in much the same way as him,[145] writing: 'This raises ... the question of whether, with

---

141 See Harich 1975, p. 48 ff.
142 Harich 1975, p. 59.
143 Harich 1975, p. 60.
144 During a panel discussion in Vienna in 1979, Harich stated: '... and there are large parts of *Capital* by Marx as well as parts of Engels's works where they attach importance to natural resources for human production and human life and advocate for those resources to be protected from destruction' (Harich/Herbig/Illich/Welsh 1979, p. 72).
145 Harich speculated that if Marx were alive today, he would regard the transition phase of socialism as superfluous due to the high level of relations of production in the industrial states. 'At the same time, however, he would also abandon the society of abundance as the type of society he designed communism as in his *Critique of the Gotha Program*. This can be assumed owing to the fact that Marx, at the very start of the same document, placed so much importance on both labour and nature being recognised as the source of all wealth in society. ... Today, Marx would no longer insist that "the springs of co-operative wealth

the current state of development of productive forces, it would not be in line with Marx's philosophy to, by means of a transition to zero or ... organic growth, bring the satisfaction of human needs into alignment with the protection and conservation of the biosphere once and for all. Under capitalist conditions, this is an impossibility'. He goes on to say: 'Communism readily allows zero or organic growth. ... In contrast to this, if a socialist society decided to do this and, specifically for this purpose, introduced a comprehensive system of rationed distribution which aligns the satisfaction of human needs with the conservation of the biosphere, while at the same time eliminating market relations, money, and the "performance principle", it would already be a communist society'.[146]

Thus Harich undertook a revision of Marxism under ecological premises, meaning he can, as was already the case in 1956, be considered a revisionist.[147] Harich lamented that the GDR economists and officials who were fixated on growth defined the dangers invoked by the Club of Rome as Western problems, basing their assessment on the West German Communist Party (DKP). The DKP saw the findings of the Club of Rome as endangering jobs in West German industry and suspected that a new capital campaign was behind it. According to Harich's analysis, in the eyes of these economists and officials, the Club of Rome and the environmental movement was nothing more than a new 'form of bourgeois ideology'.[148]

Lastly, he commented on his position 'regarding the class nature of the Club of Rome'. In his view, despite the fact that the Club of Rome was bankrolled by Western businesses, the findings should not be ignored. That said, they should not be blindly accepted. Harich saw the report as an act of 'bourgeois charity', which may in fact have been a bad investment on the part of the industries commissioning the report given that it did not produce the desired results. 'Meadows recommends zero growth as the lifeline to prevent our demise. This means that, without realising it, let alone explicitly expressing it, he came to

---

[must] flow more abundantly". He would be much more likely to strive towards communism as the crucial precondition for tackling the environmental crisis, even if this meant taking recourse to Babeuf' (Harich 1975, p. 201f.).

146 Harich 1975, p. 62.
147 For Harich, demanding that nuclear energy be abolished was also breaking a taboo. Harich considered this an incalculable risk, and thus called for this position to be renounced, something that went against the views of many communists. He believed that energy saving measures would ultimately be the end of nuclear energy anyway. See Harich 1975, p. 66ff.
148 See Harich 1975, p. 82.

the conclusion that the survival of homo sapiens on this planet hinged on the rapid elimination of capitalism'.[149]

Finally, Harich called for the class question be incorporated into the Club of Rome's report to prevent it from being instrumentalised by capitalism for the purpose of pure scaremongering. Accordingly, the next chapter of Harich's book was entitled 'Ökologische Krise und Klassenkampf' (The ecological crisis and the class struggle). In this chapter, Harich combined the archistic concept of the 'dictatorship of the proletariat' with the conclusions he believed had to be drawn from the Meadows Report:

'The fall of the bourgeoisie, the creation of a dictatorship of the proletariat and the realisation of communism are the prerequisites for being able to push through the demands made by the Club of Rome in society'.[150]

This made it clear that Harich now wanted the Marxist transition to communism to be manifested as a communist end state under ecological premises. By doing so, he was transcending the dogmatised historical determinism of Marxism-Leninism and departing from the historical goal of luxury communism for all. This is one of the main reasons that Harich should be regarded as an unconventional thinker or an oppositionist in the 1970s, too.

Harich believed that, under the leadership of the working class, the following measures had to be taken to save humanity: the population explosion has to be stopped, economic growth limited, nature protected from industry, resources conserved, the North-South divide eliminated and total disarmament achieved. Aware of the necessity of this, the proletariat would play the central role as the subject of the transformation and would be prepared to go without – at least this is what Harich believed. However, this could only succeed if capitalism were to be overthrown by revolution, since 'with capital accumulation and the valorisation of capital being the key principles behind the existence of capitalism, it cannot make the transition from expanded to simple reproduction'.[151]

Following Babeuf, Harich argued for 'ascetic communism', a form of communism that reconciled human needs and the protection of the biosphere, 'which, in turn would make life in the industrial regions simpler, more modest, less hectic and, in so doing, would fulfil the not entirely unfounded yearning for a simpler life that rolled in with the wave of nostalgia'.[152] And this clearly demonstrates that *Communism without Growth?* satisfied a key criterion

---

149 Harich 1975, p. 86.
150 Harich 1975, p. 109.
151 Harich 1975, p. 111.
152 Harich 1975, p. 128.

for political utopia, namely that it was oriented towards the future. Harich distanced himself from the antimodernist, regressive nostalgia wave which spread like wildfire during the post-materialist transformation. Although he welcomed the renunciation of consumption and the material frugality, as a dialectical materialist thinker, he rejected the backward-looking romanticisation at the same time.

In the following passage of dialogue, Harich expresses his views on rationing and the social question:

> DUVE: But it is a communism of rationed consumer goods that you are attempting to propagate.
>
> HARICH: Capitalism also rations consumer goods, through prices, which results in inequitable rationing, such that the rich remain free to indulge in all pleasures, entertainment and vices, while the masses have to tighten their belts.[153]

Rather than demanding luxury for all as the nineteenth and early twentieth century utopias had, because of the ecological crisis, Harich placed a return to the asceticism of the modern utopias at the heart of his utopian concept of communism. This

> ... would not be a paradise, but rather 'merely' a home based on ecological reason under conditions of strict social equality. But this is genuinely the best that it will ever be possible to achieve. We will have to jettison all the wild fantasies of a life of unlimited luxury that have been associated with the term communism up till now. Thus: Back to the days of Babeuf![154]

This takes us to the sixth chapter in the book, which was entitled 'Kommunismus als Lösung' (Communism as the solution). Here, Harich proposed specific solutions and strategies for transformation. He attributed a progressive political structure to the actually existing socialist states, believing they provided the optimal conditions for a transition to rationed communism. At the same time, however, Harich broke with a dogmatic Marxist-Leninist philosophy of history by predicting that this transition might first take place in the capitalist West. Here, he refused to speak of building socialism, instead arguing

---

153   Harich 1975, p. 129.
154   Harich 1975, p. 132.

that, in light of advanced relations of production, it was necessary to dismantle capitalism. According to Harich, those living in the Eastern Bloc had been forced to bear much hardship during the post-World War II reconstruction phase, while, during the same period, the citizens of the industrialised capitalist countries had been able to engage in excessive consumption. Now the standard of living in the Eastern Bloc had slowly started to improve, making it harder to convince people of the benefits of a more ascetic lifestyle, particularly if those in the capitalist West were to continue to live extravagantly.[155]

Harich also called for regulation to ensure goods were produced in a more environmentally sustainable manner – which would involve more bureaucracy:

> Before entering into production, all inventions must be subject to legal proceedings which would either approve them for use or condemn them to be rejected. In this process, the economists could take on the role of the defence and the ecologists the prosecution. Judges were to be appointed by policymakers, policymakers with great foresight, sustained by global responsibility, in fact a Marxist leadership.[156]

What remained unclear, however, was what processes would be used to appoint the various representatives of the prosecution and the defence, how or to what degree this could be democratically regulated and which mechanisms would be in place to prevent such processes – of which there would surely be many – becoming a pure farce. The flaw in this administrative concept can be described in terms of a critique of bureaucracy: When an institutionalised bureaucracy has to decide whether inventions are translated into actual products, there is the immanent risk of the apparatus operating autonomously and of unregulated decision-making. These processes would run into problems at the very latest when, out of political necessity, products have to be manufactured that do not satisfy the environmental criteria. Moreover, based on theory alone, it is never possible to fully gauge all the potential practical consequences – whether positive or negative.[157]

---

155 See Harich 1975, p. 134 ff.
156 Harich 1975, p. 149.
157 In an interview with the *Kölner Stadt-Anzeiger* in 1978, Harich countered the accusation that the communism he described would involve huge bureaucracy: 'This view is, if you really think it through, not as bad as it seems. For one thing, the administrative apparatus of modern industrial societies, whether capitalist or socialist, is far larger and more com-

Harich also attacked private car ownership. His conclusion that a 'privately owned motor vehicle ... is a means of consumption that is both antisocial and damaging to the environment, and most certainly anti-communist',[158] is plausible, as is the expansion of the public transport network and the increase in walking and bicycle riding, he calls for. At this point, however, it becomes clear that *Communism without Growth?* is a utopian counter-model to reality, a reality in which it is impossible to imagine life without private car ownership, whether socially, politically or economically – and this was all the truer in 1975 than it is today.

In any case, according to Harich, the material decadence of the industrialised world was not compatible with environmental conservation. Only by eradicating the inequalities between these developed states and the poor countries of the Global South would it be possible to achieve this. On the other hand, this would, in turn, not be compatible with capitalist imperialism. Consequently, introducing communism in the industrialised countries is the only way of liberating the Third World, although the aim must not be to industrialise these countries, but for their economies to be based on small-scale production instead. The large-scale industrial goods that the countries of the Third World currently need would then have to be imported from the industrialised countries of the Global North. The global market and money would be 'abolished and replaced with a global system of more equitable distribution'.[159] In return, all the poor countries have to do is to strictly regulate their birth rates and better protect the environment. If necessary, a few individual industrial plants could be built – on the proviso of environmental and human sustainability. But the formerly poor countries would no longer be dependent on the West as everything would belong to everyone:

> In a world built on communist principles, every production plant in every industrialised country would, without exception, cease to be privately owned by some corporate overlord but would instead become the property of the people. They would, however, also no longer be the property of the people of the respective country whose workers and engineers are

---

plex than that of a communism without growth. In addition, bureaucratic activities have the advantage that they neither waste raw materials nor do they cause damage to natural life cycles' (BStU, MfS, AP, 4578/71, vol. 7, p. 28 ff.). In this context, Harich recalled the post-war period when the distribution of food via ration cards was the least of everyone's worries.

158   Harich 1975, p. 156.
159   Harich 1975, p. 165.

employed in the factories. Instead, they would be owned by all people equally, the social property of the whole of humanity.[160]

By eliminating the competition on the global market, production locations could be appointed based on environmental sustainability considerations (criteria here might be, for instance, the right climate or the availability of raw materials). A centralised administration would coordinate all this: 'The global economic council would develop a global economic plan with quota requirements ... for all ... industrial products, and for the individual members of society there would be ration cards and coupons, and that would be that'.[161] Harich did not see his concept as 'barracks' communism in which people remain enslaved. On the contrary, the achievement of the common good and the happiness of each individual would be an integral part of his concept:

> In communism, neither elemental autochthonous modes of production nor technical perfection or efficiency are absolute values per se. Communism is committed to the happiness of mankind. Communism will emerge from the victory of the world revolution of the proletariat as a global system of centrally controlled mutual assistance and satisfaction of demands, liberated from goods exchange, competition, balances of trade and such like, geared solely towards providing the optimum benefit for all.[162]

Harich did not argue for uniformity of all people, but rather envisaged preserving country-specific traditions, albeit modified for ecological purposes:

> There would be local distinctions according to the different traditional lifestyles and habits. Rice would continue to be the staple food in South Asia, just as the Russians and the British would continue to have a preference for drinking tea rather than coffee. The Bavarians will have their *Weisswurst* sausages and the Chinese their shark fin soup. But the communist global economic plan, based on humanity's collective ownership of all means of production on the planet, with its indicators geared towards 'organic growth' ..., would, according to the principle of equality, allocate to each individual the consumer goods required for a decent life,

---

160   Harich 1975, p. 166.
161   Harich 1975, p. 167.
162   Harich 1975, p. 168.

no more, but also no less, irrespective of whether that individual lives in India, the US or any other country in the world.[163]

Consequently, at this juncture, for Harich it was not a question of compulsory absolute asceticism but rather of people managing their resources in a sustainable and ecological manner. Harich believed that, to achieve this, more locality would be just as important as more globality.

As a result of a heart attack, Harich was unable to conduct the seventh and final interview in his book. Instead, under the title 'Kritik der Bedürfnisse und der Kommunismus Babeufs' (A critique of needs and Babeuf's communism) the chapter comprised a series of letters Harich had written to Duve. In these letters, he welcomed the authoritarian structure of the actually existing socialist states and distanced himself from Havemann, Sakharov and other dissidents. In addition, he turned against the ideas underlying the Prague Spring: 'I evidently have nothing in common with pluralism, with the demand for more freedom and such like; quite the contrary, in fact'.[164] In saying this, he was clearly distancing himself from much of the GDR opposition who regarded the Prague Spring as a key event when it came to shaping their identity.

Despite all the coercion envisaged in *Communism without Growth?*, Harich regarded human happiness as his highest aim, limited only by the imperatives of the ecological crisis. To accuse him of eco-Stalinism, as many did, would be misguided.[165] All the more so because the term is an oxymoron due to the fact that a fixation on growth, which recklessly destroys the environment, is one of the main driving forces and characteristics of Stalinism. In fact, it would be more fitting to use the term 'eco-Leninism', which is a far more accurate description of Harich's model, given that his focus was on the creation of a central power with a steering and regulatory function, which it would fulfil without using *arbitrary* terror as an instrument of power – but where the withering away of the state would then be impossible.[166]

---

163   Harich 1975, p. 170.
164   Harich 1975, p. 172.
165   Only if we were also to describe the actually existing socialism of the post-Stalinist epoch as Stalinism and were to impose on this social system an economic policy along the lines of Harich's, could we refer to this as 'eco-Stalinism'. The problem then would only be the fact that the GDR of the 1970s cannot be equated with the intensely Stalinist 1930s Soviet Union with its mass terror. In this sense, his model is not Stalinist but rather dictatorial – not totalitarian but authoritarian. Harich's utopia is thus not Stalinist but rather archistic, in line with Lenin's 'dictatorship of the proletariat'.
166   See Amberger 2011b, p. 13f.

Even rigorous proposals such as the forced re-education of people in terms of their material needs, for example by 'shutting down entire branches of production accompanied by statutory mass rehabilitation programmes'[167] do not capture the essence of Stalinism but are the hallmarks of an (utopian) eco-dictatorship. From an economic point of view, the Stalinism of the 1930s was geared towards the ruthless expansion of the country's infrastructure.[168] To this end, both nature and human beings were unscrupulously destroyed. In his utopia, however, Harich proposes the protection of both nature and people and, to this end, he calls for the economy to be dismantled. To achieve this, he envisages undemocratic coercion – but not destruction and death. His focus was on mandatory regulation of consumption by the world state: 'The proletarian state must ... have the instruments of power at its disposal to be able to control individual consumption using criteria provided by the environment'.[169] Given the stage of development of the productive forces at the time, Harich still considered a form of communism feasible that was 'more complete' than the one Babeuf and Marx had in mind.[170] In his utopia, Harich deliberately refrained from fleshing out many of the details, such as the exact distribution of food, an employment service for young people, waste collection etc. According to Harich, in real life, people would resolve these issues themselves. For him, the key was to surmount Western pluralism, which, he believed was incapable of inflicting any damage on capital and was thus not in a position to halt the destruction of the environment. Only a swift revolution and the construction of communism would be able to resolutely put a stop to the destruction of the environment.[171]

2.3   Situating Communism without Growth? *in Utopian History*

2.3.1   The Book's Position in Relation to Post-materialist Discourse

Harich's book undoubtedly made a vital contribution to the history of political utopias in the twentieth century. He deliberately makes reference to utopian history to be able to develop convincing alternatives using a critique of the present. His work meets the criteria of a classical utopia. But, more than that: Harich draws on archistic utopias at a time when anarchistic and post-modern

---

167 Harich 1975, p. 179.
168 Incidentally, in the 1940s, Harich welcomed the 'enormous proliferation and development of "co-operative wealth" that was achieved by perfecting technology and increasing labour productivity qualitatively' (Harich 1949, p. 59).
169 Harich 1975, p. 179.
170 See Harich 1975, p. 202.
171 See Harich 1975, p. 205f.

utopias shaped the zeitgeist.[172] He did not entirely negate the latter, but rather adopted elements of them in his archistic blueprint.

The most prominent of these components was ecology. In this regard, Harich drew both on the ideas of asceticism depicted in the modern archistic utopias and on the contemporary return to nature. Contrary to the SED's growth policy, Harich called for sacrifice. In view of communism's promise of prosperity, this was an exceedingly risky approach as '[t]he call for abstinence is an old motif, which was mainly used to ward off the material demands of the general population with the objective of maintaining social injustice'.[173] However, Harich's focus was not social injustice but rather radical social levelling for the benefit of nature and the survival of humankind.

Harich watched with concern as, in the 1970s, dystopian scenarios were published and received with great acclaim.[174] He was unable to read the bleak predictions with the necessary academic distance and consequently fought with missionary zeal for radical environmental protection measures. Along with the Club of Rome reports, Gordon Rattray Taylors' *Doomsday Book* was another particular source of concern for Harich. Taylor predicted an imminent catastrophe and spoke of the collapse of the global ecosystem. Coining the term 'superpollution', he added another superlative and painted a bleak, austere picture of a future that had marked parallels with Harich's utopia – albeit portraying a hopelessness that far exceeded Harich's. Taylor states:

> For my part, I think man will surmount most of the dangers ..., but at tremendous cost and by a very narrow margin. In doing so, I fear, he could create a way of life which would scarcely be worth living. By a tremendous technological effort, he may succeed in detoxifying the soil; he may clean the air enough to breathe, and purify at least some of the water. He may avert starvation by giving up beefsteaks in favour of algae and converted petroleum and sacrificing unnecessary luxuries as sugar and alcohol. He may have to do without the private car and forgo the luxury of a full-length bath. He may have to life in domes and tunnels in the Arctic, or on islands in the sea, giving up the pleasures of owning a garden or the smell of grass after the rain. If, by drugs or conditioning processes, people are led to accept such a life without too much regret, what kind of a victory will that be? Science-fiction writers of the more serious sort, from

---

172 With *Communism without Growth?* Harich 'successfully revived the tradition of the closed archistic utopia' (Heyer 2007b, p. 548).
173 Idler 1999, p. 71.
174 For more on the publication and reception of dystopias, see Radkau 2014, p. 182.

George Orwell onward, have warned us of a nightmare world in which man continues to exist, but desperately, frustrated and unfulfilled. ... It is this kind of solution which seems to me most probable. What kind of solution will this be? A world in which everyone has to work many hours a week to re-establish an approximation to the conditions which, at a more reasonable level of population, nature would provide free of charge would make a mockery of technology. This would be a technological treadmill, on which man has to pedal furiously just to remain in the same place. And even this solution only conditions to be possible if population growth is eventually brough under control and the level stabilized.[175]

In light of this apparently inevitable prospect, the only options were asceticism or death. Here, the time factor plays a pivotal role for both Taylor and Harich: the sooner we can break away from civilisation's ostensible achievements, the more tolerable a future we will be able to create. Both for his analysis of the existing circumstances and in his search for solutions to the crisis, Harich drew on Western contemporary literature. He was very well read in this area despite the fact that these books were never published in the GDR. This afforded him the opportunity to think outside the box far more than other critics of the system, let alone ordinary people. In Harich's quest for solutions, Taylor's book served as a real source of inspiration. Proposals such as reducing transport costs by producing locally[176] or changing eating habits by consuming unfamiliar foods, for instance, can be found in both books.[177] With regard to stemming population growth, Taylor also presented proposals which Harich went on to develop further. To quote Taylor:

> In Japan, a situation has been reached in which it is positively embarrassing to have a large family. Such attitudes are created by education, both at school and in the larger sense of what the new media carry. At the same time, the government must provide incentives, rather than disincentives, as at present.[178]

Similarly, in terms of institutional concepts, there were also clear similarities between Harich, who proposed a global authority, and Taylor, who called for

---

175   Taylor 1972, p. 23.
176   See Taylor n.d., p. 287.
177   See Taylor n.d., p. 295.
178   Taylor 1972, p. 259.

the establishment of permanent global and climate policy institutions with an analytical, monitoring and planning function.[179] Taylor also pre-empted Harich's critique of the growth policy of the SPD and SED with his conviction that socialist and social democratic governments would neglect the environment because they perceived an economic upswing as more important. This applied as much to the socialist/social democratic governments in the West as to Soviet Russia's political system. Also typical of the post-materialist discourse was Taylor's rejection of mass consumption, artificially created needs and the 'throw-away' mentality. Taylor maintained that consumption only suppressed the desire for fundamental happiness, serving as a substitute drug. People lacked opportunities for personal growth and their work alienated them from their environment. According to Taylor, industrial progress had to be curbed and regulated. He called for a complete change in thinking with a more sceptical approach to technology – but stopped short of 'Luddism'.[180] In his critique of consumption, Harich also drew on Wolfgang Menge, renowned, among other things, for writing the *Ein Herz und eine Seele* (One heart and one soul) television series. Menge's 1971 book *Der verkaufte Käufer* (The sold buyer) in which he denounced the artificial creation of needs and resource-intensive mass production with its 'throw-away' mentality,[181] furnished Harich with basis for his theory that saving the environment was incompatible with the capitalist mode of production.

Closely linked to ecology is another overlap with post-materialist utopia: the (near-mythical) connection with nature. Harich did not see himself as someone who, in response to an oversaturation of Western civilisation, aspired to the romantic notion of 'getting back to nature'. He saw this aspiration as being un-communist, viewing it as regressive – yet claimed its very existence was evidence that, even in the West, counter-currents to consumerism were gradually emerging. And while rejecting the neo-anarchism of some members of the 1968 generation, he did welcome their critical stance on consumer society. That said, he argued that these currents of the extra-parliamentary opposition protest movement were pursuing the wrong strategy. He viewed the earlier attacks by the Baader-Meinhof gang on department stories as tactically unwise. Although he sympathised with their motives:

> [s]etting fire to department stories doesn't achieve anything apart from risking the lives of innocent people. It can only be politically damaging;

---

179 See Taylor n.d., p. 335 f.
180 See Taylor n.d., p. 381 f.
181 See Menge 1973, p. 29 ff.

that much is certain. But a communist global economic plan, imbued with the spirt of the department store fire-raisers ..., would be beneficial for humankind from an ecological point of view.[182]

Harich believed that people should take a conciliatory approach to dealing with nature, something which was inherent in the ecological communism derived from Marx. It would be more accurate to describe Harich's stance on this matter using Martin d'Idler's concept of 'nature rationalism' than the idea of nature mysticism. Harich saw himself as an unmistakably dialectical thinker without any kind of spiritual or esoteric notions.

Another overlap between Harich's utopia and the post-materialist discourse is in the interrelated areas of women's emancipation, sexuality and the model of the family. The idea that the reproductive function of sexuality should be subordinate to the primary purpose of pleasure has already been discussed elsewhere. In the book itself very little is said about the role of women. A few years later, however, Harich describes his views on the issue in considerable detail, declaring this to be an extension of his concept of feminism.[183] The end result was published under the title *Das Weib in der Apokalypse* (The woman in the apocalypse) in a Helmut Gollwitzer jubilee edition in 1978. In this article, Harich presents a correlation between the habitus of masculinity and the apocalypse. To do this, he draws heavily on the French author Françoise d'Eaubonne[184] and the Soviet writer Valentin Grigoriyevich Rasputin. Pre-empting his later struggle against the Nietzsche renaissance, Harich criticises the destructive mechanisms of the patriarchal world order and praises d'Eaubonne's 'synthesis of the complete emancipation of women and strict ecologism'. This impressed Harich and he approvingly quoted her demand: 'In order to be able to pass our planet on to the humankind of tomorrow, it must be ripped from the man of today'.[185] Harich pinned his hopes on the principle of motherly love, in other words on the notion that today's mothers will act to save their children from the apocalypse. In this context, he did not rule out illegal measures and expanded on the views he expressed in 1975 about the Baader-Meinhof department store attacks: 'From this point of view, it is worth considering the current phenomenon of female terrorists. Having succeeded in raising awareness of the problem of the environment, it could now mature

---

182 Harich 1975, p. 124 f.
183 See Harich 1994b, p. 140.
184 For more on the works of Françoise d'Eaubonne, see Radkau 2014, p. 201 f. For an important account of her situatedness in utopian history, see Saage 2003, p. 359 ff.
185 Harich 1979a, p. 682.

into a mass movement, admittedly one which, rather than committing senseless acts of terror against individuals, could involve, for instance, slashing the tyres of all parked cars or sabotaging the sale of aerosols and in general smashing the entire self-destructive toolkit of our misguided civilisation to pieces.'[186]

Harich now even placed masculine society above capitalism when it came to resistance, stating:

> It has a much longer history than capitalism and even if capitalism is overcome, it is far from guaranteed that [masculine society] will wither away, and certainly not automatically. Socialism serves only as the basis for this. First of all, a form of communism will have to be created, in which consumption too will be regulated differently, no longer according to merit, but according to need. It is only communism that will be able to recreate primitive human society on a higher level – as 'negation of negation' –, a society which, according to Bachofen, Morgan, Engels and more recently also Bornemann, is composed along matriarchal lines.[187]

This meant a radical change in his philosophy under the influence of feminism.

Again, Harich rejected the demands of the anti-authoritarian left (e.g. Herbert Marcuse's) for a liberal communism of abundance, in order to ultimately briefly outline his utopia, now expanded to include feminism:

> But on our finite planet with its limited resources and natural life cycles, in themselves not indefinitely resilient, all the time-honoured chimeras of absolute freedom from repression, an absence of rule or government, the withering away of the state and the likes are no longer relevant. For we will never experience an abundance to satisfy our every need. ... The only alternative to our own demise is this growthless, homeostatic communism adapted to protect the biosphere, a system that is capable only of reproducing the bare necessities of life and allocating identical rations to every individual. For this, we need authoritarian entities, wise, strict and just. But, these will also be matriarchal entities, which will protect the general feminisation of society, which will guarantee that everyone's life will be well worth living, judging by today's standards. After millennia of being oppressed, women have learnt to get around their lack of power and protect the weak. Women are the promise of peace and the

---

186 Harich 1979a, p. 684.
187 Harich 1979a, p. 685 f.

end of exploitation and violence incarnate. Women have always had a caring and protective relationship with nature, never violating its cycles in order to increase output. Thus, in the feminine communist order, for the sake of the protection of nature, work will be reduced to that which is absolutely necessary only, since in the perennial dusting, washing up and laundry, the master pattern for all forms of recycling has long since been found. Objects of daily use will outlive generations, stress and haste give way to soothing pleasure, the rest of the day filled with playful creativity, rivalry will only be found in the fields of music and poetry, affection will replace performance. Nobody can expect more than this. But what can be expected is a great deal and is valuable enough, and thus worth fighting for.[188]

In Harich's utopia, family, sexuality and the emancipation of women thus merged into a communist matriarchy[189] which seeks to guarantee the preservation of the environment. These ideas blend seamlessly with the Western post-materialist discourse of the time.

From a history of philosophy perspective and in relation to anarchism and its notions of a grassroots democracy community, however, certain discrepancies can be identified between Harich's ideas and this discourse. The post-materialist utopias broke with the historical determinism of earlier utopias. The society that was outlined in these utopias no longer represented an historical end point, but rather a dynamic, changeable – and thus vulnerable – entity. Here, the dangers and inherent contradictions were described in detail, with probably the most vivid depiction to be found in Ursula K. Le Guin's *The Dispos-*

---

188   Harich 1979a, p. 686.
189   A recent definition illustrates the direction of Harich's thinking: '... despite the considerable differences, matriarchies, both historical and actually existing, are essentially shaped by life-sustaining, environmentally friendly, egalitarian, cooperative, nonviolent and responsible relations, which have proven effective for long periods of time as well as under difficult environmental conditions. Patriarchal civilisation everywhere, in contrast, is characterised by a conflicting shaping of relations, which emerge in the form of social contradictions, while the originally matriarchal society is violently subjugated, destroyed and transformed. Thus, from the very beginning, patriarchal civilisation is a belligerent countermodel ("system of war") to the matriarchal system, although to this day it still requires the remnants of the matriarchy as a "second culture". A "pure" patriarchy without these matriarchal remnants is thus aspired to but ultimately cannot be achieved because it would succumb to its own "sterility". This dialectic constitutes the true development of the patriarchy, including capitalism as its modern, radicalised version' (Werlhof 2009, p. 148).

sessed.¹⁹⁰ Harich did not call into question the proposed concept of archistic global eco-communism. His social order was self-contained, with the contradictions of the present having been resolved.

The aim of post-materialist discourse was to defeat consumer society and its alienating mechanisms and constraints. Post-materialist discourse sought to emancipate human beings and create an awareness of the individual as an alternative to the false façade and supposedly bogus existence in consumer society. In some cases this involved individuals engaging in an existentialist exploration of their own personal potential, often with the help of narcotics and stimulants. Here, too, the gap between Harich's utopia and the discourse was huge, as Harich was against all forms of hedonism – and thus also drug use. Although he does not say so explicitly in his utopia, in his 1971 *Kritik der revolutionären Ungeduld*, Harich writes:

> Just as a side note: The latest development will also probably come down to anxious parents attributing their children being spared the harrows of drug addiction to the influence of the M.L. [Marxist-Leninists, author's addition], including the recent rampant Stalinist renaissance among left-wing students. The *Paradise Now* ideology is not capable of erecting barriers against such temptations as drugs. Quite the contrary, it helps to tear them down, whereas Stalin worship and hash are probably not very compatible.¹⁹¹

Harich thus took an extremely conservative stance on this issue, which was possibly due to the limited range of empirical experience he had. However, probably the most important difference between *Communism without Growth?* and the new anarchistic utopias can be seen in the area of governance and elites. Harich wanted to create an absolute world state, rather than establishing grassroots democracy and small-scale self-administration. Harich's concept contains several elements that follow Morelly and Babeuf's line of theory. On the other hand, there are also many aspects that can be seen in actually existing socialism: a dictatorial system of government, a centrally planned economy, the sublation of basic civil and human rights for the sake of a higher purpose, or the leadership claims made by a small 'vanguard'. When it came to the institutional framework, Harich did not take an opposing position to those in power, by no means did he challenge the claim to power on the

---

190 For insight into the significance of the work in utopian history, see Saage 2003, pp. 211–32, Waschkuhn 2003, p. 210 ff.
191 Harich 1971, p. 99.

part of the SED and its apparatus. Instead, he directed his criticism exclusively at their growth-oriented economic policy. There were three reasons for this:

1) As already discussed, Harich had no desire to be a dissident. 2) He had learned a lesson from his 1956/57 defeat, and 3) he regarded *Communism without Growth?* as an offering to Brezhnev, a form of policy advice from a Marxist environmental lobbyist.[192]

Harich's aim was to make his concept become reality as quickly as humanly possible. To achieve this, he sought allies, ideally from among those in the same camp as him when it came to world politics, but not necessarily – as his acknowledgement that countries in the West could also make a rapid transition to communism proves. Harich's thinking thus went against the dogma that actually existing socialist states would establish communism more quickly than capitalist countries, reasoning that the only possibility was a 'transition to a super state that was based on the sublation of all individuality' and that could also happen in the West first.[193]

For Harich, étatism and coercion as a means to an end were part of this. Humans needed to be re-educated to the point where they had fewer needs. Heyer regarded this re-education by a state elite as reminiscent of Babeuf: 'A small group knows, in blind obedience and contrary to the opinion of the majority, what is good and right. And when "re-education" is not enough, that is when repression starts'.[194] But Harich did not limit the function of this world state to the issue of economic growth and consumption. He also incorporated the population problem, attempting to revise the established Marxist pattern of argumentation by taking a letter from Engels to Karl Kautsky about the potential population regulation under communism and reinterpreting it in alignment with his own interests. Heyer was critical of this dubious course of action: 'Harich didn't invent this kind of reading of the tea leaves. This method has already been used to reinterpret Jesus as a member of the greens, a socialist, a teacher or astronomer, and Marx and Engels, too, have frequently experienced, or rather suffered, such treatment. That said, it is natural for us to ask why one has to invoke Marxism, if this is ultimately reduced to a quote from a letter. Harich, however, derives from the passage what is probably the most powerful means of repression of his whole leviathan: the regulation of the birth rate'.[195] This goal is the most debatable of all Harich's ideas, Heyer claims:

---

192   See Harich 1994b, p. 140.
193   See Heyer 2009, p. 12.
194   Heyer 2009, p. 13.
195   Heyer 2009, p. 14.

> There can be no doubt that the encroachment on family structures as well as the family planning that Harich calls for crosses the line of twentieth century totalitarian systems. What is not clear from Harich's book, however, is who lays down the rules about birth and why, what should happen to women who become pregnant without permission, whether a huge-scale sterilisation programme will be applied (even forcibly) to women after the birth of their first child, for instance. These passages thus opened the doors to dystopia as much as to the methods of total repression of individuality that history (in particular that of the twentieth century) chronicles in all its brutal intensity. The difference between this and fascism on this point is – and there can be no doubt that this must be attributed to Harich – at most a few degrees.[196]

While there may be some overlap between Harich's ideas and the authoritarian political right, Harich cannot be described as a fascist or an eco-fascist. Quite the contrary, he was a Marxist who was known for his extremely rational dialectic thinking and who later retracted the radicalism of his ideas. In so doing, he made it clear that the radical nature of his ideas did not reflect his personal wishes but were a necessity, something that had to be endured in order to save humanity and nature. Another illustration of Harich's anti-fascism is an anecdote from the Stasi files about a conversation he had with Klaus Höpcke on 10 August 1978. In Höpcke's own words, he was able to dissuade Harich from becoming involved with the work of the Green Party in West Germany, because 'from recent publications about the "Green Party" in the FRG, he concluded that Höpcke's warnings about former and current Nazis being involved with this party were warranted. Harich's previous assessment that this party was a melting pot for all left-wing forces proved to be inaccurate and he would abandon any personal endeavours in support of this party he might have implied'.[197]

2.3.2 Harich, Gehlen and the 'New Man'

Although Harich had read and commented on a variety of texts from Western post-materialist discourse that were critical of authority – and indeed he was far more knowledgeable than either Bahro or Havemann in this field[198] – he preferred to resurrect Babeuf's archistic utopia. This was also related to his aversion to anarchism.

---

196 Heyer 2009, p. 15.
197 BStU, MfS, AP, 4578/71, vol. 8, p. 42f.
198 See Heyer 2009, p. 45.

His rejection of the anti-authoritarian concepts of the West German APO (extra-parliamentary opposition, a political protest movement) was evident in his 1971 book *Zur Kritik der revolutionären Ungeduld*. Here he criticised the anarchist strategy of using all available means to fight the state: 'Anarchist violence is intended as popular pedagogy but is devoid of considerations of political utility and is thus no more than misdirected, frittered and squandered. And these tendencies to use its energy senselessly is something anarchist violence shares with the peaceful activities of anarchy, with all the absurdity with which it believes it can "destabilise institutions".'[199]

The phrase 'destabilising institutions', frequently used by the 'New Left', was coined by the conservative pioneer of the 'formed society' Arnold Gehlen, who saw it as a threat to the bourgeois order, its vales and institutions. In *Zur Kritik der revolutionären Ungeduld*, Harich expresses his views on Gehlen's thinking. He agrees with him that norms are necessary for interpersonal relationships and institutions to preserve order. Like Harich, Gehlen also deplored anarchism. However, his rationale for rejecting it was its anti-communist conservatism, while Harich advocated archistic socialism or communism. Harich, for instance, was also critical of the fact that Gehlen neglected the historical process in his teachings on institutions. After all, institutions could become historically obsolete and thus superfluous. For Harich, things that belong to the past could most certainly be relinquished, which is why it made no sense to him to wish to protect institutions at any cost.[200]

Harich and Gehlen's common adversary was the Frankfurt School, the intellectual centre and trailblazer of the anti-authoritarian movement in the Federal Republic. As different as Gehlen and Harich were, one thing they had in common was their rejection of institutional critique of Critical Theory. Despite all their differences, they exchanged letters between East and West Germany for decades, a correspondence that outlasted even Harich's time in prison.[201] Karl-Siegbert Rehberg observed: 'The most fundamental point of agreement

---

199   Harich 1971, p. 40.
200   See Harich 1971, p. 45 ff.
201   See Harich, A. 2007, p. 350. See also Rehberg 1999, p. 467. According to Peter Christian Ludz, Harich publicly referred to Gehlen as early as 1956: '*Harich* ... attempted to combine *Karl Marx*'s thinking with elements of *Arnold Gehlen's* cultural anthropology. *Gehlen's* influence came to the fore in *Harich's* presentation on "Rationality in Kant's conception of freedom" at the Conference of the Philosophy Section of the Germany Academy of Sciences, Berlin (8–10 March 1956). *Harich* asks *Gehlen* about the motives for the "specifically human impulse structure" – a question directed at Marxist anthropology. ... In so doing, *Harich* once again took up the concept of labour as the central category of Marxist thinking. However, until his imprisonment, he had not managed to convincingly bring

between them was their belief in the need for stabilisation, both being of the opinion that without this man, "deficient being" as he was, would not survive. This view became more evident as well as politically tangible in Wolfgang Harich's (and of course Gehlen's) criticism of the student movement of 1968 and the demands for emancipation that writers of Critical Theory – particularly Theodor Adorno – also had a bearing on'.[202]

Harich's enthusiasm for Gehlen's anthropology stemmed from his conviction regarding the need for institutions, which he believed were imperative for imperfect humans to be able to live in a community.[203] This influence could also be seen in *Communism without Growth?*: Since humans were 'deficient beings', and since they were therefore not capable of saving the environment or the world drawing on their own resources, stronger institutions were needed to mould them and guide them on this path.[204]

The anti-authoritarians of the Frankfurt School, however, largely saw these institutions as something negative, believing them to infantilise and incapacitate human beings, who were the real cause of fascism. Harich deliberately obscured this critique of bureaucracy, and this very aspect is the main shortcoming of his utopia: If the new world government is not subject to democratic control, who can ensure that it does not become a force in its own right? Who will control the elite that is to show the way, and why should such an elite know better than the ordinary people themselves what is good for them? If we accept Gehlen's concept of man as a 'deficient being'[205] it follows that these elites

---

together his philosophical considerations and his political demands in a manner that would have seriously shaken up dialectical and historical materialism in the GDR' (Ludz 1976, p. 269).

202   Rehberg 1999, p. 446.
203   See Rehberg 1999, p. 450 f.
204   'Institutions protect the indirect relationship that human beings have to forge with other human beings and with themselves. Gehlen considered institutions improbable and hard-won stabilisations, whose historical capacity for governance he saw as beginning to unravel in the twentieth century. He sensed that his own affirmative but pervasive analysis of these institutions, which should hold true without question or thinking, contributed as much to their relativisation and threat as the critique of institutions that he so detested. But this signified the author's conservative fears ...' (Rehberg 2002, p. 166).
205   'First and foremost, humans are "deficient beings", characterised by an inability to adapt and a lack of specialisation, primitive organs (e.g. a lack of hair covering), a lack of escape and attack organs – in fact by a "perilous lack of real instincts" and "their incomparably long need for protection" that continues throughout infancy and childhood. People are "world-open" beings, meaning they need to take action, beings that depend on approval and are thus also capable of language and symbolisation and rely on their responsive world and "self-productivity". However, it is precisely because of this "incompleteness" that this "open" being also needs compulsory stabilisation. For Gehlen, "self-discipline,

must, at the very least, have fewer deficiencies than those being governed. But who is to decide this and legitimise their rule?

These contradictions show that Harich's eco-communist utopia called for a 'New Man'.

> What qualities are possessed by such a person who, according to Harich's ideas, understands freedom in the Hegelian sense as the realisation of necessity and who has needs that always converge with environmental requirements? To put it in a nutshell, the 'New Man' in Harich's ecological world state has transcended the boundaries of expert specialism to become a polymath who begins to approximate the ideal of the Renaissance and German *Bildungshumanismus*. The only type of human Harich could envisage understanding the interdisciplinary problem of the ecological crisis and acting accordingly was one with such broad and comprehensive knowledge and not the parochial expert. But is such an approach enough to regulate the structures of individuals' needs, not only objectively, but also subjectively in the interests of ensuring the ecological survival of humanity? It is no coincidence that Harich laments the absence of a theory of needs in Marxism-Leninism, such as that provided, to some extent, by Arnold Gehlen's philosophical anthropology. Harich accepts the sublation of dualism in favour of an interplay between the first (biological) and second (socio-cultural) nature of humans in the sense of the 'variability and plasticity of the human motivational structure'. This shows that he does not aspire to the genetic and technical manipulation of human beings, but rather – as can already be observed in Marx – to the premise of philosophical anthropology that the biological needs of human beings can be masked and directed by the socio-cultural imperative. It is thus the purpose of the future environmental leviathan and its institutions to educate human beings, on the basis of communism, such that their needs converge *a priori* with the requirements of the global ecological equilibrium.[206]

The parallels between the two philosophers were not limited to their rejection of anti-authoritarians, however. They also shared common ground in their critique of consumer society: 'It seems that in Harich's magnum opus *Communism without Growth?* he ultimately ... wishes to have Gehlen as an ally in the fight

---

education and upbringing, cultivation as a means of getting in and staying in shape" are all conditions of human existence' (Rehberg 2002, p. 152 f.).
206 Saage 2008, p. 155 f.

against Western consumer fetishism, as Gehlen had already made observations about asceticism in the early phase of West Germany's so-called economic miracle'.[207]

In his 1949 book *Man in the Age of Technology*, Gehlen describes the transformation of humans over the course of industrialisation. According to Gehlen, the concomitant mass consumption and the widespread availability of luxuries changed the intellectual and moral constitution of human beings. And this results in man's 'loss of a feeling of reality'. Consequently, '[i]n keeping with a psychological law, desire correspondingly becomes unrestrained – another root of the prevalent disposition to keep quiet and keep consuming'.[208] According to Gehlen, there was an: '... astonishing absence, in our time, of any ascetic ideals. This must seem strange to the historically informed, since in all previous times marked by sharp advance in the demand for luxuries, ascetic ideals always existed as a counterweight to that advance, and were never basically challenged. The individual who renounced the goods of this earth always enjoyed a moral authority, whereas today he would be thought mentally defective'.[209]

As a result of industrialisation, the many items that had previously been deemed luxuries then became mass goods. These had to be consumed for the system of industrialism (Gehlen did not draw a distinction between capitalism and actually existing socialism) to continue to exist. There was no longer any room for asceticism, the alienation was complete.[210] A statement made by Harich in the summer of 1979 serves as a useful comparison: 'I have always found the wasteful world of consumption in the West repugnant, not least because it is so devoid of culture .... I have been a sworn enemy of the entire way of life in the West from the moment I arrived'.[211]

And, in an interview with the daily newspaper the *Frankfurter Rundschau* to mark Gehlen's death, Harich said that he saw him as a rare type of conservative that one could learn from. He gave Gehlen credit for his philosophical accomplishments and commended him for having always defended the Soviet Union. Harich called for those on the left to develop more conservative values, i.e. for them to do everything within their power to preserve man and nature.[212]

---

207   Dornuf 1996, p. 83.
208   Gehlen 1980, p. 55.
209   Gehlen 1980, pp. 105–6.
210   'The system not only presupposes the right to well-being; it also tends to exclude its contrary, that is, the right to renounce well-being, particularly insofar as the system itself produces and automatizes the need to consume. Here, perhaps, lies the root of all currently dominant forms of unfreedom', Gehlen 1980, p. 108.
211   Harich 1979b, p. 18.
212   See BStU, MfS, AP, 4578/71, vol. 7, p. 82 ff.

2.3.3 Asceticism Now! Utopia and Reality

A political utopia contains, on the one hand, a critique of the present and, on the other, the image of a well-thought through alternative that extrapolates possible development trends from precisely that criticism of the status quo. In the early modern era, these works comprised almost exclusively critique, the scenarios they depicted were all set on far distant islands, and they described parallel societies, which did not necessarily mirror the author's wish for the future. With the shift away from the spatial, from the island utopia to a temporal utopia, which took place during the Age of the Enlightenment,[213] this purpose changed. Utopias became blueprints for the future, scenarios which seemed achievable and which only featured the depravity of the present in descriptions of the past.

With the advancing development of the capitalist mode of production, the suffering of the masses increased. The more their social circumstances declined, the more meaningful the social utopias became. The genuine hardship people were experiencing intensified the desire for alternative forms of society, and utopias provided them with ideas as to how to actually build the communities they envisaged. Much, however, remained vague. Very few utopian writers described their scenarios in terms as concrete as Babeuf's, who saw the revolution as a means for transformation. This was something that earned high praise from Marx and Engels, who believed it was precisely this radical will to make the utopian scenario reality that the majority of other social utopian writers lacked. Babeuf had a clear claim to validity for his utopian visions.

Marx and Engels sought to underpin their transformation strategy, to give it theoretical legitimacy, using their theory of self-defined scientific socialism and the methodology of dialectical materialism.[214] But they underestimated the possibility of their project failing. The anthropological components, the imponderables, the compulsiveness of humans and the contradictions between the individual and the collective were – partly because they had never actually been scientifically researched[215] – given short shrift in their works.

Dystopias, in contrast, stirred up fears of the scenarios depicted becoming reality. They projected the negative potential of progress and modernity. Desirable images became frightening images, a transformation which simply had to be prevented, particularly as noticeable tendencies in that direction

---

213 Above all associated with Louis-Sébastien Merciers *The Year 2440*. See Saage 1990, p. 17 f.
214 See Engels 1989.
215 Academic disciplines such as anthropology, psychoanalysis and (mass) sociology did not develop until the twentieth century, and to some extent were built on the foundations of Marxism.

could already be seen. Here, the antagonism between the individual and the (overpowering) collective became all the more apparent. In the dystopia, the nonconformist individual was demoralised and incapacitated by a society that was forcibly made to conform and the ruling bureaucratic apparatus and elites.[216]

In post-materialist utopias, this self-reflective nature of the genre was embraced. The tension between individual and community remained unchanged, the latent risk of forced collectivism continued to exist. The earlier desirable image of equality and the frightening dystopian image of complete levelling of society were artificially abolished. The isolation of modern man in Western capitalism was rejected, but equally, the (forced) collectivism of the archistic utopias was not favourably received either. Attempts were made to show the problems a future community could experience stemming from the tension between the individual and the collective against the backdrop of human frailties. After the failure of the in some cases brutal re-education measures of the twentieth century, the idea of the 'New Man' barely resonated. A utopia without a 'New Man', on the other hand, inevitably resulted in (irresolvable) contradictions.

Communism without Growth? contained none of these self-reflective components that were characteristic of post-materialist utopias. Harich did not distance himself from authoritarian actually existing socialism in his book. All he wanted was for it to be modified in accordance with his ecological ideas. He ignored the contemporary criticism of the concept of the 'New Man' and, as we have shown, continued to use the idea in his work. Moreover, he advocated the very aspect of socialism that the anti-authoritarian post-materialists rejected: the creation of the 'New Man' through state-controlled re-education. In doing so, he renounced the self-reflective elements that twentieth century utopian discourse had gone to great lengths to include and that made it possible to defend the genre against harsh conservative critique.

In light of the ecological crisis, Harich felt there was no time for such self-reflective thinking. In his view, urgent action was imperative, and this meant creating the 'New Man' as quickly as possible. As to the institutions and the authoritarian state, Harich welcomed them already.

This distinguished Harich from the anarchists, who, in his opinion, were not going to be able to save the world because this would involve abolishing vital institutions immediately. In his *Zur Kritik der revolutionären Ungeduld* published in 1971, Harich attacked anarchism from a Marxist position. He referred

---

216   For a seminal work on this, see Elias 1985, p. 144 ff.

to the anarchist belief in the acceleration of the historical process as 'opium for socialists'. This notion cropped up almost everywhere among the left-leaning groups, although among the anarchists it took an ideal-typical form. According to Harich, like with religious heterodoxy, there was a mixture of 'desire and ignorance', each of which fed off each other.[217] That said, he still adhered to the idea of the withering state as a final aim shared by both the communists and the anarchists.

Harich believed that the difference between the anarchists and the communists lay in their approach. While anarchists fought against the state, communists attacked the economic basis of the class divisions, and the state as no more than a real-life manifestation of this. Thus, the anarchists were fighting against the symptoms, the superstructure, while the communists were tackling the problem at its roots, i.e. the economic foundation. In the process, according to Harich's critique, the anarchists naively rejected coercive measures being taken by the state during the transition phase. 'Faced with the task of building, in the service of the revolution, an accurately and systematically functioning machinery of oppression and keeping this operational for as long as the power relations between the classes make the activities of outside and inside adversaries a genuine danger, faced with this prosaic responsibility, their enthusiasm faded away – that is all'.[218]

Harich, who, in 1956/57, had been sentenced to ten years imprisonment by the GDR's organs of political repression on account of his oppositional behaviour, was therefore singing the praises of that very same apparatus. What he failed to recognise was the possibility that bureaucratic institutions could become independent entities. For Harich, this problem could be easily resolved, as he outlined in an article published in the *Frankfurter Rundschau* on 7 November 1977. He wrote that in his communism, there would no longer be any privileges, causing the incentive for careerism within the apparatus to disappear. Here, leadership functions would be taken on by idealists only.[219] He overlooked the fact that the pursuit of power and decision-making authority can also be an incentive for careerism. In any case, Harich did not view the actually existing socialist states as being ruled by rigid, monolithic, bureaucratic regimes driven by the desire to hang on to their own power. Rather, he saw them as transitional systems with a dynamic progressive orientation, threatened by imperialism, heading towards the final goal of communism.

---

217 See Harich 1971, p. 13 f.
218 Harich 1971, p. 28.
219 See BStU, MfS, AP, 4578/71, vol. 7, p. 71 ff.

On the other hand, he did not join the anarchistic quest for the immediate and ill-considered destruction of Western parliamentary democracies, despite the fact that he saw these as bastions of the bourgeois capitalist system. In Harich's view, these parliamentary democracies could and must be used as platforms for the left and also be defended as a historical achievement against any attack from the right. The left must never again be allowed to fail as it did in 1933.

Harich condemned the purported naivety of the anarchists in their belief that reason, solidarity and similar values were *a priori* qualities, inherent in every human being. He did not believe this to be true. He held a more pessimistic view of mankind and for that very reason he advocated coercion. In taking this position, he was, in his own way, also naive, particularly when it came to the rationality he assumed the centralist authorities of communist provenance to possess.[220] This could be seen in the lack of separation of powers, the lack of checks and balances in *Communism without Growth?*.

A paper he wrote condemning anarchism in 1971 also featured some early thoughts on the environment. Even at this early stage, Harich had already identified capitalism's waste of resources as a problem:

> According to the historical materialist premise behind Marx's analysis of society, the reason for this appalling abuse and scourge stems much more from the fact that the capitalist relations of production and ownership structures have, since time immemorial, enabled the bourgeoisie to exploit the proletariat and, based on this, have in our time, stopped being suitable for the stage of development in the productive forces. This is why the bourgeoisie is only capable of sustaining these relations and structures artificially, by means of terror or ideological manipulation, and the price is the senseless waste and destruction of material resources and ultimately life-threatening consequences for humanity as a whole. Thus, these relations must first be abolished – by sublating capitalist private ownership, by transferring the means of production to socialist collective ownership –, before we can even begin to conceive of society in its entirety being changed for the better. The destruction of the structures and institutions of the superstructure that hinge on capitalism is a problem that needs to be dealt with later. As long as this superstructure continues to exist, it would be senseless to pre-empt a solution to this problem.[221]

---

220   See Jäger 1973, p. 144.
221   Harich 1971, p. 66.

Consequently, patience is required during the transition phase as building communism could take centuries.[222] Just a few years later, in *Communism without Growth?*, Harich contradicted his own precept, claiming that the time for this had now run out. He no longer believed that a withering of the state would occur, which meant that the transition phase – the era of the dictatorship of the proletariat, brought about through revolutionary means – would therefore be the final state. In 1975, Harich wrote: 'Communism will thus never survive without state authority and codified law, as the classics of Marxism-Leninism believed, ultimately concurring with the anarcho-communists on this point'.[223]

This shift in Harich's thinking was, by his own admission, sparked by Gordon Rattray Taylor's *Doomsday Book*, which Harich read in 1971. 'In the finite system of the biosphere, in which communism will need to establish itself, human society can only transition to a permanent homeostatic state which, as much as it will not allow the dynamics of capitalism or those of socialism to progress, will also prohibit unlimited freedom of the individual. Any thoughts of a future withering of the state are therefore illusory'.[224]

Yet, Harich called for such a state to be created as quickly as possible, in order to preserve as many freedoms as possible. He believed that the sooner this was achieved, the more humane the world would remain. The longer it takes to come up with a solution to the problem, the more drastic the means required to remedy that problem. 'According to Harich, the communist eco-Leviathan also drew its legitimacy from the fact that it helped to prevent eco-fascism'.[225] He was not opposed to preserving human freedoms (with the exception of the freedom of consumption and family planning), and in fact wanted, through rapid transformation, to retain as many of those freedoms as possible.

Harich's claim to validity was absolute. In his 1971 *Zur Kritik der revolutionären Ungeduld* he still rejected any kind of immediate transformation. Just

---

222 See Harich 1971, p. 82.
223 Harich 1975, p. 161.
224 Harich 1975, p. 161.
225 Heyer 2009, p. 17. 'This is the choice we are confronted with: Eco-fascism or a homeostatic growthless communism with a state authority. Faced with this choice, a liberal must tend towards pessimism. I am not a liberal' (Harich 1980, p. 77), and elsewhere in the book: 'HARICH: ... If the volte-face happens soon, the space of freedom for the individual will, accordingly, remain, far and wide. However, the longer this U-turn is delayed, the more likely harsh authoritarian measures will be the only way of accomplishing this. Thus, if this is something we want to avoid, we must embark upon the path of this volte-face as soon as possible. ... A MAN: Then I just want to say one thing: this darn well reminds me of 1984. HARICH: Unfortunately, very much so, yes' (Harich, Herbig, Illich & Welsh 1979, p. 78).

four years later he had completely reversed his position on the issue. He now believed that there was no longer enough time for a transition phase spanning generations. And he also broke with another, perhaps more significant dogma of Marxism-Leninism: the assumption that the proletariat had to be the subject of the revolution. In his ecological utopia, he assigned this role to the whole of humanity. Some camps on the left strongly criticised him for this, accusing him of betraying the working class. Hofbauer noted: 'The enclosedness of all of society by nature, something that was already acknowledged by Hegel, and the proven interdependencies between nature and humans, necessitated this conclusion. In crises threatening the existence of humanity – and only in such crises – would humans take priority over class'.[226]

For Harich, it was worth sacrificing this dogma to save the world.

2.3.4 Harich's Book from a Biographical Perspective

Many of Harich's ideas can be relativised (or at least explained) if we position *Communism without Growth?* within the author's biographical context and also take into account later statements and modifications. In light of the contradiction that the exact same Harich, who was so harshly punished in 1957 for demanding democratisation, then went on to pen such a seemingly undemocratic utopia in 1975, we must ask ourselves whether, in the almost 20 years between these two events, Harich's thinking really was so radically transformed or whether this was a perfectly consistent development. If we take the demands Harich made in the 1950s and factor in statements and comments made in the final phase of his life relativising these demands, a more cohesive picture of Harich as a philosopher emerges than we might have originally assumed on first examining his life's work.

A good example of such an unnuanced view can be seen in series of comments by Wolfgang Leonhard, who stated in 1996 that the ideas Harich presented in 1956 were also in keeping with his own ideas at the time, yet he was, at the same time 'noticeably' appalled by *Communism without Growth?*. Not because he doubted the need for urgent ecological reforms in any way – in fact he considered these to be a matter of utmost priority –, but rather because, to achieve this, Harich propagated a dictatorship in the name of fairness and equality, run in a dictatorial fashion along the lines of Robespierre's or Babeuf's, a total rationing of all goods, the elimination of the world market, centralised distribution of industry and the resettlement of humans in accordance with ecological principles. These functions were to be performed by a centralised dictatorship.

---

226 Hofbauer 1996, p. 51.

Harich reiterated this in an interview with the *Spiegel* on 11 June 1979: 'I firmly maintain that there are global circumstances that can only be addressed by a central authority and this must be equipped with dictatorial powers. For me this represented a shift from a once humanist, democratic socialist reformer to an ecological Stalinist. I was shaken to the core by Harich's transformation.'[227]

Leonhard's assessment may very well be understandable from his position of moral indignation, but it only scratches the surface. Firstly, in 1956 Harich was already an advocate of democratic centralism. Secondly, he was also committed to protecting freedoms in 1975.[228] And thirdly, the term 'ecological Stalinist' is an oxymoron.[229]

What should we make of Leonhard's proposition that the Harich of 1956 had been a humanist and democratic socialist reformer? Harich's ideas were, without a doubt, altered by his sentence and subsequent imprisonment. His loyalty to the SED and the GDR, however, was not affected. Quite the opposite in fact. Leonhard's view implies that this sense of loyalty was already present in 1956, although in the mid-1950s, Harich was quite clearly not unconditionally and unquestioningly devoted to the SED. Unlike Leonhard,[230] however, he did not break with the GDR entirely, but rather only sought to reform the system for the purpose of achieving greater legitimacy among the population of the GDR and West German workers. Ideologically, Harich also maintained his Marxist-Leninist line, while Leonhard switched to West German social democracy. This means that in 1956, Harich did not adhere to social democratic ideas in any way, despite the fact that he sought to make contact with the SPD.

His motive here was not ideological conviction but rather the belief that, without the SPD, his political ideas for the two German states would not be

---

227 Leonhard 1996, p. 230. See also Maschke 1979.
228 '"Rationing bureaucrat", "shortage administrator", and "eco-Stalinist" were all the expletives they used and they were most certainly intended to be insulting. This third accusation weighed heavily. Of course, it completely missed the point of Harich's philosophical thinking. Here, his logic was razor sharp. The longer it took to tackle the ecological crisis, the more authoritarian the mechanism needed to resolve the threats to humankind' (Hofbauer 1996, p. 49). The quicker the necessary change was implemented, the fewer the restrictions on freedoms.
229 Stalinism is just one form of authoritarian or totalitarian rule. Harich himself drew the distinction by always rejecting the accusation of eco-Stalinism but not that of the eco-dictatorship. See Prokop 1996, p. 61.
230 Leonhard, who at the time was himself a sceptical young member of the SED, fled in the early 1950s to the Federal Republic via Yugoslavia. He describes this journey in detail in his bestseller *Die Revolution entlässt ihre Kinder* (Child of the revolution).

achievable. Thus he was driven by a Marxist understanding of necessity – the same motive that was also behind *Communism without Growth?*.²³¹

In his 1956 'manifesto', Harich retained the SED's claim of being the vanguard of the proletariat. He simply added elements of grassroots democracy, with the aim of motivating the working population and better integrating them into the system. Harich rejected the claim of the apparatus to omnipotence, upgrading the individual without positioning them above the party. Although he was not able to resolve the contradiction between the individual and the collective, he could still attempt to make socialism somewhat more 'humane' and thus more attractive and, at the same time, put it forward it as a model for a unified Germany.

The democratic socialist ideas Harich had expressed in his *Plattform* faded during his time in prison. On the other hand, they never complied with what the anarchists understood the term grassroots democracy to be either but were in fact rooted in Soviet democratic elements of Marxism-Leninism. Consequently, the break with democracy that Harich allegedly made later was in fact only a shift within his Marxist thinking, a change of course towards an étatist tradition, and was not a radical abandonment of liberal-anarchist ideas of socialism after all. Against this backdrop, his reckoning with (neo-)anarchism in *Zur Kritik der revolutionären Ungeduld* did not constitute him renouncing his own ideas from 1956 but was in fact a rejection of Western European anarchism, which propagated something entirely different to his *Plattform*.²³²

Harich was a Marxist, not an anarchist, and this also shaped his ideas about democracy and dictatorships. His thoughts continuously oscillated between these two poles. While in 1956, the pendulum swung toward Marxist concepts of democracy, in 1975 it moved in the opposite direction, revealing him to be a proponent of an étatist socialist dictatorship. And then, as his works show, the pendulum swung back again. This latter shift resulted from the time he spent in the West in 1980 and his real-life experience with the grassroots democracy of the Greens as well as through his study of feminism. Although Harich intensively pursued the Western environmental discourse, he was also very interested in the feminist works of his time and became profoundly know-

---

231   Here, too, he sought out contact with the SPD, this time through Freimut Duve, because he did not believe his environmental policy objectives could be implemented without the SPD. The view that cooperation between the communists and the social democrats was a necessity, even transcending the Cold War bloc borders, was a constant in Harich's thinking.
232   Manfred Jäger speculated that, with this work, Harich was only 'distancing himself from the enthusiastic exuberance of his younger years' (Jäger 1973, p. 138).

ledgeable on the subject.[233] In this way, the Western post-materialist discourse influenced Harich's thinking, increasing both the breadth and depth of his ideas.

During the almost two years Harich spent in the West, his relationship with the post-materialist environmental movement was also empirically strengthened. In 1979, shortly after arriving in Austria, Harich gave an interview for the Vienna *Neues Forum* journal in which he expressed his intention to become involved in the green movement and his wish to play the role of mediator between the political wings.[234] During this time, he had actually begun to self-critically scrutinise his own étatist model:

> With regard to centralism, it goes without saying that I have learned a substantial amount since writing my book, not least thanks to the works of *Carl Améry* and *Jona Friedman*, which appeared *after* my own book, and have as a result modified my own position. Nowadays, I, too, am an advocate of a local, where possible far-reaching autarchy, and this will undoubtedly both require grassroots democratic solutions in the political sphere and give rise to such solutions. But the global conditions for this will have to be created by a power centre equipped with dictatorial authority, a function which, given an advancing world revolution, will in all likelihood be taken on by a reorganised UN. ... In a nutshell: It will all come down to finding a happy medium between extremely autarchist solutions, such as those envisaged by Améry and Jona Friedman, and my – admittedly equally one-sided – centralism.[235]

Although just a few years later, Harich returned to the GDR resigned. The anti-étatist ideas he was confronted with in the West, however, continued to influence his thinking. In early 1989, he noted:

---

233 'It has to be said that Harich was the leading expert on Marxism in the Western European and Anglo-American environmental literature of his day. In the later years, he extended this prominence to feminist literature and social philosophy, meaning his thinking was shaped by the names and works of Françoise d'Eaubonne, Simone de Beauvoir, Betty Friedan, Marie-Louise Janssen-Jurreit, Anja Meulenbelt, Marilyn French, Irmtraud Morgner etc. By addressing feminism, he tackled what was, after ecology, both quantitatively and qualitatively, the second most important line of tradition in postmodern thought, which he sought to tie in with the Marxist "classics". And here too, it can be said that, at an early stage, books and theories became the focal point of his interest, which are today interpretatively classified as utopian discourse' (Heyer 2009, p. 37 f.).
234 See Harich 1979b, p. 18.
235 Harich 1979b, p. 19.

> I made great effort to understand the grassroots democratic concepts of the Greens and other alternative parties, and adopted a conciliatory attitude towards the democratism of the SPD and the SPÖ [Social Democratic Party of Austria], once I had seen – thanks to Eppler, Duve, Johano Strasser and Paul Blau – that, among the ranks of these parties, the change in thinking when it came to environmental threats was moving forward far more rapidly than among the communists.[236]

Harich described his own process of rethinking which came after *Communism without Growth?* as having occurred in three phases: phase one was the expansion of his thinking to include feminism while phase two comprised his empirical experience in the West. The third phase began with the change of political course brought on by Gorbachev and, for Harich himself, also entailed taking recourse to Lenin:

> I am trying to link the genuine, authentic Leninist concept of democracy to the main needs of the present and the future. ... Lenin understood the relationship between dictatorship and democracy not as one of mutually exclusive opposites. For him, the dictatorship against the minority ... was at once a broad-based democracy for the majority ....[237]

In 1989, Harich held the view that this formula needed to be applied politically to the environmental problems at the time. Using Lenin's terminology, he thus realigned his eco-utopian concept: 'As I said, democracy and dictatorship are not mutually exclusive. The eco-dictatorship is certainly not something we will be able to do without.... But this dictatorship will be exercised democratically, by the majority; not by a wise, ecologically educated dictator and his praetorian guard and certainly not within a monolithic system imposed from above and taking decisions at its own discretion, even those with neither direct nor indirect bearing on the environment'.[238]

Harich surmised that the majority of the population was suffering as a result of the discernible environmental damage and they would thus see this eco-dictatorship as legitimate.

Just 15 years later, Harich was self-critical about *Communism without Growth?*. At the time the book was written, driven by his communist conviction,

---

236 Harich 1994b, p. 141.
237 Harich 1994b, p. 141.
238 Harich 1994b, p. 142.

Harich felt that a state socialist rescue concept would be the best way of tackling the threat society was faced with. At that point, the Club of Rome's warnings were still new and, in Harich's view, the initial reactions tended towards the illusionary.[239] At the same time, however, he simply replaced these self-confessed illusions of the 1970s with new ones, which reflected the hope placed in Gorbachev's policy:

> I am confident that, if, in the socialist states, we see, combined with a broad education of the masses about ecological issues, a process of opinion building where political and social questions are discussed freely, irrespective of their controversial nature, and as a result are addressed and resolved, as is currently happening in the Soviet Union, there will be an adequate majority in favour of promoting the power of socialism to be put predominantly in the service of the survival of humanity.[240]

In saying this, Harich was granting the actually existing socialist countries the pioneering role again, provided they were capable of becoming more democratic. Consequently, he pinned his hopes on a democratisation of the system and on the majority of the population becoming subjects of environmental transformation.

Just a few months later, the one-party rule of the SED had been brought to an end by the revolutionary events. Over the course of the transformation of the system, many new parties and groups emerged, among them an East German Green Party (not to be confused with *Bündnis 90*). Harich wrote in *Keine Schwierigkeiten mit der Wahrheit* (No difficulties with the truth) that he had been approached from certain 'quarters'[241] within this new party, asking him to draft the party manifesto, which, in late December 1989, he went on to do. In this document, he demanded:

> ... a global conference on ecological security ... with the aim of putting a stop to environmentally destructive production and consumption everywhere and restructuring the global economy for the benefit of the Third World. The Common European Home must help to put a stop to the self-destruction of the human race. It must not drive it further forward by

---

239 See Harich 1994b, p. 143.
240 Harich 1994b, p. 144.
241 Harich 1993a, p. 255.

means of increased consumer excesses or by accepting the hardship and suffering of the majority of the world's population.[242]

At this early stage already, which was considerably earlier than the majority of other political actors in the GDR, Harich both predicted and called for German reunification. He also incorporated this in the document he wrote for the Green Party, where he linked it with a utopian vision:

> Irrespective of the required economic restraint, the decommissioning of the environmentally destructive industries that is such a necessary step for the survival of the human race, the rejection of the pressure to perform and the freedom to do as one pleases, the unified Germany that we hope for must guarantee full employment, security for the poor and the weak and social protection for everyone – at a modest material level, with a healthy lifestyle and complete satisfaction of ambitious intellectual and cultural needs. And for this, all in all, public ownership of the main means of production is the most fitting socioeconomic foundation. Because this is the united Germany we aspire to, because this is our vision of its internal and external composition, it goes without saying that we, the Greens, reject all attempts to put the GDR economy back on its feet that are in any way akin to capitalist restoration. We are against accepting Western loans, against foreign capital investment, the creation of any form of private company, against selling our land to speculators, against the propagation of competition and pressure to perform, and against joint ventures, especially those which lead to an increase in automobile production, for example, at a time when, for environmental reasons, we should be doing away with private car ownership to ensure the survival of plants, animals and humankind on our planet.[243]

At a party conference in February 1990, the East German Green Party rejected Harich's draft manifesto in favour of a different one. Harich remarked that this was because they did not consider his central demand for German reunification as an 'issue pertinent to the time'.[244]

---

242 Harich 1993a, p. 163.
243 Harich 1993a, p. 165 f.
244 Harich 1993a, p. 256. Andreas Heyer remarked that the antidemocratic position Harich took during the Nietzsche debate and the public reading of Walter Janka's memoirs at the time were one of the reasons his proposal was rejected, because it caused him to be discredited in civil rights activism circles. See Heyer 2010c. See also Amberger 2011b, p. 20 f.

Harich was one of the first to recognise the relevance and timeliness of the 'German Question'. But the actual course of the unification process turned out differently than he had imagined and the victory of capitalism in the Cold War forced him to rethink his ideas on the environment. This is clearly illustrated by an article he had published in 1991 in the journal *Z* on the Club of Rome Report that was topical at the time.

The report suggested that ecological transformation was feasible. Building on this, Harich therefore called for 'purposeful intent and action capable of taking into account factors that are open to influence'. Bringing to mind Gehlen's anthropology, he continued: 'And one such factor that is open to influence, because it is not determined by the imperative of instinct, because it is also adaptive, but at the same time has a permanent instinct for self-preservation – is humankind'.[245] Harich thus surmised that through education and an understanding of the need for survival, the 'New Man' could become reality.

In view of global problems coupled with the geopolitical opportunities presented by the end of the Cold War, referring to the Club of Rome, Harich called for a new world order. His view was that the left had to become aware of these problems and accept them, because only then would they stand a chance of overcoming their serious identity crisis. To achieve this, however, they would need to put their ideological premises to one side and renounce violence or rather the possibility of left-wing dictatorships.

At this juncture Harich made a radical break with the concept of the eco-dictatorship. Placing it in historical context, he called for:

> ... the resolute renunciation of violent methods of struggle and, among other things, the rejection of theories of undemocratic dictatorship of any type. And here the latter point in particular should be emphasised, as the aforementioned idea of a growthless, homeostatic communism in its original (and only well-known) form from 1974 onwards, was contaminated by the notion of an eco-dictatorship. Therefore, referring to the Club of Rome's understanding of democracy suggests the – erroneous – suspicion that this continues to be adhered to. In Brezhnev's and Honecker's 'actually existing socialism', they never even considered, whether because they were unable or unwilling, the offer with which they were naively wooed, appealing to their sense of responsibility, to leave the instruments of power at their disposal untouched, or indeed

---

245 Harich 1991, p. 63.

> to justify the choice to use such instruments – while rejecting Western consumer norms – as a precautionary measure to prevent future mortal dangers. Just as with all other forms of dissidence, they repressed, persecuted and slandered the offer. After their system collapsed, antidemocratic concepts, uncoupled from their still non-capitalist socioeconomic foundation, could only give rise to imperialist, possibly right-wing extremist cravings for dictatorship. What would be conceivable is the fascistoid caricature of an eco-dictatorship that, with the help of short-lived technological pseudo-solutions, creates a national conservation park (at best only prospering in the medium term) as pleasant surroundings for the master race, which, entrenched behind walls and barbed wire, keeps a desperately advancing flood of people from the South and the East at bay, if need be even with nuclear genocide. No, thank you![246]

Harich could not have been clearer in situating his utopia in a specific historical and political context, at the same time denying the contemporary relevance of his archistic utopia after the demise of the GDR.[247]

This quote also underlines the fact that *Communism without Growth?* was written a good 15 years earlier, intended as an offer to Brezhnev and Honecker to implement a different ecological form of socialism. As in 1956, Harich once again directed his request to the party leadership in Moscow, and once again, it was rejected.[248] However, what is also evident here is that both of his proposals were developed for the purpose of transformation. Moreover, it demonstrates Harich's ability to abandon his own ideas, even going as far as to refute them and to constantly rethink his strategies.

Another example of this was Harich's departure from the possibility of imposed asceticism, with him now favouring voluntary and democratically legitimised abstinence:

> The idea of the eco-dictatorship came, incidentally, from an inadequately historically informed memory of the beginning of World War II. From one day to the next, in Hitler's Germany, on 1 September 1939, strict rationing

---

246 Harich 1991, p. 67.
247 That said, he did not dismiss his book entirely as, shortly before his death, Harich expressed the wish for *Communism without Growth?* to be reprinted and published with the addition of all his correspondence with different institutions and authorities in the East and the West. See Harich, A. 2007, p. 172 f.
248 Scientists in the Soviet Union were more open to the problems raised by the Club of Rome than their peers in the GDR. See Hermand 1991, p. 146 f.

of food and other consumer goods was introduced and, being no longer allowed to buy fuel, car owners were prevented from driving their own vehicles. If the population was prepared to accept such restrictions in the name of pursuing criminal aggressive ambitions – and this was the only bearable, albeit not exactly enjoyable aspect of the war at the time –, then it hardly seemed far-fetched to demand of a red dictatorship which was committed to other, opposing objectives to those of the brown dictatorship of the Nazi Party, that in light of the environmental crisis, it implement analogous measures to put an end to the self-destruction of homo sapiens. ... But to think like this is, in fact, fundamentally wrong. Even the historical starting point is incorrect. In its war – a war which began in 1939 and which for once was actually justified – without abolishing democracy, Britain imposed the necessary sacrifices with a broad consensus between the Conservatives, Labour Party and the Liberals. Further, the Club of Rome is pushing for a democratic consensus of all political powers to tackle the global catastrophes that are already emerging.[249]

Moreover, in 1991, even more explicitly than in *Communism without Growth?*, Harich declared the subject of the new world revolution: in his view, it had to be all people. He believed that this would result in moral pressure, which even the most reactionary of capitalist circles would be unable to escape because after all they, too, would be offered cooperation.[250]

Here, Harich assigned the then newly reunified Germany a potentially leading role. He hoped that this new Germany would pursue the Club of Rome's objectives. In concrete terms, according to Harich, this meant that the standard of living in the West would have to be aligned with that in the East. After all, Germany's Basic Law guaranteed 'equal living conditions'. And, in accordance with the constitution and the Club of Rome, a step like this would serve as a role model for the whole world and thus represent genuine atonement for the atrocities of World War II.[251]

In the early 1990s, Harich was a member of a sectarian KPD. In 1993, he wrote an article in the party organ *Die Rote Fahne* under the title 'Communist Parties do not need a parliamentary ban', in which he criticised the fact that many communist parties were deprived of important opportunities for development as

---

249 Harich 1991, p. 67 f.
250 See Harich 1991, p. 69.
251 See Harich 1991, p. 71 f.

a result of the adoption and continuation of the ban on parliamentary groups imposed by the Russian Bolsheviks in 1921:

> And thus for two decades, since the first UN Conference on the Environment in Stockholm, since the first Club of Rome report, across all its branches, German communism has lacked a radical ecological faction, which would in time have had an internal effect and enabled the party to develop an appropriate understanding of the era, including the corresponding realignment, and would have been able to effectively and beneficially counteract the known aberrations within the Greens, or even make the founding of this party unnecessary altogether. The incorporation of environmental maxims in new draft programmes don't make up for what has been missed. They have come too late, seem insincere, and their logic is sometimes entirely incompatible with other programme messages. For this reason alone, they are likely to fall prey to the routine of one department, call it a 'working group' if you like, or other. As a side note, any substitute for the long overdue feminist faction is even less feasible.[252]

This was probably Harich's last article on the topic of the environment.

3 How *Communism without Growth?* Was Received

3.1 *Reactions from SED Circles*

The official government response to the Club of Rome reports in the GDR was dismissive. The problems of growth were declared to be ether a purely Western issue or denounced as a propaganda instrument of the West used to discredit the socialist upturn. It was occasionally pointed out that in the GDR, too, environmental policy was not quite what was aspired to. It was believed, however, that these shortcomings would disappear with the continued development of socialism and the victory over the class enemy.[253] The suggestion that the GDR

---

252 Harich 1993b.
253 One example of this: 'A tendency that is inextricably linked to imperialism is to senselessly waste the goods of this planet to satisfy the artificially created needs of a minority. And this is one of the reasons neo-Malthusian sentiments were aroused. The impulse to imitate must be dampened. Nature, according to the apologists of imperialism, imposes class differences on humankind. For, if everyone wants to live like the well-off – to exploit human beings and natural resources in the same way –, this would result in disaster. Of

itself implement urgent measures to regulate growth was rejected against the background of the ongoing system rivalry. The GDR defined itself as a socialist state. In the eyes of the SED, this meant that there were no mechanisms of the capitalist mode of production and consequently no waste of resources either owing to the artificially created needs. And even if any of this did exist, it was created by the class enemy and imported into the GDR. To a certain extent, this was in fact true, if we look at the influence of Western youth culture, for instance. That said, in the GDR, too, labour power was traded as commodity, as were the goods of nature. The relationship between goods and money prevailed, accompanied by a growth-oriented economy – a fact that was, incidentally, picked up on by many left-wing oppositional intellectuals in the GDR.

The Club of Rome reports were rejected. However, the way in which they were dismissed and the frequency with which this happened indirectly showed that they also had an impact in the GDR. Appearing against this backdrop, Harich's *Communism without Growth?* was a significant thorn in the side of the party as it was the first time an avowed Marxist from the GDR had acknowledged the findings of the Club of Rome and called for the state leadership to take measures, something it simply was not in a position to do.

Publicly, Harich's book was largely ignored. In the GDR, it 'was only available in the "locked libraries" of classified literature for special research purposes'.[254] The grounds for this can be found in the Stasi files; for instance in an 'assessment' for the GDR Institute for International Politics and Economics (IPW) written on 27 January 1976, accessible today as an unofficial review. This document describes Harich's work as an important contribution to the debate sparked by the Club of Rome, offering substantial food for thought and many talking points. He was commended for the anti-capitalist orientation of his book and for referring to communism as the only solution.

According to the critics, however, Harich's argumentation was not underpinned by 'established findings' based on Marxism-Leninism specifically with respect to: 1) the transition to communism; 2) Harich's Maoist tendencies, and

---

course, there is an alternative. Growth that is geared towards the needs of the people, and the creation of a reasonable structure of production and consumption cannot come from the anarchic structure of today's capitalist profit economy. The alternative can only be the result of an upheaval in capitalist relations of production and the – consciously and effectively applied – knowledge that comes from the inexhaustible source of socialist-oriented science and is applied through socialist planning. Such planning is only possible on the basis of socialist relations of production; for these relations are the only way to meet objectives that safeguard life for mankind for all eternity' (Grosse and Puschmann 1973, p. 137).

254   Prokop 1997, p. 145.

3) Harich's openness to convergence theory. In addition, 4) the revision of Marxism-Leninism was viewed as a threat.

It was claimed that, by questioning the leading role of the Soviet Union, Harich was laying the GDR open to attack from the class enemy. Moreover, he was providing grist for the mills of those who opposed peaceful coexistence with the West. The fact that Harich based his book on the Club of Rome reports rather than Marxism-Leninism was said to be a methodological error. As a result, he arrived at the wrong concept of communism, in other words: zero-growth communism. Harich insinuated that those living in socialist states had the same consumption tendencies as those in capitalist societies. His ideas could be misappropriated by anti-communists as he also criticised GDR scholars, for instance, and publicly named 'revisionist authors'. That said, in this regard, his book was deemed considerably more nuanced and clinical than those of the 'renegades and traitors (Havemann, Sakharov and others)'. Nevertheless, Harich's key message was rejected: 'However, Harich's main shortcoming was his propagation of the notion that communism was a society of asceticism, of poverty, of limiting needs, of "total rationalisation" and "distribution via ration coupons". The imperialist press seized these ideas and exploited them for their own anti-communist propaganda'. The evaluation came to the conclusion that the book should not be published in the GDR but that it would be a useful subject for discussion among an interested expert audience.[255]

The Stasi files also contained another short discussion on the book: a note by HA XX (Main Directorate XX for State Apparatus, Culture, Churches and Underground) dated 16 January 1976. The document was a brief report on an 'initial review' praising Harich for being an unwavering communist. 'Of particular note is that Harich appears not to exclude the possibility of the most advanced capitalist states making a direct transition from capitalism to communism at some point in time'. It was acknowledged that Harich was very well informed when it came to the environmental discourse. According to the report, the book was 'good for stimulating the discussion on these issues among Marxist-Leninist scholars ...'. The publication of the book was well received in the West, too, although an independent GDR edition was seen as obsolete 'because the problems it raises are not issues that are at the heart of the political ideological work'.[256]

Thus, Harich's achievement was acknowledged behind closed doors but concealed from the public. He did not lose heart, however: 'He began to pester the

---

255   BStU, MfS, AP, 4578/71, vol. 8, p. 328 ff.
256   BStU, MfS, AP, 4578/71, vol. 8, p. 346 f.

Central Committee Department of Sciences with petitions demanding that a scientific committee be set up to deal with these issues. Harich was tireless in his letter writing to the GDR's different "organs" of the state'.[257]

In the late 1970s, he wrote innumerable letters to the GDR Ministry of Culture calling for them to publish important current ecology books (such as those by Meadows and Taylor, for instance) in the GDR, and he hoped that a modified GDR edition of his own book *Communism without Growth?* would be published, too.[258] The response he received from the Ministry took the form of a letter written by Karl-Heinz Selle rejecting his request since the Western books he had referred to were pseudo-scientific and based on bourgeois ideology, and because the GDR leadership was already addressing environmental issues, thus rendering a broad 'public discussion' on this question superfluous.

At a meeting with the leading editors of the SED's theoretical organ, the monthly newspaper *Einheit* on 6 January 1977, Harich asked to be taken seriously as an ecologist and to be allowed to work on an environmental strategy for the GDR. The official taking the minutes at this meeting noted:

> For him, this was much more about coming out of isolation, something which he saw as the reason for any mistakes he might have made, and he asked me to help him. I told him that, to my knowledge, comrade Scheel had recommended him for further work and asked him his view on this. He responded that he would accept the offer 'as a pedant checking footnotes for the publisher', but, if I were able – as he anticipated – to assign him a more important role, he would gladly accept. He acknowledged that

---

257 Harich, A. 2007, p. 172. For example, between August 1976 and June 1977, he penned five petitions on the topic of aerosols and CFCs. In addition, he proposed the creation of a GDR pendant to the Club of Rome, a 'Club of Berlin or something similar'. He envisaged this being staffed by GDR scientists and being attached to the Central Committee of the SED. In fact, he offered to work for the institution himself. See BStU, MfS, AP, 4578/71, vol. 8, p. 189 ff.

258 See BStU, MfS, AP, 4578/71, vol. 6, p. 1. During a meeting with his colleagues at the Academy of Sciences, he even suggested specific changes. According to the minutes, Harich expressed the wish to be able to publish a modified version of the book in the GDR, as it 1) could make a contribution to the growth debate in the GDR, which had so far been on the flimsy side and 2) he wanted to avoid the danger of being labelled an oppositionist by the Western media if the book was only published there. Harich then presented a list of changes to be made to the GDR edition, which would also be compliant with copyright: 'a) the omission of Duve's reactionary foreword'; b) a new, critical foreword by a GDR academic; c) 'followed by the publication of the text of the interview with Duve'; d) a new postscript by Harich with self-critical commentary, 'highlighting points bringing together all the Marxist concepts'. See BStU, MfS, AP, 4578/71, vol. 8, p. 294 ff.

he could not be tasked with presenting issues pertaining to growth 'to the outside world' because this would mean that: 'Honecker was building on zero growth'. He thus consented to accept any task we gave him; repeatedly and explicitly emphasising: 'All I ask of you is to please make use of me!'[259]

Although his pleas fell on deaf ears, Harich persevered, albeit in vain, with his petitions and letters.[260] In a letter to Höpcke on 20 November 1978, for instance, he wrote:

> I am simply opposed to the so-called peaceful use of nuclear energy. Although I view this as a global problem and not one that is specific to the GDR, and by arguing so I am striving to counter attempts to place nuclear power stations at the centre of any kind of agitation directed against the GDR. However, if the recent referendum in Austria, which prevented the construction of the Zwentendorf nuclear power plant – in my opinion one of the most important historical events in recent times and cause for hope for the future – is completely ignored by our mass media, then I can only strongly object. Incidentally, I see this as sheer ignorance on the part of our media – ignorance that has undermined their own credibility and thus people's trust in the party and the state as well. Thirdly, I flatly reject reliance on private cars as well as the resulting expansion of the road network on environmental protection grounds and I am therefore a declared opponent of the construction of a new motorway between Berlin and Hamburg, as was agreed by the GDR and the FRG just a few days ago.[261]

During this time, Harich also frequently corresponded with the 'Minster of Books'. He hoped that this would enable him to introduce his ecological ideas and thus also Western knowledge on the issue of the environment to the SED. Höpcke listened to what he had to say and did what he could to help him. The documents from the Federal Commissioner for the Records of the State Security Service of the former German Democratic Republic (Stasi Records Agency, BStU), for instance, contain a confidential summary of the situation written by Höpcke on 31 July 1978 in which he outlines how best to proceed with Harich following a meeting with him on 11 July 1978. Höpcke writes that,

---

259   BStU, MfS, AP, 4578/71, vol. 8, p. 243 ff.
260   See Harich, A. 2007, p. 173 ff.
261   Harich, A. 2007, p. 180.

for Harich, literature was just a secondary occupation and that his primary concern and focus was the environment. He rejected Harich's request to publish Western environmental books in the GDR on ideological grounds. Harich criticised the DKP for only half-heartedly broaching the issue of the environment, e.g. when it came to the subject of promoting cars.

> In response to my counterquestion of whether he seriously wanted to suggest solutions that would result in hopeless isolation, he shrugged his shoulders and said he didn't know how to tackle the problems either. He said he would have to deliberate on it and come up with some suggestions. The trick will be to impose a combination of social and environmental solutions. What personally affects and concerns Harich is evidently the fact that he senses how little impact his ecological endeavours are having. ... He is forced to see himself as a failure in terms of both his internal and external environmental endeavours; thus, his words on the crisis that affect the very roots of his existence, which he begged me to take seriously and – should I think it right to do so – convey to others, too.

Harich still hoped to be heard in GDR and be considered for a role as an intellectual environmentalist. In Höpcke's words, Harich lamented that, on the one hand, he was not able to publish unimpeded in the West and yet his ecological proposals were not heard or taken seriously in the GDR either. This placed him 'in a hopeless situation ... What Harich needs is obviously a gratifying activity in the field of the ecology that gives him the feeling, in the narrowest or the broadest sense, that he, Wolfgang Harich, is contributing to socialism. ... As an aside, it also came up that he was still deprived of his academic titles, his professorship and doctorate.[262]

However, Harich's needs could not be met and thus, in a letter to Höpcke on 31 December 1978, he wrote with resignation that, as a result of being ignored, he was considering the possibility of leaving the GDR. The fact that he carried out this wish just a few months later can without a doubt be put down to him having been disregarded. Harich described this himself in another interview with the *Spiegel* in 1979. In the interview he said that the SED had offered him a job working with an interdisciplinary commission on environmental issues but that this commission had not fulfilled his expectations as its primary purpose was to provide ideological defence against Western environmental accusations. In addition, it was never intended for Harich to have contact with the other

---

262   All quotes taken from: BStU, MfS, AP, 4578/71, vol. 8, p. 49 ff.

scholars involved in the Commission.[263] In other words, the plan had been to co-opt Harich and, at the same time, to isolate him, which is something he was not prepared to allow to happen.

The SED leadership saw Harich's book as an affront to their economic policy. His proposals were rejected outright something which Harich very much acknowledged:

> In early 1979, even the Vice President of the Academy of Sciences of the USSR, Fedoseyev, made a statement against Harich's views. Behind closed doors, the SED Politburo became agitated on several occasions, a fact that was expressed in the form of anonymous attacks on the 'zero-growth' concept in presentations at Central Committee plenary sessions. Wolfgang Harich marked up all the passages in *Neues Deutschland*, the official organ of the SED for which he had a subscription, which he perceived as an attack on him. For instance he highlighted a passage in a paper by Werner Lamberz which had been published on 10/11 January 1976, in which the author wrote: 'Where anyone could hope to find a "written record of what has been achieved", in other words "zero growth" in the economic and social policy of the GDR, remains a mystery. People who want to hang the capitalist crisis around our necks, who want to deter us from the main goal to achieve a continual increase in the material and cultural standard of living have no influence on the GDR. Speculations on this made by Western prophets are utterly groundless. This is why they only exist in such journalistic organs of the so-called free world that have been ruined by anti-communist follies. Our path is clear and unambiguous as the General Secretary of the Central Committee of our Party, comrade Erich Honecker, reaffirmed in the recent Central Committee congresses' Harich also found plenty to mark up in a review by Harald Wessel. The review was from a book published by Reclam *Von Babeuf bis Blanqui* [From Babeuf to Blanqui], written by Joachim Höppner and Waltraud Seidel-Höppner, under the telling header: 'Eine geistige Quelle für die aktuelle Situation' [An intellectual source for contemporary debate]. Harich marked the following passages in Wessel's review: 'If you read the introduction by the two authors and, for instance, the stirring original texts penned by Gracchus Babeuf (1760 to 1797), it is instantly recognisable how anti-historic and absurd this attempt to depict Babeuf as an advocate of a "theory of zero growth in a socialist system" is

---

263 See Harich 1979c.

... However, Babeuf advocates with the same vehemence that the working classes must be provided with everything that is vital for life. This is impossible with "zero growth".[264]

In the years that followed, Harich's book remained unpublished. Instead, various articles appeared discrediting the Club of Rome as described above and also containing criticism of *Communism without Growth?*, be it indirect or even blatant. Symptomatic of the 'learning pathology' (Richard Saage) of the GDR and the disregard for Harich's warnings and opinions were a number of books that I will now describe in brief. What these publications, as well as the works with similar intent outlined in the Introduction, had in common were a fundamental rejection of a 'barracks' communism and an insistence on prosperity at any price. These works thus show that, for the SED, there did not appear to be any practical alternative.

The first such publication is *Gibt es Grenzen des ökonomischen Wachstums* (Are there limits to economic growth?) written by Harry Maier and published in 1977, two years after Harich's utopia. In the book, the author argues that capitalism is in serious crisis, while socialism, on the other hand, is showing healthy growth. According to Maier, the Meadows Report fits very nicely in this context, which is precisely why it had been so widely distributed and extensively marketed. Maier goes on to say that the Meadows Report takes crisis-stricken capitalism out of the firing line by diverting the criticism of the status quo in a direction that is less dangerous for capitalism. This is the reason why Maier considered the Meadows Report to be mere ideology.[265]

Maier claimed to have identified the following ideological tricks in the Club of Rome reports. Firstly, they attempt to present the limits of capitalism as if they were limits to the development of productive forces and secondly, the crisis of capitalism is depicted as a crisis of the whole of humanity.[266] In reality, however, the rational approach taken in the socialist system makes it superior. For example, it primarily uses raw materials that can be found in the socialist states themselves, it develops the available capacities and strives to reduce consumption without simultaneously causing a decline in productivity.[267]

The extensive growth that had been observed in the socialist states up till then was not an end in itself (as it was in capitalist societies), but rather was

---

264 Prokop 1997, p. 146.
265 See Maier 1977, p. 15 ff.
266 See Maier 1977, p. 33 f.
267 See Maier 1977, p. 46.

intended to serve the development of socialism. This was now well advanced, such that it gradually became possible to make a transition to 'intensive expanded reproduction'.[268] According to Maier, growth is needed to achieve communism, and he was critical of anyone who argued against that. In this sense, the following quote can also be interpreted as being critical of Harich:

> Incapable of understanding this correlation, the 'ultra-left' theorists identify with the 'melancholy era of capital' by simply repeating the theories about the 'limits of economic growth', believing every word of the predictions. They call on socialist countries to abstain from economic growth and preach an ascetic 'barracks' communism built upon the restriction and bureaucratic regulation of the satisfaction of the workers' needs. It is no coincidence that the ideological structure of this belief is identical in every way to the official bourgeois theories on this issue: the crisis of capitalism is reinterpreted as a crisis of humanity and the limits to growth that capital is coming up against are stylised as universal human limits. Underlying these beliefs are grave doubts about the ability of the working class along with other working people allied with that class to guarantee effective needs-based growth of the socialist economy and thus put an end to the capitalist social system's overexploitation of both workers and the natural environment. In light of the successes in improving the cultural and material living standards of workers, the 'workhouse' communism the 'ultra-left' theorists entrust to the working class do not even warrant a pitying smile. It distorts both socialism's successes in the economic rivalry with imperialism, achieved thanks to unparalleled creativity and incredible drive, and the goal of the revolutionary workers' movement to build a communist society which guarantees every member of society the opportunity to develop their social, productive, intellectual and aesthetic assets and abilities.[269]

Maier did not mention Harich by name but it can certainly be surmised that he was familiar with his critique of growth and that the passage quoted above was referring to this.

This stands in contrast to Rolf Dlubek, who, in 1978, in an article for the *Marx-Engels Jahrbücher* openly named and criticised *Communism without Growth?*.

---

268   See Maier 1977, p. 62ff. Maier accused the Club of Rome of veiling stagnation with their demands for reduced growth. And now argued, no less apologetically, in the same manner. For, from the mid-1970s an economic depression also hit the Comecon countries.
269   Maier 1977, p. 70f.

The following passage taken from the article deals with Harich's book and can, as such, be considered an indirect review of the publication in the GDR:

> The experiences in all socialist countries confirm that only by fully developing the merits of socialism can the preconditions for the gradual transition to communism be achieved. ... For all these reasons, it has nothing to do with Marxism when attempts are made to trump a reactionary utopia of 'zero-growth' capitalism with a theory of 'communism without growth' as Wolfgang Harich did in his book, which he declared, among other things, to be a contribution to the 100th anniversary of the *Critique of the Gotha Programme*. Influenced by the Club of Rome reports ... the author abandoned these key Marxist positions. Despite polemic attacks on imperialism and the multinational corporations, he ultimately rejects the notion that the environmentally harmful consequences of the scientific-technical revolution are rooted in the capitalist system rather than in science and technology itself. He only allows one choice: either a transition to the so-called zero-growth scenario or the end of mankind. The purpose of communism should not be to ensure the increasing domination of humans over nature. Its superiority should, in contrast to capitalism, be rooted in its ability to transition to zero growth! This utterly false viewpoint leads to a change in direction against the entire Marxist-Leninist concept of communism. Marx's conclusions in the *Critique of the Gotha Programme* according to which the productive forces must be qualitatively better developed for communism and all sources of social wealth must flow from this are declared by Harich to be untenable. In so doing, he distorts the Marxist-Leninist concept of communism, attributing it with a land-of-plenty belief of sorts and he sees the significant development of productive forces as only necessary for high material consumption, and not for the further development of the relations of production, the expression of the new nature of work and the all-round development of the personality. Moreover, he also relies on the primitive concept refuted by Marx and Engels according to which the essence of communism comprises the egalitarian regulation of distribution. .... Subsequently, he declares the development of the productive forces to be already perfectly sufficient to enable the transition to what was supposed to be communism, and the socialist countries, like 'all industrialised capitalist countries, ready for the seamless realisation of communism'. He essentially makes a mockery of his own concept when, in the same breath, he explains that, to achieve this, people in the East must 'sacrifice much' and that those in the West must 'sacrifice very, very much indeed!' It was therefore no coin-

cidence that the bourgeois press in West Germany gave this book a level of publicity that no Marxist-Leninist work would have been granted, given their desire to use the book in the prevailing deep crisis of imperialism to obscure the alternative, to once again conjure up the spectre of communism, vilify it as a 'future of asceticism, rationing and discipline imposed by a world state apparatus of coercion'. Flying in the face of all imperialist, social democratic, right and left-wing revisionist misrepresentations and defamations ..., 60 years of practical experience with communist and socialist development in the Soviet Union and the countries affiliated to it unmistakably confirms the increasingly appealing scientific view substantiated by Marx, Engels and Lenin: as much as socialism and communism do not mean ascetic egalitarianism, neither do they imply exclusive ownership of material goods, anarchic chaos or a barracks existence.[270]

Thus, Harich was branded a revisionist and the seriousness of his ecological warnings was denied. Over the next ten years, the final decade of the GDR's existence, the SED still did not deviate from its line of argument that the ecological problem recognised by Marx and associated exclusively with capitalism played only a minor role for socialism, although it did acknowledge that it had grown in importance in recent years. However, the blame was placed squarely on capitalism's shoulders, while the socialist states in contrast endeavoured to preserve the environment.

In 1983, *Zur Dialektik des Geschichtsprozesses* (The dialectics of the historical process) was published, a book written by two GDR philosophers Wolfgang Eichhorn I and Adolf Bauer. Symptomatic of the situation at the time, the authors write: 'The scope of tasks the working class is expected to take on in the class struggle is growing. Today, the socioeconomic interests of the workers have been joined by ecological interests, which include an environment that is valuable for human health, in particular decontaminating *water, soil and air* and/or preventing the pollution thereof in the first place, and maintaining the all-important equilibrium of the biosphere'.[271] Here, in relation to socialism, two problematic circumstances came to light: the socialist productive forces were only in an emergent phase and the system rivalry with capitalism required too many resources, which the authors believed would be better invested in the conservation of the environment. Here, the authors even criticised the GDR's high military spending, although they did insist that this was

---

270 Dlubek 1978, p. 41f.
271 Eichhorn I and Bauer 1983, p. 264.

necessary.[272] Eichhorn I and Bauer maintained that the more the technical and material potential of the socialist states developed, the more it would be possible to invest in environmentally sustainable production, and they validated their view with reference to the party line: 'The 25th Congress of the Communist Party of the Soviet Union, along with the 9th and 10th Congresses of the SED, made an enormous contribution to tackling these tasks by defining comprehensive measures for the complex, rational exploration, use and replenishment of natural resources, concentrating on the development of progressive technologies and highly effective technical methods for waste purification and recycling as well as by calling for ideal ways to forecast the damaging effects of the increased production output on the environment'.[273]

Based on its own pronouncements, the SED had already been a red-green party for a long time. And environmental protection was also institutionally embedded in the GDR. However, this had barely any impact on the conservation of nature in reality: quite simply, there was neither the money, the genuine will nor the opportunities for this.[274] Although Eichhorn I and Bauer did not explicitly refer to these weaknesses, reading between the lines, they also acknowledged their existence:

> In contrast to capitalism, however ... the socialist system allows for the establishment of a fundamental congruence between the standards and the actual environmental degradation .... That said, even in socialism, the legal configuration cannot take precedence over the economic substance of this process. Most importantly, this means that when resources policy and the economic process of reproduction are linked, the specific interests of the different businesses, social groups and also individual workers as producers and consumers, which are part of this interplay, are both duly considered and influenced.[275]

---

272 See Eichhorn I and Bauer 1983, p. 267 ff.
273 Eichhorn I and Bauer 1983, p. 283 f.
274 In the same year, *Die Zeit* wrote about Harich's ideas and the actually existing socialist reality: 'Years ago already, in his book *Communism without Growth?*, Wolfgang Harich called for the GDR government to force the people to behave responsibly, in other words in an environmentally sustainable manner. Instead of chasing after the prosperity of the West with their tongues hanging out, they would be better off improving the attractiveness of their country by making its natural environment healthy. He even called for pollutive two-stroke cars such as those made by Trabant and Wartburg to be dispensed with and for public transport to be developed instead. Exactly the opposite has happened' (Menge 1983).
275 Eichhorn I and Bauer 1983, p. 266.

Herein lies the difference with Harich, making it quite clear why his ideas were not compatible with the SED's realpolitik. In the first part of the quote there are considerable similarities with Harich's views, while in the second, the disparity is evident: the two authors called for the protection of the environment to give due consideration to the economy and consumers – Harich, in contrast, believed there was no time for this.

In the 1970s and 1980s, the protection and conservation of nature was therefore also designated an SED objective. But Harich's 'barracks' communism was of no help when it came to the legitimation of the GDR and the SED. They were simply unable to deviate from the goal of a communism of abundance until the very end. And for this reason, attempts were made to link environmental protection to the socialist ideal. In 1985, for example, a book entitled *Mit der Natur in die Zukunft* (With nature into the future) was published. In this book, whose title speaks for itself, realpolitik was linked with an ecologically balanced form of socialism. The author of the book, Rolf Löther writes: 'The energy supply of the future will be based on nuclear and solar power. Nuclear energy is a natural resource that even from today's perspective will still be available for thousands of years to come, while solar energy is even seen as one of our inexhaustible resources'.[276] In light of these high hopes, we can imagine just how severe the ideological and economic damage wreaked by the Chernobyl disaster must have been for the GDR. Harich had already warned against nuclear power in the 1970s, but the SED could not do without this form of power generation. In 1986, the MCA permanently destroyed the belief in a nuclear-powered communism. From then on, the fear of nuclear power outweighed the hope (not least because the GDR's only nuclear power plant in Lubmin near Greifswald was a Soviet-type reactor). Harich's criticism of humans' abuse of the environment in the actually existing socialist states increasingly turned out to be true. For the SED, on the other hand, it became more and more difficult to conceal the true magnitude of environmental destruction.

In sum, in terms of how *Communism without Growth?* was received by the GDR's intellectual and political elites, it can be said that they acknowledged the existence of the book, and then rejected it. Its very essence contradicted the growth policy of the actually existing socialist states and it also made reference to Western eco-discourse. However, Ehrhart Neubert was mistaken when he wrote: 'Despite the originality of bringing the environmental issue up to date, in doing so he provided the SED with ideological support in the event that it needed to defend the idea of the dictatorship of the proletariat against

---

276   Löther 1985, p. 139.

the Eurocommunists'.²⁷⁷ Although it was Harich's intention to help the SED, there was never an occasion where the SED or politically aligned scholars used the book to defend the party against Eurocommunism. They had their own set of arguments for this – especially since environmental protection was not one of the Eurocommunists' central demands, meaning the extent to which it legitimised the dictatorship of the proletariat against the Third Way that the Eurocommunists envisaged would have been rather limited.

3.2   Reactions to the Book in the West

When *Communism without Growth?* was published in the FRG in 1975, it sparked a contentious discussion, and the 11,000 copies of the book that were sold bear witness to this.²⁷⁸ The book was also translated into Spanish and Swedish.²⁷⁹ Even the history of the publication made a good anecdote for Harich:

> Then in 1975, when I began to have heart problems and the doctors here in the GDR warned me of the unsterile conditions in the operating theatre of Sauerbruch, the Rowohlt-Verlag and Augstein [founder of the *Spiegel* magazine Rudolf Augstein] covered part of the cost of my operation in Geneva. And for this I was obviously incredibly grateful. But not so much to the publishing house because Rowohlt was looking to be compensated by not paying me the royalties for my book *Communism without Growth?*. I said this was not something I would even consider as it brings foreign currency into the GDR via the Copyright Office. I simply can't do that. The book is not going to be published here, this will only place me in an even worse light. And old Rowohlt held this against me.²⁸⁰

Although Rowohlt still went on to publish the book, what the story shows however, is that critics of the SED who published in West Germany were subject to the laws of the capitalist book market and, at the same time, were forced to take the transfer of foreign currency to the GDR into account. It also reveals the minor privileges that Harich was able to enjoy, in this case heart surgery in Switzerland.

---

277   Neubert 2000, p. 213.
278   See Harich, A. 2007, p. 170.
279   See Prokop 1997, p. 145.
280   Harich 1999, p. 377. In his autobiographical work *Ahnenpaß*, Harich describes how he had already made acquaintance with Rowohlt in the early 1940s and that in the late 1940s they had had a brief falling out, because Rowohlt had published the memoirs of the NSDAP functionary Hjalmar Schacht. See Harich 1999, p. 220.

Communism without Growth? became a subject of discussion as much in the mass media as in political journals. In the Berlin weekly *HOBO*, a predecessor journal of today's *zitty*, H. Schreiter devoted an article in vol. 46/1975 to Harich's book and reactions to it in the Federal Republic. His article was a polemic against the tone of the Western reviews. He wrote: 'It's the same old ploy over and over again: a long-winded discussion about the ascetic version of communism, which is generally equated with a society characterised by extreme hunger; then speculations about how much trouble the author will be in with the "authorities", who he actually dared to refer to as the "authorities" (what a nerve!); and finally, they use a hand-carved cubit to measure how far the author has deviated from the orthodox Marxist line'.

The preface by Duve reminded Schreiter of the those added to Kafka, Camus and Proust's respective GDR editions to make them more palatable. 'You would not be wrong in thinking that the majority put the book aside after reading the preface because they found everything they wanted to know in that chapter alone'. The preface did little more than reflect Duve's powerlessness: 'Because, during their discussion, Harich's formidable intellect enabled him to effortlessly ward off Duve's childish attempts to portray him as a dissident, the latter ultimately laid a proverbial cuckoo's egg in the shared nest of the manuscript in the form of an infamous preface'.

However: 'Once the critics are freed ... from the suspicion that the preface was enough, a much more serious suspicion arises: the fear of uncomfortable, hard-to-sell truths'. The majority of them would go on to choose the more pleasant path: 'Instead providing a detailed depiction of a communist dictatorship of distribution, regardless of how this is envisaged, because this is easy to grasp, it is so nice and shocking, and it fits so well into Dr John Doe's idea of a communist reign of terror.'

Yet, this goes beyond the intention behind the book, because: 'The crux of Harich's train of thought is not the rediscovery of the food ration card; rather his book comes to the conclusion that only a communist world society is capable of setting reasonable limits ... and achieving equitable distribution ....'

Schreiter then goes on to praise the utopian elements of *Communism without Growth?*: 'The fact that Harich had the courage to interrogate the socialist present about its future prospects is what I consider his biggest accomplishment'.[281] But, aside from this polemic, what did the reviews that were criticised

---

281   BStU, MfS, AP, 4578/71, vol. 7, p. 101ff.

by Schreiter actually contain? In an article in *Die Zeit*, Wolfgang Roth writes that Harich had much to offer those searching for heresies in the works of Eastern European critics of the system. 'Entire broadsides filled with heresy are being launched'. These heresies culminated in the shift away from the golden future that communism would provide. That said, despite all the criticism it came under, Harich's book did not serve to satisfy anti-communist appetites as Harich himself remained a loyal supporter of the actually existing, authoritarian version of Marxism-Leninism and could thus not fill the role of 'stooge' of 'democratic socialism'. What is more, he also identified threats that affected the West as much as they did the East. Harich did not present the West's political-economic systems as an alternative. Quite the opposite in fact. Roth commended the author for managing to portray the magnitude of the threat accurately, without embellishment. Roth was also full of praise for Harich's consistent critical examination of the GDR's political system and he pointed all the proponents of the Western system to Harich's work as an example of how to be critical of their own ideals. Something he did find fault with, however, was Harich's belief in zero growth, accusing him of economic naivety, as zero growth already existed but was not remotely beneficial to nature. Roth suggested that it was better to oppose Babeuf-style authoritarian communism with 'a real alternative to a growth-oriented society that practices democratic self-constraint'. That said, he described the many contradictions in Harich's *Communism without Growth?* as having made a stimulating contribution to the debate. 'Especially when we seek to argue forcefully against Harich does it become clear how absurd it is to hope that environmental requirements and a major economy based predominantly on profit could be reconciled.'[282]

The *Spiegel* came to a similar conclusion: 'In fact, it seems that Wolfgang Harich – along with Robert Havemann ... – is one of the few communist philosophers to take the "limits to growth" seriously and to accept the thesis that if humanity were to maintain its current level of industrial and demographic expansion, it would breathe its "last breath" a century from now (Harich). He is certainly the first prominent communist to seriously think through the political and philosophical consequences of the Club of Rome analysis – coming to the conclusion that the "old communist dream of humankind" would have to be "massively scaled back".'

Critics concluded that Harich had turned his back on the Marxist dream of abolishing the state.

---

[282] Roth 1975.

There is no doubt that Harich is serious about his concept of communism – referred to by Freimut Duve as 'a total police state controlling global supply'. However, we also sense a subtle irony in Harich's words. His future 'ascetic distributive state' (Duve) is, at least in part, a mirror image of the state in which Harich lives, a state which once threw him in jail, in other words the GDR. This state is unlikely to be particularly thrilled to recognise itself in Harich's image of a future communist global police state. And Harich, the author, is most certainly aware that the SED men did not like to be addressed as 'the authorities'. Nevertheless, Harich is fervently committed, with almost overpowering zeal, to the 'authoritarian structures of our system' – a repugnant situation for him, but all the more so for the 'authorities' ruling over him.[283]

Reading between the lines, characteristics of the utopian concept can be seen in the reference to and critique of the reality of the GDR and the (ironic?) utopian counter model serving as a mirror being held up to the SED.

Carl Améry also makes a connection with the history of utopia in his review of the book in the *Süddeutsche Zeitung* on 13 September 1975. In an article entitled 'Stalin: The Stone Guest', Améry commends Harich for being one of the first Marxists in the East or West to take the Club of Rome seriously. He describes Harich as having broken with the Marxist optimism about the future, returning to Babeuf, whose *Conspiracy of the Equals* will become the master template, not Fourier's mystical early socialism and certainly not the materialist utopias which had 'nurtured the pathos of the labour movement in the past'. Améry claimed that, on the one hand, Harich showed Marxism without eschatology, but, on the other, he had also revived and eternally justified Stalinism, which Améry referred to as a 'moral deficit'. Even so, he still considered the book a 'landmark', exposing the 'inadequacies' of Marxism.[284]

In a discussion aired by radio and television broadcaster *Norddeutscher Rundfunk* (NDR) on 2 November 1975, Manfred Hertwig applauded his 1956 'companion' (Hertwig and Harich were both arrested on the same day in 1956) for daring to contradict the SED ideologues with regard to the Club of Rome. Hertwig found two aspects of the situation paradoxical, however – the first, the fact that, in the GDR, it was ironically an outsider who broached the necessary environmental modification of Marxism, thus exposing the rigidities of Marxism-Leninism, and second, the fact that Harich, who had served time in

---

283   *Spiegel*, no. 31/1975.
284   BStU, MfS, AP, 4578/71, vol. 7, p. 112 f.

prison for making democratic demands, was now extoling the virtues of the authoritarian state. Hertwig advised the SED not to worry that Harich might using his arguments to incite the masses against the party, as the people would favour growth and consumption.[285]

In edition no. 36/1975 of the SPD newspaper *Vorwärts*, Romain Leick reviewed Harich's book in an article entitled 'Schmale Kost für Sozialisten' ('Meagre fare for Socialists'). Leick praised Harich's incisive dialectical thought, which easily dealt with Duve's quips. 'What has proven to be more important is whether, when thinking about the relationship between the state and the people or between nature and man, we, like Duve the social democrat, proceed from the constituent parts to the whole or, like Harich the communist, from the whole to the constituent parts'.

Harich adhered to Marxist thinking and accordingly

> ... deems not the emancipation of man, but that of man*kind* to be important, not the domination of the physical worker but of the working *class*. In terms of its logic, such a dialectic is very convincing. Politically, however, it leads those in power into the temptation of committing the most extreme brutality against individuals in the name of global responsibility.

And this is something which also applies to the relationship between nature and human beings:

> He believes that nature does not exist solely for humankind, but by and of itself; expressed in Hegelian terms: it exists in its own right. Nature relates to humans as the general to the specific. Assuming the primacy of the former, the eco-dictatorship appears to be the social order that is most suited to nature.

Leick comes to the conclusion that 'Harich's communism no longer rests on the dictatorship of the proletariat but on that of the environmentalists'.[286] On 9 October 1975, Jürgen Rühle reviewed Harich's book for *Die Welt*. He assumed that it was not being published in the GDR because Harich's criticism of industrial societies in both the East and the West was reminiscent of Sakharov's convergence theory. That said, for the West, the substance of his ideas was of questionable relevance, because the problems outlined by the Club of Rome

---

285 BStU, MfS, AP, 4578/71, vol. 7, p. 108 ff.
286 BStU, MfS, AP, 4578/71, vol. 7, p. 124 f.

had purportedly already been resolved there: 'The Western world, and also the majority of developed countries with which we have economic relations, have already moved beyond the apocalyptic projections of the Club of Rome. The tropical rainforest in the Amazon is being exploited but not cleared; the dwindling oil supplies in the Middle East will be replaced by sources in Alaska and the North Sea in the near future; environmentally friendly nuclear power plants are under construction; population growth has been curbed in the most densely populated countries of the world, such as India and especially China; asphyxiated by exhaust fumes, we are designing more efficient and more comfortable forms of short and long-distance public rail transport'.[287]

Rühle believed that Harich wanted to reframe the fact that the Eastern Bloc was lagging behind as an advantage: 'As a vision for the future, we are being proffered the Stalinist model of a brutal system of domination and rationing, which not only envisages distributing ration cards and fuel allocations for all eternity, but also proposes resettling entire nations (citizens of India to the GDR, for instance). ... In this strict form, even for Brezhnev and Honecker, this is alarmingly pure neo-Stalinism'.[288]

In the *Zeitschrift für Politik*, Georg Stadtmüller argues that

> ... in the book, H. declares himself as a 'Marxist' and claims to be taking a Marxist 'approach' to his philosophising. And yet, at the same time, he negates pretty much all of Marx's most important doctrines: the immiseration of the proletariat, the collapse of capitalism, the withering of the state and the interrelated emergence of the 'New Man' in the future affluent society (according to Marx!). H. refrains from referring to these predictions because, due to the course of historical events since the start of the nineteenth century, they have been sufficiently rebutted. Harich justifies such deviations from the Marxist 'classics' with the simple assertion that, if he were alive today, Marx would think just as he (Harich) does.[289]

According to Stadtmüller, Harich draws 'on the ideas of the French utopian Socialist *Gracchus Babeuf*' – although without identifying *Communism without Growth?* as a utopia.[290] Despite all his criticism, Stadtmüller ultimately also

---

287 BStU, MfS, AP, 4578/71, vol. 7, p. 104. It is noteworthy that Rühle saw the Chinese population policy as a Western achievement.
288 BStU, MfS, AP, 4578/71, vol. 7, p. 105.
289 Stadtmüller 1977, p. 206.
290 From the reviews it is clear that at that time, the book had not yet been classed as utopian discourse.

found something positive to say about Harich's book stating that '... it comprised deliberations, reflections and postulates of a philosophising mind, who, as a result of his disengagement from the official party interpretation of Marxism-Leninism, had raised suspicion among the custodians of pure party doctrine. Harich is one of the most remarkable representatives in the reformist "neo-Marxist" ideological landscape'.[291]

In his commentary, Günter Gaus recalls the period in which the book was published and Harich's intellectual habitus. Gaus describes how he visited Harich in his Berlin flat in 1976.

> Harich gave barely a word of introduction, mentioning only that I had been the editor-in-chief under Augstein, and then went straight on to talk about his most recent book *Communism without Growth?*, asking me whether I had read it. At least that's how I recall this first meeting in spring 1976. The impression I had of Harich on that day was that of a rather shy man who, wanting to rid himself of this self-consciousness, moved immediately on to the most familiar territory for him, his own books. My cursory reading of Harich's ecology book meant that I had missed the fundamental issues of communist doctrine that it addressed. I therefore limited myself to discussing the issue of how to control the guardians of a social life that was suited to natural resources. Who controls the controllers? Harich engaged in a discussion on this subject, sometimes with a certain self-irony, but on the whole, I felt, with a considerable degree of gravity. And of course, behind all this, hides the revival of Stalinism. Whether or not my own memory of the meeting is inflated when I speculate that Harich saw this revival as inevitable if the world was to survive, I am not sure.[292]

Praise for Harich's break with the dogmas of Marxism-Leninism and the rejection of his eco-communist proposals at the same time was also a common thread running through reactions to the book from Western intellectuals such as Herbert Gruhl, Carl Amery and Johano Strasser, all of whom explicitly referred to Harich's utopia in their own books, albeit drawing different conclusions.

CDU politician Herbert Gruhl, who became a pioneer of the Green movement in the 1970s, was one of the few authors besides Harich to draw on the

---

291 Stadtmüller 1977, p. 206.
292 Gaus 1999, p. 293f.

archistic utopian tradition.²⁹³ In his book *Ein Planet wird geplündert* (The ravaged planet), which was published shortly after *Communism without Growth?*, Gruhl already referred to Harich's utopia:

> Of course, the question of how much freedom we even have left is something we often hear, even today. The freedom to bring about our own downfall is always there. If we want to escape this inevitability, however, there are very few options that remain open to us within the limits of this planet. In fact, these limits are particularly evident in the excessive and irresponsible use of economic freedom. Similarly, Soviet communism has the potential for destruction that is far too great to be able to readily provide the solution to 'growth', as Wolfgang Harich proposes in his book *Communism without Growth?* (1975).²⁹⁴

Gruhl was probably the first to refer to Harich's utopia in a book that was part of Western environmental discourse.²⁹⁵ In 1984, social democratic visionary Johano Strasser conducted an in-depth analysis of Harich's philosophy. in his book *Die Zukunft des Fortschritts* (The future of progress), which he co-authored with Klaus Traube and in which he made a plea for liberal, emancipatory and socialist alternatives to industrial society.²⁹⁶ It was against this backdrop that Strasse and Traube presented their critique:

> Despite the differences when it came to the details, Gruhl and Harich (who have since clearly revised their views on many points) were still

---

293 'Based on the clear threat to humanity posed by the global environmental crisis, three concepts were proposed, all with vastly different ideological and philosophical origins when it comes to eco-dictatorship. The concepts were developed by West German conservative Herbert Gruhl, East German dissident Wolfgang Harich and American liberal Robert Heilbronner (and certain other comparable personalities from the context of French right-wing extremism could be added to this list, too). There is, however, no preponderance of repressive utopias of social order' (Schwendter 1994, p. 15).

294 Gruhl 1975, p. 287 f. Erich Fromm also commented on Harich's book shortly after his best-seller *To Have or to Be?* was published in 1976, referring to Harich as one of the few Eastern Bloc authors to critically analyse the issue of growth. See Fromm 2013, p. 143.

295 During a lecture in Vienna in 1979, Harich defended Herbert Gruhl against the accusation directed at him by the then Research Minister Volker Hauf that his views increasingly resembled fascist ideas, Harich stated: 'I see it as my duty to Dr Gruhl, from whom I am separated by very profound differences of opinion and who I regard as representing an unachievable bourgeois solution to the ecological problem, to nonetheless say, even in relation to him, that the conclusion that his views "resemble fascism" is completely indefensible and unwarranted' (Harich 1980, p. 72).

296 See Strasser and Traube 1984, p. 230.

essentially in agreement on one key point, this being the more or less openly expressed belief that an environmentally sound society of the future would have to restrict freedom and self-determination to ensure survival. Their predominantly scientific, biologistic position on the problems created by industrial society's expansion dynamics is the reason why the solutions they put forward in the aforementioned books neglect key aspects of the problem and, in particular, misjudge the opportunities for emancipation and autonomisation of human beings that an ecological alternative would provide. Gruhl, like Harich, is a pessimist at heart.[297]

According to Strasser and Traube, both Gruhl and Harich sought to back up their solutions with historical references. Gruhl's inspiration was the Spartan Polity and Harich's was Babeuf's egalitarian communism. Both adopted an anthropocentric world view, to which everything was subordinate and which they seemed to find legitimate at any cost: 'Harich and Gruhl are portrayed here as representing a type of ecological thinking that tends to reduce the problems of industrial society to the issue of guaranteeing the biological existence of humankind and thus almost inevitably arrives at democratically disputable solutions'.[298]

Strasser and Traube, however, deemed the price of such solutions too high and the abuse of power an inherent danger.[299] Bearing this in mind, rather than going from the frying pan into the fire, they called for a more restrained approach:

> The objective predicament, in which both Gruhl and Harich believed themselves to be, did not, in fact, exist and, consequently, their anti-emancipatory pessimism is by no means justified either. Owing to their

---

297   Strasser and Traube 1984, p. 231.
298   Strasser and Traube 1984, p. 232.
299   'Dire need and danger have often been used as a pretext for increasing centralist powers, even going as far as to justify absolute dictatorial power, and equally often, the benefits of installing an emergency dictatorship have proven to not even come close to outweighing the costs. The restrictions to freedom and the centralisation of power and decision-making authority, which are purportedly necessary in the interests of the public, seem to make it more likely that the interests of the majority of the population will be systematically distorted or ignored entirely. The concept of the eco-dictatorship should, however, not be rejected only because it is inhumane. It is also based on the incorrect assumption of fundamental shortages that impact all areas of life. As we have shown, this premise is only accurate if we accept that industrial expansion continues in a straight line and if we disregard opportunities for completely new human wealth' (Strasser and Traube 1984, p. 233).

> pessimism, Gruhl and Harich became eco-technocrats; they expected betterment, if need be by means of a drastic cure imposed from above; in Harich's case this would be achieved through science and the collective wisdom of the Politburo, and in Gruhl's through a charismatic figure that was willing to build a new Sparta through blood, sweat and tears. And Harich never said a word about the incredible waste that went hand in hand with the establishment of yet more extensive bureaucratic apparatus ....[300]

Strasser and Traube did not see the expansion of dictatorial powers as being the way out of the crisis, but rather considered more democracy and emancipation to be the solution. Harich's concept was not regarded as a genuine alternative and was thus rejected.

Carl Amery took a similar critical stance on *Communism without Growth?* in a book he published in the mid-1980s. He knew Harich personally, having met him in West Germany in March 1978 when they had discussed the problems of growth but had failed to reach any consensus.[301] Based on this, in his 1985 book *Die ökologische Chance* (The ecological opportunity) Amery conceded that Harich was 'a very skilful and resolute political operator' who had firmly committed to the Club of Rome's findings and made this the focus of his activity. He also praised Harich for his harsh judgement of those communists who were advocates of growth policy.[302] But he also highlighted the contradictions and dangers inherent in Harich's utopia, acknowledging at the same time, however, that these were an intellectual achievement:

> With a flick of the wrist, Harich sweeps fundamental questions of Marxist theory to one side. His communism of distribution ... requires ... centralised authorities with immense powers. It requires constant policing of perennial global food queues. And, most importantly of all, it demands sacrifice, the total and immediate forgoing of the most noble centrepiece of Marxist ethics: its eschatological hope, the end of alienation. The Stalinist system, retrospectively crowned with the laurel of heroic justice, will become the permanent fate of humankind. It would be strange if this clever man had not understood this. ... Wolfgang Harich is not, to put it mildly, exactly a friend of humanity, but more a friend of ... law and order .... And here lies the real danger of his theory. Even a man like Harich, who

---

300 Strasser and Traube 1984, p. 233.
301 See Harich, A. 2007, p. 78.
302 See Amery 1985, p. 334f.

has such a poor existential understanding of his fellow human beings, must be aware that a humanity deprived of all hope of wealth and freedom ... will hit back by unequivocally refusing to produce. This retaliation – or attempt to retaliate – will, in turn, necessitate very extreme forms of repression. It is of course utterly unrealistic for Harich to expect the West, by plebiscite as it were, to become such an economy .... One day – for instance following an economic and ecological collapse of the industrial system – the call for Babouvist distributive justice is much more likely to constitute the key ideological justification for the ultimate, the global central power. The only heavy industry that would then be necessary – arms production ... – could also be justified on this basis and the eternal survival of the last global parasites would also have a secure theoretical basis. After all, this would result in permanent global civil war – or at least permanent deception, permanent fraud, permanent preferential treatment of those who are more equal than the Babouvist equals. This model ... takes both a moral and anthropological approach. Using an ecological pretext to demand unlimited central power sidelines the most important anthropological and ecological objections to central authorities' forms of production and organisation. ... Irrespective of this, it is highly unlikely that the implementation of this model will be possible.[303]

While Amery found Harich's concept thought-provoking, he did not believe his utopian vision was anything to be aspired to. In fact, in light of the potential dangers, which Harich either failed to see or was not willing to consider, Amery believed it should be rejected outright. In this context, Amery rightly points to the authoritarian traits that Harich and Gehlen share.

Lastly, Ralf Bambach saw the associated view of humanity as a possible means of understanding Harich's motivation: 'W. Harich's ... recommended recourse to Babouvist ideas of regulation, which is based on a belief in the fragile nature of the human ecosphere, once again manifests the – euphemistically expressed – authoritarian socialists' fear of the purported deficit of communicative rationality'.[304]

The examples quoted demonstrate just how varied the response to *Communism without Growth?* was, ranging from outright rejection of an ostensibly eco-Stalinist text to an intensive discussion of the contradictions inherent in growth in industrial society, contradictions that Harich analysed so precisely. At that time, the articles and reviews made barely any reference at all to the book's utopian content.

---

303   Amery 1985, p. 336 ff.
304   Bambach 1991, p. 4.

CHAPTER 3

Rudolf Bahro's *The Alternative in Eastern Europe*

1   Bahro's Life: Exploring the Realms of the Possible

Rudolf Bahro, who was born on 18 November 1935 in Bad Finsberg, a Lower Silesian spa town, came from humble beginnings. He lost his mother and both siblings while fleeing Silesia, and after the end of World War II, grew up with his father in a province of Brandenburg. As early as 1954, after a two-year application period that was standard at the time, Bahro's political convictions led him to join the Socialist Unity Party (SED).[1] In the same year, he embarked on a philosophy degree at Humboldt University,[2] graduating five years later, after completing his dissertation on Johannes R. Becher. As a student, in 1956/57, Bahro was witness to the political quarrels among the Marxist intellectuals at the university. Later he described his own involvement as having been half-hearted: 'Towards the end of the 1950s, I was … involved in the mutual interrogation that took place at the Philosophical Institute at Humboldt University. At the time, I didn't clearly express my unwavering support for Robert Havemann, hiding behind trivial political differences of opinion'.[3]

Nevertheless, Bahro's critical involvement was enough to make him a subject of observation for the state police for a time, an operation that was soon discontinued due to its insignificance, however.[4] A year after Bahro's graduation, the Volk und Welt publishing house, which focused on modern poetry by young writers, printed a short volume of (largely) political poems by Bahro as part of its *Antwortet uns*[5] (Answer us) series. In his poetry, Bahro impassionedly invoked the development of communism in the German Democratic Republic

---

1   Bahro spoke about his motivation in an interview for the *Spiegel* in 1995: 'I was 16 when I decided to support the party. I was won over by a teacher in my secondary school, who went on to become the headmaster of the school. It was his sincerity and uprightness that convinced me' (Bahro 2007c, p. 501).
2   In the same year Harich's position at Humboldt University came to an end.
3   Bahro 1990, p. 554f. Elsewhere, he reported having only noticed Harich's arrest in passing when he was a student and not having fully comprehended the gravity of it. See Grimm 2003, p. 267.
4   See Herzberg and Seifert 2005, p. 40ff. *Rudolf Bahro. Glaube an das Veränderbare* (Rudolf Bahro. Faith in the possibility of change) by Guntolf Herzberg and Kurt Seifert is the most extensive and detailed Bahro biography written to date.
5   For more information on the history of this series, see Henze 2012. Also see Amberger 2012a.

(GDR). In one of his poems, he deals with the relationship between the intelligentsia and the workers, calling upon his fellow students to adopt the role of the revolutionary vanguard:

> TO THE STUDENTS OF MY UNIVERSITY
> [...]
> How do you want to prove yourself later?
>   As a teacher? Ah, so you want to be a doctor ...
> So what? I want: for doctors, too, to fly the flag of the proletariat!
> [...]
> Marx is with us. Resurrected in us, Lenin's breath casts the serenity of
>   quiet dreamers into chaos: Young thinkers – let us go to the class
>   front![6]

The poem illustrates Bahro's fierce loyalty to the SED and the GDR at the time. It is therefore unsurprising that, after graduating, he became an active agitator for the collectivisation of agriculture in Oderbruch, where he also married his first wife Gundula Lembke.[7] Shortly after this, Bahro took on a post as editor of the Greifswald University party newspaper and for a while became an unofficial collaborator for the Ministry for State Security (Stasi). In 1962 he returned to Berlin where he worked as a staff member and personal advisor to the Chairman of the Governing Board of the East German Science Union.[8] Until then Bahro had been a loyal, if partially critical member of the SED. Subsequently, according to Guntolf Herzberg,[9] Bahro gradually started to loosen his ties to the party line.[10] In 1995, Bahro himself stated:

---

6   Bahro 1960, p. 11.
7   See Herzberg and Seifert 2005, p. 54 ff. This was not to be Bahro's only marriage, not to mention extramarital affairs. He also fathered a number of children. For more on this, see the chapter entitled 'Glück und Unglück: Rudolf Bahro und die Frauen' (Happiness and unhappiness: Rudolf Bahro and his women) in: Herzberg and Seifert 2005, pp. 545–62.
8   See Herzberg and Seifert 2005, p. 70 ff.
9   Bahro and Guntolf Herzberg, who later became his biographer, had known each other since 1976. See Herzberg 1988, p. 69. 'Herzberg was also involved in revising Bahro's work. He was monitored by the Stasi as part of an aptly codenamed operation: *Korrektor* (*copy-editor*). In the process of this operation, the Stasi discovered a total of 95 of Herzberg's contacts. Having been banned from working as a philosopher and faced with a lack of prospects in the GDR, in 1983, he had no choice but to apply for an exit visa. In spring 1985, Herzberg and his family left the GDR' (Eisenfeld and Eisenfeld 1999, p. 106). Herzberg described the situation in his own words: 'The only real harm the Stasi did to me was when they deliberately spread information about me being on their staff, which drove a wedge of suspicion between ... Bahro and I' (Herzberg 1988, p. 77).
10 See Herzberg and Seifert 2005, p. 76.

> For me, the turning point was the 15th anniversary of the GDR in 1964. I passed by the bleachers with the parade in the morning of 7 October, where I read the slogan: 'What is made by the hands of the people, belongs to the people'. And that same afternoon, it suddenly clicked. In that moment, I knew they didn't want to go any further, all they wanted to do, forever and a day, was to increase their power and strengthen the role of the party.[11]

And yet, Bahro gave the impression of being an opportunist, becoming deputy editor-in-chief of the student newspaper *Forum* in 1965 where he headed the culture section. In the same year, the 11th Plenum of the Central Committee, dubbed the 'clear-cutting plenary', took place. This symbolised the end of the more relaxed cultural policy that had been pursued since the wall was built in 1961 and brought in its wake the prohibition of innumerable films and books with content that highlighted the political, cultural and social contradictions in the GDR.[12] In his role as cultural editor, Bahro was directly impacted by the restrictive implications of this watershed.

Refusing to accept this new 'ice age', Bahro wrote articles that did not exactly find favour everywhere.[13] Indeed, his rebellious behaviour caused a stir when Bahro 'in the editor-in-chief's absence, approved the printing of Volker Braun's play *Kipper Paul Bauch*, which was opposed by various members of influential circles'.[14] He lost his position at *Forum* and faced disciplinary action: From May 1967 Bahro worked as a research assistant for sociological issues at the engineering firm VVB *Gummi und Asbest* in Berlin-Weißensee. The position was actually intended as a demotion, but in reality provided Bahro with empirical insights into the relations of production of 'actually existing socialism'. The disciplinary measure enabled Bahro to gather the knowledge which formed the basis of the social analysis part of *The Alternative in Eastern Europe* (henceforth: *The Alternative*). The backwater where Bahro had been placed proved to be a stroke of luck in another respect. He was able to conduct research there and work on his theories undisturbed and without arousing suspicion.[15]

---

11   Bahro 2007c, p. 501.
12   Among the works affected by this were Frank Beyer's Film *Spur der Steine* (*Trace of Stones*) and Werner Bräunig's book *Rummelplatz*. For more on this, see Agde 2000; Mittenzwei 2003, p. 215 ff.; Ruben 2005, p. 40.
13   See Herzberg and Seifert 2005, p. 80.
14   Herzberg and Seifert 2005, p. 84.
15   See Herzberg and Seifert 2005, p. 88 ff.

This isolation was not something Bahro had chosen and initially he continued to try and voice his opinions.[16] However, he soon changed his strategy and withdrew. According to Bahro, the events which unfolded in Czechoslovakia in 1968 played a pivotal role here. Like other critics of the SED's policy, he had also pinned his hopes on an emancipatory movement in Germany's south-eastern neighbour.[17] The Czechoslovakian reform communists were endeavouring to democratise their country. They wanted to expand actually existing socialism to include civil liberties and elements of the market economy and, according to Stefan Wolle, they drew on 'more of a traditional social democratic way of thinking'[18] to do so. Bahro had such high hopes, but these were dashed by the suppression of the Prague Spring by the 'socialist brother states'. This destroyed not only Bahro's hopes of an emancipatory movement but also every illusion he had that the actually existing socialist system could change. To use Bahro's own words, 'the incursion ... finally opened my eyes'.[19] The crackdown on the Prague Spring shaped his thinking and his actions ultimately motivated him to write *The Alternative*. Some of the ideas that came out of 1968 Czechoslovakia were also incorporated into the book.[20]

Between 1967 and 1969, Bahro wrote several texts, which were published in West Germany in 1979 in a volume entitled ... *die nicht mit den Wölfen heulen* (They who don't howl with the wolves ...). The book, which appeared shortly after *The Alternative* and was printed by the same publishing house, provides us with insights into Bahro's personality. Among other things, it includes a music theory essay on the revolutionary impetus of Ludwig van Beethoven. Bahro wrote the piece at the point in his life when he himself had made a final break with the actually existing socialist system. Against this background, what he subjectively perceived to be his political watershed appears to have influenced his view of the classical composer. For instance, regarding Beethoven's disappointment over the increasing reactionary tendencies after the 1815 Congress of Vienna, Bahro comments:

> And this raises the crucial question of *what* a person should do with their disappointment. Whether they should also let go of their ideals as a result of their lost illusions and betray a revolutionary subjectivism that after

---

16 For instance, in early 1968, Bahro wrote a letter to Walter Ulbricht describing problems in the production process. He never received a response to the letter. See Bahro 2007a, p. 81.
17 See Land and Possekel 1998, p. 26.
18 Hertle and Wolle 2004, p. 139.
19 Bahro 2007c, p. 501.
20 See Herzberg and Seifert 2005, p. 102.

all remained in alliance with the great laws in place of the romantic one ... Whether, under the Hegelian pretext of aspiring to a gradual improvement of the status quo, they strip this ideal down to 'only' the absolute, i.e. utopian moments (without which it is not 'ideal'), thus in reality scarcely declaring it a utopia ... Or whether they unwaveringly inquire about the new conditions of the struggle and ready themselves for the next historic hour.[21]

This is a blueprint of what drove Bahro himself, and also provides an early explanation as to why he opted for utopia as a means to express his motivation. At this early juncture, he had already said that without utopianism, revolutionary impetus would lose its ideal nature, making the goal completely unachievable, and that a revolutionary process without utopianism would inevitably ossify. This reminds us of Bloch's *Principle of Hope*, an impression that is reinforced by another statement Bahro made about utopia that shows that he saw it as a process and not an end state: 'But humanity will not stop forming and deploying its vanguard for as long as the absolute, yet rational, visions that shone out of the climactic moments of the great revolutions are not achieved in their entirety (and we know this will never happen). Once the current status of the existing system has firmly taken root, the most passionate and the most impatient will once again break away and, in their thoughts and their emotions, begin to strive for the next level'.[22]

At the same time, Bahro makes another defiant statement, which appears to be directed at the opponents of the Prague Spring: 'But often even the ahistorical memory of the origins of a movement is a threat to its usurpers and traitors, and a source of strength to its heirs'.[23] Here, Bahro already sets out his strategy: He wanted to confront the 'traitors' he identified in the upper echelons of the Politburos of the different state parties, using original Marxist works.[24] Thus, just as the medieval heretics confronted the autocratic church dignitaries with biblical quotes, Bahro was seeking to compare actually exiting socialism with Marxist classics and use the result against the ruling classes of his time. He himself later stated that *The Alternative* was 'designed to be a venomous response to the tanks'.[25]

---

21   Bahro 1979, p. 11 f.
22   Bahro 1979, p. 64.
23   Bahro 1979, p. 65 f.
24   Critical GDR intellectuals had been making this connection with the (purportedly) 'original' Marx and the works of Lenin, Luxemburg and other Marxist classics since the 1950s. This approach continued to be used into the autumn of 1989, the year of the Peaceful Revolution.
25   Bahro 2007a, p. 86. Here, he was referring to the tanks that rolled into Prague in 1968.

In order to be able to continue his work unhindered and avoid attracting unnecessary attention for his rebellious behaviour, thus endangering his conspiratorial work, Bahro retained his membership of the SED. Officially applying to submit his dissertation also enabled him to continue working in secrecy, as it meant he did not arouse any suspicion when conducting research.[26] In his thesis, published in West Germany in 1980 under the title *Plädoyer für eine schöpferische Initiative* (A plea for creative initiative), Bahro presented suggestions for improvement when it came to the potential of young cadres in GDR enterprises. Included in Bahro's sociological study was an extensive appendix of interviews he had conducted. He submitted his thesis in 1975. Since the Stasi were already monitoring him, and were aware of the incendiary nature of the text, they began to 'take steps to prevent Bahro from defending his thesis'.[27] Ultimately, it was ensured that his work was definitively rejected, despite that fact that the original advisor awarded Bahro the distinction 'cum laude' for it.[28] Bahro went on the offensive, sending his thesis to the East Berlin publishing house Dietz-Verlag asking that they publish it, a request they declined, however.[29] Since Bahro's academic career in the GDR had been brought to a conclusive end, he went on to position *The Alternative*.

A detailed description of the origins of this book will be provided later. At this juncture a brief outline will suffice. All in all, Bahro spent almost nine years working on his oeuvre. The manuscript was already brought to the attention of the Stasi in 1974.[30] Bahro was aware of the danger and adjusted his strategy accordingly. This included establishing contact with the *Spiegel* and giving them an interview in 1977, which, ultimately, provided the grounds for

---

26 See Herzberg and Seifert 2005, p. 115 ff.
27 Wording from a Stasi interim report from 10 July 1975. BStU, MfS, HA XX, no. 2065, p. 8.
28 See Herzberg and Seifert 2005, p. 122 ff. Bahro submitted this thesis as part of his doctoral degree, which he completed in 1980 under thesis adviser Oskar Negt at the University of Hanover. See Herzberg and Seifert 2005, p. 128.
29 See Herzberg and Seifert 2005, p. 131. In 1976, a few self-printed copies of what would later become *The Alternative* were also circulated under the title *Berlin, Hauptstadt der DDR* (Berlin, the capital of the GDR). See Bahro 1977b, p. 90.
30 The Stasi had been aware since September 1974 'that Rudolf Bahro had prepared a theoretical work with subversive content ... under the title: *Zur Kritik des real existierenden Sozialismus* [A critique of actually existing socialism]'. This is the reason why Bahro had been subject to investigation in the VAO *Konzeption* since November 1974 'on reasonable grounds of suspicion of "incitement against the state" in accordance with section 106 of the StGB [German Criminal Code]'. In February 1975, the Stasi then deployed the unofficial collaborator 'Rolf Anderson' to acquaint himself with Bahro. See BStU, MfS, HA XX, no. 2065, p. 9 f.

his imprisonment.[31] In his biography on Bahro, Herzberg stated that, all told, the Stasi procrastinated for far too long and he provided a possible explanation for this:

> On 9 November [1976 – author's addition] HA XX/OG drew up ... an 'action plan to open investigation proceedings against Bahro that would lead to imprisonment and conclude' the operative procedure *Konzeption*. Had this been implemented quickly, the end result might have been the imprisonment of an unknown 'dissident' and the book would not have been completed, meaning there would have been no copies of the work, the six lectures would not have been held, likewise the *Spiegel* interview – the damage caused by this alone would have been minimal for the GDR. However, the plan also involved unauthorised searches of the homes of Volker Braun and Martin Stade, a request to Stefan Heym to hand over the first manuscript of Bahro's book to the police or Stasi and – should he refuse – a legal search warrant was envisaged. All this would have resulted in more trouble, which was something the GDR leadership could ill afford.[32]

It is important to remember that Biermann had only just been deported and this was followed by an exodus of intellectuals and cultural professionals. These circumstances caused quite a headache for the state and the party, as revealed in a *Spiegel* article that appeared at the time:

> Kurt Hager, member of the Politburo responsible for cultural policy, did propose a gentler approach – but his attempt was in vain. In the end, the so-called security faction around Werner Lamberz, Paul Verner and the editor-in-chief of *Neues Deutschland*, Joachim Herrmann, prevailed .... The grounds the SED gave for Bahro's arrest comprised a very harsh yet utterly improbable allegation: suspected 'intelligence activities'. The party leadership hoped that this perfidious move would have a two-fold effect.

---

31   See Herzberg and Seifert 2005, p. 153 ff. Years later, Bahro himself was self-critical about this course of action: 'My first Enlightenment Intensive was very important to me. One of my most momentous experiences was when, out of the blue, I remembered that on 22 August 1977, when the *Spiegel* announced that *The Alternative* had been published, and that was reported in the news, that I, alone in my apartment, had let out this huge victorious cry. I had completely forgotten about that. I had pushed it to the back of my mind. Until that memory came to me, I had not acknowledged the vainglory and the hunger for power that had been behind my actions ...' (Bahro 1998, p. 103 f.).

32   Herzberg and Seifert 2005, p. 168.

Firstly, the aim was to suppress any discussion of theories that were so inflammatory for the regime – something that, if the bureaucrats in the Politburo were to portray Bahro as an ideological dissident or counter-revolutionary, would have been virtually unavoidable anyway. Secondly, by branding all critics as Western spies, the SED wanted to intimidate any of Bahro's potentially like-minded colleagues in the GDR. At the same time, the intention was to make it difficult for Eurocommunist parties in France and Italy to show solidarity with Bahro and his critique of Eastern Bloc communism.[33]

Bahro's plan to beat the system at its own game worked. Through their actions, the SED (and consequently the Stasi) provided the tangible evidence for Bahro's theories. *The Alternative* is composed of three parts. In Part One, Bahro describes the development of actually existing socialism. In Part Two, he analyses the anatomy of the actually existing socialist system and, lastly, in Part Three, he describes a communist alternative and outlines a strategy for its implementation. Commenting on the book, Herzberg writes:

> Strictly speaking, in terms of its objective, *The Alternative* is a daring, carefully engineered construction of communism and the most logical publisher would certainly have been the East Berlin Dietz-Verlag. The SED Politburo, however, wasn't keen on the book's factual foundation.[34]

Since the actual content of *The Alternative* did not provide sufficient legal grounds for arrest, Bahro was detained on the basis of Paragraph 100 of the German Criminal Code, which referred to 'subversive associations' – a very elastic concept.[35] The trial that followed was in the end nothing more than a farce. Bahro was accused of intelligence activities and the disclosure of secrets and was sentenced to eight years in prison.[36] Despite fierce protests from various countries in the West, the unpopular dissident was imprisoned at 'Bautzen II' political prison.[37] On the thirtieth anniversary of the GDR, thousands of prisoners were given amnesty, among them Rudolf Bahro – on the condition that he leave the GDR immediately. In so doing, the SED leadership planned to rid

---

33   'Geistige Leere', in: *Spiegel*, no. 36/1977, p. 34.
34   Herzberg and Seifert 2005, p. 189.
35   See Herzberg and Seifert 2005, p. 193.
36   See Herzberg and Seifert 2005, p. 244 ff.
37   See Herzberg and Seifert 2005, p. 282.

itself of its irksome critic. Bahro accepted the offer and left the GDR for West Germany on 17 October 1979.[38] In hindsight, he referred to his decision as having been too self-serving:

> In 1979, I left the GDR without actually having to. I had good reasons for doing so but they were not entirely unselfish. Ultimately, I myself was not even aware of some of my own motives.[39]

Bahro's life after his release from prison is of only marginal relevance to any analysis of *The Alternative*. That said, it is important to at least touch on this period as the ecological and post-materialist dimension of Bahro's ideas and actions did not reach maturity until he had moved to West Germany. An examination of this period also provides us with insights into the eco-utopian character of *The Alternative*.

Shortly after arriving in the Federal Republic, Bahro became involved in the green movement, seeing this milieu as providing him with an opportunity to play his part.[40] He was heavily involved in the beginnings of the Green Party and is one of its most prominent founders. Bahro was primarily concerned with further developing his ideas and seeing them come to fruition on the basis of ecological considerations. He hoped to be able to unite the green and socialist movements in order to reconcile Marxism with ecological concerns.[41] This was a new start for Bahro and he certainly had no intention of playing the part of the East German dissident.[42] He refused to take a public stand on issues and problems relating to the GDR. For Bahro there was no going back. On the contrary, in fact, he sought to make West Germany his new home, while, at the same time, making sure he did not forget the GDR:

---

38 See Herzberg and Seifert 2005, p. 314 ff.
39 Bahro 1990, p. 555. Immediately after leaving for the West, he expressed a different view in an interview for the *Spiegel*. During the interview, Bahro reported that his emigration made the oppositional activities of his supporters easier, and that *one* Havemann was enough when it came to criticising the system. See Bahro 2007d, p. 400 ff.
40 He did not, however, find himself drawn to the West German left: 'In the years after leaving the GDR, Bahro emphasises a universal understanding of the world in which the communist approach was only one part of a broader view' (Ferst 2005, p. 5). 'When Bahro ... arrived in the West, he struggled to find a single person on the left who sympathised with such ideas. As a result, he become involved with the environmental groups, which ultimately led to the emergence of the Greens' (Hermand 1991, p. 146).
41 See Herzberg and Seifert 2005, p. 329 ff., Bahro 2007d, p. 413.
42 See Bahro 1980a, p. 7.

Rudolf Bahro was keen to feel totally at home and so jumped headfirst into life in the Federal Republic. It can be assumed that this was his way of also staying very close to the GDR; he didn't want to cut ties, he wanted reconciliation. He would probably prefer to be known as a pan-German. This was possibly the most striking thing about him.[43]

In West Germany, Bahro wanted to consolidate the left and the Greens under one umbrella, at the same time remaining open to environmentally minded conservatives.[44]

For Bahro, key milestones in this process were the two socialist conferences (in Kassel in May 1980 and in Marburg in February 1981) at which his desire to break with the left became apparent. With ecology becoming increasingly important to him, Bahro was intent on getting out of the leftist political milieu. For him, it was about two ideological breaks: the first with the bloc mentality of the East-West conflict and the second with the industrial system – while those on the left he saw as allies remained stuck in Marxism.[45]

Subsequently, spiritual and religious elements played a role in Bahro's thinking, which also meant a change in the agents of transformation: 'In the process, the concept of the *Invisible Church* emerged as a philosophical and political formula as early as November 1979, which was to replace his earlier vision of a *League of Communists* as actors of change'.[46]

On this subject, Reinhard Spittler writes: 'The years from 1979 to 1983 can probably be regarded his most productive because this was when he succeeded in creating the strongest and most fundamental theoretical link between his thoughts on emancipatory communism and his theological ideas. Everything that came after 1983 simply involved fleshing out, clarifying and reinforcing what he had already developed'.[47]

---

43 Hofmann 1980. The SED leadership, however, did not trust Bahro's word, and continued to try and monitor him while he was in the West. See Knabe 2001, p. 192.
44 'Once he arrived in West Germany, Bahro turned to the Greens. As is already evident in *The Alternative*, Carl Amery introduced Bahro as "a covert member of the Greens". Bahro was interested in the entire alliance, from Dutschke to Gruhl, which crossed all the existing socio-political frontiers at the time. He believed that such a broad alliance was the only way to tackle the ecological crisis from a political perspective' (Ferst 2005, p. 38).
45 Herzberg 2007, p. 11.
46 Herzberg 2007, p. 12.
47 Spittler 2007, p. 350 f.

It was during this period that Bahro wrote his book *Elemente einer neuen Politik. Zum Verhältnis von Ökologie und Sozialismus* (Elements of a new policy. The relationship between ecology and socialism; later published in English as part of *Socialism and Survival*). And it was here that this thought process became apparent. Bahro believed that Marx's theories could still serve as the basis for a contemporary analysis of capitalism, but were no longer enough to resolve the problems of the day. The environmental crisis at the time could not be tackled at the level of the national state – it was a problem of global dimensions, and as such could only be overcome at the global level.[48] Bahro also urged the leftists among the Greens to take the primacy of the environment seriously. Bahro did not, however, limit his ecological endeavours to theory, but took his search for new paths to many different levels – even seeking to unlock the potential of the esoteric and spiritual realms.

> In the early 1980s, Bahro was especially concerned with the emotional conditions of the individual and social forces that bound people to ways of life and modes of behaviour that, intellectually, had already been recognised as antiquated. He practiced what could be defined as entering into a different and, more importantly, less fear- and resentment-driven consciousness. Bahro increasingly saw experimenting with meditational practices and engaging in the creation of communitarian and subsistence-oriented communities as the junction to, and very embodiment of, social and individual practice that is more future oriented.[49]

In the early to mid-1980s, Bahro gathered first-hand experience of the West German commune movement. In his search for ways to implement his concrete utopian concepts, he ended up on uncertain terrain: his visit to the Indian cult leader Bhagwan in 1983, for instance, attracted fierce criticism.[50] On the one hand, Bahro was actively involved in all manner of things; on the other, he did not fit in everywhere and was constantly coming up against barriers which, in turn, resulted in conflict. He was extremely active in what at the time was a very strong peace movement, was also elected to the Green Party National Council and was keen to connect the grassroots movements with the party to create a strong transformational project, an endeavour that saw him at loggerheads with pragmatists like Joschka Fischer. Bahro was unable to gain acceptance for

---

48   See Bahro 1980a, p. 10.
49   Schubert 2002, p. 504. For a seminal account, also see Schölzel 1998.
50   See Herzberg and Seifert 2005, p. 386 ff.

his ideas and, in 1985, he resigned himself to the situation and left the Green Party.[51] Bahro then began work on his book *Logik der Rettung* (Avoiding Social and Ecological Disaster).

> This work, which was published in 1987 with the subheading *Wer kann die Apokalypse aufhalten? Ein Versuch über die Grundlagen ökologischer Politik* [Who can stop the apocalypse? An essay on the fundamentals of environmental policy] was, at least on the surface, not a huge success, with just a few copies being sold. There were, however, good reasons for this – the main one being that the public could no longer follow him. Bahro demanded no less of people than they make a complete break with the way of life they had pursued so far. He wanted to rebuild society from the ground up, with a 'prince of ecological change' as head of state.[52]

Herzberg reasoned: 'Very few will have finished the book. Bahro's ideas about who and what could stop the apocalypse and how humanity could find salvation in theocracy will have come across as simply too spiritual, too religious, too fanciful'.[53]

In Arnold Schölzel's eyes, Bahro 'shifted the problem of an emancipated society into the realm of esotericism and religious faith, which leaves no scope for argumentation and thus can never represent an alternative to any form of reality'.[54] Joachim Radkau was also critical of Bahro's attempts to gain a foothold in the West. Instead of following the course of *The Alternative*, he lost his way:

> [F]or the rest of his life Bahro's political capital rested on the book: all the more curious, then, that his further thinking was not marked by the same intellectual discipline. ... even sympathetic Greens found his later writings increasingly unreadable. As with so any of his contemporaries on the left, once he threw off the Marxist straitjacket, he lost his intellectual bearings and allowed himself to be carried along by shifting trends.[55]

Bahro's apocalyptic predictions met with very little resonance among the Greens. Radkau noted:

---

51   See Spittler 2007, p. 344.
52   Herzberg 2007, p. 15.
53   Herzberg 2007, p. 20.
54   Schölzel, p. 76.
55   Radkau 2014, p. 192.

Bahro himself could speak like a prophet, as when he declared at the Green meeting in Hamburg in December 1984: 'The race against the apocalypse can be won only if this becomes a great age of faith, a Pentecostal season in which, as far as possible, the living Spirit pours out over everyone'. That was too much for ex-pastor Antje Vollmer, who accurately pointed out that Bahro had forgotten one thing: 'You don't make yourself a prophet, but are made into one when people follow you and trust in what you say'. Indeed! One of the marks of a prophet is his spiritual and human trustworthiness for disciples: something sorely lacking in Bahro, who was self-enamoured to the point of autism ... and when he left prison for the West he displayed a restless need to make up for the lost time – intellectually, spiritually and sexually. Even Petra Kelly, who until then had been intellectually close to him, ran out of patience shortly after the Greens entered the Bundestag (1983), when Bahro, with his horror of any bureaucratization, tried to foil a plan for more efficient running of the party offices. And in late 1983 the minutes of the Green parliamentary group record: 'It was generally held against Rudolf Bahro that he would promote a doomsday mood'. The Green Bundestag group did not offer a suitable sounding board for an apocalyptic prophet. But even people with religious feelers increasingly regarded him as a loose cannon. ... With all his eccentricity, he belonged to a type of the age, more often found in the lower ranks of the eco-scene than at the top: a man who, in his own eyes, was 'searching' for something. In the eyes of the critical observer, however, he latched indiscriminately onto contradictory spiritual trends – from cool Japanese Zen meditation to the sweat lodges of Indian shamans.[56]

And Evelyn Finger wrote in an article for *Die Zeit* on 10 November 2011:

> Bahro was in prison for a year before he was able to leave for West Germany. His mistake then was to start criticising the system again once he got there. He warned of a crisis of capitalism and developed a programme against the 'logic of self-destruction'. From then on he was perceived as a dangerous mad man in the West, too.[57]

Bahro marginalised himself and the public ultimately lost interest in him. A contemporary, Marko Ferst, describes how Bahro positioned himself in relation to society:

---

56 Radkau 2014, pp. 192–93.
57 Finger 2011, p. 27.

Rudolf Bahro once said publicly that he was not a dissident, that it was not him that deviated from society. With his critique of the ossified political circumstances in the GDR, of the dictatorship of the Politburo as a disastrously excessive bureaucratic entity, Bahro could count on the support of the majority of GDR citizens. In the GDR he really wasn't a dissenter or a dissident. ... But his dissidence does begin to show its face even in the GDR, at the point in *The Alternative* where he discusses whether our social metabolism is compatible with the preservation of nature, whether industrialism has not, in fact, already exceeded a beneficial degree in many countries. ... He only really becomes a dissident when he publishes his second magnum opus *Avoiding Social and Ecological Disaster*. Here, his position does not diverge from East and West German society on every point but the essence of his political and spiritual message certainly does.[58]

The process of socio-political change that the GDR underwent in 1989 provided Bahro with a way out of his isolation. He immediately turned his attention to events in the GDR and the public took notice of him again. He wanted to go back to the GDR to warn the population against adopting the Western lifestyle and saw the revolutionary situation there as an opportunity to embark on a new path of ecological revolution.[59] Convinced by his own ideals, he soon returned to the GDR where, in early December, he took the floor at the Extraordinary Party Congress of the SED. Here, he attempted to present economic policy proposals to those of his comrades present at the congress, all of whom were in an extremely agitated state due to the revolutionary events. On top of the fact that some of the SED cadres saw Bahro as a provocative character anyway, the ideas he postulated at the congress could not have been more misplaced. He called for the deindustrialisation of agriculture, for instance, and criticised the growth mindset of GDR premier Hans Modrow.[60] In his 30-minute speech, he warned that the market economy and industrial society could not overcome the ecological crisis, and the only solution was to return to an equilibrium between humanity and nature.[61] This is why he also spoke out against environmental protection under capitalist relations of production, which he claimed harboured a dangerous premise: 'The so-called environmental protec-

---

58   Ferst 2005, p. 33.
59   See Herzberg and Seifert 2005, p. 450.
60   See Herzberg and Seifert 2005, p. 457 ff.
61   See Bahro 2007e, p. 177. On this, also see Schubert 2002, p. 504 f.

tion that goes hand in hand with industrial expansion does well to disguise this dangerous model'.[62] Bahro advised the SED against adopting the principles of Western capitalism in the GDR. His speech went down like a lead balloon, eliciting statements of disapproval, which, in retrospect, former member of the SED Politburo Klaus Höpcke found a shameful state of affairs: 'Today, the PDS [Party of Democratic Socialism] would do well to learn lessons from the Bahro episode at the [SED] party congress 15 years ago'.[63]

Bahro urged delegates at the Extraordinary Party Congress to be self-critical rather than to pass the buck for the failure of the GDR to scapegoats such as the old Politburo or Erich Honecker.[64] Bahro believed that apportioning blame in this way only told half the story. Later, he went as far as to offer to testify as a witness for the defence in the trial against Honecker – despite the fact that Honecker had demanded Bahro receive a ten-year prison sentence.[65] For Bahro this was a question of identity: his view of the GDR had, in many respects, changed dramatically since 1977, but, like Harich, he did not want to propagate the negative image of the GDR in the period following the Peaceful Revolution, let alone reinforce it.[66] He also emphasised this in an interview with the *Spiegel* in 1995:

> I was of the opinion that it was absolute nonsense to write off the entire GDR as an illegitimate state. I spent decades investing all my positive energy here, I have nothing to hide. Nor can I deny my own contribution to the repression that took place here. That's just how things were in those days, all in good faith, but that still doesn't mean it was right of course. SPIEGEL: So far, the GDR elite has stubbornly refused to acknowledge the role it played in the failure of socialism. The majority are taking refuge in silence. BAHRO: Indeed there is denial here. I think this comes from feelings of guilt. This is wrong. SPIEGEL: What would be the right thing to do then? BAHRO: I think the key factor is the PDS, because they do in a sense control the attitude towards the GDR. But the way

---

62 See Bahro 2007e, p. 182.
63 Höpcke 2008, p. 161.
64 See Bahro 2007e, p. 172.
65 Bahro reported having made an offer to Honecker's lawyers to testify as a witness for the defence in the trial against their client. Erich Honecker wrote a letter of thanks to Bahro for his offer, to which Bahro responded post-haste to ask of Honecker that he concede that the conflict with Bahro in 1977 was an internal GDR and SED problem, in other words that both parties to the conflict wanted the same thing and that this was just a difference of opinion. Honecker did not take Bahro up on his offer. See Bahro 1998, p. 82.
66 See Ferst 2005, p. 43.

the PDS does this is something I find downright stupid: small-minded clientelist politics that only looks after the vested interests of the underdog.[67]

Like Harich, Bahro had a detached, albeit not outright dismissive relationship with the SED's successor party. This became clear in his last major work, an essay he wrote for Sahra Wagenknecht, a member of the Communist Platform of the PDS. In this essay he called for there to be a stronger focus on ecology. By now, Bahro saw himself as having been completely liberated from materialism and as having left all political constraints behind him. Thus, in his essay, he declared his allegiance to Nietzsche and expressed his surprise about Harich's hatred of the philosopher.[68] Bahro advised the left to no longer adhere to the bourgeois traditions and values of the French Revolution as these were the cornerstone of modern capitalism and represented the beginnings of imperialism. Now was the time to reconstitute secular and spiritual power.[69] Quoting from Bahro's work, Guntolf Herzberg writes: 'First and foremost, communism is the principle of a comparatively unimportant economy. So, instead of a society of abundance, it embodies the positive antithesis: simple reproduction as a condition of life ..., "letting go so that we may rest lightly upon the Earth" ... "broadening our consciousness is the true task of mankind" ...'

Herzberg concludes: 'And here he built a bridge between "the spiritual realm" and "communism", in a bid to interpret communism "once and for all" as a "practice of grace" – with which he would presumably have left the last communist member of the PDS filled with consternation'.[70]

But this is unlikely to have bothered Bahro: politically and legally rehabilitated, the centre of his life was now the Institute for Social Ecology at Humboldt University of Berlin, an institution that was set up especially for him and at which he held a distinguished professorship.[71] Here he focused on developing alternatives to industrial society. The work of the Institute did not conform to the Western model of academic research and Bahro deliberately pushed back the boundaries, incorporating elements of spiritualism and esotericism in his research.

---

67 Bahro 2007c, p. 504.
68 See Bahro 2007a, p. 148.
69 See Bahro 2007a, p. 157.
70 Herzberg and Seifert 2005, p. 573.
71 Herzberg and Seifert 2005, p. 503 ff. This institute no longer exists today, having been closed down after Bahro's death.

In view of the global destruction of the environment and the ineffectiveness of political rescue measures, he sees the sole cause as lying in three human traits: greed, the thirst for knowledge, and the desire to produce. Consequently, what is required is the reverse: self-limitation in terms of knowledge and actions. And, to consolidate all this in the consciousness, Bahro has to return to Laozi and religion – an approach which to his mind is entirely logical, but which many members of his unprepared audience (the majority of whom know him only as the author of *The Alternative*) fail to understand.[72]

Besides the Institute for Social Ecology, Bahro was also involved in a second project. Drawing on his first-hand experimental experience of communes in the 1980s, he co-founded *Lebensgut*, a place of 'real-life utopia' in Pommritz, a village in the East German state of Saxony. According to its homepage, this cooperative project started:

> ... when, in 1991, then Minister President of Saxony Prof. Kurt Biedenkopf was invited by the visionary Rudolf Bahro to give a lecture entitled 'An Economic Order for Gaia. Ways Out of the Ecological Crisis' at Humboldt University of Berlin. At the end of the post-talk discussion, they concluded that, especially in East Germany where so many people from every profession were unemployed and suffered from the resulting lack of purpose, the conditions in the village were perfect for experiments on the creation of a society of the future. Biedenkopf signalled his willingness to create the regulatory framework for such a project to be launched. ... Rudolf Bahro's Institute for Social Ecology developed a concept on how a green economy, new sociality and free human development might interact.[73]

Bahro's thinking, his institute and *Lebensgut* together formed their own independent realm, a microcosm in which he, his colleagues and supporters were able to experiment and search for alternatives to the realities of industrial soci-

---

72 Herzberg 2007, p. 198. 'During the lectures he held in Berlin from 1990 he spoke of a great many intentions, but above all, it was the mission he aspired to that became clear – to criticise the prevailing mindset of unbridled production and consumption, to initiate a change in consciousness and to replace the ungodly scientific technical world and its environmentally exploitative behaviour with a vision of a spiritual life in harmony with nature, and indeed with the universe' (Herzberg 2007, p. 319).

73 Lebensgut 2010.

ety. This did not protect him from conflicts with the outside world, however. Probably the most significant of these erupted in the early 1990s when several statements Bahro made in an interview in the *junge Welt* daily provoked impassioned reactions. The interview saw to it that, from that point on, Bahro was branded an eco-fascist by certain camps on the political left. He said: 'What concerns me is the question of how human and especially white Northern civilisation has developed such a self-destructive nature'.[74] Having already referred to 'white Northern civilisation', he then went on to give even more cause for anti-fascist opposition:

> On the whole, as a left-wing party, the Greens are a disappointment to the West German population, and the reason for this is that they do not attend to this national, let's say 'völkisch' element, for want of a better word. In actual fact, there is something in the depths of the Volk that calls for a Green Adolf. And the left is afraid of it, instead of realising that a Green Adolf would be entirely different to the infamous Adolf. It has nothing at all to do with whether it is a man or a woman. It is a question of structure. That is the German element in this green movement. The political left and the extreme 'left-wing left' have never managed to get beyond defence mechanisms and feelings of resentment towards this aspect of reality. They have never accepted it.[75]

In an essay entitled *Horde, Stamm und Staat* (Horde, tribe and state) Bahro expanded on this argument, addressing the issue of Germany and his own sense of 'being German'. The nation-states played an important role for him and he was critical of the (Western) leftists who rejected this idea or even suppressed their own nationality. In this regard, he saw himself as following the tradition of left-wing patriots such as Johannes R. Becher, who aspired to a 'good' Germany, which they juxtaposed with a 'bad', in other words fascist Germany. Here, Bahro drew, as he so often did, on Hölderlin and his concept of German national consciousness.[76] Bahro's stepson Erik Lehnert[77] later spoke

---

74 Bahro 2007b, p. 438.
75 Bahro 2007b, p. 440.
76 See Bahro 1998, p. 89.
77 Lehnert himself faced similar accusations. In July 2009, the left-leaning magazine *Konkret* printed an article accusing Lehnert of being 'the head of a right-wing radical ultranationalist *Institute for State Policy* (*Institut für Staatspolitik*, IfS). The IfS is seen as the most important "training facility" of the New Right scene, operating in the same grey area between conservatism and neofascism where the weekly *Junge Freiheit* and the student magazine *Blaue Narzisse* also propagate the reemergence of the Right' (Burschel 2009).

in his defence, claiming that Bahro had not intended his comments in the way they had been received and that he felt misunderstood and unfairly treated by the allegations and misinterpretations of his words.[78]

Bahro aspired to a cross-front approach for the benefit of the environment and used this to appeal to the political right[79] whose interest in green issues he saw as an area of common ground. Lehnert justified his stepfather's approach as follows:

> The key question here is whether … Bahro believed in inner-worldly salvation. … The claim that Bahro is an eco-fascist has a kernel of truth if you define fascism as a form of political governance based on a holistic concept that is a panacea for all of society's problems: Bahro was a worst-case scenario thinker who did not see the symptoms as the cause. The 'prince of ecological change' and the establishment of an 'upper house' were meant to help mitigate the worst-case scenario, or even prevent it from happening in the first place.[80]

On 5 December 1997, Bahro passed away after a battle with cancer. The eulogy was given by Jochen Kirchhoff, one of his colleagues at the Institute for Social Ecology. Kirchhoff spoke about how important Beethoven's music was to Bahro and used this as an opening to try and describe Bahro's character and elucidate what motivated and drove him:

> For a long time, Beethoven was like some kind of guru for him, a much-admired role model and master rolled into one, an all-round human being, if you like. A lesser-known essay about Beethoven that Bahro wrote in 1967/69 showed the true Bahro. And the picture of Beethoven as a musician and as a person that Bahro painted with such passionate brushstrokes, can easily be interpreted as an – albeit idealistically depicted – self-portrait. Rudolf Bahro wanted to be just like Beethoven ….[81]

---

78 See Lehnert 2007, p. 376.
79 See Lehnert 2007, p. 381.
80 Lehnert 2007, p. 390 f. The Bahro quotes Lehnert used were taken from his *Avoiding Social and Ecological Disaster*.
81 Kirchhoff 1998, p. 269.

2   The Origins of *The Alternative*

2.1   *Frustration*

To glean additional insight into Bahro's utopian concept and the utopian intentions of his book, the following section will summarise the origins of his magnum opus.

The Alternative in Eastern Europe was published in 1977 in West Germany. It was a long journey, one which, as already mentioned, began in the 1960s. The suppression of the Prague Spring meant that many critical, educated young people lost hope in a liberalisation of actually existing socialism. Bahro, too, was disappointed – and furious. He plotted revenge, but initially had no idea how to carry out his plan other than by means of blind, aimless, ineffective actionism. Ultimately, he resorted to writing a book which he hoped would cause problems for the SED leadership. Later, he revealed in an interview that the writing process had gradually quelled his anger:

> I deliberately took a two-pronged approach, in other words, after 1968, I was determined to take some form of action against them. Although, in the years immediately following '68, I was angrier than I had been after writing the first chapters of *The Alternative*. And, at that point, I was angrier than when I had completed the final proof. The writing process liberated me. My reaction to this incursion was one of genuine hatred.[82]

To be able to work on *The Alternative* undisturbed, Bahro chose to lead a double life. In private, he was writing his subversive book, but professionally and publicly his behaviour was inconspicuous. When Bahro made the decision to write the book, Ulbricht was still head of state in East Germany, soon to be replaced by Honecker. By that time, however, Bahro had long stopped pinning his hopes on a change in leadership and government. For him it was not the individuals but rather the structures that were crucial – and these largely remained unchanged under Honecker. Bahro opposed the existing system (although he was not against the GDR and socialism in general),[83] which is why he analysed

---

82   Grimm 2003, p. 274. If the conversation log by unofficial collaborator 'Rolf Anderson' in March 1975 is accurate, then Bahro's strategy had been more than successful. Having vented his anger through his writing, Bahro had come to terms with the incursion. 'Rolf Anderson' summed up Bahro's words: 'He said that at the time he had opposed the incursion of troops from the socialist countries but, over the years, (he) had had a change of heart and had come to the conclusion that this occupation had actually been inevitable and in fact had secured peace in Europe' (BStU, MfS, HA XX/9, no. 879, p. 166).

83   In an interview given in 1995, he said looking back that in all of his critical analyses of the SED, his motive had always been to improve socialism. See Grimm 2003, p. 266.

it in painstaking detail. At the same time, however, he completely conformed in order to be able to write his book.

He identified and explicitly pointed out contradictions between what the founders of Marxism had written and the development of actually existing socialism. Bahro saw the bureaucratic apparatus that pervaded the entire country and he observed the inequalities, the deeper causes of which he sought to identify, while: '… in 1972, the SED [declared] that the GDR was a "new type of class society", in which the "classes and social strata co-existed, bound together in friendship, led by the working class", meaning the antagonistic contradictions had been eliminated. The SED thus abandoned the concept of a "socialist human community" proclaimed by Ulbricht, at the same time glossing over the actually existing contradictions and social stratifications, the conflicts between the working population and the ruling elites'.[84]

In the GDR, a new upper class had taken shape, socialist elites who enjoyed privileges and made sure the system continued to function. 'The majority of these privileged functionaries were former workers or white-collar employees … but, to be granted a position, what tended to be more important than qualifications was loyalty to the party leadership; as a result, the frequently observed contradiction between expertise and political narrow-mindedness created new problems'.[85]

Bahro saw this crippling structure of the apparatus as the central problem of 'actually existing socialism'[86] and sought to tackle this issue head on with *The Alternative*.

2.2 *Mentors and Companions*

Bahro worked on his book for almost nine years, adopting five areas of thematic focus from his own independent studies: 1) the Russian Revolution and the

---

84 Weber 1991, p. 140 f.
85 Weber 1991, p. 65.
86 In short, the origins and meaning behind this term are as follows: 'The term "real socialism" (or actually existing socialism) was introduced at the International Conference of the Central Committee of the SED on the 125th anniversary of the publication of the *Manifesto of the Communist Party* in Berlin in March 1973. "Actually existing" socialism was a synonym for "true" socialism. It represented a deliberate departure from other forms and made it possible to conceal damage to the system and to dilute contradictions. The Conference wrote off "several Marxisms" and "models of socialism" as a form of revisionism. … The USSR and actually existing socialism remained the benchmarks. The socialist idea was reduced to the legitimation of iron principles – the global historical mission of the working class, the property question, the dictatorship of the proletariat and the role of the communist party' (Klein, Otto and Grieder 1996, p. 401).

history of the Soviet Union, 2) world history and the history of Christianity, 3) psychology and psychoanalysis, 4) theories of the political economy, and, lastly, 5) political literature.[87] 'Bahro studied Isaac Deutscher's biographies of Stalin and Trotsky particularly intensively, describing his reading of these works as his "Trotskyist phase" .... He also maintained an interest in Yugoslavia's self-governing socialism and the Chinese Cultural Revolution ...'.[88]

Despite studying this subversive, undogmatic canon, Bahro was still unable to completely detach himself from the ideological conditioning of his philosophy degree, as Herzberg noted:

> The structural disadvantage of an education of this type stemmed from the dogma that, because Marx and Engels inherited everything from their predecessors, those predecessors became obsolete and irrelevant to the present, and the advances in theoretical thinking ended with Feuerbach (who, according to Engels's dictum, was seen as the 'escape from classical German philosophy'), meaning it could only take place within Marxism and later Leninism. This led to a total negation of philosophy and history that was not rooted in Marxism. Bahro, along with all other students of philosophy, bore this ideological burden .... What Bahro still found appealing, however, was Hegel and the utopian socialists and communists. During the 1970s, while writing *The Alternative*, Bahro read work by so many more authors than he mentions in the book, but, even here, historians play no more than a peripheral role, although his knowledge of the Asiatic mode of production and the associated form of governance referred to as 'oriental despotism', as well as the history of Russia does of course come from historical studies. He was also fascinated by the French Revolution, which (although I cannot provide any evidence of this) he studied, without actually incorporating this knowledge directly into any of his works.[89]

---

87   'He borrowed these works from friends and acquaintances, including Günter Baumgart, Volker Braun, Wolfgang Heise, Harry Goldschmidt, Werner Tzschoppe and Rudi Wetzel, and also got hold of some of the publications from the public library. By 1972, Bahro had essentially finished his literature degree. The extensive copies of excerpts from the books he had borrowed alongside his own books served as a direct basis for his work' (Herzberg and Seifert 2005, p. 137).

88   Herzberg 1998, p. 5.

89   Herzberg 2007, p. 316f. The debate surrounding the reception of Hegel's social and political ideas and the associated evaluation of pre-Marxist German philosophy (particularly idealism) shaped the philosophical discourses in the GDR throughout the 1950s. While Bloch, Harich, Lukács and others interpreted idealism as an important pillar of Marxism,

In his examination of the socioeconomic conditions of actually existing socialism, Bahro drew on the works of Marx, Engels and Lenin, as well as the ideas of Karl August Wittfogel, adopting the latter's concept of the Asiatic mode of production for his analysis of actually existing socialism. Looking back at his sources of inspiration, Bahro writes:

> The use of the term 'Asiatic' to refer to the mode of production used, for instance, by ancient Egyptians, Indians, Chinese, even the Incas stems from Marx's *Foundations of the Critique of Political Economy*. I have Siegfried Wollgast to thank for giving me, at some point in the mid-1960s, the passing hint that this could provide means of understanding the conditions of actually existing socialism. He was probably also the one to point me in the direction of Karl August Wittfogel's *Oriental Despotism*. I did not reveal him as my source ..., because I did not want to burden him with yet another confrontation. Wittfogel had found the experience of the Russian Revolution so traumatic that, when it came to the Asiatic restoration, he had become an unrestrained eulogist of the Western capitalist path.[90]

The concept of the Asiatic mode of production was pivotal for *The Alternative*. Bahro made a connection between the actually existing socialist economy and this explanatory concept, and based on the results, went on to adapt his utopian strategy for overcoming actually existing socialism accordingly. Manfred Hertwig defined the concept as follows: 'In the Asiatic mode of production, referred to by Karl August Wittfogel as "orientalist despotism", the skimming off of the surplus product or exploitation is not typically carried out by a group that owns the means of production but rather by a broad bureaucratic caste of public officials led by a despotic government. ... From an objective perspective, the state bureaucracy was necessary for the organisation of common tasks, but its power acquired a momentum of its own .... thus resulting in a pronounced relationship of servitude between the population and the state, which was transplanted into Russia throughout the two centuries of Mongol rule. Tsardom thus began life as the Golden Horde's tax collector'.[91]

After having sifted through and taken extracts from the majority of his research literature, in 1972, Bahro began to flesh out *The Alternative*. At the same

---

Stalinist hardliners like Kurt Hager regarded idealism as irrelevant. While these debates were taking place, Bahro was a philosophy student at Humboldt University. See Amberger 2013, p. 563f.

90   Bahro 1990, p. 550.
91   Hertwig 1977, p. 1095.

time, he also continued work on his thesis which, although thematically similar to his magnum opus, was of a quite different character in terms of its methodology and purpose and addressed a different target audience, too.

He completed the first draft of *The Alternative* in mid-1973 already, producing seven copies of the book. Shortly afterwards, East Berlin hosted the *World Festival of Youth and Students*. Bahro's intention was to try and get some copies of his text out of the country via foreign visitors attending the festival, an endeavour in which he was unsuccessful, however. He therefore distributed the manuscripts among his friends and acquaintances, asking them to provide him with constructive criticism. If we look at the names of those who read his manuscript (not all of whom Bahro knew personally as the document was also passed along to others), we can conclude that, even before 1977, *The Alternative* had been seen by circles who were critical of the SED. The conspiratorial circle of readers (also including those who read a later version of the manuscript) comprised many of the GDR's most renowned cultural professionals and intellectuals: individuals who, according to the Stasi files, actively contributed to 'the creation or dissemination of Bahro's miserable anti-socialist effort' including scholars Friedrich Behrens and Guntolf Herzberg. Those who were familiar with Bahro's book included the writers Volker Braun, Günter de Bruyn, Stefan Heym and Ulrich Plenzdorf. And those identified by the Stasi as being in possession of one of the manuscripts were Klaus Hilbig (editor-in-chief of the national television network in the GDR), several renowned professors such as Dieter Klein, Harry Maier and Harry Nick, and the film director Konrad Wolf.[92]

In his speech at the Extraordinary Party Congress of the SED in December 1989, Bahro also spoke about *The Alternative*. He used the opportunity to publicly thank those who had helped him with the book, specifically naming:

> *Ursula Beneke*, who was in the employ of the biology library at Humboldt University at the time; in the cellar of the library we made the 70 copies of the book that went on to be the first to appear in the GDR. ... My friends *Werner Busold* and *Werner Naujok* worked with her to distribute the book .... *Rudi Wetzel* ... was my editor for every chapter of the book, from start to finish; he was indispensable, also because it was through his contacts that I was able to find a publisher. My friends *Marianne* and *Dieter Lorf* ... were also by my side for many years. *Fritz Behrens* stored the book at the Bund publishing house of the German Trade Union Confederation, after

---

92 Some of these manuscripts went straight into the hands of the Stasi through a 'voluntary surrender of works of art'. See BStU, MfS, HA XX/9, no. 1747, p. 4 ff. See also Herzberg and Seifert 2005, p. 138 f.

> *Harry Goldschmidt*, a Swiss musicologist living in the GDR, had transported it across the Wall. Harry Goldschmidt ... supported me throughout the ten years it took for me to write the book from 1968 to 1977. As did *Volker Braun* .... The initial impetus, however, came in the mid-1960s from *Walter Besenbruch*, who was like a political father to me. ... And *Werner Tzschoppe* was like an older brother throughout those long years .... In that final year before I left, I often sat with *Guntolf Herzberg*. ... And certainly not to be forgotten, the man who drove me to improve the quality of my concept, especially the rationality of the vision in the final part of the book, which was initially somewhat flimsy, my sceptical teacher of over 20 years: *Wolfgang Heise*. Finally, I want to thank *Gundula Bahro* ... who made sure that a first version of the book got to Switzerland.[93]

Bahro took a meticulous approach to writing *The Alternative*, taking on board objective criticism from those he trusted. This meant that the first manuscript, completed in 1973, was not identical to the final version. On the contrary, in fact: Wolfgang Heise and Werner Tzschoppe had been fiercely critical of the text, which prompted Bahro to substantially revise it.[94] However, this did not happen immediately because, at the same time, he was busy completing his thesis, meaning he only changed individual elements of the book owing to time constraints. Only after submitting his thesis was he able to devote all his energy to revising *The Alternative*, especially rewriting the third part.[95] Heise, however, was not only critical of Bahro; he was also supportive.

> Up until just before the completion of *The Alternative*, we met regularly. Even though he was largely critical of my text. He had read the first version of *The Alternative* and thoroughly criticised it, not from a party perspective, but factually, and he did me a tremendous service in the process. Firstly, after reading the analytical sections, where he had marked a lot

---

93   Bahro 2007e, p. 175 ff.
94   Many years later Bahro felt he still owed a debt of gratitude. In 1993, at a colloquium in honour of the late Wolfgang Heise (who had died in 1987), Bahro said of him: 'When he read my first draft of *The Alternative* in 1973, he advised me not to get it published. That was him wanting to protect me again: He said I would only end up being ground down in the mills of the Cold War. Put it to the back of your shelf. ... Despite the fact that he thought I shouldn't get it published, he then spent hours giving me a detailed criticism of the entire text. ... He found the last part of the book sketchy, and I agreed with him, and went on to rewrite it entirely. That was the most important and direct impetus that I received from Heise' (Bahro 1998, p. 252).
95   See Herzberg and Seifert 2005, p. 140.

of passages, he asked: Who is this Brezhnev, with whom and with whose peers you are in constant discussion? And that was when I knew I had to cut the whole central polemic against his [Brezhnev's] behaviour that angered me so much. Such a step could only benefit the whole endeavour. And, even more importantly, he refused to accept the final part 'A Strategy for a Communist Alternative', saying it was too sparse, too thin. So, I radically revised it. Although many others from the GDR made it quite clear to me even before I came back from the West, telling me: the first two analytical parts, we are with you there, but the conclusion: that's far too optimistic. We simply don't believe that this could really be possible. However, thanks to Wolfgang Heise's critique, in particular, that part was vastly improved.[96]

In late 1976, Bahro found out that the Stasi knew about his plans to publish the book and were acquainted with the manuscript. This meant that he needed to be quick with his revision of the third part. With this in mind, he took leave and attempted to travel to the Harz region in secret to finally finish the book. Since Bahro had not managed to distribute a large number of copies of the book in the GDR and thus achieve the commensurate resonance, he was keen to publish in the Federal Republic instead. With the Stasi already on his heels, this proved to be difficult. In the end, however, he did manage to do so, partly because the SED leadership and the Stasi were unable to agree on a strategy.[97]

Although the state organs were well informed about every step Bahro took, they failed to arrest him before his book was published: 'Despite the sound information they had and the criminal findings, *right up until the last minute*, the Stasi had no clear position on whether or not they should arrest Bahro. Of course the SED leadership had the final say; the Stasi was only able to consider the various options'.[98] As a result, Bahro was able to publish the book in the West virtually unimpeded and it quickly became a bestseller, making him world famous overnight.[99] The SED leadership had backed itself into a corner.

---

96 Grimm 2003, p. 275. See also Spittler 2007, p. 339.
97 See Grimm 2003, p. 280.
98 See Herzberg and Seifert 2005, p. 171.
99 A brief recap of the events that led up to this: 'On 22 August – a Monday, carefully timed to coincide with the day the *Spiegel* comes out – the book's author, who had up till then been anonymous, outed himself .... As planned, the *Spiegel* had published a long article, including significant passages of the book, then in the evening, a pre-prepared self-interview was broadcast on *RIAS II* (Radio in the American Sector). The next day, both the ARD and ZDF put out extended broadcasts that had been recorded in the author's Weißensee apartment a few days before his identity was revealed. *RIAS Berlin* broadcast a six-episode sum-

2.3　His Dissertation

In the early 1970s, Bahro was writing two books at the same time: he was working on *The Alternative* in secret, while officially writing his thesis. He regularly used this latter endeavour as a pretext for applying for sabbaticals and other postgraduate 'perks', which he then used to work on *The Alternative*. The content of the two books was also very similar, meaning that Bahro did not have to work on two entirely different subject matters. Bahro saw it in the same way, as can be gleaned from a report written in March 1975 by an unofficial collaborator who went under the name of 'Rolf Anderson'. According to the report, Bahro said: 'Anybody who can read would also be able to deduce from the current doctoral thesis how he [Bahro – author's addition] envisaged the organisation of a fundamentally new society'.[100] Given the similarity between these two books, it would now be pertinent to briefly turn to the thesis.

The Stasi made sure that Bahro's thesis was rejected, preventing him from receiving his doctorate.[101] In fact, Bahro did not manage to publish his thesis and receive his doctorate until he moved to West Germany where, in 1980, his thesis was published under the title *Plädoyer für eine schöpferische Initiative. Zur Kritik von Arbeitsbedingungen im real existierenden Sozialismus* (A plea for creative initiative. A critique of working conditions in actually existing socialism). In his thesis, Bahro lamented the fact that sociologists in the GDR had, up till that point been focusing predominantly on the working class, while barely any attention had been paid to the situation of the qualified staff working in production. It was this gap he sought to fill with his thesis.[102] The research goal was to identify the reasons behind the demotivation that university graduates showed after having worked in production for just a short time. Bahro concluded that there was a lack of opportunities for personal development

---

mary of *The Alternative* – intended specifically for the GDR population – and, as everyone had expected, the author was arrested. Left-wing West German intellectuals immediately began to declare their solidarity, while those interviewed in the East began to distance themselves. Book sales soon exceeded all expectations (hitting around 300,000 copies), other publishers clamoured to get licenses to translate the book (and succeeded, as it was soon translated into all major European languages as well as Japanese). One of the most renowned Marxists, Ernest Mandel, described *The Alternative* as the most important Marxist book in 30 years – and thus a book written by someone who was until recently a completely unknown Marxist found itself in the international spotlight' (Herzberg 1998, p. 1).

100　BStU, MfS HA XX/9, no. 879, p. 170.
101　See Herzberg and Seifert 2005, p. 121 ff.
102　See Bahro 1980b, p. 15.

and, to address this, he proposed that the production process be tailored to the cadre's individual personal development needs. He argued that the cause of this demotivation dilemma was in fact rooted in training: 'The excellent qualifications promise to deliver opportunities for enjoyment in life, but these promises are ultimately only partially fulfilled. This is the likely explanation as to why we see psychological reactions of disappointment, dejectedness and fatigue emerging particularly frequently among the scientific practitioners in the enterprises'.[103]

Bahro lamented that, although the means of production was state owned, it was not yet adequately democratised. He claimed that this gap could be bridged if democratic progress were to happen from the bottom up, emanating from the workplace, gradually eliminating the traditional division of labour. This would enable the state of development, the creative initiative and consciousness of human beings to grow and advance. And, in Bahro's view, this progressive change in 'developed socialism' would only be possible by eliminating the traditional division of labour.[104] He expresses this belief both in his thesis and in *The Alternative*. Another concept the two books have in common is that of 'surplus consciousness', although he does not elaborate on this as much in his thesis as he does in his magnum opus.[105] Bahro was critical of the praxis: 'Under the pressure of the norms that stimulate the creation of new knowledge within the institutionalised scientific sphere, a very one-sided concept of privileged creativity is cultivated which easily becomes the opposite of the general emancipation of human creativity and exacerbates the psychological impact of the aforementioned dilemma experienced by scientific practitioners. And yet, creativity or the capacity to produce is such a fundamental human capacity that we have to ask ourselves whether, by following anthropological studies, we are even going back far enough.'[106]

---

103 Bahro 1980b, p. 13f.
104 See Bahro 1980b, p. 19ff.
105 Only after submitting his thesis did Bahro delve further into this field of research so that he could finish *The Alternative*. Guntolf Herzberg wrote that Lucien Sève's *Marxist Theory and the Psychology of Personality* had inspired Bahro with regard to the importance of 'the creation of consciousness' when he was rewriting *The Alternative* in 1976/77. Bahro drew on Sève for his concepts of 'superfluous consciousness', the 'surplus product' of 'intellectual production', which is, in turn, divided into 'compensatory' and 'emancipatory' interest. These concepts gave Bahro a tool with which to capture and analyse the role of the subject in his critique of actually existing socialism. See Herzberg and Seifert 2005, p. 141f.
106 Bahro 1980b, p. 34f.

He criticised bureaucratism and the associated traditional division of labour and its hierarchical structure, arguing that this was the main reason that young cadres became demotivated so quickly.

> The essence of *bureaucratism* is that the governing system functions such that it prevents those within the system from duly executing their work, for instance through excessive and damaging administrative management. ... The problem, however, is that, provided individuals remain subsumed by the traditional division of labour, this risk will continue to be an inherent part of large organisations; and it will take more to manage it than simply differentiating between manifestations. Rather, what is needed is far-reaching changes to the social organisation of labour coupled with a better quality development of socialist democracy.[107]

2.4   Bahro and Dutschke

While Bahro was working on his thesis and *The Alternative*, in West Germany, one of the spokespeople of the protests of 1968 was writing his own doctoral thesis. As chance would have it, the two (non-conformist) Marxist philosophers were exploring the same topic and ultimately came to similar conclusions. Like Bahro, Rudi Dutschke also focused on the influence of pre-revolutionary Tsarist Russia on the development of the Soviet Union. Dutschke's thesis, which was on the subject of 'The Difference between the Asiatic and European Path to Socialism', was published as a book entitled *Versuch, Lenin auf die Füße zu stellen* (An attempt to stand Lenin on his feet) in 1974. A year later, Bahro had just finished the first part of *The Alternative* and was preparing to revise it when a copy of Dutschke's book came into his possession. Two years later Bahro reported having intentionally left the first chapter of *The Alternative* unaltered, in order to avoid being influenced by Dutschke's book.[108] Around the same time, Dutschke also came upon Bahro's as yet unpublished manuscript. Later, Dutschke's widow described this event:

> During a visit to East Berlin in 1976, someone handed Rudi a typed manuscript that was being circulated underground. The author was anonymous. Rudi read the manuscript and was surprised. It reminded him so much of his *Versuch, Lenin auf die Füße zu stellen* that he initially thought someone was trying to rile him, thinking it might have come from the

---

107   Bahro 1980b, p. 78.
108   See Bahro 1977b, p. 72, Herzberg and Seifert 2005, p. 140.

Stasi. I asked him why the Stasi would want to publish such a work. But Rudi couldn't come up with a reason. Six months later, Wagenbach publishing house wanted to print the manuscript and asked Rudi to write the preface. Rudi agreed but insisted this be done under a pseudonym because he was still not sure where the work came from. The book project fell victim to internal disputes within the publishing house. Sometime later, in August 1977, Rudi read in the magazine for culture and politics *das da* that the book was to be published by the Europäische Verlagsanstalt publishing house under the title *The Alternative in Eastern Europe*. The name of the author would not be announced until shortly before distribution. His name was Rudolf Bahro, an SED functionary. For the first time we really knew there were critical thinkers within the party and state apparatus. And at last one of them had been brave enough to go public.[109]

Despite his respect for Bahro's achievement, Dutschke did not believe that he had written *The Alternative* without recourse to Dutschke's own insights into the West. He believed parts of book had been plagiarised and still complained in the diaries he wrote in 1978 that Bahro had not named him as a source or at least as an inspiration for the book.[110] Nevertheless, Dutschke campaigned for Bahro to be released from prison. He wrote letters, participated in conferences and in 1978 co-organised a major Bahro congress in West Berlin. He endeavoured to generate as much publicity for the prisoner as he possibly could.[111]

After Bahro's release from prison and his exile to West Germany, the two men met and also attended various events together – although they did not always see eye to eye, as the following episode clearly shows: A panel debate in Düsseldorf on 14 November 1979 saw Bahro, Dutschke, Wolfgang Leonhard and the 83-year-old Karl August Wittfogel all in attendance, with this being the first time the latter had stepped on German soil since 1933. In his presentation, he tore the Soviet Union to pieces, declaring that, even under Brezhnev, it was still

---

109 Dutschke, G. 1998, p. 422 f. Rudi Dutschke was not keen on writing the preface as he wanted to avoid making Bahro's work even more vulnerable to attack from the Stasi than it already was. Dutschke wrote: 'If the book had been covertly published with an introduction written by me, the Stasi would have used the fact that this was something that had come from outside, from others, from me, to sideline it and denounce it, or at least this is my firm belief' (Dutschke, R. 1978, p. 89). Dutschke also provides a detailed account of the events described from his own perspective.
110 See Dutschke, G. 1998, p. 435, Dutschke, R. 2005, p. 295.
111 See Dutschke, G. 1998, p. 438 f.

a 'bloody Mongolian swampland' that was incapable of breaking with Stalinism. Bahro then unexpectedly rejected Wittfogel's line of argument. Dutschke's widow recalls:

> With a friendly smile, Bahro intervened with an undisguised attempt to give the old man a roasting. He claimed Wittfogel's concept was 'a thought that went against the march of history'. He declared that Wittfogel had turned anti-Soviet trauma into anti-socialist hysteria. Rudi listened to Bahro's words in visible horror, and Wittfogel's response was irritation and perplexity: 'I do not see being opposed to the gulag as being hysterical, but I was and I remain a socialist'. Leonhard took the microphone and responded to Bahro: 'But in your book *The Alternative*, your criticism of actually existing socialism was far harsher'. Bahro continued unperturbed: 'The political left in the West could not make a graver error than to portray the Soviet Union as it is today – turning towards the West – as the enemy'. ... But Bahro was not finished there, and he went on to claim that the centrally planned economy of the GDR was at least as efficient as the Federal Republic's social market economy. He substantiated this with statistics from the GDR, the deceptive nature of which he himself had exposed in his book.[112]

This perhaps also tells us something about Bahro's attitude towards Wittfogel: He drew on Wittfogel's theories for *The Alternative* without mentioning him as a source, a step he justified by claiming that he had wanted to protect Siegfried Wollgast. Yet, this would not actually have been necessary, because, at the time, there was already a public debate in the GDR about Wittfogel and the Asiatic mode of production, something which Bahro neglected to mention, however.

---

112 According to Jürgen Rühle, Bahro saw Wittfogel 'as an "*hysterical anti-communist*" and as such unquotable .... Moreover, at the time Bahro wrote his book, both implicit and explicit criticism of Wittfogel was doing the rounds and there was also extensive controversy around the Asiatic means of production' (Gransow and Gransow 1981, p. 406). The German communist Wittfogel was forced to leave his homeland in the 1930s. He fled to the US via England. While living as an émigré, he developed ideas about the correlation between the Asiatic means of production and the Soviet system type. These ideas culminated in his 1957 book *Oriental Despotism*. In Wittfogel's eyes, the Soviet Union was not even "proto-socialist"' (see Gransow and Gransow 1981, p. 404).

3   The Alternative

Bahro's *The Alternative in Eastern Europe* consisted of three parts: the first two parts were devoted to criticism and analysis and the third comprised his utopian vision. In the book, he subjected the status quo to scrutiny and criticism, juxtaposing it with a deliberately utopian alternative. In his introduction, Bahro already provides his own definition of the utopian aim of communism: 'We were planning to create a new and higher civilisation! … its image has nothing in common with the illusion of a "perfect society" free from contradiction'.[113] In this explanation, we can already see one of the characteristics of post-materialist utopias: The new society is not defined as being in a state of perfect harmony. The dialectical historical sublation of the contradictions of the time that Bahro sketched out based on his Marxist-Leninist understanding of history also envisaged the emergence of new contradictions in the future, which would, in turn, be subject to dialectical sublation in the process of history, and so on and so forth. His utopia was thus not defined or conceived as an historical end state.

In fact, Bahro saw the society of the future as being extrapolated from the possibilities of the present, with the central themes being the fault lines between people's way of life and nature, issues around ecological behaviour and lifestyle: 'There is no need today to preach poverty, but rather to indicate the extent and – far more important – the true horizon of further human development on this planet. Who can stand up for this new direction, if not the communist movement, in the broadest sense of this term?'[114]

According to Bahro, before this movement could move forward, however, it first had to address its past. And he took it upon himself to conduct such analysis in the most sober and factual manner: 'Any mere resentment at the existing conditions is to be avoided as far as possible'.[115]

3.1   Criticism and Analysis

With this in mind, Bahro devoted Part One of *The Alternative*, which he entitled 'The Non-Capitalist Road to Industrial Society', to the history of communism. He endeavoured to explain why the humanist and emancipatory elements of Marxist theory had not sufficiently evolved in actually existing socialism, turning to pre-revolutionary Russia in search of reasons. In Part Two, he builds on this by examining 'The Anatomy of Actually Existing Societies' in which he

---

113   Bahro 1978, p. 7 f.
114   Bahro 1978, p. 8.
115   Bahro 1978, p. 13.

analyses the omnipresent bureaucracy in terms of the mechanisms of its functioning and depicts the negative effects it had on the development of socialism.

For Bahro, even in *The Alternative*, it was about so much more than just criticising actually existing socialism. Right at the start, in the Introduction, he is critical of the governments in both the East *and* the West for the 'alienation and subalternity of the working masses'.[116] Even at this early stage, he had already begun to prepare the ground for the criticism of industrial society that he would go on to develop in his later works. At the same time, however, he defended the defended the Soviet Union's catch-up industrialisation under Stalin.

3.1.1   The Asiatic Mode of Production and Alienation

In his analysis of actually existing socialism, Bahro draws on Marx's works, albeit critically, saying that, while Marx may have recognised the 'Asiatic mode of production' and the associated form of government commonly known as 'oriental despotism', he failed to connect it with the socialism of the future. Marx tended to assume that the socialist transformation would begin in the most advanced industrialised countries.[117] But of course things turned out quite differently in the end, with the first major socialist revolution taking place in 1917 in what was at the time a scarcely industrialised Russia. Bahro came to the conclusion that the October Revolution, instead of binging about socialism in Russia, had given rise to a unique stage of socialism that he labelled *proto-socialist*, i.e., ... socialism in an embryonic stage'.[118] This stage was characterised by pronounced étatism, that is to say by its archistic structure. In Bahro's words: 'There is no more striking antithesis between Marx's communism and the actually existing socialism of the Soviet bloc, even from the theoretical standpoint, than in the character of the state. While I would repeat here that I am simply recording a fact, not making any accusation, I shall show how our countries are ruled by a state machine such as Marx sought to smash in the revolution, not to let it rise again in any form or under any pretext'.[119]

For Marx and Engels, the commune marked the beginning of socialism, not its end. In reality, this concept was standing on its head: 'Let us now turn our

---

116 Bahro 1978, p. 8.
117 See Herzberg and Seifert 2005, p. 175.
118 Bahro 1978, p. 22. At this point he saw things moving firmly in the direction of actually existing socialism. He therefore concluded that this was the point at which we needed to start again. Accordingly, in 1988, Bahro described *The Alternative* as 'my utopia of the Russian Revolution' (Kirchhoff 1998, p. 269).
119 Bahro 1978, p. 31.

minds back to actually existing socialism with its cultivation of social inequalities that goes far beyond the spectrum of money incomes; with its perpetuation of wage-labour, commodity production and money; with its rationalization of the traditional division of labour; with its almost clerical family and sexual policy; with its high official dignitaries, its standing army and police, who are all responsible only to those above them; with its official corporations for the organization and tutelage of the population; with its duplication of the unwieldy state machine into a state *and* party apparatus; with its isolation within national frontiers – and it is quite evident how incompatible this is with the conceptions of Marx and Engels'.[120]

Unlike Harich, Bahro thus did not see this system as a model to be aspired to. Nor did he see it as representing socialism or communism. To substantiate this, he explored the relations of production, demonstrating that the socialisation of the means of production in the original Marxian sense had not taken place. In Bahro's view, the prerequisites for this were the elimination of alienated wage labour or the goods for money principle it was based on, the abolition of the traditional division of labour[121] and of the state through the 'appropriation of the means of production by the associated workers', as well as the international brotherhood of mankind. After the revolution, these prerequisites had given way to power politics and were thus no longer deemed feasible. He therefore accused the 'trained ideologues' in the Eastern Bloc of generally having 'no more than a wry smile' for these original Marxist aims while referring to real-life problems. He emphasised this with the observation that 'Marx's communism does in fact contain utopian elements'.[122]

Bahro criticised the author of *Capital* for a view of history that was focused 'too one-sidedly on capitalist private property': 'What Marx did not foresee was the notorious fact, as it has since transpired, that the unification of philosophy and the proletariat, of socialism (as science) and the workers' movement,

---

120   Bahro 1978, p. 37.
121   The issue of the division of labour was particularly important to Bahro's analysis and utopia. Here too, he drew on Karl Marx, who, in the first volume of *Capital* wrote that, '... the division of labour brands the manufacturing worker as the property of capital. ... What is lost by the specialized workers is concentrated in the capital which confronts them. ... This process of separation starts in simple co-operation, where the capitalist represents to the individual workers the unity and the will of the whole body of social labour. It is developed in manufacture, which mutilates the worker, turning him into a fragment of himself. It is completed in large-scale industry, which makes science a potentiality for production which is distinct from labour and presses it into the service of capital', Marx 1976, p. 482.
122   See Bahro 1978, p. 30 ff.

would turn out very similar, after the revolution, to the earlier case of the third estate, from which the bourgeoisie came to power',[123] the counterpart of which is bureaucracy.

> No one shows as clearly as Bahro that, and indeed why, even under historically favourable conditions, the *abolition* of capitalist private property as a *necessary* prerequisite is not, contrary to the belief held since Marx, an *adequate* condition for the development of a classless society. The key to understanding this can be found in the analysis of bureaucratic domination. This should no longer be interpreted ... solely as a result of movements or deformations in the superstructure of the political state and a consequence of underdeveloped productive forces ..., but rather should be seen as a form of organisation of social labour, including, and indeed especially ... in the case of developed material productive forces[124]

In light of this unwanted development, Bahro called for Marxism to be revised, adjusted to the prevailing 'tremendous productivity of "late capitalism" in the USA, Japan and Western Europe. Marx would have been the first to have revised himself, so as to give revolutionary practice a better basis'.[125] According to Bahro, negative phenomena rooted in the pre-capitalist era, which had survived the radical change in the relations of production, included first, the patri-

---

123 Bahro 1978, pp. 42–3. According to Bahro, the cause of this error in judgement was Marx's Eurocentric perspective and his Hegelian roots. See ibid.
124 Schäfer 1978, p. 37. In as early as 1918, Ernst Bloch, a contemporary of the Russian Revolution wrote about the dangers bureaucratic state socialism posed for Germany: 'Each nation ... can only expect to receive the socialism warranted by its degree of civil freedom, its liberalism. If the Prussian mentality that we have seen in this war remains as strong as it is now, even a later socialist revolution, which would be highly unlikely in the event of a favourable outcome of the war for the Prussians, would not bring true freedom and democracy. It is much more feasible that this [revolution], like Lenin, will inherit the tendency towards power-grabbing, and even worse than this, it will create that "giant prison" that interestingly not only ordinary people but also the academic state socialists in Germany imagine the organisational magic of cooperatively regulated production and consumption management to be' (Bloch 1985b, p. 198). And in another of Bloch's texts published in the same year, he writes 'Empirically, freedom has not yet been fully thought through to the end in Germany; even in Marxism a latent state socialism still looms which – just as the despotism of the rulers of the principalities morphed into the despotism of the state or the Fatherland – is moving the Prussian state in the direction of an absolute cooperative mindset with no deeper personal freedom and utopian ideas' (Bloch 1985b, p. 448).
125 Bahro 1978, p. 44. Here we are struck by an analogy with Harich, who, speaking of his own ideas similarly claimed that if Marx had still been alive he, too, would have altered his thinking along these lines.

archy and the associated oppression and exploitation of women,[126] second, the oppression of the manual workers by the intellectuals, and third, the fact that the towns and cities had power over and lived at the expense of rural areas. Bahro believed that these problems, while stemming from cultural and pre-bourgeois developments, continued to exist under actually existing socialism, even significantly influencing the shape of society.[127]

Bahro attributed the emergence and rigidity of actually existing socialism to the Asiatic mode of production. In his view, these roots were virtually non-existent in the GDR and Czechoslovakia, since, in both of these countries, capitalism and industrialism had already been developed before the era of actually existing socialism. He argues that, after World War II, the Soviet Union's social order was imposed on these two countries, making them unsuitable objects of analysis, given that the wrong turn originally stemmed from Asia.

> The October revolution, already, ... was and is above all the first anti-imperialist revolution in what was still a predominantly pre-capitalist country, even though it had begun a capitalist development of its own, with a socio-economic structure half feudal, half 'Asiatic'. Its task was not yet that of socialism, no matter how resolutely the Bolsheviks believed in this, but rather the rapid industrial development of Russia on a non-capitalist road. Only now, when this task is by and large completed, is he struggle for socialism on the agenda in the Soviet Union.[128]

Despite his criticism, Bahro drew a dividing line: He did not hold Lenin and Stalin responsible for the development, instead blaming their successors. He believed that Lenin and Stalin had no other option but to take the political path they took.[129] 'All these analyses and assessments reveal Bahro as a late Leninist. ... Besides Antonio Gramsci and Rosa Luxemburg, Lenin was undoubtedly

---

126 A link which August Bebel already established in the nineteenth century in his *Woman and Socialism* (first edition 1879). See Bebel 1910.
127 See Bahro 1978.
128 Bahro 1978, p. 50.
129 A position which he also maintained in his controversial four-lecture series on Stalinism at Humboldt University in 1990. During these lectures, he spoke about the totalitarian form of Stalinism and the gulag, in particular, as having been inevitable given the Soviet Union's chosen path of catch-up industrialisation. Here, Bahro took an even more lenient view on Stalinism than in *The Alternative*. Thomas Schubert speculated that Bahro did this because he was disappointed about the failure of his ideas and the impending global victory of capitalism. See Schubert 2007, p. 228. Legitimising Stalinism using economic rationale reveals a contradiction, because this means legitimising terror. Yet, at the same

one of Bahro's very own role models …'.[130] Although, through his reading of the works of Isaac Deutscher and Roy Medvedev, Bahro was well aware of the crimes committed under Stalin, he still defended Stalin's murderous economic policy with its destruction of natural resources. He saw the catch-up industrialisation with its millions of victims, and terror against anyone who (allegedly) deviated from Stalin's course, as inevitable from a philosophy of history perspective, and thus legitimate.[131] This line of thinking was something of a balancing act: 'By attempting to reduce the socialism that had been achieved to date to "proto-socialism", Bahro was trying to avoid the disillusionment that inevitably occurs when dealing with the reality of socialism'.[132] Gert Röhrborn regarded Chapter One of *The Alternative* purely as an apologia for Leninist practice and a critique of Stalin's successor: 'Bahro's primary aim was to describe the Soviet Union's path to socialism, which he had identified as non-capitalist and which was paradigmatic for all actually existing socialist countries, as an objective necessity. Industrialisation by means of a state monopoly capitalism without a capitalist mode of operation *had* to take place in order to overcome the semi-Asiatic character of Russia that had been postulated by Marx'.[133]

In later years, Bahro's appeared more self-reflexive when he spoke about his belief in authority: 'Of course I got into the Party by authoritarian means and I had authoritarian ideas myself. In my book *The Alternative*, the idea was obviously to save socialism here by reforming from above. And I still would have had this tendency even during the Nazi era if I had been born a generation earlier, or indeed during any other period of time, whether earlier or later, so long as nothing had been processed, nothing has at least been realised and dealt with'.[134]

On the other hand, Bahro's combination of critique and defence of Stalinism made it difficult for his denouncers in the GDR to criticise his book without entering into a discussion about the content of *The Alternative*. This presumably was one of the reasons why he was taken to court over alleged intelligence activity rather than his works.

---

time, there are recent studies that cast doubt on the economic advantages of this system of slavery over a free, motivated well-paid labour force. For a discussion of this issue in more recent academic literature, see Hedeler 2010, pp. 7–47.

130 Herzberg and Seifert 2005, p. 176 f.
131 See Herzberg and Seifert 2005, p. 177.
132 Nolte 1981, p. 46.
133 Röhrborn 2008, p. 115 f.
134 Quote from Lehnert 2007, p. 387.

3.1.2 Critique of the Elite and Social Structure of Actually Existing Socialism

In *The Alternative*, Bahro did not yet voice wholesale opposition to industrialism and its 200-year history as he went on to do in later works. He did, however, already reject further economic growth as a mere end in itself and also explored the ecological problems at the time. Bahro criticised resource consumption in the industrial states for exceeding the amount nature can regenerate and for being too high in light of the poverty of the rest of the world. Moreover, the North-South divide this resulted in was, in his view, something the rich countries sought to uphold using arms. However, pure redistribution of wealth was not a satisfactory solution and on its own would not result in human emancipation. For this to happen, there would first need to be a break with the traditional division of labour and this would require the related division into intellectual and manual labour to be completed abolished: 'Even the richest peoples, therefore, if they could throw off the capitalist shell tomorrow, would still face a long struggle to take control of their technical and social apparatus from within, i.e. to divest the function of regulation and administration bit by bit of their immanent character of domination'.[135]

Bahro viewed industrial states as being 'closest' to socialism from a material perspective, in other words, it was there that socialism had to be implemented as a matter of urgency. Yet, according to Bahro, because of their high level of prosperity, it was also in these very countries that such an undertaking was most difficult, which is why he said that 'mature industrialism' was the necessary basis for fully developed socialism or communism.[136]

Bahro also believed that in some states, such as the Soviet Union, there were progressive elements within the bureaucracy that are needed for the development of their infrastructure. Now that socialism had been consolidated there and the country was at an advanced stage of industrial development, it was time for it to abandon its bureaucratic structures. However, previous attempts to move in this direction had failed on account of the firm embeddedness of industrial despotism.

> The constancy of state despotism can be explained ... mainly by the antagonistic nature of the productive forces themselves, in other words by the fact that they are organised on the basis of the division of labour and the character of the class structure and state resulting from these social rela-

---

135 Bahro 1978, p. 125.
136 Bahro 1978, p. 125.

tions .... Bahro's analysis of the key structures of this non-capitalist, state-organised class society based on developed industrialism draws primarily on the example of the GDR. In the analysis, he focuses mainly on the form of social planning and control, the stratified structure of this society and its state-party bureaucracy as the driving mechanism.[137]

Bahro believed that it was more than just the stage of industrial development that was instrumental in the transition to socialism: '... the question of what exactly constitutes maturity is naturally settled not only by technical criteria but rather by social movements'.[138] According to Bahro, social movements require a social fabric which, in turn, is reflected in the class structure or stratification of that society. The communist ideal is a classless society. Accordingly, pre-communist societies, including actually existing socialism, still had a class structure. Bahro saw the division of labour as pivotal for the development of these societies.[139] This results in social contradictions that made historical progress possible by means of the class struggle. Bahro ascribed utopia a leading role in this process[140] and he fulfilled one of its criteria by calling for forward-thinking: 'If those too brusquely ejected from an earlier age have always turned time and again to the past, in search of the lost paradise, similar illusions today are assured of a rapid and bitter end. The "guarantees of harmony and freedom", if they exist, can only be attained the other side of industrialism, which means by the social mastery of the material basis industrialism has created'.[141]

Bahro believed this had to be overcome as, even in actually existing socialism, it resulted in the working class not controlling the surplus value it created. On the contrary, in fact, the workers were confronted with this surplus value is in conflict with the workers, and thus it comes about 'that this now concentrated objectified labour becomes the means of commanding the living labour – for the overall purpose of increasing this alienated wealth both quantitatively and qualitatively'.[142]

In capitalism, the bourgeoisie has power of disposal over the workers. In actually existing socialism, this is no longer the case. In this system, accord-

---

[137] Spohn 1978, p. 17 f.
[138] Bahro 1978, p. 125.
[139] 'The law of the division of labour lies therefore at the root of class division'. Bahro 1978, p. 140.
[140] 'Even Marx and Engels gave us no prognosis for these new relations of domination. It is up to us to get to their root, in the full spirit of the young Marx's proclaimed intent, to make social conditions dance by singing them their own tune' (Bahro 1978, p. 138).
[141] Bahro 1978, p. 127.
[142] Bahro 1978, p. 151.

ing to Bahro, bureaucracy takes the place of the bourgeoisie, even extending its control further. '... [T]here is no field in which actually existing socialism has made greater progress than in the breadth, depth and diversity of the bureaucratization process'.[143] Through its power of disposal over state property, the apparatus controls the workers, at the same time making the social hierarchy permanent.

> The almost total disempowerment of the working class inhibited the formation of a genuinely socialist labour organisation. And with the continuation of 'the traditional division of labour' imposed 'from above', *social stratification that is in line with this division of labour* was unavoidably perpetuated, despite all the ideological commitment to achieve a classless society.[144] The bureaucracy and the hierarchy it entails thus correlated with the vertical division of labour.

Bahro did not oppose a qualitative division of labour accompanied by specialisation, but rather was against hierarchies in the labour process.[145] This was the reason why the bureaucratic apparatus assigned people a position in the multi-tiered hierarchy to which they were to assimilate.

> 'Plan together, work together, govern together!' echoes the slogan from the loudspeakers, meaning that everyone is to show more system-conforming activity in his due place. But as soon as anyone dares to overstep the limits of the prevailing regulations and institutions, they invariably hear the government's true message: 'Cobbler, stick to your last'. And this is at all levels, not simply political life.[146]

Thus, in actually existing socialism, the elemental contradiction of utopian history between the individual and the collective is found in dystopian form. Bahro identified several consequences of this, including a lack of motivation and subalternity,[147] on the one hand, and the ruling class's leadership claim, on the other. He argued that, only once this traditional division of labour was

---

143   Bahro 1978, p. 159.
144   Korte 1980, p. 21.
145   'It is not just the mere differentiation of work functions and their requirements, but rather the subjection of individuals to these, that creates social stratification and the bureaucratic phenomenon' (Bahro 1978, p. 165).
146   Bahro 1978, p. 176.
147   He took this term from Gramsci.

eliminated would true human emancipation be possible.[148] 'In the context of advanced industrialism, this means that the complex vertical hierarchical structure of technology that accompanies the social production process was no longer manifest in social inequality and social hegemony'.[149]

According to Bahro's assessment at the time, the ruling bureaucracy felt insecure in its position of power, with the increasing level of education causing them particular cause for concern. They attempted to counter this problem by means of a strategy of depoliticisation, manifested in the form of trivialities, in bread and circus offers and by expanding compensatory consumption, writes Bahro. Consequently, he was critical of economic planning geared towards quantitative increases, which he viewed as being oriented exclusively towards the Western range of goods and consumerism. This reminded him of the story of the hedgehog and the hare, with actually existing socialism playing the role of the hare, always only arriving at the goal once the West had already moved on.[150] In terms of economic policy, rather than coming up with a viable alternative, the industrial capitalist system of the West, with all its ecological problems, was being emulated. Bahro saw the bureaucracy as attempting to maintain social harmony by satisfying compensatory consumption using the West as a role model.[151]

From a political economy perspective, among those Bahro drew his inspiration from were two GDR economists, Arne Benary and Fritz Behrens, who had come into conflict with the SED leadership. As early as in the 1950s, they

---

148   See Bahro 1978, p. 206 ff. In this context, he made a very interesting reference to the history of utopia: 'Fourier had already realized that "the people would give themselves over to leisure if they had at their disposal an adequate *minimal existence*, an ensured supply of food and a decent livelihood, since the civilized mode of production is too repugnant". And Fourier ... concluded: "In the socialist order, therefore, labour must offer as much stimulation as our festivals and entertainments do today." "The remedy against idleness and other burdens that might destroy the association lies in the research and discovery of an attractive system of production that transforms labour into an enjoyment, guaranteeing that the people persist in labour and hence achieve the *minimal existence* aimed at." This attractive system of production, moreover, was for Fourier a question of the *social organization and division of labour*, in no way one of its technical level (and the error lies, I believe, in this complete neglect of technique)' (Bahro 1978, p. 206).
149   Spohn 1978, p. 11.
150   See Bahro 1978.
151   'For Bahro, there is a close relationship between the subalternity into which people are forced by the bureaucratic system and defining subalternity on the basis of patterns of consumption and leisure behaviour of subalternate masses in Western class societies' (Korte 1980, p. 30 f.).

had both already fleshed out several ideas as to the form the planned economy might take in the future, none of which met with much enthusiasm 'from above'. Indeed, the two economists found themselves facing disciplinary sanctions as a result.[152] Bahro in fact made direct contact with Behrens after he had expressed his interest in casting a critical eye over the manuscript of *The Alternative*, and in August 1976, they met in person.[153] Although Bahro had taken on some of Behrens's economic policy ideas, the economist was not happy with the end product. During a later interrogation by the Stasi, Behrens reported being familiar with Bahro's manuscript, but stated that he found the economic part of the book weak and, although it contained social criticism, he considered the text, as a whole, not to be against the system as such.[154]

Bahro had no direct contact with Benary, who took his own life in 1971. Bahro did, however, draw on Benary's economic policy ideas: Benary's

> particular contribution is an attempt to explain the relationship between socialist consciousness – which, according to Marxist theory, is linked

---

[152] Benary was Behrens's student. In 1956, they worked together on *Überlegungen zum Verhältnis von Wirtschaft und Staat in der Planökonomie* (Considerations on the relationship between the economy and the state in a planned economy). This was met with resistance at the highest level: Ulbricht called the text revisionist. From then on Behrens had a strained relationship with the SED leadership and was politically and academically stigmatised. Following a lecture he gave in Frankfurt in 1968 which was critical of the SED, Behrens came under increasing fire, ultimately leading to his early retirement in 1970. Behrens then worked at home on several manuscripts about the actually existing socialist economy, an undertaking he concealed, however, not getting the texts published until 1992 under the title *Abschied von der sozialen Utopie* (Farewell to the social utopia). See Janke and Krause 2010, p. 8. To some extent, these texts have post-materialist utopian characteristics. However, since they were not published until after the collapse of the GDR, they are not included in the present work.

[153] See Herzberg and Seifert 2005, p. 142 f.

[154] See Herzberg and Seifert 2005, p. 144. In his *Abschied von der sozialen Utopie*, Behrens states: 'As the "revolutionary" critic Bahro sees himself as, he justifies ... the hierarchical elite structure of actually existing socialism. The words of Brecht apply to Bahro: "for anyone making a new beginning who has not mastered tradition will easily fall back under the sway of tradition". Bahro has not mastered the tradition of the workers' movement. He is not familiar with the dialectic of the hierarchy and its criticisms. Just as – from a technological perspective – the structure of the labour process is determined by the character of the social productive forces, so, too, is the structure of economic and indeed political decision-making processes defined by the relations of production, by peoples' relationships within material production. If the latter is hierarchical, so, too, are the decision-making processes, taking on the form of the oft-invoked and ill-reputed leadership pyramid where decisions flow from the top down' (Behrens 1992, p. 112). See also Janke and Krause 2010, p. 14 f.

to the leadership role of the party and its permanent task of educating the population – and spontaneity – which tends to be viewed by Marxism as 'anarchistic' and considered a flaw – by arguing that spontaneous action on the part of the workers was essential, as was their full responsibility, autonomous decision-making power and operative independence in the production process. Benary's key statement is as follows: 'This is why the full development of creative activity includes the full development of spontaneity, of spontaneous action.' He seeks to express, perhaps more forcefully than Behrens, that the 'only objectively given and thus pivotal driving force of technical and economic progress' is not the party and its educational ideology, but rather the workers and their creative activity and initiative.[155]

Bahro also dedicated himself to conducting a sociological analysis of the GDR. His intention was, on the one hand, to reveal the true (numerical) ratio between the bureaucracy and the working class.[156] On the other, he was searching for a transformational subject that would be able to surmount 'proto-socialism'. Bahro believed he had identified a paradox in the ideology of actually existing socialism: He argued that, according to the ideology, the system was legitimised through the working class, which was led by the vanguard in the form of the state party. However, 'Beyond capitalism, the concept of the working class not only loses its operative sense, it now becomes available for decking up this or that new special interest, particularly for the pseudo-legitimation of the substitute bureaucratic power'.[157] Bahro was critical of the fact that Marx's idea of the

---

155 Herzberg 2006, p. 460 f.
156 In 2008, Wilfriede Otto summed up the situation that prevailed in late 1977: 'If we round the numbers off we have 8.5 million employed people, 7.5 million of whom are manual workers and white-collar employees. Of the almost 800,000 people working in agriculture, around 600,000 were members of agricultural cooperatives. Around 400,000 men and women worked in the service sector of the production cooperatives for tradespeople and private tradespeople. The private retail and hospitality sector comprised 720,000 people. The level of education among the GDR's population had changed. A total of 75 percent of under 35s had obtained an upper or lower secondary school leaving qualification. A million GDR citizens had graduated from university or from vocational school or technical college. There has been a radical generational change in the entire structure of the population. As many as 50 percent of citizens were born after 1945. ... The number of young workers who identified with the GDR fell by more than 20 percent from 1975 to 1979. This change in the demographic structure is reflected in the fact that, since the early 1970s, new SED memberships have mainly been recruited from the 18–25 age group' (Otto 2008, p. 150 f.).
157 Bahro 1978, p. 184.

proletariat becoming an historical vanguard was already a false utopian hope: 'In actual fact, the Marxian concept of the proletariat expresses the utopia that communism will follow on from capitalism in its stage of free competition after a brief transition period'.[158] Bahro, however, saw the contradiction as being between the subalterns and their functionaries, with the latter having ceased to be workers.

On the subject of the recruitment of bureaucrats, Bahro writes: 'Subservience to those above, severe discipline towards those below, and only in the third place competence – this is the prevailing order of selection criteria. The result is that the productive and creative elements suffer from an increase of mediocrity, indeed incompetence, dishonourable behaviour and insecurity in official positions, not to speak here of the political standardization that is required'.[159]

Ultimately, this is how creative potential is destroyed, something that Bahro had already lamented in his dissertation. Careerism is the logical consequence. And with this comes a specific type of actually existing socialist human, characterised by 'conservative mediocrity, people who can outshine through "creative" conformity (in the favourable case), correct accomplishment of any orders they are given (on the average), or unfruitful officiousness (at the negative end of the scale)'.[160]

This type of human has developed its own social habitus, a behaviour that is far removed from the socialist claim to equality: 'There is a real class division in common morality .... It is possible to be addressed by a superior in the familiar form, without being able to answer back similarly. Marxist Bolshevism has nowhere been more completely laid to rest than in the realm of social communication between social strata with unequal powers in co-determination'.[161]

---

158   Bahro 1978, p. 193. At another point in the book, he states that Marxism is more of an academic theory than one for the masses: 'The workers – individual exceptions apart – were never Marxist I the strict sense. Marxism is a theory based on the *existence* of the working class. It was always left intellectuals who found themselves in a position to understand Marxism as a whole' (Bahro 1978, p. 197).
159   Bahro 1978, pp. 212–13. With the start of the Honecker era there was also a shift within the upper echelons of power: the experts who had entered the Politburo and the Central Committee under Ulbricht (who primarily worked on economic policy) were gradually replaced by 'a series of young party leaders who were pursuing typical bureaucrat career paths and were responsible for solving political tasks in particular'. According to Hermann Weber, technocrats were thus supplanted by bureaucrats. See Weber 1991, p. 132.
160   Bahro 1978, p. 224.
161   Bahro 1978, p. 225.

Although Bahro was angry about the material privileges of the nomenklatura, he did not see this as the main problem. The key issue for him was the privileges that came with the guaranteed positions of power in politics, industry and culture. 'By the mere fact that certain sections, groups and strata claim for themselves, as their major occupation, a life-long universal and creative activity in politics science and art, thus monopolizing that work which inherently leads to the development of the individual's essential powers – by this fact they condemn other groups and strata to occupational limitation, if not to the stultification of their brains'.[162] Bahro thus caricatures Marx's and Engels's original aim, according to which, in a socialist society, even professors and architects have to act as 'professional porters'.[163]

In reality, the vast majority of ordinary East German people lived subaltern lives, which was a fundamental contradiction with the Marxist claim to human emancipation. Bahro described the antagonism inherent in this: 'People and functionaries – this is the unavoidable dichotomy of every proto-socialist society'.[164] The state apparatus had become set in its world view. When errors occurred, the cause was only ever sought outside the system. This ossification led to widespread resignation. And the problem here was that the Marxist ideology that could have alleviated the situation had been appropriated by the system and used to legitimise it. Marxist ideology could thus no longer serve as a revolutionary impulse. Consequently, truly committed communists were out of place in the SED, unable to achieve anything other than attract negative attention or, alternatively, assimilate.[165]

Bahro blamed the problem of bureaucratisation on Marx and Engels, saying it was a result of their naivety. His critique was more or less in line with Robert Michel's concept of the 'iron law of oligarchy'.[166] The role played by the working

---

162 Bahro 1978, p. 181.
163 Bahro 1978, p. 208.
164 Bahro 1978, p. 241.
165 See Bahro 1978.
166 For more on this 'iron law of oligarchy', see Amberger 2010a, p. 75 ff. In the early twentieth century, Michels addressed the organisational dilemma of the socialists. He argued that transformation was impossible without organisation but, on the other hand, it was inevitable that in every organisation an apparatus would grow commensurate with the degree of the organisation's success. Even if they had previously been workers, the bureaucrats develop their own apparatus habitus. Michels believed that both the reformational and the revolutionary path to socialism was blocked by this problem. See Michels 1916. Bahro described the same problem in the context of the GDR intelligentsia: 'In any case, the transformation of the intelligentsia into a bureaucracy is the predominant tendency. University and technical education, particularly the former, is precisely the entrance ticket to a bureaucratic career, in no matter which branch' (Bahro 1978, p. 215).

class and its vanguard party in the establishment of socialism was something Bahro questioned: 'That the proletariat is to be something beyond this, i.e. the actual collective subject of universal emancipation, remained a philosophical hypothesis, in which the utopian component of Marxism was concentrated'.[167]

At this point, he therefore still regarded utopia as a supposed weakness, although he later went on to draw on it to develop his own strategy. Did he do this to fill the gaps in his own concept, to gloss over the contradictions? Or does this apparent contradiction show that utopia is not rigid, that it is bound to a specific time, that it is in fact dynamic?

Much like Marx and Engels, Bahro also wanted to harness the driving forces of social utopia to start making his model of society reality. With this in mind, he focused specifically on the transition phase and what had till then been the Marxist agent of that transition: The fact that, after the victorious revolution, the working class had to adjust its consciousness immediately, was something Bahro regarded as a problem. He refused to believe that this was happening because he assumed that at this point new conflicts over resource allocation would arise, as a result of which he came to the conclusion that: 'The whole problem of general emancipation must be placed on a new basis, as far as its practical political form is concerned'.[168]

The problems described above and the contradictions of actually existing socialism which came to light were quite obvious to Bahro. Despite all the efforts made by the bureaucracy to maintain subalternity, efforts he himself described, it was precisely here that Bahro saw the starting point for change.[169] Bahro's hope was that anyone with any intelligence would no longer be able to ignore these contradictions.[170] The narrowness of the centralist, bureaucratised and alienated world of work was incompatible with the increasing level of education and consciousness in large parts of the population. This 'overpro-

---

167   Bahro 1978, p. 198.
168   Bahro 1978, p. 202.
169   'The historical task which I have in mind is the *overcoming of subalternity*, the form of existence and mode of thought of "little people". At its core, this means the abolition of the traditional vertical division of labour, and the revolution of the entire orientation and structure of needs that is bound up with this. It proceeds by way of a radical change in all our customary institutions and modes of procedure in society and in the economy' (Bahro 1978, p. 271).
170   Bahro's critique of the bureaucracy and its inhibiting effects on free development reminds us of Callenbach's *Ecotopia*, which criticises the bureaucratisation of science in the USA. Callenbach wrote that the rigid structure of the science establishment with its established, respectable and experienced scientists largely prevented access for young and free-thinking academics. This meant that the US missed out on significant innovative potential. See Callenbach 1978, p. 35.

duction of consciousness' had be put to good use. The required 'second cultural revolution' had already begun. As part of this process 'man will found his existence on his consciousness, on the "highest mode of existence of matter", and concentrate on the social organization of this noosphere so as to regulate his natural relationship anew from this point of departure'.[171]

The bureaucracy was no longer in a position to sufficiently co-opt educated people, resulting in a growing awareness among the latter that would allow them to become the agent of the transformation. The subaltern, on the other hand would be unable to take on this role because they were traditionally 'conservative' and would not be capable of looking and striving towards the future. This is why, in terms of the agent of transformation, Bahro concluded:

> New perspectives only arise if, in a more general social crisis, a fraction of the upper strata or classes, or more effectively, a new 'middle class', organizes the mass of the oppressed for a reformation or revolution. It is

---

171 Bahro 1978, p. 257. On the term noosphere: 'The intellectual sphere – the noosphere –, a term Bahro borrowed from Pierre Teilhard de Chardin, can be traced back to the one book written by him that was available in the GDR (*The Phenomenon of Man*). Bahro was deeply impressed by the biological world view of this Jesuit paleontologist. In the last century, during the inter-war years, in particular, Teilhard developed a concept stemming from the biological sciences on how life, thought and intellect developed in the cosmos in an evolution of materials. Besides the incredible force of dispersion and of the sheer empty space in the universe, Teilhard saw a phenomenon of corpuscle creation, as he called it. The universe has a tendency to furl or roll in on itself. From this tendency, the universe concentrates on solar systems with the planets. After multiple attempts on Earth in manifold life forms, this cosmic tendency to roll in on itself ultimately ended up developing the human brain. Like the universe, the human brain is made up of corpuscles and thus corresponds with the cosmos. With the appearance of the first hominids, the threshold of our consciousness was reached. Beyond a certain level – a level that was reached with homo sapiens – this consciousness transcends itself and creates a new layer around the globe, the sphere of thought and emotion, the noosphere. At several key points in *The Alternative*, Bahro refers to this noosphere. Bahro sees the purpose of the communist awakening as being situated in the social phenomenon that Teilhard identifies – the development of a collective consciousness. But this awakening has become stalled in actually existing socialism and is a "termite mound" rather than a "living cell", Bahro states quoting Teilhard' (Spittler 2007, p. 337). Representing Marxism-Leninism, Kurt Hager wrote the following on this subject: 'One concept which is currently very widespread is Teilhard de Chardin's, according to which, biological evolution led to the emergence of thought and this enabled man to produce tools. The idealistic and theological character of this concept is reflected in the fact that for Teilhard de Chardin, the emergence of thought is an expression of the spiritual nature of the universe and it takes place like a miracle, in one fell swoop' (Hager 1975, p. 39).

necessary to go back to the origin of inequality, domination and exploitation if we are to understand this mechanism of progress, which proceeds from the *totality* of a social system full of contradictions and is not produced just by *one* of its poles.... The formation of the new historical power bloc is therefore always the formation of a *structured* organism, in which several elements of the old society combine into a new quality.[172]

3.2   *Utopia in* The Alternative

As shown, links to political utopia can already be identified in the first two parts of *The Alternative*, which primarily comprise a diagnosis of the time. But it is really only in Part Three, entitled 'The Strategy of a Communist Alternative', that Bahro fleshes out his actual vision for the future. For Bahro, this was the most significant part of his book, a fact that he emphasises during a self-interview recorded shortly before his arrest:

> Part Three is now the most important to me, despite the fact that the preceding analysis remains essential and will thus probably receive more recognition than the alternative concept. Analysis does not suffice. Theory must not stop at practical political consequences. This is an outline of a programme that can mobilise those who do not want to continue as before. I would like my book to provide the impetus for broader self-understanding and to encourage people to hold together in the struggle to find a new perspective in actually existing socialism.[173]

Bahro wanted his work to be programmatic, at the same time also acknowledging the 'risk of utopianism'. With this claim to validity, he publicly ignored Marxism's ban on utopia and images. He deliberately chose a vehicle which in itself signalled oppositional impetus.[174] That said, Bahro did not turn against

---

172 Bahro 1978, pp. 148–49.
173 Bahro 1977, p. 73.
174 Bahro was aware of this. In reference to Marx, he wrote: 'The utopians who preceded him had ... constructed a state of affairs that did justice to human nature. But they could never say how this "natural" society was to arise out of the existing circumstances. This was the very barrier that caused Marx to pause for a moment at the time of his transition to communism, where Engels came to his aid for the first time with the concrete insights he had acquired in England about the dialectic of bourgeois society and the revolutionary role of the proletariat. The more he immersed himself in the political struggles and economic contradictions of bourgeois society, the more clearly Marx saw that there was no purpose in dreaming up a model of a new society, but that the true point, as he and Engels jointly expressed it, was rather to discover and promote the real movement that sublates the existing state of things' (Bahro 1977, p. 24).

Marxist utopian critique per se, as the unofficial collaborator 'Rolf Anderson' reported in August 1977. The collaborator raised the subject of Ernst Bloch in a discussion with Bahro, who stated: 'Although Bloch may have been a utopian philosopher, he was at least a Marxist one. He had worked out how to use images and allegories to bring communism to a broader public. ... However, what Bloch failed to recognise was that the October Revolution had not yet achieved socialism and he therefore saw historical necessities as aberrations of a supposedly already existent socialist formation'.[175]

Bahro's aim was therefore not to replace scientific Marxism with utopia. Despite his affinity for the genre, he still regarded utopia as unscientific. For him, the purpose of utopia was in fact to gradually overcome the entrenched structures. And he regarded the effectiveness and power of imagination and visualisation inherent in utopia as the means to achieve this.

Bahro justified the claim to validity of his utopian concept as follows: 'Marxists have a defensive attitude towards utopias. It was so laborious to escape them in the past. But today utopian thought has a new necessity. For that historical spontaneity that Marx conceived as a process of natural history and which our Marxist-Leninists celebrate in the name of objective economic laws, *must* be overcome'.[176]

The ossified, unreformable and deadlocked system of actually existing socialism had to be dismantled, and this required the progressive power and dynamism of utopia. Scholar of Marxist utopianism Vincent Geoghegan highlights that Bahro, like Ernst Bloch, Andre Gorz and Herbert Marcuse, believed that without a future perspective Marxism was 'blind'.[177]

For Bahro, continuing along the same path would not lead to the historical goal. He therefore called for the achievement of what he felt was needed: '... general emancipation ..., since in the blind play of subaltern egoisms, lack of solidarity, the antagonism of atomized and alienated individuals, groups, peoples and conglomerates of all kinds, we are hastening ever more quickly towards the point of no return'.[178]

Despite Bahro's statement that his main motivation was to revive utopianism for the sake of its concrete character, its revolutionary power, *The Alternative*, particularly Part Three, also meets the criteria of the classical utopia. And, to quote Bahro, who purposely designed his utopia in this way: 'The ques-

---

175   BStU, MfS, HA XX/9, no. 880, p. 162.
176   Bahro 1978, p. 253.
177   See Geoghegan 1987, p. 135, 'Bahro's thought must be seen as a powerful and original contribution to the whole question of a Marxist utopianism' (Geoghegan 1987, p. 110).
178   Bahro 1978, p. 254.

tion accordingly arises as to how ... the organization of society, the system and the mode of function of its institutions, should accordingly be constructed'.[179]

Bahro outlines a strategy for this that he subdivides into a 'minimum programme' and a 'maximum programme', in other words into Blochian short and long-term goals (*Nahziele* and *Fernziele*), although he did not fully commit to these goals, appealing instead for flexibility when it came to the sequence of these transformational steps.[180] And he saw his utopian thoughts as providing inspiration and a foundation for debate on this. This was his claim to validity. Bahro did not therefore call for his strategy to be implemented to the letter. For him, utopia served as a stimulus for action and discussion. Bahro writes: 'Communism is not only necessary, it is also possible. Whether it becomes reality or not must be decided in the struggle for its conditions of existence'.[181] For this reason, his starting point is not one of dogmatic historical determinism. Instead, he establishes a direct connection with Marx, suggesting that people still create their own history.[182] Bahro thereby fulfils a typical criteria of post-materialist utopias, which is also evident in Ernst Callenbach's *Ecotopia*, one of the classics of the genre. Callenbach makes it clear that, from a philosophy of history perspective, *Ecotopia* does not represent a historical end point, but rather is in a permanent process of development accompanied by constant debate.[183]

As mentioned above, Bahro's priority was people's emancipation from the constraints of modern industrial society. Characteristics of post-materialist utopian discourse can be identified throughout his utopian concept. This is also how Bahro's community ideal, which is reflected in his ideas about architecture and form of settlement, is to be understood. When it came to the relationship between the individual and the collective, Bahro believed that individuality could only be experienced in small groups, where people felt heard and needed – in contrast to the individual of the time who suffered from isolation.

Bahro outlined a utopia that sought primarily to overcome the social constraints of industrial modernity:

---

179   Bahro 1978, p. 273.
180   See Bahro 1978, p. 406 ff.
181   Bahro 1978, p. 453.
182   'Men make their own history, but they do not make it just as they please; they do not make it under circumstances chosen by themselves, but under circumstances directly encountered, given and transmitted from the past', Marx 1979, p. 103.
183   See Callenbach 1978, p. 36.

> The cultural revolution can create the preconditions for the great majority of people to be effectively associated in problem-solving collectivities, above all by the redivision of labour. The share of necessary routine work that falls to each person must thus be inserted in his overall time-schedule, so that continuous concentration on psychologically productive activities becomes possible, and there is increasing room for the free choice of objects, i.e. for commitment to this or that creative group.... Given the greater scope for deployment of people with an all-round education, we can assume that the dissociated spheres of activity such as labour, hobbies (a wretched word, which defines free activity in terms of the lack of social ties that presently characterizes it), domestic living, recreation, friendship and love, would be more closely and more frequently linked together in groups such as these.[184]

In other words, people would live in communes, something that would give each individual more self-esteem and would benefit the common good at the same time. These communes, however, would not be economically self-sufficient. Instead, the supply of resources would be controlled by society as a whole: 'This requires, firstly, central material balances which are met by tasks set by the plan for the various communes, according to their average productivity, and secondly, the maintenance of an insurance fund which is only at the economic disposal of the centre. Large-scale investments, furthermore, in so far as they have effects on the goal and conditions of production at a trans-communal scale, are to be disposed of by the society as a whole and allocated to the communes, providing these with all the resources they require'.[185]

The approach Bahro takes in his utopian model of society is geared towards the notion of 'biological organisms' that share a single central brain. Similarly, society, too, needs some form of control centre or central nervous system, which is why a purely decentralised syndicalist model is not a viable option. Instead, a hierarchical system is required, but, according to Bahro, this hierarchy must not be reflected in the social structure.[186] At the same time, Bahro argues against pure centralism:

> Immediate centralization of power of disposal is not only identical with socialization, but unmistakeably erects a barrier against it. And total centralization without organic gradation will always remain a theoretical con-

---

184 Bahro 1978, p. 298.
185 Bahro 1978, p. 446.
186 See Bahro 1978, p. 436 f.

ception of compulsive characters devoid of imagination. What is ultimately central in the sense of the overall social level is simply decision over the (ethical) value concept by which the association is to govern its development.[187] Thus, centralisation will no longer be implemented within a (closed) state apparatus but rather will be a fundamentally democratic oeuvre carried out by everyone.[188]

Bahro's communist utopia is therefore neither an ideal-type anarchistic utopia, nor an archistic one. In fact, it is a hybrid of the two, with a slight bias towards anarchism:

> In a developed communist society, individuals are equally and simultaneously present at all levels of subjective interest. There is a 'top' and a 'bottom', but in a system that no longer defines *people* in these terms. In this way any jealousy on the part of the 'bottom' would be meaningless.[189]

This principle is reflected in the political system described in Bahro's utopia. The multiple individual communes represent individual units that make up the whole. The communes delegate representatives to the National Assembly. But it is not this latter body that is the highest instance. That function is performed by the 'League of Communists':[190] 'Only the League of Communists can and must rise above all these particular limitations, and not least above the particularity of time – i.e. above the merely present interests of the association. The League of Communists is precisely the organization that corresponds with the universal tendency of individual interests'.[191] To put it bluntly, this means that the delegates the communes send to the National Assembly are responsible for the nitty gritty administrative work, i.e. for the routine, day-

---

187   Bahro 1978, p. 438.
188   'The mediation of the *overall social* connection can only become the common work of free individuals if this is not a separate activity that confronts all other necessities of mediation in an abstract and commanding way' (Bahro 1978, p. 439). Bahro also expressed clearly anti-étatist views elsewhere in his book: 'To persist in étatism or press forward to general emancipation, forward to the cultural revolution – that is the alternative' (Bahro 1977, p. 356).
189   Bahro 1978, p. 440.
190   Although Bahro does not mention this explicitly, here he clearly draws on the historical 'League of Communists', which developed in 1847 based on the 'League of the Just' and for whom Marx and Engels wrote the 'Manifesto of the Communist Party'. The Manifesto set out the tasks expected of the communists as well as their tactical approach. See Grebing 1981, p. 41 f.
191   Bahro 1978, p. 448.

to-day political work. The 'League of Communists', on the other hand, provides impetus and sets the course for the development of society as a whole. This council of intellectuals in the guise of a new type of party is to represent the political vanguard without affectation and should thus be the 'collective intellectual', not the 'super-state apparatus': 'The concept of the collective intellectual is the quintessence of all ideas about the political leadership function and internal constitution of the communist party that were elaborated from Marx and Engels, via the young Lenin, Rosa Luxemburg and Gramsci, down to the new approaches to Marxist thought of today'.[192] The most important function the 'League of Communists' will have to fulfil is 'the unification, coordination and direction of intellectual and moral efforts for elaborating a strategy and tactics of cultural revolution'.[193]

Bahro did not set out the institutional structure of this 'League of Communists' in detail, instead leaving it open: 'Whether this League will be formed as a new party alongside the old, or whether it will take the shape of a renovated old party, we cannot prescribe to history'.[194] In any case, its members certainly had to be self-critical and alert in order to prevent a new version of the old

---

192 Bahro 1978, p. 362. He took the concept from Gramsci: 'With his "League of Communists" he sought to avoid the mistakes of the old cadre party and ensure the organisation of political action – like Gramsci, he used the concept of the "collective intellectual" ..., while he defined the intellectual (singular) as Gramsci did, as "all thinking people are at least potential intellectuals, and can acquire the ability to think dialectically beyond the hierarchy of social connections and become involved in this as active experimenters and constructors." Accordingly, the "intellectual" has become a normative concept' (Herzberg 2006, p. 47).
193 Bahro 1978, p. 376.
194 Bahro 1978, p. 346. Nevertheless, it was still necessary to split the state monopolistic parties in order to weaken them: 'The split is a transient moment of the historical process. It is directed not against the idea of the party, but rather against its apparatus, against its decay into the state that is embodied in the party apparatus. Society is again to have a leadership that is not located in the apparatus .... The leaders must live in society and share in its everyday life, so that they cannot avoid taking direct notice of the real needs and requirements of the masses' (Bahro 1978, pp. 356–57). Bahro thus ascribed an identity to his left-wing oppositionist readers that clearly differentiated them from SED functionaries: 'Those who simply reproduce the existing conditions and defend themselves terroristically against all progressive criticism, are communists neither objectively nor subjectively, whatever doctrine they might profess to express. The ruling party apparatuses have as little in common with communism as the Grand Inquisitor with Jesus Christ' (Bahro 1978, p. 357). Bahro considered the SED apparatus to be ossified and completely incapable of breaking new ground. 'There is also no communist *leadership*. Appearances here are deceptive. The General Secretary is the highest ranking subaltern in the whole society, the most polished product of the bureaucratic hierarchy. ... The whole system of political institutions ... is incapable of actively changing itself' (Bahro 1978, p. 359).

apparatus emerging. In addition, the interests of all social strata must be properly taken into account to prevent inequality from developing again, in order words the 'weak' must be protected.

According to Bahro, the National Assembly would have to be just as cooperative and collectivist as the 'League of Communists', with the principle of reason functioning as the main lever for integrating the different branches of power: 'The most difficult thing remains *control over the local and particular special interests, i.e. over those of the communes and of the unions within the communes, associated for the various subordinate functions* – if this control is to have a social character, and be effective enough not to break down and conjure up the rebirth of repressive state agencies with their whole sorry retinue of bureaucratic planning, accounting and reporting expenditures. The principle of solidarity requires quite decisively that every commune, indeed every organized interest, should demonstrate a normal degree of effort, and this not just in possible critical situations'.[195]

At the end of Part Three of *The Alternative*, Bahro ultimately provides a very vivid depiction of his utopia, initially elaborating on the structure of society: 'Association of individuals into unions in which they pursue the various specific purposes that make up the process of their social life; association of these unions with subordinate functions into communes as complex territorial units that embrace the process of social life in its all-round character; finally association of the communities into the society – naturally specialized at certain points in the framework of planned division of labour: this is communism from the angle of the *organization* of the social connection. The principle of association replaces the centralist superorganization which is constitutively hostile to individuality and initiative, and is in fact a legacy of class domination from the Asiatic formation through to the capitalist'.[196]

The essence of Bahro's concept of association was to establish what decisions had to be taken at central level. These were, first and foremost, issues relating to common requirements and economic planning: 'To this extent, central controls, i.e. controls proceeding from the overall interest, will probably always be needed. The assortment of goods supplied, as opposed to the *conditions* of production, cannot and must not be freely chosen by the individual branch and factory, by any internal criterion of utility'.[197] Commodity planning would thus continue to take place centrally because this is a task that a society

---

195   Bahro 1978, p. 449.
196   Bahro 1978, p. 440.
197   Bahro 1978, p. 441.

organised along purely decentralised anarchistic lines would be unable to fulfil. Here, centralised – not centralist – planning was imperative, underpinned by people's belief in a cognisant community.

Bahro saw this as a perfect commune concept, and he depicted it as a utopia: 'We can see how a population, basing itself on the organs it has set up, can share in the various activities from planning and statistics through to street cleaning and garbage disposal, from applied research to the dispatch of products, from teaching of various kinds and levels to the repair of machinery, from the construction of new buildings to the distribution of objects of use and the performance of services, while the general arts and sciences become as much the general occupation of all as the exchange between the sexes, between generations, and individual or group enjoyment of the most varied forms of partnership, which will more than ever before become a source of pleasure'.[198]

Bahro made the principle of association the foundation of his model of society and structured all units, from the commune to world order, in accordance with this: 'association instead of subordination of individuals to their various subjective and objective purposes; association of their unions (not least of course of the basic units of the labour process) essentially into territorially grouped communes, as the decisive mediating links of the totality; association of communes into a national society; association of nations in a contentedly cooperating world; mediation to each higher unity by delegates elected from the base'.[199]

Bahro's utopian concept of a future world thus rested on cooperation between a family of nations on equal footing. He was critical of the contemporary model of development aid, arguing that poor countries did not need charity and patronage, but rather recognition and equality: 'But the cultural revolution must create the broad social basis, beyond the laws of national and bloc interest, on which a massive and economically effective development aid can be established on a scale appropriate to the magnitude of the North-South antithesis'.[200]

Consequently, the nations – which would thus not be done away with – would cease to wage war against one another, instead organising the exchange of goods and raw materials on an egalitarian basis. Similarly, Bahro's thoughts on architecture and urban planning also showed clear links with utopian history. *The Alternative* was written at a time when the SED was establishing its residential construction programme. In light of the real housing shortage in

---

198 Bahro 1978, p. 442.
199 Bahro 1978, p. 453.
200 Bahro 1978, p. 432.

the GDR, the aim of this socialist housing programme was to create blocks of high-rise flats for millions of people. In his social alternative, Bahro juxtaposed this construction style against a different ideal of communist living that drew on utopian history: 'Socialist communes could reproduce at a higher level the human scale in building that was attained in the architecture of the ancient polis and the medieval city, instead of simply placing layers of isolated cells on top of one another to give aesthetically formless aggregates, against which the human form shrivels to the size of an ant'.[201]

Bahro was openly opposed to metropolitan life (although or perhaps because he was living in Berlin at the time). For him, it embodied the antagonism between the city and the countryside which he sought to overcome. He regarded urban life as being at odds with the principle of the commune and coexistence based on solidarity, as, rather than truly living together, residents of modern cities were subjected to isolation. He countered this lifestyle with a utopian settlement concept that did not include cities and agglomerations:

> The commune would have the properties of a social microcosm, particularly if we imagine in the distant future the dissolution of the present urban agglomerations, which already lead to absurd results in many places. It goes without saying that there would be patterns of energy economy, of traffic and communications which would cross through the communes. The same would certainly apply also to certain (though not many) institutions of the superstructure. In general, what would remain would be the branch-oriented specialist flow of information, which could be looked after by relatively independent scientific branch institutes that could also be consulted by the communes. The communes would have set for them the output of their industry for society, according to assortment and quality, in due relation to their input in resources (the above-mentioned reserves taken into account). In this way the communes would also be the economic units for the full complexity of accounting. Their councils of elected delegates would have to take the same decisions, with some restrictions, as the government of the nation as a whole, which would similarly be based on the delegate system.[202]

This concept displays some important elements of post-materialist utopias: Despite its coherence, it is not a holistic model, instead remaining dynamic

---

201   Bahro 1978, p. 442.
202   Bahro 1978, p. 443.

and capable of development and change. Besides this, Bahro also fulfils the decentralisation criterion by ensuring that the communes are economically self-sufficient, while at the same time enjoying substantial freedom to determine their own lives through grassroots democracy. So '… the communes would be able to study and influence not simply the question of taxes for general social purposes (for the state budget can be financed almost entirely via the communes), but also the whole economy of the community. And at the same time, the communal delegates in the national assembly would have from the start, as a result of the microcosmic character of the communities they represented, the social power and competence also to decide the general plan for the associated communes'.[203]

Despite the existence of the overarching 'League of Communists' and the elements of centralised economic planning he includes, Bahro's aim is clearly for his concept to be distinctly anti-étatist: 'The positive economic of the cultural revolution can be summarized in a single concept: *to create that new organization of labour and social life on which it will at last be possible to base a community that deserves the old name of a free association of individuals in solidarity*. This is a society in which there is no longer any domination of man by man, since the ground is removed for those social inequalities based on subordination to subaltern work functions'.[204]

Closely linked to the issue of equality are Bahro's statements on property and the mode of production. The goal of simply improving the social situation was not enough for Bahro. He called for social barriers to be dismantled: 'All people must obtain the real possibility of *access* to all essential realms of *activity*, and moreover right up to the highest functional level'.[205]

But here, too, the political makeup of his utopian society demonstrated that equality was paramount. Bahro argued against ideological indoctrination and patronage from above. Accordingly, he did not intend his transformative leading elite to look down on the rest of society: 'The cultural revolution would contradict itself if it led to a new vanguard establishing itself in the old administrative monopoly of education and opinion forming. … The building of a society free from domination can only be brought about if it is not drawn up in an exclusivist political spirit, but arises rather in open communication with the masses'.[206]

---

[203] Bahro 1978, pp. 443–44.
[204] Bahro 1978, p. 405.
[205] Bahro 1978, p. 273.
[206] Bahro 1978, p. 300.

Bahro placed his faith in grassroots democracy, which he saw as making use of the achievements of modern means of communication. This approach was a clear indication of Bahro's foresight: 'Now that the problem of a general assembly of the people is solved from the quantitative and technical aspect by modern computers and means of mass communication, it would be possible at least in principle for all individuals to participate regularly in deciding on the distribution of new value, in establishing future perspectives for society, and fixing prognoses'.[207]

All that was needed was for the computers to be repurposed, taken out of the hands of the ruling powers, who used them to repress the people. This would ensure transparent use of the means of communication, thus ensuring they were not misused. They would no longer serve as an instrument of power wielded by the apparatus behind closed doors.

When Bahro wrote these words, computer technology was still in its infancy. It was the era of the typewriter, and a global network was still inconceivable. During the years that passed between Bahro penning these words and the advanced computer technology we have today, we have seen a phase during which the technical means of mass communication was first developed via the Internet and ultimately made accessible to people from all walks of life. Today, Bahro's prognosis that the democratisation of the means of mass communication would contribute to more transparency and the democratisation of society as a whole appears to be within reach.[208] In this respect, he joins the line of utopian authors that integrated visions of technical progress in their outlines, including, for instance, Edward Bellamy with his work *Looking Backward: 2000–1887*, a utopian novel which, in 1888 predicted the evolution of a type of radio as a means of mass communication. Or George Orwell, who, in 1948, forecast the dangers of video surveillance, among other things.

Consequently, in Bahro's utopia, technology also plays an important role at the political and administrative level. His interest in the potential of engineering led him to make a direct link between technology and science. The technical intelligentsia in Bahro's utopia '... have greater opportunities in the context of

---

207 Bahro 1978, p. 301.
208 Bahro writes: 'It would only need public access to more generalized information, with the entire society having an elementary right to this, and the use of the mass media to discuss the various possible solutions. This need in no way means that every individual must expressly pronounce his opinion before the whole society, which would in any case not be possible. Those interest groups that objectively exist in a differentiated society will have their formally elected spokesmen and not least also those selected informally' (Bahro 1978, p. 303).

a democratization of the decision-making process for bringing their particular demands to public attention and carrying them into practice. Thus for example the natural scientists and engineers can easily present their particular interests in more comprehensive ultra-modern and thus expensive technical equipment as having absolute social necessity, not only subjectively (as a result of their highly developed powers of expression), but also objectively'.[209]

Their knowledge was thus a gateway that enabled them to participate. That said, Bahro's utopia was not technocratic, but rather post-materialist, meaning that science and technology played an important, but not the most important role. For this reason, the idea of 'the primacy of ecology' (Saage) also applies to Bahro's utopia. Bahro aspired to the creation of an equilibrium between people and nature, which is why he proposed, for example, repairing and renovating properties instead of constructing new buildings, as well as reducing wear and tear and establishing extensive spare parts production. For Bahro, people had priority over the economy and profit. Profit should not be to the detriment of people's health. With this in mind, he proposed that new industrial plants be built that, if at all possible, no longer produced emissions that were harmful to humans and the environment, that material and energy savings be made by means of quality maximisation, that disposable products and advertising be banned and that changing fashions be adapted to product lifespan. Bahro also called for comprehensive recycling and an end to the resource-intensive arms industry.[210]

Bahro's ecological utopian ideas were quite clearly part of the post-materialist discourse of his time since he called for a break with the focus on material needs: 'Instead of establishing in a pseudo-Marxist fashion the particular consciousness that necessarily arises from the existing conditions, with a view to satisfying the corresponding alienated needs, the question to be asked is what realities have to be created so as to break through the vicious circle of reification and change the content of needs'.[211]

Bahro manifested a decidedly post-materialist attitude when he questioned the modern way of life in its entirety: 'The whole nature of expanded reproduction that European civilization has brought about in its capitalist era, this very avalanche of expansion in all material and technical dimensions, is beginning to exhibit a runaway character. The success that we had with our means of

---

209   Bahro 1978, p. 352.
210   Both parties locked in the conflict of the Cold War would, even in peacetime, use their military strength to wage war on man and the environment. See Bahro 1978, p. 430.
211   Bahro 1978, p. 256.

dominating nature is threatening to destroy both ourselves and other peoples, whom it relentlessly draws into its wake. The present mode of life in the industrially most advanced countries stands in a global antagonistic contradiction to the natural conditions of human existence. We are feeding off what other peoples and future generations need for their own life. At the very least, our wastage of all easily accessible resources increases their necessary labour and this keeps their liberation under the old historical constraints. The present problems of resources and environment are the by-product of only two centuries of industrial activity by a small fraction of humanity. Based on the economic principle of profit maximization, still a powerful governing force under actually existing socialism, this is an essentially quantitative progress leading into a bad infinity. It must cease, because if the planet is to remain inhabitable at the portion of the earth's crust that can be ground up in industrial metabolism with nature is limited, despite all possible extension and acceleration of this process'.[212]

According to Bahro, post-materialist planning and production will result from a change in priorities: 'In general the scope of the plan will be able to retreat a great deal, once an economy that is no longer oriented primarily towards growth, but rather to quality, has established balance between production and consumption'.[213]

Bahro wanted planning to be environmentally sustainable, something he referred to as *'giving the reproduction process a harmonious character'*.[214] The aim should not be for humanity to adjust to modern civilisation, but rather for that very civilisation to be overthrown, to make a break with the industrialism and blind faith in progress that were destroying the natural foundations of life. In Bahro's mind, there was no other way to resolve the contradiction between nature and industry.

Bahro believed that, if we could not prove ourselves capable of making this change, we would face the dystopia of an eco-dictatorship: 'If the development of the next few decades is going to lead to 10 or 15 thousand million individuals, as present extrapolations would suggest to be the likely limit, all aiming at the same maximum levels of consumption and waste products as the most developed countries, then the coming generations will have to produce oxygen for the atmosphere, water for the rivers, and cold for the poles'.[215] We are heading straight towards environmental disaster and if we fail to change course

---

212 Bahro 1978, p. 262.
213 Bahro 1978, p. 427.
214 Bahro 1978, p. 428.
215 Bahro 1978, pp. 262–63.

in time, we will be forced to endure an eco-dictatorship 'under the blows of catastrophic collapses of civilization, under the sign of barbaric struggle and dictatorship'.[216]

Given the growth crisis, Bahro, like Harich,[217] also called for a radical revision of Marxism:

> Communists must modify their understanding of ... a surplus of material goods as the presupposition for communism. Far as the great teachers of socialism and communism were from reducing the task of socialist accumulation to the maximum production of material goods, their formulations still mirror an epoch in which the working masses were never sure of their minimal existence in food, clothing, housing and education. Today, when late capitalism even spares its unemployed these insecurities, to a large extent it is readily apparent that we do not need socialism simply to ensure well-being – as long as the resources don't run out.[218]

Accordingly, Bahro was fiercely critical of the SED's economic policy: 'Per capita consumption of raw material and energy, per capita production of steel and cement, are the criteria *par excellence* of a totally alienated progress'.[219] He also criticised the fact that the GDR was taking the easy approach of engaging in competition with the West instead of embarking on the tougher path of its own independent development, despite the fact that this might go against the material needs of its own population. According to Bahro, this policy would ultimately run aground: 'If our aim is to catch up with capitalist standards then we shall have our work cut out for a long time to come in dealing with our own problem of "growth". In so far as the communists simply adapt themselves to these highly particular interests, they are precisely not what they give themselves out to be: champions of general emancipation'.[220]

---

216 Bahro 1978, p. 266.
217 By way of comparison: commenting on this contradiction in 1979, Wolfgang Harich said: 'The longer this waste and environmental degradation continues, the more severe the measures required will be. What will be the benefit of these measures? They will guarantee a decent life for the masses – and thus be to the detriment of the rich. And this is where the danger of eco-fascism becomes evident. This is the choice we are faced with: eco-fascism or homeostatic, zero-growth communism based on a state authority' (Harich 1980, p. 77).
218 Bahro 1978, pp. 268–69.
219 Bahro 1978, p. 263.
220 Bahro 1978, p. 264.

Bahro insisted on no less than a complete break, in terms of economic and cultural policy, with the path being pursued by industrialism, calling instead for a different, global, post-materialist approach to politics.[221] The concept of labour Bahro described in his utopia was also based on rationalised economic policy, characterised by the reduction of production to the most essential goods and the removal of luxury goods and single-use products, advertising, the transport of goods over long distances, etc. 'The first condition concerns the de-bureaucratization and genuine socialization of the activity of management, the participation of all individuals in disposal over the reproduction process. The second condition bears on the elevation of the collective worker to the level of the given principles of science and technique of the time, which are at work in the production process'.[222]

According to Bahro's concept, each and every individual must be capable of doing each and every job, something that would require a massive increase in the general level of education. In Bahro's utopia, the concept of work depicted this as something positive: he even portrayed seemingly unpleasant activities as useful, arguing '... that the complete liquidation of simply physical and schematic work – which is anyway an extremely questionable goal, and one which is ... not even desirable from a biological standpoint – lies in an unforeseeable future. From a humanist standpoint, it is only labour that is too heavy for the body or monotonous (unskilled, one-sided) that must disappear; all other kinds can then serve as a rational balance'.[223]

His positive concept of work also included the requirement that everybody participate equally in every task that arose, with even high-level functionaries 'acting as porters'.[224] The belief that technical progress would solve all of

---

221 *'The communist association, as a social body that will be master of its problems without having to strangle its individual members, can only be a system of quantitatively simple reproduction, or at most very slow and well thought out expanded reproduction, of men, tools and material goods.* Only in this way can a relative surplus of the goods that are needed for life come into being on a world scale; given the continued dominance of the old economy with its permanent "revolution of rising expectations", drive forward by the latest needs for luxury of the time, society must *always be too poor* for communism. On this basis, it will still be held against communists in a hundred years' time that they want to make poverty universal' (Bahro 1978, p. 265).
222 Bahro 1978, p. 276.
223 Bahro 1978, p. 276.
224 Labour is divided so that everyone bears the burden, even political leaders. This is in line with the positive concept of work that can be found in the modern utopias penned since More's *Utopia*. See More 1795. The record of the conversation with the unofficial collaborator 'Rolf Anderson' from March 1975 explicates Bahro's concept of work: 'He advised me to reread Engels's *Anti-Düring* as carefully as possible, adding that, just like Mr Eugen

humanity's problems and make a 'golden' future possible was something Bahro considered entirely inflated.[225] In future, people would no longer be tied to one task. The high level of universal education would see to it that nobody would have to spend their entire lives performing the same mindless job again.

Bahro painted a vivid and detailed picture:

> The conditions of labour could be rapidly and continuously improved, if those who construct the machines also worked at them for prolonged periods. The entire apparatus of management and administration could be freed both from many control functions and from the ignorance of detail that increases with the number of levels, if its personnel again had a hand in the whole range of task and problem-oriented activities (the continuity of management would be maintained by systematic multiple occupancy of positions). We can just as well imagine the everyday situation in a hospital ..., in which the entire staff consisted of people with full medical training, or other pertinent qualifications, who also took part in all nursing and ancillary work, and in social and economic functions as well ....[226]

Additionally, Bahro called for a process of equalisation of wages in order to overcome the disparities in the value attached to different occupations. The performance mentality that was so deeply ingrained in the population had to gradually be eliminated. According to Bahro, the payment of a unified wage would help achieve this: 'We could make the whole system very much more simple and cheap if we based it on the assumption that all individuals were to receive this average amount in their capacity as members of society. What is the purpose for example, of the millions of calculations and book jugglings of income tax and social insurance payments?'[227]

Düring, some of our people can only imagine that an architect needs a porter. They cannot imagine that, in a vertical division of labour, the architect, the porter, the politician, the administrator, and all men with an unimportant job are participants in the production process based on the division of labour, just as Engels explicitly establishes in *Anti-Düring*' (BStU, MfS, HA XX/9, no. 879, p. 162).

225   As he was not, however, opposed to progress per se, but rather denounced 'alienated progress' (Bahro 1978, p. 263) and, in this context, called for a radical shift in thinking: '*The idea of progress in general must be interpreted in a radically different way from that to which we are accustomed ...*' (ibid.).
226   Bahro 1978, p. 280f.
227   Bahro 1978, p. 396f.

Bahro argued that in actually existing socialism, the wage differences were used to try to incite workers to increase their performance. His approach, in contrast, moved away from the relationship between goods and money and the system of wage labour. In his utopian concept, he outlined a completely different worker remuneration model that factored in both individual and collective well-being.

Instead of paying workers with money, he proposed compensating them with a time equivalent for the work performed. Bahro was thus advocating a fundamental post-materialist change in values: the aim of human endeavour would no longer be to accumulate material goods, but instead it would be to acquire the maximum amount of free time. Bahro thus went further than Harich since he did not necessarily see zero growth as the key criterion. He believed that quantity would automatically lose its relevance as a factor in social development because the desire to accumulate material goods was the main obstacle to general human emancipation.[228]

Bahro's text can also be clearly categorised on the basis of the functional requirements of classical utopias that Saage elaborated in reference to More's *Utopia*:

> All labour resources are to be mobilised. The unearned wealth of the clergy and the aristocracy ceases to exist, removing the basis of the feudal system. In addition, there is a strict ban on luxury items. With no more conspicuous consumption, the economy is focused on a predictable and constant demand for goods, and science and technology are extremely popular because their power to increase labour productivity is, at least to some extent, to be used for the common good.[229]

If we replace the early modern terminology used here with contemporary pendants from Bahro's time, there are clear links to the utopian tradition defined by More.

---

228   Bahro 1978, pp. 402–3. 'The problem as to the possibility or impossibility of an unlimited satisfaction of needs will prove devoid of any object, merely a reaction to the present conditions, once we break out of the production cycle of compensatory interests. For then the expansion of material consumption beyond a certain threshold will be of disservice to those who pursue it. It will be recognized as an obstacle to the self-realization of individuals.' Anyone who continued to gear their lives towards 'unproductive consumption' will become an outsider: 'Such people are then viewed with the same mixture of sympathy and mild disdain with which we are already accustomed to consider people in sufficiently prosperous countries who "live for food"' (ibid).

229   Saage 2010, p. 16.

Bahro saw disposable time as an important basis for transformation and believed that the economy had to be geared towards the achievement of this goal.[230] With this in mind, he proposed that labour be organised more efficiently. All work tasks were to be assessed for their utility and purpose, the administration was to be radically trimmed down, and the work to be performed distributed among the resulting available labour force.[231] This suggestion had, in fact, already been made in *Utopia*, where More lamented the idleness of large swathes of the population – from beggars to the nobility or the clergy. If all these people were to work together and, according to More, the 'many trades that are both vain and superfluous and that serve only to support riot and luxury' were to be rationalised away, 'a small proportion of time would serve for doing all that is either necessary, profitable, or pleasant to mankind'.[232] In More's *Utopia* the labour that is to be performed is divided among almost all inhabitants, which reduced the time each person spent working to a minimum. Other elements also contributed to this, including the fact that housing renovation was given priority over new construction, clothing was uniform, robust and practical, etc.[233] In More's classical utopia, all these savings served the purpose of ensuring the maximum amount of 'disposable time' for everyone.

---

230 'If it is to give individuals and collectives "disposable time", time for development and self-realization, time for increased feedback into the economy, then the first condition is that there is sufficient labour-time available in general. The reproduction process must be organized in such a way that the plan does not lay claim, right from the start, to the entire available labour-power, for the satisfaction of social needs, since it is impossible without a reserve of labour-power, without a buffer of this kind, to uncouple a sphere of free and mentally productive activity from the realm of necessity. This is not a mere technical economic question, but a genuine question of political economy. Available labour-time will be expanded by raising productivity without raising output, and by making superfluous, through the equalizing of material and cultural conditions of existence, the greater part of the gigantic apparatus of control over all individual and particular interests' (Bahro 1978, p. 299).

231 When it came to working hours, Bahro specifically considered a rapid introduction of a 30-hour week: 'In order to make a significant change here, it would be rational to keep the five-day week of approximately forty hours but plan for only $5 \times 6 = 30$ hours of better prepared and hence optimally effective production. This would mean covering the 24 hours of the day where necessary with four production shifts. The last quarter of the existing capacity could be balanced out, at the overall level, by a number of non-manual employees twice as great as the number of workers employed in immediate production spending six weeks of the year on the shop floor' (Bahro 1978, pp. 421–22).

232 More 1795, pp. 57–8.

233 See More 1795. In More's book, these cuts were due to the material scarcity of the time. In the utopias of the thriving industrial age, in contrast, asceticism and the prohibition of luxury was no longer practiced, as material hardship and supply bottlenecks appeared

Marx, too, had this objective in mind and Bahro drew on this when he called for working hours to be reduced under communism.[234] But Bahro believed that, as long as compensatory patterns and the subaltern way of life continued to prevail, reducing working hours alone would not suffice. As a basis for socioeconomic development, he therefore proposed 'a reduction of necessary labour-time, so as to make this more precise with respect to the present situation: *priority for the shortening of psychologically unproductive labour-time within necessary labour-time*'.[235]

More specifically, he demanded a '*new economy of time*'[236] to resolve the contradiction between the individual and the collective:

> This is *the* economy of time which Marx had in mind for the realm of freedom: the appropriate allotment of for all-round development and satisfaction on a social as well as an individual scale .... This new economy of time will also save costs (*abstract labour-time*), but in the first place it will secure *concrete living time*. Its 'goal function' comes to be the maximization of 'time for development', 'time for the productive appropriation of culture'.[237]

---

to be surmountable through the development of the productive forces. With the discovery of the *Limits to Growth*, this notion of sacrifice typical of the early modern utopias experienced a renaissance under different circumstances.

234 In the first volume of *Capital*, Marx wrote: 'The intensity and productivity of labour being given, the part of the social working day necessarily taken up with material production is shorter and, as a consequence, the time at society's disposal for the free intellectual and social activity of the individual is greater, in proportion as work is more and more evenly divided among all the able-bodied members of society, and a particular social stratum is more and more deprived of the ability to shift the burden of labour (which is a necessity imposed by nature) from its own shoulders to those of another social stratum. The absolute minimum limit to the shortening of the working day is, from this point of view, the universality [*Allgemeinheit*] of labour. In capitalist society, free time is produced for one class by the conversion of the whole lifetime of the masses into labour-time', Marx 1976, p. 373.

235 Bahro 1978, p. 415.

236 For more details on this, see: Himmelmann 1981, p. 79ff. Although Gerhard Himmelmann welcomed this approach, he saw it as not properly thought through: 'Bahro's concept of the "economy of time" appears, ... when it comes to the issue of the transition from financial accounting to a universal working time budget and from an economy based on commodities to one based on use value, problematic and poorly thought through, from both a theoretical and practical perspective. Bahro fails to provide any new arguments to back up the theoretical coherence and practical opportunities for the application of these new forms of accounting' (Himmelmann 1981, p. 85).

237 Bahro 1978, pp. 415–16.

This is the primary objective of economic planning in Bahro's model of society. Bahro saw the resulting surplus labour time as creating scope for individual and social emancipation and the need for economic regulation disappearing with social progress.

In his utopia, Bahro envisages the workers being better integrated in their factories, and, by virtue of increased transparency and participation, they would identify with their places of work more closely than is the case now. A sense of being needed to perform one or even multiple meaningful tasks is expected to motivate workers.[238]

Bahro did not provide a detailed description of how the future would be structured and organised, thus meeting one of the criteria of post-materialist utopias: 'How exactly the organization of work within the factory would be shaped under conditions of such disposability and mobility of individuals, we can confidently leave to later practice, and in the meantime to utopian predictions. The realization of equality in the division of labour will bring about so natural a solidarity and discipline of individuals in the best possible execution of the necessary labour that repressive controls will become completely superfluous and the effectiveness of the collective, governed in the first place by quality and the saving of raw materials, will reach an optimum simply from the collective's own internal regulation'.[239]

With the aim of reducing labour time in general, Bahro proposed a *'a new definition of need'*. It is here that the post-materialist substance of his utopia is especially evident. At this juncture, Bahro makes a complete break with the Western consumer ideal and modern commodity society. Bahro was of the view that rich individuality calls for other use values as well. However, the required change in values had to come from society itself and could not be imposed from above. And a *'calculation for a new economy of time'* was needed for this. The aim was for the economy to be orientated towards the use value rather than the exchange value of a commodity. This meant that quality would have come before quantity and, consequently, things would have to be produced differently, i.e. no longer geared towards quantity over quality, but rather for the purposes of the common good, with the aim of gaining 'disposable time': 'what is needed ... is a transition at the primary level of economic accounting from measurement in terms of value, or rather price, to direct measurement in terms

---

[238] Against this background, Bahro posed the following question: 'Why shouldn't the worker who repairs his own car himself not also repair his production machine? If necessary he must be given systematic instructions for this' (Bahro 1978, p. 420).

[239] Bahro 1978, p. 425.

of time equivalents'.²⁴⁰ Bahro believed that although economic calculations based on time equivalents are difficult to achieve, they are nonetheless essential, and he argues that, up till then, there had only been half-hearted attempts to implement this approach.

When it came to the distribution of goods, Bahro drew on an approach which has frequently been used throughout the history of utopia (e.g. in Bellamy's *Looking Backward: 2000–1887*): the same consumption credit for everyone. According to this approach, each member of society receives this share of the nation's wealth to purchase goods as services as compensation and reward for the work performed. The amount is the same for everyone, but there are differences when it comes to the labour time:

> No addition for creative and development-promoting work. If society pays the costs of education and lets each have his share in consumption during the education period too ... Restrictions are needed only on individuals who culpably shirk for long periods from making their contribution to reproducing the conditions of life. Compensation, however, is due for heavy work, monotonous work, unpleasant work, night-work, in short for all work that acts against the possibilities of development (as long as this is not shared more or less equally among all).²⁴¹

To ensure that the unpleasant work also gets done, Bahro relies on incentives: 'Society must bring into the correct proportions the supply and demand for labour-power in the various more or less attractive branches and activities. If no-one can be found for important activities, on account of their unpleasantness for the individual, it is not unfair to allocate additional income for these jobs until the places are taken ...'.²⁴²

Accordingly, those who are willing to carry out unpleasant tasks have to invest less labour time to receive their share of consumption than those who perform more pleasant activities.

It is then up to each individual how they choose to spend their credit. Bahro gave a few concrete examples that are rather strongly reminiscent of a passage from Bellamy's utopia:²⁴³ 'Individuals could choose between means of satisfac-

---

240 Bahro 1978, p. 433.
241 Bahro 1978, p. 397.
242 Bahro 1978, pp. 397–98.
243 The exact wording in Bellamy's utopia was: '... although the income is the same, personal taste determines how the individual shall spend it. Some like fine horses; others ... prefer pretty clothes; and still others want an elaborate table. The rents which the nation receives

tion and development that are very different in their concrete use-value and purpose, as to which of these they wanted to spend their individual share of the surplus product on. Assuming a supply in approximate proportion to these needs (however much they might change), I can consume my share according to my inclination primarily on a comfortable home or on travel abroad, on *haute cuisine* or an extensive library'.[244]

Bahro assumed that his utopia would require a new type of human. And, in order to create this 'New Man', he aspired to a very high level of universal education and demanded comprehensive single-track tertiary education for everyone.[245] But here Bahro did not mean school-like education based on the needs of the economy, but rather an education that turned out critical thinkers with an interest in culture.[246] Bahro thus composed an alternative to the reality that he saw: 'The cultural revolution and its educational policy must draw the lesson from the uncontestable experience that people who grow up within the possibility of political-philosophical and artistic practice are condemned to subalternity, even if they become specialized scientists'.[247]

Thus, only when the majority of individuals, having acquired the capacity for critical thinking, recognise and manage to overcome their own subaltern position will Bahro's utopia become a possibility. Bahro thus saw this as an intergenerational process of transformation.[248]

---

for these houses vary, according to size, elegance, and location, so that everybody can find something to suit' (Bellamy 2007, p. 64).

244 Bahro 1978, p. 398.

245 And this also places him in the tradition of utopian thought: 'The concept of education itself is based on a utopia, emanating from the opportunity for human development and fulfilment in an emancipated society. Learning and science are principles that have remained constant from Comenius to Flitner, and Platon to Asimov. In utopias like this, the education of man plays the central role, being assigned the main responsibility for social change. Conversely, the fact that social conditions must be right to be able to acquire knowledge has also always been common knowledge' (Faulstich 2005, p. 301).

246 'The entire educational process must be organized in such a way that the youthful development of all people leads up to the summit of art and philosophy, the emotional and the rational bridges from the subjective microcosm to the totality. If this is a utopia, it is Marx's utopia too' (Bahro 1978, p. 286).

247 Bahro 1978, p. 287.

248 The unofficial collaborator 'Rolf Anderson' reported on this in March 1975: 'Marx and Engels assume that a fundamentally new society must be created and envisage a transition phase which is historically short but temporally long. (Bahro, for his part, sees the transition from capitalism to communism during the socialist phase as lasting 200–300 years)' (BStU, MfS, HA XX/9, no. 879, p. 161). Bahro also wrote in *The Alternative* that the process of transformation could take centuries. See Bahro 1978, p. 22.

As this transformation progresses, the time would ripen for communist emancipation: 'The essentially aesthetic motivation, oriented to the totality and to the return of activities to the self, will enable man (who had an excellent early childhood) to appropriate for himself in a meaningful way the fundamental *instruments* of spirit and feeling: language (more than one) for mastery of the quantitative, cybernetics for mastery of the structural aspect, and the technical capacities for the artistic expression of self. These four pillars alone require a strict syllabus that insists on a controlled appropriation'.[249]

Consequently, children may also be forced to learn, as this is something they would be grateful for later on (having learned to play a musical instrument, for example). The approach thus did not correspond with the anti-authoritarian notions of education as free self-realisation that dominated Western post-materialist discourse.

This is also evident from the education system Bahro describes as part of his utopian concept: 'Since it will be far more possible in the future than before to complete the overall general polytechnical training in a special branch of the technical division of labour, there will be no real break between a "delayed matriculation", as it were, and specialization. Education time will also generally neither be a deduction from ordinary production time, nor will young people be exempted from simple labour – something which is the greatest educational nonsense'.[250]

When it came to the creation of the 'New Man', Bahro assumed that the biological factor, the genetic make-up of the individual, did not play a major role in a person's ability to achieve the maximum possibly level of education. In other words, virtually anyone could reach an academic standard of education. This was a scenario Bahro desired to see and he was willing to accept dystopian elements to achieve it. Those who were *a priori* not suited to achieving such an academic education, for example, would be detected before birth and weeded out by means of eugenics: 'Genetic and other pre-natal injuries can in part be foreseen early enough to avoid births of this kind with minimal complications; their occurrence can in part be prevented altogether, or at least we can stem the present growth in their number, which is the product of a particular stage in medical and hygienic progress'.[251]

Given that the biological factor only played a marginal role, the reasons behind the significant discrepancies in educational achievements and poten-

---

249   Bahro 1978, p. 288.
250   Bahro 1978, p. 289.
251   Bahro 1978, p. 290. Here too Bahro proved his foresight as such processes are now well established in Western societies.

tial must lie elsewhere. Bahro saw them as being rooted in early-childhood education. And it was thus this context that he took as his starting point for the creation of the 'New Man'. Conventional education that maintained the reproduction of subalternity had to be replaced. Parents had to become enlightened and self-reflective to avoid repeating the mistakes made in their own upbringing:

> Public opinion must discriminate against all those customary practices of socialization that produce anxiety in the child, disturb a trusting orientation to the social and the natural environment, poison initiative with feelings of guilt, devalue achievements, break the child's will and turn its energies back on itself, where they form the basic model for mistrust, spitefulness, aggression and substitute behaviour of all kinds. The result will be a remarkable growth in the consciousness and capacity for responsibility of the next generation of children. We shall then see how great is the potential to educate people right up to the highest level.[252]

Here, once again Bahro's thought process was entirely in keeping with the postmaterialist discourse of his time.

Children are not to be coerced, but instructed. Their training and education will be financed by the community, which they will be required to pay back later, as a form of quid pro quo, by integrating into society and performing their own work. Any individual leaving the collective, not playing their part, refusing to integrate and perform their duties is considered to be displaying antisocial behaviour and a lack of solidarity. Although this does not result in any form of legal punishment, the individual in question would not receive the consumption 'credit'. Here, a certain contradiction between the individual and the collective remains: those who do not integrate are classed as antisocial. What are these individuals supposed to live off? Surely crime is the only option left for them to secure the means to live? Bahro disregarded this scenario, providing for a suitable place in his utopia for each and every individual.

When it comes to child-raising, Bahro's utopia sees love and sexual morals as playing a role:

> Society must finally provide young people with the framework for a comprehensive collective and individual understanding of themselves, at the right time, and of the great task that they face in bringing eroticism, edu-

---

252 Bahro 1978, p. 291.

cation and marriage as far as possible into harmony with one another .... It is most probable that the less proscription there is on the needs of sexual love, the more happy intimacy in youth, the more humane will be the general educational climate for the next generation .... The present problem in this field must be whether we cannot unburden and improve the family situation, which is still completely indispensable for the socialization of children, in such a way that the absolute identification of marital union and exclusive erotic partnership is demolished in public morality.[253]

Bahro thus questioned the notion of the nuclear family being the only form of sustainable loving relationship, calling for free love, albeit while retaining the option of a monogamous partnership as a possible voluntary form of cohabitation in the future. This objective could only be achieved by means of a process of transformation: 'Work, family, school – all these must be superseded and raised to a higher level from inside, not simply destroyed. It is pure subjectivism to try and begin for example with the 'abolition' of the family and marriage, instead of adapting its internal and external conditions of existence to the new possibilities'.[254]

The cultural revolution was to begin by transforming the way children are raised in families.

Bahro counterposed the traditional family model with a new form of cohabitation: 'Besides the unions for work and educational purposes, the articulation of the population in communes would be one of the most important concerns of cultural-revolutionary practice. For everything indicates that the transition from the present small family towards larger unions, though in no case units to be organized by the state, is the key to the immediate progress essential in two closely connected fields, whose backwardness would inevitably be a severe hindrance to the overall process of a transformation of civilization: the liberation of women and also the liberation of children, or more precisely the securing of the psycho-social conditions for an educational process that does not impose barriers on development'.[255]

In other words, Bahro is also addressing the role of women in his utopia, arguing that women were shouldering multiple burdens due to the concurrence of professional and family duties. Only once 'the small family is abandoned as the reproduction unit' would they be emancipated from this situation.

---

253   Bahro 1978, pp. 291–92.
254   Bahro 1978, p. 293.
255   Bahro 1978, p. 444.

In the commune, housework and childcare is socialised, thus making a common struggle against the remnants of patriarchal traditions possible.[256]

But how exactly did Bahro envisage the transformation of society in the direction of his utopian vision? As previously mentioned, Bahro saw upbringing and education as playing a key role in the creation of the 'New Man'. Thus, he did not see the property question as being the lever of transformation, nor the contradiction between capital and labour. Instead, he regarded education as the driver of change. He developed a concept of social restructuring on an intellectual basis, which did not, however, mean that the intellectuals alone would lead the process and the less educated would follow. After all, as has already been remarked, Bahro demanded that even professors should regularly 'act as a porter', just as engineers should work at the machines they develop. His expectations of political leadership were no different.[257] When it came to the transformation, Bahro had a gradual process of the withering of the state in mind. The process would involve power gradually being passed on to society, reciprocating the dismantling of the power of apparatus.[258]

Bahro considered intellectuals to be the key agent of transformation, with their education and knowledge constituting the best possible starting point. 'That is not a demand, but a reality. What one can and must demand is that these elements do not merely act in their own special interests, but gather and organize around them all forces with a desire for change.'[259]

During the transformation, the intellectuals would represent an interim elite and would organise themselves into a 'League of Communists'. Bahro saw this body as constituting an intellectual centre, although, reminiscent of Gramsci's definition, his definition of the 'intellectual' was very broad:

> The League of Communists must therefore be open to all those who have the need to go beyond the pursuit of their immediate interests, having recognized that the barriers to their self-realization bear a social character. By this action they act as intellectuals. This is of course a use of the concept that goes beyond the traditional social structural sense. It

---

256 See Bahro 1978, p. 446 f.
257 'The leaders must live in society and share in its everyday life, so that they cannot avoid taking direct notice of the real needs and requirements of the masses' (Bahro 1978, p. 357).
258 'In principle, this means a division of social power, the installation of a progressive dialectic between state and social forces, and not just temporarily as within the party process itself, but rather for the whole duration of the transition. The result will be a situation of dual supremacy, in which the étatist side gradually becomes less dominant' (Bahro 1978, p. 361).
259 Bahro 1978, p. 328.

assumes that all thinking people are at least potentially intellectuals, and can acquire the ability to think dialectically beyond the hierarchy of social connections and intervene in these as active experimenters and constructors.[260]

Accordingly, in its 'work of knowledge', the 'League of Communists' would take a participatory, non-hierarchical, transparent, grassroots and pluralist approach. Political party currents and wings were part and parcel of this. Decision-making in Bahro's utopia would take place from the bottom up.[261] All of these elements were in keeping with post-materialist thinking: a move away from seclusive elites (i.e. a comprehensive dynamisation of society), the increase in grassroots decision-making and, related to this, broad participation of the population in political processes. Bahro envisaged a 'party constitution that is open towards all genuine social forces' with neither nepotism nor secrets. The members of the 'League of Communists' would encourage idealism, not careerism, as the party would no longer serve as a career stepping stone.[262] Much like the state, the party too would be restricted to administrative functions in the service of society, which itself must serve as basis of the anti-étatist initiative towards transformation.[263] Bahro was well aware of the risk of, at the end of the cultural revolution, a new seclusive elite simply taking over where the old one left off. He hoped this scenario could be avoided by means of democracy, transparency and participation.[264] He refrained from making tangible suggestions as to how such an undesirable development could be prevented, however,[265]

---

260   Bahro 1978, pp. 363–4.
261   See Bahro 1978, p. 365.
262   See Bahro 1978.
263   '... the party itself must place control of the bureaucracy and state machine by social forces at the centre of its policy' (Bahro 1978, p. 371).
264   'This is the field of representation of the various corporate interests, by professional group, sex, age group, level of education, leisure pursuits, etc., which can bring their claims into non-antagonistic comparison all the more easily, the more openly these can be recognized and expressed, and are weighed against one another by public opinion in general. Here, plurality and diversity must fully prevail, precisely so that these interests are not anachronistically driven to set themselves up as universal interests and form into political parties. The trade unions will continue to have the greatest importance in this connection' (Bahro 1978, p. 353).
265   At one point in the book, he formulated this more specifically: 'Viewed from the formal aspect, the communal (territorial) organization which presently balances the centrally directed industrial branch organization and the other pervasive bureaucracies only in an artificial constitutional sense, would have to be the medium-sized planning and directing instance, via which in particular all central controls would have to pass on their way down to the basic units of the various primary activities of the reproduction process' (Bahro 1978, p. 442).

relying mainly on idealism instead. Bahro pinned his hopes on the progressive, corrective power of young people, 'if we are to avoid the force of everyday habit leading yet again into the production of subaltern modes of behaviour'.[266]

Bahro's proposed transformation also pertained to the actually existing socialist states where private ownership of the means of production had been (formally) abolished. When it came to the capitalist West, he simply briefly outlined that, because of its different starting point, the process there would have to take a different course. These countries had bourgeois democracies based on a class structure which was reflected in the political party landscape and which Bahro regarded as anachronistic. Nonetheless, he still devised a strategy for these states:

> In the economically developed capitalist countries, the transformation can certainly be introduced by a bloc of different parties, who represent the existing differentiation within the revolutionary camp.[267]

In the society of the future, class antagonisms are eliminated, leading Bahro to the conclusion that one party is enough. Vincent Geoghegan considers this line of argument to be contradictory: The assumption that this one party must assume leadership in the historical process reveals that Bahro's history of philosophy continues to be shaped by the 'vulgar determinism' of Marxism-Leninism. According to Geoghegan, with this way of thinking Bahro was undermining his own strategy of transformation.[268]

4   Bahro and Utopianism

4.1   *Up to 1980*

The interpretation of *The Alternative* as a post-materialist utopia outlined above will now be extended and fleshed out based on other texts Bahro wrote during the same period. His dissertation, which he worked on parallel to *The Alternative*, primarily comprised analysis in the field of industrial sociology and contained very few utopian passages. By and large, his dissertation was an empirical study with a few concrete proposals for improvement,[269] but unlike

---

266   Bahro 1978, p. 375.
267   Bahro 1978, p. 350.
268   See Geoghegan 1987, p. 120.
269   See Bahro 1982a, p. 71.

The Alternative, it did not put forward an all-embracing alternative to actually existing socialism in itself. The only element of possible relevance here is the image of the work of the future that Bahro paints in his dissertation: 'As work becomes the psychologically productive consumption of an individual's own abilities, it can take on the character of a positive desire. As a result, the stimulation to work primarily becomes a question of building on the individual's inherent desire for personal fulfilment and development, and this, in turn, requires new advances in the socialisation of labour, in the expansion of possibilities for individuals to appropriate the general productive forces'.[270]

Bahro thus saw labour, provided it fed into the emancipatory process of education of the no longer alienated individual, as being instrumental to the reorganisation of society, to the transformation his utopia envisaged. This reorganisation '... means the removal of all social barriers between leadership functions and activities involved in the execution of work. The subordination that technology calls for ultimately loses the last of its authoritarian character because individuals are then able to continuously (which will not necessarily mean hourly or daily but pre-arranged in accordance with an individual economy of economy of life) swap places. Skill will then become solely a question of acquiring experience in open collectives which, for the individual, constitute the polytechnical unity of education and work processes'.[271]

Bahro elaborated on his utopian ideas in the six lectures he gave on *The Alternative* just before his arrest. At the very outset, he defines his claim to validity and specifies the aim behind *The Alternative*:

> The aim of my critique of actually existing socialism is to develop a *radical communist alternative*, one that goes to very roots of the economy, an alternative to the politbureaucratic dictatorship that keeps our social processes of work and life in shackles. I put forward suggestions for the programmatic positions of a new League of Communists, something I believe must be created all over in order to pave the way for and spearhead the transition from 'actually existing' to true socialism. ... An alternative such as this pertains to more than just a few individual elements. In fact, it involves the upheaval of the entire social setting, the dissolution of the existing form of society, it must, in all its complexity, at the very least be outlined, if not described in its entirety.[272]

---

270 Bahro 1980b, p. 133.
271 Bahro 1980b, p. 148.
272 Bahro 1977, p. 9f.

Bahro distanced himself from the renowned opposition in the Eastern Bloc, since in his view, although they lamented their defeat in Prague in 1968, all they demanded in the aftermath was the defence of human rights. In doing so, they were thus focussing on the social superstructure rather than the socioeconomic basis. What Bahro did deem necessary was an overarching concept and the organisation of the opposition across the entire Eastern Bloc. This was something that required planning and ultimately a theoretical foundation.[273]

Bahro defined the target group of his utopian concept as follows: 'My vision is not addressed to a crypto-communist sect, but rather to anyone living in our countries who is hoping for emancipation from modern material and state slavery, irrespective of their official position or how they have portrayed themselves up till now'.[274]

This included non-Marxist groups, such as Christians, for whom the Sermon on the Mount was important. According to Bahro, this whole group should carry out a peaceful cultural revolution. 'The aim is to actually create the social conditions for the free development of *each and every single person*, something which, in accordance with the Communist Manifesto, is the *prerequisite* for freedom for everyone'.[275]

Bahro's belief was that, in actually existing socialism, the exclusionary nature of the system structure had resulted in political disenfranchisement among large parts of the population, with the party ruling over and stifling emancipatory forces: 'That party and its apparatus now occupy the very position which should be taken by the vanguard of emancipatory interests'.[276] He believed this vanguard would do a better job. That said, he failed to include a strategy for preventing renewed oligarchisation. Here, Bahro relied entirely on the spiritual and moral discretion of the intellectuals, who would listen to the voice of reason and retract their own interests. For this same reason, he also dismissed the related question of whether, once it had liberated itself from the tutelage of the upper class, society would immediately accept being subordinated to a new elite for the sake of an ideal for the future. One critic argued: 'The suspicion remains that, society could, albeit unintentionally, end up in the next straitjacket, one that serves the purposes of the cultural revolution'.[277]

Here, much like Harich, Bahro also failed to provide a self-critical analysis of his own utopian construct, neglecting to consider the possibility of it fail-

---

273 See Bahro 1977, p. 13.
274 Bahro 1977, p. 15. See also Ferst 2005, p. 35.
275 Bahro 1977, p. 16.
276 Woods 1986, p. 145.
277 Weis 1981, p. 39.

ing in practice. The fact that Bahro had not adequately factored in the risk of another wrong turn on the path to communism is also evident when we look at his conception of humanity.[278] Although Bahro accepted that people would not change of their own accord, he nevertheless assigned this educational task to a vanguard party. The new elite would, of its own accord, foster universal and critical consciousness – thus subjecting its own elite position to the permanent scrutiny of critical minds.

Bahro wanted to break up the sole domination of one party, to install another, which would make everything better. For things to carry on as they were was out of the question because, in Bahro's eyes, the contradiction between the original emancipatory task of the current party and its actually existing form of organisation destroyed the potential of communism and had an obstructive effect. Committed communists would either be turned into bureaucrats, co-opted and thus stunted, or, if they were unwilling to integrate, perceived as a danger. In Bahro's words: 'In a party such as this, the communists are working against themselves and against the people'. And for this reason, the apparatus must be challenged and destroyed, and from its ashes, the League of Communists, a new, different form of organisation must rise.[279]

Bahro drew his inspiration for this new form of organisation from Gramsci.[280] Consequently, he called for the party to be open and transparent towards the outside world. Even the new League would inevitably require an administration, but, unlike the current apparatus, this administration must not be allowed to take centre stage and dominate everything around it. Bahro did not desire a '... superstate to control the actual state and administrative apparatus from outside and above, but rather an intellectual catalyst for holistic behaviour among all grassroots groups, providing people with the ability to control the decision-making process from within'.[281]

---

[278] Although he did not completely overlook the risk: 'The communist alternative aims at a transformation which penetrates into the deepest layers of culture. Such an upheaval in no way relies on the naive illusion that power has to be passed into the hands of the opposition for history to then be able to change course. Society cannot be ambushed with the cultural revolution as it can be with a coup' (Bahro 1977, p. 47). An article from the same year in the *Spiegel* says: 'Bahro does not accept the objection that he has utopian dreams of "New" Humans. Although he acknowledges that a quasi-religious movement would be required to achieve his cultural revolution, in the long term, he sees no alternative to his ascetically purified socialism: "If we do not forego further material expansion, we are doomed"' (*Spiegel*, no. 35/1977).

[279] See Bahro 1977, p. 34f.

[280] On this see Gramsci 1980, p. 222ff.

[281] Bahro 1977, p. 39.

Instead of managing the status quo through an almost military party apparatus, the League should be the collective intellectual, the conveyer and the collector of ideas. 'The main function of this League of Communists will be to lead society into the cultural revolution so that it undergoes planned but not imposed change, in other words practical change underpinned by predominantly positive needs'.[282]

Along the same lines as Harich, Bahro too drew on Marx in his critique of growth:

> Unless the explosion of material needs can be halted, communism will not only be impossible from an economic perspective, but also from a psychological one. When Marx made a surplus of goods a necessary condition for communism, he was first and foremost referring to the absolute subsistence minimum, in other words no more than what is needed to live. In the industrialised world, the driving dialectic has shifted from production and need to the means of enjoyment and development.[283]

Bahro's *The Alternative* was thus opposed to consumerism and quantitative growth in both the actually existing socialist and industrial capitalist states. As such, *The Alternative* was quite clearly Bahro's response to the ecological discourse of the time, to the critique of the Club of Rome.[284]

Bahro made growth subordinate to the primacy of acquiring leisure time: Once industrial development has reached a level of maturity where it is capable of meeting people's most important needs, then

---

282 Bahro 1977, p. 39.
283 Bahro 1977, p. 40 f.
284 During an interview in 1995, Bahro made this clear in retrospect, stating: 'While I was still in the GDR, I was impressed by the signals received from the Club of Rome through Soviet publications: that we are eating into our resources too much and putting too much pressure on the Earth. At that point, I already proposed taking a new path – under socialism and under the conditions of a difficult class struggle – a path that would have to result in unilateral disarmament, and here I mean industrial rather than military disarmament. The two are connected anyway. Without military disarmament there can be no genuine ecology' (Grimm 2003, p. 283). Bahro's interest in the problem of the environment is confirmed by a Stasi report on him from 21 January 1975, which says: 'There were several occasions when Bahro addressed, for example, issues of ... environmental pollution. He was constantly trying to discuss these issues with the colleagues. He pursued these discussions with great passion and they were always based on political and ideological perspectives'. Further: 'Socialism was not an alternative to the capitalist consumer society. Socialism was no better at solving the problems of environmental pollution than capitalism. Bahro frequently conducted these discussions in this form, which could no longer be clearly dated' (BStU, MfS, AOP, no. 17596/81, vol. 2, p. 13 f.).

> ... economic planning [must] gradually, but decisively, be switched to the priority of all-round development of the people, increasing their opportunities for happiness. ... This does not imply the reverse scenario, with zero growth becoming the goal, but that there is a new criterion which replaces quantity at the top. ... It will at last mean no longer allowing wealth to be defined by late capitalism .... A socialist society will provide individuals with the general freedom for self-realisation and personal growth and development, even in the realm of necessity, which, economically speaking, means it will end the domination of objectified labour over living labour. People will no longer live, learn, consume, relax, enjoy solely to provide the labour force needed for the next production cycle.[285]

Bahro relied on a federal system of communes and close interpersonal contacts and relationships. Communism would be organised according to this principle, all the way up to the level of a global society. Bahro thus deliberately took a different path to Harich, vehemently rejecting 'the abhorrent idea of a hyperbureaucratic world government'.[286]

In 1980, after Bahro had emigrated to West Germany, another of his books was published: *Elemente einer neuen Politik. Zum Verhältnis von Ökologie und Sozialismus* (Elements of a new policy. The relationship between ecology and socialism). This work along with all of Bahro's subsequent texts can no longer be seen as a work of utopian thought opposing the GDR. In the following section, therefore, the only parts of these books I will refer to are those relating directly to the utopian content of *The Alternative*. Bahro's political impact as a member of the Greens in the Federal Republic transcended the topic of utopia, however.

Suffice to say that in 1980, Bahro's aim was to turn the nascent Green Party into a melting pot for all those seeking tangible alternatives to industrial society, both in the East and the West. Here, Bahro's goals went far beyond what already existed, showing very clear links with post-materialist utopia. According to Bahro, the purpose of the ecological movement had to be to put an end to the artificial dynamics of needs. Without this, true socialism would remain inconceivable. As such, Bahro saw the socialist and environmental movements as highly compatible.[287]

In the early 1980s, Bahro addressed not only the question of the environment but also the question of peace. Much like Harich and Havemann, he called

---

285   Bahro 1977, p. 44.
286   Bahro 1977, p. 46.
287   See Bahro 1982a, p. 32.

for the reunification of Germany, but under different conditions. According to Bahro, the aim should be 'a bloc-free and alliance-free Germany and Europe'.[288] To achieve this, Bahro drew up another programme that involved a reorganisation of the global system:

> We must therefore determine afresh our material demand ... For this we require first of all a debate that embraces the whole of society, with the aid of the means of mass communication ... The point is to agree on a social order in which production oriented to need is possible. Political culture will only survive if a broad agreement as to how we want to change can be arrived at in good time. If things come to a terrible end in the form or wars of distribution and civil wars, forced rationing and eco-fascism, this will not be primarily because there are interested parties and ideologists who actively support these alternatives.[289]

In other words, like Harich, although Bahro was opposed to eco-fascism at the time, he saw it as inevitable, unless a radical change in lifestyle, underpinned by a broad democratic basis was to be implemented immediately.[290]

In a book entitled *Was da alles auf uns zukommt. Perspektiven der 8oer Jahre* (Everything the future holds for us. Prospects for the 1980s), also published in 1980, Bahro fleshed out the details of this programme. He called for capitalism to be eradicated and its entire process of reproduction abolished. This required a broad movement which, at that time, was still in a nascent state.[291] Bahro

---

288   Bahro 1982a, p. 103.
289   Bahro 1982a, p. 104.
290   Later he wrote that people had to endure this dictatorship as a consequence of their actions: 'Bahro illustrates in the *Avoiding Social and Ecological Disaster* that Western democracy will clearly quickly end up in a state of emergency, with the corresponding government, a dictatorial junta, when the environmental disasters head our way. People will increasingly be objectified and the overall state of society will thus deteriorate. An emergency government like this will make our spiritual failure quite clear. All manner of philanthropic justifications and honourable motives can easily be distorted and used for nefarious goals. We will eventually be grateful for police-controlled rationing, because that would safeguard the means of living for some time at least. All this will not emerge from the perfidious meetings among ruling groups, but will result from the non-existent willingness to start, at the right time, to work towards an emancipatory society which attempts to limit itself from an ecological perspective' (Ferst 2005, p. 31). See also Grimm 2003, p. 291.
291   'Just like in the 1950s, when, faced with the threat of the atomic bomb, people began to grasp that the class struggle could not be waged at this level, today, the ecological crisis, the general crisis of our civilisation, has also induced people from all manner of social strata to seek solutions beyond their specific class interests ...' (Bahro, Mandel and von Oertzen 1980, p. 32).

made the assumption that, in the following 30 to 50 years, the world would run out of resources. This would automatically stop growth, and capitalism would thus reach its limits. Against this backdrop, Bahro was also sceptical about the possibility of this change averting the problems thanks to new technologies, seeing a temporary reprieve as the best that could be hoped for.[292]

The book records a conversation about the situation in the Eastern Bloc between Bahro, Ernest Mandel and Peter von Oertzen. Although, after leaving for West Germany, Bahro claimed to have no interest in taking on the role of GDR expert,[293] it was this very role that he adopted during the discussion. Bahro believed that the world market adversely effected the economies of the Soviet Union as well as all the states that fell within its sphere of influence. Another factor that had a stifling impact on the Eastern Bloc economies was the bureaucratic management of the economy, which Bahro saw as having an inhibitive effect and as hampering mass initiative. Bahro lamented this as he predicted that by weakening the actually existing socialist economy, there would be a real danger of the existing imbalance tipping further towards the West and capitalism being able to function without the corrective role of the East.

When it came to the process of transformation and the agent of that transformation, Bahro maintained the position he set out in *The Alternative*:

> When it comes to the level of education, the GDR is the most Marxist in Eastern Europe. Marxism is organised within the party. These elements are essential. ... It is precisely these elements that, once they come to the fore, create something entirely different to the Leninism, they were criticised for. The situation in the USSR is worse because there, Marxism suffered a devastating defeat due to Stalinism, ultimately at the hands of the firing squad. These firing squads did not wreak havoc in Poland, Hungary, Czechoslovakia, or the GDR. The potential is there.[294]

Bahro envisaged a two-stage process: First there had to be a democratic revolution against the politbureaucracy, and only then would it be possible to usher in and forge ahead with a process of transformation. When it came to Bahro's notion of how this should be achieved, in other words his apparently elite concept of the intelligentsia, he attracted criticism from his interlocuters, to which he responded:

---

292   Bahro, Mandel and von Oertzen 1980, p. 64.
293   See Grimm 2003, p. 281.
294   Bahro, Mandel and von Oertzen 1980, p. 127 f.

> It is true that I did not envisage the change in the countries of Eastern Europe as stemming from grassroots democracy, nor, given my experiences with reality there, would I do so now. ... We cannot yet allow ourselves to hope ... for the creation of a society without domination to happen in one step alone. I cannot ... guarantee that at a later, more advanced stage, there will not be renewed confrontations of this type, a monopolisation of these positions of power, and we will not end up having to go through the same thing all over again. But there is still no way round this next stage.[295]

So Bahro was well aware of the contradictions and the risks, but he pinned his hopes on practical implementation, the objectives of which were to be based on the anarchistic utopian tradition.

Elsewhere, Bahro elaborates on his concept of the transformational subject further, drawing, as the SED did, on Marx's concept of the proletariat. This was something which Bahro believed, as described in *The Alternative*, had developed in the wrong direction in the political sphere. As with the concept of communism, he wanted to return to what he supposed was the originally intended purpose of the proletariat. Bahro clearly saw the proletariat as a revolutionary agent. But he adopted a very broad definition of it, ultimately seeing almost everyone as alienated, both in terms of their work and their (subaltern) way of life. Their alienation was that of the whole of society, stemming from the traditional division of labour. For Bahro, overcoming this was pivotal, a view that can also be found in Karl Marx' 1847 *The German Ideology*:

> For as soon as the division of labour comes into being, each man has a particular, exclusive sphere of activity, which is forced upon him and from which he cannot escape. He is a hunter, a fisherman, a shepherd, or a critical critic, and must remain so if he does not want to lose his means of livelihood; whereas in communist society, where nobody has one exclusive sphere of activity but each can become accomplished in any branch he wishes, society regulates the general production and thus makes it possible for me to do one thing today and another tomorrow, to hunt in the morning, fish in the afternoon, rear cattle in the evening, criticise after dinner, just as I have a mind, without ever becoming hunter, fisherman, shepherd or critic.[296]

---

295 Bahro, Mandel and von Oertzen 1980, p. 30 ff.
296 Marx and Engels 1975b, p. 47.

4.2 Post-1980

In *Avoiding Social and Ecological Disaster*, published in 1987, Bahro took his criticism of industrial society all the way to the limits of social and human existence, musing on post-industrial transformations that embraced all political systems. In this work, his criticism of actually existing socialism was of marginal importance and limited relevance.[297]

In the late 1980s, the prediction Bahro had made a decade earlier became reality, with capitalism on track to emerge victorious over actually existing socialism in the ideological struggle of the Cold War, should the latter fail to correct its course. In the postscript Bahro added to the GDR edition of *The Alternative* published in 1990, he wrote: 'In those days, the view of both friends and foes was that my analysis was good, but my conclusion was purely utopian, and now utopia has partially become reality. ... On the other hand, it is clear that a perestroika imposed from above has its limits, both in reality and of course also in my book'.[298]

Bahro seemed disappointed about the process of transformation in the GDR in 1989/90. In his eyes, both the population and the government of the GDR were compliantly and opportunistically striving for capitalism – probably at least partly because in 40 years, they had acquired neither backbone nor truth. Bahro was also critical of the SED cadres, who he accused of joining the chorus of shallow criticism of Stalinism.[299] He was dismayed that the GDR had missed its chance to develop in an alternative direction:

> What was less inevitable, and this is the reason why for the SED and its people the course of events now seems to have become something of a tragicomedy, is us missing out on the last five years, a time during which Mikhail Gorbachev attempted the type of reformation that so many of us

---

[297] In the mid-1990s Bahro wrote of his own book: 'So I've gone from *The Alternative* to *Avoiding Social and Ecological Disaster*, which calls for an "assembly" based on a canon of values beyond that of late bourgeois society and of which the "eco-communist" perspective developed here is but one, albeit increasingly important, facet. In the *Avoiding Social and Ecological Disaster*, I describe what was depicted in *The Alternative* as a specific bottleneck of "actually existing socialism" as a general bottleneck of the technology-obsessed human race. I now have the impression that just as *The Alternative* has not been superseded by the ideas of some socialist theorists or other in the 20 years since its publication, neither has the *Avoiding Social and Ecological Disaster*, in the ten years since it appeared, been supplanted by some ecological theorists or other. This applies, as is probably quite clear, to *political* theory. *Philosophically*, I was never original, nor was or indeed am I advanced' (Bahro 2007a, p. 95).

[298] Bahro 1990, p. 548.

[299] See Bahro 1990, p. 549.

had awaited for decades. And thus we have missed the chance that would have been bigger in the GDR than in the Soviet Union to follow our own independent path, a path that I referred to throughout the final part of my book as the 'Strategy of a Communist Alternative'. The hour of the League of Communists is gone. We have embarked upon another path, one which calls for a different type of leadership.[300]

Here, the author himself once again elucidates the spatial and temporal context of *The Alternative*. The book was a review of the historical development of actually existing socialism. It pre-empted certain developments, at the same time ignoring other tendencies and risks. It also becomes clear that, in the 13 years between 1977 and 1990, *The Alternative* did not succeed in becoming 'The Bible' of the oppositional movement.

Bahro's last, longer text *Das Buch von der Befreiung aus dem Untergang der DDR* (The book on escaping the demise of the GDR) also has utopian elements. The book, a 140-page essay, was written in the mid-1990s and addressed Sahra Wagenknecht, then a young exponent of the communist platform of the PDS.

Bahro begins the book by deliberately drawing on the eco-communist content of Part Three of *The Alternative*, the aim being to help the PDS recognise the inherent link between communism and ecology and make it part of their programmatic position. Bahro saw Marxism-Leninism's reduction of the idea of communism to the economy as undesirable and incompatible with ecology because it focussed on the 'original source', namely economic growth. As an 'ism', Marxism had failed; according to Bahro, modern 'isms' were largely unsuited for overcoming the ecological crisis.[301] Similar to Harich in his later years, Bahro identified the patriarchy as one of the fundamental evils from an anthropological perspective: 'Only from the prevailing pursuit of power of the ego, which is synonymous with the advance of the patriarchal class society, does a scarcity of resources arise, and in its wake this alluring market and explosion of material needs. Social antagonisms are the cause, not a consequence of scarcity'.[302]

With hindsight, Bahro noted that *The Alternative* already contained economy of time approaches:

> Let go, so that we may rest lightly upon the Earth, become part of the 'outer' of the two essential poles of the emancipatory programme. When

---

300 Bahro 1990, p. 554.
301 See Bahro 2007a, p. 37 ff.
302 Bahro 2007a, p. 64 f.

I wrote *The Alternative* I was unable to see this connection as clearly. However, I did have an idea which was consistent with this, that being the return to the original communism. In contrast to today's exuberant deliberations on a minimum wage for all ... I proposed a single income level for everyone ... Based on the criterion of the *Critique of the Gotha Programme*, it was intended to be 'communist', not 'socialist'. A crucial prerequisite was the quantitative equality of needs coupled with qualitative inequality.[303]

Since then, however, Bahro has relativised the utopia he conceived in 1977. In retrospect, he felt it was overly subjective:

I was admittedly so deeply engrossed in the utopia of socialism, of communism 'with a human face', which was supposed to solve my biggest personal problem: The fact that GDR communism, which I too had ordered, was so unloved by the people – no matter what it looked like. 'The Communist Party of Czechoslovakia – loved by the nation!' – this was the dream I had taken from the Prague Spring.[304]

In any case, by now, Bahro had changed his view on utopia. One of his students, Marko Ferst, recalls that in the 1990s Bahro had rejected concrete utopian concepts, instead focusing on achieving transformation through inner mindset:

I once confronted Rudolf Bahro, saying that his book, *Avoiding Social and Ecological Disaster*, actually needed a second part focussing on the potential form of a concrete utopia for a sustainable society. It was about more than a few theoretical parameters. He insisted that an individual's perspective on change was the most important matrix, and everything else would lead from there.[305]

4.3 A Post-materialist Philosophy of Praxis

Bahro's utopian thinking at the time of writing *The Alternative* can clearly be categorised as part of post-materialist discourse. At the same time, it was linked with the call for the actual implementation of utopia. In a television interview for the ARD broadcaster on 23 August 1977, Bahro said:

---

303   Bahro 2007a, p. 65.
304   Bahro 2007a, p. 77 f.
305   Ferst 2005, p. 44 f.

> I have no plans to form a party tomorrow. History doesn't work like that, nor does politics. However, providing the communist opposition, for which there is potential in every actually existing socialist country, ... with a theoretical basis, that is the real purpose of my book.[306]

Bahro thus combined a post-materialist utopia with one based on a philosophy of praxis in the tradition of Marx, Gramsci or Bloch. In Helmut Korte's view, overcoming alienation and social inequality was '... the practical aim of and the basis for Bahro's fundamental criticism of the societies of "actually existing socialism" ... He addressed the problems ... in a manner that was not abstract and theoretical, but practical, "on the ground": in the struggle for the creation of a classless, emancipated society in those places where the power of capital – in one way or another – is broken'.[307]

In his review of *The Alternative*, philosopher Manfred Hertwig, too, acknowledged Bahro's call for a philosophy of praxis. He wrote that the plain language the book used meant that it was accessible to a large number of people, and it was exactly this that made it a threat to the SED elites. In keeping with this, Bahro sought to provide a theoretical basis and establish a philosophy of praxis through *The Alternative*. The radical social change he had conceived required a 'new communist party. Bahro drew up programmatic ideas for a new "League of Communists" worded more specifically and precisely than anything drafted by opposition groups in the Eastern Bloc so far'.[308] Hertwig establishes a link between Bahro's agents of transformation and his own biography. He thus expresses his view on Bahro from the rare perspective of a dissident from an earlier generation:

> Some people in the Western world might still be surprised to learn that, in his preparations for radical change in the Eastern Bloc, Bahro is pinning his hopes on a group that '*the party apparatus is forced to nourish and keep alive*', in other words the ideologues. ... The more this group manages, through its work and the contradictions therein, to read Marx and Lenin properly, the more lasting the influence of the distinctively subversive spirit and temperament of these revolutionaries on so many people. What Bahro writes here did in fact become reality in the GDR of 1956/57.[309]

---

306 Bahro 1977, p. 100.
307 Korte 1980, p. 12.
308 Hertwig 1977, p. 1093. And this includes the 'Harich group'. This is remarkable, given that in 1956, Hertwig himself was a member of the so-called 'Harich group', something he spent two years in prison for. In 1959, after his release, he moved to Hamburg.
309 Hertwig 1977, p. 1099.

According to Hertwig, with the development of his strategy of transformation, Bahro does not have his head in cloud-cuckoo-land at all, but in fact draws on the actual situation observed in 1956 and the experiences of the Prague Spring. Hertwig continues:

> Albeit somewhat belated, Marx had found a better pupil in Bahro than he could ever have wished for. He [Bahro] was certainly no dogmatist, he was more of revisionist heretic. But in his analysing and de-dogmatising ... he adopts Marx's methods .... Against all the odds, there are still prizes to be won using this method, albeit only from the confines of a GDR prison.[310]

Someone else who expressed praise for Bahro's pursuit of a philosophy of praxis was theologian Helmut Gollwitzer. In his opinion, what was special about *The Alternative* was Bahro's frequently overlooked strategic concept, in other words his utopia. Bahro's concrete approach appealed to Gollwitzer:

> Finally, the aim of communism is being taken seriously again, brought down to earth from the heaven of ideals, back to 'concrete conceivability' .... Anyone who dismisses Bahro as a dreamer is simply showing their cynicism and this has already destroyed their socialism. Setting a goal that is not 'utopian' but can feasibly be achieved on this earth and analysing the steps required to accomplish this is of the utmost importance in the current situation. The resignation with which we shift this aim onto a 'bad utopia' not only contradicts the socialist concept; it also goes against what needs to be done in the context of today's threat to humanity. ... We will only succeed in escaping from this if we stop persisting with sceptical reserve ... and instead make our aims as radical as our criticism of barbarism.[311]

Bahro's attempt to escape reality, which remained stuck in the very same reality at the same time, was also referred to in a positive light by political scientist Wolf-Dieter Narr, who saw this revival of utopia as vital and was critical of the fact that it had been discredited by Marx and Engels and marginalised by their successors. He believed that the accompanying ban on images had led to a lack of creativity in the practical implementation of actually existing socialism. Bahro had finally left this unimaginative state behind without losing sight of real life:

---

310 Hertwig 1977, p. 1099.
311 Gollwitzer 1978, p. 34.

Reviving the discussion about objectives, especially for the purpose of analysis – that is the challenge Bahro is facing, among other things. He also engages in the extremely arduous task of developing a concept for an alternative society, and not some kind of cloud-cuckoo-land construct either. At long last, theory is being put into practice again, and will not wither away or become an atrophied abstract remnant simply because the masses, who will never grasp it anyway, have not yet grasped it.[312]

The trade unionist Heinz Brandt was similarly full of praise for Bahro's approach, guided as it was by a philosophy of praxis: 'What amazes me so much about the work of Rudolf Bahro is that practical theory and theoretical practice are in unison. I am opposed to a way of thinking that only interprets without striving for change'.[313]

In other words, the design of Bahro's political utopia was, on the one hand, in line with classical utopias since More. On the other hand, Bahro intended it to be a set of specific instructions for practical implementation. For him, these two planes were not mutually exclusive. His utopian concept comprised a direct claim to validity and call for implementation combined with tactical instructions for action. This distinguished him from authors whose utopias were not directly connected with a demand for their implementation.[314]

For the strategic implementation of his objectives, Bahro devised a 'minimum programme', in other words small steps such as the abolition of privileges and piecework pay, and a 'maximum programme' comprising a longer-term eradication of subalternity achieved by means of a restructured division of labour.[315] His approach thus follows the dualism of short-term and long-term goals that Bloch called for. In *Abschied von der Utopie?* (Is this goodbye to utopia?), Bloch comments on the difficulties of such an undertaking, arguing that a long-term utopian goal alone, with no short-term goals and without engaging in practical work 'in the Devil's inn or beer house ... was null and void, pure nonsense in some abstract distant future'. If, however, we only have short-term goals, Bloch continues, in other words only engage in the political administra-

---

[312] Narr 1978, p. 54 f.
[313] Committee for the Release of Rudolf Bahro (ed.) 1979, p. 82.
[314] Here I am referring in particular to those utopian texts which (to some extent) were only designed to serve as warnings or as theoretical frameworks for exploring different possibilities, as was the case with the dystopias of the early and mid-twentieth century, for instance.
[315] See Spohn 1978, p. 27.

tion of the status quo, and fail to link this to a long-term (socialist) goal, this will achieve nothing at all. After all: 'There are no rungs, no steps, without a ladder'.[316]

Bahro's aim was not to attempt a second revolution or to turn back the clock to 1917. Nor did he want immediate revolution, calling instead for his 'cultural revolution' to be understood as a process. In the words of Fritz Vilmar: 'Bahro's *The Alternative* is not about revolution or reform (in other words first revolution and only then reform), it implies either revolution without democratisation, without reform – which would then not constitute a socialist revolution – or structural, radical, democratic, in other words long-term reform with a revolutionary effect'.[317]

For Bahro, a philosophy of praxis meant nothing other than the original method proposed by the young Marx, which saw – and this is particularly evident in the eleventh *Thesis on Feuerbach*[318] – theory and practice as belonging together – not in the form of practice substantiating theory, but where theory is also animated. Bloch argued that Marx was the first to take this approach, as the philosophers who came before him had cultivated an arrogant, detached view.[319] The analogy with Bahro is quite clear here: as the vanguard the intellectuals were not to position themselves above the ordinary people. They should instead be embedded in the very heart of society, translating the needs of the people into political strategy and guiding and advising on practical implementation. 'In other words: real practice cannot take a single stride without having consulted theory economically and philosophically, a theory advancing with great strides'.[320]

Bahro created a synthesis of classical utopia, a philosophy of praxis as defined by Marx, Gramsci or Bloch and the post-materialist utopian discourse of his time. With a view to making advanced industrialism a thing of the past, he employed short and long-term goals, i.e. concrete steps combined with a far-reaching utopian concept. In keeping with post-materialism, he also called for the future economy to be organised on the basis of time equivalents, instead of financial and material capital. Bahro believed this would help liberate individuals from the alienating constraints of wage labour. The use values would acquire a different social significance, and man and nature would exist in productive harmony. This would occur 'through the primacy of simple reproduction,

---

316   Bloch 1980 p. 71f. On this, see also Amberger 2010b.
317   Vilmar 1981, p. 128.
318   See Marx 1975, p. 5.
319   See Bloch 1986.
320   Bloch 1986, vol. 1, p. 277.

through a radical reduction in the material and energy input and by tailoring products towards functional quality'.[321]

The influence of post-materialist discourse in *The Alternative* can also be seen when it comes to the role and emancipation of women, although Bahro only touches on this topic briefly. One of the working groups at the 1978 Bahro congress discussed this thematic focus at length, coming to the following conclusion:

> Bahro's significance for us as women ... lies in his concept of comprehensive individual self-realisation. ... He calls for the small family to be abandoned, housework to be socialised and the population to be divided into communes, a process in which the leading role would fall to women. Moreover, there would also be the possibility of direct united representation of interests against the patriarchal tradition .... That said, his ideas about the abolition of traditional family structures did not go far enough for us as they were reduced to the economy. ... Consequently, Bahro's strategy for overcoming the subalternity of women also falls short by 'transforming women's emancipatory struggle from a hopeless and tense ideological rebellion into an issue of practical economics', as he sought to do .... Indeed, Bahro neglects the fact that patriarchal behaviour ... does not stem solely and directly from economic conditions, nor can it be resolved in this context.[322]

Another aspect that drew criticism was the fact that, although Bahro's utopia envisaged the liberation of women from the shackles of the patriarchy, this emancipation was led by men and conducted in a masculine manner.[323] This is very similar to his strategy of general emancipation 'from above'. In terms of sexuality, Bahro's concept of freedom corresponded more with that of the French Revolution than the form proposed by the 1968 generation, an approach which Bahro rejected.[324] For Bahro, it was therefore more about liberated love than hedonistic 'free love'.

Bahro's philosophy of praxis approach ensured that he also incorporated the actual achievement of his utopia in his model. Here though, there is also

---

[321] Spohn 1978, p. 27.
[322] Committee for the Release of Rudolf Bahro (ed.) 1979, p. 216f.
[323] 'Women were not depicted as emancipatory subjects because the specific potential for emancipation created by women was disregarded in his analysis of forces of resistance' (Committee for the Release of Rudolf Bahro (ed.) 1979, p. 217).
[324] See Heyer 2009, p. 44f.

a flaw in his utopian concept, for when it comes to the associated dangers and risks, Bahro's observations are patchy at best. The crucial question of what would happen to those individuals who rejected the transformation was left unanswered, with Bahro apparently going on the assumption that through a process of education and emancipation everyone would welcome the communism of his utopia. This is where *The Alternative* differs from Callenbach's *Ecotopia*. In the latter, those who wanted to continue with their old way of life simply remained outside the utopian state. Ursula Le Guin, too, relocated her anarchistic utopia to the *Planet of the Dispossessed* which, with its traditional way of life, was juxtaposed with a home planet, which served as an antagonist.

A contradiction in *The Alternative* pointed out by Röhrborn also highlighted the disparity between the allocation of labour in the collective and the individual decision about the type of work: the free development of the individual was thwarted by the social relationship. And Bahro had not resolved this contradiction. Moreover, in Röhrborn's view, there was a danger that even a communist transformation like the one proposed by Bahro would not being immune to taking a wrong turn and heading in the direction of a dictatorship,[325] not least because Bahro's concept of transformation was designed as a radical change 'from above'. 'He did not have faith in individuals' capacity to achieve such far-reaching emancipatory change themselves'.[326]

Although Bahro made strategic proposals, like Harich, he remained vague when it came to the details of the political institutions and system. This was something Peter von Oertzen was also critical of: Bahro 'refers to an association of communes, but says nothing about political groupings let alone parties, nor does he say a word about guaranteeing certain political and social rights. It can be assumed, however, that he is against the repression of such rights, something that is reflected in almost every word of his book. And he clearly neglects to tell us anything about the tangible formal organisation of this association of communes, quite in contrast to his very concrete, detailed analyses of the socialist economy and its process of transformation. And I think this is no coincidence. Among those on the left who see themselves as revolutionary Marxists, there is a kind of barrier to any form of nuanced examination of reality and the idea of actually existing democracy, irrespective of whether you put this term in quo-

---

325   See Röhrborn 2008, p. 120f.
326   Röhrborn 2008, p. 122. Working Group 6 at the Bahro Congress in West Berlin came to the same conclusion: 'When it came to the question of the role of the intelligentsia in the transformation of society, Bahro remained Leninist. He thus distrusts his own premise, in other words that mass "surplus consciousness" exists in actually existing socialism' (Committee for the Release of Rudolf Bahro (ed.) 1979, p. 194).

tation marks or not'.³²⁷ In von Oertzen's opinion, Bahro intentionally avoided describing the institutions in his utopia in too much detail, and this was down to his fear of confronting Western democracy.³²⁸

Bahro's utopia can thus also be seen as rooted in a philosophy of praxis in the sense that the future shape of communism was entrusted to the actual revolutionary process. Thus, to some extent, Bahro's concept also fulfilled the post-materialist utopian criterion of an openness of history.

5 *The Alternative* as an Alternative?

5.1 *Impact in the* GDR

Essentially, when examining how *The Alternative* was received in the GDR, we can draw a distinction between two audiences: first, critics of the system that were for the most part organised in conspiratorial circles, and second, the SED and the state organs that went with it. This dualism in the response to *The Alternative* was already evident before the book was even published: Bahro initially circulated his work among a small number of cultural professionals and intellectuals in the GDR and in 1975 he distributed a few manuscripts among friends and acquaintances. Two years later, before the book had been published in West Germany, he sent a number of manuscripts, under the pseudonym Dr R. Walser, to select GDR figures. East German filmmaker Thomas Grimm assumes that the majority immediately redirected this correspondence to the SED or the Stasi.³²⁹ Both audiences were therefore already aware of Bahro's text at this early point in time, albeit on a small scale to begin with.

5.1.1 The State Authority's Reactions

I will begin by examining the reactions of those targeted by Bahro's criticism. Following the publication of his book, Bahro was arrested and later sentenced to a number of years in prison. In early July 1978, an article about Bahro's arrest and sentencing appeared in the official party newspaper of the Central Committee of the SED, *Neues Deutschland* (New Germany). This was a somewhat

---

327 Committee for the Release of Rudolf Bahro (ed.) 1979, p. 44.
328 Bahro did not see Western democracy as an alternative. 'What is more, for him, democracy could only exist beyond bourgeois society, in other words in socialism. He sees the real function of democracy as being to provide opportunities for debate, guarantee freedom of expression and such like, and to support the decision-making process' (Heyer 2009, p. 44).
329 See Grimm 2003, p. 267f.

unusual occurrence as the names of dissidents and other opponents of the regime were seldom disclosed in the GDR media. The article in *Neues Deutschland*, too, was no more than a brief press release stating the official verdict:

> Rudolf Bahro appeared before the first criminal division of the Berlin city court on charges of treason for collecting communications as well on charges of betrayal of state secrets. ... It was established beyond doubt that, in the course of his treacherous activities, the accused made intentionally fabricated reports, gross misrepresentations and false allegations using sufficiently well-known conspiratorial state security means, methods and channels made available by hostile groups working against the GDR. In the process, he cooperated intensively with correspondents from the West German mass media. ... During the trial, it was further proven that Bahro satisfied his greed by accepting DM 200,000 in payment for these anti-socialist and subversive activities. On 30 June 1978, Bahro was sentenced to 8 years imprisonment for his crimes pursuant to paragraphs 98 and 245 of the German Criminal Code (StGB).[330]

This reflected the official SED position on Bahro.[331] This was not, however, the state authority's only reaction to his book. Several copies of *The Alternative* did the rounds in the Central Committee of the SED, for instance. An economics professor at Humboldt University of Berlin at the time, Hermann von Berg, who also had close links to the SED,[332] reported having-

> ... received a total of 36 copies from Dietrich Spangenberg ... and *Spiegel* editor Ulrich Schwarz. He distributed these copies in the Central Commit-

---

330 Quoted in Herzberg 1998, p. 2.
331 The political motivation behind Bahro's sentence was indirectly admitted a few years ago by a high-ranking Stasi official: 'It should be pointed out, however, that at the behest of the SED, a political examination of Bahro's views and specifically the content of the book was prevented. In assessing the Stasi measures against Havemann and Bahro, we must not overlook the fact that their political reputation and their views were used against the GDR during the Cold War' (Schmidt 2003, p. 644).
332 Not long after this, the once cordial relationship fell apart when von Berg was suspected of being the author of the *Spiegel Manifesto*, a piece published in 1978 in West Germany that was critical of the SED. It was treated as a GDR opposition text, although this later turned out to be a false assumption. The self-proclaimed 'German Alliance of Democratic Communists' which wrote the paper – and here the parallels with Bahro are unmistakable – did not actually comprise members of the opposition at all but in fact SED scientists and other high-ranking members who were close to the very same Hermann von Berg. To this day, the identities of the members of the Alliance remain unknown, and, over the years,

tee ..., the State Planning Committee, the Council of Ministers, Humboldt University (and he also listed one or two other organisations). In response to my question of whether he wasn't taking a huge risk passing the book on, he just laughed and told me: We all know one another and can talk openly about things like this ....[333]

The book was also circulated among members of the security service. It was part of the training for those Stasi cadres responsible for dealing with Bahro, with opposition circles and with preventing Western support for the GDR opposition. But even in Stasi circles, the book could only be accessed by those who were directly involved. In other words, not every Stasi employee got to read *The Alternative*; confiscated copies had to be handed in. Although it was theoretically possible for a member of the Stasi to read the book, they were not allowed to pass on any of the content, nor could they discuss it outside the Ministry.[334] So even within the Stasi, where the SED placed only the most loyal of supporters, the party leadership feared Bahro's ideas.

The archives of the Stasi Records Agency (BStU) contain an 'assessment' dated 30 November 1976 of the study '*a critique of actually existing socialism*' that was produced for the Stasi.[335] This 16-page text can be understood as an internal, strictly confidential review of the book. At the very beginning of the assessment, Bahro's work is described as 'an extremely ingenious and dangerous anti-communist – and above all anti-Soviet – counter-revolutionary platform'. Bahro attacked the prominent role of the SED, the state form of the dictatorship of the proletariat, the historical mission of the working class, the nature of actually existing socialism as a historical transitional phase to communism and the pioneering role of the CPSU, or in other words the Soviet Union. The Stasi regarded Bahro's text as 'capable of reaching a very broad audience', which was exactly what Bahro intended. This made Bahro so much more than just an unconventional thinker or a critic of the system. It would be more accurate to describe him as 'a sworn and ingenious enemy of the socialist state and social order, the working class, the party and its Marxist-Leninist politics'. Bahro saw himself '... as ... a spiritual leader, responsible for setting the course

---

there have been numerous theories and tales about the authors of this publication, some of which even insinuated that members of the KGB might have behind it. See Vesper 2008, p. 22.

333   Herzberg and Seifert 2005, p. 619f.
334   The source of this information was a former employee of the Main Directorate for Reconnaissance of the Ministry of State Security (*Hauptverwaltung Aufklärung*).
335   See BStU, MfS, AOP 17596/81, vol. 1.

of the counter-revolutionary movement' and 'fundamentally questioned the entire development of socialism since the Great October Socialist Revolution'.

His study goes beyond simply listing the reasons for 'a radical change' of actually existing socialist conditions. 'He also fleshes out the main features of a strategy of counter-revolutionary upheaval, thus providing instructions for counter-revolutionary action'. The report did not interpret Bahro's book as Marxist critique, and did not even attribute it socialist characteristics, instead describing it as (purely and simply) anti-communist. The SED leadership did not see Bahro's arguments as Marxist critique either, as seen in a letter from Albert Norden to Erich Honecker, for instance. On 6 July 1978, Norden, a member of the Politburo of the SED Central Committee sent a letter to Honecker furnishing him with quotes from the Western press:

> Dear Erich, in connection with the Bahro case, the rabble-rousing in the FRG against the GDR has reached new dimensions. ... Bahro's crimes are being celebrated as the 'duty of a critical left-wing author' who has 'renounced his allegiance to a morally and politically corrupt caste of bureaucrats'.[336]

Within the party – in keeping with the prevailing principle of 'democratic centralism' – the political view of Bahro and his book was stipulated from above. The party leadership's position was to be adopted by all party members. Criticism from the party grassroots was neither welcome, nor permissible according to party rules. However, this position on Bahro no longer met with approval throughout the SED. Not all members saw Bahro's ideas as pure anti-communist, as Wilfriede Otto reported:

> The Alternative was a prohibited publication, which no one was allowed to discuss within the party, yet which was discredited in party communications and by party functionaries as 'nonsense'. At least those who perceived Bahro as a utopian communist showed reflectiveness and despondency.[337]

The SED leadership was faced with the problem that not all members of the party were willing to adopt the view of the leadership without having read Bahro's *The Alternative* themselves.[338] The actions of top-level party function-

---

336 Quoted in Eberle and Wesenberg 1999, p. 155 f.
337 Klein, Otto and Grieder 1996, p. 418.
338 See Otto 2008, p. 159.

aries in this regard also caused internal party tensions in the years that followed. This meant that during the second half of the 1980s, Gorbachev's ideas of glasnost and perestroika fell on the fertile ground that Bahro had had a hand in preparing.

As described above, Bahro's book was most certainly acknowledged and discussed among the GDR political elite, although it was not officially addressed. That said, public statements about the book, albeit disparaging ones, were made by certain scholars close to the SED, including cultural scientist Hans Koch,[339] who, three months after *The Alternative* was published, stated –

> ... at a conference of cultural officials in the Eastern Bloc ... that Bahro's book exemplified 'impatience, weakness and faint-heartedness when it came to the complex, protracted and contradictory processes that were part of creating the fundamental prerequisites for the gradual transition to communism'.[340]

Koch thus accused Bahro of revolutionary impatience and a lack of understanding of the SED's long-term strategy for achieving communism. In so doing, Koch indirectly admitted that, in the GDR itself, the 'prerequisites for the gradual transition to communism', in other words to socialism as the preparatory stage for communism based on the philosophy of history, had not yet been achieved. He thus unwittingly agreed with Bahro's analysis of actually existing socialism, at the same time revealing that the SED leadership's fears of Bahro's arguments were not unfounded.

From a power politics point of view, this public silence made sense, given that a fundamental debate about the legitimacy of the party was not in the interests of the SED leadership. Moreover, because of the relationship of de-

---

[339] In as early as 1957, Koch could already be seen as a dogmatist: 'Cultural functionary Hans Koch did not initiate the official examination of Georg Lukács until summer following the delays that were typical of the apparatus, with a view to banishing him from the GDR and branding him as *revisionist*, despite the fact that, up until that point he had been recognised as a Marxist authority on literature and aesthetics' (Herzberg 2006, p. 246). At the time *The Alternative* came out, Koch was Director of the Institute of Culture and Arts Studies at the Academy of Social Sciences of the GDR and member of the *Volkskammer*. In 1981, he became a member of the Central Committee of the SED. Five years later, he committed suicide, the first high-ranking official ever to do so, a fact that was highlighted by the GDR media in their coverage. See Müller-Enbergs, Wielgohs and Hoffmann (eds.) 2000, p. 445f. 'Koch was not just a member of the SED Central Committee, he was a leading cultural functionary in the GDR ...' (Mertens 2004, p. 68).

[340] Kroh 1988, p. 24.

pendency on the Soviet Union, a debate like this would not have been feasible in the late 1970s anyway.

5.1.2 The Relevance of the Book for the GDR Opposition

Bahro's book was primarily aimed at GDR citizens with a high level of education[341] and 'surplus consciousness'. He surmised that people like this could be found not only among the functional elite but particularly in circles of left-wing critics of the system. Bahro sought to gain the support of these individuals as initiators of a broad mass movement. He also called for an end to the ideological disunity that prevailed on the left, which was evident in his rejection of Trotskyism:[342]

> However, we have to free ourselves from the old orthodox Marxist sectarianism. We cannot learn the way from an opposition that once, much to its own ever-increasing irritation, lost the fight against the rise of Stalinist despotism. After 1917, during a certain phase of rejection of the domination of the apparatus, every revolutionary communist saw themselves as Trotskyite. But in reality, this position is historically futile. We don't want to re-establish the old norms, we want to create new ones. We are no longer dependent on internal party constellations but instead must consciously rely on the support of broad societal forces, forces which, at once naive and cunning, wave the words of the constitution and UN resolutions in front of the faces of the political police. We don't have to *identify* with, for instance, Sakharov's school of thought, and someone like Solzhenitsyn stands for the very opposite of what we stand for.[343]

Bahro thus defines the political framework for the GDR's left-wing opposition. For those critics of the SED who largely operated underground in small Marxist circles, this was likely to have been instrumental in shaping their identity. Moreover, the quote bears witness to the fact that Bahro's utopia was forward-looking and did not indulge in nostalgia.

---

341   Korte pointed out the disadvantage of this strategy: 'Bahro's *The Alternative* is not an easy read – far from it! In each and every line, the reader can almost feel the tremendous endeavour of the concept. The author did not make it easy for himself, or for the reader. Reading *The Alternative* takes time and knowledge – criteria which, unfortunately, not everyone in this society fulfils' (Korte 1980, p. 8).
342   This meant that he furnished himself with an argument that defended him in the face of the damning accusation of Trotskyism often used against left-wing critics.
343   Bahro 1977, p. 49 f.

Bahro played an important role for this part of the opposition. He was the epitome of courage, becoming, like Havemann, something of a role model. By hook or by crook, *The Alternative* was smuggled into the GDR, where it was reproduced, read and discussed in secret.[344]

> The fact that the political opponents of the SED were so keen to discuss *The Alternative* could mainly be put down to their desire to find a workable political form of oppositional action. What could not be achieved with theory was instead achieved through protest against Bahro's imprisonment. ... Although, his book failed to deliver specific instructions for action, Bahro nevertheless had a long-term impact when it came to the history of ideas. The basic model for the transformation of GDR socialism followed a ... concept of social change based on anticipating the future in small groups, groups which Bahro referred to as 'the first seeds of the new league'.[345]

The environmental groups of the eighties, in particular, found several points of reference in Bahro's texts.[346]

Critics of the system read Bahro's book not only to get a sense of inner satisfaction, seeing it as an articulation of their permanent malaise,[347] a theory

---

344 See Neubert 2000, p. 234. 'In October 1979, the Stasi identified nearly 90 GDR citizens who had come into contact with Bahro's *The Alternative* and expressed their solidarity with his texts in one way or another. Among them were 33 supporters and seven individuals who had been directly involved in the production of the book' (Eisenfeld and Eisenfeld 1999, p. 105f.).

345 Neubert 2000, p. 234.

346 'For this reason, he saw social change as being linked with society's betterment in terms of moral evolution – that would take the form of a move away from a political economy to society based on political ecology. Both elements cropped up in a variety of ways in the theoretical frameworks of the GDR opposition and, combined, represented an almost ideal-typical model of social change. ... The group-oriented anticipatory political ecology could be found among the Christian anarchists ... of the 1980s, in Falcke's group theory ... and in the theory of catastrophe developed by Hans-Jürgen Fischbeck .... Even if it is not always possible to identify a direct link with Bahro, this compatibility shows what subversive strength, what power to criticise the system this theory possessed' (Neubert 2000, p. 234). Elsewhere Neubert writes: 'Bahro offered another ideological concept to reconcile ecology and the economy. The radical nature of his critique of industrial society followed the familiar path of Marxist criticism of capitalism and at the same time downgraded the unpopular reality of the political economy in the GDR. In 1977, the year *The Alternative* was published, this was nothing new, ... but it brought the Marxist intellectuals closer to the subject' (Neubert 2000, p. 232).

347 'Combined with the use of the term subalternity, his ruthless disclosure of the workings of

which they could relate to. More than this, they also interpreted it as an appeal for them to take action themselves. In this sense, we can conclude that Bahro's philosophy of praxis approach did in fact reach small circles. Admittedly, the book did not spark the mass movement Bahro had hoped for but, in individual cases, it did motivate people to act:

> Despite the fact that the engagement with *The Alternative* did not result in the immediate implementation of his theories, it did drive the opposition to reflect on its self-perception. Frequently, this intellectual debate turned into practical actions of solidarity in support of political prisoners. The Leipzig Marxist-Trotsykist opposition group headed by Saar and Langrock produced flyers calling for Bahro's release and for his book to be published and attached a banner demanding his freedom to the Monument to the Battle of the Nations (*Völkerschlachtdenkmal*) during the autumn Trade Fair in Leipzig, leading to their arrest in 1978 and lengthy prison sentences in 1979. ... In Berlin, several Bahro reading circles sprung up and carried out their meetings in both private and church premises.[348]

Some elements of Bahro's strategy could also be seen in the 1980s opposition movements. In six lectures published on *The Alternative* under the title *Ich werde meinen Weg fortsetzen* (I will continue along my path) Bahro writes:

> The time is ripe to bring together those individuals who wish to become involved, without too much conspiring but more through knowledge and under the protection of a specific interested public. Admittedly, to begin with this will be less of a mass movement and more about theoretical, ideological and propagandistic activities. But we have to start somewhere.[349]

If we look at the activities of the 1980s civil rights movement, we can identify this very same strategy: besides the more or less covert meetings that took

---

the apparatus's rule and its self-interest, gave a name to the consciousness characterised by paralysing immaturity which prevailed in the GDR and clearly showed starting points for alternative action' (Röhrborn 2008, p. 119f.). This feeling of being incapacitated was described by Guntolf Herzberg, who himself felt like this at the time. See Herzberg 1988, p. 69f.

348 Neubert 2000, p. 321.
349 Bahro 1977, p. 54.

place in people's private apartments, nonconformist citizens of the GDR were increasingly becoming brave enough to meet in public, generally under the protection of the church. Churches hosted blues services, punk concerts, readings, prayers for peace etc., but discussion circles and individuals producing samizdat publications also met on their premises. These activities were the basis of the 1989 mass movement which brought about the end of the one-party rule of the SED. In this sense, Bahro's strategy proved to be a success.[350]

From the perspective of the strategy's content, i.e. its political, ecological and post-materialist objectives, in the real context of 1989/90, his strategy failed, however. For the majority of people in the GDR who read the book, the first two parts of *The Alternative* validated their own subjective perceptions, their feelings and, more than that, it provided them with a convincing counter-theory to the official ideology. In some cases, the book also gave them the impetus to become involved themselves. What they completely ignored, however, was Bahro's post-materialist utopia.[351] In other words, *The Alternative* was at once a success and a failure in the GDR.

One case, in particular, deserves additional mention here: in covertly penned texts, which were hidden away only to be published after the Peaceful Revolution, the abovementioned GDR economist and SED critic Fritz Behrens discussed the problem with Bahro's work. One of these texts was Behrens's own critical commentary on *The Alternative*, a text which was published for the first time in 2010. This commentary, which was actually written in February 1979, was entitled *Über Alternativen* (About alternatives) and highlights the problems a proponent of emancipatory socialism had with the Leninist elements of Bahro's utopia.

Behrens criticised Bahro for justifying the development of Stalinism and also found fault with Bahro's model of society, which envisaged neither an economy based on workers' self-management nor a bottom-up democracy, but instead an elite 'League of Communists'. Although Bahro called for workers to have more of a voice, he stopped short of advocating for complete self-determination. In Behrens's words:

---

350 See Hosang 2009.
351 'In Part III he outlined the grassroots democratic and ecologically oriented communist alternative that gave the book its name – which he referred to as a "cultural revolution" – which, however, the vast majority of readers either ignored or failed to understand' (Herzberg 2007, p. 10). See also Neubert 2000, p. 233. We should not, however, forget those readers who actually did acknowledge and understand Bahro's *The Alternative*, although they have rejected it.

In Bahro's model, not only does society maintain its hierarchical and elitist structure, but the party, albeit renamed the "league", remains the brains behind emancipation, whether existing or future.[352]

Behrens claimed that Bahro was contradicting himself by defining actually existing socialism as both 'proto-socialist' and transformable. He argued that the cultural revolution was not the right path to take, instead calling for a political revolution that abolishes state ownership immediately rather than through a process of transformation towards 'workers' self-management'. He did not consider Bahro's approach to be anarcho-syndicalist, instead seeing him as pursuing a centrist elite strategy and accusing him of failing to move on from Leninism: 'Like Lenin, Bahro sees state monopolism as an interim stage en route to socialism'.[353]

Behrens, who had also briefly met Bahro and read his manuscript before it was published in the West, came to the conclusion that, due to its inherent contradictions, Bahro's concept of transformation was doomed to fail:

> All in all, Bahro is calling for indirect and thus civic and parliamentary democracy. By rejecting communal self-management based on direct democracy, he is perpetuating the very "subalternity" he seeks to eradicate.[354]

By rejecting cooperative, egalitarian self-management, Bahro is preserving the domination of one class over another. Yet, according to Behrens, class rule can allow for no more than bourgeois democracy. Behrens considered the book to be normatively important, but argued that from an economic perspective it suffered from serious flaws:

> Bahro claimed to have 'revealed the (political and economic) essence of actually existing more starkly than any other attempt so far' .... But, in reality, all [the book] entails is a technocrat polemicising against a bureaucrat, and when it comes to the economy, the only thing that both are committed to is a vulgar economy![355]

---

352 Behrens 2010, p. 159.
353 Behrens 2010, p. 163. 'Like supporters of Leninism, Bahro did not deem the masses to be the at the centre of historical conflict; they remained at the receiving end of an elite that was at the pinnacle of the party hierarchy, and which, thanks to its information advantage, understood what allegedly needed to be done' (Behrens 2010, p. 167).
354 Behrens 2010, p. 165.
355 Behrens 2010, p. 166.

Despite the criticism he voiced, Behrens's view was that the actually existing socialist states needed to facilitate a discussion of Bahro's theses to stimulate a critical discourse and set the learning process in motion. He kept his own thoughts under wraps, however.

5.2   Reception of Bahro's Work in the West

The appearance of *The Alternative* on the West German book market received considerable media attention. In addition to the public broadcasters, the biggest weekly newspapers, such as the *Spiegel* and *Die Zeit*, also reported the book's publication, making Bahro and his work an overnight sensation. Subsequently, West Germany's fragmented political left, too, went on to address the subject in a variety of different ways. The main players on this side of the spectrum were the Social Democrats, who at the time formed the West German government along with the Free Democratic Party (FDP) and who were thus also the subject of Bahro's critique. Besides this political mainstream, there was a whole raft of left-wing groups and parties that were the lingering remnants of the 1968 movement, ranging from the Red Army Faction (RAF) to the rivalling communist 'K Groups', from the West German Communist Party (DKP) to the new social movements.[356]

Since the previous section describes reactions to the book from those close to the SED, now would be a plausible juncture to focus on reactions among members of the DKP, which was (both ideologically and financially) very close to the SED. In this sense, the DKP's views can be seen as an indirect representation of the SED's position. This small party had to make itself heard above all the other Marxist organisations in the Federal Republic, i.e. it had to struggle for hegemony in the left-wing discourse. In light of this, it had no choice but to take a view on Bahro. Since the party was structured according to the hierarchical principle of 'democratic centralism', one representative text on Bahro is sufficient and here I will draw on the text entitled 'Comments on Rudolf Bahro's *The Alternative*' by Jürgen Harrer, which appeared in a volume of collected works published by Pahl-Rugenstein, a publishing house connected to the DKP.[357]

Harrer prefaces his critique with the caveat that his text was not meant as a commentary on the political case of Bahro, but was intended solely as a critique of *The Alternative* as the critical Marxist work Bahro declared it to be. He

---

356   Gerd Koenen aptly described the character of this time in his book *Das rote Jahrzehnt* (The red decade). Koenen 2007.

357   At the time, the Pahl-Rugenstein Verlag publishing house was indirectly financed through the SED. See Kirbach 1989. From 1979 Harrer worked there as an editor and since 1990 he has headed the Papyrossa Verlag publishers.

accuses Bahro of playing capitalism down and glossing over it throughout his book, while diminishing socialism and its achievements at the same time.[358] In his critique, he includes many abbreviated passages from *The Alternative*, quoting selectively and out of context, ultimately portraying a distorted version of Bahro's theses. Harrer criticises Bahro for levelling the differences between the capitalist and socialist systems and for catering to anti-Russian cliché with his references to the Asiatic mode of production. He accuses him of having written a book devoid of scientific basis and of measuring actually existing socialism against his own utopia.

> Although the book is highly eclectic, ... at the same time, Bahro's reasoning is characterised by a levelling of differences between the systems. This can be seen in his rejection of the theory of social formation, his failure to factor in the relations of production and ownership, and his adoption of the most influential bourgeois social theory at the time: the theory of industrial society.[359]

Bahro rejected Marxist social formation theory, yet at the same time referred to himself as a critical Marxist, something Harrer saw as being incompatible. In his social systems analysis, Bahro ignored the relations of production and ownership, reducing everything to the development of the productive forces. For Harrer, this did not go far enough and neglected the socio-historical contradictions.[360]

---

358 See Harrer 1978, p. 54f.
359 Harrer 1978, p. 59. In order to explain this theory – one protagonist of which is Daniel Bell – reference was made to a definition provided by Bruno Flierl, a GDR architect at the time: 'The bourgeois concept which is currently the most widespread and at the same time the most effective, and which has taken on particular importance when it comes to creating architectural and urban development concepts, is the theory of the "industrial society" and the "post-industrial society". This concept describes society as a whole and the development of that society on the basis of scientific and technical progress in the productive forces, beyond social structure, beyond the relations of production and the superstructure of a specific historical social formation, i.e. beyond the social forces and groups whose role and position is determined by this superstructure, and above all, beyond the classes, where capitalism and socialism are but variants and "modalities" of this so-called "industrial society". This is ultimately also the reason why, despite increasingly relying on economic and social research, and analyses and forecasts of architectural and spatial environmental design, proponents of the theory of "industrial society" are not in a position to properly interpret the scientific and technical development processes of our time, many of which they actually experienced first-hand, or the impact these developments had on society and architecture' (Flierl 1973, p. 10).
360 See Harrer 1978, p. 61f.

Harrer goes on to defend the development of the productive forces in the Soviet Union, claiming this comprised state-led modernisation achieved through mass initiative.[361]

Lastly, Harrer levels criticism at Bahro's depiction of the proletariat and the hopes he pinned on the intellectuals. Bahro's mistake here, according to Harrer, was to reduce the social structure of society to the factor of education. By reducing the working class to mere physical workers, he abandoned the Marxist path.

> Of course, this programme already existed before Bahro, and went by the name Godesberg. Bahro, in contrast, exhorted the working class to ignore the desire to satisfy their growing material needs .... Such positions also allowed an edition of the *Frankfurter Allgemeine Zeitung* (11.1.77) to concede the attribute of a 'significant achievement of a Marxist thinker'.[362]

In his analysis of *The Alternative*, Harrer agreed with the accusation made by the SED that Bahro had composed a 'bourgeois ideology'. He equated criticism of the way of life in industrial societies with criticism of the (economic basis of) the GDR. This clearly placed Harrer in the same category as the actually existing socialist opponents of the Club of Rome, whose reasoning he agreed with.

The SPD's reaction to *The Alternative* was quite different to the DKP's – both in terms of how they dealt with it as well as the actual substance of their reflections on the book. There was no unified 'official party' position, but Bahro did not meet with complete rejection from the SPD either, although his ideas were not exactly welcomed with open arms. The most revealing window on the SPD's position on *The Alternative* is provided by the reactions from the intellectuals in SPD circles, who reflected extensively on the feasibility of Bahro's utopia.

In this context one book in particular stands out: a collected volume by Hans Kremendahl and Thomas Meyer published in 1981 and entitled *Menschliche Emanzipation. Rudolf Bahro und der Demokratische Sozialismus* (Human emancipation. Rudolf Bahro and democratic socialism). This book was published as a 'study text for the University Initiative Democratic Socialism (HDS)' and includes contributions from a conference held in May 1980, at which Bahro was a guest. By their own admission, the publishers wanted to address the

---

361   Harrer 1978, p. 62. It seems paradoxical that Bahro, himself having worked for many years in industrial production in the GDR and therefore familiar with the practical 'functional context', should have a less thorough understanding of it than his West German critics.
362   Harrer 1978, p. 80 f. This refers to the SPD's 'Godesberg Program' of 1959, which is regarded as the party's renunciation of Marxism.

issue of Bahro and his works because he constituted a fascinating and potentially integrative figure for the whole of the political left in West Germany. The majority of the articles in the book referred directly to *The Alternative*, most of them even focusing on the third part of the book, i.e. Bahro's utopia.

Kremendahl did not view Bahro's strategy of transformation as a blinkered approach restricted to the issue of the means of production, but instead saw it as describing a holistic transformation which, from the perspective of a history of ideas, was heavily influenced by Rousseau and the young Marx. The problem he saw, however, was that Bahro's goal risked being misused to legitimise violence and coercion. This was a flaw Bahro's utopia shared with older social utopias and actually existing socialist systems. In making his plea for utopia, Bahro does not question the extent to which actually existing socialism is also the result of attempts to achieve utopia.[363] By opting for the utopian genre, Bahro is thus employing the wrong tool. Here, Kremendahl reduces the concept of utopia to the positive utopias that were popular until the early twentieth century. He overlooks the self-critical potential of the post-materialist utopias, which Bahro himself also neglects to properly consider. Kremendahl also criticised Bahro for turning his back on the class struggle and turning to post-materialism.

> Bahro thus made himself more of an advocate – in both the East and the West – of the needs of intellectuals, the well-educated, 'leading cadres' and members of the middle classes than of the proletariat. This is the reason behind Bahro's affinity with the Greens.[364]

Instead of making the proletariat the centre of revolutionary emancipation, Bahro placed the 'underchallenged intelligentsia' at the heart. Nevertheless, he still retained his Marxist historical paradigm: for Bahro, the historical process was based on 'objectivity' and there was a 'contradiction' that had to be 'sublated'.

> The Marxist-Leninist characteristics of the process remain, with Bahro changing only the executor. By ascribing vanguard status to the intelligentsia, Bahro ran the risk of the 'needs of the well-educated members of society potentially being treated as those of society as a whole'.[365]

---

363   See Kremendahl 1981, p. 148 f.
364   Kremendahl 1981, p. 151.
365   Kremendahl 1981, p. 152.

According to Kremendahl, Bahro believed that human characteristics were not inherited but rather instilled. This contentious and very optimistic theory defined his conception of man. At the end of the day –

> ... the assumption that a perspective on society as a whole can be based on the ability to sublate the division of labour is rather doubtful. There is simply too great a risk of this failing due to human imperfection, due to the fact that the actual (as opposed to the supposedly 'real') needs of the vast majority are not being met. ... Eliminating the diverse talents, dispositions and needs will be nigh on impossible.[366]

A similarly risky move was shifting social pluralism from the political realm to the non-political realm. According to Bahro, the political sphere should only comprise the 'League of Communists', which was designed to act as the big social harmoniser.[367] The whole idea demonstrated dystopian characteristics:

> The leadership function of the party envisaged by Bahro was to be far more powerful and more extensive, penetrating deeper into society, with a much firmer, all-encompassing grasp on people than is currently the case under actually existing socialism.[368]

Bahro was unable to resolve the contradictions between the new elite he had conceived and the danger of a re-oligarchisation:

> On closer examination, Bahro's notion of creating a new and better unity party is no more than an impractical attempt to take the Leninist party model and start from scratch again – to establish, if you like, a vanguard party with better, less self-interested, less power – obsessed individuals.[369]

Kremendahl's final verdict was very matter of fact:

> Right down to its fundamental assumptions, Bahro's concept of a political system inherently contains a seed of self-destruction, of a backslide

---

366   Kremendahl 1981, p. 153.
367   See Kremendahl 1981, p. 156 f.
368   Kremendahl 1981, p. 157.
369   Kremendahl 1981, p. 157 f.

to centralism and monism, and is highly unlikely to be in a position to facilitate fundamental political reform of the system of actually existing socialism.[370]

Despite the apparent unsuitability of his concept in practice, Kremendahl nevertheless saw it as a valuable source of inspiration for the debate on democratic socialism:

> Rudolf Bahro is an important social critic and an inspiring utopian. ... One thing his work is not, however, is a guide for a realistically feasible process of societal transformation, particularly in Western societies.[371]

Hans-Heinrich Nolte came to a similar conclusion in his essay for the very same collected volume. Nolte criticised the fact that Bahro's utopia remained too distant a goal and that he failed to provide concrete details on the transformation. On the notion of *The Alternative* as a utopia he wrote:

> As a utopian critique of contemporary socialist societies, Bahro's book has value. But this was not the function that *The Alternative* had for the masses in the West and nor could it be seen as such; it was interpreted as a utopia for a world society and thus also for our own society. In this sense, Bahro's book is not especially compelling. His utopia is not based on a concrete, precise or verifiable transformation of an existing world system, but instead focuses on the development of one region only. Even in a utopia, the diversity of the world system must be reflected in a diversity of social, economic and political constitutions that are systematically linked with one another.[372]

Fritz Vilmar, on the other hand, did not see Bahro's labour concept as 'utopian' at all, pointing to –

> ... the tendencies in the United States, in Italy, in Scandinavia, and even in the Federal Republic of Germany to offer workers more highly skilled work because they are no longer prepared to repeatedly perform senseless

---

370 Kremendahl 1981, p. 159 f.
371 Kremendahl 1981, p. 161 f.
372 Nolte 1981, p. 52. In terms of its geographical and political scope, Nolte viewed Bahro's utopia as severely limited. This putative shortcoming is one shared by almost every utopia, however.

> tasks to a high standard. And this development is, in my view, something that cannot be brought to an abrupt end at any given point during the course of "the emancipation of labour" through means that conserve the existing system. In this sense, if we understand Bahro's concept as long term – which is really the only way it can be seen – it is by no means a negative utopia, but rather a 'real utopia', in other words it is consistent with tendencies that can be observed in real life.[373]

Thomas Meyer, in contrast, argued that *The Alternative* lacked concrete utopia and pragmatic political short-term goals. Only once Bahro had fleshed these out would the practically useful aspects of *The Alternative* be revealed. Bahro thus has only two options: he either had to sacrifice some of his demands and focus on more concrete definitions of his short-term goals, or he perseveres with his utopia and refuses to engage with actual politics. The following would then apply to him: 'Anyone who declares his daily job to be the development of abstract utopia has, in reality, opted out of the political process of shaping society'.[374]

Peter von Oertzen, however, already commended Bahro's ecological utopian approach as early as 1978:

> Statements about 'the production target of rich individuality', 'redefining demand', 'reproduction' and 'economic planning' are, in my view, of particular relevance to the current discussion about 'growth' and 'quality of life' .... Here, for the first time, someone has proposed a reasonable economic solution to the dilemma of growth fetishism and ascetic zero-growth ideology.[375]

Von Oertzen saw a gap in the discussion about democratic socialism that Bahro's book could help fill. Heinz Brandt was also full of praise for Bahro's visions of the future,[376] seeing *The Alternative* as a contribution to ecological discourse. Unlike Nolte, he interpreted Bahro's utopia as a global concept:

373　Vilmar 1981, p. 126.
374　Meyer 1981, p. 178.
375　Von Oertzen 1978, p. 63.
376　'A combination of "abolishments" was intended to fuel the "far-reaching transformation of the needs structure"; he recommends "a series of immediate measures" which are not only suitable for "putting a stop to mass compensatory needs", despite being cheap, but which also "go beyond this" by accelerating the transformation, as they "appeal to the longing for social justice", in other words they are both right and proper' (Brandt 1978, p. 168).

Rudolf Bahro has provided us with a planetary alternative to this competition between lemmings, to the East-West growth frenzy, to the threat of ecological catastrophe.... [This book contains] an understanding of socialism that applies as much to the highly industrialised West as to Eastern Europe. Thus, the bitter struggle against this understanding is being waged as much by multinational companies as by the nomenklatura in the Eastern Bloc.[377]

Brandt thus remarks:

If Bahro lived in Brussels, he would – like Ernest Mandel – be an esteemed university lecturer, prohibited from entering either East or West Germany. His books would be banned over there [in the East] and barely known over here [in the West]. If he lived here, he would be prohibited from working, he would have sparse print runs, and a miserable wage. But, since he lives in the GDR, he is in solitary confinement over there and his book is a bestseller over here.[378]

Other writers from the socialist trade union scene, such as Joachim Bischoff and Klaus-Dieter Lühn, however, took Bahro's critique of growth to task. They rejected the radical break with growth that Bahro called for,[379] something they argued Bahro himself had contradicted: on the one hand, they argued, the cultural revolution will not come about if the aim is to eliminate the compensatory needs ad hoc and by decree. Overcoming these needs is a longer-term process and as long as this process is ongoing, growth will be inevitable. On the other hand, for Bahro's maximum demands to be fulfilled the entire economy would have to be restructured, and this cannot be achieved by halting growth. Thus, Bahro represents a regressive viewpoint.[380] Bischoff and Lühn found the

---

[377] Brandt 1978, p. 176.
[378] Brandt 1978, p. 170.
[379] See Bischoff and Lühn 1978, p. 190f.
[380] 'Bahro's fundamental idea that a break with "extensive growth" was necessary is neither new nor is it pioneering. He reproduced theoretical misconceptions, the ultimate social reason for which was certain antagonisms in modern social formations, whether capitalism or actually existing socialism, and which sporadically attract excessive attention in socialist theory. Bahro's concept is not founded in Marxism. On the contrary, Marx persistently and resolutely fought against theorists who see modern antagonisms as being rooted in the principle of the division of labour and believe these contradictions in social development can only be overcome by fettering the productive forces. Bahro's *The Alternative* presents precisely this type of concept, one which is on the whole retardive' (Bischoff and Lühn 1978, p. 191).

concept of 'compensatory needs' vague and hence dangerous. They raised the question of where existential needs stopped and compensatory needs began. Was this not also dependent on the given stage of development society was in? And who decides where the dividing line is? Here, the authors saw the risk of a dictatorship over allocation, which they countered with the alternative of a broad social debate about the structure of needs. They also perceived Bahro's ideas on the division of labour as posing a risk of imposed asceticism, as they would essentially 'restrain the development of productive forces'.[381]

In 1981, Hermann Scheer, who went on to be awarded the alternative Nobel Prize in 1999, criticised *The Alternative* for lacking in practical relevance. He claimed that Bahro placed too much emphasis on the utopian long-term goal, and this was at the cost of concrete short-term goals.[382] According to Scheer, when it came to the transformation of society, Bahro relied on the subjective factor as the driving force. He overlooked the risk posed by unrestrained subjective development, that being the emergence of a radical egocentricity and an erosion of social solidarity in its wake. He argued that politically regulated limits for individual self-realisation must be set. To prevent the re-emergence of a ragged class structure, an institutional framework was thus required. In Scheer's view, subalternity would not necessarily be overcome by means of the decentralised social structure Bahro had in mind, citing as evidence small human communities, such as village populations, where, alongside pure labour, there were also hierarchies. Thus, it is not the size of an organisation that is most important, but rather its internal democracy. Scheer regarded the SPD and parliamentary party democracy as successful examples of this.[383]

A final publication that illustrates how *The Alternative* was received among social democrats is *Die Zukunft des Fortschritts* (The future of progress), written in 1984 by Johano Strasser and Klaus Traube. These two authors were full of praise for Bahro, who they regarded as a farsighted thinker, given the fact that very few authors in the East had embarked on the process of rethinking faith in progress.[384] In the course of this process, those passages from the works of Marx that included a critique of the alienation and traditional division of labour took on new significance. As an Eastern Bloc visionary, Bahro 'convincingly demonstrated'[385] the topicality of these problems and their unresolved nature. He took up the critique of alienation from Volume 1 of Marx's

---

381 See Bischoff and Lühn 1978, p. 192f.
382 See Scheer 1981, p. 143.
383 See Scheer 1981, p. 144ff.
384 See Strasser and Traube 1984, p. 14.
385 Strasser and Traube 1984, p. 43.

Capital, developing it further and, in the process, proving that today, the separation of manual and intellectual labour did not have to be connected to private capital.[386] Strasser and Traube also recognised the post-materialist content of Bahro's utopia: 'It appears that people are starting to reflect on the idea that there are other vital things in life than just ownership and consumption'.[387]

As the above examples show, reactions to *The Alternative* from the social democratic milieu were far from homogenous. For some authors, Bahro's work was too focused on long-term goals, while others saw the book as containing direct links with realpolitik. He was accused both of being backward looking and of looking too far into the future. Consequently, we can safely say that the third part of *The Alternative* has fulfilled at least one criterion of utopian research: its relevance for contemporary discourse.

To develop this argument further, I will now reflect on the reaction to the book from the West German Maoists. This group was insignificant when it came to parliamentary representation, but in the 1970s, it nevertheless played a clearly discernible role within the political left, especially in the context of what were known as the K Groups. The journal *Theorie und Praxis des Marxismus-Leninismus* (Theory and practice of Marxism-Leninism), the theoretical wing of the KPD,[388] also printed a critical examination of Bahro's *The Alternative*. This group of Maoists were opposed to Soviet post-Stalinist communism, which they referred to as imperialist and revisionist.[389] They thus welcomed Bahro's critique of Soviet-type actually existing socialism, with the emphasis being on the 'Soviet', as the Maoists rejected the other elements of Bahro's critique just as vehemently as the defenders of post-Stalinist actually existing socialism. Reviewer for *Theorie und Praxis des Marxismus-Leninismus*, Werner Heuler, also only shared Bahro's views to a certain extent. Initially, he called for critical solidarity with Bahro, who he said had become the victim of the 'reactionary Prussian traditions of the GDR' where he was being held in a 'fascist prison'.[390] He then went on to critically examine the content of *The Alternative*. Heuler believed that the GDR's backwardness was to blame for Bahro's utopianism:

---

386 See Strasser and Traube 1984, p. 117.
387 Strasser and Traube 1984, p. 305f.
388 They previously also had the suffix AO (structural organisation) in their name, not to be confused with KPD/ML, which had their own section of the GDR. For more on this, see Wunschik 1998.
389 See Koenen 2007, p. 281 ff.
390 Heuler 1977, p. 118.

> It is striking that, on almost every point, Bahro's position corresponds with the position that Karl Marx and Friedrich Engels referred to in the *Communist Manifesto* as 'critical-utopian socialism and communism'. The only explanation for this is the underdevelopment of the class struggles in the GDR, as a result of being cut off from the experiences of the international workers' movement, especially those of the revolutionary struggle of the people of the Third World and of China's Great Proletarian Cultural Revolution.[391]

Heuler was critical of Bahro's failure to identify either the proletariat or the peasantry as a revolutionary class.[392] He called Part Three of *The Alternative* a 'bourgeois utopian perspective'. He ridiculed Bahro's idea of a non-violent transformation:

> Everything ... will develop in a peaceful manner and – given that classes no longer exist in his concept – without a class struggle. Bahro paints a harmonious picture, virtually free of contradiction .... The more Bahro talks about the future, the more he loses sight of the realities of the class society. The 'future society' that he imagines is depicted in detail. He dreams of a socialist system without a working class and without a communist party organised along democratic centralist lines. He imagines a transition from capitalism to communism without a dictatorship of the proletariat and without a proletarian state, which he sees as being replaced by an 'Association of Communes' based on a society where class harmony prevails. ... He does not even attribute any significance to the struggle against social-imperialist foreign rule, for independence and unity for Germany. It is this failure to consider the national question in particular that will make it very difficult for him, as a representative of a bourgeois democratic, oppositional movement, to connect with the working class and the masses once it is obvious, even to him, that they have made an appearance.[393]

Bahro was mistaken, as the class struggle in the GDR was real, just as real as the 'struggle for national independence'. According to Heuler, with these struggles, the working class would lead the people to victory, bringing foreign rule to

---

391 Heuler 1977, p. 121.
392 At the same time, despite his criticism of the content of his ideas, he was full of praise for Bahro's courage in opposing the status quo.
393 Heuler 1977, p. 137.

an end and, as the true 'dictatorship of the proletariat', it would bring about national unity against a backdrop of socialism. This will be the transition phase, moving towards the 'final goal of a communist, classless society'. The author of *The Alternative* does not recognise this historical context, however: 'We hope that Rudolf Bahro will be prepared for and in a position to continue his fight, to learn, to overcome his flaws and unite with the working class and masses in their struggle'.[394]

The Trotskyists' reactions to the book were less impassioned. As mentioned above, Ernest Mandel held a very positive view of *The Alternative*, seeing it as making a significant contribution to the discourse of the time. Pierre Frank, who was Trotsky's personal secretary for a time, also considered Bahro's analysis of actually existing socialism to be plausible, albeit not exactly innovative. He praised its Marxist goals and strategy, which opposed the privileges of the actually existing socialist elites and contained measures 'for the creation of a truly socialist society'.[395] Frank saw Bahro's programme as building on the ideas Marx had developed in his *Fundamentals of a Critique of Political Economy*. Bahro adapted Marx's arguments to the broader problems of the present (e.g. education, women's emancipation or the environment), and believed that they should be discussed and used by the Fourth International.[396] That said, he was still critical of Bahro's philosophy of history perspective and the associated justification of Stalinism, as well as Bahro's abandonment of the notion of the proletariat as the Marxist revolutionary subject. In contrast to Bahro, Frank argued that workers were perfectly capable of selecting the necessary 'specialists' themselves, something they had demonstrated many times over the course of history. In other words, they had no need for the patronage of an intellectual vanguard.[397]

As the various reactions demonstrate, the political left in West Germany was splintered into many different camps and currents. Yet, with the exception of the DKP, they still showed their solidarity with Bahro, despite the fact that his ideas did not always meet with approval. This situation resulted in the West German left temporarily coming together around the table for a four-day congress. Although the organisers failed to achieve their objective of overcoming the fragmentation of the left, they nevertheless managed to assemble a large number of participants from various different camps in West Berlin.[398]

---

394   Heuler 1977, p. 138.
395   Frank, P. 1978, p. 42.
396   See Frank, P. 1978, p. 44.
397   See Frank, P. 1978, p. 50 ff.
398   See Nawrocki 1975.

Of course, the GDR's state security was also very interested in the event, given its objective of mobilising broad-based solidarity among the political left for Rudolf Bahro who, at the time, was in a GDR prison. Between 1979 and 1983, the Stasi filled eight dossiers with around 1,500 pages on Bahro sympathisers based in West Berlin alone.[399] For the Stasi, the effort was not unwarranted: in late August 1977, Bahro was arrested; on 15 February 1978, the *Committee for the Release of Rudolf Bahro* was formed; on 30 June 1978, Bahro was sentenced, and five days later, the Committee organised a protest rally in front of the West Berlin *Gedächtniskirche* with Ernest Mandel, Jakob Moneta, Heinz Brandt, Helmut Gollwitzer and future German Chancellor Gerhard Schröder among the speakers and Gerulf Pannach and Christian Kunert, former members of the banned East German political blues band *Renft*, performing some of their songs; in October, the Committee made preparations for the aforementioned congress, which was ultimately held on 16–19 November at the *Technische Universität Berlin* (TU Berlin). Around 8,000 participants attended. On 10 December 1978, the International League for Human Rights awarded Bahro the Carl von Ossietzky Medal. Two months later, on 2 February 1979, the Bahro Committee reconvened. One of its main initiatives was an 'Appeal to the State Council of the GDR to provide a general amnesty for political prisoners to mark the state's thirtieth anniversary'. The 10,000 signatories of the appeal included prominent figures such as Simone de Beauvoir, Jean Paul Sartre, Wolf Biermann, Romy Schneider and Heinrich Böll. Following the appeal, several protests were held in Berlin and Marburg over the summer, and these continued until Bahro was released.[400]

Many prominent figures expressed solidarity with Bahro and also aired their views on the content of *The Alternative*. Helmut Gollwitzer described the book as –

> ... without a doubt, the most important theoretical work about the nature of society and the laws of motion in the Eastern Bloc to come out of the region since World War II. More in-depth and more concrete than any other analysis of post-capitalist societies before it, Bahro's *The Alternat-*

---

399 See Klepper 1998, p. 10. The Stasi had also planted informants at the congress. For the purpose of preventing the dissemination of statements and outcomes and to avoid the emergence of any campaigns in the GDR, participants of the congress were barred from entering the GDR or East Berlin during the period after the congress. The Stasi obtained information about the participants through informal staff. See Klepper 1998, p. 13.

400 See Klepper 1998, p. 10 ff.

ive captures the conditions of human emancipation in socialist society, at once obstructive and offering immense promises of hope.[401]

The Alternative caused 'Herbert Marcuse to make the momentous remark that it set out the only feasible way out of the apparently hopeless spiral of modern capitalism to date'.[402]

In a letter to Harich, Amery wrote that he saw *The Alternative* as so much more than just a book opposing the GDR. With his book, Bahro had tackled 'political ecology', unwittingly responded to *Communism without Growth?*, and had thus bridged a gap. Instead of advocating equality, Bahro called for freedom. Amery preferred this to Harich's dictatorial model. He saw Harich's approach as being destined for failure because the functional mechanisms of actually existing socialism were not capable of solving the ecological crisis. Here, Bahro's concept was more sophisticated.[403]

Lastly, in 1978, the Marxist theoretical journal *PROKLA*[404] published a special issue (issue 31) with a focus on Bahro. One article, written by Wilfried Spohn, was entitled 'Geschichte und Emanzipation. Bahros Beitrag zu Sozialismus-Diskussion' (History and emancipation. Bahro's contribution to the socialism discussion). The author commended *The Alternative* and its potential as a source of inspiration for the political left in the West, transcending all camps and currents. That said, Bahro's ambitions would not come to fruition in West Germany because, even among large parts of the political left in the West, he had been reduced to his function as a GDR critic of the SED. Spohn went on to criticise Bahro's Western critics such as Joachim Bischoff, whose article

---

401 Korte 1980, p. 5. Gollwitzer emphasised that utopianism must remain more important than all forms of analysis or empiricism: 'The fact that he adapted the previous understanding of material "abundance" in communist society from quantitative to qualitative, which was precisely what was needed given today's growth problem ..., is also pointed out. Bahro's outline of the "cultural revolution" required for survival is, to some extent, an initial attempt at filling the yawning gap in today's Marxist theoretical work. Instead of stonewalling any attempt to testing the unchartered "utopian" waters, what is called for is a far-reaching constructive critique that does justice to his intellectual courage, which was no less impressive than his existential courage. For me this is what makes it more important to engage with Bahro's Part III than with Part II, which criticises "actually existing socialism"' (Gollwitzer 1978, p. 36f.).

402 Hosang 2007, p. 280.

403 See Amery 1978, p. 39 ff.

404 The then editors of the journal included Elmar Altvater, Gerhard Armanski and Jürgen Hoffmann. *PROKLA* was published by Olle and Wolter, the self-same publishers of Bahro's later books.

on Bahro lacked substantive analysis and aimed solely to discredit Bahro for being an anti-Marxist and 'representative of a "bourgeois-utopian reactionary socialism"'.[405] Bahro's critique of actually existing socialism stands out not only because he rejects the idea that the social systems in the Eastern Bloc are actually socialist, thus placing his hopes in a true proletarian revolution in these countries, but also because he 'very specifically identifies the elements of social domination that will have to be eliminated for socialism and social emancipation to come to fruition'.[406] Spohn also focuses on the utopia Bahro sets out in Part Three of *The Alternative*: Bahro 'makes it abundantly clear which direction a socialist-communist transformation of social relations must take and is thus likely to become a theoretical focal point for a communist opposition in Eastern Europe'.[407]

In another article in the *PROKLA* special issue, Gert Schäfer also voices criticism of how *The Alternative* and its author is perceived on the left of Germany's political spectrum: there are those who want to pigeonhole Bahro *a priori* (e.g. anarchist, Trotskyist, utopianist, anti-communist) and condemn him. At the same time, there are also those on the left who have expressed their moral solidarity with Bahro, but who reject his goals as unrealistic. Then again, there are also the 'thinkers', who, for the most part are still unable to rise above placing him into existing pigeonholes.[408]

However, it was not only in West Germany that Bahro came to people's attention. The circumstances of his arrest made headlines around the world, which also saw his book enter the limelight. Publisher of *The Alternative*, Tomas Kosta took stock in April 1978:

> In specific terms, less than eight months since the book was published, the situation is as follows: the book now has a total circulation of 80,000 copies; so far we have the foreign rights for the US, the UK, France, Italy, Spain, Denmark and Sweden; purchasing the rights for Japan is also a distinct possibility. All foreign language editions will be available at the upcoming Frankfurt Book Fair, in other words just a year after the German edition was published. In terms of media response, so far we have filled nine binders with press clippings and transcripts of television and radio broadcasts. We do have to draw a distinction between the reports and commentaries on Bahro's political case and articles about *The Altern-*

---

405 Spohn 1978, p. 7.
406 Spohn 1978, p. 24.
407 Spohn 1978, p. 30.
408 See Schäfer 1978, p. 34.

ative. There have now been around 200 reviews; all the major newspapers, journals, West German broadcasting and television stations have dealt with the issue at great length ..., as has the local press. The same applies to other German-speaking countries, as well as France, Italy, Spain, England, Sweden, Denmark and the Netherlands. We now have two big binders of reviews. ... From 19 September 1977, in other words just three weeks after it was published, *The Alternative* made it into the *Spiegel* bestseller lists, where it stayed in the top ten for weeks. Even today it still features in the top 20 non-fiction books. In October 1977, the book retailers' professional journal *Buchhändler heute* described *The Alternative* as "one of the most relevant books of the autumn". ... And the media response when it comes to the political circumstances surround Bahro is even more extensive; we needed three big binders just for the press clippings covering the period from 23 August to 4 September 1977, and this included a lot of very detailed articles from major foreign publications ....[409]

Besides this huge media response, there were also all manner of symposia, conferences and congresses, with well-known participants attending from all over the world, including leading members of West European communist parties. On top of this, innumerable letters were written, petitions conducted, solidarity campaigns launched, and Bahro was awarded a whole raft of prizes and accolades, and this is just a fraction of the publicity that surrounded the author and his book.[410]

The support for Bahro from among the Western European Eurocommunist parties[411] is particularly noteworthy here. Some elements of these parties had been trying to escape the influence of the Soviet Union. When Bahro was arrested, leading Eurocommunists declared solidarity with him, including figures such as Santiago Carillo Solares, the General Secretary of the Communist Party of Spain, and Lucio Lombardo Radice, a leading member of the Italian Communist Party,[412] both of whom welcomed the fact that Bahro's approach

---

409   Kosta 1978, p. 120 ff.
410   See Kosta 1978, p. 122 f.
411   Bahro, too, was influenced by Eurocommunism, which gave hope to the critics of the SED in the GDR. This caused problems for the SED as it was unable to break with these parties or conceal the new direction they were taking. This culminated in the SED grudgingly publishing the results of the Eurocommunism conference that took place in East Berlin in 1976 in its official organ *Neues Deutschland*. According to the contemporary witness Thomas Klein, for once, this was an issue of the newspaper that members of the opposition and critics of the system were happy to buy. See Klein, Otto and Grieder 1996, p. 410 ff.
412   See Julius 1977, p. 114 f.

was rooted in a philosophy of praxis.[413] The French Communist Party also distanced itself from the SED, writing of Bahro and *The Alternative* in its newspaper *L'Humanité*:

> 'Many of his opinions ... do not coincide with our own'. Nevertheless, Bahro's book is 'a remarkable piece of work and deserves attention because it confronts us with crucial questions', questions which 'cannot be evaded'. 'In any event', the party newspaper continues, 'we state loud and clear that we certainly do not agree with how he has been treated, in other words his imprisonment under the official pretext of him being involved in "espionage"'.[414]

But, in the West, it was not only the political left that expressed their views on Bahro. Other intellectuals also made their opinions public. For instance, Polish economist Włodzimierz Brus, who was lecturing at Oxford at the time, argued that Bahro's utopianism was the Achilles heel of *The Alternative*, blaming the GDR economists for the flaw:

> This escape into utopianism is all too typical of an otherwise sensible peasant's son and activist in a party which is one of the more pragmatic of the governing communist parties in Eastern Europe! Incidentally, Bahro makes no secret of this: 'But today utopian thought has a new necessity', he writes on page 253 of his book. And yet his book barely even mentions the GDR's current reform efforts – neither in terms of the ideas behind them nor the actual measures they entail. It is difficult to say why Bahro fails to provide an analysis of the attempts to reform the economic system so far .... Whatever the reason – this fact alone is part of the material and economic reality in the GDR that pushes an individual towards utopianism in pursuit of much-needed change and offers no hold on the slippery world of sterile thought. Do you, fellow scholars of the economic sciences, perhaps bear part of the blame for the mistakes and naivety of Rudolf Bahro?[415]

---

413 'Bahro sees Marxism not only as a method of analysis and a means of acquiring and consolidating knowledge, but also an instrument to facilitate the transition from protosocialism to socialism in revolutionary political practice. In other words, a philosophy of praxis, an acknowledgement that serves to advance change' (Lombardo Radice 1978, p. 13).
414 Quoted from *Spiegel*, no. 53/1977.
415 Brus 1978, p. 26f.

Brus did not consider utopia's progressive function, seeing utopianism merely as something negative, a shortcoming that detracted from Bahro's analysis and blocked his view of the real possibilities for change.

In an article about Bahro and *The Alternative* in the weekly newspaper *Die Zeit*, Gunter Hofmann acknowledges the post-materialist content of the book:

> We cannot talk about Rudolf Bahro without mentioning utopia in Germany, specifically the lack of it and the yearning for it. ... In terms of its substance, the utopia he brought from the GDR can be applied anywhere. It consists of the dream of rich individuality ... This utopia is not limited to visions of doom, cultural pessimism and a critique of civilisation. Bahro tirelessly beats the drum for setting the salvation of our civilisation in motion and urges people to take action. One of these heroes is Karl Marx. ... What fascinates him most about Marx is that he was both an analyst and a protagonist, that he researched sources at the London Library and was involved in politics at the same time.[416]

The *Frankfurter Allgemeine* was another newspaper to acknowledge the utopian aspects of *The Alternative*: 'no German communist has written about utopian thought with such skill, authenticity, anger and yet vivacity in a long time'.[417]

The *Spiegel*, for its part, dedicated several articles to the subject of Bahro, one of which is of particular relevance to how his utopia was received. The article appeared in September 1977 under the headline 'Pfeffer in offene Wunden' (Salt in the wound). It concluded that Bahro's book merely analysed how the system functioned and in no way did it represent an attack on the SED elites, the political system or human rights violations in the GDR. Bahro wanted to preserve the country's 'economic structures, to retain public ownership and stabilise the system', in doing so achieving stability in the GDR.

> He also continued to cling to the utopian elements of Marx's concept of communism, which of course had long since been superseded by the ever-growing international division of labour, the problems of the developing world and the environment.

Bahro's utopian objectives were characterised as anachronistic, while his role as an opposition figure was emphasised:

---

416   Hofmann 1980.
417   Quoted from *Spiegel*, no. 37/1977.

Bahro's courage to publicly put not just his citizenship but even his physical existence on the line will certainly secure him an honorary place in the history of the German workers' movement, irrespective of the misinterpretations he made on account of his communist idealism.[418]

A review published by the monthly business magazine *Manager-Magazin* makes this point even more clearly. The article claims that Bahro did not tell his Western readership anything new when it came to bureaucratic dictatorship. 'That said, it is certainly still interesting and beneficial to read an experienced insider's analysis by of the typical behaviour of the comrades in actually existing socialism who so often find themselves engaged in bureaucratic rivalry'. The fiercest criticism of Part Three, the utopian part of the book, came from reviewer Ernst Helmstädter, who, also recognising the utopian character of the book, immediately rejected it: 'The irrationality of this utopian goal is surpassed by the futility of the means proposed by the author'. Helmstädter went on to list a number of Bahro's programmatic proposals, stating that he found the idea of a working time budget (in place of money) warranting particular criticism: 'economic concepts such as this are not even worthy of mention. Not a word is said about the economic mechanisms that would facilitate a better form of socialism. These are secondary ...'. Helmstädter concluded:

> The book is definitely worth reading. It is well written, despite being peppered with linguistic monstrosities from the language of Marxism ... My utmost respect goes to the author for his personal accomplishment of completing this book under the difficult conditions of internal exile. But is it an alternative? No, it is not. Neither for the East or the West.[419]

As the select reviews presented in this chapter show, reactions to *The Alternative* overwhelmingly focused on the aspects of the book's content that were critical of the system. Contrary to Bahro's hopes, the majority of attention this book received did not go to its utopian elements, although the majority of the reviewers did in fact acknowledge and mention it. Depending on the author's standpoint, the utopian content was either welcomed as an innovative contribution or branded a flaw.

---

418   *Spiegel*, no. 39/1977.
419   Helmstädter 1977, p. 192 f.

CHAPTER 4

Tomorrow: Robert Havemann in Pursuit of the Third Way

1   The Life of Robert Havemann

A multitude of scholars have studied the life and impact of the best-known member of the GDR opposition. The Robert Havemann Society, for example, has been exploring Havemann's unpublished works since 1990. These very scholars have brought forth countless publications examining and analysing the dissident's life. In addition to these works, Stasi files also contain research reports about Havemann's past that were part of their unsuccessful campaign to unearth damning facts about his life to undermine his credibility. There are also several biographical articles in publications on the history of the philosophy of the German Democratic Republic (GDR) as well as in various newspapers and journals. And while no comprehensive academic biography about Havemann similar to Bahro's *Glaube an das Veränderbare* (Faith in the possibility of change) has been written to date, much of his life has in fact already been sufficiently researched thanks to the many individual publications and articles. That said, at this point, an outline of his life that looks at the origins of Havemann's *Morgen* (*Tomorrow*) and his utopian ideas is nevertheless needed in view of this book's importance as a reflection of both his character and his life, with all its ups and downs.

Robert Havemann was born to educated bourgeois parents on 11 March 1910 in Munich. His mother was a painter and his father a teacher who worked as an editor and writer at the same time.[1] Marxist and communist ideas did not feature in Havemann's upbringing at all, but, as a young man, he had a keen interest in the sciences, as the first major biographical essay about him, *Dokumente eines Lebens* (Documentation of a life), published in 1991, reveals.[2] When Robert was two, his family moved to Bielefeld but he eventually returned to Munich in 1929 to study for a degree in chemistry. It was here that Havemann and Klaus Piper, who would go on to publish many of his works (including

---

1   Robert Havemann's son Florian Havemann wrote that his grandfather Hans was the editor-in-chief of the *Hannoversche Zeitung*. See Havemann, F. 2007, p. 81.
2   For more on this and the following, see also: Draheim and Hoffmann 1991, p. 13 f., Hurwitz 2012.

Tomorrow), became friends, although their families had in fact known each another for much longer. Two years later, Havemann moved to Berlin to continue with his studies. Up until this point, he had not shown any enthusiasm at all for political issues, but this was all to change in Berlin, when he was given a copy of Friedrich Engels's *Anti-Dühring*. The link this book made between the sciences and Marxism sparked Havemann's interest and politicised him to such an extent that he volunteered to work as a helper of the Communist Party.[3] Whether, as he later claimed, he actually became a member of the Communist Party of Germany (KPD) at that time is doubtful. What is undisputed, however, is that he helped the Communist International with conspiratorial campaigns[4] and, as a staunch anti-fascist, became involved in two illegal resistance groups against the Nazis: *Neu Beginnen*[5] and *Europäische Union*.[6]

After completing his chemistry degree, Havemann went on to do his doctorate in Berlin in 1935. In late 1943, Havemann was sentenced to death by Freisler's People's Court for his involvement in the *Europäische Union* resistance group, only receiving a stay of execution because a number of important scientists fought for him, giving him research assignments that were indispensable for the war effort.[7] Shortly before the end of the war, Havemann, along with Erich Honecker and many others, was liberated from Brandenburg prison.

---

3   See Draheim and Hoffmann 1991, p. 20 ff. In retrospect, Havemann himself wrote: 'It was through mutual friends that I became part of the communist movement, the communist party. And from the very start this happened in quite an unusual way, through me having been incorporated into the so-called intelligence wing of the Comintern apparatus' (Havemann 1978, p. 37).

4   It is reported that in 1957 Havemann had his party membership backdated from the time he joined the SED in 1951 to the time he joined the KPD in 1932. According to Allertz 2006, p. 17 ff., during that period Havemann had not in fact been a member of the KPD but rather had only helped the party. Stasi briefing document HA IX/11 from 3.12.1976 on enquiries about 'HAVEMANN's political past' states in reference to the period before 1933: 'In personnel files since 1951, HAVEMANN repeatedly made the claim – something that has now also been reported by Western publications – that he had been a member of the KPD since 1932. While there are no documents to substantiate this claim, there are none that refute it either'. BStU, MfS, AU, 145/90, vol. 6, p. 366. Similarly, the Stasi was also unable to find any evidence of his collaboration with *Neu Beginnen*, whereas his involvement with *Europäische Union* can be clearly proven. See BStU, MfS, AU, 145/90, vol. 6, p. 367, Havemann, F. 2007, p. 219. For more on Havemann's contact with the KPD/Comintern, see Hurwitz 2012, p. 8 f., p. 220, p. 254.

5   For more on *Neu Beginnen*, see Draheim and Hoffmann 1991, p. 26 ff.

6   For more on *Europäische Union*, see Draheim and Hoffmann 1991, p. 50.

7   There are various controversies surrounding the reasons for this. Florian Havemann remarked, for example, that although his father had been involved in the resistance, he was also

Robert Havemann was clearly elated when, in 1946 in a *RIAS* (Radio in the American Sector) broadcast he enthused about the creation of a 'new free socialist Germany',[8] and he soon went on to become a staunch member of the Socialist Unity Party (SED). His optimism over the possibility of a 'friendship among nations' and socialism after the end of fascism was also reflected in a report he wrote about a visit to China, in which he painted an indiscriminately positive picture of Mao Zedong, the Soviet Union and the Communist leaders.[9]

After his release from prison, even before the arrival of the Western Allies, Havemann came into contact with the 'Ulbricht group' and was made head of the Kaiser Wilhelm Institute (KWI).[10] Once the KWI, which was located in the western part of Berlin, had been transferred to the American military administration, Havemann was dismissed from his position as president, but continued to work at the Institute. As a scientist, Havemann knew how to position himself between the occupying powers at this time. The nascent Cold War hampered this approach, however, and forced him to nail his political colours to the mast. This saw him dismissed from the KWI for good. As a reason for his dismissal, his employers cited an article about the atom bomb that he had published in *Neues Deutschland*, and that was alleged to be critical of the US. Havemann made a final move to East Berlin, where, in 1950, he became Commissarial Director of the Institute for Physics and Chemistry at Humboldt University, a position he held until 1964.[11] As a scientist and pacifist, in the early 1950s, Havemann became an active opponent of the atom bomb, although he recognised the benefits of civilian use of nuclear energy.[12]

---

    carrying out research on poisonous gas for the Nazis at the same time and was a member of the National Socialist German Lecturers' League. He also had contacts with the Gestapo. See Havemann, F. 2007, p. 143 f. Here, Bernd Florath states that Havemann exploited his Gestapo contacts to help the *Europäische Union*. Florath insisted that there was no question about Havemann being an informant for the Gestapo. Nor did he knowingly have any contact with the Comintern before World War II. Moreover, the Gestapo knew nothing about Havemann's membership in *Neu Beginnen*, which is why he was the only member of the Berlin leadership not to be arrested. Those who were arrested would not have turned him in due to the conspiratorial rules they adhered to. Despite its best efforts, the Stasi never managed to discredit Havemann as a collaborator and Nazi informer. See Florath 2006, p. 20. On this see also Skiba 2006, p. 61 ff. and Schmidt 2003, p. 643.

8   Havemann 1990, p. 87.
9   See Havemann 1990, p. 98 ff.
10   See Hoffmann 1991, p. 64 f.
11   See Hoffmann 1991, p. 75 ff.
12   See Hoffmann 1991, p. 94. In relation to this, it is also worth referring to an article by Havemann published by the *Tägliche Rundschau* newspaper on 8 July 1954. In the article, Havemann expressed how pleased he was that the world's first nuclear power station

However, it was not only in the context of nuclear power that Havemann, in his capacity as an eminent scientist, came into contact with politics. Indeed, he had already had encounters with the Gestapo even before 1945 and had had contact with members of various secret services after his liberation from prison. In a brochure published in 2006, Arno Polzin addressed this aspect of Havemann's biography. Polzin had discovered that, from 1946 to 1952, Havemann had worked as a secret informant for Soviet intelligence, where his mission was to spy on Trotskyist and social democratic members of *Neu Beginnen*. He is reported to have supplied very little important information, however.[13] From 1953, Havemann cooperated with the Stasi, where, once again, he served as a secret informant from 24 February 1956. His code name, 'Leitz', was one he chose himself.[14] In his brochure, Polzin also described how Havemann's gradual departure from the party line in the 1950s and early 1960s was a fact that was registered by the Stasi. The Stasi noted Havemann's first critical statements in 1956, but his shift away from the party was not documented in the files until 1963 and the beginning of his abandonment backdated to 1956.[15] From early 1959, the Stasi began to have doubts about Havemann's credibility and four years later the various instances during which he had shown a lack of discipline were collected and recorded for the first time as part of an 'operative procedure' (*Operativer Vorgang*, OV) and a plan of action decided against him. The last meeting with secret informant 'Leitz' was on 14 November 1963, after which time the Stasi ended the collaboration.[16]

It was surprising that Havemann never publicly owned up to his cooperation with the Stasi in later years, particularly given that he addressed his Stalinist

---

      had gone live in the Soviet Union. Incidentally, Havemann's scientific and technological optimism was something he remained true to into the 1970s in the context of the Club of Rome debates. See Hoffmann 1991, p. 111 f.

13   See Polzin 2006, p. 23 ff. Polzin reported on the intensity of cooperation with the Stasi and on denunciations Havemann was responsible for, indicating that there had been a total of around 60 meetings since 1963. Havemann's main job was to make contact with and recruit Western scientists. See Polzin 2006, p. 9 f. 'However, he also reported on internal university issues, on individuals from the university, on the general mood in the different HU faculties, and he quite clearly provided information which incriminated certain individuals. The reports were both about character flaws and political views and possible plans to leave the country' (Polzin 2006, p. 29). Havemann did not unknowingly give this information but rather 'was well aware of the intelligence nature of his Stasi contacts' (Polzin 2006, p. 34).

14   See Polzin 2006, p. 28.
15   See Polzin 2005, p. 12.
16   See Polzin 2005, p. 38.

past[17] in his published works. On this subject, Bernd Florath, who was part of Havemann's inner circle in the 1970s, reported that among his closest friends, it was known that Havemann was ashamed of his collaboration with the Stasi. Although he never spoke openly and explicitly about it, any allusions he made were unambiguous.[18]

Up until 1964, Havemann was a loyal top official, occupying various different posts over the years. He held (voluntary) positions at the university and was also Chair of the Peace Council of the GDR, a member of the *Volkskammer*, a member of the Presidium of the Cultural Association of the GDR and Chair of the 'Motorsports Science Club' at the German Motorsports Association (ADMV), among others.[19] Moreover, he was regarded both nationally and internationally as the GDR's most respected scientist.[20]

At the same time, after the 20th Congress of the Communist Party of the Soviet Union in 1956, he dared to express his first public criticism of dogmatism. At an event about the Congress, organised by his university's party organisation, Havemann praised his Soviet comrades for breaking with the cult of the personality, and called for dogmatism in science to be eradicated in the GDR, too.

> This combination of critical intellect, mixed with optimism, was unusual. The speaker who followed Havemann accused him of insulting the party. During the break, many avoided Havemann like a leper. ... But Ulbricht ... had the last word: 'Well, I'd just like to say that the only one here who has shown us what really matters now is Comrade Havemann'. The atmosphere changed in an instant. Those who had just given Havemann a wide berth, were now patting him on the back, although they couldn't forgive

---

17 Havemann was a dyed-in-the-wool Stalinist, as the following episode from the early 1950s is testament to: 'At a conference about a paper by the "genius Stalin" he questioned whether the sciences in the Western world were even viable, whether some of them could even be rightfully called sciences' (Herzberg 2006, p. 540f.).

18 See Florath 2006, p. 20.

19 See Hecht 1991, p. 133f. and p. 174.

20 'As a scientist, he founded two new research institutes in the GDR: one centred on magneto-chemistry and the other on photochemistry (with the unachieved long-term goal of photosynthesis). He was also given several roles at the university, including vice rector, vice dean and head of department. As a chemist, he belonged to a number of scientific boards and committees. He certainly enjoyed this recognition and represented the official policy of the SED with the utmost dedication. And for a scientist he wrote an almost incredible number of political articles – on nuclear technology, on the threat of war, against West German imperialism and militarism, on the glorification of the GDR's political system' (Herzberg 2005, p. 339).

him the humiliating failure. Havemann received a request from *Neues Deutschland* to write an article titled 'Gegen Dogmatismus, für den wissenschaftlichen Meinungsstreit' (Against dogmatism and for a scientific exchange of views). Published a few days later, the article triggered a huge dispute. The main point of attack was the following remark by Havemann: 'Philosophy is not a science in its own right with its own specific object. Its object is every object, but defined within the specific scientific research carried out in each individual field'.[21]

Havemann's intention was not, however, to call Ulbricht's position or that of the SED into question. His aim was much more to represent the interests of those (natural) scientists who were prevented from conducting independent, unbiased research because of the ideological constraints placed on their disciplines.[22] Guntolf Herzberg commented on this:

> Politically, the professor was ... a thoroughly Stalinist-minded poster child for the SED, but as a scientist he was able to defend himself against the pretensions to regimentation of the Marxist philosophers.[23]

An illuminating example of the smouldering conflict between Havemann, this prominent figure who no longer toed the line, and the leading SED functionaries was the events that transpired at the Third University Conference of the SED in February/March 1958, during which Hager criticised Havemann for the 'conciliatory' stance he had taken in 1956. After himself having been berated, Havemann hit back by criticising Hager and Ulbricht, both of whom then attacked Havemann again, who at that point was forced to be self-critical. Havemann's career weathered the crisis,[24] and in 1959, the Institute for Chemistry at Humboldt University even put him forward for the National Prize, which he

---

21 Prokop 2000, p. 134f. See also Herzberg 2006, p. 203f. and 543f.
22 See Mittenzwei 2003, p. 231f.
23 Herzberg 2006, p. 429f. Siegfried Prokop suspected that in 1957, after the members of the 'Harich group' were sentenced, Havemann underwent an internal transformation. Initially he endorsed the sentences handed down to Harich and the others, but then increasingly felt solidarity with the prisoners, something that he ultimately publicly expressed in the *Kulturbund* (Cultural Association of the GDR). This brought him into conflict with Hager and may well have been the start of his departure from Stalinism. See Prokop 1997, p. 123.
24 'In actual fact, these allegations would have been enough to bring about the final split with Havemann as well. But, compared to Harich, Havemann was a much more important figure. He had already been sentenced to death by the Nazi regime. After he was liberated

was indeed later awarded. Up until 1963, he refrained from attracting attention with critical political statements, instead concentrating on his successful scientific research.[25] He publicly welcomed the erection of the Wall in 1961 and never really distanced himself from this position, even in his later years as a dissident. He connected it with the call to critics of the system to remain in the GDR and fight for a different form of socialism.[26]

Despite his silence, the antagonisms intensified.[27] In the words of Hubert Laitko: 'If we take a bird's eye view, Robert Havemann's life in the GDR seems like an inexorably mounting conflict between him and the political system'.[28] He presumed that Havemann's break with the SED must have been painful, and that throughout the 1950s, he never saw himself as a subservient party soldier but as playing a key role in 'shaping' socialism in the GDR. 'From the very beginning, he was thus accustomed to being on equal footing with the functionaries of the party apparatus and, under this premise, assuming responsibility in the GDR wherever he felt it was necessary. Why then would he have recognised the party apparatus's claim to a monopoly over the reconstruction achievements of the GDR in which he himself had invested so much? This position – which, although implying willingness to, at his own discretion, be part of a collaborative undertaking, still ruled out any form of blind subordination to the will of others – would, in the long run, inevitably collide with existing circumstances'.[29]

Numerous statements give an idea as to the type of person Havemann the functionary was. He possessed influence and standing, he had a luxurious apartment and summer house in a prestigious residential area for government officials on Werlsee in the Grünheide municipality of Brandenburg.[30]

---

from Brandenburg Prison by the Red Army, he agreed to cooperate with the Soviet intelligence services. From February 1956 to October 1963 he worked for the Stasi as "secret informer Leitz".' (Prokop 2000, p. 139).

25   See Herzberg 2006, p. 550 ff. In his political statements, he never criticised the SED but, as in the postscript of the GDR edition of Robert Jungk's book *Children of the Ashes*, he targeted the USA's foreign policy. See Havemann 1961, p. 340.
26   See Havemann, K. and Widmann 2003, p. 35.
27   'Havemann's dilemma was that to resolve the shortcomings of cooperation between philosophers and natural scientists, he had to become more and more involved in politics' (Mittenzwei 2003, p. 233).
28   Laitko 2010b, p. 37.
29   Laitko 2010b, p. 41.
30   Linguist Manfred Bierwisch, a contemporary of Havemann, remembered him as a 'hedonist who, in an unpretentious manner, loved and enjoyed comforts and luxury, such as the opulent wine cellar in the summer house at the lake in Grünheide, which he owned on top of his extravagant apartment ...' (Bierwisch 2007, p. XIV).

Moreover, he cultivated a habitus which set him apart from the majority of the other functionaries, who tended to come from working class families and had been raised with different economic and moral notions of a 'good life' than Havemann, who, as the offspring of a bourgeois family, had studied, had contacts with the secret services and enjoyed a reputation as an international scientist. Consequently, Havemann was perceived by some of his comrades as arrogant, opinionated, money-minded and craving recognition. Typifying this attitude was Robert Allertz's criticism of Havemann for collecting titles and 'official positions like others collect stamps', yet at the same time as not having any particular scientific ambition: although he was a professor with a full teaching position, he generally never spent any longer than about three hours a day at the university. In 1965, the Central Party Commission issued an opinion on Havemann stating that he did not respect the rules and statutes in the desired manner, nor did he maintain the necessary discipline, instead behaving in a 'highly individualistic' manner and demonstrating 'anarchistic tendencies', remarked Allertz.[31]

In a police report on a drink driving offence committed by Havemann on 1 December 1955, it states that in an encounter at a checkpoint, he looked down on and insulted the policeman. Havemann was quoted as having said: 'For us, you are just such little people!'; and then he simply left without even being given permission to do so.[32] Hartmut Hecht also accused Havemann of having a slightly exaggerated opinion of himself:

> There is no doubt that his assured self-importance, which was, of course, so well fed by his success and all the official awards and distinctions he received in fields where his intellect was unapologetically accepted, often went too far. And this was most certainly the case when it came to philosophy.[33]

Havemann's departure from the SED was thus very much a result of his personality and his social aspirations.[34] Although he had the same aim as his

---

31 See Allertz 2006, p. 20 ff.
32 This report can be found in Hoffmann 1991, p. 115.
33 Hecht 1991, p. 129.
34 'As long as Havemann saw himself as a representative of a progressive scientific community and was also recognised as such, he largely suppressed his doubts, adhering, as was expected of him as a member of the SED, especially of the university party leadership, to party discipline. On the other hand, owing to his many personal abilities and virtues, he was also a vain man, who did not deal well with setbacks and failure. The fact that,

comrades, he no longer wanted to submit to their instructions about how to get there and risked the situation escalating when, in a series of lectures about the relationship between philosophy and the natural sciences, he expressed criticism of the influence of dogmatism. In 1963, the conflict between Havemann and the party leadership finally came to a head. In essence, the conflict was about the series of lectures he had held at Humboldt University under the title *Naturwissenschaftliche Aspekte philosophischer Probleme* (Scientific aspects of philosophical problems), in which he spoke about the obstructive or even destructive influence of political dogmatism on the freedom of the sciences. Given that this lecture series became something of a crowd puller for critical students from all manner of disciplines and universities, it quickly attracted the attention of those who were the target of Havemann's criticism.[35]

Indeed, the lecture series was the main reason why Havemann's academic and political career came to an end. It was not this, however, that was the reason for his dismissal, but rather the fact that he gave an unauthorised interview for the *Hamburger Echo*, which was released on 11 February 1964.[36] His dismissal was swiftly followed by the dismantling of his scientific and political career:

> At a session of the Central Committee Secretariat on 12.3.1964, the occasion of an interview with Havemann in the *Hamburg Echo* resulted in decisions regarding his removal as head of department and dismissal from his post as professorial chair at Humboldt University, and the order to conduct party proceedings against him at the subsequent extraordinary conference for party activists at HU ... and meeting of the party's

---

after so many years of recognition, the party no longer accepted him, dropped him in an instant, was an insult to his narcissistic ego. His lifestyle and his interests, his quest for self-affirmation also saw him come into contact with intellectuals with different views, leading him to gradually distanced himself inwardly from the party and its rules' (Herzberg 2005, p. 362).

35 '1,250 people ... attended his lecture' (Klein, Grieder and Otto 1996, p. 354). For a more detailed account of Havemann's dismissal from the Academy of Sciences, see Florath and Müller 1996, Bierwisch 2007, p. XIIIf. and Wilke 2010, pp. 27–35.

36 See Laitko 2010a, p. 657. Even now, Robert Allertz still officially blames this for his dismissal: by leaking information on internal matters and research results to a Western journalist, Havemann violated the duty of confidentiality written in his employment contract, and through his public demands for political change in the West German press, he seriously violated the code of conduct to which a political official is bound and as such was no longer tenable. See Allertz 2006, p. 28f.

chemistry committee. Hager issued the usual press releases regarding Havemann's dismissal. The grounds for his dismissal were given as follows: breach of fiduciary duty; the grounds for the party proceedings: non-compliance with the regulations. This decision by the Secretariat was approved by the Politburo on 17.3.1964. At its session on 16.7.1964, the Central Committee Secretariat upheld the decision to deny Havemann's appeal against his removal from the party on 13.3.1964.[37]

In his memoires, published in 1996, Kurt Hager recalled that at the time Havemann constantly criticised the (mistakes made by the) SED leadership. The all-important split, however, occurred at a conference for party activists at Humboldt University on 14 February 1964: Hager addressed both the decisions made at the 5th Party Conference and Havemann's views. 'The differences of opinion would not necessarily have resulted in a split, had Havemann not begun to disseminate his views via the Western media'. After he had given an interview to the *Hamburg Echo* in which he spoke about the flaws in the creation of socialism and about de-Stalinisation, 'emotions ran high'. On top of this, he also gave an interview to the *Spiegel*.

> Walter Ulbricht stated that Havemann could no longer be tolerated, he had relocated his professorship to the West. ... Emotions played a major role in these decisions. Havemann's appearances in the Western media made any further discussion with him about politics or ideology impossible. He had violated a moral code. Communists were forbidden from airing their differences with their own party in the Western media.[38]

That said, at the time, Hager was still not prepared to support the publication of the lecture manuscripts in the GDR, and rejected Havemann's April 1964 request to do so.[39] This prompted Havemann to publish his manuscripts

---

37   Klein, Otto and Grieder 2006, p. 69 f. Havemann said that he had been deceived. The journalist had not introduced himself as a journalist but rather as an interested member of the audience at the lecture. However, the SED leadership now had the reason they had been looking for to take the desired action against Havemann.

38   Hager 1996, p. 282. Hubert Laitko did not rule out the possibility that Ulbricht, whose New System for Economic Management and Planning (NÖSPL) had at that time been criticised by the orthodox SED cadres that made up a majority in the apparatus, 'had sacrificed his comrade Robert Havemann to pacify his opponents within the party with a demonstration of "revolutionary vigilance"' (Laitko 2010a, p. 657).

39   See Polzin 2006, p. 21.

the same year in West Germany under the title *Dialektik ohne Dogma?* (Dialectics without dogma?). Hubert Laitko aptly described this step as a 'journalistic watershed'.[40] Havemann was now irreversibly excluded from the GDR ruling elite. According to Havemann's last wife Katja, in the period that followed, the Stasi started 'the rumour ... that Havemann was under the influence of drugs'.[41] The 'Leitz' file remained but was converted into an 'operative procedure'.

The conduct of the ruling classes made Havemann popular among those sections of the population who were critical of the system, and this made him increasingly untouchable.[42] The 11th Plenum of the Central Committee of the SED which took place in 1965 – dubbed the *Kahlschlagplenum* or 'clear-cutting plenary' – also contributed to Havemann's status:

> The party functionaries did Havemann one last big favour by referring to him as one of those individuals who posed a particular risk to the socialist social order, the other two being Stefan Heym and Wolf Biermann.[43]

Robert Havemann had thus lost all his offices and with them his social status as a member of the nomenklatura. As a result, he was offered various new posts, although he refused these on the grounds that he was overqualified. In a report written at the time, the Stasi stated:

> Prof. Havemann rejected serious job offers from the Ministry for the Chemical Industry for no valid reason, and as such it became clear that he wanted to continue his amoral lifestyle in Berlin. In 1966, he applied for ... a pension for victims of Nazism.[44]

Havemann received this pension from 1967 onward. Havemann, who also went through a divorce from his wife in 1966,[45] withdrew to his weekend residence,

---

40 Laitko 2010a, p. 656.
41 Havemann, K. and Widmann 2003, p. 37.
42 See Havemann, K. and Widmann 2003, p. 37 ff.
43 Havemann, K. and Widmann 2003, p. 49 f.
44 BStU, MfS, AU, 145/90, vol. 2, p. 274. This was a pension for those persecuted by the Nazi regime (VdN).
45 In relation to the records of the divorce in 1966, the Stasi wrote 'that the marriage ... had been happy until around 1954', after which time there followed a 'process of estrangement', and that from 1958 Havemann slept 'only' at Grünheide. 'From 1958 up until the divorce in 1966, the only time he visited his former apartment in Berlin, at Straussberger Platz

while the state leadership did not dare to lock up or deport the died-in-the-wool antifascist. For Havemann, the Prague Spring of 1968 and its suppression was to become a major source of inspiring indignation. In a letter to Bloch, Havemann described the day that Czechoslovakia was invaded as the 'darkest day in the history of socialism since Stalin'.[46]

After all these setbacks, finally in 1970, Havemann resurfaced with the publication of his book *Fragen, Antworten, Fragen* (Questions, answers, questions), which was well received by the public. The book was published by his childhood friend from Munich, Klaus Piper, and became an immediate success in the West, with its impact also spreading to the GDR.[47] Along with his friend Wolf Biermann, Havemann became a landmark and a kind of 'mecca' for artists and intellectuals who were critics of the system. Grünheide was somewhere young people in particular[48] congregated, among them Bernd Florath, Jürgen Fuchs, members of the banned rock band *Renft* and also Havemann's future wife, Katja.

The Stasi described Havemann's lifestyle as 'amoral'. And, taking the SED's moral standards as a yardstick, this would certainly be an accurate description of life in Grünheide. In his book, *Havemann*, Florian Havemann described the veritable orgies that took place there. Given that the scientific authenticity of his descriptions is not necessarily reliable, however, I will instead draw on accounts from writer and human rights activist Siegmar Faust, who, upon his early release from Cottbus Prison (also thanks to Havemann's support) after 400 days, became part of 'the notorious Biermann-Havemann circle like a trophy of their victory'. However, by his own admission, Faust did not feel comfortable in this group as he 'soon discovered its dark side, which ... Florian Havemann ... had meticulously described in his thousand-page family saga

---

       19, was to have lunch, to spend occasional afternoons or to receive guests'. The report concluded: 'Character witnesses described Prof. Havemann's behaviour as being characterised by inconsiderateness, egotism and self-importance' (BStU, MfS, AU, 145/90, vol. 2, p. 296). The court record of Havemann's divorce, which was reprinted in a high-profile report for the *Berliner Zeitung* at the time, stated: 'For a long time, not only was Mrs Havemann not an equal partner in the marriage, but at times she was subjected to degrading treatment. Havemann saw his wife as no more than the "caretaker of the household". Havemann's demeaning treatment of his family went as far as to demand that his wife and children treat his lovers as members of the family. He described his licentious lifestyle as a "new way of living together", which was entirely in keeping with his views on "personal freedom"' (Quoted in Hecht 1991, p. 190).
46   Havemann 1990, p. 233.
47   See Havemann, K. and Widmann 2003, p. 55.
48   See Havemann, K. and Widmann 2003, p. 75 ff.

Havemann'.⁴⁹ These details do not need to be rolled out again here, however. Suffice to say, that those who gathered at Grünheide were, on the one hand, endangering their social position by having contact with Havemann, yet at the same time enjoyed a certain degree of protection from reprisals thanks to Havemann's media contacts.

Havemann had since begun to celebrate bearing the alleged stigma of an outcast. In the early 1970s, the GDR was fighting for recognition. The Basic Treaty between the Federal Republic of Germany (FRG) and the GDR and the Helsinki Final Act allowed Havemann to feel even safer. He was not afraid of direct repression or imprisonment, and in fact focused on secretly cultivating contacts with Western journalists and diplomats which enabled him to publish regular articles in major West German political journals.⁵⁰ When asked why he would remain in the GDR while carrying out his publishing activities via Western capitalist media and publishing houses, Havemann responded in volume 1 of the *Europäische Ideen* journal in 1973 that he was 'an ally of the GDR and a staunch socialist'. He was afraid that leaving the GDR for the West would undermine his 'credibility'. Besides, he would not be able to 'advocate for the GDR' to the same extent from there. He described the main readership of his works as GDR citizens who saw themselves as critical socialists.⁵¹

Havemann deliberately went on the offensive. In *Fragen, Antworten, Fragen* he wrote: 'I was and still am against any conspiratorial political activity if the aim is to fight as a communist in one's own country. Things were different under conditions of fascism. There was no other option then. But, as a communist in the GDR, political operations must be conducted openly and legally'.⁵² For Havemann, this included condemning those who left the GDR for the West despite their not facing great adversity, as he held out hope that a united opposition would in fact be able to change the conditions in the East.⁵³

---

49   Faust 2010, p. 24.
50   See Havemann, K. and Widmann 2003, p. 71f.
51   See Havemann 1980a, p. 194.
52   Havemann 1970, p. 32. In 1978, Havemann commented on Harich in this context. According to Havemann, Harich's mistake was his having acted in secret in 1956 because he ultimately wanted to offer a complete programme. 'To be politically effective, you must never conceal your thoughts and ideas, but instead do everything to ensure that they become known as soon as possible and certainly at the initial stage of their development' (Havemann 1978a, p. 80f.).
53   In this context, Florian Havemann reported on an event which took place in the early

The top state and party functionaries were suspicious of Havemann and Biermann's entourage. On 15 November 1976, they dealt them a major blow: an arrest warrant was issued for Havemann, and, the very next day, Biermann was stripped of his citizenship.[54] Not long after this, Jürgen Fuchs and *Renft* musicians Gerulf Pannach and Christian Kunert were also arrested.[55] These moves were seen as a 'coming straight from the top', decisions made at the highest political level.

Besides the arrests and deportations, Havemann was also held in isolation at his Grünheide property, a step which cost the state considerable sums of money and manpower: over 300 guards and an entire Stasi department were tasked with keeping Havemann under observation. The aim was to force him to leave the country 'voluntarily', and a strategy was mapped out that was designed to wear him down and that included measures ranging from house arrest to discrediting his anti-fascist past to destroying his marriage.[56] The assumption was that Havemann was installed by the West and controlled from outside as an enemy of the state, and the crackdown against him was correspondingly tough:

1970s: 'My father knew that I wanted to get out of there. I had told him so. And his answer was: "If you don't leave my property immediately, I'll get the police"' (Havemann, F. and Jochum 2002).

54 'According to Kurt Hager, Biermann's denaturalisation was a unilateral decision made by Erich Honecker .... After he was removed from power, he said that he "could perhaps have made a different decision" back then. This was not even considered, however. At the meeting of the Politburo on 16 November 1976, everyone present consented to the measure' (Mittenzwei 2003, p. 283). For more on Biermann's denaturalisation, also see Havemann, F. 2007, p. 351f., Pleitgen, Fritz: Die Ausbürgerung, München 2001, Zwerenz, I. and Zwerenz, G. 2004, p. 239.

55 See Havemann, K. and Widmann 2003, p. 130ff.

56 See Havemann, K. and Widmann 2003, p. 164ff. According to a Stasi plan dated 31.1.1978, Havemann was supposed to have made himself seem 'both implausible and at the same time preposterous to his opponents' and he was permanently prevented from committing 'hostile acts'. All contact between him and the outside world was to be severed in order to ultimately 'force him to focus solely on himself and his family problems in future' (BStU, MfS, AU, 145/90, vol. 5, p. 240f.). Even in its classified assessment, the Stasi assumed that Havemann was being controlled by the West and sought '... to provide proof that his activities, steered by the enemy, aimed at deliberate organisation of political underground activity in the GDR' (BStU, MfS, AU, 145/90, vol. 5, p. 241). Even negative impacts on Havemann's marriage were to be taken into consideration: 'By using existing or recruiting and introducing new unofficial collaborators to HAVEMANN's wife, the conditions are to be created to systematically separate her from Havemann through extramarital affairs and to place more psychological pressure on him and to prevent him from engaging in hostile activities. Here, such circumstances as HAVEMANN's excessive jealousy, his continual distrust of his wife, intermittent marital disputes, the need of HAVEMANN's wife to have friendship with others etc. are to be deliberately exploited' (ibid, p. 246).

by summer 1977 the state had made certain that Havemann and his family were holed up in Grünheide with their contact to the outside world reduced to a bare minimum. And this indeed had repercussions: Robert Havemann's relationship with his wife Katja suffered from the isolation, and the Stasi saw the rift between Havemann and his wife as proof that their strategy had been a success.[57]

Yet Honecker and Mielke were not content to stop at house arrest, because, despite all the measures taken against him, Havemann still repeatedly managed to get his texts to the Western media. In spring 1979, the house in Grünheide was searched, Havemann's work materials were ransacked and some permanently confiscated[58] (including some preliminary work for *Tomorrow*). The official grounds for the search of Havemann's house were that the customs office was conducting a preliminary investigation under the Foreign Exchange Act. But the real reason behind the search was actually a Stasi operation that could be traced back to Mielke and Honecker.[59]

Soon after this, the house arrest was lifted.[60] The SED's actions against critics, artists and intellectuals – particularly those from Havemann's milieu – meant that by the time Havemann came out of isolation, barely any of his former friends were left: Biermann, Fuchs, Pannach, Kunert, Eva-Maria Hagen and many others were now all living in West Germany. This led Havemann to begin to look for new interlocuters and friends and one of the places he found them was in the context of the church. Barely ten years later, some of

---

57 See Vollnhals 2000, p. 70.
58 See Havemann, K. and Widmann 2003, p. 230 ff.
59 See Vollnhals 2000, p. 78 ff. 'In reality, this was all about the politically motivated punishment of a critic of the regime. Owing to his prominent status, a conviction for incitement against the state, the criminal offence they could actually have accused him of, was prevented, however, meaning a minor offence had to serve as the basis for his punishment and criminal prosecution' (Vollnhals 2000, p. 108 f.). In an internal communication, Mielke admitted that prosecuting Havemann for a customs offence was a strategic move. See Vollnhals 2000, p. 127.
60 However, soon after this, criminal law regarding the transfer of written works to the Western media was strengthened: 'On 28 June [1979 – author's addition] the GDR *Volkskammer* adopted draconian laws with strict penalties for any helpers or sympathisers of opponents or critics of the GDR regime. Even passing manuscripts and "non-confidential messages to the Western media" could and can be punishable with up to 12 years imprisonment' (Kroh 1988, p. 32). This provided the public prosecutor's office with a law they could use to legally prosecute the transfer of any text with critical content. The main impetus for the adoption of this law was Bahro, Havemann and Stefan Heym, but it also effected a large number of other authors, for whom this law essentially constituted an indirect publication ban. This meant that whatever the GDR publishers did not want to print, simply did not appear anywhere. See Mittenzwei 2003, p. 291 f.

these new acquaintances would go on to become important civic rights activists during the Peaceful Revolution, including, for instance, Bärbel Bohley, Lutz Rathenow, Gerd Poppe and Rainer Eppelmann,[61] with whom Havemann initiated the peace movement's *Berliner Appell* (Berlin call to action) in 1982.

Not long after this, on Good Friday of the same year, Robert Havemann passed away at his residence in Grünheide. 'This was the last of the prominent critics of the regime from the communist, anti-fascist tradition'.[62]

Countless obituaries appeared in the Western press. On 11 April 1982, Siegmar Faust wrote in the *Berliner Morgenpost* that, despite all his negative experiences, Havemann remained a Marxist. 'He was one of the last credible and honest communists and his legacy will continue to live on. We dissidents and those with different faiths and beliefs will continue to take our hat off to him'.[63] In the *Volksblatt Berlin* on the same day, Hartmut Jennerjahn remarked that Havemann had repeatedly called for open and free debate under 'actually existing socialism'. Jennerjahn also noted certain critical aspects, however:

> 'In the opinion of some, no less critical GDR citizens, however, his extensive isolation prevented him from taking a sober view on reality, and he occasionally lost himself in utopias'.[64] And, as Hartmut Jäckel pointed out in the *Tagesspiegel* dated 11 April: 'Robert Havemann never abandoned his belief in utopia and that this belief would ultimately be victorious. For Havemann, who was not ready to be satisfied with expectations alone but who was filled with and driven by conviction, Ernst Bloch's dialectically constructed *Principle of Hope* did not go far enough. Havemann's dialectic was to act through the written and spoken word, to change the world and to correct his own mistakes and those of others'.[65]

2 The Origins of *Tomorrow*

Robert Havemann was an extremely self-confident bon vivant. On the one hand, this meant he did not behave in a submissive manner towards the SED leadership. The other consequence of this, however, was that he could

---

61 See Havemann, K. and Widmann 2003, p. 289f., Havemann, F. 2007, p. 125f.
62 Kroh 1988, p. 36.
63 Quoted in: BStU, MfS, AU, 145/90, vol. 23, p. 317.
64 BStU, MfS, AU, 145/90, vol. 23, p. 319.
65 BStU, MfS, AU, 145/90, vol. 23, p. 321. A long version of this obituary by Jäckel was also published in Deutschland-Archiv, no. 5/1982, pp. 452–55.

not, or did not always want to, play the role of the family man and father. These two sides are particularly evident in *Tomorrow* and at the time the book came out. *Tomorrow* was published in 1980, and, although Havemann had put everything down on paper in an incredibly short period of time, various political and personal setbacks resulted in a publishing lead time of several years.

Havemann had already been grappling with utopia for some time. He addressed the issue as early as 1965 in a manuscript for a lecture titled 'Kommunismus – Utopie und Wirklichkeit' (Communism – utopia and reality). Over the following 15 years, he would occasionally return to this topic again. However, since Havemann preferred to pen short statements or express his views verbally,[66] he never committed any longer utopian texts to paper during this period – although this was something he always intended to do.

In an interview printed in the *Westdeutsche Allgemeine Zeitung* in September 1975, speaking about his next book project, Havemann said:

> I want to focus on a new socialist utopia. ... I am on friendly terms with utopia. There is nothing derogatory about the concept. Without utopia, there is no progress. Utopia means imagining a world where the brutality and inhumanity with which we all live are no more.[67]

Five years passed between Havemann making this statement and the publication of *Tomorrow*. There are various explanations as to why Robert Havemann ultimately wrote the book. Bizarrely, there are two individuals who each claim that they were the driving force, despite the fact that they are both very critical of the book – his son Florian and his widow Katja (who is not Florian's mother, but Robert Havemann's last wife).

Florian Havemann, who, even today, has a complex relationship to his father and who cut off all contact with him after fleeing to West Germany in the 1970s,

---

[66] If we are looking for evidence of Havemann the political writer (rather than natural scientist), several books fit the bill. However, the vast majority are collections of texts or interview or lecture transcripts. Besides *Tomorrow*, the only other of Havemann's publications that takes the form of a complete book is the autobiographical *Fragen, Antworten, Fragen* (Questions, answers, questions). Vollnhals is hitting the nail on the head when he says that Havemann was not a writer of lengthy theoretical texts, that this was not in 'his nature'. 'A rigorous, self-contained argumentative analysis and critique of "actually existing socialism" against the background of Marxist theory or a well-founded historical depiction of this fool's errand is not something the reader can expect to find' (Vollnhals 2000, p. 18).

[67] BStU, MfS, AU, 145/90, vol. 4, p. 161.

published his own personal account in the *Spiegel* in 1978. In this article, he accused his father of being lazy about writing. In his book, *Havemann*, published in 2007, Florian Havemann referred back to the *Spiegel* article, placing it into the context of *Tomorrow*. He suspected that his father had in fact written the utopian chapter of the book in 1979 –

> ... after I remarked in the *Spiegel* that his way of thinking was beginning to take on utopian characteristics, but that it was not utopian in the classical sense. Well, there you go. Maybe this was the very thing that spurred him. But also the fact that, in my descriptions of him as a philosopher, I accused him of dilettantism.[68]

Whether it was really provocation from his son that incited Robert Havemann to write his utopia, is not known. What we can assume, however, is that this is unlikely to have been the only decisive factor. Indeed, in late summer 1979, his marriage was also in a critical state. Katja Havemann had moved out of the summer residence in Grünheide, taking their daughter Franziska with her. It was during this time that Havemann wrote *Tomorrow*, which is said to have taken him a mere six weeks. In retrospect, Katja Havemann surmises that the book was heavily influenced by this personal crisis. Under the cloud of his marital crisis, Robert Havemann reflected on relationships, free love and morals and incorporated these ideas into *Tomorrow*. His loneliness led him to stop all the 'organised revelry', instead using his time to at last write the utopia which he had begun before the house arrest but which had remained untouched since then.[69] According to Katja Havemann's interpretation, the utopian part of *Tomorrow* is a very subjectively written reflection of a specific period in time. In her view, Havemann's utopia was not primarily driven by political reasons, but rather it was the result of the author processing a personal crisis. Morris-Keitel disagrees with this interpretation of the book:

> If, in retrospect, Katja Havemann is attempting to reduce this utopia to something personal or a far better coming of age story, she is doing so from today's perspective, which has nothing in common with the socio-political and historical context of the 1970s and thus with the eco-socialist issue that is Robert Havemann's main concern.[70]

---

68 Havemann, F. 2007, p. 302.
69 See Havemann, K. and Widmann 2003, p. 296.
70 Morris-Keitel 2004, p. 37.

Havemann worked on his book in secret and with absolute focus, always afraid of having to stop before reaching his goal:

> *Tomorrow* was intended to be, if not his legacy, at least his magnum opus, a book that would leave the position between party power and dissidence that he had occupied throughout his life far behind. Nobody saw Havemann working. His desk remained untouched. And this was precisely the impression he wanted to give. When he was alone, he worked on his manuscript which he always carried with him. Katja Havemann had hidden a carbon copy in Neubarnim.[71]

In *Tomorrow*, Robert Havemann briefly touches on the origins of the book. After Biermann was deported in 1976, he 'interrupted' his work on the as yet unfinished manuscript. Thereafter he was under house arrest and a number of his friends and acquaintances had to face reprisals. Although 1979 saw the end of Havemann's isolation, this was soon followed by the house search, during which 'a copy ... of the first four chapters' was seized. The Stasi did not get hold of a copy of the original, but the last part of the fourth chapter was lost and Havemann had to rewrite it.[72]

The report on the house search conducted on 19 April 1979 can be found in files at the Stasi Records Agency (BStU). According to this report, numerous documents and publications from the period between 1971 and 1978 were seized:

> Moreover, the examination of the documents seized revealed firm evidence of Havemann's intention to publish further works in the West. This essentially comprised:
> 1. The completion of a book that Havemann had started writing and in reference to which he informed 'Wilke in a letter written on 20.8.1978 ... that he had already completed three out of ten chapters, in which he addressed the subject of 'socialism in freedom as an opportunity to break through capitalism's ecological crisis'. Among the material seized during the search of the property was a 30-page, four-chapter manuscript with the title *Freiheit Demokratie Kommunismus – Utopie und Wirklichkeit? von Robert Havemann* (Freedom democracy communism – utopia and reality? By Robert

---

71   Havemann, K. and Widmann 2003, p. 297.
72   Havemann 1980b, p. 59f.

Havemann) containing chapters headed 'Actually existing socialism' and 'Why actually existing socialism cannot avert the crisis', which were particularly critical of socialist democracy and the planned economy in the GDR and which denigrated the domestic policy of the party and state leadership in the Soviet Union.[73]

Elsewhere, the aforementioned texts were described as –

> Four pages of a typewritten original and three pages of copies of a manuscript titled *Freiheit, Demokratie, Kommunismus – Utopie und Wirklichkeit* by Robert Havemann, started on 13.9.1973, as well as a 27-page document dealing with this subject over the following chapters:
> 1. The end of our time
> 2. Why capitalism cannot avert the ecological crisis
> 3. Actually existing socialism
> 4. Why actually existing socialism cannot avert the crisis.[74]

According to this information, Havemann had already started preliminary work on *Tomorrow* in September 1973, just a year after the Meadows Report was published.[75] However, he also expressed his views on the subject of utopia in the period between 1973 and 1980. In 1978, for example, under the headline '"Does everyone have to have a car?" Havemann's communist utopia' issue no. 40 of the *Spiegel* printed a text which already contained some of the key elements of *Tomorrow*.

Havemann managed to finish the manuscript for *Tomorrow* and, with the help of the Austrian ambassador, who received the manuscript from Havemann's messenger Thomas Klingenstein, the book made it via the diplomatic route to the Munich Piper-Verlag publishing house, which had already known about Havemann's book project for quite some time. The archives of the Robert Havemann Society contain publisher's files from Ernst Piper's collection containing, among other things, a note written on 18 March 1980 stating that Havemann had announced the publication of his book and had requested 'the lowest possible retail price and a paperback edition'.[76]

---

73 BStU, MfS, AU, 145/90, vol. 13, p. 143 ff.
74 BStU, MfS, AU, 145/90, vol. 13, p. 333.
75 Although Havemann did not actually complete his utopia until about six years later, this meant that *Tomorrow* was started at the same time that Bahro and Harich wrote their utopian books.
76 For this and the following quotes: RGH/RH 392.

In a letter written on 9 April 1980, Havemann proposed various titles for the book. Interestingly, Havemann had originally wanted the utopia to feature, not as a subheading, but rather as part of the main title, something which was not the case in the end.

The last title he had proposed was *Terra Utopie. Die Hoffnung zu überleben* (Terra Utopia. The hope of survival), which, according to Havemann, he and his wife Katja had come up with. Enclosed with the letter was a piece of notepaper documenting Havemann's search for a title: 'Utopia – The Path to the World of Tomorrow', 'Utopia – The Path to Tomorrow', 'The End of Our Time: Destination Utopia', 'Actually Existing Utopia. The Path and the Destination', 'How Will We Survive the End of Our Time', 'Between Yesterday and Tomorrow. The Land of Utopia', 'Utopia – (how) will we survive our time?' and lastly: 'Terra Utopia – how we (can/will) survive (our time)'. Based on this source, it is undeniable that Havemann's intention with the book was quite clearly to write a political utopia and he wanted this to be referred to explicitly in the title.

The Stasi files also contain a transcript of a RIAS interview from 3 September 1980 with Ernst-Reinhard Piper, the editor of *Tomorrow*. Piper did not believe that utopia served as a form of escapism for Havemann, but rather embodied hope and optimism. By his own admission, Piper had edited the manuscript and passed the edited version back to Havemann for him to proofread. Havemann 'then, after making some minimal changes, sent the book back to the publisher and this was the form it was published in'.[77]

This was essentially Havemann signing off on the final version of *Tomorrow*. The publisher put the book on market in September 1980. On 28 August, the *Stern* published a preprint and *Die Welt* announced on 1 September 1980 that *Tomorrow* would be published the following day.[78] From Ernst Piper's private collection, it emerges that his father, Klaus Piper, chose the final book title in April 1980. In the publisher's catalogue, however, the book was entered with the subtitle *Die Weltsysteme am Scheideweg* (The world system at a crossroads) and as having had a print run of 25,000 copies despite the fact that it was ultimately published with the subheading *Die Industriegesellschaft am Scheideweg* (Industrial society at a crossroads).[79] On 20 October, Ernst Piper wrote to Havemann to tell him that 10,000 copies had already been sold and that he intended to print the same number again.

---

77 BStU, MfS, AU, 145/90, vol. 8, p. 459.
78 See BStU, MfS, AU, 145/90, vol. 8, p. 456.
79 See RGH/RH 392.

Shortly beforehand, Havemann eagerly awaited the publication. He was not worried about any political or legal repercussions, and the Stasi files bear witness to this: in a report written on 15 August 1980, it states that they were able to unofficially record Havemann's expectations regarding the SED's reaction to the publication of *Tomorrow*. 'Among other things, Havemann said the following:

> My book will appear on 5.9.1980. An advance copy of a number of passages will be printed in the *Stern*. The whole thing will be a test of strength. I personally will be able to tell from the reactions whether there has been a change of heart in the "upper echelons". In my book, I have clearly addressed the internal problems in the GDR, the best thing for "them" to do is not to react at all.
> - If I am fined – I will file a lawsuit.
> - If they put me under house arrest – the Western press will show up and start a riot.
> - If they seize my accounts – I will buy five cars over there and sell them here.
> - If, to top it all off, they lock me up – they ought to know that I couldn't care less.
>
> You see, my friends, they have nothing they can really attack me with'.[80]

3 Havemann's Classical Utopia

3.1 *Critique of Industrial Society and World Systems*

In *Tomorrow*, Havemann's main focus is on the economic and ecological fiasco that the Club of Rome outlined. He posits that the vast majority of the Meadows Commission's forecasts would not entirely come true. On the other hand, Havemann also firmly believed that the trend Meadows described did undoubtedly exist and that humanity could therefore simply not continue as before, otherwise they would be heading towards 'an economic and ecolo-

---

80   BStU, MfS, AU, 145/90, vol. 10, p. 177. And despite the stricter legislation, Havemann was right. The SED and the Stasi proceeded cautiously: 'On 21 August 1980, via the ZAIG [the Stasi's information department] the Stasi informed Honecker, Hager and Herrmann from the Politburo, as well as the head of the Central Committee's Culture Commission, Ursula Ragwitz, that Havemann was about to publish another book with the Munich Piper-Verlag. His last book *Tomorrow. Industrial society at the crossroads*, a socialist ecological polemic with strong utopian elements was published in September without the permission of the Bureau for Copyright ...' (Vollnhals 2000, p. 129).

gical crisis' from which there would be no return. Havemann saw political decisions as vital for change, whereas economic decisions were secondary. He also believed in the primacy of the political over the economic sphere.

The arms race, global social inequality with the West's wastefulness, on the one hand, and famine in the 'Third World', on the other, as well as the obsession with luxury goods and the squandering of resources, ultimately resulting in huge mountains of rubbish – these were all developments that were condemned in *Tomorrow*. Contrary to the opinion he had expressed in the 1960s, Havemann now began to question the safety of nuclear power stations. He saw the energy issue as being a pivotal problem for the decades to come. He predicted, for example, that oil shortages in the US would lead them to take military action in the Middle East within the next 20 or 30 years. But the political and economic costs of these wars would far outweigh the success.[81]

Based on the assumption that it was impossible for seven billion people to enjoy the standard of living which prevailed in the West without permanently destroying the very foundation of their existence, Havemann asked, in reference to the Meadows Report the following (while at the same time making statements about his understanding of humanity):

> Why does humanity behave like the driver of a car racing towards a precipice whose only action to prevent the inevitable is to blindfold himself instead of putting his foot on the brakes? Might it perhaps be a congenital human weakness that the worries and the passions of the present blind us to the worries that lie in the future? I don't believe in such theories. ... I see humankind's ability to anticipate the consequences of its actions – albeit to a limited extent – as one of the fundamental differences between humans and animals. ... The fact that the warnings contained in the Meadows Report have so far failed to have any significant effect ... has other reasons, reasons rooted in the political economic structure of the social systems that exist in today's world and in the huge tensions and contradictions between them.[82]

He thus placed responsibility for the inability to come up with solutions on the industrial societies in both the East and the West as well as on the Cold War and the competition between the systems of capitalism and actually existing socialism, without actually blaming one world system or the other entirely.

---

81   See Havemann 1980b, p. 7 ff.
82   Havemann 1980b, p. 25.

Like Harich, Havemann, too, came to the conclusion that capitalism would not be able to avert the global crisis because, in order to continue to exist, it was still condemned to growth. Capitalism lives off consumption rather than use. It is shaped by short-lived fashions and trends, by compulsive consumption, which results in a huge, futile waste of resources that is intrinsic to the system.[83] From this, Havemann concluded:

> Capitalism, its internal structure and its very essence is completely incapable of overcoming the major impending crisis, because to do so, it would have to give up capitalism and that is something it cannot do. It has reached its end. It is living on borrowed time.[84]

Havemann did not reserve his criticism solely for capitalism, however. In fact, he also challenged actually existing socialism, describing it as the result of a long and misguided process, whose shortcomings could be traced back to Tsarist Russia. The October Revolution came too early, which meant that a –

> ... social system [emerged] that in actual fact ought to be described as socialist feudalism if this weren't such an absurd notion, i.e. a state with a completely pyramidal hierarchy .... A state with no legal remedy for despotism other than the degrading form of complaint, which is invariably 'processed' and thus dealt with by the very authority the complaint is directed at in the first place. A state where freedom of the press, freedom of speech and freedom of opinion only exist for those who say what those at the top want to hear. A state that suspends all the rights and freedoms won and defended with great sacrifice by the exploited members of bourgeois capitalist societies .... A state where all foreign literature is forbidden unless ... special dispensation has been granted, as with a few isolated cases.[85]

Havemann criticised the fact that the SED's policies were too fixated on emulating and aspiring to the Western lifestyle. He sarcastically commented that the SED leadership imitated everything from the West and as such would only turn its back on its growth-oriented economic policy if the West were to do the same first.

---

83   See Havemann 1980b, p. 33 f.
84   Havemann 1980b, p. 35.
85   Havemann 1980b, p. 41.

> No other nations are more devoted to its beloved growth than the actually existing socialist countries. Because the standard of living here is still lagging so far behind that of comparable capitalist countries ..., phrases like 'catch up' and 'take over' have become emotive terms on the political scene, words which express both the fervour of despair and embarrassing absurdity in equal measure.[86]

Havemann regarded the GDR's planned economy as undynamic, arbitrary, even chaotic – the 'prices do not correspond to the value', the costs are not covered, and this results in a downright waste of resources.

> However, as long as actually existing socialism (AES) with its pyramidal hierarchy continues to exist in socialist countries, and as long as it perpetuates its equally pyramidal pricing system with mass poverty and solitary peak of commodity prices for the luxury class, it will continue to compete with capitalism, only trying to reproduce the latter's economical absurdities, without being able to use a single advantage of its competitive system. It will hopelessly fail to fulfil its historical mission to show the whole world that socialism is fundamentally different from capitalism, and not only politically but also in terms of its economic objectives. And actually existing socialism might become even blinder to the impending global economic and ecological crisis than is the case with its hallowed economic role model.[87]

Havemann was critical of the fact that the SED's price policy was creating a growing social cleavage in the GDR. The low wages of broad swathes of the population, on the one hand, and the high prices of luxury goods, on the other, allowed the black market to prosper, causing illegal employment to become even more widespread. In Havemann's eyes, the system was to blame for this, a system which offered luxury goods to the privileged, financed by exploiting the workers. And the whole economy suffered in the process.[88] In his view, the only solution was to 'abolish private ownership of the means of production and thus eradicate the domination of one class over the others'[89] – although Havemann did not view the SED leadership and its followers

---

86 Havemann 1980b, p. 52.
87 Havemann 1980b, p. 57 f.
88 See Havemann 1980b, p. 64 f.
89 Havemann 1980b, p. 66.

as the ruling class, but rather as rulers who were at the mercy of Moscow. For Havemann, therefore, the Soviet Union was the key to change, the key to power.

Havemann predicted that capitalism would be incapable of overcoming the global crises. In his view, the situation with actually existing socialism was different, albeit not much better: 'If it managed to achieve world dominance, it might be capable of freezing the current barbaric state of the world into a Harich-style police system. This would not be the solution to the crisis, however. All it would achieve would be a decline into barbarism. The only path that would take us through the great disaster that lies ahead, without leading to our demise along the way, is the path of true, liberal socialism'.[90] In short, a Third Way. In order to embark on this path, however, we must finally acknowledge the crisis and come up with a concept for an ideal world of the future. Havemann believed that it was crucial to visualise this future in order to be able to begin implementing it, to not have to give up the hope of creating another world. He described this as 'our only salvation'.[91] These were Havemann's reasons for choosing utopia as his medium.

At the same time, Havemann's book also has elements of the classical utopia, with characteristics such as a critique of the status quo and a fictitious countermodel.

3.2   *The Third Way via Utopia*

Havemann's contextualisation of both the model of the classical utopia and Bloch's concept of concrete utopia is evidenced in the chapter titled 'Utopia und Hoffnung' (Utopia and hope). Here, Havemann urges people not to give up the 'principle of hope' as the principle of human existence despite the mortal perils created by man, because without hope there can no longer be resistance. Clearly echoing Bloch, Havemann states: 'The principle of hope is the only thing that can move the world ahead'.[92] For Havemann, utopia served to provide the principle of hope with images and substance:

> Thus, the substance of all hopes, big and small, is always utopia. ... With utopia, in our minds we create a world in which the brutalities and inhumanity of today's world are eliminated. In other words, utopia is a way of critically examining the world in which we live. It is, therefore, not only the new and the unprecedented that we imagine for our utopia that

---

90   Havemann 1980b, p. 66.
91   Havemann 1980b, p. 67.
92   Havemann 1980b, p. 72.

is of significance. In fact, the very things that do not exist in our utopia are also important. In utopia, our world is sublated in three different ways: nullified and vanquished, preserved and not lost, and elevated to a higher level.[93]

The latter was in keeping with Havemann's interpretation of Marxist dialectic. In his eyes, socialism or rather communism was the greatest utopia of the twentieth century, and actual developments in Eastern Europe and China caused serious damage to it. 'Yet, in spite of everything, in spite of all the bitter disappointments, the concept of socialism maintained an intriguing lustre, namely the hope that the exploited and the disenfranchised would one day triumph over the power of their exploiters after all and create a new, just and humane social order'.[94]

Havemann believed that Engels's *The Development of Socialism from Utopia to Science* had been misinterpreted by the Marxist dogmatists. Contrary to their conjecture, Engels in fact believed it was impossible to conceive a utopia without a thorough political economic analysis of the existing circumstances, as had been the case with the early utopianists. But Engels had not objected to utopia per se. 'In fact, today we really ought to call Engels's opus "From utopian socialism to a socialist utopia based in science".'[95] And with these words, Havemann was also expressing what he aspired to achieve with the utopian concept he put forward in *Tomorrow*.[96]

Following his analysis of the global political and economic situation and the utopian part of the book, Havemann includes a chapter titled 'Die Reise in das Land unserer Hoffnungen' (The journey to the land of our hopes) with over 100 pages. In this chapter, Havemann conjectures, based on the philosophy of history, that there were alternatives to the course of the October Revolution and the development of actually existing socialism, and that his utopia had the potential to be implemented beyond Marxist-Leninist historical determinism.

The utopian chapter in *Tomorrow* takes the form of a report recounting a fictitious journey that Havemann took with his family to 'Utopia'. He describes the entrance to this country as being located beyond the Yugoslav border,

---

93 Havemann 1980b, p. 72 f.
94 Havemann 1980b, p. 73.
95 Havemann 1980b, p. 74.
96 According to his son Florian, however, there were pictures of Lenin, Mao and Stalin displayed in his parents' home. 'But Marx? There were no pictures of Marx in the Havemann house. The Marx books all sat unread on the bookshelves, volume after blue volume. My father was, however, a fan of Engels, who actually represented the beginnings of all this Marxism' (Havemann, F. 2008).

not far from Ljubljana (although the account describes a car journey via the Czechoslovak Socialist Republic and Austria with no border controls). Once the reader has entered Utopia, however, the geographical location no longer plays a role. Based on this, Havemann's utopia can be defined as a temporal utopia as, once the reader steps over the border, the entire Earth becomes a utopia, a utopian space projected into the future (Havemann always uses the past tense when writing the passages in his travelogue that talk about his present). At the border, the protagonists dispense with all their material belongings, including their cars, and are met by three citizens of Utopia, a man (Bertram), a woman (Anna) and boy called Felix – the same name as Havemann's grandson in Hamburg.[97]

First of all, Havemann describes the process of discovery which is enhanced by the new types of drugs taken – drugs that (unlike real drugs) have no harmful effects on people's health nor are they addictive. People can therefore happily get high on these safe drugs – a desire that undoubtedly fulfilled Havemann's subjective needs. Against this background, the scientist and bon viveur extoled the 'creative power of mental confusion, which Plato already described as far superior to colourless rationing'.[98]

This attitude to drugs is *one* component of the post-materialist way of life in Utopia. Here 'to be' is far more important than 'to have', and, in Havemann's view, being able to enjoy the experience of one's own sense of 'being' to the full undoubtedly called for drug use. He thus also evoked the role of science, which, in future, would benefit humans just as much as labour and technology. In addition, there was a distinct environmental awareness.

Havemann's utopia can be categorised as falling within the anarchistic utopian tradition. For 'In Utopia there is no state, nor is there a government, a police force, or any form of administration of the people. All that is left is the almost fully automated administration of things'.[99] Where earlier cities were agglomerations of human evil, harbouring destructive tendencies as well as human isolation and smog, in Utopia these have been eradicated. Consequently, there is also no capital city. Havemann describes how, in the past, the cities were home to workers that produced pointless and superfluous items and the functionaries of the bloated bureaucracy who controlled and managed the workers. This has now all become superfluous because in Utopia, industry is efficient and computerised, meaning there is very little need for human labour power.

---

97   See Havemann 1980b, p. 78 ff.
98   Havemann 1980b, p. 81.
99   Havemann 1980b, p. 90.

The Havemann family is then shown how agriculture works in Utopia: diverse crop species grow in big fields intersected by streets (for electric commercial vehicles) and supplied by a branched irrigation system. There are also huge greenhouses, which are heated throughout the year using waste heat from industry. This waste heat is produced by 'large-scale, fully automated industrial equipment, indeed an entire array of such manufacturing machinery', located underneath the huge agricultural installation. In the winter, the waste heat is channelled into the greenhouses and in the summer, it goes into the nearby Adriatic. No-one needs to work in this industrial plant as it is fully automated, as is the sowing and harvesting. Farming is strictly organic: there are no parasites in the greenhouses and naturally resistant crop varieties, developed and tested by researchers, are grown on the fields. These varieties are not genetically modified but rather intrinsically resistant varieties. This is one of the few jobs for which humans are actually needed; but they are not forced to work, they do so voluntarily and with great enthusiasm.[100] No-one is forced to work in Utopia[101] – who would even impose such an obligation? There is no money, ergo there are no wages either. There is still work to be done, but the people of Utopia are free to engage in those activities and jobs which they find enjoyable. In Utopia, exchange values are no longer produced, with utility values being used instead. 'It is only necessary for people to work where the development of processes and relevant technologies has not yet been completed'. Once this has been achieved, everything works automatically and research is focused on the development of new technologies.[102]

Havemann also described the industrial institute which was part of the production facilities underneath the large-scale agricultural installation. The underground industrial plant covers 25 square kilometres and includes a street (with side streets), leading to a nearby port. This port is used to supply the facility with raw materials and the finished goods are then transported from here. No visitors are allowed to enter the facility and only a small number of experts actually work there. Utopia has no industrial plants above ground, instead having opted for a small number of large-scale facilities underground. The plant visited by the Havemann family primarily manufactures microelectronics. Sup-

---

100 See Havemann 1980b, p. 98 ff.
101 'In addition, there are of course many, often complex jobs in industry and agriculture that require highly specialised technical and scientific training. But no-one devotes themselves to such activities because they are under economic pressure to do so but because each and every individual chooses their field of their work according to their interests and changes field whenever they please' (Havemann 1980b, p. 182).
102 See Havemann 1980b, p. 105 ff.

plemented by two subsidiaries, the plant covers the entire global production for this industrial sector, a quantitative feat made possible by products being manufactured with ever longer service lives.[103] Industrial products last for several decades and this long service life and minimum wear means they acquire the 'beauty of living, growing creatures'.[104]

Many products of the capitalist era are no longer produced or needed in Utopia, and here Havemann is referring first and foremost to cars and roads, which have become superfluous because people no longer have to drive to work. Cars are no longer needed for travel in Utopia, nor are airplanes because people's lives no longer have the same sense of urgency or haste. In Utopia, travelling means moving at a slow pace to discover the world.[105] Motorised vehicles are only used for medical purposes and to supply the population.

> There are still trains ..., which are used to transport certain raw materials, if this is required for technical reasons. The majority of products and goods are transported by sea. In general, dedicated underground transport systems move goods from the ports ... first to the major distribution centres and then on to the smallest ones, Utopia's supermarkets, where all the industrial products people need in their daily lives are available. These large, well organised storage warehouses have neither sales staff ... nor any form of control or security staff. Even the constant replenishing of stocks happens automatically through the upstream on-demand distribution centres.[106]

None of this requires a vast amount of effort, however, as the long service life means that the demand for consumer products tends to be limited. Thus, the system of distribution of goods Havemann describes in his utopia resembles that which has traditionally featured in utopias over history. Depicting a visit to a *Kinderdorf* or 'children's village' – the most popular form of settlement in Utopia – Havemann describes how the residents take their meals and the food they consume. Meals were prepared centrally and eaten privately:

---

103 See Havemann 1980b, p. 110ff. Unlike capitalism, where engineers are concerned with designing products with the shortest possible lifespan so that more and more has to be consumed, according to Havemann, researchers in Utopia work on designing products that are as durable and long-lasting as possible. When it comes to so-called 'integrated wear and tear', also known as 'planned obsolescence', the French documentary *The Lightbulb Conspiracy* made in 2010 makes for interesting viewing.
104 Havemann 1980b, p. 114.
105 See Havemann 1980b, p. 114f.
106 Havemann 1980b, p. 116.

> The two main meals, lunch and dinner, were prepared in a large-scale highly automated kitchen, using both fresh vegetables and meat and pre-cooked meals and preserved food. Individual portions were packaged in transparent containers, which were transferred via an underground transport system to 20 different distribution centres in thermally insulated containers. Families then came to these centres with little carts to collect their food, returning their clean, empty containers at the same time. There was always a wide variety of different dishes. Many followed an almost vegetarian diet. Meat consumption was relatively low.[107]

Havemann then provides a detailed description of housing construction and architecture in Utopia. In addition to the *Kinderdorf* settlements which were like little agglomerations, the landscape was characterised by a well-meant, intentional urban sprawl:

> Houses were basic constructions but came in assorted styles and designs. They were assembled from prefabricated parts that come in shapes and dimensions that, when combined, allow for a seemingly inexhaustible number of variations. Wherever we looked there were gardens with fruit and vegetables growing, and of course there were also flowers and fanciful shrubs and exotic trees. Quite a few also had very respectably sized greenhouses. We even saw proper farms, which, in many respects, resembled our own, where animals were also kept, from chickens and all manner of poultry to pigs, cows and horses.[108]

Energy in Utopia is produced by small-scale decentralised nuclear fusion plants powered by hydrogen obtained from regular water. As a result, there are no more problems with shortages of raw materials, and overhead power lines are no longer needed. Overall, significantly less energy is consumed and required, because the resource-intensive arms industry has become a thing of the past, for example. Nor are there any nuclear power stations in Utopia. This is not because of safety, which is not an issue 'if they are properly designed and operated' – at least according to Havemann the scientist – but rather due to the unresolved issue of final storage and disposal of spent radioactive fuel.[109]

Another classical utopian feature is the long-lasting clothing that the citizens in Havemann's Utopia wear, manufactured using newly developed arti-

---

107 Havemann 1980b, p. 130 f.
108 Havemann 1980b, p. 124.
109 See Havemann 1980b, p. 120 ff.

ficial textiles which only need water to be washed and dry quickly and easily in the air. The clothes have a timeless design, are comfortable and durable, writes Havemann. The material 'looks like soft suede but feels quite different and, as we discovered later, was also very light and breathable yet so durable that it could not be torn or damaged no matter how hard you tried'.[110] In contrast to the uniform clothing found both in modern utopias and dystopias, different patterns could be cut from the Utopian textile fabric described in *Tomorrow*, and the textiles could be dyed to suit individual tastes, meaning there was no standard look.

The final stop on the Havemanns' journey through Utopia was one of the larger *Kinderdorf* settlements: 'In a gently sloping valley we saw hundreds of houses and huts of all different types and sizes in the midst of a park-like landscape, in which an almost circular lake was nestled'.[111] The settlement thus very much coincided with the model of post-materialist utopias: the individual and the community blend seamlessly into one another, anonymity and isolation in the big city no longer exists, but nor does the concept of a closed utopian city for which More's *Amaurotum* provided the blueprint.

Havemann describes the settlement as follows:

> With its houses, gardens and parks, the *Kinderdorf* covered a total area of almost three square kilometres and was home to around five and a half thousand people, including three and a half thousand children of all ages from one-year-old toddlers to 18-year-olds. A total of 1,200 "parents" taught and raised the children, meaning each set of parents had an average of six children at home. Then there were another 500 adults, some of whom worked as teachers, while others helped with the technical administration or in the kitchen, or assisted in the scientific and technical departments and in shops.[112]

---

110 Havemann 1980b, p. 80. See also Havemann 1980b, p. 110 and p. 159.
111 Havemann 1980b, p. 124.
112 Havemann 1980b, p. 125. 'Since Utopia's population has been virtually constant for a long time, this must mean that every woman gives birth to an average of two children. The majority of women have their children between the age of 20 and 40, and almost none of these women separate from their children, instead remaining in the *Kinderdorf* settlements with them, until they are between 10 and 15 years of age. ... Many of the biological fathers of these children also lived in the settlement, some with the mother of their children and some with other women. As a result, upbringing, learning and further education in Utopia had become people's main occupations, with each and every individual spending the biggest part of their lives alternating between being a teacher and a student, or even being both at the same time' (Havemann 1980b, p. 126 f.).

The younger members of Utopia's population lived primarily in these automated *Kinderdorf* settlements, while the rest of the population lived in houses dotted about the countryside. The global population was double the size it was in 1980 and yet there were no supply problems whatsoever. Moreover, the demographic structure of society was fundamentally different and people lived to a much older age.[113]

The change in age structure and the concept of labour in Havemann's Utopia leads to the question of whether a 'New Man' is needed for the system to function. Here, Havemann builds on an anti-authoritarian, educated, healthy 'New Man', with a thirst for knowledge. Not one who has come about through eugenics or human breeding, but through education and upbringing. The people of Utopia acquire knowledge from the cradle to the grave. Thanks to high-level automation, they have much more free time, which they use for education. The knowledge they acquire is passed on continually: 'From an early age into their advanced years, each and every individual is both a student and a teacher'.[114]

Havemann described the education system:

> The first school-like lesson takes place when a child is just four years old. ... The number of different classes a child can choose to take increases as they grow older. The level of education and knowledge reached by the time an individual leaves the *Kinderdorf* at between the age of 18 and 20 was very high .... It was not even comparable with our educational goals, neither from a quantitative nor a qualitative perspective. There was also considerable scope for artistic education. Painting, drawing, sculpting, pottery, making music and composing, dancing and miming, singing, acting, filming, writing poetry, even the first attempts at writing short stories, fairy tales and novels, were all taught and practiced in courses and small groups. Various different languages were taught, as was the international world language of course. People studied the great literature of the history of the world and these books were also available in a well-stocked library. History, especially cultural history, were among the most important subjects. But maths and the sciences, too, were taught to an advanced

---

113   'With a global population of approximately six billion people, we have around 750 million children under the age of 18. That is almost 13% of the total population. ... Up until the age of 100, we have a very low death rate of around 5%. That means that 95% of those born live to 100 or longer. Only after this does the death rate gradually increase so only around 85% of the 100-year-olds live to over 120. Thereafter, mortality increases rapidly with relatively few people reaching the age of 150 or 160' (Havemann 1980b, p. 125f.).

114   Havemann 1980b, p. 109.

level, and well-equipped laboratories and workshops had been set up for this purpose. The difference to our teaching and learning methods, I would say, lies in the fact that the aim is actually not to accumulate knowledge. There are no tests, no questions are asked, and nobody receives any grades. Nor are there records of achievement or any form of qualification. In Utopia there are no longer any titles, not even for older, highly qualified specialists. The aim of all lessons and upbringing was not knowledge, but rather education.[115]

To be able to experience the world empirically, the 'families' would leave their *Kinderdorf* every few years to travel until they found a new one that they liked.[116] They were not tied to a specific workplace or job since:

Here, as Marx already predicted, there are no painters, no poets – nor are there technical physicists. What there are, however, are people who engage in painting and write poetry, people who work as technical physicists. But rather than pursuing just one of these professions, they can potentially pursue all of them, even at the same time.[117]

In short: in education, progressive educational methods prevail. The aim is for people to learn how to think. Consequently, there are barely any specialists any longer, but instead a large number of universal scholars. Here, it is quite clear that Havemann is referring to his own struggle for free sciences, not dictated by politics. His fictitious experiences during a school philosophy seminar should be interpreted against this background. It is here that his long-standing call for a 'dialectic without dogma' becomes reality:

Our group of philosophers had 15 members – eight girls and seven boys. To my great relief, I found that we weren't studying some kind of beatific philosophical doctrine. The head of the group told us that the first hurdle every philosophical circle has to surmount is to acquire an understanding of what the term philosophy even means. For the people of Utopia, for a long time this term had described a way of thinking that belonged firmly in the past. It was difficult for them to understand that since the first development of culture, many millennia ago, people had completely bought into the most fantastical doctrines and stories – often to the point

---

115 Havemann 1980b, p. 131.
116 See Havemann 1980b, p. 132.
117 Havemann 1980b, p. 133.

of being fanatical and intolerant towards anyone who thought differently – and still clung onto these even when their incompatibility with scientific findings became quite obvious. So as not to simply dismiss these apparent paradoxes as pathological perversities of human thought, which they certainly were not, the group began to work on exploring the origins of philosophy.[118]

Thus, what Marx called for in the *11th Thesis on Feuerbach*,[119] and what Bloch, Bahro and Havemann insisted on, had at last become reality. That said, Havemann assumed that even in utopia, there would still be human misfortune. Despite having eradicated the bourgeois relations of ownership and production, despite the emancipatory development of education and the world of work, there could still be no complete harmony 'as long as humans and human culture continued to exist'.[120] Havemann's communist utopia is thus not devoid of internal contradictions: interpersonal problems continue to exist, just without the burden of all things material.

In *Tomorrow*, the issues of love and sexuality played a disproportionately important role. As mentioned above, Havemann wrote the book at a time when he was going through a serious marital crisis, and, as a result, his wife interpreted the opus as a form of self-therapy. We can clearly recognise that Havemann used the book to process his relationship troubles and desires. At the same time, he also incorporated his ideas regarding the post-materialist utopian discourse that prevailed at the time,[121] which made the book so much more than just a form of private therapy for its author.

Gender relations in Utopia are based on the elimination of patriarchy by eradicating the material dependence of women on men. The essence of this new matriarchy, which is not intended to represent dominance of women over men but rather the abolition of patriarchal structures and mentalities, lay in feminine and maternal characteristics – much like in Harich's *Das Weib in der Apokalypse* (The woman in the apocalypse). For Havemann, 'the feminine is at the centre of our life because it is from here that all life and love emerges'.[122]

---

118 Havemann 1980b, p. 155.
119 See Havemann 1980b, p. 157. The *11th Thesis on Feuerbach* states: 'The philosophers have *interpreted* the world in various ways; the point however is to *change* it', Marx 1975, p. 5.
120 Havemann 1980b, p. 123.
121 He put love above work, for instance. See Havemann 1980b, p. 133.
122 Havemann 1980b, p. 149.

When it comes to love and sexuality, this meant that women could behave in a less constrained manner. The taboos associated with the patriarchal society have been eradicated: adultery does not exist as a concept, incest is no longer stigmatised and homosexuality is nothing unusual either.[123] These ideas are in keeping with the post-materialist zeitgeist of the 1970s and were also the subject of highly controversial discussions during the early years of the West German Greens, for instance.[124]

Anna, the main female protagonist in *Tomorrow*, provided an account of love in Utopia: 'There are no sexual taboos here whatsoever, and this, of course, also includes physical love. This is not something we regard as the gratification of a sexual urge, but rather as a form of art, a field of discovery rather than biologically programmed instinct, the highest form of self-experience through the experience of identity with a partner'.[125]

Given that these are qualitative criteria of love, since the latter has not been reduced to sexual gratification, there is no need to introduce Malthusian means of birth control – not even the pill.[126] Fidelity and infidelity no longer exist in Havemann's Utopia because, as a category, love is at the centre of everything: people simply love whoever they want to. This can be one person, or many. Partnerships can comprise two or more people and last as long as the love between the partners continues. Relationships based purely on sex or group sex in the old sense, however, no longer exist, 'as in our society, the motives that led to these phenomena in yours no longer exist. This is because, in our world, the character of human relationships has been cleansed of so much of the filth and smut that had besmirched everything that was human in your society, poisoned by conditions of covetousness, possessiveness, a craving for admiration and thirst for power. In our society, love and sexuality are no longer separated.[127] Thus, when love ends, although there is no longer

---

123 See Havemann 1980b, pp. 91 and 136 ff. 'There are very clear facts in support of the notion that homosexuality has nothing to do with biology, but that it being a taboo is rooted in the social sphere' (Havemann 1980b, p. 137).

124 '... the Greens would probably have made even deeper inroads if they had reached out to such milieux instead of alienating them with chaotic affectations, debates on the decriminalization of paedophilia, and contempt for the motherhood of women' (Radkau 2014, p. 206).

125 Havemann 1980b, p. 140.

126 See Havemann 1980b, p. 90 f.

127 Havemann 1980b, p. 142. 'Sex without love always implies subordination. The fact that this was virtually the norm in your time is down to one very simple reason: material dependence. There were almost no relationships between people that were free of material dependence, often reciprocal, whereas relationships between men and women almost always involve one-sided dependence of the woman on the man. This basic evil of your

vengefulness or jealousy, as these have been overcome along with the materialistic patriarchal society, those effected still feel the same sadness they always felt.[128]

The contradictions that remain in Utopia are no longer rooted in the material, in the desire to have possessions. According to Havemann, society's awareness of these antagonisms is the ontological basis of the system. He created a model of the future that comprised the components of political utopia that were critical of the present.[129]

The synthesis of freedom and community is fundamental for the utopian society described in *Tomorrow*. It probes the tense relationship between the individual and the collective, bringing them into balance. There is no forced community as there was in the older utopias but people are not isolated either – even within a forced collective – as they are in dystopias. One example of this is taking meals, which does not take place in large groups – although the citizens of Utopia can of course choose to eat together if they wish – as that would be tantamount to 'feeding the masses'.[130] In Utopia, post-materialism is embedded in norms: tranquility is considered the reason for the lack of meaning in 'having possessions': 'In Utopia, not having is what constitutes wealth'.[131] Havemann went as far as to claim that Utopia was the kingdom that Jesus Christ would have described as his own.[132]

However, Utopia was not a theocracy like all forms of institutionalised religion; its rituals and ceremonies had disappeared, 'almost imperceptibly petered out'.[133] That said, the wisdom of the ancient religions continued to be cherished as a source of inspiration. The research on this no longer focused on refuting religious and philosophical works, however, but rather on gaining insights and knowledge from them.[134]

---

time destroyed every burgeoning love time and again and ultimately made you all incapable of loving; in each and every one of you, it maimed the most wonderful thing about being human' (Havemann 1980b, p. 143).

128   See Havemann 1980b, p. 144.
129   'There is much from the past – which was your present – that lives on in us in a thousand different forms to this very day, often quite hidden. Added to this are the new contradictions of our lives. If we had failed to thoroughly examine your time and really understand it, we would never have been able to overcome it and today would not find ourselves in utopia but rather in a world of brutal savagery' (Havemann 1980b, p. 130).
130   See Havemann 1980b, p. 146.
131   Havemann 1980b, p. 165.
132   See Havemann 1980b, p. 175.
133   Havemann 1980b, p. 157.
134   See Havemann 1980b, p. 158.

The attitude towards culture is similar: in Utopia, there are countless small amateur dramatic groups. Culture is not elitist but rather a common good, and there is a world language that allows global communication.[135] Something that was rather progressive – given that this has been virtually implemented today (with the exception of the property question) – was Havemann's concept of media technology and communication. If people in Utopia want to listen to music, all they have to do is press a number on a cordless telephone and ask for the song. This request is then transmitted wirelessly to loudspeakers concealed in the wall and the song is played immediately. Besides music, this system also allows people to access information and all kinds of images. Television programmes have ceased to exist, having been replaced by high-resolution displays on which people can retrieve and view whatever information they require.[136]

After returning from Utopia, Havemann wrote in his travelogue that this society was by no means complete or comprehensive as:

> Every utopia shares the same flaw that, in our minds, it is only possible to eradicate that which, in our barbaric society, is inhumane, unjust and incongruous and infringes upon human freedom and dignity. As a result, it is possible that … our criticisms and accusations … do little more than scratch the surface and, instead of getting to the root of the actual disease, only make out a few of its symptoms. These shortcomings in our powers of judgement, as well as the fact that the eradication of our social order in the new, future social order will be more – both quantitatively and qualitatively – than our society has the mental capacity to conjure up, means that tomorrow's reality will be different in many respects, and will certainly be much more fanciful than we can even imagine.[137]

In light of this, Havemann did not connect his utopia with any absolute demand for implementation or claim to validity. What was more important for him was extrapolating a better society from today's conditions while demonstrating that it was possible to set a positive and conceivable goal for humanity. The aim of his utopia was

> to help overcome the growing hopelessness and defeatism which were paralysing the progressive forces the world over. Its purpose was to put an end to the fragmentation into a hundred sects by visualising a common

---

135 See Havemann 1980b, p. 97 f.
136 See Havemann 1980b, p. 85 f.
137 Havemann 1980b, p. 178.

goal, albeit a distant one. It sought to convince people that we are capable of tackling the impending risk of self-destruction and demise, thus giving us the courage to take up the fight for this.[138]

Havemann believed his utopia was achievable, naming a number of areas where he believed this to be the case. *In terms of technology*, the current level of knowledge would be largely sufficient to ensure fully automatic supply for the people and 'new, as yet unknown or inconceivable technical miracles are not prerequisites for achieving the utopian technology'.[139] By dispensing with armaments and airplane and automobile construction, maximising product service life and giving primacy to 'optimum use value', the demand for energy and raw materials will be significantly reduced. In the case of raw materials, one way this will be achieved is by optimising recycling systems and using alternative energy sources.[140]

Politically, he saw a (cultural) revolution as being the path to implementing utopia: 'The question as to whether there is a possibility of such a utopia being achieved is thus initially reduced to the possibility of such a revolution happening'.[141] From his Marxist perspective, Havemann came to the conclusion that class antagonisms had intensified since the late 1960s, and that this had resulted in a historical situation developing which, in this form, was unprecedented in history – even in the Russia of 1917. And this was because only now were the existing relations of production increasingly becoming an obstacle to the developing productive forces.[142]

Havemann believed that, in light of the global threat of nuclear weapons, the transformation could no longer function as a revolution against the state.

---

138   Havemann 1980b, p. 179.
139   Havemann 1980b, p. 179.
140   See Havemann 1980b, p. 179 f.
141   Havemann 1980b, p. 185.
142   See Havemann 1980b, p. 185 ff. 'It was not until the late 1970s and now, at the beginning of the 1980s, that we have started to see the beginnings of a structural crisis of capitalism bearing the distinctive traits that are characteristic of the birth of the revolution that Marx postulated. Essentially, there are three main elements that determine the structure of this crisis: (1) The economic imperative to continue economic growth; (2) The resulting waste of all natural raw materials and the inevitable catastrophe this leads to, as well as the accompanying environmental pollution; (3) The continuous reduction of the workforce brought about by the constantly evolving full-scale automation achieved through the use of microelectronics, a workforce which, under pressure from rising mass unemployment, is prevented from enjoying the fruits of the technical progress achieved through their labour, fruits that are manifested in the form of higher wages and fewer working hours' (Havemann 1980b, p. 187).

This might have been possible at the end of World War I, but would no longer be feasible at the end of a Third World War. He thus saw a peaceful transition to a new society as the only option: 'The new revolution will not be able to overturn state power because it has been weakened by external enemies; it will not be the result of an upheaval or a putsch. The revolution will only be victorious if it is driven by the strength of the solidarity of the broad masses, who have recognised that revolution is everyone's salvation from the gravest danger'.[143] Havemann identified four development stages as prerequisites for this transformation:

> 1. The revolution ... does not mark the start of a lengthy process of evolution, it is in fact its end. 2. During this process, the working class gradually acquires economic power through self-organisation and, with the help of these organisations (trade unions and parties), participates in political processes. 3. In the meantime, under pressure from this new class, elements of a new society already begin to emerge. And all this culminates in 4. The working class draws up a political and economic programme that gains the support of the vast majority. As Marx put it: Ideas become a material force once they are understood by the masses. Under these conditions, the revolution happens without a single drop of blood being spilled.[144]

Havemann conjectured that the path of transformation would be different in the East and the West because of their different relations of production and ownership. After World War II, the unwanted Soviet system was grafted onto the actually existing socialist states. Havemann did, however, see one positive aspect of the development in the East in that private ownership of the means of production – which he saw as the root of all evil – had been eradicated. Unfortunately, private owners were replaced by new owners in the form of a state monopoly.

> These relations of production, which were not *yet* socialist, are a suitable counterpart to the 'politbureaucratic dictatorship'. But the transition from this politbureaucratic dictatorship to the dictatorship of the proletariat, as it was described by Rosa Luxemburg in line with Karl Marx's thinking, is only *one* step – one step to complete the incomplete revolution.

---

143 Havemann 1980b, p. 190.
144 Havemann 1980b, p. 197.

It is undoubtedly a difficult step to take. But it has already been done once before: in 1968 by the Czechoslovak Republic, under its own steam! And previous historical experience shows us that great revolutions rarely achieve their goal in just one step.[145]

Havemann thus hoped for transformation from within actually existing socialist societies, based on the previously socialised means of production, and here he was in agreement with Bahro and Harich. Like Bahro, he based his hopes on the experience of the Prague Spring, which had proved that actually existing socialism could be transformed into democratic socialism without bloodshed – it was not the ongoing 'completion of the socialist revolution' that had been bloody but rather the violent restoration.[146]

When it came to the capitalist West, Havemann assumed that other conditions prevailed. Here, he saw the split within the workers movement and the sectarianism on the left as obstructing the agent of transformation.[147] He called for the left to adopt a strategy of 'unity in diversity', a principle coined by Palmiro Togliatti, in other words for a pluralist left, uniting a variety of viewpoints under one roof.[148]

In his opinion, parliamentarianism could not be the sole way of exercising power, but could only serve as the extended arm of the movement in the legislative field. Havemann believed that the groundwork needed to prepare for new laws and for the revolution would take place elsewhere:

> The fronts on which this battle will be waged will essentially be the major industrial enterprises, where the trade unions will fight for almost everything for the development of the new society in the lap of the old – and it will not be until after this that the front will shift to the public forums where the battle against the ideology of the still dominant class will be waged .... Equally important are all the social institutions that serve to provide the public with information about economic, technical financial and administrative changes, as well as scientific analysis of this informa-

---

145   Havemann 1980b, p. 202f.
146   See Havemann 1980b, p. 203.
147   Havemann was critical, for example, of the West German Greens, accusing them of having become a sect which believed that its ideology was the panacea for world improvement. He claimed that focusing on tackling environmental pollution would not solve the problem as long as capitalism itself remained unchallenged. See Havemann 1980b, p. 204.
148   See Havemann 1980b, p. 206.

tion. ... Other crucial areas of public life where our battle is being fought are art and literature, theatre, film – in fact all forms of cultural production and reproduction.[149]

Havemann's concept of transformation includes elements which had already been articulated by socialist pioneers of the Third Way, such as Eduard Bernstein, Karl Kautsky, Rosa Luxemburg, Antonio Gramsci or the Austrian Marxists. But his concept was also reminiscent of the model of economic democracy developed by Fritz Naphtali, as well as Yugoslavia's attempts at council communism, notions of worker self-administration and other ideas about the objectives of and paths to democratic socialism or socialist democracy.

4   Havemann's Utopian Ideas and Their Place in Utopian History

4.1   Tomorrow *in the Context of Havemann's Political Works*

In this section, the utopian elements of Havemann's political works[150] will be described and analysed in terms of their form and possible transformation over the decades. In the 1950s, Havemann was among the politically active scientists who took part in philosophical debates. He saw dialectical Marxism as a method rooted in a philosophy of praxis and also strongly recommended it to other scientists, as he did, for example, in his 1957 text *Unsere Philosophie und das Leben* (Our philosophy and life).[151]

This period also saw the start of Havemann's gradual departure from the path the party was on. He became increasingly aware of the discrepancy between the party's dogmatic interpretation of dialectical Marxism – which it used to legitimise its rule – and his own personal expectations of it as a method employed in critical (natural) sciences. In his view, this dogmatism hampered the freedom of the sciences, sometimes leading to disastrous developments, which in turn had resulted in the actually existing socialist states being left behind in the battle of the systems.[152] In a series of lectures held in 1963/64,

---

149 Havemann 1980b, p. 208.
150 'The sheer breadth of Havemann's works range from poetry to texts emanating from his research activities as a physical chemist, the content of which thus probably only reaches an audience involved in this specialist field. Alongside his extensive correspondence, today it is the political and philosophical texts he penned that are especially valuable, texts that are testimony to the controversies and conflicts of the last century' (Florath and Theuer 2007b, p. x).
151 See Havemann 1971, p. 43 ff.
152 'To this day there are still people who, citing dialectical materialism, refuse to recognise

later published as transcripts under the title *Dialektik ohne Dogma?* (Dialectics without dogma?), Havemann demands that 'our philosophy not be determined by what we already know, but rather be the key to new knowledge'.[153] In his view, this also involved permanently questioning the findings of previous research: 'I believe that modern materialism in particular must question itself, and that constant reflection on the doubts in the fundamental nature of modern materialism is essential for continued historical development'.[154]

Havemann saw it as wrong and indeed politically inept

> ... to keep the people ignorant of how things truly are .... A government can only be successful in what is very important work if it is able to rely on the active and dedicated support of all members of society. Yet this support can only be secured if the popular masses are constantly informed about all the goings-on and problems in their lives. The concept of the collectivity must not be reduced to leadership activities. It has to extend to society in its entirety.[155]

In as early as 1964, Havemann refrained from placing the individual in an isolated and disenfranchised position relative to the collective, instead portraying them as an active participant in a democratic socialist society. On this he wrote:

> We must not force people into a mould and impose officially approved views on them, as doing so will only tempt them to think in a schematic and superficial way. We must provide comprehensive information to increasingly equip people to grasp the true circumstances. We must initiate a broad debate on all the questions of our time. Only by doing so will the immense power of the popular masses make a productive and creative contribution and not be discharged in destructive conflicts.[156]

Here, we can already see the approach adopted in *Tomorrow*, where people are equipped to perform creative non-alienating jobs from a young age. Havemann did not start from the position of a schematic form of historical determinism.

---

cybernetics as a scientific discipline. If it had been up to these advocates of dialectical materialism, the Soviet Union would never have had sputniks. It only had them because natural scientists and physicists continued to work despite the endless objections that came from philosophers' (Havemann 1968, p. 14).

153   Havemann 1968, p. 19.
154   Havemann 1968, p. 33.
155   Havemann 1968, p. 52.
156   Havemann 1968, p. 52.

Instead, he believed that people had to 'try and influence the possible before it becomes reality. We shape and transform the world by changing its possibilities. In this way we make that which we are striving for reality'.[157] Primitive communism, which imposed equality out of suffering and poverty was, for Havemann, a thing of the past. 'Modern communism can only be communism if it provides freedom and, at the same time, is not based on shared suffering, labour and exertion'.[158] As early as 1964, Havemann had already taken a utopian approach, writing

> ... that the aim of our endeavours must be a society the survival of which does not require moral codes because all members of that society can see what is needed .... Communism is humanity's long-standing dream of a society which is not made up of one part enjoying the very rights that the other part is deprived of. It is the dream of a humane world where everyone has the same rights and opportunities, where people can be good without having to sacrifice themselves.[159]

A good 15 years before *Tomorrow* was even published, Havemann had already decided that a society free of conflict and contradiction was unrealistic. He did believe, however, that a fundamental change would be possible if the material antagonisms based on exploitation were to disappear. The old morals obscured these contradictions and made the system more stable. For Havemann this also included, for instance, interpersonal problems, such as the patriarchy and the bourgeois institution of marriage. He believed that this set of traditional morals had to be dismantled and replaced by socialist morality.[160]

---

157 Havemann 1968, p. 97.
158 Havemann 1968, p. 106.
159 Havemann 1968, p. 119 f. When it came to morality, Havemann wrote that it served to protect any and all regimes from revolutions by hiding social reality. Havemann saw moral standards as 'making a mockery of the good. They are the means for preserving the wickedness in our lives. Because society is "amoral", it has a need for morals' (Havemann 1968, p. 119).
160 See Havemann 1968, p. 120 ff. 'Socialist morality is a morality of change, of transformation, of a revolution of all social relations, in other words on the basis of increasingly widespread human solidarity' (Havemann 1968, p. 126). In thinking this way, Havemann clashed with the GDR under Ulbricht, something the Stasi noted, too: 'The contempt for the role and identity of women had its impact both on Mrs Havemann and on the children's upbringing. Mrs Havemann stated that moral standards barely featured in the children's upbringing' (BStU, MfS, AU, 145/90, vol. 2, p. 270). Havemann was said to have had 'liaisons with women' and in conversations expressed 'his views on free love'. 'The moral deprav-

According to Havemann, it was impossible to build socialism based on a simple plan, it would have to emerge from popular consciousness, an awareness of necessity, as this 'is more than an industrial and economic process, it is to the greatest extent also a process which occurs in our minds, a process of growing consciousness'.[161] For the GDR, this level of consciousness was a long way off, as the process of transformation was a lengthy one and the former consciousness, which was still so deeply engrained in people's minds, could not be eliminated overnight. Havemann saw the SED's approach as correspondingly helpless and misguided:

> For a planning practice which attempts to implement deterministic detailed control of societal processes, Havemann had nothing left but superior ridicule. That said, for him, this did not mean that people were powerless, at the mercy of a game of chance where a given possible historic development can become reality. For Havemann, the dialectic that helps us understand the relationship between necessity and chance, possibility and reality was not a vademecum of fatalism.[162]

In keeping with the Marxist tradition of thought, he saw people's social behaviour as the result of their material reality and consequently came to the conclusion that the negative characteristics that people sometimes possess were caused by social factors.[163] In as early as 1964, he displayed post-materialist tendencies, criticising the fact that people had been reduced to the consumption that was generated by the system itself: 'People are becoming utter slaves to their needs'. And 'The more developed the economy becomes, the deeper the cultural barbarism goes'.[164] Against this backdrop, even Havemann called for an end to the dependence on material needs, for people to turn towards the notion of 'being' and away from the notion of 'having'.[165]

---

ity that Prof. Havemann showed women, is also reflected in his attitude towards social etiquette, his clothes and his attitude towards work' (BStU, MfS, AU, 145/90, vol. 2, p. 273).
161   Havemann 1968, p. 126.
162   Laitko 2010b, p. 34 f.
163   See Havemann 1968, p. 144.
164   Havemann 1968, p. 149.
165   'In light of the despoliation of man and nature in the countries of the Third World and the resulting prosperity of the industrial nations, he recommended a general lack of needs as a desirable goal for humanity, saying this was the only path towards true social wealth. By taking this stance, as a Marxist, it was clear that Havemann envisaged the transformation of the natural sciences, which for centuries had been almost exclusively understood in terms of technology, into social sciences, thus advocating at an early stage demands

The 'desire to have' is, first and foremost, an expression of alienation. *Havemann* thus recognises the phenomenon of alienation even in socialist societies. Consequently, alienation becomes a universal phenomenon which applies to all social orders in the industrial world. *Havemann's* critique was thus extended and transformed from being a critique of the existing system of domination by the SED to an all-encompassing social critique, which in this form, situated in the framework of the ideological dogma while calling that very dogma into question, opens up completely new perspectives.[166]

In the mid-1960s, Peter Christian Ludz judged Havemann's utopian ideas as being in some respects naive and overly one-sided in their critique of capitalism. He argued that in parts of his work, Havemann uses utopia as a gap filler in his line of reasoning.[167] According to Ludz, '*Havemann* construes the utopia of the original Marxism as an ascetic communism of needlessness, which distances itself from *Khrushchev's* communism of prosperity as clearly as it takes up certain concepts found in Chinese philosophy'.[168] Havemann's *Dialektik ohne Dogma?* to some extent already describes a form of post-materialist ascetic communism:

> With such a vision, Havemann remains within the horizon of existentialist Marxism. With such a vision, however, he is also moving closer to certain ideas found in Chinese communism. And ultimately, with such a vision, he is approaching one of the schools of intransigent Western social

---

which were not made again until the seventies and early eighties during the environmental movement' (Morris-Keitel 2004, p. 32).

166 Ludz 1976, p. 294.
167 'For *Havemann*, egalitarian existentialist freedom is a key normative foundation for scientific and social science analysis. Its transformation into a tangible interpretation of society as a whole fails, apparently inevitably, owing to its complexity. Whenever social science issues are being addressed, this causes *Havemann* to move time and again between two sides: from the tangibility of his scientific thinking and the philosophical reflection of the resistance, which is the foundation of positive critique of dialectical materialism, to the programmatic language of utopian speculation, whenever social science issues are being addressed ...' (Ludz 1976, p. 296).
168 Ludz 1976, p. 269f. In his review, Hubert Laitko contradicts Ludz at this point: '"Aesthetic" is not really the right word here: Havemann created the ideal of a materially sufficient society whose members have abandoned the boundless desire to possess and are now focusing their interest in human coexistence on the acquisition and development of spiritual and cultural wealth, which enjoys the secure and undisputed status as a public good' (Laitko 2010b, p. 29).

and cultural critique influenced by the philosophy of the Enlightenment and the ideas of young Marx, as represented by *Theodor W. Adorno, Max Horkheimer* and *Jürgen Habermas*, for instance ... Accordingly, *Havemann* tenaciously advocates the moral demand to detach social relationships from material dependence. .... No doubt, *Havemann* himself recognises the fundamentally moralistic incentive and the normative character of his utopia of future communism. He explicitly rejects the mere utopia of a 'perfect society', which so often finds its pendant in a mechanistic concept of the possibilities for completion of a still incomplete society. ... A social philosophy based on specific social sciences data would need to interpret the dialectic of conflict and cooperation that is a distinctive characteristic of industrial social systems. However, this remains in the dark, ignored in favour of a utopian ethical rallying cry.[169]

This statement by Ludz highlights the pros and cons of Havemann's utopian approach. On the one hand, the latter always cut short the critique and analysis of the existing circumstances in favour of an indiscriminate anti-capitalism; on the other hand, his utopia was always morally and normatively loaded despite all his technological fantasies and he used this to legitimise his utopia. Havemann's utopian thinking was shaped by this dichotomy to the very end.

The utopian content of *Dialektik ohne Dogma?* is remarkable in many respects. Firstly, it must be stressed that Havemann developed elements of post-materialist utopia at a time when, even in the West, this genre was still in its infancy (by way of comparison: Aldous Huxley's *Island*, published in the English original in 1962 and in German under the title *Eiland* in 1973, is widely seen as one of the first post-materialist utopias). Also worth noting is the fact that Havemann was already reflecting on the limits to growth almost a decade before the Meadows Report appeared and already had a communism that did not aim at economic prosperity in mind.[170] And thirdly, it is striking that

---

169 Ludz 1976, p. 297.
170 'He did not believe that the only reason for the transition to communism was the need for social justice, but rather saw the demand for ecological stability as an equally important incentive. In his fifth lecture, which was devoted to the problem of the finiteness and infinity of time, there is a remarkable but scarcely noticed passage. ... This passage sounds as though it anticipates the first Club of Rome report, which forecast that, over the medium term, a global ecological collapse of the world system was a real possibility if the existing growth trend were to continue unchanged. Havemann's reflections could be interpreted as meaning that he saw the transition to communism as a path of evolutionary transformation, transporting society from an economy of limitless growth to a stationary, ecologically stable economy, thus avoiding the catastrophe of the "great rupture". For him,

Havemann already publicly expressed these ideas before his break with the SED. In other words, it was here that he laid the foundation for his utopian thinking in later years and indeed the post-materialist elements from *Tomorrow* can clearly be identified in his publications and lectures at the start of the 1960s. This supports the supposition that the utopia he wrote in 1980 was not a purely subjective book about his personal relationships, but in fact a serious contribution to utopian discourse.

This theory was also underpinned by a text Havemann wrote on the subject of utopia at the time when he had just started to gravitate towards the opposition. This text was an undated typewritten manuscript found in the Stasi files and titled *Kommunismus – Utopie und Wirklichkeit* (Communism – utopia and reality), which Havemann had planned to present in Salzburg in 1965, a trip he ended up not making, however, because he was afraid of being refused entry to the GDR on his return. The paper was later edited and included in the book *Rückantworten an die Hauptverwaltung 'Ewige Wahrheiten'* (Responses to the central administration 'eternal truths') which appeared as an anthology in West Germany in 1971.

Something the manuscript contained, but which of course did not feature in this published version, was various deletions and notes in the margins, handwritten by Havemann. These are discussed (in the paragraphs) below. The notes provide an insight into Havemann's engagement with the concept of utopia:

> The world in which we find ourselves is always cruel and inhumane in comparison with the world which appears possible to us. This real possibility of a better world is the reflexive response to our active critique of the existing circumstances. Each and every phase of history thus has its own utopia, which is used to understand and replace the reality of this phase (marginal note from Havemann: replace with 'which is used by the phase itself to understand and replace itself'). Thus, all utopias of a future, fairer world (marginal note: 'are but') reflections of the respective social relations. ... At the same time, they are also all (note: 'always') a constituent part of the larger, purely human utopia, following the law to which we have been bound. ... But the utopia of communism has so far been (replaced by: 'is') shaped far too strongly by the capitalist epoch alone. ... After the 20th Congress of the CPSU, the communist utopia began (note:

---

the communist ideal comprised the moral desiderata of social justice and the economic desiderata of securing the survival of humanity coming together in a programmatic vision' (Laitko 2010b, p. 27 f.).

'however') to be guided by its own reality. The revolution is at constant risk of losing its credibility once it begins to implement its objectives.[171]

Subsequently, Havemann described a 'Marxist utopia' that possessed the 'strength of the unattainability of the moral society it created'. The historical development of actually existing socialism

> ... brought about the situation, at once fantastical and tragic, that the communist utopia was put at fault and robbed of its credibility by the political practice of the very countries that had already embarked on the path of communism. ... However, when a society claims that, to a large extent, it constitutes the achievement of its own utopia, it destroys all faith in its future. ... Yet, even in the age of communism, we will only ever be on the path to this world of social harmony.[172]

In the mid-1960s, Havemann experienced his own personal turning point. Not only was his career in ruins; so, too, was his marriage to Karin. The reports the latter made to the Stasi about her husband clearly revealed Robert Havemann's penchant for luxury and indulgence, for women and alcohol, and this indirectly helps us understand his utopian thinking. In 1966, Karin stated:

> Since he increasingly recklessly indulged in his own interests and pleasures only, demanding complete freedom for himself, we could not even find a basis for friendship that might replace the love. ... Even the 'shared' summer residence belonged to him alone and he even denied me the right to my own room, instead letting his friends use my bed in my absence. On the rare occasions that we had a conversation about this, something he tried his best to avoid, he never admitted that he was in the wrong.... He even forced me to endure serving the girlfriends he had stay overnight in his cottage.... He showed no evidence of understanding that not only was he hurting me, but his actions were especially distressing to the children who were present. He constantly created theories to justify his behaviour. Not only did he disregard any criticism directed at him, but in fact reacted very strongly and irrationally or circumvented serious questions with arrogance and laughter. The contempt he showed for the identity and role of a spouse had a direct impact on the status of the mother. For

---

171 BStU, MfS, AU, 145/90, vol. 11, p. 222.
172 BStU, MfS, AU, 145/90, vol. 11, p. 223.

him, being a role model, played no part at all in child-raising. There were virtually no 'moral standards' to speak of and, for many years, through his direct influence, he managed to alienate his son from his own mother. Particularly in the last two years he encouraged antagonisms between the children and society and their school commitments. Moulding the character of his children was really not remotely important to him or was based on very individual standards (modesty, non-conformity, respect, discipline etc.).[173]

This report was undoubtedly very subjective and reflected a significant amount of personal disappointment. Nevertheless, it did show that, even in his private life, Robert Havemann attempted to implement his hedonistic notions about life,[174] which inevitably clashed with the GDR's social conventions. In any case, the concepts he articulated in *Tomorrow* about aspects such as freedom, love, family or raising children barely deviated from the statements made by his estranged wife, the only difference being that while he presented them in a positive light, she presented them in a negative one.

In the aforementioned report, Karin Havemann also referred to financial issues, complaining that Robert Havemann deprived her in this respect, while allowing himself a life of luxury:

> On the other hand, huge sums were spent on alcoholic beverages, expensive installations (a mosaic bathtub and flooring etc.), power consumption (around 1,000 marks in just a year) for his little house, without ever having consulted with me about the larger purchases. ... Yet he insisted that more and more be saved on food and demanded in an increasingly dictatorial manner – either in writing or via the housekeeper – that we use an ever-larger share of my income, with no concern for my own obligations. He is of the opinion that the life insurance policy I purchased in 1962 was actually paid for with his money and was to be treated as a shared savings account, in other words it should now be cancelled, while he, in contrast, still owned four cars at the end of 1965 (he dragged his feet about the sale of a Volga, for example, because he allegedly could not find, i.e. did not look for, the required papers). At the moment he still has two cars to his name.[175]

---

173   BStU, MfS, AU, 145/90, vol. 12, p. 24.
174   On this see Hurwitz 2012, p. 11 f.
175   BStU, MfS, AU, 145/90, vol. 12, p. 25. In those days, Havemann was very enthusiastic about technology and a passionate car driver: 'For this keen car driver being elected head of the

These assertions bear witness to the strongly subjective character of Havemann's utopian concept. His personal notions of an ideal society were clearly distinguishable in *Tomorrow*, including, for instance, freedom from paternalism – whether political or on a personal level.

In the years after 1965, Havemann entered a period of personal crisis which did not come to end until the late 1960s, partly thanks to the success of his book *Fragen, Antworten, Fragen* (Questions, answers, questions), published in 1970, in which he also expressed his utopian ideas.[176] 'Havemann writes that instead of continuing to focus on the emptiness and hopelessness of consumer societies such as those that had developed in both the West and the East, a forward-looking society must transform what has till now been utopian into tangible reality, which would allow us to create a socialist system where personal objectives and those of society as a whole go hand in hand'.[177] In his book, he appealed for a socialist democracy that included the achievements of bourgeois democracy but that eradicated private ownership of the means of production.[178]

> The completion of the socialist revolution is thus only possible with a second revolutionary transformation which affects both the foundations and the superstructure, with the changes in the foundations enabling the changes in the superstructure, making what was previously utopian a tangible reality and, conversely, the shifts and changes in the superstructure opening up new opportunities for the foundations to be remoulded. Only once socialist democracy is completed, which is tantamount to a cultural revolution, will the new society see its new goals with absolute clarity. Stalinism has no new goals. It is blinded by capitalism.[179]

General German Motorsport Association [ADMV] meant more than just having a nice title. Indeed, it gave Havemann an opportunity to personally live out his fascination with science and technology. He loved vehicles, especially big motorbikes' (Hecht 1991, p. 140). Draheim and Hoffmann reported that in as early as the 1930s, Havemann enjoyed motorbiking through Europe with his wife, taking photos of the places they visited. See Draheim and Hoffmann 1991, p. 30. This makes it all the more remarkable that in *Tomorrow* he abolishes private car ownership and pushes for the discovery of a slower pace of life.

176 'The vision of a democratically organised communism based not on coercion but rather on citizens' free self-awareness was something Havemann had advocated since the start of the seventies and, increasingly joining forces with Wolf Biermann, had conveyed in numerous statements which also had an effect on the GDR via the Western media' (Vollnhals 2000, p. 19).
177 Morris-Keitel 2004, p. 33.
178 See Havemann 1970, p. 60.
179 Havemann 1970, p. 153f.

Havemann was already critical of the conditions in the actually existing socialist industrial society in which he lived in 1970:

> ... in this truly ominous time, overshadowed by the threat of the super bomb, Stalinist 'goulash communism' aspires to nothing more than the modern convenience of refrigerators, washing machines, cars and television sets, whose flickering make-believe world ever more completely transforms people into increasingly perfect slaves to the consumer needs that target them, washing away the final remnants of independent thought from their minds, the last of their individual idiosyncrasies and interests. Do we as European socialists and communists really want to embark on this depressing path of becoming fat bourgeois citizens, a path that will lead us permanently away from the history of our time into the tarnished corner of global history? Our historical mission is the completion of the socialist revolution.[180]

Havemann could see no alternative in the capitalist system and Western freedom was no more than a chimera for him, an obfuscation of the dominance of capital and so that was not an option either. Havemann believed, in the spirit of Rosa Luxemburg, 'that without socialism there could be no freedom and without freedom there could be no socialism'.[181]

In 1969, Havemann wrote an essay for the volume *Das 198. Jahrzehnt* (The 198th decade) titled 'Der Sozialismus von morgen' (The socialism of tomorrow). In this essay, Havemann called for a socialist market economy as a transformational interim step:

> When the state withers, the market will disappear, too. For the market will become superfluous to the extent that social consumption will replace individual consumption. After all, there will be no market under communism.[182]

Indirectly influenced by the worldwide events of his time, Havemann pinned his hopes on the Western protest movement.

> Right now, with its political contradictions, with the Wall, with its stifling of the arts and literature and bourgeois puritanism, the GDR is a serious

---

180 Havemann 1970, p. 155.
181 Havemann 1970, p. 253.
182 Havemann 1969, p. 204.

impediment to the nascent revolutionary movement. On the one hand, the movement needs to distance itself from the GDR. On the other hand, it must acknowledge that in this part of Germany, capitalism and fascism have been buried once and for all. When will this lamentable situation finally change? It will certainly change, and quite radically at that, if the Dubček spark is finally ignited across the whole of Eastern Europe and the USSR. And then we will be able to say: the future of socialism has begun.[183]

Much to Havemann's disappointment, this development did not materialise in the period that followed. Quite the contrary happened in fact: the suppression of the Prague Spring and the waning student movement in Western Europe moved his model of transformation from the domain of the possible firmly back into to the domain of the utopian. His short-term goal became a distant one. Yet Havemann still held on to his belief. Shortly afterwards, the Meadows Report was published and it was this very report that must have given Havemann, a scientist with philosophical ambitions, the incentive to reflect on technical and social ways out of the dilemma that industrial society found itself in. In so doing, he simply could not get past the utopia that so fascinated him. In an interview with the *Stern* on 22 October 1975, Havemann described himself as '... a utopianist in that I believe that for us to move forward with the development of history, it is necessary to be able to envisage abolishing one's own circumstances, to imagine how different the world in which we live could be. ... Modern capitalism lives on growth – this is essentially already apparent in Marx's works – except of course that Marx believed that the limits to growth would arrive much sooner'.[184]

In another article written in the same year, Havemann refers to the Club of Rome explicitly, stating:

> The renowned Meadows Report by the Club of Rome proves that such exponential growth cannot continue unbridled. The sources of energy and raw materials available on Earth are not infinite and impose insurmountable limits on this unbridled growth. Yet, since capitalism cannot continue to exist without growth, a major economic crisis lies ahead of us that could easily culminate in the universal disaster of a nuclear war.[185]

---

183 Havemann 1969, p. 212.
184 Havemann 1977, p. 94f.
185 Havemann 1975, p. 20.

While, according to Havemann, Western capitalism was gradually starting to grasp the magnitude of this crisis, the Eastern Bloc was still blindly running down the wrong path of development, a path the West had already left behind. By way of illustration, he cited private motor vehicles, describing the car as harmful, inefficient, dangerous and a nuisance. In his view, it could easily be replaced by far more efficient technologies. This would, however, contradict capitalism's logic of profit and, since actually existing socialism sought to emulate the West, the automobile was unquestioningly accepted here, too. That said, unlike capitalism, socialism offered clear opportunities to develop alternatives. What was lacking, however, was the desire to do so. And it was for this reason that Havemann stressed just how important it was that socialism become a serious and genuine alternative to capitalism if it were to survive.[186]

In *Tomorrow*, Havemann afforded technology an important role in securing the survival of humanity in the future. In the book, however, people no longer served technology, instead technology served people and the environment. Havemann already developed this concept in the aftermath of the Meadows Report. An undated typewritten manuscript from around that time, with the title *Kann die Technik den Menschen ausrotten?* (Can technology eradicate humanity?) can be found in the Stasi files. The document must have been written after 1975 as it makes reference to Harich's concept of an eco-dictatorship. Havemann writes that mankind already had the requisite technical knowledge to be able to safeguard the existence of all members of the current population, and possibly even a few more in the future.

> In other words, if we apply our technical and scientific knowledge intelligently, it is possible to bring about a boom in human culture the extent of which even the boldest of imaginations would struggle to envisage. Right now, we are making virtually no progress towards this goal. ... Hopefully the hydrogen fusion reactor will have become our inexhaustible source of energy before we reach the point where all our oil and coal reserves are depleted. This would ward off the mammoth crisis for a few decades. Hydrogen power will also mitigate environmental pollution. Those who are alive today will have a lucky escape. At least this is what many hope, and they will leave the horrible end for future generations. What they fail to grasp is that what they are doing is the very thing that will bring about

---

186   See Havemann 1975, p. 22 ff.

this horrible end with absolute certainty, and possibly even sooner than they expect in all their irresponsibility.[187]

Hence, for Havemann, all this technical progress was not worth much unless it were accompanied by a shift in society's thinking and a process of emancipation, a universal change in consciousness. Otherwise, he predicted, we might see the emergence of 'Wolfgang Harich's barbaric world police state, in which "zero growth" is achieved by sheer force using methods of state repression'.[188] The Stasi files also contain a transcript of a broadcast from 1 April 1975 titled 'From the Communist World' (broadcast from London, broadcaster not given), in which the first part of Havemann's essay is read. This text, which had no specific title, discussed 'the triangle of tension between socialism, capitalism and freedom'.[189]

In the text, Havemann remarks that the Meadows Report proved the incompatibility of exponential growth and the finite nature of resources. And for this reason 'a major and profound transformation of political economic conditions'[190] was needed to ensure the continued existence of humanity. The second part of the essay was read in a broadcast from the same location on 8 April 1975. Here, Havemann first criticised the automobile as one 'of the biggest polluters of the environment'.[191] He envisaged a utopian alternative. After all

> ... a group of experts can design a system of automated modes of transport in the blink of an eye, a system that will enable everyone to reach all their local destinations more quickly and at virtually no risk, and at a fraction of the cost and material and energy currently consumed by cars. This would mean, however, that the automobile industry, currently one of the cornerstones of capitalist industry, would no longer have a role to play. The previous private consumers would be replaced by a small number of mainly state customers, and not only the roads and motorways but also all means of transport on those roads would be part of the infrastructure. The consumption of individual passenger cars would be replaced by social consumption. The free-market economy would have lost its biggest, most powerful partner.[192]

---

187 BStU, MfS, AU, 145/90, vol. 11, p. 301.
188 BStU, MfS, AU, 145/90, vol. 11, p. 302.
189 BStU, MfS, AU, 145/90, vol. 4, p. 74.
190 BStU, MfS, AU, 145/90, vol. 4, p. 78.
191 BStU, MfS, AU, 145/90, vol. 4, p. 82.
192 BStU, MfS, AU, 145/90, vol. 4, p. 82.

Embarking upon such a path was virtually impossible under capitalism, but in actually existing socialist states, too, transport policy focused on the car industry in order to be able to keep up with the West. Against this backdrop, Havemann painted a gloomy picture of the future for the actually existing socialist states: 'If in the near future the wheels produced by these factories flood onto the road networks of these countries, which, compared with those in Western Europe, are for the most part still very underdeveloped, this will rapidly, far more so than in the West, result in the most preposterous, most chaotic traffic conditions, which will show us exactly what capitalism would look like'.[193]

Havemann believed that this example could also be applied to other sectors of the economy as everyone was trying to mimic the West – something that was impossible, however, because 'the economic goals of capitalism could be achieved far more successfully in a capitalist society'.[194] Freedom, on the other hand, was for Havemann the key to socialism's success: 'The withdrawal of democratic rights and freedoms, rights which even the capitalist state must grant its citizens, ... is the underlying cause for the economic failure of socialism so far, as well as for the increasingly poor reputation socialism has worldwide and the resulting pathological fragmentation of all left-wing and revolutionary forces the world over'.[195]

Two years before *Tomorrow* was published, Havemann already set out the core elements of his post-materialist utopia in an article for the *Spiegel*, where he wrote:

1. I do not believe that communism ... can be defined as every man having to possess an electric razor and every woman an electric hair curler, or each and every member of society having a television or a car or a motorbike or speedboat or a cottage in the forest etc., etc. ... I believe that the essential prerequisites for communism are first and foremost that no one should be afforded special privileges ....
2. It is essential that this is not a communism of hardship and suffering. ... It must provide complete social protection for each and every individual, for each and every member of society. ...
3. All individuals must be equal when it comes to the freedom to make their own decisions. They must have the freedom to venture

---

193   BStU, MfS, AU, 145/90, vol. 4, p. 82.
194   BStU, MfS, AU, 145/90, vol. 4, p. 83.
195   BStU, MfS, AU, 145/90, vol. 4, p. 84.

wherever they want, to move to another town, to another country, to take journeys, to choose where they work, choose their own interests, according to their own personal taste and desires ....
4. And something I consider crucial is that all people have access to the great cultural values of humanity, ... so that they can at last see that there is such tremendous wealth of magnificent literature and spiritual beauty and can discover profound wisdom and the great philosophers in the history of all countries. ... It is my belief that if we could imagine a world without arms and without the senseless waste of capitalism, then this form of communism would have been achievable for everyone long ago.[196]

In his book *Ein deutscher Kommunist. Rückblicke und Perspektiven aus der Isolation* (A German communist. Retrospectives and perspectives from isolation), which was also published in 1978, Havemann writes that capitalist growth is not 'true growth ...', but rather an increasing waste of valuable productivity',[197] which must be countered by an alternative in the form of rational planning.

> The aim of the socialist economy is not to expand production, to increase consumption, but rather quite the opposite; the aim is to increase leisure time, to continuously reduce the amount of time needed for work, to create more autonomy for people to make decisions about their own lives .... Of course, this often begs the question: Will people know what to do with all this freedom? What will they do when they have so much time and do not have to work? If work is reduced to two months a year or a few hours a day, what will they do then? One thing they will definitely not do is what people living under capitalism do or what they are doing here now: sitting at home, building a little place to live, having drinks with a friend or getting drunk. I have nothing against people enjoying time together, even taking pleasure in wine and alcohol, but there is a far greater pleasure that people will devote themselves to and that is learning new things, discovering the world, expanding their knowledge, discovering and learning how to appreciate art, or even working with children or becoming a teacher.[198]

---

196   Havemann 1978b.
197   Havemann 1978a, p. 85.
198   Havemann 1978a, p. 87 f.

Havemann saw the ability to envisage utopia as conducive to the achievement of this socialist goal and, in expressing this view, also surreptitiously announced the forthcoming publication of *Tomorrow*:

> Creating such a communist utopia is, in my view, one of the most important undertakings of our time. I have devoted myself to this issue for a long time. I believe we must develop new goals before we can agree on the how to get there. Socialism is one path that will lead us to the goal, a goal that is of course fantastic and huge and utopian. And like all other utopias, it is also the manifestation in which we imagine eradicating all the barbarity we are forced to suffer today. Thus, our utopia, too, is always biased and shaped by the wretchedness of our present lives.[199]

On 3 October 1979, the Danish newspaper *Politiken* printed an interview with Havemann under the headline 'Die DDR kann trotz allem sozialistisch werden' (Inspite of everything, the GDR can still become socialist). This interview, conducted by journalist Kastholm Hansen, can also be found in the Stasi files. In the interview, Havemann predicts that '... something is going to happen in the next few years in the countries in the east because the economic crisis is becoming increasingly evident here ..., and this is precisely because we do not have socialism. this is the real crisis in the GDR – the very fact that we have not learned from the west's mistakes but rather are still trying to create the same consumer and throwaway society. .... but the true goal of the socialist economy is of course not external growth but internal growth – growth in quality, in other words producing things that last longer, growth in leisure time, growth in human development. these problems are discussed in the west but not here'.[200] And he continues: 'hope and utopia, these two things belong together. a form of hope that compels people to move forward – and utopia: *principiis obsta* ... ... which means we must create a new concept of the future, influence things that do not even exist! utopia is the mental sublation of today's wretchedness – but only once utopia has entered the minds of an entire generation, only then can something happen – as marx said: an idea becomes a material force when it seizes the masses.[201]

As shown above, in the months and years before *Tomorrow* was published, Havemann repeatedly expressed positive views about utopia and its potential

---

199   Havemann 1978a, p. 102.
200   BStU, MfS, AU, 145/90, vol. 10, p. 85f. Editorial notice: This concerns an internal information document where everything was written in lower case.
201   BStU, MfS, AU, 145/90, vol. 10, p. 86.

to change society. He saw utopia as the catalyst for transformation. He saw the degradation of utopia as a meeting of 'the opponents and enemies of socialism with the ideologues of actually existing socialism':

> They make fun of the simple-minded, those who believe that socialism is possible without the repression of dissidents, without the police system and the Wall. They claim you can have either freedom or socialism, but never both at the same time. And their proof for this claim is actually existing socialism.[202]

Havemann also described the importance of utopia for social progress in a reply published in the *Spiegel*, in which he defended his 'wishful thinking' towards his critics represented by philosopher Rudolf Schottlaender:

> How can a historian of his calibre get so upset about wishful thinking, which is after all the all-important, ever active impetus for all changes in the life of each and every individual and humanity as a whole? ... Bloch called this the principle of hope. And Marx is in clear agreement. He said that one of the fundamental differences between humans and animals is that everything humans create and construct has already been created in their minds first, and only then do these things become reality in their hands. Everything new, all the changes that we make sprang from our hopes and wishes and were already – often a long time ago – fantastic reality in our own minds.[203]

This principle also applied to the present:

> Even the incomplete 'real' socialism will break free of its rigidity again and finally overcome its Stalinist degeneration. Over and over I struggle to understand how many of our contemporaries deem the conditions under which we are currently living unalterable.[204]

In this context, Havemann repeatedly made reference to his main utopian influence: Bloch's *Principle of Hope*. In the Stasi files, there was also a transcript of a television interview with Havemann conducted in September 1980.[205] In

---

202 Havemann 1999, p. 162.
203 Havemann 1979, p. 98.
204 Havemann 1979, p. 100.
205 The interview was broadcast on 19 September 1980 on FS II [Austrian television chan-

the introduction to the broadcast, referring to the utopian content of *Tomorrow*, the announcer says: 'How this potential beautiful human world is described to the point of naivety, however, exposes our tragic present more than the hard facts'.[206] And, referring to his own utopia, Havemann's exact words in response to this:

> ... a world is portrayed in which all the cruelties of the world in which we live are removed from our thoughts. This is, after all, the essence of utopia. Utopia does not mean describing a world in exact terms, a world that on this point will be exactly like this and on that point will be exactly like that, precisely how it is described in the utopia. Utopia simply illustrates the inhumanity of our time by removing it from our thoughts. ... People living together is the essence of utopia, not a life dedicated to some kind of work, to some arduous burden, physical or otherwise.[207]

Havemann was optimistic and described his book as motivating people to survive. In the few short years of Havemann's life left after *Tomorrow* was published, his support for utopia did not wane. In a commemorative volume to mark the 70th birthday of his old friend and publisher Klaus Piper, in 1981, Havemann expressed his views on the literary genre of socialist realism:

> Here too, the world is not portrayed as it actually is, instead being depicted as the author would wish it to be. Yet, this yearned-for world is not described as an as yet unachieved utopia, but is instead depicted as though it has already become reality. ... The idea that the chosen path is the wrong one and that there could be negative consequences of this grave mistake does not even enter into the minds of the socialist realists.[208]

---

      nel, since 1992 ORF 2] at 22.20 hrs. The same interview can also be found in the file BStU, MfS, AU, 145/90, vol. 10, p. 205 ff. The file contains a transcript of the tape recording made on 21 September 1980, which declares it to be an interview broadcast on 19 September 1980, 22.20 on *Aspekte*, a cultural programme broadcast on the West German TV channel ZDF.

206   BStU, MfS, AU, 145/90, vol. 8, p. 463.
207   BStU, MfS, AU, 145/90, vol. 8, p. 463.
208   Havemann 1981, p. 139.

The function of utopia as social criticism, highlighted by Havemann on numerous occasions, was therefore something he felt was lacking in socialist realism and he could thus not really warm to the assertion that the GDR was a real-life utopia, for which no socialist counter-utopias were required. Quite the opposite in fact: for Havemann the Marxist, the development of socialism was directly linked to the existence of utopias.

4.2   Situating the Book in Utopian History

Tomorrow undoubtedly corresponds to the model of the post-materialist utopia. In fact, Havemann's book fits into this context even more than Bahro's *The Alternative* or Harich's *Communism without Growth?*. It is clearly reminiscent of some of the most significant works of this genre, especially Callenbach's *Ecotopia*. It would, however, be oversimplifying things to insinuate that Havemann's only influences were from utopian history. Havemann was a Marxist and as a result was most certainly familiar with the pre-Marxist social utopias. But at the same time, his book also draws heavily on anarchistic utopian discourse. In *Tomorrow*, Havemann combines elements from post-materialist utopia with aspects of the anarchistic utopian tradition and the long-term Marxist goal of a classless society.[209]

4.2.1   Tomorrow: Between Marxism and Utopia

Throughout the extensive works of Marx and Engels, we find very few places where they describe the classless communist society. They did not see it as useful or productive to depict detailed utopian images. Quite the opposite, in fact. The Marxists who came after them, however, broke through the invisible barrier of the ban on images so that they could provide the proletariat with a goal worth striving for. A good example of this is August Bebel's *Woman and Socialism*.[210] But also in texts that did not include a visual representation of the future, even before World War I, communists outlined the contours of the kind of socialism they imagined and/or the kind they did not want. This was evident in the debate between Lenin and Rosa Luxemburg over the concept of the 'dictatorship of the proletariat', for example. Besides this, ideas developed by Kautsky, Bernstein and, in his later years, Engels also featured in the discussion about the paths to socialism.

Havemann's concept of transformation drew on these early twentieth century debates combined with post-materialist aspects. His model of socialist

---

209   See Saage 2008, p. 157.
210   See Heyer 2006b, p. 32.

democracy stems primarily from Luxemburg. That said, with its Marxist dimension, the utopian model of society in *Tomorrow* is more reminiscent of Bebel's utopia in *Woman and Socialism*, the first edition of which was published in 1879 and quickly became a bestseller. The author continued to update the book even in later editions, adding the chapter 'Woman in the Future', a welfare communist utopia, for instance. In this part of his book, Bebel broke with the Marxist ban on images, focusing deliberately on utopia as the goal to inspire his social democratic readers. His utopian model was shaped by an unreserved faith in the potential of technical scientific research and development. Bebel pinned his hopes on industrial growth, and thus saw large-scale socialist companies as the basis for prosperity and education.[211]

In Bebel's socialist society of the future, labour was obligatory, but should not be alienated or too strenuous. Ideally, people should be able to choose their place of work, as labour should be pleasant and emancipatory. A democratically legitimised and controlled administrative apparatus, which should be kept as lean as possible, would essentially be responsible for running the economy and for managing the distribution of goods.

Much like Havemann's, Bebel's utopia was also based on the potential and hopes of technical progress. Yet, while Havemann took up these ideas with the aim of reconciling a pleasant life with the worthwhile protection of the environment, a century earlier life in material abundance was still deemed the ideal. That said, Bebel cannot be accused of having conceived of the consumerist, throwaway society of excess such as it exists today, because his utopia relied on durable products with as little wear and tear as possible, as well as on making trends and fashions in clothing and home furnishings a thing of the past. Wastage had to be avoided. Bebel predicted that managing things in this way would give people more peace, relaxation and pleasure. There would be clean, light and safe workplaces as the pressure on capitalist companies to rationalise would no longer exist. Bebel relied on electricity, which he assigned a messianic impetus. Electricity was to ensure progress, quality of life and the accelerated development of socialism. What is remarkable is that at the beginning of the twentieth century, Bebel was already advocating regenerative energy sources such as wind energy and hydropower, as well as solar power in North Africa, which have since gone on to become part of everyday life.[212] Here, too, there are clear parallels with Havemann's utopia. And the same applies to settlement type: Both utopias describe how cities are gradually replaced by decentralised

---

211   See Bebel 1910, p. 266.
212   See Bebel 1910, p. 370 ff.

settlements.²¹³ In addition, Morris-Keitel remarked that Havemann's matriarchal 'concepts are largely based on August Bebel's work *Woman and Socialism* (1887)'.²¹⁴

The argumentation regarding the issue of nutrition in the context of population growth follows a similar pattern. In his book, Bebel picks up on the Marxist critique of Malthusian warnings of overpopulation. Much like Havemann a century later, Bebel believed that the problem was not population growth but rather the social inequality inherent in capitalism. If the capitalist mechanisms no longer existed, there would no longer be anything stopping significantly higher food production. According to Bebel, thanks to technical progress, food production could be increased almost infinitely. Bebel writes: 'In matters of nutrition, chemistry has an inexhaustible field for development'.²¹⁵ The parallels with *Tomorrow* are remarkable: Havemann, too, was of the opinion that, in a socialist society, assuming all technical possibilities were developed at the same time, feeding ten billion people would present no problem at all.

However, the two utopias are not entirely identical, with differences arising from the prevailing zeitgeist at the time each of them was written. While *Tomorrow* demonstrates pronounced post-materialist traits, in Bebel's work, materialism rooted in technical optimism dominated. However, in the context of the conditions of their respective eras, the possibility of the world being changed by humans to their own advantage resonates as an ideal in both Bebel's *and* Havemann's works.²¹⁶

---

213   See Bebel 1910, p. 432. This model is also observed in Friedrich Engels's *Anti-Dühring*, a book that had a strong influence on Havemann's political thinking. Engels: 'The present poisoning of the air, water and land can be put an end to only by the fusion of town and country; and only such fusion will change the situation of the masses now languishing in the towns, and enable their excrement to be used for the production of plants instead of for the production of disease. ... It is true that in the huge towns civilisation has bequeathed us a heritage which it will take much time and trouble to get rid of. But it must and will be got rid of, however, protracted a process it may be' (Engels 1987a, p. 282 f.).
214   Morris-Keitel 2004, p. 38.
215   Bebel 1910, p. 280.
216   'Who can even say where the line should be drawn when it comes to our knowledge of chemistry, physics and physiology? Who will dare to predict what huge undertakings humanity will carry out in the centuries to come in an attempt to bring about significant changes in countries' climatic conditions and their land utilisation? Today, in the capitalist form of society, we are already witness to activities that would have been considered impossible and indeed incredible a hundred years ago. Wide isthmuses are broken through and oceans connected. Mile-long tunnels are dug into the bowels of mountains to connect countries separated by the highest of peaks, while other tunnels dug under the ocean floor to shorten distances, avoid the disruption and hazards faced by the countries separated by the sea. So, at what point will someone say: "This far and no further!"' (Bebel 1910, p. 402).

Yet, Bebel was not the only one to influence Havemann's utopian thinking. Bloch also played a role. 'He appropriated the idea from one of them and the method from the other',[217] wrote Heyer aptly. Bloch was an important influence for the GDR's left-leaning SED critics across all generations. His *Principle of Hope* was put in the same context as the possibility of another form of socialism. In *Tomorrow*, this concept features explicitly. The link Bloch claimed to exist between freedom and socialism can also be found in Havemann's texts. Bloch's call for 'no democracy without socialism, no socialism without democracy: this formula implies, *mutatis mutandis*, a connection'[218] is reflected at many junctures throughout Havemann's works. Similarly, Bloch's position that, in practice, the rigidity of Marxism could only be countered by utopia[219] also appears in *Tomorrow*.

Even with regard to the faith in technology and promises of prosperity of socialism, there are clear parallels between the two, despite the fact that in 1980, Havemann incorporated post-materialist ideas into his utopia.[220] In so doing,

---

217 Heyer 2006a, p. 106.
218 Bloch 1985c, p. 394. In as early as 1918 Bloch wrote: 'Socialism without a loosening of the regulations that govern associations, without far-reaching democracy, including in the lives of the individuals, is no more than Prussianism of a different order' Bloch 1985b, p. 390. In *The Principle of Hope* he wrote: 'All freedom movements are guided by utopian aspirations', Bloch 1986, p. 7. And in May 1956, he stated: 'Every form of socialism is designed according to the measure of democratic freedoms on which it can build, freedoms that are incorporated into the system and, more importantly, continued to be guaranteed. This means that civil liberties are not only embraced, in fact made up for, but are in fact perfected and implemented meticulously without capitalists, by bringing an end to the capitalists', Bloch 1985c, p. 365.
219 In as early as 1923, in the *Spirit of Utopia*, Bloch called for Marxism to be enriched with elements of social utopia, so that it could remain organic. The picture he painted of socialism was very similar to that depicted by Havemann later: the private economy gives way to cooperative production and only then can the true private sphere unfold. 'Only in this way will the community, freely electing itself, have space *above* a society that merely disburdens and a communistically restructured social economy, in a structure without violence because without classes', Bloch 2000, p. 246.
220 In the *Principle of Hope* (written between 1938 and 1947), Bloch wrote: '... the technological possibilities, indeed realities of today are being artificially curbed by means of a superannuated economic system. The social balance of power releases technology only for the purposes of war, for the production of means of death; but the power of this production alone already indicates how lavishly the manufacture of food as a means of life could prosper' (Bloch 1986, p. 898). This reveals his faith in technology and chemistry as a means of achieving the kingdom of freedom. He also believed that neither monopoly capitalism nor state capitalism could use technology and chemistry to promote human emancipation. They were only capable of increasing overproduction. What was essential, however, was the socialisation of the means of production. See Bloch 1986, p. 899.

he left behind – albeit not entirely – the technological promises of salvation which he had supported during his years as an acclaimed scientist during the Ulbricht era.[221]

Tomorrow thus shows clear influences of classical Marxism. This distinguishes it from Western post-materialist utopias, although Havemann did in fact draw on the roots of these utopias as well. Havemann went further than the Marxist utopias by incorporating ecological, post-materialist approaches as well as by drawing on elements of anarchistic utopia in an attempt to give Marxism new impetus.

Another book that is part of the shared origins of *Tomorrow* and the Western post-materialist utopias in utopian history is William Morris's *News from Nowhere*.[222] The parallels between *Tomorrow* and this classic of the anarchistic utopian tradition written in 1890 are quite apparent, which at the very least suggests that Havemann was (very) familiar with the book.

The parallels start with the clothes people are wearing, which in each case are classic, plain and unadorned, lightweight in keeping with the season.[223] Other similarities can be seen in the people themselves, who in both books, thanks to their contented lives, are able to reach a much older age than the contemporaries of each of the authors.[224] When it comes to architecture and settlement type, too, *Tomorrow* reminds us of *News from Nowhere*: Morris describes a rural way of life with small, pretty houses amidst splendid gardens shaping

---

221 A young adult book published in 1961 describes the very euphoria of the Ulbricht era: 'And the world of tomorrow will be rich, far richer than the wildest dreamers could ever have dreamed, so rich that every reasonable wish of each and every person will be fulfilled. ... The face of the Earth will change to suit the wishes and purposes of humankind. ... The immeasurable energies which shine from the sun onto the Earth or which lie dormant inside the nuclei of atoms will be made universally accessible. The laws of nature, studied by science and applied by technology will be confidently mastered by humans. And flowing from all this are all manner of unforeseeable riches which man will possess in the future. But the best part is that this world of the future, which is more alluring and wonderful than any utopia, is anything but a utopia! It is the reality of tomorrow, which is emerging from the reality of today. ... In about two or three decades, when the young people of today are just about "middle-aged", their world will have changed beyond recognition – for the better, of course! And, without having been truly aware of it, they, too, will have changed – they will have become people of a new era, who know how to make the best of this world. ... The people want ... to exploit the wonderful treasures and forces of nature, transforming them into wealth that they can all share in, not just a select few, elected by no one' (Böhm and Dörge 1961, p. 12 f.).
222 See Morris-Keitel 2004, p. 25 f.
223 See Morris 1995, p. 16. On Morris's utopia, see Heyer 2006b, pp. 38–53, Saage 2002b, pp. 157–82.
224 See in Morris 1995, p. 16, p. 64 f.

the landscape. People live with whoever they wish – with no constraints or quantitative specifications. As in Havemann's utopia, in Morris's, too, cities are abolished along with all the suffering they bring, while smaller towns are in abundance.[225]

In contrast to his contemporary utopianists in the late nineteenth century, most of whom dreamed of total control of nature and agricultural cultivation of the wilderness, Morris describes an understanding of nature similar to that found in the post-materialist discourse: there is evidence of elements of forest romanticism as the protagonist enjoys the cool quiet of the 'green forest'.[226] The wilderness is portrayed in a positive light and nature is considered a gift to be treated with care. Morris criticises industrial society's instrumental understanding of nature, which '… was always looking upon everything, except mankind … – "nature," as people used to call it – as one thing, and mankind as another, it was natural to people thinking in this way, that they should try to make "nature" their slave since they thought "nature" was something outside them'.[227]

Like the utopia in Havemann's *Tomorrow*, Morris's utopia has no government, no state, no laws and consequently no authorities. There are no state requirements when it comes to education, and the children learn through their curiosity and inquisitiveness, which gives them immense enjoyment. Work is no longer a burden, but rather a 'pleasant spell',[228] preferably to be celebrated in a community. In place of factories there are 'Banded-workshops; that is, places where people collect who want to work together'.[229] Accordingly, there is no centrally planned economy and in the production of goods, it is the use value that is important and not the exchange value. With respect to technology, too, there are clear parallels between the two books: both authors rejected 'Luddism', all the while dreaming of a post-industrial age that combined *Handwerksromantik*, a romanticisation of artisanry, with technological optimism in such a way that heavy work would continue to be performed by machines,[230] while enjoyable work would be done manually – with people relearning traditional crafts and perfecting those skills under new socioeconomic conditions.[231]

---

225 See Morris 1995, p. 25, p. 67ff. 'As to the big murky places which were once, as we know, the centres of manufacture, they have, like the brick and mortar desert of London, disappeared' (Morris 1995, p. 71).
226 Morris 1995, p. 30.
227 Morris 1995, p. 187.
228 Morris 1995, p. 50.
229 Morris 1995, p. 48.
230 See Morris 1995.
231 'The universal decentralisation of the economy and the dismantling of the throwaway

Love and relationships is another area where similarities can be identified between Havemann and Morris. Although Morris does not explicitly describe polygamy, homosexuality or incest, his utopia does transcend the bourgeois conventions of his time to achieve gender equality. Moreover, the role and function of mothers is held in particularly high esteem.[232] Connected to the fact that women are now no longer treated as the private property of men are that the moral 'follies about the "ruin" of women for following their natural desires in an illegal way, which of course was a convention resulting from the laws regulating private property'[233] had been relegated to the past. This very same rationale for abolishing bourgeois moral values can be found in Havemann's writing.

On a final note, the words written by Gerd Selle about *News from Nowhere* can also be applied to Havemann's utopia:

> After all the destruction of the environment and damage to human relationships caused by capitalism, things are rebuilt, newer and better. The overexploitation of people and nature ceases to occur, all forms of alienated labour are abolished, and the productive power of technology is no longer abused at the same time. With the elimination of capitalism and the introduction of socialist work culture, the negativity of the age of technology is overcome. In other words, the technological progress that during the capital valorisation process was deformed into a destructive force is returned to its human purpose in utopia.[234]

4.2.2   Links to Classical and Post-Materialist Utopia

There is no doubt that *Tomorrow* corresponds to the model of the classical utopia. The book comprises a critique of the existing circumstances and an ima-

---

society reveal other advantages. This is demonstrated for example by the long shelf life of consumer goods, although Havemann, like William Morris in *News from Nowhere* (1890) before him, explicitly refers to the aesthetic principle of the beauty of self-made objects, of which people can, at last, be proud again' (Morris-Keitel 2004, p. 39).

232   '... this is universally recognised ... that all the ARTIFICIAL burdens of motherhood are now done away with. A mother has no longer any mere sordid anxieties for the future of her children ... [S]uch anxieties as these are a part of the mingled pleasure and pain which goes to make up the life of mankind. But at least she is spared the fear (it was most commonly the certainty) that artificial disabilities would make her children something less than men and women: she knows that they will live and act according to the measure of their own faculties' (Morris 1995, p. 64).

233   Morris 1995, p. 84.
234   Selle 1981, p. 21.

gined better world, combined with a strategy of transformation.[235] Havemann's works are a smorgasbord of the different elements of utopian history. During their search of his house in Grünheide in 1979, the customs authorities created a list of the books from Havemann's private library 'which are subject to confiscation by the customs authorities of the GDR'. In other words, the list only included Western literature and as such does not indicate which of the utopias published by GDR publishers or before 1949 were part of Havemann's library (which makes it impossible to prove, for instance, that Havemann owned works such as *Utopia, Looking Backward: 2000–1887* or *News from Nowhere*). Alongside works of fiction and various works of left-wing literature, the customs authorities also listed the following more or less utopian works: Andrei Sakharov's *How I Imagine the Future*, Rudolf Bahro's *The Alternative* and *Eine Dokumentation* (A documentation), Ulf Wolter (ed.): *Antworten auf Bahros Herausforderung des realen Sozialismus* (Responses to Bahro's challenge of actually existing socialism), Otto Rühle (ed.): *Texte des Sozialismus und Anarchismus* (Texts on socialism and anarchism) (including texts by Proudhon, Bakunin, Blanqui and Weitling), Ernst Bloch's *Widerstand und Friede* (Resistance and peace), Erich Fromm's *Das Menschenbild bei Marx* (Marx's concept of man), and Aldous Huxley's account of his psychedelic experience under the influence of drugs *The Doors of Perception*.[236] Besides these, there were also books by Marxists such as Trotsky or Bukharin that were not published in the GDR, texts on the environmental debate in the West and books with a Eurocommunism orientation. The list produced by the customs authorities reflects both Havemann's political thinking in general and the theoretical building blocks of *Tomorrow* more specifically.

Firstly, we can assume that Havemann, condemned to professional inactivity, had not only collected all the titles in the list but had actually read them, too. Secondly, it is likely that he also discussed the content of these books with

---

235 In *Tomorrow*, Havemann was critical of the present and developed a utopian alternative. 'In doing so, Havemann joined the tradition of cooperative socialism, highlighted the chances of emancipation and free personal development for all, and sought recourse to the communal mentality. Havemann bundled these different elements together and – as part of a modified refraction of Marxism – transformed them into a utopian scenario. What is crucial here is that, thirdly, Havemann went beyond this framework of conditions. For the utopian space he envisaged was not only a goal but also demonstrated the ways and means that could be used to make the alternative he presented reality in the medium term, or at least to get close to it. In doing this, he brought the intended normative effect of the utopia into the text itself, which served as the medium for conveying this into reality' (Heyer 2009, p. 22 f.).

236 See BStU, MfS, AU, 145/90, vol. 13, p. 336 ff.

the numerous guests he welcomed to his house. And thirdly, it seems reasonable to suspect that this was not the only literature they discussed. Given that Havemann already took recourse to utopian works in the 1960s, it would be safe to say that he was also familiar with utopian classics published in the GDR. One thing that does not feature in the list at all, however, are Western post-materialist utopias.

Richard Saage is correct in his assessment that Havemann's *Tomorrow* is relevant for utopian research for two reasons:

1. Entirely in keeping with the classical utopian tradition, it offers something which Marx and Engels always rejected – a detailed description of a fictitious alternative society that includes not only the economic and political, but also the interpersonal, cultural reproduction and its anthropological basis.
2. Havemann's approach clearly resembles those structural features of the so-called post-materialist utopia which espoused the cause of anarchism, ecological equilibrium and women's emancipation. Indeed, Havemann's utopia *Tomorrow*, written in 1980, can quite easily be assimilated into the utopian paradigm of the classical tradition, albeit on the basis of the post-materialist interpretation, of course.[237]

According to Saage, Havemann underpinned his utopia 'with post-materialist elements which were quite alien to classical Marxism: the end of quantitative economic growth which corresponded to the efficient and rational use of energy resources, the use of regenerative energy sources, the use of energy-efficient transport systems (e.g. the abolition of cars), a ban on conspicuous consumption, emancipation of women, the creation of decentralised communes free from domination, creative self-expression of the individual in a harmonious society of unity in diversity, the abolition of cities, which equated to large-scale naturalisation of settlement areas, etc. And of course, Havemann did not overlook the signum of all classical utopias: the "New Man"'.[238]

Let us examine all these elements in detail. In terms of resolving the antagonism between ecology and economy, Havemann fulfilled the criteria of post-materialist discourse. He did not, however, break with his Marxist and scientific tendencies and as a result avoided becoming entangled with nature mysticism or anthroposophical esoteric ideas as Bahro had in his later years, for example. Martin d'Idler's statement that Callenbach's *Ecotopia* was characterised far more by 'nature rationality' than nature mysticism applies even more explicitly to *Tomorrow*.

---

237 Saage 2008, p. 158.
238 Saage 2008, p. 159f.

In his utopia, Callenbach criticises the people's subjugation of nature that was enshrined in the Christian world view. Callenbach juxtaposes this world view with the ideas of nature worship, which he also considered a potential solution when it came to the pursuit of an equilibrium between man and nature. *Ecotopia* managed without big cities, instead being based on sprawling suburbia and ecological restoration. This represented a major break with More's utopian tradition, in which the planned city was the ideal. However, Callenbach (and indeed Havemann alongside him) was not entering new territory when it came to utopian history but was, in fact, continuing – whether consciously or otherwise – in the tradition of early anarchistic utopianists such as Lahontan, Diderot or Morris.[239]

Even more apt than d'Idlers concept of 'natural rationality' is the distinction Sandra Thieme draws, in reference to *Tomorrow*, between a naturalist and sociocentric understanding of nature: while Callenbach tended towards the naturalist in his ideas, Havemann adopted a sociocentric approach to examining ecological problems: 'Through technological progress and social restructuring, an ecological society can be achieved that has no deficits. Thus, the two models represent opposing positions in the ecology debate …'.[240]

Havemann, Thieme writes, pinned his hopes on thermonuclear fusion as a decentralised source of energy. Thieme had her doubts about this, because it was a technology that was far from fully developed, was currently only feasible as a centralised mega technology and would, once again, result in radioactive waste. Another thing she had her doubts about from an ecological perspective was the fact that, when it came to agriculture, Havemann advocated industrial monocultures instead of ecological farming.[241] Ultimately, she came to the conclusion that he could not be an orthodox environmentalist: 'Wherever nature is supposed to satisfy social needs, it is used, shaped and "optimised" accordingly. Within the scope of their technical capabilities, the utopianists make use of the plasticity and versatility of nature, something which can be seen particularly clearly in the agricultural sector'.[242]

Here, it becomes clear that Havemann had remained a Marxist with an instrumental understanding of nature:

---

239 See Saage 2003, p. 197.
240 Thieme 2000, p. 205. 'Havemann argues … in a typical socio-centric manner. … Norms and objectives are not derived from scientifically determined nature, but rather from the social sphere, including from the need to survive' (Thieme 2004, p. 205).
241 See Thieme 2004, p. 125.
242 Thieme 2004, p. 129.

> In people's hands, nature is ... a malleable material, a resource; encroachment on nature is inevitable, but should be limited such that it does not destroy the foundation of human existence. Of course, the concept of domination of nature plays a central role in Havemann's *Tomorrow*. ... However, the author regards the idea of the planet remaining habitable for everyone, including future generations as one of society's long-term needs.[243]

Havemann searched for the Third Way and not only from a global political perspective but also in terms of utopian history. In his works, we can detect elements of classical utopia, of utopias based on technological optimism, but also of a post-materialist utopian tradition. This is rooted in his self-perception as a Marxist scientist and, in turn, in the utopian content of Marxism. Havemann thus sought to sublate the contradiction between the promise that technology would bring salvation and its dialectical antagonism in the form of industrial overexploitation, drawing on the medium of utopia to do so.

This is also reflected in how *Tomorrow* addresses the topics of speed, travel and transport: 'The underlying theme of his utopia is the "life journeys" of people as autodidacts, who seek sense in interpersonal relationships. These are characterised by post-materialist needs such as moderation, conscious enjoyment instead of intoxication, a slow-moving pace and caution, joie de vivre and curiosity'.[244] Travel contributes to self-experience and self-improvement. Time plays no role, the constraints inherent in industrial society are overcome. The motto of modernity that 'time is money' no longer applies in Havemann's Utopia. The hectic pace of life is replaced by an unhurried one. This is made possible by rationalising and automating production, while at the same time dispensing with putatively superfluous industrial products. Travel was now no longer for business purposes, but nor did it serve as short-term regeneration for the individual in the form of an annual package holiday.

> While the production process is highly technological in utopia, in other parts of society, such as the transport sector, for instance, things are completely different. Here, there is a huge discrepancy between high-tech and pre-modernity. Moreover, despite the fact that it is critical for the existence of utopia, technology seems to be separate from everyday life. It exists as an almost self-perpetuating system – a kind of 'black box' con-

---

243 Thieme 2004, p. 208.
244 Röhrborn 2008, p. 96.

trolled by just a small number of engineers which automatically supplies the required products in the right number each time.[245]

The production and distribution of goods in *Tomorrow* are, on the one hand, reminiscent of classical utopias rooted in the communism of abundance such as Bellamy's *Looking Backward: 2000–1887*. On the other hand, we can also identify elements of post-materialist utopian discourse, abstaining from consumption, for instance. That said, it should also be emphasised that the condemnation of *wasteful* luxury is a core element of utopian history. The majority of post-materialist authors pick up from here with no major break in discourse.

A clear example of the post-materialist criticism of consumption that prevailed in the 1970s can be found in Erich Fromm's book *To Have or to Be?*, published in the US in 1976 and appearing in Germany in the same year under the title *Haben oder Sein*. There are considerable overlaps between this book and Bahro and Havemann's utopias. Fromm writes, for example 'By *being* or *having* ... I refer to two fundamental modes of existence, to two different kinds of orientation toward self and the world, two different kinds of character structure the respective predominance of which determines the totality of a person's thinking, feeling, and acting'.[246] He combined this with a contemporary criticism of consumption: 'Modern consumers may identify themselves by the formula: I am = what I have and what I consume'.[247] And the result of this was that man became passive.

Much like Havemann, Fromm, too, saw knowledge as the key to critical thinking, rather than being a matter of the mere accumulation of alleged truths. In this context, *being* meant more profound qualitative knowledge, while *having* stood for additional quantitative knowledge.[248] Parallels could also be seen between Fromm and Havemann when it came to sexuality and the role of morals in modern society. Fromm believed that the creation of sexual taboos served the purpose of breaking the human spirit and believed this to be at the essence of how societies of exploitation and oppression worked. 'What matters is that new forms of propertylessness will do away with the sexual greed that is characteristic of all having societies'.[249] The two books are not identical but they are certainly akin to one another. Their similarity shows just how close *Tomorrow* is to Western post-materialist (utopian) discourse.

---

245   Thieme 2004, p. 199.
246   Fromm 2013, p. 21.
247   Fromm 2013, p. 24.
248   See Fromm 2013, p. 26 f.
249   Fromm 2013, p. 68.

Thieme writes

> ... that in utopia, a post-materialist lifestyle is cultivated. ... Here, post-materialist primarily means that existing needs are satisfied with far fewer resources. This is thanks to the change in the mode of production which was now oriented towards use value and equal distribution of social wealth. This is inevitably accompanied by a shift in the consciousness of the population that enables people to view this lifestyle positively and be able to forego the current abundance of goods.[250]

This shift in consciousness was connected with the elimination of the patriarchal elements of today's society. Similar to Bahro and Harich, but also to post-materialist utopias in general, Havemann developed a utopia based on matriarchal principles. 'In Havemann's book, the matriarchy functions as an indicator of more advanced social development'.[251] Sexual liberation against a backdrop of feminism is a core element of matriarchal approaches in post-materialist utopias. 'These are utopias which no longer regulate the individual, and equal rights for women are seen as a key element of this'.[252] In *Tomorrow*, Havemann broke with virtually all the sexual taboos of Western society. 'Thus, on the one hand, Havemann depicts passions as having been shifted to the individual where they also take shape in the first place. On the other hand, these passions are satisfied in the collective, or at least in compliance with the new norms and values that are created voluntarily as a means of social cohesion'.[253]

According to Heyer, Havemann derived his matriarchy from Engels's *The Origin of the Family, Private Property and the State* as well as Bebel's *Woman and Socialism*. 'In this respect, Havemann was discrediting what was known as the sexual revolution of the 1960s and '70s given that it did not manage to emancipate women, but rather fostered atomisation (as a negative form of individualisation). Consequently, according to Havemann, modern feminism relied on a false premise ....'[254]

---

250 Thieme 2004, p. 134. 'Without abandoning his Marxist position, Havemann, recognising the historical context and economic developments, clearly prioritised ecological problems over the issue of class, although in his utopia he sought a solution for society as a whole in the de facto connection between the two problem areas' (Morris-Keitel 2004, p. 37).
251 Heyer 2010b, p. 31.
252 Heyer 2009, p. 31.
253 Heyer 2009, p. 31.
254 Heyer 2009, p. 32.

It was therefore not the modern individualisation of women and their equal participation in the structures of the patriarchal industrial society that represented the true emancipation of women, but rather women's self-discovery in the role of the mother – needless to say not in the spirit of a patriarchal society as the protector of home and hearth. 'On this issue, Havemann's thoughts were more progressive than post-materialist utopian discourse, as the latter generally assumes that state-of-the-art technologies will free women from the task of giving birth. When the so-called feminist utopias proclaim a matriarchy, new mechanisms of suppression are in fact hidden within'.[255]

Florian Havemann's claim that *Tomorrow* should be primarily considered a sexual utopia[256] unjustly marginalises the importance of this work in utopian history. In his opinion, Robert Havemann gave his sexual fantasies free rein in the book. And, there do indeed appear to be parallels with Callenbach, whose *Ecotopia* Waschkuhn saw in a similar light, saying 'that the liberated sensuality in his concept was certainly shaped by male fantasies (particularly with respect to the nurse named Linda and her massage techniques)'.[257] Nevertheless, both authors used political utopia to voice criticism of the elements of patriarchal structure in Western industrial societies, at the same time presenting alternatives.

The new matriarchy was also accompanied by another type of society related to the form of settlement, the architecture, political administration and the position of the individual in the collective. The individual is liberated from the chains of the present, especially the political and economic paternalism, but also from the archistic utopias' promise of happiness based on forced collectivism and their attempts at implementing actually existing socialism. The decentralised settlement structures meet this demand and illustrate a line of tradition that draws on the Russian anarchist Peter Kropotkin (1842–1921): 'It

---

255 Heyer 2009, p. 32.
256 'It is a utopia of culture and upbringing, love and desire, of fidelity and of course infidelity, of homosexuality and lesbian love, of incest and the prohibition of incest, which no longer exists in his dreams, of the matriarchy that exists in this country, but has no ability to dominate at all. It is a technological utopia, because everyone is adequately taken care of in this country of Utopia. It is an ecological utopia, because a solution has been found for all the problems of our industrial society. Yet, even though the subtitle of the book *Industrial Society at a Crossroads – Criticism and Actually Existing Utopia* suggests something else, both of these in fact only play a marginal role, as, more than anything else, this is a social utopia. But even then, it only offers a template, a framework for something else: for a sexual utopia, which seems to be the real essence, the driving force behind the creation of all this ...'. (Havemann, F. 2007, p. 151).
257 Waschkuhn 2003, p. 202.

was from him that Havemann took the idea of mutual assistance and solidarity, the limited anarchist social organisation (anarchy in the sense of the absence of hierarchical power structures), which led to cooperative socialism where it become compatible with Rosa Luxemburg's concept of freedom'.[258]

Kropotkin wrote a utopian account of the principles of anarchism: 'We imagine a society where interpersonal relationships are regulated by mutual obligations, voluntarily entered into and capable of being dissolved at any time as well as willingly accepted traditions and customs – no longer imposed by law, the legacy of a past under oppression and barbarism, and no longer controlled by authorities, whether elected or inherited. ... In any case, certainly not an authority that imposes its will on others'.[259]

Havemann was not the only author of political utopias in the second half of the twentieth century to draw on Kropotkin. It would in fact be no exaggeration to say that his anarchistic ideas influenced the entire utopian discourse of the time. One reason for this was the fact that the Stalinist systems discredited the archistic utopian tradition. Any author who wanted to continue to write positive (communist) utopias had no choice but to dissociate themselves from these regimes and thus also from the étatist, anti-individualist utopias. And given that this latter type of utopia was criticised due to its tutelage and, to some extent, even enslavement of the individual by the ideology of the collective, post-totalitarian utopias had to resolve this contradiction. Recourse to this combination of the free individual and a society based on solidarity, similar to that found in anarchistic utopias, particularly Kropotkin's, was well suited to this purpose and acquired increasing significance.[260]

The division of society into 'free associations' reflects this separation from any kind of state socialist ideas. 'Administration of justice, law-making and the monopoly on violence are not assigned to a political authority ... but are instead the responsibility of each individual'.[261] Havemann's *Tomorrow* fits with this

---

258 Heyer 2010b, p. 32. 'Kropotkin, the anarchist who yearned to replace laws of central government with consensus of local communities, certainly hoped to locate a deep preference for mutual aid in the innermost evolutionary marrow of our being. Let mutual aid pervade nature and human cooperation becomes a simple instance of the law of life' (Gould 1988, p. 18).
259 Kropotkin 1994, p. 65.
260 See Saage 2003, p. 383 ff., Heyer 2006, p. 74 ff.
261 Thieme 2004, p. 202 f. '... In *Tomorrow*, Havemann does not, however, explore the question of how freely associated individuals manage to make collective decisions regarding the structure of social life. The impression that arises is, therefore, that social and political life functioned "automatically", with no social friction and in the form of a "pre-stabilised harmony"' (ibid).

structuring of society in keeping with the model of post-materialist utopias. 'The principles of decentralisation and self-determination are also proposed for ecological anarchism. Autonomous, self-governing and self-sustaining political and economic entities, often conceived in the form of communes, are intended to replace the growth-oriented, global capitalist economy.'[262]

And this model can be seen in Havemann, Bahro and Callenbach's works, or even in B.F. Skinner's *Walden Two*.[263] The balance in relations between the individual and the collective or man and the environment is based on changed behaviour and a changed way of life. In this context, Havemann, too, took recourse to the 'New Man', an abandoned motive in utopian history. It is important to recall here that this concept had fallen into disrepute following the real attempts at moulding human beings within utopian discourse, which is the reason why this was seldom used in post-materialist utopias any longer. This concept did not assume that people were malleable but rather that the utopian model could be adapted to this 'deficient being' (Arnold Gehlen). In utopian studies, a consensus rightly prevails that in *Tomorrow*, Havemann envisaged a 'New Man' who was to serve as the basis for this utopia – but who was ultimately not so very different from today's man and would thus develop quite freely without needing to be forced.

Saage, for instance, situated Havemann's 'New Man' in the same line of tradition as Friedrich Schiller.[264] And Heyer, too, in reference to *Tomorrow*, described the 'New Man'

> as an engineer, teacher, hero, liberator. In Havemann's book, citizens of Utopia reach twice the age they do today, everyone is an artist, with opportunities for them to realise their full potential. At the same time everyone develops the ability to make the right decisions. However, utopias of this type always end up with a paradox: On the one hand, the 'New Man' is the mainstay of the utopia, ensuring through his basic anthropological configuration that things function smoothly. On the other hand, this 'New Man' does not exist until utopia, with its common good, its educational programme, its ability to tap into all cultural, civilisational and human

---

262 Idler 1999, p. 42.
263 See Waschkuhn 2003, p. 196 ff.
264 'This concept of the "New Man" thus follows certain trajectories, as Schiller depicted in his letters on the aesthetic education of people. The "New Man" acquires his development prospects by overcoming the hard dualism between body and soul, mind and body, socio-cultural and animalist nature: His spiritual dimension would embrace the sensual side, and the sensual side the spiritual. The "New Man" shaped by this equilibrium can expect to double his life expectancy compared to man in the society of origin' (Saage 2008, p. 160 f.).

potential, has been reached. Utopia, and this is the basic message of this antagonism, cannot be reached exactly as it is described. But, and this is what Havemann's line of argument aims at too, the concepts outlined can have a normative impact on their own present by describing a possible goal for people to work towards.[265]

Similarly, Morris-Keitel also saw the 'New Man' as a fundamental condition for Havemann's utopia to function.[266] And Ferst, too, was of the opinion that *Tomorrow* was based on a new, less aggressive human with educational aspirations.[267]

Lastly, Thieme argued that Havemann's utopia did not in fact rely on the morally perfect man, in other words the 'New' Man:

> Contrary to conservative and liberal fears about utopian models, the individual should in no way be subordinate to an all-powerful, 'levelling' collective. First and foremost, the collective or the community plays a protective role and makes up the social foundation for individuals to realise their full potential. Following from this, the assumption is that a positive sociability can only be achieved on condition that individuals can live self-determined lives in a milieu of psycho-social protection. The question of whether a 'New Man' is needed ... can ... be answered in the negative. ... However, utopias need a shift in consciousness among the subjects, albeit not in the sense of achieving a morally perfect human.[268]

Hence, although *Tomorrow* is predicated on the creation of a 'New Man', that Man does not necessarily have to be all that New. And Havemann certainly does not envisage (eugenic) breeding to achieve this. That said, what he does assume is a different human consciousness, which he believes will result primarily from a transformation in the relations of production and ownership.

With regard to these relations, the role played by technology and science in *Tomorrow* is an important one. Despite all its many post-materialist elements,

---

265 Heyer 2010b, p. 31. See also Heyer 2009, p. 23 ff.
266 'However, Havemann leaves no doubt that such a future prospect is only possible if humanity replaces its anthropocentric addiction to waste with a resolutely biocentric commitment underpinned by solidarity. Only once humans are ready to do away with a mindset fixated on material possessions and success, only once nature is granted the same privileges that humans today claim for themselves alone, will we find opportunities to stave off the threat of irreversibility in the next few decades' (Morris-Keitel 2004, p. 40).
267 See Ferst 2005, p. 30.
268 Thieme 2004, p. 211.

the book is in fact a technical utopia that reflects the way Havemann thinks as a scientist. A good illustration of this is his model of decentralised hydrogen-based energy generation. This was not an idea he came up with from scratch for *Tomorrow*, but in fact is described almost word for word in a manuscript called *Atomtechnik im Jahre 2000* (Nuclear technology in the year 2000) written in March 1956, which can be found in the archives of the Robert Havemann Society. The text clearly reflects the hopes that prevailed during the 1950s. In the manuscript, Havemann writes: 'In the year 2000, we will generate nuclear energy with hydrogen, a substance available to us on Earth in vast and unlimited quantities in the form of water'.[269] Since energy supply would then no longer rely on coal, which is so cumbersome to transport, from then on, a decentralised system of electricity generation would be possible.

> The aim of the nuclear technology of the future will be to build small, even very small, power generators. The ideal will be that anything that consumes energy will already incorporate its own power supply. Cars will run for years without having to be refuelled. Power generation will be integrated into every vacuum cleaner, every sewing machine, every central heating system, virtually everything ....

As a result, there will be no more power supply lines and no disposable batteries. After all, 'the tiny quantities of raw materials required to produce nuclear energy in this equipment can simply be replenished every now and then ...'. And Havemann defended his images of the future against critics:

> Some will say these utopias are impossible to achieve. But I want to warn these pessimists! They have always been proven wrong and are among those people who made more of a fool of themselves than the most fanciful of utopianists.

Havemann never took ecological risks into consideration in those days, and even the *Dialectics of Nature*[270] that he thought so highly of was not taken into account when he dreamt of traveling by rocket to 'take a picnic on Venus', and using a 'nuclear pumping station' to supply the Bering Strait with warm water in order to heat 'America's north coast and the Soviet Union ... by means of an

---

269   Source (also for the following quotes from this text): RHG/RH 023/06 vol. 92.
270   The same file contains, for instance, an article by Havemann published in *Einheit* no. 9/1952 and titled *Dialectics of Nature*. On the publication of the first complete German edition of the brilliant work by Friedrich Engels, see RHG/RH 023/06 vol. 92.

artificial Gulf Stream', thus making it possible to use these areas for agricultural purposes, or ultimately even 'thawing parts of the Antarctic continent' in order to tap into the supply of ore under the permafrost.[271]

Another concept that reminds us of *Tomorrow* is the idea that in the year 2000

> ... the majority of the industrial production that is indispensable for human life will be fully automated. There will be a very small number of people managing, controlling and monitoring these machines, producing all the food, clothing and anything else required for the daily needs of the other people. As a result, people will have a lot of spare time to do what they enjoy and are interested in.

At this point, Havemann also elaborates on his concept of work, stating that in actual fact people are not born lazy and do not have to be forced to work. The situation is quite the opposite, in fact: 'The major undertakings of the human race will be voluntary endeavours, things which, viewed from the perspective of material necessity, are superfluous'. This was why in as early as the 1950s, Havemann already saw humanity's future as being bathed in golden light thanks to technical progress:

> The less time and energy the work that is essential to sustain life requires of us, the more we can dedicate ourselves to the pursuit of happiness, beauty and the unravelling of the mystery of nature. This is the purpose of the new age that is now emerging. Man's forces are a million times stronger enabling him to become the ruler of nature and create a human world guided by intelligence and knowledge and filled with happiness and beauty for everyone.

In *Tomorrow*, Havemann only managed to distance himself from these technological fantasies to a certain degree. In light of the economic development which failed to materialise by 1980 and against the background of the increasing ecological crisis, he did abandon concepts such as the picnic in space or the thawing of Antarctic. On the other hand, *Tomorrow* did not yet address

---

271   Today, this kind of thinking with respect to climate policy is called 'geoengineering' and is 'very controversial – on the one hand, because its technical feasibility is still unclear, and on the other because of the unpredictable and uncontrollable consequences, but first and foremost because it could suggest ... that we may not have to reduce emissions of greenhouse gases' (Borries 2010, p. 112).

the problem of nuclear waste either, and the discharge of warm industrial wastewater into the Adriatic Sea that he described was just as unconvincing an example of a well thought through ecological dialectic. Havemann stuck by his positive notion of technology, which he believed should serve people. This was his utopian programme and represented the reverse of the reality he perceived. It also included using technology to solve environmental problems, for instance, resolving the problem of waste through recyling.²⁷² Technology was thus subordinate to humans. And, since Havemann's utopia saw humans as living in equilibrium with nature, technology, too, was subordinate to nature.

The function it fulfils in *Tomorrow* is therefore similar to in other Western post-materialist utopias. Here, Havemann's ideas become entangled in contradictions, however. According to Heyer, the authors of post-materialist utopias

> ... assume that the technology used up till now not the right approach and consider it to have has negative effects, yet at the same time produce new technologies themselves. The notion that these are harmless just because they were created and used in utopia is illogical. Why is it not possible for utopia to be contaminated by a virus as well? For a brilliant inventor to generate possibilities for the destruction of humanity with the accidental by-products of his creation? In a nutshell: the huge technology complex – from power generation to recycling and industrial progress to biotechnology and genetic modification – is one of the greatest weaknesses of new utopias.²⁷³

In relation to this, Thieme asks the fitting question of

> ... whether domination of nature is technically possible to this degree, and whether the technical equipment required for this does not in fact create more environmental problems. It is also difficult to imagine how the cit-

---

272 See Morris-Keitel 2004, p. 38.
273 Heyer 2009, p. 28 f. And Ferst notes: 'In his social utopia of the ecological communism of the future, the majority of jobs that no one wants to do will be automated. In other words, the problem of another political economy is not quite as pressing. That said, it is highly doubtful that this path is navigable in the context of the ecological boundaries that we have far exceeded. Admittedly, Havemann assumes a very self-sufficient way of life. If we consider the ecological "rucksacks", in other words all the additional burdens that arise, much suggests that it would not be a good idea to manufacture all goods in automated factories and indeed, given the long transport distances alone, in as highly a centralised manner as he envisages' (Ferst 2005, p. 11).

izens of utopia can develop a relationship with natural processes which is not instrumental if all plants are grown with computer-controlled machines. ... The path may already have been paved for the next step towards an economic system that exploits and destroys nature.[274]

Klaus Richter and Manfred Wilke were correspondingly critical of the technical concept in *Tomorrow*:

> Havemann firmly holds to the socialist movement's old traditions of progress: perfected, automated technology used by man is crucial for the overall humane development of society. Here, although he was addressing problems that were certainly close to the newly formed environmental movement, the solution he was proposing came from an angle that seemed anachronistic to the environmental movement that was happening around 1980. This is because criticism of technology, which was almost symbolically tied to criticism of nuclear energy, served as the starting point for the green movement. Havemann's utopia could not expect a positive response from these people with their romantic tendencies to flee from technology.[275]

That said, the transport concept Havemann outlines in *Tomorrow*, his ideas about the mode of travel, were in contradictions with his belief in technology. Considering the fact that he loved to drive cars and ride motorbikes and was even chair of one of the sub-divisions of the GDR Automobile Club, the complete break with this passion seen in *Tomorrow* is all the more striking. Entirely in keeping with the Western post-materialist discourse, Havemann advocates romanticised travel and a slow pace of life.

As already described, Havemann's *Tomorrow* contains a number of elements from post-materialist utopias. There is one key aspect of the genre that has not yet been addressed, however: the renouncement of a historically determinist world view. The utopian scenario described is always understood as more of a fragile state, in other words not as the end of history, which is why its potential failure is considered, too. This failure often comprises the descent of utopian society into a new dictatorship, meaning there is always a latent risk of the latter happening. Accordingly, within this utopian genre, the strategy of transformation is also looked upon self-critically.

---

274   Thieme 2000, p. 211 f.
275   Richter and Wilke 1991, p. 233.

Tomorrow does not fulfil all these criteria of post-materialist utopia. On this point, Havemann departs strongly from the post-materialist utopian discourse in the West as he conceives his utopia as a historical end state, in which social antagonisms only exist on the interpersonal level. At no point does Havemann consider the notion of the whole system failing. Heyer: 'For him, utopia, which is definitely the better alternative to the current conditions, in fact takes on eutopian dimensions. Here, there is a clear break with post-materialist utopian discourse and at the same time a radical break with the scepticism of the alternative depicted, which has been an integral part of utopia since Thomas More. Discussions on utopia no longer feature in Havemann's work'.[276] On this point, Havemann adheres to the deterministic view of history found in dogmatised Marxism-Leninism, even

> ... finalistically intensifying it further. In the end there are only two options. Either apocalyptic demise or salvation through utopia. In *Tomorrow*, Havemann categorically rules out a middle ground. In so doing, he falls behind the standards of post-materialist production of utopia ....[277]

Many reviewers of *Tomorrow* accused Havemann of naivety when it came to the functional capacity of his model of society.[278] The reason for this was the concept of man that his utopia was based on, which was intended to make it possible to refrain from integrating powers and checks and balances. On this, Saage pointed out that Havemann had behaved incredibly naively in respect of the problem of human aggressiveness: 'Havemann appears to believe that it is not rooted in the biological evolution of human beings but rather in their socio-cultural nature. ... If it were the case, however, that, as suggested by modern evolutionary biologists, the animalistic remnants of natural aggression lie dormant in human nature, then post-materialist utopias such as Le Guin's *The Dispossessed* and Callenbach's *Ecotopia* would be more realistic than Havemann's, because they consider aggressive behaviour to be a possibility in utopia'.[279]

---

276 Heyer 2009, p. 33. See also Heyer 2010b, p. 31.
277 Heyer 2009, p. 34 f.
278 See following chapter.
279 Saage 2008. p. 161. Le Guin drew among other things on Kropotkin's political ideas – though she did not depict a paradise. Instead, according to her, 'many of the exaggerations are cancelled out by the repeated collapse of reality that is described' (Waschkuhn 2003, p. 213).

Havemann's utopian concept did not envisage any entities at all to facilitate checks and balances over power. Unlike Le Guin, he did not consider the possibility of opaque personal networks being able to be used for the acquisition and abuse of power and he completely failed to reflect on the anthropological risks to an anarcho-communist social order. Instead, he simply incorporated the criticism of his utopia in the utopia itself and then refuted that criticism and all its arguments based on his concept of man.

More specifically, this criticism could be linked to the function of the elites in *Tomorrow*, with a particular focus on the role of technicians and engineers. Thieme, for instance, saw 'the risks of a technocracy evolving, since only a small number of engineers controlled the social production process, resulting in a concentration of power'.[280] Since Havemann did not envisage any authorities at all for the integration of power or checks and balances, this results in a clear risk of a dystopian shift because: 'After all, a large part of the utopian supply system is in their hands. They are the only ones with an understanding of the technical processes and they develop innovations that are important for society. Effectively, they have a huge amount of social power at their disposal'.[281]

Röhrborn took a similarly sceptical view on the issue: 'Although they only make up one percent of the population and occupy a position that is literally essential for the continued existence of humanity, they should not derive from this any – oftentimes extortionate – special interests'.[282]

Tomorrow does not fully meet the criteria of post-materialist utopias. Indeed, it would be unreasonable to expect this, as this was a Western genre and in fact Havemann was one of the very few philosophers from the Eastern Bloc to contribute to it. Since he was isolated from society while he was writing *Tomorrow*, the book represents a substrate of his own way of thinking.[283] Owing to the elements of utopian history that can be identified in *Tomorrow*, it is also very doubtful as to whether he had even read the Western post-materialist uto-

---

280 Thieme 2000, p. 208.
281 Thieme 2004, p. 127.
282 Röhrborn 2008, p. 101.
283 'The only ones who dared visit the Havemanns were those who were essentially already resolved to turn their backs on the GDR and leave for the West. Thus, Havemann was forced to develop his ideas on his own. In his view, such a vision of the ideal future had to comprise everything research and technology had achieved and at the same time had to minimise ecological impact. It had to validate the traditional family and at the same time dissolve the family alliance. It had to permit maximum possible individuality yet recognise order. It could no longer be an "ism" without betraying communism. Even to Havemann, it was clear that requirements like this ... were at odds with all popular ways of thinking' (Havemann and Widmann 2003, p. 298).

pias of his time. In fact, there is much to suggest that Havemann combined the classics of the anti-étatist communist utopian tradition by authors such as Bebel, Kropotkin or Morris with elements of Bloch's utopian concept, ecological warnings of the time, Western anti-authoritarian contemporary philosophy and his personal experiences and desires[284] to create his own utopian model. And he deliberately designed this concept on the basis of More's *Utopia*, in other words on the basis of an ideal-type classical utopia.

5 The Reception of *Tomorrow* in the East and the West

5.1 *The East*

5.1.1 Reactions by the State

Havemann was not afraid of punishment or sanctions. Any measures the party leadership took against him ultimately only served to increase his popularity and disseminate his ideas more widely. Although the SED had recently tightened the laws against unauthorised publication of texts in the West, making them far more draconian,[285] they did not apply these laws to Havemann for the publication of *Tomorrow*.

The reaction of the party leadership to the publication of the book was more reserved, a fact that can probably be explained by its content. On the one hand, *Tomorrow* was relatively held back in its criticism of SED policy (especially with regard to the specific demand for human rights). On the other hand, the party presumably did not consider Havemann's utopia to be particularly controversial. This impression was reinforced by the Stasi's unofficial assessments of *Tomorrow*, which completely ignored the content of the book's utopian chapter. For instance, the monthly report dated 8 July 1980 stated that Havemann was about to publish a new book. This was followed by brief, unbiased information about the content which made no reference to the utopia at all. The only topics that the Stasi showed an interest in were the arms race, the Cold War and trade union policy.[286] An assessment of *Tomorrow*'s compliance with criminal law written after it was published stated: 'In this book, HAVEMANN addresses

---

284 Florian Havemann writes: 'If you scrutinise this so-called utopia, you will have a sense of it having been derived from my father's psyche alone. There is no work in Utopia because he himself has always found work to be something tedious. He fled from work whenever he could. Philosophising is a kind of escape from scientific work' (Havemann, F. 1978, p. 130).
285 In June 1979, two articles in the Criminal Code, article 106 (incitement against the state) and 129 (regulations on the dissemination of texts and materials abroad) were tightened. See Weber 1991, p. 162.
286 See BStU, MfS, HA XX/9, no. 972, p. 27.

the so-called ecological crisis of capitalism, attacks actually existing socialism as well as the socialist state system and social order in a variety of different ways and, in a relatively substantial part of the book, depicts fantastical utopian visions about the future of humanity. HAVEMANN'S anti-socialist attacks are expressed in the following statements, for instance: ....'.[287]

This is followed by quotes from the book taken from pages 37 to 66 and 199 to 230. In other words, the utopian part of the book was completely omitted and none of it cited at all. We can only speculate as to the reasons for this – either no passages were identified as 'anti-socialist' and so there were none to quote, or this part of the book was not taken seriously. The second assertion is supported by another statement from the same file referring to a RIAS broadcast made on 19 April 1981, which included an audio recording made by Havemann. The statement read: 'After repeating the hostile attacks which have already been described in detail, HAVEMANN read extensive passages from the fantastical utopian part of the aforementioned book'.[288] The Stasi did not deem these passages to be worth analysing either. After all, according to Engels, utopias and visions of the future were seen as anachronism. And the very personal, private nature of the book's content was presumably not regarded as subversive. Moreover, in *Tomorrow*, Havemann also came down very hard on the West's policies. His critique therefore addressed shortcomings and tendencies that cut across all industrial societies, irrespective of the political system.

Havemann's utopia was disregarded not only by the upper echelons of the SED but also by the party grassroots and critical intellectuals, the reformers who Havemann actually saw as being one of the target groups of his utopia. On this, Wilfriede Otto commented: 'Even after his death on 9 April 1982, some members of the intelligence services who had also been in the SED felt an affiliation with his democratic and socialist ideas, but within the party, no organised solidarity for him was forthcoming. ... Indeed, even in the citizens' groups that emerged later, representatives of which actually invoked Havemann, those who took up his aims beyond immediate legitimate political demands were few and far between'.[289]

This observation is confirmed by Christof Geisel's analysis of how the 1989/90 GDR civil rights movement responded to Havemann. According to Geisel, for the SED reformers, the eco-socialist ideas Havemann presented in *Tomorrow* were 'beyond their realms of imagination'.[290]

---

287 BStU, MfS, AU, 145/90, vol. 10, p. 346f.
288 BStU, MfS, AU, 145/90, vol. 10, p. 351.
289 Klein, Otto and Grieder 1996, p. 437.
290 Geisel 2000, p. 37.

5.1.2 Views within the GDR Opposition

Havemann attempted – with the help of his friends in the West – to publish *Tomorrow* with the support of the mass media. This meant that, besides the publication of the book itself, a whole raft of television and radio broadcasts were planned with the aim of bringing Havemann's utopian ideas to as many people as possible. Florath commented on this endeavour:

> In this way, potential readers in the GDR will have access to the text even if they can't get their hands on the book itself. That said, given the amount of broadcasting time available for consumption in the entire GDR, this media cascade will, in case of doubt, remain exactly where the political literature imported by post can be found – and that is hidden behind adverts and entertainment, behind mail order catalogues, football and glossy magazines. In order to ensure the widest possible dissemination of his comments, Havemann has also been organising more and more visually memorable images. He worked with the GDR filmmaker and member of the opposition movement Klaus Freymuth, for example, to put together a television interview to accompany *Tomorrow*, with Freymuth surreptitiously making copies of the interview in the tech labs of the GDR television channels.[291]

The copies of the book that was successfully smuggled across the border into the GDR were circulated among opposition reading circles but were not nearly as well received as Bahro's *Alternative*. At the Robert Havemann conference in 1994, Rüdiger Rosenthal gave an account of the circumstances at that time. In his words, these reading circles 'sometimes had as many as 100 participants' who met 'in dark courtyards' or somewhat 'shabby apartments'. These events were organised by people like Gerd Poppe, Frank Wolf and even Robert Havemann, who Rosenthal reported as having presented his utopia in person during such meetings: 'It was there that I witnessed Robert Havemann reading from his book *Tomorrow* in person. The meetings were all quite conspiratorial and the conditions they were held in were not the best'.[292] Unfortunately, Rosenthal did not go into detail about the content of these debates. Letters to Havemann discovered on his estate, however, showed that the book was met with a certain scepticism.

The first of these letters was written in 1981 by a 26-year-old craftsman from Dresden who had completed extended secondary school. In the letter, the man

---

291 Florath 2007, p. XXXI.
292 RHG/RH 038.

told Havemann that he found the utopian part of the book 'excessively abstract' and 'highly risky'. A 'society without production workers' or administrative management would be impossible and here Havemann agreed with Bahro. The writer of the letter went on to criticise Havemann's utopian concept of education and his ideas on issues relating to sexuality. That said, the writer welcomed the first part of Havemann's book and thus advised Havemann to avoid the 'narrative form' in his writing in future, and instead to opt for tangible criticism to reach 'a wider audience' – and, incidentally, this corresponded with the views the craftsman had heard from among his friends. His conclusion was that the book was 'interesting and worth reading'. But: 'Unfortunately your "pipe dreams" in Chapter VI weaken the overall impression quite significantly'.[293]

The second piece of correspondence found was a manuscript addressed to Havemann by the writer Karl-Heinz Jakobs, who had also come into conflict with the SED. Jakobs likewise failed to see anything positive in Havemann's utopia. For him, for example, Havemann's utopian concept of love had not been 'properly thought through'. He continued with his criticism, bemoaning that: on 'five, six pages of the 150-page description of the journey … Havemann is rip-roaring drunk'. Jakobs also struggled to understand why there was no soap in Utopia ('I really don't know what Havemann has against soap, … they wash themselves with plain water, a thought that scares me'), and he speculates sarcastically that they probably had 'no toothpaste either'.

Jakobs asks how much human sacrifice the creation of this society would have cost, recalling the countless victims of Stalinism. Referring to the *Kinderdorf* settlements or children's villages, he described an 'archipelago' in allusion to the system of Stalinist Gulags, and accused Havemann of naivety when it came to the possibility of another wrong turn in the process of transformation, something that in Jakobs's view was very likely. According to Jakobs, Havemann had outlined an 'end state' of history, an objective that Stalin had also claimed to be working towards. 'Time and again Havemann protests that the citizens of Utopia have no police. Can he seriously believe that people will voluntarily condemn themselves to the life he so euphorically describes …?' What if someone demands a car and developed roads because they 'are tired of constantly riding a donkey'? Would this not be considered 'high treason', because essentially the whole social system is being called into question? Jakobs went on to accuse Havemann of ignoring the true needs of the people of the GDR in his theorising, claiming that they were not interested in progressing towards communism, but instead in precisely those SED policy decisions that Havemann criticised

---

293   RHG/RH 022/1 vol. 79 A.

as chasing after West Germany's capitalism: more consumption, more relaxed cultural policy, fashion sense, faster cars, etc.[294]

Finally, in 2000, Christof Geisel published a study examining Havemann's impact on the opposition during the 1980s and the 1989/90 civil rights movement. As well as making use of the materials in the archives of the Robert Havemann Society, Geisel also conducted interviews with contemporary witnesses and, after viewing materials from the 1989/90 period, arrived at the conclusion that Havemann's name barely featured in any of the texts produced by the civil rights movement at the time (flyers, programmes, posters, etc.). That said, he believed that Havemann's indirect influence on these texts and demands was unmistakable.[295]

The situation was quite different with his book *Tomorrow*, however, writes Geisel: 'The disinterest that the GDR opposition of the eighties showed towards socialist-style "romantic utopia" illuminates the fact that Havemann's last book was not destined to have a major impact'.[296] Geisel described the civil rights movement as very heterogenous and for the most part much less political than Havemann and other Marxist dissidents – which was in all likelihood one of the reasons for the limited resonance that his ideas had in 1989/90. Unlike Havemann, the younger members of the opposition were not looking

> ... to build on the positive aspects of GDR history. Had the civil rights movement taken this approach, they would most certainly have seen a figure such as Robert Havemann as a mentor and an inspiration, had their self-perception not been apolitical, but rather socialist or 'romantic socialist'. At the same time, they would also have seen themselves as being capable of standing up to the state socialist monopoly with their own system of values and concepts.[297]

Havemann intended his utopia to offer hope for a better *Tomorrow*. He wanted his readers to accompany him on his journey and wanted to motivate them to make his utopia reality, at least in part. But Havemann's plan failed. Parts of his utopia were regarded 'naive or even grotesque'[298] and certainly not seen as a political guide.

---

294 All quoted from RHG/RH 023/13 vol. 111 A.
295 See Geisel 2000, p. 19 ff.
296 Geisel 2000, p. 47 f.
297 Geisel 2000, p. 54.
298 Geisel 2000, p. 48.

Geisel came to the conclusion that during the *Wende* or Peaceful Revolution, it was only the Marxist elements of the opposition that chose Havemann as a point of orientation – elements which saw themselves becoming 'increasingly marginalized over the course of the *Wende*'. Given that this group was 'no more than a disappearing minority' within the opposition anyway, 'it is probably best to refrain from linking Havemann's life and works with the demise of the GDR'.[299] And this includes *Tomorrow*.

In the appendix to his text, Geisel also included interviews with contemporary witnesses. One of these was with Bernd Gehrke, who recapitulated the view of the left-wing opposition from 1989/90 on Havemann and his utopia. According to Gehrke, the opposition movement of the 1980s had not linked the term 'alternative', which defined the identity of the movement, with Marxism. They were the new generation, while Havemann was one of the old guard. This is why *Tomorrow* was not deemed a pioneering work by this ecologically driven part of the opposition, Gehrke concluded.[300] In his interview, Reinhard Schult spoke about the texts that were discussed in the self-organised reading circles:

> Havemann was no theorist. He was a political practitioner and an agitator pushing against the system. His only theoretical work, *Dialektik ohne Dogma?*, was written too long ago and so no longer read as widely. His other stuff was, if I consider his most recent book, for example, too superficial. So, our theoretical ideas did not come from Havemann either, but rather from Bahro. *The Alternative* was read a lot, shared a lot and we conducted an awful lot of seminars on it.[301]

Lastly, in his interview, Jens Reich noted that Havemann's ecological utopia was really not of interest to the civil rights movement:

> Overall, I would agree that we really did not have any Havemann-style ideas about what form the GDR might take after the end of the gerontocracy or the politbureaucracy. On the other hand, Havemann was not a thinker like Bahro, who really tried to reform and advance Marxism. Although he [Havemann] had the same goal, he never developed a systematic approach to achieve this. The only new path Havemann com-

---

299 Geisel 2000, p. 55.
300 See Geisel 2000, p. 71ff.
301 See Geisel 2000, p. 88. Walter Janka said something similar in his memoirs, writing that, on the whole, Havemann's ideas did not reach the masses but rather just a few critical students and songwriter Wolfgang Biermann. See Janka 1992, p. 435.

mitted to paper was in the form of his eco-utopia, a kind of communist society that he saw as developing on the basis of ecological utopia. ... Consequently, Havemann's historical impact stemmed mainly from his personal views .... In terms of serving as a blueprint for the society of the future, his work was less influential. Even today it is apparent that concepts for a reformed society based on ecological principles resonate less in the East than in the West. The environmental movement in the GDR was a movement that sought to stop the country from suffocating, not a movement that wanted to change the future.[302]

Overall, it can be concluded that Havemann's *Tomorrow* enjoyed very little resonance in the GDR. Neither the state agencies nor the opposition movement took his book seriously as a utopia. If there was a response to his book at all, it referred mainly to his critique of the present.

5.2   The West

In the Federal Republic of Germany, Havemann was seen as one of the most well-known dissidents of the GDR. Everything he said tended to be reported by all the major media outlets.[303] Accordingly, the publication of *Tomorrow* was also announced in high-profile news agency reports, which appeared in many of the regional and national newspapers, and there were countless reviews of the book.[304] The first edition was published with a print run of 25,000 copies, went straight to number 22 on the *Spiegel* magazine bestseller list (no. 44/1980)[305] and was subsequently reprinted multiple times.[306]

As could be expected, the reactions to *Tomorrow* were varied and controversial to the extreme. This is exactly as Havemann had hoped and in a letter

---

302 Geisel 2000, p. 98 f.
303 The Stasi files contain a statement claiming that one of Havemann's supporters in West Germany, Manfred Wilke, had developed a marketing strategy for Havemann: 'In relation to the objectives pursued by Havemann's publications, certain observations made by Wilke in a letter to Havemann are to be highlighted. According to these observations, Havemann was interesting "only as a 'GDR dissi'" and all efforts must be made "to prevent the normalisation of his exceptional situation", "to continue to publish his books and, as in the case of Rudolf Bahro, never let the matter rest"' (BStU, MfS, AU, 145/90, vol. 13, p. 145).
304 Werner Theuer and Bernd Florath put together a large number of book reviews. See Florath and Theuer 2007b, p. 151 ff.
305 See RHG/RH 031B.
306 In 1990 by the Mitteldeutscher Verlag, for instance, and in 2010 by the Edition Zeitsprung publishing house.

to Ernst Piper dated 9 September 1980 he wrote that he was excited to see the reaction, especially from the Western leftists:

> ... from Bahro to the JUSOS [Young Socialists in the SPD] and the KPDML sects [small, radical Marxist-Leninist/communist splinter groups]. And what all the different members of the SPD have to say about it ...[307]

This section is devoted to discussing these reactions. Given the particularly high number of reviews that were published, I will focus primarily on those observations on the utopian part of the book.

First of all, it is first worth pointing out that reactions from within the Western leftist camp were not really what Havemann had hoped for. Social democrats like Richard Löwenthal regarded Havemann's reform communism as 'utopian' in the most negative colloquial sense of the word.[308] And there was no great resonance among other left-wing organisations and currents either. This is also reflected in the extensive bibliography of Havemann's works put together by Bernd Florath and Werner Theuer in 2007, which contained barely any book reviews from this side of the political spectrum.

One of the few that did exist was written by Ossip Flechtheim for *Die Zeit*, in which the author said that Havemann's utopian ideas were 'extremely original .... With its optimism, this account reminds us of Aldous Huxley's last major utopia *Island*. With a similar faith in the future, Havemann depicts a society based on a synthesis between technology and humanity'.[309] According to Flechtheim, Havemann explored the possibilities and sought a historical solution achieved through a utopia of love: 'People will say it is an impossible model. That may be so! But does that which seems impossible today not inspire us to venture to the outermost limits of possibility for tomorrow?'[310] Last but not least, Flechtheim hoped that the book would be read by a great many people.

The DKP, on the other hand, was another story altogether. Here, we can consider the views of the two party theoreticians Hans Heinz Holz and Robert Steigerwald as representative of the overall position of the party. In as early as 1977, Steigerwald wrote a book in which he already expressed his objections to Havemann's utopian ideas. He considered any attempt, even by left-wing activists, to achieve any kind of socialism other than the actually existing kind

---

307   RHG/RH 392.
308   See Richter and Wilke 1991, p. 224.
309   Flechtheim 1980.
310   Flechtheim 1980.

to be counter-revolutionary attempts that must be seen as being part of 'the arsenal used to wage psychological war against socialism'.[311] Consequently, he also attacked Havemann, accusing him of having always aligned himself with Western philosophical trends and adapted them for his own purposes. The German-American philosopher Herbert Marcuse had been his role model in the 1960s, for example.

> Of course, Havemann later adopted the 'ideas' ... of the first study of the Club of Rome regarding the 'ecological disaster' that threatened the 'East and West' in equal measure, irrespective of the social system, a notion which is in fact just a new version of convergence mythology. In short: Lenin's words are spot on when it comes to Havemann, i.e. that the revisionists always just regurgitate whatever bourgeois theory is in fashion at the time.[312]

Holz, on the other hand, published a text in 2006 criticising Havemann's utopian ideas for being no more than pessimistic ravings and denied that he followed the same tradition as Bloch's *Principle of Hope*. According to Holz, Havemann never saw utopia as something to actually try to achieve, meaning he could never have been satisfied with reality, however good it was: 'This is the argument used to deny progress, because it is something that has to happen gradually and cannot materialise from one day to the next at the wave of a magic wand'.[313]

Lucio Lombardo Radice's feature about *Tomorrow* on German radio can be regarded as reflecting the views of the Southern European arm of Eurocommunism. The transcript of the broadcast from 8 January 1981 can be found in the archives of the Robert Havemann Society under the heading 'Havemann's utopia, presented by a Roman friend: Longing for Goethe'. The landscape described in *Tomorrow* reminded Lombardo Radice of Goethe's 'Wilhelm Meister's "Pedagogical Province" where Meister's son Felix completes his education in the *Journeyman Years*. I think it is no coincidence that the lad ... in Havemann's utopia ... is also called Felix'.[314] He places *Tomorrow* alongside the works of Gruhl (*A Planet is Looted*), Bahro (*The Alternative*) and Garaudy (*Call to the Living*) and welcomed Havemann's attempt to link the question of the environment with Eurocommunism.

---

311   Steigerwald 1977, p. 11.
312   Steigerwald 1977, p. 43.
313   Holz 2006, p. 77.
314   RHG/RH 393.

Beyond the left of the political spectrum, however, there was a strong media response in the West German press. Fritz Aschka wrote an article entitled 'Robert Havemann – Träume von einer schönen neuen Welt' (Robert Havemann – Dreams of a beautiful new world) for the *Nürnberger Nachrichten* on 18 October 1980. In Aschka's words, Havemann dreamt 'of a beautiful new world in which people are free, equal and happy. The great role models shine through: Thomas More's *Utopia*, Klopstock's *German Scholars Republic*, and Franz Werfel's *Star of the Unborn*. But ... the utopia is written ... with elements of cheap science fiction'.[315] As a result, Aschka comes to the conclusion that 'the leap ... Havemann dares to take ... is too big ...', which is why Aschka also suspects escapism as being behind *Tomorrow*.

In an article by Bernd Stadelmann printed in the *Stuttgarter Nachrichten* on 22 October 1980 under the heading 'Hinter den sieben Hügeln' (Behind the seven hills), the author concludes: 'But the sum of his reflections leaves us more perplexed than hopeful, more confused than approving. *Tomorrow* ... is a fantasy world from yesterday, built with bricks from Marx and a fairy tale land, Walt Disney, Christianity and loveable anarchy'.[316]

Like Flechtheim, Stadelmann also regards Havemann's concept of transformation as stale and unoriginal: 'This world built from kitsch and fictional characters, and depicted by a writer who isn't exactly one of the most talented novelists, comes across as being more embarrassing than plausible'.

In an article for the *Handelsblatt* on 28/29 November 1980 about 'Havemann's journey to an imaginary world', Karl Peter Arens writes that this 'certainly isn't exactly everyone's dream'.[317] That said, in light of the crises at the time, Arens does consider the book to be thought provoking. Peter Erkelenz regards the book in a similar light in *Berliner Bauwirtschaft*, no. 6/1981, remarking that Havemann's utopia may very well be paradise for some people, but that it could also be interpreted as the basis for a *1984*. Ultimately though, Erkelenz sees Havemann's book as 'not warranting citation'.[318]

In his article on 24 January 1981 in *Die Welt*, Siegmar Faust states that he

> ... found this 'personal real-world utopia' so boring it was as though I had been forced to read a book written for ten-year-olds. Nonetheless, I did discover a few self-critical passages .... Of course, the environment is always to blame, whether 'capitalism' or the stalled 'revolution'. Like

---

315   RHG/RH 031B.
316   RHG/RH 031B.
317   RHG/RH 031B.
318   RHG/RH 031B.

almost all leftist intellectuals in the West, he finds the present to be 'barbaric'. So now a new Messiah arrives, providing us with more than just a ruthless 'critique of the current order', delivering us with a 'goal that we can use at any time to decide which direction our path should take'. ... Defiant, almost infantile, Havemann tries to outwit his own criticism of the system, of actually existing socialism, a criticism which in its detail is in fact occasionally very wise and astute, by doing his utmost to give the term socialism an 'alluring gloss'. ... Believing that 'true change can only be brought about by the state, the party and the government', Havemann absurdly appeals to those autocratically and illegally ruling over the 'GDR' by the grace of Moscow alone to see reason. In today's Poland people would be ridiculed for saying such things. But I would have liked to spare Havemann this ridicule.[319]

On 21 November 1980, Kurt Gehrmann then published an article in the *Neue Ruhr Zeitung* criticising Havemann's unbroken optimism: 'Anyone who knows about Havemann's personal fate, his futile attempts to ignite discussions in the GDR must ask the question of whether Havemann really dreams?'[320] In a similarly subjective review of *Tomorrow* published in the *Tagesspiegel* on 5 December 1980, Bernd Rudolf writes that he recognised 'the trauma of personal experience' as one of the book's most important influences. According to Rudolf, Havemann dealt with that trauma through his utopia, 'which, for him, was the solution to the reality that was heading straight towards destruction and demise, a reality we must escape from as long as there is still time to do so'.[321]

In his article for the *Frankfurter Allgemeine Zeitung* on 7 February 1981, Hans Herbert Götz categorised *Tomorrow* along with those more recent utopias that call unlimited economic growth into question. Like Harich, Havemann did not let other people forbid him to think. That said, Götz, too, saw the utopian chapter as *Tomorrow*'s weak point: 'This, at times quite amusing, description of utopia may well be entertaining weekend reading, but other parts of the book are of more substance'.[322] According to Götz, Havemann aspired to a future society beyond the established systems, although in the West he pinned his hopes on the unions – unlike Bahro who counted on the alternative environmental scene. Havemann's economic proposals for the Federal Republic such

---

319   BStU, MfS, AU, 145/90, vol. 10, p. 215.
320   BStU, MfS, AU, 145/90, vol. 8, p. 481.
321   BStU, MfS, AU, 145/90, vol. 8, p. 485.
322   Götz 1981.

as a 20-hour week, for example, were considered by Götz to be weak and he combined this criticism with a general rejection of utopia:

> The problems of the century cannot be solved with the 'Do-Nothing Society' propagated by Havemann and advanced by the trade unions. When – or if – we manage to give the companies and consumers in the market system the right signals, to maintain competition and bring inflation under control, we would see the waste of raw materials and other ills come to an end. This can be done if only we keep a clear head. Utopias normally make for entertaining reading. But Havemann's book ultimately shows that the economy has proven to be unsuitable material for utopias. The field is stony.[323]

While the examples give above are but a few of the many press reviews published on *Tomorrow*, they are nonetheless representative of the large majority of opinions that are not included here. In light of this, the following words in a letter from Havemann to Klaus Piper dated 28 August 1981 are all the more surprising: 'You can imagine how happy I was that *Tomorrow* was so well received after all'.[324]

The impression Havemann had was deceiving. By the 1980s, the impact of his book was no longer felt, despite the fact that it addressed the key issues being debated at the time – protection of the environment, feminism, peace. Perhaps it would have had more of a lasting effect had Havemann not passed away in 1982. Very few of the newspaper articles published after his death even mentioned his utopia.[325]

Within the academic discourse, especially the utopian discourse, however, his book most certainly did resonate. For Richard Saage, *Tomorrow* was 'one of

---

323   Götz 1981.
324   RHG/RH 393. This statement contradicts his wife's recollections. In the book she published with Joachim Widmann, she writes: '*Tomorrow* was published in spring 1980 by the publishing house belonging to Havemann's old friend Piper. He impatiently awaited the reviews. And he was disappointed. Some wrote that, in *Tomorrow*, they searched for but did not find the Havemann they knew and admired. Others thought the book was out of touch with reality. Even Havemann's friends thought he had lost touch. The book failed to spark any kind of debate across the borders of East and West Germany, as he had secretly hoped. He had overestimated the impact his text would have. He clearly realised that the cool, polite acknowledgement of *Tomorrow* in the Western press was a most respectful way of dismissing it outright' (Havemann, K. and Widmann 2003, p. 299).
325   This is the conclusion drawn following an analysis of the newspaper articles written about Havemann which are archived at the Robert Havemann Society under: RHG/RH 031B.

the most notable attempts in the GDR ... to respond to the ecological crisis by means of the classical utopian tradition'.[326]

Hubert Laitko notes that *Tomorrow* was referred to in the 'intense sustainability debates that started in the mid-1990s' and was 'regarded as "eco-socialism"'.[327]

Even in the GDR's reappraisal of history, *Tomorrow* is perceived more as an ecological utopia. Take a biography published by the Robert Havemann Society in 2007, for instance: 'The book he wrote was shaped by the long tradition of social utopias, including those penned by Thomas More, Thomas Campanella, Francis Bacon or Etienne Cabet. In his book, Havemann and his family go on a journey to the fictitious land of Utopia where he describes a society with some of the main features of socialist democracy and odd sounding fully automated technology. Besides the indirect criticism, his account directs at the reality of the GDR while addressing the issue of industrial societies endangering the natural environment at the same time'.[328]

That being said, in the context of the reappraisal of the history of the GDR, the role played by *Tomorrow* remains inconsequential. Here, it is Havemann's demand for freedom and civil rights that are most important. A good example of this is the special issue of the journal *Europäische Ideen* published in 2010 to commemorate Havemann's 100th birthday. Here, *Tomorrow* receives no more than a brief mention.[329]

---

326 Saage 2008, p. 161 f.
327 Laitko 2010c, p. 2.
328 Florath and Theuer 2007a, p. 27 ff.
329 See Wilke 2010, p. 32 f.

CHAPTER 5

Conclusions

The utopian genre is dynamic and adaptive, making it capable of surviving social crisis and upheaval. The end of utopia has been announced on more than one occasion and yet it keeps coming back in ever-new forms and will continue to do so for as long as social antagonisms prevail.

Each and every century has had its own unique contradictions and the utopian genre has always managed to adapt in response. Even in societies which were supposedly founded on an attempt to achieve real-life utopia, the genre was still adopted as a means of criticising the system, a programmatic roadmap and a means of correcting the path society had taken or of offering an alternative. The same applied to the German Democratic Republic (GDR). Over the years, for a great many reasons, a system that had officially reached its goal of creating a classless communist society lost itself in almost irreconcilable contradictions. On a political economic level, the reasons for this were largely rooted in foreign policy, but they were also associated with the treatment of the population and the working class, with social guarantees, the housing programme, arms spending and more bringing the state to its knees financially. No less serious was the lack of credibility that the whole system had. Everyone knew there were problems, even those in power who the Stasi and other bodies constantly furnished with empirical data. Yet, up until very recently, news broadcasts, the newspapers and speeches by functionaries continued to paint a rosy picture that was at odds with the population's experience and that did not align with the reality of the situation. Publicly identifying flaws and shortcomings had its risks, which is why this would become the means and the end of the opposition, a politically heterogenous group covering a broad political spectrum from anti-communists to Trotskyists, Maoists or anarchists.

In the previous chapters of this book, I introduced three of the most important members of the opposition: Rudolf Bahro, Wolfgang Harich and Robert Havemann. In other countries, these three men were widely known as critics of the system – and were thus also seen in the GDR as such (the sequence here is relevant) – they identified as politically left-leaning, they drew on utopian history and themselves wrote utopian texts. The latter is an important addition and certainly not a foregone conclusion. Indeed, they were virtually the only members of the entire opposition throughout all actually existing socialist countries to do so. The fact that they also focused on issues pertaining to the environment and growth in their utopias is something that cannot be stressed enough.

In light of this, without a shadow of a doubt, the three books analysed here make a crucial contribution to utopian discourse and also (more recent) utopian history. While Robert Havemann's subjective anarcho-communist utopia was presented as a novel, Wolfgang Harich presented us with a pretentious dystopian eco-dictatorship in interview form. Rudolf Bahro's *Alternative*, on the other hand, took the form of an analysis of 'actually existing socialism' coupled with a utopian counter-vision. We can argue that all three authors adhered to both the classic style of utopia along the lines of More's works and the type of utopia embodied by Bloch's *Principle of Hope*. While Harich revived the archistic utopian tradition, something that was particularly evident in his repeated call for a world government with a rigid population policy and centralist distribution of goods, Havemann and Bahro tended more towards the anarchistic utopian tradition. They put forward alternatives to the centralist system of the Socialist Unity Party (SED), models based on grassroots democracy that incorporated both the idea of the soviets and the commune system. All three thus adapted their utopias to the circumstances of the time in which they were written.

Although the three men were never friends, rather acting independently of one another – and sometimes even publicly against one another – as individuals, Bahro, Harich and Havemann had much in common:

1. All three saw themselves as Marxists. They adhered to the Marxist philosophy of history and believed that the GDR was (at least potentially) a better version of Germany.
2. All three clashed with the SED's policy direction and sought to overcome or at least correct this.
3. All three endured a difficult and traumatic experience in their younger years. Fleeing from Lower Silesia, Bahro lost not only his home but also his mother and both siblings. While in custody in 1956/57, Harich had the death penalty hanging over his head. Ultimately, after he was convicted, he spent eight years in prison, resulting in long-term damage to his health (including a wrongly treated heart attack and permanent medically certified paranoia). Havemann, for his part, was sentenced to death by the fascist People's Court (*Volksgerichtshof*) in 1944, only surviving thanks to a great deal of luck and his personal contacts.
4. All three were undoubtedly shaped by these extreme experiences, something that is also reflected in the self-confident manner in which they took a stand against leading SED politicians (although this did not always apply to Harich in his later life).

5. Something else all three men had in common was that they remarried several times and sometimes also engaged in extramarital affairs.
6. All three refused to be bound to the role of a father figure in a nuclear family. Despite the fact that they all had children, none of them were very involved in the upbringing of those children – albeit for different reasons.
7. All three allowed their personal lifestyles to clearly influence their respective utopias: *Tomorrow* is marked by Havemann's dandyish habitus, *Communism without Growth?* is characterised by Harich's asceticism (when it came to material luxury), which also defined his private life, and Bahro's *Alternative* reflected his ambition as an intellectual.
8. The three had (virtually) no direct contact with one another after 1964. Nor did they ever meet to discuss their ideas, whether due to personal animosities and/or because the Stasi prevented it.
9. All three initially levelled criticism at the dogmatic rigidity of actually existing socialism. Only later – indeed at almost exactly the same time – did they begin to concern themselves with the matter of the environment, which they sought to address using utopian means.
10. All three share the same fate of their works having barely any resonance today.

Despite these (and the many more) things they had in common, there was still much that distinguished Bahro, Harich and Havemann from one another, and indeed they had many differences of opinion.[1]

Firstly, they were different ages, which meant that they were at very different points in their lives when World War II came to an end. Havemann was born in 1910, studied in the Weimar Republic, experienced the rise of fascism first-hand, and indeed played an active part in the resistance from the very beginning; he took on a position as professor in the 1930s and ended up on death row in 1944, from which he was ultimately liberated by the Red Army in 1945. As a result, Havemann was already a highly respected academic and staunch anti-fascist when the Soviet Occupation Zone (SBZ)/GDR was created. Harich was born 13 years later than Havemann, meaning he experienced fascism as a child and young man, and by the end of the war, he was an aspiring intellectual, rapidly gaining a foothold in the SBZ/GDR cultural scene. Bahro, in contrast, was not born until 1935, lost his mother and siblings when fleeing Germany, and by 1945 was a penniless, homeless war child. It was not until he was in the GDR that he became an intellectual and functionary.

---

[1] See Amberger 2012b.

Examining the relationships between the different members of the trio also provides us with some interesting insights. Harich and Havemann encountered one another as early as 1956 during the discussion that took place following the 20th Congress of the Communist Party of the Soviet Union.[2] After Harich was released from prison in 1964, the recently demoted Havemann attempted to make contact with him, but Harich refused to speak with him.[3] Unlike Havemann, Harich sought to achieve his literary, and subsequently also environmental, goals by showing a willingness to cooperate, even to the point of subservience. This was also one of the main reasons why he refused to accept the role of dissident assigned to him.[4] In so doing, he distanced himself, both personally and in terms of his ideas from the internationally recognised Grünheider Community around Havemann and Biermann.[5] On this subject, Harich writes:

> I never liked Havemann, for philosophical reasons. I also found him to be an awful show-off, and all his talk of the opposition, everything he said in the Western media, all of this was no more than the usual social democratic critique of communism, but at a very low level. It was only the fact that he was a citizen of the GDR that gave his words a certain allure.[6]

Harich's ideas really had nothing in common with the goals of the Prague Spring, the search for a 'Third Way' between capitalism and actually existing socialism, *ergo* the calls for democratisation, human rights and greater freedoms. Quite the opposite, in fact. He also had a completely different lifestyle to Havemann. Harich led a modest existence, thought little of technical progress, did not drive a car, was not keen on travelling and was opposed to drugs. In each of these respects, the exact opposite applied to Havemann. And there is plenty of evidence of the derogatory remarks the two made about one another over the years. In the late 1970s, for instance, Havemann said of Harich:

---

2 See Prokop 2000.
3 'When I was released from prison he tried to contact me. At the time, I wasn't home and my mother picked up the phone and said, for goodness sake Mr Havemann will you just leave my son in peace. He has suffered enough. Nothing against you, but I will not be telling him that you called. And then she did tell me after all: Son, I beg of you, do not go and visit Havemann, he is involved in another political opposition movement. Please, for my sake, don't do it. And indeed, I did not call him. Once bitten, twice shy' (Harich 1999, p. 370).
4 See Amberger 2011b, p. 20.
5 See Amberger 2012b; Harich, A. 2007, p. 169, Prokop 2000, p. 142.
6 Harich 1999, p. 370.

Harich came back from his nine years in Bautzen a broken man, politically speaking. While he was in prison the role he took on was not a very positive one. Today, Harich is a conformist, completely devoid of political relevance.[7]

And Harich, for his part, remarked on Havemann in an article for the *Berliner Extra-Dienst* in 1976, saying that 'whether towing the line or as a dissident, he had always been no more than a mediocre scientist, as a philosopher, Havemann has always been an ignoramus, a nonentity'.[8] As a result, until the day Havemann died in 1982, the two Marxist environmental pioneers and SED critics never managed to reconcile their differences.

Harich's and Havemann's attitude towards Bahro was quite different and was burdened with less historical baggage. That said, Harich objected to Bahro's support for the Prague Spring and found very little positive to say about *The Alternative*. Moreover, shortly after Bahro went to prison, he stated:

> It is not my problem. In the *ND* [Neues Deutschland – the official mouthpiece of the SED Politburo] it said that he had been convicted for revealing state secrets. That is exactly what he did and he has gone to prison for it. Thank God there was no clemency for him as there had been for HAVEMANN. BAHRO has to be held accountable for what he has done and does not get to play the martyr.[9]

And in an interview with the *Kölner Stadt-Anzeiger* in May 1978, the view Harich expressed about the differences between his and Bahro's ideas was not much less blatant; Harich said that although he agreed with Bahro's utopian outline, he did not find his transformational subject fitting: 'I feel more of an affinity to a political apparatchik, regardless of how stubborn he may be, than the most talented of trained engineers or the smartest of business executives and in our system, if the politbureaucracy that is so unpopular in Bahro's feels the need to rein these people in a little, then this is not something I am opposed to'.[10]

That said, writing about Bahro in an article in the *Spiegel* in 1979, Harich remarked: 'I hope that this highly talented, well-read and prolific thinker is released very soon'.[11] It was clear, therefore, that he still had great respect for Bahro's ideas.

---

7   Havemann 1978a, p. 80f.
8   BStU, MfS, AP, 4578/71, vol. 7, p. 15. See also Harich 1999, p. 370.
9   BStU, MfS, AP, 4578/71, vol. 8, p. 48.
10 BStU, MfS, AP, 4578/71, vol. 7, p. 31.
11 Harich 1979b, p. 75.

And what about Bahro, what did he think of Harich? His postscript to the GDR edition of *The Alternative* published in 1990 provides us with insight into this:

> Unfortunately because of my own prejudices I have neglected to read Wolfgang Harich's *Communism without Growth?* since it came out in 1979. ... However, Wolfgang Harich showed up at an event under the Berlin Television Tower in early December 1989, which I too was attending, and he supported my fundamental position better than I could have done myself. I have to assume that we were in fact in agreement on many things. Quite irrespective of this, it is high time that we do him justice while he is alive – both in legal terms (he spent four times the number of years in prison that I did) and as a thinker whose works must be published because they are so very necessary.[12]

In the mid-1960s, Havemann and Bahro established themselves as critics of the SED. The former from 'above' and with quite the impact in the public eye, and the latter from 'below' and until 1977 very much under the radar if at all possible. When Bahro wrote *The Alternative*, Havemann was already the best-known dissident in the GDR. In summer 1977, before the publication of *The Alternative*, when asked confidentially by an unofficial collaborator whether 'he saw himself as a Havemann mark 2 and whether in future he should be addressed as Rudi Havemann or Robert Bahro', Bahro responded as follows: 'In some respects, yes, this is true but in others it is not, as his philosophical achievements are of a far superior quality and not as superficial as Havemann's manuscripts'.[13]

After Bahro was detained, Havemann publicly expressed solidarity with him. As a result, the SED leadership was nervous that the two critics would meet during the short period of time between Bahro's release from prison and his departure for the West. Indeed, both men were keen to have such a meeting. The Stasi files give an indication of just how much effort was made to prevent any such encounter from taking place. After Havemann wrote an open letter to Kurt Hager calling for Bahro's release,[14] the party leadership attempted to

---

12   Bahro 1990, p. 558.
13   BStU, MfS, HA XX/9, no. 880, p. 144.
14   See Kroh 1988, p. 27. In a *Spiegel* interview in autumn 1978, Havemann had already stated: 'Of course I would love to meet with Bahro and discuss many of his ideas in more detail. Perhaps one difference between him and I is that I consider his concept of the "subalternity" of the masses ... in the form in which he presents it, somewhat unfortunate' (Havemann 1978c).

muzzle him for the duration of the trial. The house arrest in Grünheide, which had actually been lifted in the summer of 1979, was temporarily reimposed in October of that same year for the time between Bahro's release from prison and him leaving the GDR.[15] An internal Stasi report dated 15 October 1979 stated: 'A meeting between BAHRO and HAVEMANN that was to take place in the latter's city apartment at 19.00 hrs ... was prevented by means of the relevant security measures. BAHRO informed an operational security officer that he had a scheduled meeting with Havemann'.

Despite being instructed to refrain from attending such a meeting

> BAHRO remained stubborn. For him, a meeting with HAVEMANN was an 'material and existential issue'. He did not agree with HAVEMANN's ideological position and a meeting with HAVEMANN would not focus on problems pertaining to the GDR but rather on him defending his position to HAVEMANN. In his words: 'I cannot leave the GDR without having spoken to HAVEMANN first'.

Bahro claimed '... the dispute with HAVEMANN was about the fact that there were parts of HAVEMANN's ideological position he did not condone, particularly his misjudgement regarding the role of the working class. Moreover, BAHRO's dispute with HAVEMANN was also about the fact that his application to emigrate to the [Federal Republic of Germany] FRG should not be regarded, as HAVEMANN claims, as betrayal'.[16]

In the end, however, Bahro was persuaded by the Stasi not to attend the meeting after all. Thus, no meeting ever took place between these two members of the opposition. In *Elemente einer neuen Politik* (Elements of a new policy) Bahro expressed his regret at never having got to know Havemann personally. He also praised his courage as a dissident. Moreover, Bahro endorsed Havemann's call not to surrender the GDR by annexing it to the Federal Republic.[17] At the memorial held in West Berlin on 18 April 1982 after Havemann's death, Bahro gave a speech praising Havemann for his role as a supporter of the peace movement in both the East and the West.[18]

---

15   See Havemann, K. and Widmann 2003, p. 291, BStU, MfS, AU, 145/90, vol. 5, p. 233 f.
16   BStU, MfS, AU, 145/90, vol. 10, p. 96 f. According to the Stasi file, at a birthday party in February 1980, Havemann said of Bahro that he led a 'sad and miserable existence in the FRG and would have been better off staying in the GDR' (BStU, MfS, HA XX/9, no. 972, p. 1).
17   See Bahro 1980a, p. 37 ff.
18   See Bahro 1982, p. 67.

However, the differences and similarities between Bahro, Harich and Havemann were not only evident at the personal and inter-personal level but especially also when it came to their approach to utopia. Unlike Bahro and Harich, for instance, Havemann did not design his utopia as a philosophical, discursive vision of the future with no protagonists. Instead, his work comprised an extensive fictitious travelogue with various protagonists who he even named, thus meeting the main criteria of the classic political novel.

The works of all three writers contain the key elements of utopia: they all criticise the status quo and they all outline a theoretical alternative extrapolated from the trends of the present day. All three utopias contain normative statements on types of settlement, architecture and the concept of the common good. In each case, questions centred on the fields of work, science and technology are discussed in detail. Even the 'soft' political issues, such as women, the family and child rearing, art and culture are included. The role played by and the need for a 'New Man' in each of the models of the future also features in all three utopias, as does the role and function that future elites have in the transformation and/or the proper functioning of the respective utopia.

The works of Bahro, Harich and Havemann all refer to political utopia *and* Marxism in a positive light.[19] Collectively, albeit each in their own (in Harich's case admittedly reserved)[20] way, they established their utopian concepts on the basis of Bloch's *Principle of Hope*. In other words, utopia should be at once concrete and abstract, have short and long-term goals, and should seek to make Marx's *11th Thesis on Feuerbach* reality. They were thus in keeping with Bloch's 'Programme of a Utopian-Charged Marxism'.[21] All three men intentionally broke with the Marxist *Bilderverbot*, while at the same time refusing to restrict themselves programmatically to demanding Western freedoms. '[F]reedom as the utopia of western capitalism is chloroform'[22] writes Bloch in *The Principle of Hope*. And Bahro, Harich and Havemann all followed this credo, meaning Saage's main criticism of Bloch applies to them, too, i.e. that Bloch's image of the future has associations with 'the ideas of homogeneity typical

---

19   'It would certainly not be exaggerated at this juncture to underscore the uniqueness of the way in which the GDR opposition appropriated utopia. ... Along with the "yes" to utopia, came the "yes" to Marxism. However, the latter was modified by Harich, Bahro and Havemann, which meant that it came into conflict with the official dogmatism of the GDR. As has been established, when it comes to utopia, the appropriation of Marxism was another unprecedented act that had no equivalent in either the West or the other state socialist countries in the Eastern Bloc' (Heyer 2009, p. 40).
20   See Harich 2004, p. 116 f.
21   Saage 2003, p. 423.
22   Bloch 1986, p. 584. See also Saage 2008, p. 157.

of the classic utopian tradition'.[23] In Bloch's utopia, the common good and the welfare of the individual coincide, a 'public office' deals with the remaining issues between people, operates pastoral care and manages any remaining work, which is to be carried out voluntarily. This scenario reminds Saage of Huxley's *Brave New World*, though Bloch apparently ignores the shortcomings of Huxley's utopia:

> Irrespective of the widely known political crimes committed in Stalin's Soviet Union in the name of historical progress, Bloch rejected the notion of any utopia having a claim to validity that – like utopias of the classic tradition and their post-materialist successors – accepted 'incompleteness as their fate, ... destined to only ever advance on the goal'.[24]

This flawed self-criticism of enclosed utopian visions and failure to consider the line of conflict between the individual and society is inherent in the works of Bahro, Harich and Havemann alike. One thing which distinguishes the three authors from one another, however, is how they address the question of the concept and subject of transformation. While Bahro saw his 'cultural revolution' as a continual process with progress and setbacks, naming the intelligentsia as a progressive subject, Havemann sticks with the proletariat as the subject of transformation. Like Bahro, Havemann also envisages a lengthy process but he has more confidence in the 'masses' than Bahro.[25] For this reason, within the context of actually existing socialist states, he rejects the conspiratorial strategy of a 'League of Communists',[26] as well as Harich's covert activities in 1956.

Despite the differences between them, Bahro and Havemann both envisaged a transformation 'from below'. Whether by the working class or underchallenged intellectuals, the ruling classes were to be replaced during the process of transformation. Harich, on the other hand, created his path to *Communism Without Growth* 'from above'. In keeping with archistic tradition of thought,

---

23   Saage 2003, p. 424.
24   Saage 2003, p. 426.
25   See Havemann 1978a, p. 98, Röhrborn 2008, p. 125 f., Saage 2008, p. 162 f.
26   Havemann wrote: 'This League would be an opposition counterparty, one based purely on ideology, with no economic or social foundation in society, a know-it-all party that would possibly have a much stronger claim to being the vanguard and elite cadre party. This would amount to the internal party opposition splitting off from the party and confronting it, while in actual fact its only job can be to lead the party out of its dead-end and prepare it for the huge challenges it will have to face. It is certainly not the responsibility of the opposition to confront the party, but rather to take action within its living body' (Havemann 1980b, p. 220). See also Havemann 1978a, p. 80, Ferst 2005, p. 14.

he relied on the institutions as the custodians of transformation, pinning his hopes on an understanding of necessity based on a philosophy of history. Havemann criticises him for this very approach in *Tomorrow*:

> But what state, what government anywhere in the world would be prepared to do this! Does Wolfgang Harich really believe that socialist and communist parties in the capitalist industrial countries could arouse anyone's interest with his slogans about true communism? Fortunately for the international workers' movement, we have at least reached the point where these parties have broken away from the principles behind actually existing socialism. According to Harich, however, everything which even the defenders of actually existing socialism attempt to make palatable by depicting it as a transient, short-lived evil, must be extolled and immortalised as the only cure for humanity. Harich invokes Babeuf. We are somehow reminded of the statement in Marx's introduction to the *Eighteenth Brumaire* about the reappearance of tragedy in the shape of a farce.[27]

All three authors referred to the societies that emerged following each successful transformation as communist. And indeed they were, despite the differences between them. In theoretical communism, like the closely related utopian history, both an archistic and anarchistic line of tradition can be identified. Havemann followed the anarchistic and Harich the archistic line, with Bahro falling somewhere between the two. Throughout his works, Havemann combined grassroots democracy and centralism, much as Harich had, albeit using a very different approach. The point of connection between Bahro's and Harich's thinking can be found in Lenin's vanguard concept of transformation. The latter's idea of 'democratic centralism' left distinct traces on Bahro and Harich's ecological utopian ideas, despite the fact that in the *Alternative*, Bahro frames his statements on utopia in a 'decidedly anti-Marxist manner'.[28]

Besides the strong Marxist influence on the texts, the reference to ecology is the most important similarity between the three utopias studied here. Shortly after the publication of the Meadows Report in 1972 and in the context of the discourse it fuelled on the limits to growth, Bahro, Harich and Havemann turned to political utopia as a means of finding solutions to these problems.

---

27   Havemann 1980b, p. 51.
28   Saage 2008, p. 38.

They sought ideas as to what form life, humble in terms of material possessions yet far happier from an immaterial perspective, might take and how that could be achieved.[29]

In light of this, all three utopias can be situated in post-materialist utopian discourse, which until that point had been almost exclusively dominated by US-American works. Unlike the main protagonists in the USA, however, which included writers such as Ursula K. Le Guin, Ernest Callenbach and Marge Piercy, the three GDR authors drew on Marxism, a fact that impacted the holistic nature of their texts and their penchant to draw on the philosophy of history, in particular. At the same time, they introduced influences into the discourse that went beyond the hermeneutic horizon of the Americans.

It is thus doubtful that a utopian outline like *Communism Without Growth?* would even have been conceivable on the other side of the Atlantic. And indeed, of all the many post-growth utopias, it is this text in particular that therefore occupies a special place. According to Heyer, Harich was responsible for a 'renaissance of the archistic utopian tradition to follow Burrhus Frederic Skinner's *Walden Two*'.[30] When it came to Bahro and Havemann, however, Saage felt they highly resembled 'the Western post-materialist utopias: decentralised economic entities, centralism reduced to an unavoidable minimum, a break with the dynamic of artificially created needs as well as direct democratic participation following the example of the Marxian model of the Paris Commune'.[31]

Unlike the Western post-materialist utopias, however, the works studied here are based on (dialectical) materialism. Nature mysticism, spirituality or esotericism are nowhere to be found. Religion plays a marginal role and the choice to practice religion or not is down to the individual. One thing that is clearly rejected is the hostility towards religion that prevailed under Stalinism and still had a lingering impact on the GDR. That said, a break was made with institutionalised religion and the church in general, which were relegated to the past in all three visions of the future.

Harich, on the other hand, saw the state political institutions as the sole alternative to the apocalypse and was the only one to take this position. Bahro did not completely discard the Leninist vanguard concept, instead modifying it with the addition of grassroots democracy, however. In Havemann's utopia, in contrast, there was no longer any trace of étatism. Nevertheless, he continued

---

29   See Hertwig 1977, p. 1098.
30   Heyer 2009, p. 34.
31   Saage 2008, p. 162 f.

to adhere to a technical vanguard, which was to implement his scientifically based methods of world salvation.

If we consider the characteristics of post-materialist utopia, the three books are fundamentally in agreement on the topics of ecology, feminism, decentralisation of infrastructures and the political structures of society (with the exception of Harich), criticism of consumption, the importance of regulating or halting growth and the satisfaction of non-material needs. In addition, all three utopias were based on a positive concept of work.

The books do depart from the newer utopias, however, especially when it comes to the self-reflexive nature of the utopias, their tendency to draw on the philosophy of history and the associated tension between the individual and the collective. Although, in American utopias of this type, the latent danger of coercion and disempowerment could never be completely dispelled, it was always part of the blueprint, thus making these utopias somewhat fragile constructs. In Bahro, Harich and Havemann's utopias, in contrast, this source of tension did not exist. Thus, the latter evidently do not fulfil the criterion of post-materialist utopias that Martin d'Idler describes as follows: 'Faced with the task of credibly reconciling individual freedom and collective solidarity in a utopian outline, these utopianists end up with a less altruistic image of the "New Man" and thus less perfect social harmony than the traditional utopian discourse, where perfect happiness and freedom from pain no longer seem realistic, material consumption has to be restricted in light of the limits to growth, and people's thirst for power and aggression can no longer be denied'.[32]

And yet, this is precisely what Bahro, Harich and Havemann do, albeit not deliberately. In the process, they deviate so dramatically from the concept of the post-materialist utopia that a modified understanding of the concept has to be considered. When it comes to the environmental movement, Joachim Radkau draws the distinction that it 'is usually listed among the "new social movements", but this affinity by no means precludes a sense of foreignness or animosity'.[33] Following on from this, it is possible to see the three utopias studied here as independent from the rest of the genre: they were not primarily post-materialist, but above all addressed ecological issues. Far more than was the case in US discourse, for these three GDR thinkers, the question of growth played a, if not *the*, central role – particularly with regards to the Marxist philosophy of history, whose objective, which was the achievement of the 'fount' of all things material for all people, needed to be modified. Questions pertain-

---

[32] Idler 2007, p. 208.
[33] Radkau 2014, pp. 397–8.

ing to the 'soft' policy areas were side-lined by this problem, playing a far less important role than, for instance, in Marge Piercy's works. From this perspective, it would be more fitting to use the term 'post-growth utopia' to describe Bahro, Harich and Havemann's texts than the concept of the post-materialist utopia. This also means that the three texts examined here are compatible with today's post-growth discourse, which is conducted primarily in the academic field beyond Germany's borders under the headings of degrowth and décroissance.

After three decades of utopia losing its shine, and the 'TINA' or 'there is no alternative' principle postulated by Margaret Thatcher coming to dominate the economic and social policy of the nations of the Western world (and not only there), a few years ago, change began to set in. Given that so little time has passed since then, the full impact and scope of this change cannot yet be seen. There is, however, some indication of its effect, with the popularity of 'attac's' motto 'A different world is possible' as much worth a mention here as the fact that Germany nominated '*alternativlos*' or 'without alternative' the 'ugliest word of the year' in 2010.

At the same time, 20 years after the end of Soviet-style actually existing socialism, the spectre of communism seems to pale in comparison with new crises. The notion of the 'end of history' postulated by Francis Fukuyama in the 1990s is now being called into question, not least due to the serious crisis of legitimacy of neoliberalism's economic policy and to recent environmental disasters such as the oil spill in the Gulf of Mexico or the Fukushima (Daiichi) nuclear disaster. Paradigm shifts in global politics, climate change, resource conflicts, environmental degradation etc. make ecologically utopian thinking more important than ever before. And once we free Bahro, Harich and Havemann from their GDR shackles, their ideas are still of the utmost relevance today.[34] The dichotomy between eco-dictatorship and the Third (post-materialist) Way that they represent is just as prevalent today. When it comes to how their utopias were received, however, there is certainly room for improvement. Taking the final years of the GDR as a starting point, the manner in which their works were received can be described as follows: In the GDR, the phenomenon of

---

34   In *DIE ZEIT Geschichte* magazine in 2009 Evelyn Finger wrote: 'Anybody who today bemoans the fact that Marxian doctrines in the GDR were turned into agitprop must remember that the intellectuals in the GDR who actually took a stance were themselves Marxists: Ernst Bloch, Hans Mayer, Wolfgang Harich, Rudolf Bahro. The celebrated alternative did exist, at least in people's minds – even though the struggle ... for a liberal form of Marxism and enlightened form of socialism are not compatible with today's post-utopian debate' (Finger 2009, p. 95).

the post-materialist utopia was in fact also mentioned in official publications, albeit belatedly. In 1987, for example, Dietrich-Eckhard Franz, a member of the Section on Marxist-Leninist Philosophy at the University of Jena, published a book on the social utopias of the nineteenth century with the popular science Urania-Verlag publishers, in which he also discussed modern utopias. And while he, too, maintained Engels's position on classic utopias, he did believe 'that the utopias had retained their vital force, even in the subsequent period'.[35] Franz acknowledged and described the post-materialist renaissance of the genre in the West, which took place against the background of the dangers to humans and their environment caused by capitalism: 'Yet it is this very fact that creates such incredibly fertile ground for the renaissance of utopian thinking, for the emergence of new utopias in that part of the world. These utopias are extremely diverse, spanning the entire spectrum, from hope and forced optimism on the one end to boundless pessimism on the other'.[36] What Franz neglected to mention, however, was that Bahro, Harich and Havemann had already written this very type of utopia in the actually existing socialist GDR more than a decade earlier. According to Franz, the new utopias only applied to the capitalist part of the world.

After the Peaceful Revolution, the attitude of the West German press towards the former left-wing dissidents changed dramatically. They lost their privileged status and instead often found themselves subject to criticism for their adherence to socialist ideals. Yet, they were not welcomed by the Party of Democratic Socialism (PDS), either, as Werner Mittenzwei describes: 'There was an aversion to new ideas and erstwhile reformers. As a result, Wolfgang Harich and Rudolf Bahro, who had modified but not abandoned their Marxist position, did not stand a chance in this party'.[37] Mittenzwei went on to remark on Bahro after 1990:

> He did not open up any new fronts, instead saying that he was a member of the SED, in good times and in bad. ... At a time where theories were receding and utopias being denounced, he found open-minded listeners. Although he was never in a position to assert any kind of specific orientation, he achieved influence by example. The prophetic nature of his views was at once a source of irritation and fascination.[38]

---

35 Franz 1987, p. 13.
36 Franz 1987, p. 15f.
37 Mittenzwei 2003, p. 387.
38 Mittenzwei 2003, p. 467.

Today, Bahro, Harich and Havemann are seen primarily as critics of the SED. At the same time, however, there are an increasing number of voices citing their ecological ideas. To mark Havemann's 100th birthday, for example, Hubert Laitko wrote: 'His greatness lay in the fact that, at a very early stage, he understood the existential significance of the first major diagnoses of environmental disaster for the very essence of our understanding of society'.[39] Some years ago, Christoph Geisel claimed that although Havemann had never reached the theoretical heights of Bahro's *Alternative*, '*Tomorrow*, in particular, provided highly practicable ways of achieving a synthesis of the "old" traditional socialism and "new" issues, especially those pertaining to the environment which young GDR dissidents, in particular, were troubled by'.[40] And, in his 2011 book *Ära der Ökologie* (published in English in 2014 under the title *The Age of Ecology*), Joachim Radkau portrayed Havemann as 'the most prominent visionary of ascetic ecologism to come out of East Germany'.[41] For Marko Ferst, the evolution of the three critics of the SED into environmental thinkers was 'a remarkable circumstance' – especially because this took place 'through conflict with their own state'.[42]

Several other writers also recognised the connection between pioneering ecological ideas and political utopia. In his recently published book, *The Conquest of Nature*, David Blackbourn of Harvard University, for instance, writes:

> Dissident intellectuals took up the issue of ecology from a utopian socialist perspective. Wolfgang Harich's *Communism without Growth?* (1975) ... criticized Erich Honecker's attachment to western 'norms of consumption'. Two years later Rudolf Bahro's *The Alternative* called for the 're-establishment of ecological stability' and a 'move away from the exploitation of nature by material production towards the adaptation of production to the natural cycle'. Then, in 1980, the dissident scientist Robert Havemann published an essay collection. *Tomorrow: Industrial Society at*

---

39   Laitko 2010c, p. 4.
40   Geisel 2000, p. 48.
41   Radkau 2014, p. 374.
42   Ferst 2005, p. 21. And elsewhere, he wrote: 'Havemann saw utopia as a critical examination of the world in which we live, and he had a wish. He wanted people to help, he wanted others to continue developing the outline he had attempted to sketch, to create a more diverse, more colourful image, full of new ideas. Continuing this research on the future was certainly closer to what Robert Havemann would have wanted than going to court to establish retrospectively that certain repressive action against him was indeed unjust' (Ferst 2000).

the Crossroads outlined an 'ecological crisis' that, in Havemann's view, capitalism could not and 'real existing socialism' would not address.[43]

With the problems addressed in the three books for the most part remaining unresolved to this day – with the exception of actually existing socialism – this raises the question as to the contemporary relevance of *Communism without Growth?*, *Tomorrow* and *The Alternative*. In terms of their implementation, Bahro, Harich and Havemann's utopias were based on a dual East/West strategy. In terms of facilitating a transformation of the system, for the authors, the biggest advantage of actually existing socialism lay in its material basis, in other words the elimination of the private ownership of the means of production. This part of their respective utopias has become obsolete, overtaken by history. The passages on the antagonism between the capitalist, growth-driven industrial society and the potential limits to growth, in contrast, are still relevant to this day. In fact, a whole four decades since the Meadows Report was published, this contradiction remains unresolved and continues to be the subject of debate.

Indeed, an analysis of these debates reveals that, in essence, the arguments are astonishingly similar to Bahro, Harich and Havemann's. One difference, however, is that today's discourses rarely feature the kind of holistic, historically deterministic scenarios presented by the three GDR Marxists, as the following statement by Radkau illustrates:

> For someone who believes in a grand definitive solution to the problems of the environment, all existing strategies taken individually, will appear hopelessly limited. Up to now, however, it does not look as if there is such a grand solution. Environmental protection is a never-ending process make up of steps that are never complete in themselves.[44]

Even today, solutions based on eco-dictatorship can still be found, albeit mostly in the form of dystopias.[45] With his 2010 book *Ausweg Ökodiktatur? Wie unsere*

---

43 Blackbourn 2011, p. 327.
44 Radkau 2014, p. 324.
45 For instance, this is illustrated by Elmar Altvater when he outlines the following: 'In this way, the endgame could result in an absurd scenario. The military will be deployed to ensure the provision of energy and raw materials. The use of fossil fuels is partly responsible for the greenhouse effect, the consequences of which – unusual weather patterns, droughts, floods, crop failure, species extinction – in turn, are forcing people to migrate. At the same time, however, the military are also being mobilised, as is already the case today, to protect the borders of "Fortress Europe"' (Altvater 2008). Morris-Keitel explained the

Demokratie an der Umweltkrise scheitert (Is the eco-dictatorship the solution? How our democracy is failing because of the environmental crisis), German journalist and writer Bernhard Pötter gives us an insight into the current status of this debate. In his book, Pötter also refers to Harich as a visionary of the Left, rightly pointing out that, after 1990, Harich distanced himself from the concept of eco-dictatorship.[46] The only conceivable way in which eco-dictatorship could ever become reality in the future – and here we must concur with the position Harich took in his later years – would be in the form of a fascist model. Consequently, beyond the political right, no other discernible, positively intended archistic, post-materialist utopia has been published since Harich's *Communism without Growth?*. That said, eco-dystopian scenarios have been described, including Margaret Atwood's *The Handmaid's Tale* (1985) and Dirk C. Flecks *GO! Die Ökodiktatur* (GO! The eco-dictatorship, 1994).

In light of the fact that we have not managed to overcome the crises of the growth society, indeed, if anything, these are likely to escalate (the climate crisis, resource conflict, hunger, environmental degradation, overproduction), there is still a need for utopias. For all the reasons mentioned above, it will be a long time before the archistic tradition is capable of hegemony. Provided they are of a self-reflexive nature, anti-statist, anti-authoritarian, anarchistic utopias, on the other hand, will still remain valid for the future – albeit not as concrete plans for the faithful implementation of a theoretical vision of that future but as an ideational corrective and impetus for debates about urgent problems of the time.

Morris-Keitel rightly states:

> What ecological utopias ... have in common is their ruthless criticism of the systematic, environmentally destructive exploitation of the global market. In contrast to the strategies employed by the ideologists of progress or the cynicism that characterises the representatives of postmodernism and post-history (along with their highly specific demands for utopian thought to be adaptable), ecological utopianists combine various praxis-oriented, economic counter-concepts to global capitalism which are quite clearly based on democratically enlightened and eco-social vis-

---

success of the eco-dystopian genre after 1990 as follows: 'In actual fact, literary cynicism is supposed to point the readers towards the very cynicism with which the powers that be in politics and the economy are leading society into the future, devoid of a concrete plan or prospects – and very much aware of the ecological consequences' (Morris-Keitel 2004, p. 18).

46 See Pötter 2010, p. 25.

ions of society. With this in mind, the concepts of eco-socialism that Robert Havemann emphatically defended have, if anything, become more relevant since the Peaceful Revolution, especially given that, for the majority of people, they are in many respects the only hope left.[47]

Havemann's utopia is now fraught with dangers that were perhaps not foreseeable at the time it was written – we only need to cast our minds back to his idea of channelling wastewater from industry into the Adriatic or his failure to explain how nuclear waste would be disposed of. And, even at the time, Havemann generally found himself in an outsider position in the post-materialist (utopian discourse) because of his technological fantasies designed to solve environmental problems. Nothing much has changed in that regard. As Radkau says '... there is some evidence that the way to a globally sustainable environment lies more through increased forest growth, cycling and birth control than through geo-engineering, underground CO_2 sequestration or giant wind-farms, not to speak of nuclear power plants'.[48]

Whether or not this can resolve the antagonism between the growth imperative of capitalism[49] and the finiteness of resources, remains to be seen. Ignoring this contradiction, however, or limiting the debate to 'green capitalism' only[50] would be very blinkered indeed. And for this very reason, there will continue to be a need for political utopias in the future. Against the backdrop of global crisis, the function of political utopias must be to present alternative models of society based on an analysis and/or critique of the present. Historical determinism, a dogmatic know-it-all attitude and holistic one-size-fits-all solutions are just as misplaced here as the whitewashing and denial of the crisis.

Yet, looking at the most recent climate policy outcomes, we have the impression that it is precisely this type of escapism that is most prevalent.[51] That said, in the past it is crisis scenarios which have proven to be particularly fertile ground for utopias.[52] Robert Misik describes the current state of affairs as follows:

> In any case, the biggest enemy of utopianism was always small-minded realism. Its maxims were always: Change? No chance. Good ideas? They

---

47 Morris-Keitel 2004, p. 41.
48 Radkau 2014, p. 418.
49 For more on this antagonism, see Amberger 2011a, Jackson 2009, Radt 2010.
50 For more on 'green capitalism', see Müller and Kaufmann 2009.
51 See Neef 2008, Pötter 2010, p. 16 ff.
52 See Misik 2009, p. 6.

will just fail because the system is holding steady, flying on autopilot. Reform? It's too expensive, we can't afford it. For the amount of money that has been pumped into the financial system in the last few months, we could have implemented every single good idea each and every do-gooder ever had. A billion is nothing in this day and age. Even basic income could almost have been paid out of the petty cash. And these days of flying on autopilot will only send us into the abyss. Such staid 'realism', which paralyses any kind of thinking or ideas, is no longer an option.[53]

Martin d'Idler emphasises that, given the global nature of all of today's problems and the resultant need for a global solution, future utopias must be globalised, too. In his view, the destruction of the environment, hunger, the North-South conflict and the terrorism seen in its wake are some of the challenges that utopia will have to rise to in the future.[54] And the striking thing here is that Bahro, Harich and Havemann already considered this global scale and these very problems in their utopias. In all likelihood owing to their Marxist internationalism, in as early as the 1970s, all three authors took their thinking beyond the confines of the GDR to incorporate a utopian global dimension and, in so doing, overcame, at least to some extent, the Eurocentrism of many Western Marxists.

Their utopias are at once anachronistic and highly topical. They are anachronistic because the context in which they were written has little in common with the world of today. Their exceptional relevance to the critique of growth and the development of post-growth models, on the other hand, is what makes them highly topical today.

---

53   Misik 2009, p. 7.
54   See Idler 2007, p. 276f.

Bibliography

Agde, Günter (ed.) 2000, *Kahlschlag: Das 11. Plenum des ZK der SED 1965* (2nd edition), Berlin.
Akademie für Gesellschaftswissenschaften beim ZK der SED (ed.) 1988, *Autorenkollektiv: Philosophie für eine neue Welt*, Berlin (East).
Allertz, Robert 2006, 'Sänger und Souffleur'. In *Sänger und Souffleur: Biermann, Havemann und die DDR*, edited by Robert Allertz, Berlin: 9–38.
Altvater, Elmar 2008, 'Das Endspiel. Energie gegen Klima – der Ölpreis weckt nukleare Begehrlichkeiten' in *Freitag*, no. 24, 13 June 2008: 1.
Amberger, Alexander 2010a, *Der Stalinismus: Totalitarismus oder Oligarchie?* Munich.
Amberger, Alexander 2010b, 'Politik ist nicht alternativlos', in *Neues Deutschland*, 10 June 2010: 15.
Amberger, Alexander 2011a, 'Abkehr vom Wachstumsdogma. Zwei neue Publikationen zur Thematik erschienen' in *Neues Deutschland*, 18 April 2011: 9.
Amberger, Alexander 2011b, 'Die Wandlungen des ökologischen Harich', in Alexander Amberger & Siegfried Prokop, *Ein 'rot-grünes' Deutschland? Über eine Vision Wolfgang Harichs 1989/90*, Helle Panke e. V. (ed.): *hefte zur ddr-geschichte*, no. 123, Berlin: 5–24.
Amberger, Alexander 2011c, 'Der konstruierte Dissident. Wolfgang Harich und seine Rolle als Oppositioneller' in Alexander Amberger & Andreas Heyer, *Der konstruierte Dissident. Wolfgang Harichs Weg zu einem undogmatischen Marxismus*, Helle Panke e. V. (ed.): *hefte zur ddr-geschichte*, no. 127, Berlin: 5–31.
Amberger, Alexander 2012a, 'Versachlichung', in *Neues Deutschland*, supplement to the Frankfurt Book Fair, 10–14 October 2012: 18.
Amberger, Alexander 2012b, 'Wolfgang Harich und die aus-der-Bahn-Geworfenen. Das Spannungsfeld Bahro-Harich-Havemann' in *Wolfgang Harichs Politische Philosophie*, edited by Andreas Heyer, Hamburg: 36–54.
Amberger, Alexander 2013, 'Ernst Bloch in der DDR' in *Hoffnung–Utopie–Marxismus, Deutsche Zeitschrift für Philosophie*, vol. 61, no. 4 (October 2013): 561–76.
Amery, Carl 1978, 'Gnade und Ungnade: Angst machen sie beide …. An Wolfgang Harich' in *Solidarität mit Rudolf Bahro. Briefe in die DDR*, edited by Hannes Schwenger. Reinbek bei Hamburg: 38–46.
Amery, Carl 1985, *Die ökologische Chance*, Munich.
Babeuf, Gracchus 1975a, 'Gracchus Babeuf an Charles Germain', in *Von Babeuf bis Blanqui. Französischer Sozialismus und Kommunismus vor Marx*, vol. 2, by Joachim Höppner & Waltraud Seidel-Höppner, Leipzig: Texts: 53–70.
Babeuf, Gracchus 1975b. 'Manifest der Plebejer', in *Von Babeuf bis Blanqui. Französischer Sozialismus und Kommunismus vor Marx*, vol. 2, by Joachim Höppner & Waltraud Seidel-Höppner, Leipzig: Texts: 70–80.

Babeuf, Gracchus 1988. 'Bürger Geschworene! Verteidigungsrede vor dem Schwurgericht in Vendôme', in ibid. *Die Verschwörung für die Gleichheit*. Hamburg: 31–102.

Bahro, Rudolf 1960, *In dieser Richtung. Gedichte*. Berlin (East).

Bahro, Rudolf 1977. *'Ich werde meinen Weg fortsetzen'. Eine Dokumentation*. 2nd expanded ed. Köln/Frankfurt am Main.

Bahro, Rudolf 1978, *The Alternative in Eastern Europe*, translated by David Fernbach, London: New Left Books.

Bahro, Rudolf 1979, *'... die nicht mit den Wölfen heulen. Das Beispiel Beethoven und sieben Gedichte'*. Köln/Frankfurt am Main.

Bahro, Rudolf 1980a, *Elemente einer neuen Politik: Zum Verhältnis von Ökologie und Sozialismus*. Berlin (West).

Bahro, Rudolf 1980b, *Plädoyer für eine schöpferische Initiative: Zur Kritik von Arbeitsbedingungen im real existierenden Sozialismus*. Köln.

Bahro, Rudolf 1982a, *Socialism and Survival*, translated by David Fernbach. London: Heretic Books.

Bahro, Rudolf 1982b, *Wahnsinn mit Methode: Über die Logik der Blockkonfrontation, die Friedensbewegung, die Sowjetunion und die DKP*, Berlin (West).

Bahro, Rudolf 1990, 'Nachwort 1989/90', in *Die Alternative. Zur Kritik des real existierenden Sozialismus*, Berlin: 545–559.

Bahro, Rudolf 1998, *'Apokalypse oder Geist einer neuen Zeit'*, 2nd augmented edition, Berlin.

Bahro, Rudolf 2007a, 'Das Buch von der Befreiung aus dem Untergang der DDR (1995)', in *Rudolf Bahro: Denker–Reformator–Homo politicus*, edited by Guntolf Herzberg, Berlin: 23–164.

Bahro, Rudolf 2007b, 'Das Stammesbewußtsein liegt nun mal tiefer als das Klassenbewußtsein. Gespräch mit Frank Schumann in der Jungen Welt, 3./4. November 1990', in *Rudolf Bahro: Denker–Reformator–Homo politicus*, edited by Guntolf Herzberg, Berlin: 436–442.

Bahro, Rudolf 2007c, 'Die wollen nur Macht – SPIEGEL-Interview (No. 26/1995)', in *Rudolf Bahro: Denker–Reformator–Homo politicus*, edited by Guntolf Herzberg, Berlin: 498–509.

Bahro, Rudolf 2007d, 'Ich weiß, ich kann völlig abrutschen - SPIEGEL-Interview (October 1979)', in *Rudolf Bahro: Denker–Reformator–Homo politicus*, edited by Guntolf Herzberg, Berlin: 397–414.

Bahro, Rudolf 2007e, 'Was ich dem außerordentlichen Parteitag der SED sagen möchte' in *Rudolf Bahro: Denker–Reformator–Homo politicus*, edited by Guntolf Herzberg, Berlin: pp. 172–189.

Bahro, Rudolf, Mandel, Ernest & von Oertzen, Peter 1980, *Was da alles auf uns zukommt. Perspektiven der 8oer Jahre*, 2 volumes, Berlin (West).

Bambach, Ralf 1991, 'Gracchus Babeuf (1760–1797)' in *Klassiker des Sozialismus*, volume 1, edited by Walter Euchner, München: 37–49.
Barthel, Horst 2001, 'Umweltpolitik in beiden deutschen Staaten', in *Hefte zur ddr-geschichte*, Nr. 69, edited by Helle Panke e. V., Berlin.
Bebel, August 1910. *Woman and Socialism*. Translated by Meta L. Stern (Hebe), New York: Socialist Literature Company.
Becker, Holger 1994, 'Als Schlapphüte auf ZK-Ticket reisten. Wie war das mit Wolfgang Harichs "Stasi-Kontakten"?', in *Neues Deutschland*, September 28, 1994: 3.
Behrens, Fritz 1992, *Abschied Von Der Sozialen Utopie*, Berlin.
Behrens, Fritz 2010, 'Über Alternativen (Februar 1979)', in *Man kann nicht Marxist sein, ohne Utopist zu sein. Texte von und über Fritz Behrens*, edited by Dieter Janke & Günter Krause. Hamburg: 147–171.
Bell, Daniel 1976, *The Coming of Post-Industrial Society*. United States: Basic Books.
Bellamy, Edward 2007. *Looking Backward: 2000–1887*. Oxford: Oxford University Press.
Bierwisch, Manfred 2007, 'David gegen Goliath – Havemanns ungleicher Kampf gegen die Dogmatiker', in *Robert Havemann Bibliographie. Mit unveröffentlichten Texten aus dem Nachlass*, edited by Bernd Florath & Werner Theuer, Berlin: XIII–XV.
Biesterfeld, Wolfgang 2006, *Utopie. Arbeitstexte für den Unterricht*, Stuttgart.
Bischoff, Joachim & Lühn, Klaus-Dieter 1978, 'Aufhebung der Subalternität oder die Reise nach Innen', in *Antworten auf Bahros Herausforderung des 'realen Sozialismus'*, edited by Ulf Wolter, Berlin (West): 180–196.
Blackbourn, David 2011. *The Conquest Of Nature: Water, Landscape, and the Making of Modern Germany*. United Kingdom: Random House.
Bloch, Ernst 1980, *Abschied von der Utopie? Vorträge*, Frankfurt am Main.
Bloch, Ernst 1985a, *Geist der Utopie*. Zweite Fassung, Frankfurt am Main 1985.
Bloch, Ernst 1985b, *Kampf, nicht Krieg. Politische Schriften 1917–1919*, Frankfurt am Main.
Bloch, Ernst 1985c, *Politische Messungen, Pestzeit, Vormärz*, Frankfurt am Main.
Bloch, Ernst 1986. *The Principle of Hope*, 3 Volumes, translated by Neville Plaice, Stephen Plaice & Paul Knight. Cambridge Mass: MIT Press.
Bloch, Ernst 2000, *The Spirit of Utopia*, Stanford: Stanford University Press.
Böhm, Karl & Dörge, Rolf 1961, *Unsere Welt von morgen*, 4., überarbeitete und erweiterte Auflage, Berlin (East).
Borries, Friedrich von 2010, *Klimakapseln. Überlebensbedingungen in der Katastrophe*, Berlin.
Brandt, Heinz 1978, 'Die Alternative, die aus dem Kerker kam', in *Antworten auf Bahros Herausforderung des 'realen Sozialismus'*, edited by Ulf Wolter, Berlin: 165–179.
Brus, Wlodzimieruz 1978, 'Ein symptomatisches Werk. An die Wirtschaftswissenschaftler der DDR', in *Solidarität mit Rudolf Bahro. Briefe in die DDR*, edited by Hannes Schwenger, Reinbek bei Hamburg: 24–30.

Buhr, Manfred & Klaus, Georg (ed.) 1985, *Philosophisches Wörterbuch*, 2 volumes, 13. Auflage, Berlin (West).

Burschel, Friedrich C 2009, 'Hitler erlösen', in *Konkret*, available at http://www.konkret-verlage.de/kvv/txt.php?text=hitlererl%F6sen&jahr=2009&mon=07.

Callenbach, Ernest 1978, *Ecotopia*, London: Pluto Press.

Carver, T 1996, *Marx: Later Political Writings*, Cambridge: Cambridge University Press.

Deutsche Akademie der Wissenschaften zu Berlin (ed.) 1956, *Das Problem der Freiheit im Lichte des wissenschaftlichen Sozialismus. Konferenz der Sektion Philosophie der Deutschen Akademie der Wissenschaften zu Berlin*, 8–10. of March, Berlin (East).

Dlubek, Rolf 1978, 'Zur Bedeutung des Gothaer Programms für die Entwicklung der Theorie von der kommunistischen Gesellschaft und ihren zwei Phasen', in *Marx-Engels-Jahrbuch* 1/1978, edited by Institut für Marxismus-Leninismus beim ZK der KPdSU and Institut für Geschichte der Arbeiterbewegung, Berlin (East): 17–51.

Dornuf, Stefan 1996, 'Gehlen-Rezeption von W. H.', in *Ein Streiter für Deutschland. Auseinandersetzung mit Wolfgang Harich*, edited by Siegfried Prokop, Berlin: 77–87.

Dornuf, Stefan & Pitsch, Reinhard 1999, 'Harich tragikótatos oder Einleitung in eine späte Gedenkschrift', in *Wolfgang Harich zum Gedächtnis. Eine Gedenkschrift in zwei Bänden*, volume 1, edited by Stefan Dornuf & Reinhard Pitsch, München: 7–22.

Draheim, Dirk & Hoffmann, Dieter 1991, 'Kindheit und Jugend – Student und Antifaschist', in *Robert Havemann. Dokumente eines Lebens*, edited by Dieter Hoffman et al., Berlin.

Dutschke, Gretchen 1998, *Rudi Dutschke. Wir hatten ein barbarisches, schönes Leben*, München.

Dutschke, Rudi, 1978, '... und geistig Dir nicht den Rücken brechen läßt. An Nico Hübner.', in *Solidarität mit Rudolf Bahro. Briefe in die DDR*, edited by Hannes Schwenger, Reinbek bei Hamburg: 86–99.

Dutschke, Rudi 2005, *Jeder hat sein Leben ganz zu leben. Die Tagebücher 1963–1979*, Köln.

Eberle, Henrik & Wesenberg, Denise (ed.) 1999, *Einverstanden, E.H., Parteiinterne Hausmitteilungen, Briefe, Akten und Intrigen aus der Honecker-Zeit*, Berlin.

Eichhorn I, Wolfgang & Bauer, Adolf 1983, *Zur Dialektik des Geschichtsprozesses. Studien über die materiellen Grundlagen der historischen Entwicklung*, Berlin (East) 1983.

Eisenfeld, Peter & Eisenfeld, Bernd 1999, 'Widerständiges Verhalten in der DDR 1976–1982', in *Opposition in der DDR von den 70er Jahren bis zum Zusammenbruch der SED-Herrschaft*, edited by Eberhard Kuhrt, Hannsjörg F. Buck & Gunter Holzweißig, Opladen: 83–131

Elias, Norbert 1985, 'Thomas Morus' Staatskritik', in *Utopieforschung*, volume 3, edited by Wilhelm Voßkamp, Frankfurt am Main: 101–150.

Engels, Friedrich 1987a [1878], 'Anti-Dühring', *Collected Works of Marx and Engels*, Vol. 25, London: Lawrence and Wishart: 5–309.

Engels, Friedrich 1987b [1925], 'Dialectics of Nature', *Collected Works of Marx and Engels*, Vol. 25, London: Lawrence and Wishart: 311–619.

Engels, Friedrich 1989 [1880], 'Socialism: Utopian and Scientific', *Collected Works of Marx and Engels*, Vol. 24, London: Lawrence and Wishart: 281–325.

Euchner, Walter 1993, 'Einleitung: Opposition als Gegenstand politikwissenschaftlicher Forschung', in *Politische Opposition in Deutschland und im internationalen Vergleich*, edited by Walter Euchner, Göttingen: 7–20.

Falck, Paul 1999, 'Der Philosoph, der in die Kälte kam', in *Wolfgang Harich zum Gedächtnis. Eine Gedenkschrift in zwei Bänden*, volume 1, edited by Stefan Dornuf & Reinhard Pitsch, München: 104–124.

Faulstich, Peter 2005, 'Reaktivierte utopische Potentiale', in *Erwägen, Wissen, Ethik*, No. 16, Stuttgart: 300 f.

Faust, Siegmar 2010, 'Robert Havemann (1910–1982). Ein Leben in zwei Diktaturen.', in *Gerbergasse 18*, No. 56: 24 f.

Ferst, Marko 2000, 'Morgen im Land Utopia. Zum 90. Geburtstag von Robert Havemann'. Available at: http://www.umweltdebatte.de/morgenimlandutopia.htm.

Ferst, Marko 2005, 'Die Ideen für einen Berliner Frühling in der DDR. Die sozialen und ökologischen Reformkonzeptionen von Robert Havemann und Rudolf Bahro', in *Hefte zur ddr-geschichte*, No. 91, edited by Helle Panke e. V., Berlin.

Ferst, Marko 2010, 'Eine Reise ins grüne Utopia', in *Neues Deutschland*, 6/7 March 2010: 21.

Fetscher, Iring 2004, Karl Marx/Friedrich Engels Studienausgabe *volume v: Prognose und Utopie*, Berlin.

Fest, Joachim 1991, *'Der zerstörte Traum. Vom Ende des utopischen Zeitalters'*, 3rd edition, Berlin.

Finger, Evelyn 2009, 'Ein Bannfluch gegen die Vergangenheit', in DIE ZEIT *Geschichte, Themenheft Karl Marx*, No. 3/2009: 92–95.

Finger, Evelyn 2011, 'Lernen von den Versagern', in *Die Zeit*, No. 46/2011, November 10, 2011:27

Flechtheim, Ossip 1980, 'Ins Land der Hoffnungen. Zeugnisse von Zukunftsoptimismus', in *Die Zeit*, No. 52/1980: 12.

Flierl, Bruno 1973, *Industriegesellschaftstheorie im Städtebau*. Berlin (East).

Florath, Bernd 1994, 'Rückantworten an die. Hauptverwaltung Ewige Wahrheiten. Wolfgang Harich ohne Schwierigkeiten mit der Wahrheit', in *Utopie kreativ*, No. 47–48/1994: 58–73.

Florath, Bernd 2006, 'Aufklärung oder Zersetzung?', in *Neues Deutschland*, April 22./23 2006: 20.

Florath, Bernd 2007, 'Havemann, der Publizist' in: *Robert Havemann Biliographie. Mit unveröffentlichten Texten aus dem Nachlass*, Berlin: XIX–XXXI.

Florath, Bernd & Müller, Silvia (Eds.) 1996, *Die Entlassung. Robert Havemann und die Akademie der Wissenschaften 1965/66*, Berlin.

Florath, Bernd, & Theuer, Werner 2007a, *Robert Havemann. Biographie, Lebensdaten, Dokumente*, Berlin.

Florath, Bernd, & Theuer, Werner 2007b, *Robert Havemann Bibliographie. Mit unveröffentlichten Texten aus dem Nachlass*, Berlin.

Frank, Mario 2001, *Walter Ulbricht. Eine deutsche Biografie*, Berlin.

Frank, Pierre 1978, 'War der "real existierende Sozialismus" historisch notwendig?', in Wolter, Ulf (Ed.), *Antworten auf Bahros Herausforderung des 'realen Sozialismus'*, Berlin (West): 42–56.

Franz, Dietrich-Eckhard 1983a, 'Babeuf, François-Noël', in Lange, Erhard & Alexander, Dietrich (Eds.), *Philosophenlexikon*, Berlin (East): 58–62.

Franz, Dietrich-Eckhard 1983b, 'Morelly', in Lange, Erhard & Alexander, Dietrich (Eds.), *Philosophenlexikon*, Berlin (East): 673–676.

Franz, Dietrich-Eckhard 1987, *Saint-Simon, Fourier, Owen. Sozialutopien des 19. Jahrhunderts*, Leipzig, Jena, Berlin (East).

Fried, Albert & Sanders Ronald (eds.) 1964, *Socialist Thought: A Documentary History*, United Kingdom: Anchor Books.

Fromm, Erich 2013 *To Have Or To Be?*, United Kingdom: Bloomsbury Academic.

Gaus, Günter 1999, 'Besuche bei Wolfgang Harich', in Dornuf, Stefan & Pitsch, Reinhard (Eds.), *Wolfgang Harich zum Gedächtnis. Eine Gedenkschrift in zwei Bänden*, volume 2, München: 290–295.

Gehlen, Arnold 1980 [1957], *Man in the Age of Technology*, translated by Patricia Lipscomb, New York: Columbia University Press.

Geisel, Christof 2000, 'Robert Havemann und die oppositionellen Bürgerbewegungen der DDR', in Geisel, Christof & Sachse, Christian, *Wiederentdeckung einer Unperson. Robert Havemann im Herbst 89 – Zwei Studien*, Berlin: 19–112.

Geoghegan, Vincent 1987, *Utopianism and Marxism*, London: The Chaucer Press.

Gollwitzer, Helmut [1978], 'Die menschliche Herausforderung, der Bahro sich gestellt hat. An Wolfgang Abendroth', in Schwenger, Hannes (Ed.), *Solidarität mit Rudolf Bahro. Briefe in die DDR*, Reinbek bei Hamburg: 31–37.

Götz, Hans Herbert 1981, '"Der reale Sozialismus ist kein Sozialismus". Robert Havemanns Reise nach "Utopia"', in *Frankfurter Allgemeine Zeitung*, 7. Febuary 1981: 12.

Götze, Frank 1996, 'W.H. – Rezensent und Kritiker', in Prokop, Siegfried (Ed.), *Ein Streiter für Deutschland. Auseinandersetzung mit Wolfgang Harich*, Berlin: 110–121.

Gould, Stephen Jay 1988, 'Kropotkin was no crackpot', *Natural History*, vol. 97, no. 7: 12–21.

Gramsci, Antonio 1980, *Zu Politik, Geschichte und Kultur*, 2. Auflage, Frankfurt am Main.

Gransow, Bettina & Gransow, Volker 1981, 'Orientalische Despotie: Diskussionsstand in der DDR', in *Deutschland-Archiv*, No. 14/1981: 401–418.

Grebing, Helga 1981, *Geschichte der deutschen Arbeiterbewegung*, 11. Auflage, München.

Grimm, Thomas 2003, *Linke Vaterlandsgesellen*, Berlin.

Grimmer, Reinhard et al 2003, 'Sicherheitspolitik der SED, staatliche Sicherheit der DDR und Abwehrarbeit des MfS', in: Grimmer, Reinhard et al (Eds) *Die Sicherheit. Zur Abwehrarbeit des MfS*, volume 1, 3., corrected and supplemented edition, Berlin: 44–238.

Grosse, Hermann & Puschmann, Manfred 1974, *Qualität des Lebens. Ausweg oder Irreführung?*, Berlin (East).

Gruhl, Herbert 1975, *Ein Planet wird geplündert. Die Schreckensbilanz unserer Politik*, Frankfurt am Main.

Günther, Hans 1985, 'Utopie nach der Revolution', in Voßkamp, Wilhelm (Ed.), *Utopieforschung*, volume 3, Frankfurt am Main: 378–393.

Gutzeit, Martin 1997, 'Möglichkeiten und Formen abweichenden und widerständigen Verhaltens und oppositionellen Handelns und die friedliche Revolution im Herbst 1989', in Drechsler, Ingrun et al. (Eds), *Getrennte Vergangenheit, gemeinsame Zukunft*, volume 2: Opfer, Opposition und Widerstand, München: 115–195.

Hager, Kurt 1956, 'Der Kampf gegen bürgerliche Ideologien und Revisionismus', in *Deutsche Zeitschrift für Philosophie*, No. 5–6/1956 (published 1957): 533–538.

Hager, Kurt 1975, *Engels' 'Dialektik der Natur' und die Gegenwart*, Berlin (East).

Hager, Kurt 1996, *Erinnerungen*, Leipzig.

Handel, Gottfried 1983, 'Bloch, Ernst', in Lange, Erhard & Alexander, Dietrich (Eds.), *Philosophenlexikon*, Berlin (East): 107–111.

Harich, Anne 2007, *'Wenn ich das gewußt hätte' ... Erinnerungen an Wolfgang Harich*, Berlin.

Harich, Wolfgang 1949, 'Arbeiterklasse und Intelligenz', in *Neue Welt*, No. 7/1949, S: 57–70.

Harich, Wolfgang 1956, 'Über das Verhältnis des Marxismus zur Philosophie Hegels', in *Deutsche Zeitschrift für Philosophie*, No. 5/1956: 559–585.

Harich, Wolfgang 1971, *Zur Kritik der revolutionären Ungeduld*, Basel.

Harich, Wolfgang 1975, *Kommunismus ohne Wachstum? Babeuf und der 'Club of Rome'*, 2. Auflage, Reinbek bei Hamburg.

Harich, Wolfgang 1979a, 'Das Weib in der Apokalypse', in Baudis, Andreas (Ed.), *Richte unsere Füße auf den Weg des Friedens: Festschrift für Helmut Gollwitzer zum 70. Geburtstag*, München: 681–687.

Harich, Wolfgang, 1979b, 'Der Stern von Zwentendorf zog mich her', in *Neues Forum*, No. 307/308 (July/August 1979), Wien: 7–19.

Harich, Wolfgang, 1979b, 'Ich hatte alle gegen mich', in *Der Spiegel*, No. 24/1979, retrieved from https://www.spiegel.de/politik/ich-hatte-alle-gegen-mich-wolfgang-harich-a-dbf155c1-0002-0001-0000-000040349947.

Harich, Wolfgang 1980, 'Kommunismus heute', in Forum Alternativ (Ed.) *Dokumentation der Parallelkonferenz zur U.N.-Konferenz über Wissenschaft und Technik im Dienste der Entwicklung UNCSTD vom August 1979*, Wien.

Harich, Wolfgang 1991, 'Weltrevolution jetzt. Zur jüngsten Veröffentlichung des Club of Rome', in *Z. Zeitschrift Marxistische Erneuerung*, No. 8/1991: 63–72.

Harich, Wolfgang 1993a, *Keine Schwierigkeiten mit der Wahrheit*, Berlin.

Harich, Wolfgang 1993b, 'Kommunistische Parteien brauchen kein Fraktionsverbot' retrieved from http://rotefahne.eu/1993/05/harich-fraktionsverbot/.

Harich, Wolfgang 1994a, 'Kritische Anmerkungen zur Rolle der PDS', in Bisky, Lothar/ Heuer, Uwe-Jens & Schumann, Michael (Eds.), *Unrechtsstaat? Politische Justiz und die Aufarbeitung der DDR-Vergangenheit*, Hamburg: 47–50.

Harich, Wolfgang 1994b, *Nietzsche und seine Brüder. Eine Streitschrift*, Schwedt.

Harich, Wolfgang 1999, *Ahnenpaß. Versuch einer Autobiographie*, Edited by Thomas Grimm, Berlin.

Harich, Wolfgang 2004, *Nicolai Hartmann – Größe und Grenzen. Versuch einer marxistischen Selbstverständigung*, Würzburg.

Harich, Wolfgang, Herbig, Jost, Illich, Ivan & Weish, Peter 1979, 'Klapp off, Rom! Diskussion bei der Anti-UNO', in *Neues Forum*, No. 309/310 (September/October 1979), Wien: 70–78.

Harrer, Jürgen 1978, 'Anmerkungen zu Rudolf Bahro: Die Alternative', in Brockmeier, Peter & Rilling, Rainer (Eds.), *Beiträge zur Sozialismusanalyse*, volume 1, Köln: 54–83.

Havemann, Florian & Jochum, Dieter 2002, 'Da war die Mauer, und da war ich', in *Konkret*, No. 9/2002.

Havemann, Florian 1978, 'Alle machen aus meinem Vater einen Fall', in *Der Spiegel*, No. 44/1978: 121–130.

Havemann, Florian 2007, *Havemann*, Frankfurt am Main.

Havemann, Florian 2008, 'Aber Marx war kein Marxist ...', in *disput*, February 2008.

Havemann, Katja & Widmann, Joachim 2003, *Robert Havemann oder Wie die DDR sich erledigte*, München.

Havemann, Robert 1961, 'Nachwort', in *Strahlen aus der Asche*, edited by Robert Jungk, Berlin (East): 335–340.

Havemann, Robert 1968, *Dialektik ohne Dogma? Naturwissenschaft und Weltanschauung*, 3rd edition, Reinbek bei Hamburg.

Havemann, Robert 1969, 'Der Sozialismus von morgen', in Grossner, Claus et al (Eds.) *Das 198. Jahrzehnt. Eine Team-Prognose für 1970 bis 1980*, Hamburg: 199–212.

Havemann, Robert 1970, *Fragen, Antworten, Fragen. Aus der Biographie eines deutschen Marxisten*, 2ND edition, München.

Havemann, Robert 1971, *'Rückantworten an die Hauptverwaltung "Ewige Wahrheiten"'*, edited by Hartmut Jäckel, München.

Havemann, Robert 1975, 'Freiheit als Notwendigkeit', in Dutschke, Rudi & Wilke, Manfred (Eds.), *Die Sowjetunion, Solschenizyn und die westliche Linke*, Reinbek bei Hamburg: 16–28.

Havemann, Robert 1977, *Berliner Schriften*, edited by Andreas W. Mytze, München.
Havemann, Robert 1978a, *Ein deutscher Kommunist. Rückblicke und Perspektiven aus der Isolation*, edited by Manfred Wilke, Reinbek bei Hamburg.
Havemann, Robert 1978b, '"Muß jeder ein Auto haben?" Havemanns kommunistische Utopie', in *Der Spiegel*, No. 40/1978: 73.
Havemann, Robert 1978c, '"Scharlatane in den Schlüsselstellungen" Havemann über den Regimekritiker Rudolf Bahro', in *Der Spiegel*, No. 40/1978: 70.
Havemann, Robert 1979, Vom Archipel Gulag redet man eben nicht. Der DDR-Dissident Robert Havemann verteidigt sich gegen seine Kritiker, in *Der Spiegel*, No. 15/1979: 98–105
Havemann, Robert 1980a, *Ein Marxist in der DDR. Für Robert Havemann*, edited by Hartmut Jäckel, München.
Havemann, Robert 1980b, *Morgen. Die Industriegesellschaft am Scheideweg. Kritik und reale Utopie*, München.
Havemann, Robert 1981, 'Fragen nach dem Sinn des Begriffs Realismus', in *Für Klaus Piper zum 70. Geburtstag, Festschrift*, March 27, 1981, München: 137–145.
Havemann, Robert 1990, *Warum ich Stalinist war und Antistalinist wurde. Texte eines Unbequemen*, edited by Dieter Hoffmann & Hubert Laitko, Berlin.
Havemann, Robert 1999, '10 Thesen zum 30. Jahrestag der DDR', in Eberle, Henrik & Wesenberg, Denise (Eds.), *Einverstanden E. H.*, Berlin: 158–165.
Hecht, Hartmut 1991, 'Philosoph und Kritiker', in Hoffmann, Dieter et al, *Robert Havemann. Dokumente eines Lebens*, Berlin: 116–190.
Hedeler, Wladislaw 2010, *Ökonomik des Terrors: Zur Organisationsgeschichte des Gulag 1939 bis 1960*, Hannover.
Hedeler, Wladislaw 2011, *Jossif Stalin oder: Revolution als Verbrechen*, Berlin.
Helmstädter, Ernst 1977, 'Ein weltfremder Ketzer', in *Manager-Magazin*, No. 11/1977: 192–193.
Henze, Eyk 2012, 'Haushalten oder Aushalten. Zur Ökonomie einer Lyrikreihe in der DDR', in Böick, Marcus, Hertel, Anja & Kuschel, Franziska (Eds.), *Aus einem Land vor unserer Zeit. Eine Lesereise durch die DDR-Geschichte*, Berlin: 113–122.
Hermand, Jost 1991, *Grüne Utopien in Deutschland. Zur Geschichte des ökologischen Bewußtseins*, Frankfurt am Main.
Hertle, Hans-Hermann & Wolle, Stefan 2004, *Damals in der DDR*, 2nd edition, München.
Hertwig, Manfred 1977, 'Der "aufrechte Gang" in Richtung Sozialismus', in *DeutschlandArchiv*, No. 10/1977: 1093–1099.
Herzberg, Guntolf 1988, 'Einen eigenen Weg gehen. Oder weggehen', in Kroh, Ferdinand (Ed.), *"Freiheit ist immer Freiheit ..." Die Andersdenkenden in der DDR'*, Frankfurt am Main und Berlin (West): 59–87.
Herzberg, Guntolf 1998, "Rudolf Bahros 'Alternative' – zur Entstehungsgeschichte des Buches", in *Horch und Guck*, No. 22, 1/1998, Berlin: 1–9.

Herzberg, Guntolf 2000, 'Harich, Wolfgang', in Veen, Hans-Joachim et al (Eds.), *Lexikon Opposition und Widerstand in der SED-Diktatur*, Berlin und München: 174–175.

Herzberg, Guntolf 2005, 'Robert Havemanns Probleme mit der marxistischen Philosophie', in Rauh, Hans-Christoph & Ders (Eds.), *Denkversuche. DDR-Philosophie in den 60er Jahren*, Berlin: 337–366.

Herzberg, Guntolf 2006, *Anpassung und Aufbegehren. Die Intelligenz in der DDR in den Krisenjahren 1956/58*, Berlin.

Herzberg, Guntolf (Ed.) 2007, *Rudolf Bahro: Denker–Reformator–Homo politicus*, Berlin.

Herzberg, Guntolf & Seifert, Kurt 2005, *Rudolf Bahro. Glaube an das Veränderbare*, Berlin.

Heuler, Werner 1977, "Über Rudolf Bahros Buch 'Die Alternative – Zur Kritik des real existierenden Sozialismus'", in *Theorie und Praxis des Marxismus Leninismus*, No. 1–2/1977:117–140.

Heyer, Andreas 2006a, 'Die Erneuerung des utopischen Diskurses im Spannungsfeld von Marxismus-Kritik und dem Durchbruch der postmodernen Problemlagen', in Kinner, Klaus & Wurl, Ernst (Eds.), *Linke Utopien – die Zukunft denken. Diskurs*, No. 21, Leipzig: 87–111.

Heyer, Andreas 2006b, *Die Utopie steht links! Ein Essay*, Berlin.

Heyer, Andreas 2007a, 'Die Last der Verschwörung – Gracchus Babeufs Theorie der Freiheit und Gleichheit', in *Utopie kreativ*, No. 195 (January 2007): 5–19.

Heyer, Andreas 2007b, 'Wolfgang Harichs Demokratiekonzeption aus dem Jahr 1956', in *Zeitschrift für Geschichtswissenschaft*, No. 6/2007: 529–550.

Heyer, Andreas 2008a, *Der Stand der aktuellen deutschen Utopieforschung, volume 1: Die Forschungssituation in den einzelnen akademischen Disziplinen*, Hamburg.

Heyer, Andreas 2008b, *Der Stand der aktuellen deutschen Utopieforschung, volume 2: Ausgewählte Forschungsfelder und die Analyse der postmodernden Utopieproduktion*, Hamburg.

Heyer, Andreas 2009, 'Ökologie und Opposition. Die politischen Utopien von Wolfgang Harich und Robert Havemann', in Helle Panke e. V. (Ed.) *Philosophische Gespräche*, No. 14, Berlin.

Heyer, Andreas 2010a, *Der Stand der aktuellen deutschen Utopieforschung, volume 3: Theoretische und methodische Ansätze der gegenwärtigen Forschung 1996–2009*, Hamburg.

Heyer, Andreas 2010b, "Freiheit und genossenschaftlicher Sozialismus in Robert Havemanns 'Morgen'", in Bois, Marcel & Hüttner, Bernd (Eds.), *Beiträge zur Geschichte einer pluralen Linken*, Heft 2, Rosa-Luxemburg Stiftung, Berlin: 30–33.

Heyer, Andreas 2010c, *Studien zu Wolfgang Harich*, Norderstedt.

Heyer, Andreas 2011, 'Harichs Weg zu einem undogmatischen Marxismus 1946–1956', in

Amberger, Alexander & Ders, *Der konstruierte Dissident. Wolfgang Harichs Weg zu einem undogmatischen Marxismus*, Helle Panke e. V. (Ed.), hefte zur ddr-geschichte, No. 127, Berlin: 32–63.

Heym, Stefan 1990, *Stalin verlässt den Raum. Politische Publizistik*, Leipzig.

Heym, Stefan 1997, *Nachruf*, Auflage 69.–70th ed. Frankfurt am Main.

Himmelmann, Gerhard 1981, 'Ökonomie der Zeit – Anmerkungen zu Bahros Konzept einer alternativen Ökonomik', in Kremendahl, Hans & Meyer, Thomas (Eds.), *Menschliche Emanzipation. Rudolf Bahro und der Demokratische Sozialismus*, Frankfurt am Main: 79–85.

Hoeft, Brigitte (Ed.) 1990, *Der Prozeß gegen Walter Janka und andere. Eine Dokumentation*, Reinbek bei Hamburg.

Hofbauer, Hannes 1996, 'Der ökologische Harich', in Prokop, Siegfried (Ed.), *Ein Streiter für Deutschland. Auseinandersetzung mit Wolfgang Harich*, Berlin: 42–52.

Hoffmann, Dieter 1991, 'Physiochemiker und Stalinist', in Hoffman, Dieter et al., *Robert Havemann. Dokumente eines Lebens*, Berlin: 65–115.

Hofmann, Gunter 1980, 'Ein Held unserer Zeit?', in *Die Zeit*, No. 45/1980.

Hollitscher, Walter 1980, *Bedrohung und Zuversicht. Marxistische Essays*, Wien.

Holz, Hans Heinz 2006, 'Philosophischer Dilettantismus und politische Schwärmerei', in Allertz, Robert (Ed.): *Sänger und Souffleur. Biermann, Havemann und die DDR*, Berlin: 72–78.

Höpcke, Klaus 2008, *Über linke Heimatliebe. Texte um die Jahrtausendwende*, Berlin.

Höppner, Joachim & Seidel-Höppner, Waltraud 1975a, *Von Babeuf bis Blanqui. Französischer Sozialismus und Kommunismus vor Marx, volume 1*, Einführung, Leipzig.

Höppner, Joachim & Seidel-Höppner, Waltraud 1975a, *Von Babeuf bis Blanqui. Französischer Sozialismus und Kommunismus vor Marx, volume 2*, Texte, Leipzig.

Höppner, Joachim 1985, 'Babouvismus', in Buhr, Manfred & Klaus, Georg (Eds.), *Philosophisches Wörterbuch*, volume 1, 13th edtion, Berlin (West): 193–196.

Hosang, Maik 2007, 'Bahros Begriff der Conditio Humana oder Über menschliche Grundlagen ökologischer Gesellschaften', in Herzberg, Guntolf (Ed.), *Rudolf Bahro: Denker–Reformator–Homo politicus*, Berlin: 280–286.

Hosang, Maik 2009, "Ein ostdeutscher 'Prophet'?", retrieved on June 24, 2009.

Hurwitz, Harold 2012, *Robert Havemann. Eine persönlich-politische Biographie, Teil 1: Die Anfänge*, Berlin.

Idler, Martin d' 1999, *Neue Wege für Übermorgen. Ökologische Utopien seit den 70er Jahren*, Köln.

Idler, Martin d' 2007, *Die Modernisierung der Utopie. Vom Wandel des Neuen Menschen in der politischen Utopie der Neuzeit*, Berlin.

Jackson, Tim 2009, *Prosperity Without Growth: Economics for a Finite Planet*, London: Routledge.

Jäger, Manfred 1973, *Sozialliteraten. Funktion und Selbstverständnis der Schriftsteller in der DDR*, Düsseldorf.

Janka, Walter 1989, *Schwierigkeiten mit der Wahrheit*, Reinbek bei Hamburg.
Janka, Walter 1992, *Spuren eines Lebens*, Reinbek bei Hamburg.
Janke, Dieter & Krause, Günter 2010, 'Einleitung', in Janke, Dieter, & Krause, Gunter (Eds.), *'Man kann nicht Marxist sein, ohne Utopist zu sein' Texte von und über Fritz Behrens*, Hamburg: 7–20.
Jordan, Carlo & Kloth, Hans Michael 1995, ARCHE NOVA. *Opposition in der DDR. Das 'Grün-ökologische Netzwerk Arche' 1988–90*, Berlin.
Judt, Matthias (Ed.) 1998, *DDR-Geschichte in Dokumenten*, Bundeszentrale für politische Bildung, Bonn.
Julius, Liselotte 1977, 'Nachwort', in Bahro, Rudolf, *'Ich werde meinen Weg fortsetzen'. Eine Dokumentation*, 2., erweiterte Auflage, Köln/Frankfurt am Main: 113–128.
Kaminsky, Annette 1999, *Illustrierte Konsumgeschichte der DDR*, Landeszentrale für politische Bildung Thüringen (Ed.), Erfurt.
Kinner, Klaus & Wurl, Ernst (Eds.) 2006, *Linke Utopien – die Zukunft denken*. Diskurs, No. 21, Leipzig.
Kirbach, Roland 1989, 'Von den Genossen verlassen', in *Die Zeit*, December 22, 1989, retrieved from https://www.zeit.de/1989/52/von-den-genossen-verlassen
Kirchhoff, Jochen 1998, 'Rede auf der Trauerfeier für Rudolf Bahro', in *Apokalypse oder Geist einer neuen Zeit*, edited by Rudolf Bahro, 2nd expanded edition, Berlin: 265–270.
Klein, Thomas, Otto, Wilfriede & Grieder, Peter 1996, *Visionen. Repression und Opposition in der SED (1949–1989)*, 2 volumes, Frankfurt an der Oder.
Klenke, Olaf 2007, 'Die Wende des VIII. Parteitages und das Problem der Effizienz', in Helle Panke e. V. (Ed.), *hefte zur ddr-geschichte*, No. 109: *Die SED in Konfliktsituationen. Die siebziger Jahre*, Berlin: 5–12.
Klepper, Peter 1998, "Operativ-Vorgang 'Kongreß' gegen das Bahro Komitee", in *Horch und Guck*, No. 22, 1/1998, Berlin: 10–22.
Knabe, Hubertus 2001, *Der diskrete Charme der DDR. Stasi und Westmedien*, Berlin, München.
Koenen, Gerd 2007, *Das rote Jahrzehnt. Unsere kleine deutsche Kulturrevolution 1967–1977*, 4th edition, Frankfurt am Main.
Kolakowski, Leszek 1974, *Marxismus – Utopie und Anti-Utopie*, Stuttgart.
Komitee für die Freilassung Rudolf Bahros (Ed.) 1979, *Der Bahro-Kongreß. Aufzeichnungen, Berichte und Referate*, Berlin (West).
Korte, Helmut 1980, *Bahro zur Einführung*, 2nd edition, Hannover.
Kosta, Tomas 1978, 'Brief seines Verlegers', in: Schwenger, Hannes (Ed.), *Solidarität mit Rudolf Bahro. Briefe in die DDR*, Reinbek bei Hamburg: 119–124.
Kowalczuk, Ilko-Sascha 1999, 'Gegenkräfte: Opposition und Widerstand in der DDR – Begriffliche und methodische Probleme', in Kuhrt, Eberhard, Buck, Hannsjörg F. & Holzweißig, Gunter (Eds.), *Opposition in der DDR von den 70er Jahren bis zum Zusammenbruch der SED-Herrschaft*, Opladen: 47–75.

Krauß, Matthias 2008, "Die überraschende Entdeckung. Die DDR im Spiegel der 'Utopia' von Thomas Morus", in *Neues Deutschland*, October 11–12: 21.
Kremendahl, Hans 1981, "Rudolf Bahros 'Alternative' – menschliche Emanzipation und politische Strategie", in Kremendahl, Hans & Meyer, Thomas (Eds.), *Menschliche Emanzipation. Rudolf Bahro und der Demokratische Sozialismus*, Frankfurt am Main: 147–163.
Kroh, Ferdinand 1988, 'Havemanns Erben – 1953 bis 1988', in Kroh, Ferdinand (Ed.), *"Freiheit ist immer Freiheit ..." Die Andersdenkenden in der DDR*, Frankfurt am Main, Berlin (West): 10–58.
Kropotkin, Peter 1994, *Der Anarchismus. Ursprung, Ideal und Philosophie*, 2nd edition, Grafenau.
Kuczynski, Jürgen 1973, *Das Gleichgewicht der Null. Zu den Theorien des Null-Wachstums*, Berlin (East).
Kuczynski, Jürgen 1993, *Frost nach dem Tauwetter. Mein Historikerstreit*, Berlin.
Laitko, Hubert 2010a, 'Chemiker–Philosoph–Dissident', in *Nachrichten aus der Chemie*, No. 6/2010: 655–658.
Laitko, Hubert 2010b, 'Denkwege aus der Konformität. Bausteine zu Robert Havemanns intellektueller Biographie in den 1950er und frühen 1960er Jahren', in Helle Panke e.V. (Ed.), *Pankower Vorträge*, No. 146, Berlin.
Laitko, Hubert 2010c, 'Die Sozialismuskonzeption Robert Havemanns im Wandel', in *Standpunkte der Rosa-Luxemburg-Stiftung*, No. 20/2010, Berlin.
Land, Rainer & Possekel, Ralf 1998, *Fremde Welten: Die Gegensätzliche Deutung der DDR durch SED-Reformer und Bürgerbewegung in der 80er Jahren*, Berlin.
Lebensgut 2010, 'Vision' retrieved from http://www.lebensgut.de/html/vision.htm
Lehnert, Erik 2007, 'Der Ökofaschist. Bahro als Reizfigur der Linken und seine Auseinandersetzung mit dem Problem von Staat und Gesellschaft in der ökologischen Krise', in Herzberg, Guntolf (Ed.), *Rudolf Bahro: Denker–Reformator–Homo politicus*, Berlin: 370–395.
Lenin, V.I. 2014, *The State and Revolution*, annotated and introduced by Todd Chretien, Chicago, IL: Haymarket Books.
Leonhard, Wolfgang 1996, 'Begegnungen mit Wolfgang Harich', in Prokop, Siegfried (Ed.), *Ein Streiter für Deutschland. Auseinandersetzung mit Wolfgang Harich*, Berlin: 223–232.
Leonhard, Wolfgang 1958, *Child of the Revolution*, translated by C.M. Woodhouse, Chicago: Henry Regnery.
Leonhard, Wolfgang 2006, 'Die bedeutsamste Rede des Kommunismus', in *Aus Politik und Zeitgeschichte*, No. 17–18/2006: 3–5.
Lombardo Radice, Lucio 1978, 'Den Marxismus auf den Marxismus anwenden. An deutsche Freunde', in Schwenger, Hannes (Ed.), *Solidarität mit Rudolf Bahro. Briefe in die DDR*, Reinbek bei Hamburg: 11–15.

Löther, Rolf 1985, *Mit der Natur in die Zukunft*, Berlin (East).
Ludz, Peter Christian 1976, *Ideologiebegriff und marxistische Theorie. Ansätze zu einer immanenten Kritik*, Opladen.
Maier, Harry, 1977, *Gibt es Grenzen ökonomischen Wachstums?* Berlin (East).
Malthus, Thomas Robert 1809, *An Essay on the Principle of Population, as it Affects the Future Improvement of Society*. Volume 1, United States.
Markov, Walter & Soboul, Albert 1989, *1789. Die Große Revolution der Franzosen*, 3rd edition, Köln.
Marx, Karl 1975 [1845], 'Theses on Feuerbach', *Collected Works of Marx and Engels*, Vol. 5, London: Lawrence and Wishart: 3–5.
Marx, Karl 1976 [1867], *Capital: A Critique of Political Economy*, Vol. 1, translated by Ben Fowkes, London: Penguin.
Marx, Karl 1981 [1894], *Capital: A Critique of Political Economy*, Vol. 3, translated by David Fernbach, London: Penguin.
Marx, Karl 1989a [1875], 'Critique of the Gotha Programme', *Collected Works of Marx and Engels*, Vol. 24, London: Lawrence and Wishart: 75–99.
Marx, Karl 1989b, 'Economic Manuscripts, 1861–63 (Continuation)', *Collected Works of Marx and Engels*, Vol. 32, London: Lawrence and Wishart.
Marx, Karl 1979 [1852], 'The Eighteenth Brumaire of Louis Bonaparte', *Collected Works of Marx and Engels*, Vol. 11, London: Lawrence and Wishart: 99–197.
Marx, Karl and Friedrich Engels 1975a [1848], 'Manifesto of the Communist Party', *Collected Works of Marx and Engels*, Vol. 6, London: Lawrence and Wishart:. 477–519.
Marx, Karl and Friedrich Engels 1975b [1847], 'The German Ideology', *Collected Works of Marx and Engels*, Vol. 5, London: Lawrence and Wishart: 19–539.
Maschke, Günther 1979, 'Harich. Ein ökologischer Stalinist', in *Frankfurter Allgemeine Zeitung*, June 2, 1979: 21.
Meadows, D, Meadows, D, Randers, J & William W. 1972, *The Limits to Growth. A report for the Club of Rome's project on the predicament of mankind*, New York: Universe Books.
Menge, Marlies 1983, 'Für Filter fehlen die Devisen', in *Die Zeit*, no. 12/1983: 63, retrieved from https://www.zeit.de/1983/12/fuer-filter-fehlen-die-devisen.
Menge, Wolfgang 1973 *Der verkaufte Käufer. Die Manipulation der Konsumgesellschaft*, Frankfurt am Main.
Mertens, Lothar 2004, *Rote Denkfabrik? Die Akademie für Gesellschaftswissenschaften beim ZK der SED*, Münster.
Mesarović, Mihailo & Pestel, Eduard 1975, *Mankind at the Turning Point. The Second Report to The Club of Rome*, United States: Dutton Books.
Meyer, Fritjof 1975, 'Sozialistische Opposition gegen den Staatskapitalismus in Rußland', in Dutschke, Rudi & Wilke, Manfred (Eds.), *Die Sowjetunion, Solschenizyn und die westliche Linke*, Reinbek bei Hamburg: 155–184.

Meyer, Thomas 1981, 'Abstrakte Utopie, konkrete Utopie und konstruktive Praxis', in Kremendahl, Hans & Ders. (Eds.), *Menschliche Emanzipation. Rudolf Bahro und der Demokratische Sozialismus*, Frankfurt am Main: 164–180.

Meuschel, Sigrid 1991, 'Wandel durch Auflehnung. Thesen zum Verfall bürokratischer Herrschaft in der DDR', in Deppe, Rainer, Dubiel, Helmut & Rödel, Ulrich (Eds.), *Demokratischer Umbruch in Osteuropa*, Frankfurt am Main: 26–47.

Michels, Robert 1916, *Political Parties: a Sociological Study of the Oligarchical Tendencies of Modern Democracy*, London: Jarrold & Sons.

Misik, Robert 2009, 'Wir bauen uns eine bessere Welt', in *Der Freitag*, No. 11/2009: 6

Mittenzwei, Werner 2003, *Die Intellektuellen. Literatur und Politik in Ostdeutschland 1945–2000*, Berlin.

Morelly, Étienne-Gabriel 1846, *The Code of Nature* (Denis Diderot was still given as the name of the author for this edition), Leipzig.

More, Thomas 1795, *Utopia*, London: printed for D.I. Eaton, At The Cock And Swine.

Morris, William 1995 [1890], *News from Nowhere*, edited by Krishnan Kumar, Cambridge: Cambridge University Press.

Morris-Keitel, Peter 2004, *Die ökologische Katastrophe abwenden!*, in Helle Panke e. V. (Ed.), *Pankower Vorträge*, No. 68, Berlin.

Müller, Tadzio & Kaufmann, Stefan 2009, *Grüner Kapitalismus. Krise, Klimawandel und kein Ende des Wachstums*, Berlin.

Müller-Enbergs, Helmut/Wielgohs, Jan & Hoffmann, Dieter (Eds.) 2000, *Wer war wer in der DDR? Ein biographisches Lexikon*, Bundeszentrale für politische Bildung, Bonn.

Narr, Wolf-Dieter 1978, 'An einen hilflosen Antikapitalisten in der Bundesrepublik – auch an mich selber', in Schwenger, Hannes (Ed.), *Solidarität mit Rudolf Bahro. Briefe in die DDR*, Reinbek bei Hamburg: 47–56.

Nawrocki, Joachim 1975, 'Mehr arbeiten für stabile Preise', in *Die Zeit*, No. 38/1975: 20 f.

Nawrocki, Joachim 1978, 'Bahro-Kongreß: Die Linke bleibt in sich zerstritten', in *Die Zeit*, No. 48/1978: 8, retrieved from http://www.zeit.de/1978/48/Bahro-Kongress-Die-Linke-bleibt-in-sich-zerstritten.

Neef, Wolfgang 2008, 'Umweltkrise als Technikchance?' in *Der Freitag*, January 18, 2008: 18.

Negt, Oskar 1998, *Marx*, München.

Neubert, Ehrhart 1999, 'Was waren Opposition, Widerstand und Dissidenz in der DDR? Zur Kategorisierung politischer Gegnerschaft', in Kuhrt, Eberhard, Buck, Hannsjörg F. & Holzweißig, Gunter (Eds.), *Opposition in der DDR von den 70er Jahren bis zum Zusammenbruch der SED-Herrschaft*, Opladen: 17–46.

Neubert, Ehrhart 2000, *Geschichte der Opposition in der DDR 1949–1989*, 2nd revised edition, expanded and corrected edition, Bundeszentrale für politische Bildung, Bonn.

Nolte, Hans-Heinrich 1981, 'Bahros Sozialismuskritik und Perspektiven von Emanzipation im Weltsystem', in Kremendahl, Hans & Meyer, Thomas (Eds.), *Menschliche*

Emanzipation. Rudolf Bahro und der Demokratische Sozialismus, Frankfurt am Main: 42–57.

Oertzen, Peter von 1978, 'Ihr Urteil über die SPD ist eher kühl', in Schwenger, Hannes (Ed.), *Solidarität mit Rudolf Bahro. Briefe in die DDR*, Reinbek bei Hamburg: 59–64.

Otto, Wilfriede 2008, 'SED-Mitglieder im politischen Spagat zwischen neuem Gesellschaftsvertrag und politischem Spannungsfeld', in Prokop, Siegfried (Ed.), *Der versäumte Paradigmenwechsel. 'Spiegel-Manifest' und 'Erster Deutscher im All' – die DDR im Jahr 1978*, Schkeuditz: 137–160.

Parteihochschule beim ZK der KPdSU (Ed.) 1974, *Politische Ökonomie*, Volume 4, Berlin (East).

Pitsch, Reinhard 1999, 'Nekrolog auf Wolfgang Harich', in Dornuf, Stefan & Pitsch, Reinhard (Eds.) *Wolfgang Harich zum Gedächtnis. Eine Gedenkschrift in zwei Bänden*, Volume 1, München: 27–36.

Polzin, Arno 2006, *Der Wandel Robert Havemanns vom Inoffiziellen Mitarbeiter zum Dissidenten im Spiegel der MfS-Akten*, 2nd revised edition, Berlin.

Popper, Karl R. 1997, *Vermutungen und Widerlegungen: das Wachstum der wissenschaftlichen Erkenntnis*, Teilband II, Tübingen.

Pötter, Bernhard 2010, *Ausweg Ökodiktatur? Wie unsere Demokratie an der Umweltkrise scheitert*, München.

Prokop, Siegfried 1996, 'Wolfgang Harich – Leben und Werk', in Prokop, Siegfried (Ed.), *Ein Streiter für Deutschland. Auseinandersetzung mit Wolfgang Harich*, Berlin: 14–25.

Prokop, Siegfried 1997, *Ich bin zu früh geboren. Auf den Spuren Wolfgang Harichs*, Berlin.

Prokop, Siegfried 2000, 'Der Harich-Havemann-Disput im Jahre 1956', in *hochschule ost: leipziger beiträge zu hochschule & wissenschaft*, No. 3–4/2000, Leipzig: 131–143.

Prokop, Siegfried 2005, "Was befähigt Marxisten? Verschollenes Dokument entdeckt: Wolfgang Harichs 'Vademekum für Dogmatiker'", in *Neues Deutschland*, July 9/10 2005: 14.

Prokop, Siegfried 2006, *1956 – DDR am Scheideweg. Opposition und neue Konzepte der Intelligenz*, Berlin.

Radkau, Joachim 2014, *The Age of Ecology: A Global History*, translated by Patrick Camiller, Cambridge: Polity Press.

Radt, Peter 2010, *Fetisch Wachstum. Philosophisch-ökonomische Anmerkungen zur Logik des Kapitalismus*, Köln.

Rauh, Hans-Christoph 2006, 'Wolfgang Harichs Versuch einer geistigen Öffnung des Marxismus', in *Deutsche Zeitschrift für Philosophie*, No. 5/2006: 751–757.

Rehberg, Karl-Siegbert 1999, 'Kommunistische und konservative Bejahung der Institutionen. Eine Brief-Freundschaft', in Dornuf, Stefan & Pitsch, Reinhard (Eds.), *Wolfgang Harich zum Gedächtnis. Eine Gedenkschrift in zwei Bänden*, Volume 2, München: 438–486.

Rehberg, Karl-Siegbert 2002, 'Mängelwesen, Entlastung und Institutionen. Arnold Gehlen: *Der Mensch* (1940)', in Erhart, Walter & Jaumann, Herbert (Eds.), *Jahrhundertbücher. Große Theorien von Freud bis Luhmann*, 2nd edition, München: 147–167.

Reich, Alexander 2009, 'Massenentziehungskuren?! Kleine Handreichung zum Klimagipfel', in *junge Welt*, December 3 2009: 15.

Richter, Klaus & Wilke, Manfred 1991, 'Opponent und Bürgerrechtler', in Hoffmann, Dieter et al, *Robert Havemann. Dokumente eines Lebens*, Berlin: 191–283.

Richter, Sebastian 2012, 'Zwischen Orden und Spott: Das vereinte Deutschland und seine DDR-Bürgerrechtler', in Böick, Marcus, Hertel, Anja & Kuschel, Franziska (Eds.) *Aus einem Land vor unserer Zeit. Eine Lesereise durch die DDR-Geschichte*, Berlin: 231–242.

Riesenhuber, Heinz (n.d.), 'Nachwort', in Meadows, Dennis et al, *Die Grenzen des Wachstums. Bericht des Club of Rome zur Lage der Menschheit*, Gütersloh: 202–213.

Röhrborn, Gert 2008, *Dissidenten als geistige Schrittmacher: Transformatorische Politik hinter der Mauer*, Saarbrücken.

Roesler, Jörg 2002, *Die Wirtschaft der DDR*, Landeszentrale für politische Bildung Thüringen (Ed.), Erfurt.

Roesler, Jörg 2003, *Ostdeutsche Wirtschaft im Umbruch. 1970–2000*, Bundeszentrale für politische Bildung (Ed.), Bonn.

Ropohl, Günter 2005, 'Die Wirklichkeit der Utopie', in *Erwägen, Wissen, Ethik*, No. 16, Stuttgart: 327–329.

Roth, Wolfgang 1975, 'Aufruf zur Askese. Wolfgang Harich reizt zu fruchtbarem Widerspruch', in: *Die Zeit*, No. 38/1975: 10, retrieved at https://www.zeit.de/1975/38/aufruf-zur-askese.

Ruben, Peter 1999, 'Der moderne Kommunismus und die soziale Frage', in Helle Panke e.V. (Ed.), *Philosophische Gespräche*, No. 1, Berlin: 5–30.

Ruben, Peter 2005, 'DDR-Philosophie unter Parteiregie. Neue Anfänge zwischen dem 5. und 8. SED-Parteitag', in Rauh, Hans-Christoph & Ruben, Peter (Eds.), *Denkversuche. DDR- Philosophie in den 60er Jahren*, Berlin: 19–50.

Saage, Richard 1990, *Das Ende der politischen Utopie?*, Frankfurt am Main.

Saage, Richard 1999, "Morellys 'Das Gesetzbuch der Natur' und die Dialektik der Anarchie", in *Utopie kreativ*, No. 100, Febuary 1999: 54–66.

Saage, Richard 2000, *Politische Utopien der Neuzeit*, 2nd expanded edition, Bochum.

Saage, Richard 2002a, 'Neue Utopien. Birst die Welt oder wächst sie zusammen? Vortrag vom 15. September 2002 bei einer Tagung der Evangelischen Akademie Tutzing', retrieved from http://www.ev-akademie-tutzing.de/doku/aktuell/upload/Utopien.htm,

Saage, Richard 2002b, *Utopische Profile, volume III: Industrielle Revolution und Technischer Staat im 19. Jahrhundert*, Münster.

Saage, Richard 2003, *Utopische Profile, volume IV: Widersprüche und Synthesen des 20. Jahrhunderts*, Münster.

Saage, Richard 2005, 'Plädoyer für den klassischen Utopiebegriff', in *Erwägen, Wissen, Ethik*, No. 16, Stuttgart 2005: 291–298.

Saage, Richard 2008: *Utopieforschung, volume II: An der Schwelle des 21. Jahrhunderts*, Münster.

Saage, Richard 2010, *Utopische Horizonte. Zwischen historischer Entwicklung und aktuellem Geltungsanspruch*, Berlin.

Schäfer, Gert 1978, 'Was heißt bürokratischer Sozialismus?', in PROKLA, No. 31 (2/1978): 33–55.

Scheer, Hermann 1981, 'Die institutionellen politischen Voraussetzungen menschlicher Emanzipation – eine sozialdemokratische Entgegnung zu Rudolf Bahro', in Kremendahl, Hans & Meyer, Thomas (Eds.), *Menschliche Emanzipation. Rudolf Bahro und der Demokratische Sozialismus*, Frankfurt am Main: 133–146.

Schivelbusch, Wolfgang 1997, *Vor dem Vorhang. Das geistige Berlin 1945–1948*, Frankfurt am Main.

Schmidt, Alfred 1999, "Die nicht-erpreßte Versöhnung. Erinnerung an eine denkwürdige Begegnung zwischen 'östlichem' und 'westlichem' Marxismus", in Dornuf, Stefan & Pitsch, Reinhard (Eds.), *Wolfgang Harich zum Gedächtnis. Eine Gedenkschrift in zwei Bänden*, volume 2, München: 488–502.

Schmidt, Wolfgang 2003, 'Zur Sicherung der politischen Grundlagen der DDR', in Grimmer, Reinhard et al (Eds.), *Die Sicherheit. Zur Abwehrarbeit des MfS*, volume 1, 3rd corrected and expanded edition, Berlin: 580–668.

Schmidt, Wolfgang 2006, 'Wem nützte es?', in Allertz, Robert (Ed.), *Sänger und Souffleur. Biermann, Havemann und die DDR*, Berlin: 93–110.

Schneider, Michael 1996, *Das Ende eines Jahrhundertmythos*, Köln.

Schölzel, Arnold 1998 'Von der Kritik zur Esoterik – Rudolf Bahro', in UTOPIE kreativ, No. 88 (February 1998): 70–76.

Schubert, Thomas 2002, 'Rudolf Bahro – ein deutsch-deutscher Denker zwischen vorgestern und übermorgen', in *Utopie kreativ*, No. 140 (June 2002): 56–62.

Schubert, Thomas 2007, "Zwischen Aufbruch und Abbruch. Die 'Stalinismus'-Vorlesungen von 1990", in Herzberg, Guntolf (Ed.), *Rudolf Bahro: Denker–Reformator–Homo politicus*, Berlin: 215–237.

Schwendter, Rolf 1994, *Utopie. Überlegungen zu einem zeitlosen Begriff*, Berlin and Amsterdam.

Scott, John Anthony 1988, 'François-Noël Babeuf und die Verschwörung für die Gleichheit', in Babeuf, Gracchus (Ed) *Die Verschwörung für die Gleichheit*, Hamburg: 7–30.

Selle, Gerd 1981, 'William Morris und sein Roman', in *Morris, William: Kunde von Nirgendwo. Eine Utopie der vollendeten kommunistischen Gesellschaft*, 2nd edition, Reutlingen: 7–30.

Sieber, Sven 2008, *Walter Janka und Wolfgang Harich. Zwei DDR-Intellektuelle im Konflikt mit der Macht*, Münster 2008.

Skiba, Dieter 2006, "Ein 'Gerechter unter den Völkern' – Fragen bleiben", in Allertz, Robert (Ed.), *Sänger und Souffleur. Biermann, Havemann und die DDR*, Berlin: 47–71.

Speth, Rudolf 2003, 'Thomas Hobbes', in Massing, Peter & Breit, Gotthard (Eds.), *Demokratie-Theorien. Von der Antike bis zur Gegenwart*, 2 edition, Bundeszentrale für politische Bildung, Bonn: 94–98.

Spittler, Reinhard 2007, 'Die Quellen von Bahros Spiritualität', in Herzberg, Guntolf (Ed.), *Rudolf Bahro: Denker–Reformator–Homo politicus*, Berlin: 333–362.

Spohn, Wilfried 1978, 'Geschichte und Emanzipation. Bahros Beitrag zur Sozialismus-Diskussion', in *PROKLA*, No. 31 (2/1978): 5–31.

Stadtmüller, Georg 1977, '[Review of:] Wolfgang HARICH, Kommunismus ohne Wachstum? Babeuf und der "Club of Rome". Sechs Interviews mit Freimut Duve und Briefe an ihn', in *Zeitschrift für Politik*, No. 24/1977: 206–207.

Stalin, Joseph 1945, 'Dialectical and historical materialism', in *History of the Communist Party and the Soviet Union (Bolsheviks): Short Course*, Moscow: Foreign Languages Publishing House.

Steigerwald, Robert 1977, *Der 'wahre' oder konterrevolutionäre 'Sozialismus'. Was wollen Havemann, Dutschke, Biermann?*, Frankfurt am Main.

Steiner, André 2007, *Von Plan zu Plan. Eine Wirtschaftsgeschichte der DDR*, Bundeszentrale für politische Bildung, Bonn.

Strasser, Johano & Traube, Klaus 1984, *Die Zukunft des Fortschritts. Der Sozialismus und die Krise des Industrialismus*, Bonn.

Taylor, Gordon Rattray 1972, *The Doomsday Book*, United Kindgom: Panther.

Theuer, Werner 2000, 'Havemann, Robert', in Veen, Hans-Joachim et al (Eds.), *Lexikon Opposition und Widerstand in der SED-Diktatur*, Berlin und München: 176.

Thieme, Sandra 2000, "Ökologische Utopien zwischen Naturalismus und Soziozentrismus am Beispiel von Ernest Callenbachs 'Ökotopia' und Robert Havemanns 'Morgen'", in Best, Günter & Kößler, Reinhart (Eds.), *Subjekte und Systeme: soziologische und anthropologische Annäherungen, Festschrift für Christian Sigrist zum 65. Geburtstag*, Frankfurt am Main: 204–213.

Thieme, Sandra 2004, *Perspektiven ökologisch-nachhaltiger Entwicklung. Zur Aktualität utopischen Denkens*, Schkeuditz.

Uekötter, Frank 2010, 'Apokalyptik als Profession? Ängste, Prognosen und die internationale Umweltbewegung', in Hartmann, Heinrich & Vogel, Jakob (Eds.), *Zukunftswissen. Prognosen in Wirtschaft, Politik und Gesellschaft seit 1900*, Frankfurt am Main: 284–300.

Ulbricht, Walter 1956, 'Zum Kampf zwischen dem Marxismus-Leninismus und den Ideologien der Bourgeoisie', in *Deutsche Zeitschrift für Philosophie*, No. 5–6/1956 (published 1957): 518–532.

Vesper, Karlen 2008, 'Nix mit Paradigmenwechsel. Das Jahr 1978 in der DDR – debattiert von Wissenschaftlern und Zeitzeugen', in *Neues Deutschland*, 9/10. February 2008: 22.

Vilmar, Fritz 1981, "Eine klassenlose Arbeitsorganisation. Bahros 'Alternative' geht auch uns an", in Kremendahl, Hans & Meyer, Thomas (Eds.), *Menschliche Emanzipation. Rudolf Bahro und der Demokratische Sozialismus*, Frankfurt am Main: 121–129.

Vollnhals, Clemens 2000, *Der Fall Havemann. Ein Lehrstück politischer Justiz*, 2nd edition, Berlin.

Walther, Joachim 1987, *Der Traum aller Träume, Utopien von Platon bis Morris*, Berlin (East).

Waschkuhn, Arno 2003, *Politische Utopien*, München.

Weber, Hermann 1991, DDR. *Grundriß der Geschichte*, completely revised edition, Hannover.

Weigmann, Gerd 2003, 'Ökologie', in Simonis, Udo E. (Ed), *Ökolexikon*, München: 147–148.

Weis, Hans-Willi 1981, 'Das theoretische und strategische Konzept der osteuropäischen Opposition und die Perspektive Bahros', in Kremendahl, Hans & Meyer, Thomas (Eds.), *Menschliche Emanzipation. Rudolf Bahro und der Demokratische Sozialismus*, Frankfurt am Main: 28–41.

Werlhof, Claudia von 2009, 'Auf dem Weg zur post-patriarchalen Zivilisation. Zu einem neuen Paradigma', in *Widerspruch*, No. 57, Zürich: 147–152.

Wilke, Manfred 2010, 'Robert Havemann und das Programm der friedlichen Revolution von 1989', in *Europäische Ideen, Sonderheft: Robert Havemann 100*, London: 27–35.

Wirth, Günter 2007, "Walter Harichs 'Ostorientierung'. Einige Bemerkungen über den Vater von Wolfgang Harich – und ihn", in *Utopie kreativ*, No. 195 (January 2007): 56–62.

Wolle, Stefan 1999, *Die heile Welt der Diktatur. Alltag und Herrschaft in der DDR 1971–1989*, 2nd revised edition, Bundeszentrale für politische Bildung, Bonn.

Wunschik, Tobias 1998, *Die maoistische KPD/ML und die Zerschlagung ihrer 'Sektion DDR' durch das MfS*, 2nd edition, Berlin.

Woods, Roger 1986, *Opposition in the GDR under Honecker, 1971–85: An Introduction and Documentation*, New York: Palgrave Macmillan.

Zwerenz, Gerhard 1996, 'Der Blick von außen', in Prokop, Siegfried (Ed.), *Ein Streiter für Deutschland. Auseinandersetzung mit Wolfgang Harich*, Berlin: 26–33.

Zwerenz, Ingrid & Zwerenz, Gerhard 2004, *Sklavensprache und Revolte. Der Bloch-Kreis und seine Feinde in Ost und West*, Hamburg und Berlin.

Spiegel Articles with No Named Author

'Bemerkenswerte Arbeit', *Spiegel*, no. 53/1977: 19, available at: http://wissen.spiegel.de/wissen/dokument/dokument-druck.html?id=40680169&top=SPI,
'Das trifft den Parteiapparat ins Herz', *Spiegel* no. 35/1977: 30, available at: http://wissen.spiegel.de/wissen/dokument/dokument-druck.html?id=40763980&top=SPIEGEL,
'Ekliges Ding', *Spiegel*, no. 31/1975, p. 86, available at: http://wissen.spiegel.de/wissen/doku-ment/dokument-druck.html?id=41458188&top=SPIEGEL,
'Geistige Leere', *Spiegel*, no. 36/1977: 34, available at: http://wissen.spiegel.de/wissen/do-kument/dokument-druck.html?id=40749177&top=SPIEGEL,
'Pfeffer in offene Wunden', *Spiegel*, no. 39/1977: 113, available at: http://wissen.spiegel.de/wissen/dokument/dokument-druck.html?id=40831347&top=SPIEGEL,
Spiegel, no. 37/1977: 3, available at: http://wissen.spiegel.de/wissen/dokument/doku-ment-druck.html?id=40831400&top=SPIEGEL,

Files from the Stasi Records Archive
On Rudolf Bahro
BStU, MfS, HA XX, no. 2065
BStU, MfS, HA XX/9, no. 879
BStU, MfS, HA XX/9, no. 880
BStU, MfS, HAXX/9, no. 1747
BStU, MfS, AOP, no. 17596/81, vol. 1
BStU, MfS, AOP, no. 17596/81, vol. 2

On Wolfgang Harich
BStU, MfS, AP, 4578/71, vol. 6
BStU, MfS, AP, 4578/71, vol. 7
BStU, MfS, AP, 4578/71, vol. 8
BStU, MfS, AP, 4578/71, vol. 9

On Robert Havemann
BStU, MfS, AU, 145/90, vol. 2
BStU, MfS, AU, 145/90, vol. 4
BStU, MfS, AU, 145/90, vol. 5
BStU, MfS, AU, 145/90, vol. 6
BStU, MfS, AU, 145/90, vol. 8
BStU, MfS, AU, 145/90, vol. 10
BStU, MfS, AU, 145/90, vol. 11
BStU, MfS, AU, 145/90, vol. 12
BStU, MfS, AU, 145/90, vol. 13

BStU, MfS, AP, 4578/71, vol. 7
BStU, MfS, HA XX/9, no. 880
BStU, MfS, HA XX/9, no. 972

Files from the Archive of the Robert Havemann Society

RHG/RH 022/1 vol. 79 A
RHG/RH 023/06 Bd. 92
RHG/RH 023/13 vol. 111 A
RHG/RH 031B
RHG/RH 038
RHG/RH 392
RHG/RH 393

Index of Names

Ackermann, Anton   5
Adorno, Theodor W.   120, 329
Allertz, Robert   284, 290–291
Altvater, Elmar   277, 394
Amery, Carl   85, 131, 154, 157, 160–161, 171, 277
Armanski, Gerhard   277
Aschka, Fritz   375
Arens, Karl Peter   375
Asimov, Isaac   230
Atwood, Margaret   395
Augstein, Rudolf   75, 151, 157

Babeuf, Gracchus   3, 34, 87–94, 97–98, 101–104, 108–109, 116–118, 123, 128, 144–145, 153–154, 156, 159, 388
Bachofen, Johann Jakob   114
Bacon, Francis   10, 378
Bahro, Gundula (née. Lembke)   163, 186
Bakunin, Michail   350
Bambach, Ralf   89, 92–93, 161
Bauer, Adolf   148–149
Baumgart, Günter   183
Beauvoir, Simone de   131, 276
Bebel, August   VIII, 14, 197, 343–346, 355, 366
Becher, Johannes R.   74, 76, 162, 179
Behrens, Fritz   185, 202–204, 262–264
Beethoven, Ludwig van   165, 180
Bell, Daniel   45, 265
Bellamy, Edward   10, 14, 219, 229–230, 354
Benary, Arne   202–204
Beneke, Ursula   185
Berg, Hermann von   86, 255
Bernstein, Eduard   324, 343
Berthold, Lothar   81
Besenbruch, Walter   186
Beyer, Frank   164
Biermann, Wolf   28, 79–80, 168, 276, 293–294, 296–297, 301, 333, 371, 382
Bierwisch, Manfred   289, 291
Bischoff, Joachim   271–272, 277
Blackbourn, David   393–394
Blanqui, Auguste   10, 144, 350
Blau, Paul   132

Bloch, Ernst   VIII, 5, 9, 11–12, 14–16, 24–26, 28, 30, 32–33, 35–36, 50, 70–71, 93, 75–76, 166, 183, 196, 210–211, 248, 250–251, 294, 298, 308, 317, 341, 346, 350, 366, 374, 380, 386–387, 391
Bogdanov, Alexander   VIII, 14, 31
Bohley, Bärbel   298
Böll, Heinrich   276
Bornemann, Ernst   114
Brandt, Heinz   250, 270–271, 276
Branstner, Gerhard   26
Braun, Volker   28, 164, 168, 183, 185–186
Bräunig, Werner   164
Brecht, Bertolt   32, 203
Brezhnev, Leonid   38, 44, 117, 136, 156, 187, 191
Brie, Michael   26
Brus, Wlodzimieruz   280–281
Bruyn, Günther de   28, 185
Bukharin, Nikolai   350
Buhr, Manfred   30, 81
Buonarroti, Filippo   89
Busold, Werner   185

Cabet, Ètienne   10, 378
Callenbach, Ernest   IX, 8, 21, 26, 207, 211, 253, 343, 351–352, 356, 358, 364, 389
Campanella, Tommaso   10, 378
Camus, Albert   152
Carillo, Santiago   279
Cohn-Bendit, Daniel   78
Comenius, Johann Amos   230

Deutscher, Isaac   183, 198
Diderot, Denis   89, 352
Dlubek, Rolf   146, 148
Draheim, Dirk   283–284, 333
Dutschke, Rudi   171, 190–192
Duve, Freimut   98, 104, 108, 130, 132, 141, 152, 154–155

Eaubonne, Françoise d'   113, 131
Ehrenburg, Ilja   70
Eichhorn I, Wolfgang   148–149
Elias, Norbert   12, 124

Engels, Friedrich   VII, 6–7, 13–15, 30–31, 57–58, 64–65, 93, 95–97, 99, 101, 114, 117, 123, 146–148, 183–184, 194–195, 200, 206–207, 209, 213–214, 223–224, 230, 244, 249, 274, 284, 309, 343, 345, 351, 355, 360, 367, 392
Enzensberger, Hans Magnus   78
Eppelmann, Rainer   298
Eppler, Erhard   132
Erkelenz, Peter   375
Euchner, Walter   1–2

Falck, Paul   77
Falcke, Heino   260
Faust, Siegmar   294–295, 298, 375
Fedoseyev, Piotr N.   144
Ferst, Marko   170–171, 174–176, 238, 242, 247, 359, 362, 387, 393
Fetscher, Iring   13, 58
Feuerbach, Ludwig   VII, 28, 78, 183, 251, 317
Finger, Evelyn   44, 174, 391
Fischbeck, Hans-Jürgen   260
Fischer, Joschka   172
Flechtheim, Ossip   373, 375
Fleck, Dirk C.   395
Flierl, Bruno   265
Flitner, Wilhelm   230
Florath, Bernd   8, 71, 74–75, 80, 285, 287, 291, 294, 324, 368, 372–373, 378
Fourier, Charles   10, 14, 154, 202
Frank, Pierre   275
Franz, Dietrich-Eckhard   92–93, 392
Freisler, Roland   284
French, Marilyn   131
Freymuth, Klaus   368
Friedan, Betty   131
Friedman, Jona   131
Fromm, Erich   158, 350, 354
Fuchs, Jürgen   294, 296–297
Fühmann, Franz   28
Fukuyama, Francis   391

Garaudy, Roger   374
Gaus, Günter   4, 81, 157
Gehlen, Arnold   IX, 72, 118–122, 135, 161, 358
Gehrke, Bernd   371
Gehrmann, Kurt   376
Geisel, Christof   2, 25, 367, 370–372, 393
Geoghegan, Vincent   210, 236

Goethe, Johann Wolfgang von   15, 374
Goldschmidt, Harry   183, 186
Gollwitzer, Helmut   113, 249, 276–277
Gorz, Andre   210
Gomułka, Władysław   73
Gorbachev, Mikhail   75, 86, 132–133, 245, 258
Gotsche, Otto   80
Götz, Hans-Herbert   376–377
Gramsci, Antonio   197, 201, 214, 234, 239, 248, 251, 324
Grimm, Thomas   162, 181, 187, 240, 242, 254
Grimmer, Reinhard   28
Grosse, Hermann   62–63, 139
Gruhl, Herbert   157–160, 171, 374
Günther, Hans   31

Habermas, Jürgen   329
Hacks, Peter   36
Hagen, Eva-Maria   297
Hager, Kurt   64–65, 71–72, 168, 184, 208, 288, 292, 296, 304, 384
Handel, Gottfried   30
Hansen, Kastholm   340
Harich, Anne   68, 70–71, 80, 84
Harich, Katharina   80
Harich, Walther   68
Harrer, Jürgen   264–266
Hartmann, Nicolai   69
Hauf, Volker   158
Havemann, Hans   283
Havemann, Florian   283–284, 294–295, 299–300, 309, 356, 366
Havemann, Franziska   300
Havemann, Karin   331–332
Havemann, Katja   293–294, 297, 299–301, 303, 377
Hecht, Hartmut   287, 290, 294, 333
Hegel, Georg Wilhelm Friedrich   13, 22, 69, 128, 183
Heilbronner, Robert   158
Heise, Wolfgang   183, 186–187
Helmstädter, Ernst   282
Henrich, Rolf   5, 26
Herder, Johann Gottfried   69
Hermlin, Stephan   28, 81
Herrmann, Joachim   168, 304
Hertwig, Manfred   75–76, 154–155, 184, 248–249, 389

INDEX OF NAMES 423

Herzberg, Guntolf   8, 70–71, 73, 76, 162–165, 167–173, 175, 177–178, 183, 185–190, 194, 198, 203–204, 214, 255–256, 258, 261–262, 287, 288–289, 291
Heuler, Werner   273–275
Heyer, Andreas   7–9, 11–12, 16, 18–20, 23, 26, 33–34, 69, 75, 87–88, 93–94, 110, 117–118, 127, 131, 134, 252, 254, 343, 346–347, 350, 355–359, 362, 364, 386, 389
Heym, Stefan   4, 26, 28–29, 32, 79, 168, 185, 293, 297
Hilbig, Klaus   185
Himmelmann, Gerhard   227
Hobbes, Thomas   94
Hofbauer, Hannes   79, 100, 128–129
Hoffmann, Dieter   258, 283–286, 290, 333
Hoffmann, Jürgen   277
Hofmann, Gunter   171, 281
Hölderlin, Friedrich   179
Holz, Hans Heinz   373–374
Honecker, Erich   32, 35, 39–40, 42–45, 55, 57, 79, 82, 135–136, 142, 144, 156, 176, 181, 205, 257, 284, 296–297, 304, 393
Höpcke, Klaus   81, 118, 142–143, 176
Horkheimer, Max   329
Huffzky, Hans   75
Hurwitz, Harold   8, 332, 383–384
Huxley, Aldous   10, 20, 329, 350, 373, 387

Idler, Martin d'   4, 10–11, 13, 16, 19–22, 24–25, 54, 66, 91, 110, 113, 351–352, 358, 390, 397
Inglehard, Ronald   172

Jackson, Tim   50, 396
Jäckel, Hartmut   298
Jäger, Manfred   126, 130
Jahr, John   75
Jakobs, Karl-Heinz   369
Janka, Walter   32, 72–74, 76–80, 82, 134, 371
Janssen-Jurreit, Marie-Louise   131
Jean Paul   78, 81, 87
Jennerjahn, Hartmut   298
Joliot-Curie, Fréderic   25
Judt, Matthias   44
Jungk, Robert   99, 289
Just, Gustav   73–74, 76–79

Kafka, Franz   152
Kant, Immanuel   119

Kautsky, Karl   117, 324, 343
Kelly, Petra   174
Khrushchev, Nikita Sergeyevich   38, 70
Kirchhoff, Jochen   180, 194
Klein, Dieter   185
Klein, Thomas   182, 279, 291–292
Klingenstein, Thomas   302
Klopstock, Friedrich Gottlieb   375
Koch, Hans   258
Koenen, Gerd   264
Kolakowski, Leszek   13–14, 71
Korte, Helmut   201–202, 248, 259, 277
Kosta, Tomas   278–279
Kowalczuk, Ilko-Sascha   1, 3
Krauß, Matthias   34
Kremendahl, Hans   266–269
Krenz, Egon   82
Kropotkin, Peter   356–357, 364, 366
Krysmanski, Hans-Jürgen   11
Kuczynski, Jürgen   59–63, 70, 99, 101
Kühne, Lothar   5, 26
Kunert, Christian   276, 296–297

Lahontan, Louis Armand   10, 352
Laitko, Hubert   289, 291–293, 327–330, 378, 393
Lamberz, Werner   144, 168
Landauer, Gustav   12
Laozi   178
Le Guin, Ursula K.   IX, 26, 115, 253, 364–365, 389
Lehnert, Erik   179–180, 198
Leick, Romain   155
Lenin, Vladimir Ulyanov   31, 57, 69, 87, 96–97, 108, 132, 148, 163, 166, 184, 190, 196–197, 214, 248, 263, 309, 343, 374, 388
Leonhard, Wolfgang   32, 69–70, 129, 191–192
Lohr (Stasi Major)   85
Lombardo Radice, Lucio   279–280, 374
Lorf, Dieter   185
Lorf, Marianne   185
Löther, Rolf   150
Löwenthal, Richard   373
Ludz, Peter Christian   119–120, 328–329
Luhmann, Niklas   9
Lukács, Georg   71, 76, 81, 183, 258
Luxemburg, Rosa   166, 197, 214, 322, 324, 334, 343–344, 357

Mably, Gabriel Bonnot de 89
Maier, Harry 145–146, 185
Malthus, Thomas Robert 50, 99–100, 318, 345
Mandel, Ernest 188, 243, 271, 275–276
Mannheim, Karl 12
Mao Zedong 285, 309
Marcuse, Herbert 114, 210, 277, 374
Marx, Karl VII, 6–7, 13–15, 28, 30–31, 35, 57–58, 63, 83, 93, 95–97, 99, 101–102, 109, 113, 117, 119, 121, 123, 126, 147–148, 156, 163, 166, 172, 183–184, 194–196, 198, 200, 204, 206–207, 209–211, 213–214, 227, 230, 240, 244, 248–249, 251, 267, 271–272, 274–275, 281, 309, 316–317, 321–322, 329, 335, 340–341, 343, 350–351, 375, 386, 388
Mayer, Hans 391
Meadows, Dennis IX, 4, 46–50, 53, 59–63, 102, 141, 145, 304–305
Medvedev, Roy 198
Menge, Wolfgang 112
Mercier, Louis-Sébastien 10, 123
Merker, Paul 32, 73–74
Meulenbelt, Anja 131
Mesarovic, Mihajlo 50–52, 64
Meyer, Fritjof 77
Meyer, Thomas 266, 270
Michel, Karl Markus 78
Michels, Robert 206
Mielke, Erich 55, 297
Misik, Robert 396
Mittag, Günter 55, 57
Mittenzwei, Werner 5, 36–37, 69–70, 74–75, 78, 85, 164, 288–289, 296–297, 392
Modrow, Hans 175
Moneta, Jakob 276
Morelly, Étienne-Gabriel 34, 89, 92–94, 116
Morgan, Lewis Henry 114
Morgner, Irmtraud 131
More, Thomas VII–VIII, 10–12, 14, 34, 88, 223, 225–226, 250, 314, 352, 364, 366, 375, 378, 380
Morris, William 10, 14, 19, 347–349, 352, 366
Morris-Keitel, Peter 8, 300, 328, 333, 345, 349, 355, 359, 394–396

Naphtali, Fritz 324
Narr, Wolf-Dieter 249

Naujok, Werner 185
Naumann, Manfred 81
Negt, Oskar 6, 167
Neubert, Ehrhart 32, 74, 76, 86, 150, 260–262
Nick, Harry 185
Nietzsche, Friedrich 81, 113, 134, 177
Nolte, Hans-Heinrich 198, 269–270
Norden, Albert 257

Oertzen, Peter von 243, 253–254, 270
Otto, Wilfriede 204, 257, 367
Orwell, George 10, 20, 111, 219
Owen, Robert 14

Pannach, Gerulf 276, 296–297
Peccei, Aurelio 46
Pestel, Eduard 50
Piercy, Marge IX, 26, 389, 391
Piper, Ernst 302–303, 373
Piper, Klaus 283, 294, 303, 342, 377
Plato 88, 230, 310
Plenzdorf, Ulrich 185
P.M. 8
Polzin, Arno 286
Poppe, Gerd 298, 368
Popper, Karl R. 4, 12
Pötter, Bernhard 395
Prokop, Gert 26
Prokop, Siegfried 8, 37, 53, 69–74, 76, 78–83, 85, 129, 288, 382
Proudhon, Pierre-Joseph 350
Proust, Marcel 152
Pushkin, Georgiy Maximovich 72–73
Puschmann, Manfred 62–63, 139

Radkau, Joachim 5, 25, 46, 55–57, 99–100, 110, 113, 173–174, 318, 390, 393–394, 396
Ragwitz, Ursula 304
Rajk, László 76
Rasputin, Valentin Grigoriyevich 113
Rathenau, Walther 55
Rathenow, Lutz 298
Rehberg, Karl-Siegbert 119–121
Reich, Alexander 79
Reich, Jens 371
Richter, Klaus 363
Riesenhuber, Heinz 50

INDEX OF NAMES 425

Robespierre, Maximilien   89, 94, 128
Röhrborn, Gert   7, 198, 253, 261, 353, 365
Roth, Wolfgang   153
Rosenthal, Rüdiger   368
Rowe, Kirsten   85
Rousseau, Jean-Jacques   19, 89, 92, 94, 267
Ruben, Peter   97
Rudolf, Bernd   376
Rühle, Jürgen   155–156, 192
Rühle, Otto   350
Russakov, Konstantin   44
Ruyer, Raymond   11

Saage, Richard   6–7, 10, 12–13, 15–23, 31, 33–36, 88, 93–94, 113, 116, 121, 123, 145, 220, 225, 351, 358, 364, 377, 386–389
Sakharov, Andrey   108, 140, 155, 259, 350
Saint-Simon, Henri   10, 14
Sartre, Jean Paul   276
Schacht, Hjalmar   151
Schäfer, Gert   196, 278
Scheer, Hermann   8, 272
Schirmer, Gregor   81
Schmidt, Alfred   83
Schmidt, Helmut   55
Schmidt, Wolfgang   28–29, 255
Schneider, Romy   276
Schölzel, Arnold   173
Schottlaender, Rudolf   341
Schreiter, H.   152–153
Schröder, Gerhard   276
Schubert, Thomas   197
Schult, Reinhard   371
Schwarz, Ulrich   255
Schwendter, Rolf   13–14, 88, 158
Seghers, Anna   32
Seidel, Helmut   26
Seifert, Kurt   8, 162–163, 167, 170, 172
Selle, Gerd   349
Selle, Karl-Heinz   141
Sève, Lucien   189
Skinner, Frederic Burrhus   358, 389
Slánsky, Rudolf   76
Spittler, Reinhard   171–173, 208
Solzhenitsyn, Aleksandr Isayevich   259
Spangenberg, Dietrich   255
Spohn, Wilfried   200, 202, 252, 277–278

Spranger, Eduard   68
Stade, Martin   168
Stadelmann, Bernd   375
Stadtmüller, Georg   156–157
Stalin, Joseph Vissarionovich   7, 31, 35, 37, 69, 77, 79, 97, 116, 154, 183, 194, 197–198, 287, 294, 309, 369, 387
Stauffenberg, Claus Schenk Graf von   82
Steigerwald, Robert   373–374
Steinberger, Bernhard   74–76
Stoph, Willi   55
Strasser, Johano   132, 157–160, 272–273

Taylor, Gordon Rattray   52–54, 110–112, 127, 141
Teilhard de Chardin, Pierre   208
Theuer, Werner   8, 324, 372–373, 378
Thieme, Sandra   8, 352–355, 357, 359, 362–363, 365
Togliatti, Palmiro   323
Traube, Klaus   158–160, 272–273
Trittel, Christina   33
Trotsky, Leon   183, 275, 350
Tzschoppe, Werner   183, 186

Ulbricht, Walter   32, 35–40, 42, 55, 57, 69, 72–78, 165, 181–182, 203, 205, 285, 287–288, 292, 326, 347

Verner, Paul   168
Vieweg, Kurt   76
Vilmar, Fritz   251, 269–270
Vollmer, Antje   174
Vollnhals, Clemens   297, 299, 304, 333

Wagenknecht, Sahra   177, 246
Walther, Joachim   14
Wandel, Peter   73
Waschkuhn, Arno   9, 17, 21, 23, 94–95, 356, 364
Weber, Hermann   28–29, 33, 182, 205, 366
Weber, Max   12
Wells, Herbert George   14
Weitling, Wilhelm   350
Werfel, Franz   375
Wessel, Harald   144
Wetzel, Rudi   183, 185
Widmann, Joachim   377
Wilke, Manfred   301, 363, 372

Wittfogel, Karl August   184, 191–192
Wolf, Christa   26, 28
Wolf, Frank   368
Wolf, Konrad   185
Wolf, Richard   74–77
Wolle, Stefan   27, 38–45, 56, 66, 165

Wollgast, Siegfried   184, 192
Wolter, Ulf   350

Zamyatin, Yevgeny   10, 20, 35
Zöger, Heinz   73–77
Zwerenz, Gerhard   80

www.ingramcontent.com/pod-product-compliance
Lightning Source LLC
Chambersburg PA
CBHW070607030426
42337CB00020B/3703